AMERICAN Home Cooking

AMERICAN Home Cooking

Over 300 Spirited Recipes Celebrating Our Rich Tradition of Home Cooking

Cheryl Alters Jamison & Bill Jamison

wm
WILLIAM MORROW
An Imprint of HarperCollinsPublishers

We gratefully acknowledge The Junior League of Charleston (South Carolina), Inc., for the use of the poems on pages 91 and 290 from *Charleston Receipts*, copyright 1950.

HarperCollins books may be purchased for educational, business, or sales promotional use. For information please write: Special Markets Department, HarperCollins Publishers Inc., 10 East 53rd Street, New York, NY 10022.

First William Morrow paperback edition published 2005

A hardcover edition was published by Broadway Books in 1999.

Designed by Vertigo Design, NYC
Photographs by Ellen Silverman

The Library of Congress has catalogued the hardcover edition as follows:

Jamison, Cheryl Alters.
American home cooking : over 300 spirited recipes celebrating our rich tradition of home cooking / Cheryl Alters Jamison and Bill Jamison.
—1st ed.
p. cm.
Includes bibliographical references.
ISBN 0-7679-0201-7 (hc.)
1. Cookery, American. 2. Cookery, American—History.
I. Jamison, Bill. II. Title.
TX715.J295 1999
641.5973—dc21 99-10814
CIP

ISBN 0-06-074764-1 (pbk.)

05 06 07 08 09 QW 10 9 8 7 6 5 4 3 2 1

To the memory of our grandmothers and
their mothers, 1842–1977:

Corrine Ellis Alters, Mayme Luthy Alters, Matilda Jane Barr, Lula Allen Cleveland, Sarah McClure Cleveland, Sarah Trone Edwards, Alma Cleek Ellis, Anna Tutt Ellis, Chellie Barr Jamison, and Gertrude Edwards Van Meter Meyer

Contents

What's on Our Table 1

Four Centuries of Home Cooking 5

Flapjacks, Grits, Hash, and Other Hearty Ways to Start the Day 15

Piled High: The American Sandwich 47

Little Whims to Whet the Appetite 65

Soup's On 87

From Sea to Shining Sea, the Catch of the Day 107

Fryers, Roasters, and Wild Turkeys 139

We've Always Gone Whole Hog 169

Beefy Passions 193

Love Me Tender: Game, Lamb, and Veal 217

Fresh from the Garden 237

Potatoes, Dried Beans, and Other Keepers 265

Sweets and Sours for the Pantry 287

Amber Waves of Grain 317

"The More Perfect the Bread, the More Noble the Lady" 339

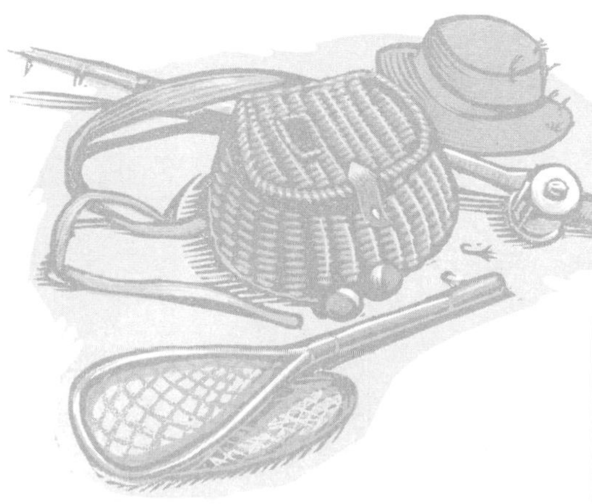

Peerless Pies, Crisps, Cobblers, and Creams 359

Cooking to Excess with Cakes, Cookies, and Candies 395

Cherry Shrubs to Mint Juleps 423

Acknowledgments 439

Selected Bibliography 441

Index 449

AMERICAN
Home Cooking

WHAT'S ON Our Table

Some of the most self-explanatory things seem to require the most explaining. Baseball, country music, and fly-fishing fall into that class, and so does our straightforward subject of American home cooking. Each of the three little words in the phrase squirms away from a quick grasp like an airborne oyster shucked skyward.

The conundrums start with the word "cooking." Many people today apply the term to anything done in a kitchen. They cook breakfast by peeling the cellophane from boxed waffles and popping them in a toaster, make lunch by zapping a frozen sandwich in a microwave, and bake a

Sunday-dinner ham by heating precooked, canned meat with a glaze of bottled sauce. We appreciate the desire for ease and expedience, but we don't cook in that fashion in these pages. The little extra effort required to use fresh ingredients and time-honored techniques simply yields too many additional rewards in flavor and fun.

We look at cooking as something like an appetizer before dinner, a taste-teasing prelude to eating, one of the most intense, accessible, and affordable pleasures of life. The hands-on, earthy process stimulates the senses, and when done with any diligence at all, it enhances the zest of the food and its enjoyment. The before and after amplify each other, making the cooking, eating, and sharing of a flavorful meal more gratifying in a creative and sensual way than any other form of entertainment we can pursue with an open door.

"Home" seems simple enough as a word and concept, but in "home cooking" the term can take on confusing connotations. For us at least, it suggests a certain style of food—what some call peasant, country, or bourgeois cooking—simple, hearty, seasonal fare brought to a peak of flavor through years of practice and perfection in thousands of home kitchens. It doesn't, in our mind, encompass everything that people cook at home. It's not combinations of convenience foods, such as tuna-noodle casserole, or even made-from-scratch versions of popular commercial treats, such as pizza, or most of all, fancy restaurant-style preparations. The question isn't whether these foods are tasty and enjoyable, but how they came to our communal table in the first place.

Some of our friends feel they are not truly cooking unless they make an elegant and complex dish, say Peking duck, or devise a series of courses with the dramatic crescendos of a Wagnerian opera. We love to dine in such a fashion, but it is *dining,* just one form of eating that's no more advanced than other forms except in the elaboration of circumstance. We don't usually cook that way at our home, or in this book, because the excess required in expense, energy, and time would cut into other opportunities for cooking and eating well. We won't get a good breakfast if we have to spend the morning inflating that duck skin.

Home cooking differs from fine restaurant cooking in multiple respects—from the sophistication of the equipment and techniques to the number of hands arrayed around a counter—but most essentially perhaps in the elementary distinction about who eats the food. Restaurant chefs cook for clients, even when they get their own fill at the stove, while home cooks prepare meals for themselves, their families, and friends. At home the pleasure of the eating and sharing becomes part of the pleasure of the making, in a way seldom realized in a professional situation. We suspect that's a major reason for the widespread problem of chef burnout, a condition we don't face in our little kitchen.

The final word, "American," you might say, at least limits our subject in a clear if broad way. Actually, it presents the opposite difficulty for us. Because the United States is a land of immigrants, a boiling pot of different cuisines if not a melting pot, almost every food on the planet is cooked in someone's home somewhere in the country. When we mentioned the theme of this book to one of our brothers-in-law, of second-generation German descent, he asked, "Isn't American

People ask me: Why do you write about food, and eating and drinking? Why don't you write about the struggle for power and security, the way others do? . . . The easiest answer is to say that, like most other humans, I am hungry. But there is more to it than that. It seems to me that our three basic needs, for food and security and love, are so mixed and mingled and entwined that we cannot straightly think of one without the others. So it happens that when I write of hunger, I am really writing about love and the hunger for it, and warmth and the love of it and the hunger for it . . . and then the warmth and richness and fine reality of hunger satisfied . . . and it is all one.

M.F.K. Fisher,
The Gastronomical Me
(1943)

I say to people I'm writing a cook book and they ask if it will tell them how to make a cake with the new better-than-butter shortening and how to use all the latest dehydrated wonders and if there will be a set of rules for balanced meals and charts showing the vitamin superiority of parsnips over nectarines.

And when I say "No, I shall write of none of these things," they are a little shocked and wonder whether the book will sell.

To this, too, the answer may well be no. But, at least, I shall have laid my cards on the table. And when I am asked further if I think this is the right time to bring out a work unconcerned with the marvels which science has placed with such a flourish on our postwar plastic kitchen tables, I can speak up with a bold and certain yes.

SHEILA HIBBEN, AMERICAN REGIONAL COOKERY (1946)

home cooking just the sum of all the foreign dishes that different nationalities brought with them?" In important and valuable ways, we answer, but not in common bonds.

Over four centuries of adaptation to a new land, immigrant Americans, with the help of Native Americans, have gradually evolved their own distinctive tradition of home cooking, a style as robust and earthy and compelling as any that preceded it on another shore. The still-developing tradition incorporates influences from around the globe—an inevitable result of our history—but it's also shaped by our soil, by the natural abundance of the waters, woods, and plains, by the interactions of multiple cultures, and most important, by the practicality and inventiveness of generations of cooks coping with a New World.

We try to capture the core of that tradition in the following chapters by focusing on a selection of dishes that we consider the best of American home cooking. Some of the dishes originated in American kitchens, but many have foreign antecedents, often two or more blended together in ways characteristic of the ethnic mix of one region or another. In a few cases, they directly replicate the basics of an older dish from overseas, but now claim a New World identity through garnishment. However they evolved, all speak today with a clear American accent, and most would require a passport to leave the country. Whether old or new, almost forgotten favorites from the past or popular comfort foods, local specialties or national staples, they appeal broadly to American tastes and represent culinary high points in our heritage. To the degree we are what we eat, the dishes are us, a living and lively legacy shared by all and accessible to all.

We approach our subject as home cooks, not as trained chefs, culinary historians, or food savants of any other kind. We include a lot of technique and ingredient tips, because they help make the preparations accessible to cooks with limited experience, and we present considerable cultural and historical background on the dishes, because it adds dimension to our appreciation of a meal, but in neither case do we seek to be comprehensive or groundbreaking. This is a cook's tour of American home cooking, focused on what's flavorful, fun, and practical, not a culinary manual or a scholarly survey of all we ate and eat. It's an invitation to pull up a chair at our national table, to relish the treasures of a delightful cuisine as democratic and spirited as the people.

Even in the case of the oldest dishes from the colonial era, we've adapted recipes to the capabilities of the modern kitchen and the nature of the finest ingredients available today. Our focus is traditional cooking—still alive and evolving—rather than historic cooking as it was practiced in the past, even though we're aware that our predecessors had advantages over us in many ways. We regret we don't have a hearth for authentic roasting in front of a flame, and that we can't make a premier syllabub as Amelia Simmons instructed in the first American cookbook, by squeezing natural, unpasteurized milk directly from the cow into the drink, but we're also grateful for the instant, steady heat of the contemporary range, and we're thrilled that the post office can deliver us an authentic Virginia ham half a continent away. We try to adapt to our limitations and rejoice in our opportunities.

Every reader is bound to disagree with some of our choices for the best, most enduring dishes. The stronger you feel about the changes, in fact, the merrier we feel about the strength of the tradition. It simply demonstrates the vigor and vitality of American home cooking. The same applies to our recipes. Unless we're considerably off course, every cook will have personal favorites among the dishes and a special way of preparing them that differs from ours. That's the glory of home cooking. The diversity expands our bounty and gives us more to celebrate together.

Representing the tastiest and truest methods we've found to prepare the selected dishes today, the recipes are our own, developed from tinkering and tweaking in our kitchen, usually over many years. While our first goal always is optimum flavor, we also strive for down-home simplicity, a direct, elemental approach to the desired flavor that's unencumbered with trendy frills or personal fancy. We accept responsibility for how well the recipes succeed in these respects, but the real credit in every case goes to other home cooks who stirred the pot before us. We acknowledge our sources of inspiration and ideas in the recipe chapters, but we're also indebted in a broader way to a number of people who sparked our passion for American cooking, including Mary Randolph, Eliza Leslie, Lizzie Kander, Irma Rombauer, Sheila Hibben, James Beard, Edna Lewis, Betty Fussell, James Villas, and John Thorne.

We're beholden too—as everyone who loves food and words should be—to M.F.K. Fisher, the great American writer who reminded the world that "hunger" is also a verb and isn't nearly as self-explanatory as it seems on the surface. Having lived through two world wars and the Great Depression, she understood hunger as deprivation, but she knew it even more keenly as a lusting to eat and enjoy and share food. Nothing bar love and death—neither a three-times-a-day experience—touches us in such basic and profound ways. Home cooks cook because we hunger, and we can't stop talking about it because our appetite abounds.

We have traveled 35,000 miles, we have eaten the fat of the land, and better still we have made hundreds of friends. We have learned that if *all* America cooked as well as the specialties of each section are cooked at their best, the American cuisine would surpass any the world has known. Maybe that time will come.

Grace and Beverly Smith and Charles Morrow Wilson, *Through the Kitchen Door* (1938)

FOUR CENTURIES OF Home Cooking

A "LAND OF PLENTY," AMERICANS LATER CALLED IT, BUT for the first English colonists it hardly seemed a hospitable home. Long accustomed to the brimming wilderness, Native Americans found a wealth of sustenance from waters awash in fish and shellfish, from untilled woods teeming with game, and from meadows burgeoning in season with edible plants. The British settlers, from a world so distant and different, barely survived extinction from starvation.

In addition to cultivating crops of corn, beans, squash, pumpkins, and melons, Native Americans harvested many wild nuts, berries, fruits, and roots, including chestnuts, black walnuts, hickory nuts, blackberries, blueberries, raspberries, cranberries, strawberries, cherries, plums, grapes, persimmons, and sweet potatoes. For meat, the forests yielded deer, bear, rabbits, squirrels, and turkeys. The skies actually darkened at times with the massive number of birds, especially during migrations of the now-extinct passenger pigeon. The rivers provided a profusion of fish, from perch to twelve-foot-long sturgeon, and the seashores boasted huge oyster beds and crabs big enough for multiple meals.

Native Americans taught the English about a few indigenous foods, particularly corn, but generally the colonists sought to preserve their own established way of life and scorned the culture of their neighbors. They had grown up in the mother country on a diet that revolved largely around wheat, dairy products, and domesticated meat, all absent in the new land. They introduced those staples as quickly and fully as conditions allowed, but they faced a variety of early obstacles that ranged from the financial structure of the Virginia venture to the obdurate soil and long, harsh winters of New England. Many died getting settled.

In adopting New World foods to survive, the colonists focused on ones that resembled familiar European products and provided comparable metabolic sustenance. Numerous similarities in ingredients helped the English to maintain traditional culinary concepts and methods developed for the Old World hearth, a massive fireplace designed for cooking. As much as six feet wide and almost as tall, the colonial hearth dominated a home when it was inside, the case in colder areas, and required a substantial outbuilding when the kitchen was detached, often the situation in the South. The size of the hearth allowed a cook to perform multiple tasks at once, perhaps simmering a soup over a gentle fire, roasting a fowl in front of a brisk blaze, and smoking a ham hung high above the flame. The first colonists often baked in Dutch ovens, an iron kettle with a lid and legs, but they preferred and gradually acquired brick ovens built into the walls of the hearth or outdoor brick bake houses.

The hearth remained central to American cooking until the mid-nineteenth century, when the cast-iron range eventually replaced it. Many cooks actively resisted the new contraption, because like the modern gas or electric range, its oven is inferior to a brick oven in bread baking, it doesn't roast nearly as well as an open, woodburning hearth, and it's incapable of smoking food. The cook gained compensating advantages in her control of temperatures and stovetop operations, but no one cared much about those potentials in earlier times. For British settlers seeking to sustain their way of life, the hearth's breadth of capability was a major strength, reinforcing the cultural continuity in the cooking styles of the mother country and the colonies.

The ultimate success of the colonists ensured that European ideas and practices formed the foundation of American cooking for the next four centuries and beyond. From the beginning, however, differences in ingredients between the New and Old Worlds produced variations in tone that gained in significance as the colonists entrenched themselves and extended their range of settlement. In a hos-

Hungry for white bread, coffee, and sugar, flesh and fowl, I came to America. . . . What I found here, in this land of refugees from hunger and oppression, remains for me a dramatic and ever fascinating story. I found, first of all, the meaning, the consumable, edible meaning, of a simple word, lost in the dictionary among thousands of others—the meaning of the word *abundance.*

ANGELO PELLEGRINI,
THE UNPREJUDICED PALATE
(1948)

Old World grains—oats, millet, wheat, rye—required a careful, patient agriculture that reworked the same fields through the centuries. Those who owned the fields and the mills that ground what was grown in them owned the culture. . . .

A corn culture is more fluid. Corn is more adaptable as both a foodstuff and a crop. Skilled Indian agriculturalists could grow three crops of corn a year, and they could grow it almost anywhere they wanted—here one year and somewhere else the next. Unlike wheat (and similar grains), corn does not require plowed fields; it can be planted around the stumps of trees in freshly cleared plots. . . .

pitable home at last, they increasingly embraced the abundance of a vast and virgin New World and began exploiting its treasures as Native Americans had done before. As attitudes and values shifted, so did American cooking, moving toward an identity of its own that reflected a growing conviction about the links between our destiny as a people and our land of plenty.

The Regional and Cultural Stew

The details of that culinary evolution, unfortunately, are not broadly understood for the country as a whole, particularly in the years before the Civil War. In the new field of culinary history, barely decades old, solid scholarship exists on some regions and times, but no one has produced yet a reliable comprehensive history of American food. That complicates our modest goal of establishing context for the recipe chapters that follow. Sometimes we must infer too much from cookbooks, our primary area of knowledge, leaving us with generalizations that oversimplify the rich complexities of life.

Even with that caveat, two patterns seem clear in the formative period of American cooking. We remained principally English in our tastes long after political independence from the crown, an abiding legacy of the colonial era. At the same time, as the country grew in territory and population, other influences became more pronounced, initially on a local and regional basis. If you look for the most flavorful and enduring food of the day, as we do in our selection of dishes, you see a convergence of contributions from varied lands—Africa, France, Germany, and Mexico as well as from Britain. The best of American cooking has long thrived on the country's regional and cultural diversity.

New Englanders, true to the name, remained stoutly British in their fare as long as the hearth ruled. They favored roasted and "boiled" (simmered) meats, savory pies and puddings, porridges, pork and beans, brown bread made with rye and "Indian" (cornmeal), and salted cod. The rocky soil and short growing season limited fresh produce, but colonial gardeners grew peas, beans, squash, cabbage, carrots, parsnips, pumpkins, and apples, and supplemented their staples with wild fruits and berries. The Yankees learned to fish, and fishing became a principal industry, but they ate little fresh seafood, viewing it as an insubstantial substitute for meat, especially their beloved beef.

The mid-Atlantic colonies shared many culinary traits with New England, but added Dutch and German overtones. Wheat grew better there than farther north, and ended up in pancakes, waffles, noodles, and dumplings as well as bread. From New York to Maryland, residents explored the bounty of the waters and developed a passion for the indigenous shad, crab, and turtle. Pork challenged beef in popularity, and replaced it almost completely on the tables of the Pennsylvania Dutch, religious separatists mainly from Germany who established one of the most distinctive cuisines in the country. While New Englanders and many Southerners ate pork primarily as a flavoring in dishes based on other foods, the Dutch preferred to roast the meat. They also enjoyed the interplay of contrasting flavors, such as fruity and salty, and built an extensive repertory of toothsome soups, pickles, and sweets.

The South prided itself on grand plantation dining, acclaimed at the time and by historians as a high point in our culinary heritage. Guests marveled at both the quantity and the quality of the food, which at one seating might include oysters or turtle soup, cured, smoked ham, roasted duck, a saddle of mutton or venison, a plenitude of vegetables, and for dessert, maybe a choice of pies or tarts and some fruit preserves. The types of food didn't generally surprise northern or English visitors, particularly in Virginia and the rest of the mid-South, but they noticed some unusual dishes and tastes.

Those flourishes came largely from the African slaves in the kitchen, who brought a tropical vitality to southern cooking at an early period. The mistress of the manor instructed her hands on the preparation of British and French dishes, but the cooks ultimately had to rely on their own sense of taste and that hailed from an entirely different place. African cooks knew subtleties of seasoning appropriate to the hot climate of the South, developed a fine, unprejudiced feel for indigenous ingredients, and introduced foods imported from their continent, including okra, black-eyed peas, eggplant, sorghum, and sesame. They had raised yams in Africa, giving them an understanding of the indigenous sweet potato, and many arrived experienced in the secrets of rice cultivation and cooking.

Their knowledge of rice created the plantation economy of coastal South Carolina, where the grain reigned, and contributed significantly to the development of a cosmopolitan local cuisine. Once the largest and wealthiest city in the South, and a worldly port, Charleston attracted French Huguenots and Sephardic Jews from Portugal and Spain in addition to the original English and Barbadian settlers and their African slaves. The blend of peoples produced a vibrant Creole cooking that featured, among a wealth of ingredients, rice, okra, tomatoes, greens, and anything that lived in the coastal waters. Some of the most popular dishes would have found little favor in Boston or London.

This was even more true of New Orleans and Cajun fare, both similar to that of Charleston except for a heavier Gallic influence. African cooks added a lot to the pot again, and early Spanish residents and later Italian immigrants threw in special touches, but country French cooking formed the basis of the brew. From gumbo to jambalaya, étouffée to rémoulade, whether it comes from the city or the bayou, it's fine Creole cuisine of the New World, as closely related to the food of Martinique as to what's served up the river in Memphis or across the sea in Marseilles.

In New Mexico, the Spanish brought hearth cooking to the Southwest before any English settled on the Atlantic seaboard, but this was the last area to be incorporated into the United States where the method had much history. The Aztecs in Mexico had acclimated the Spanish to chiles, corn tortillas, and tamales, and seventeenth-century settlers took these and other foods with them to New Mexico, where the Pueblos taught them about similar foods. Later generations of Spanish and Mexican colonists carried similar dishes and seasonings to other areas of the Southwest, from Texas to California.

Southern frontier families pushed as far west as Texas by the early nineteenth century, and in the same period, their Yankee counterparts followed the Ohio

Much has been made of the importance of corn in sustaining the original colonies, but little if anything about its immediate and subversive effect on the newborn American character. If there are no peasants in this country, it is because a peasant is wedded—as his family before him and after him—to a particular piece of land. In America, however, a man could take a bag of seed corn and an ax and head into the wilderness, to be there "as much a great lord as the other."

John Thorne, *Serious Pig* (1996)

River from western Pennsylvania into the Midwest breadbasket, which became a bastion of hearty farm cooking. A new wave of European immigrants joined both groups of pioneers, helping to swell the population of the country tenfold between 1820 and 1920. About half of the immigrants came from Germany, Austria, Ireland, and Italy, with the rest scattered more broadly among Russia, Poland, Britain, Scandinavia, Greece, and other lands. All the newcomers added elements to American cooking in varying degrees, though many tended at first to stay separate from the mainstream and to maintain their own ethnic and national food traditions to promote cultural cohesion.

> All kinds of stimulating and heating substances; high-seasoned food; rich dishes; the free use of flesh; and even the excess of aliment; all, more or less,—and some to a very great degree—increase the concupiscent excitability and sensibility of the genital organs, and augment their influence on the functions of organic life, and on the intellectual and moral faculties. SEXUAL DESIRE, again, in turn, throws its influence over the whole domain of the nerves of organic life. . . ; and when it kindles into a passion, its influence is so extensive and powerful, that it disturbs and disorders all the functions of the system.
>
> Sylvester Graham, *A Lecture to Young Men* (1834)

The Rocky Mountains posed a barrier to further western expansion, but settlers from various backgrounds breached the passes in increasing numbers by the 1840s. On the Pacific coast, they found a fresh cornucopia of foods, including olives, figs, lemons, and Old World grapes planted earlier by the Spanish, and tasty new varieties of oysters, crabs, and salmon. With its favorable soil and sunny clime, California developed over time into the produce capital of the country, a fount of salads, wines, and creative cookery. The Pacific Northwest and Alaska helped rejuvenate seafood cooking, supplementing the depleted supplies and conventional wisdom of the Atlantic coast.

Within two decades of the opening of the Oregon Trail, Chinese immigrants arrived by water from the opposite direction, the first stage of a continuing Asian influx that has introduced the country to a range of strikingly different ingredients and flavors. Most Americans ignored the Asian influence for decades, but began embracing it in the mid-twentieth century, initially on the West Coast and in Hawaii. Still gaining momentum, the Asian contribution to our cooking may someday match that from Africa, especially in the impact on our sense of seasoning.

From the original English foundation, and Atlantic seaboard roots, American food had broadened its cultural and regional base substantially by the turn of the twenty-first century. The evolution enriched our repertory, creating the potential for a distinctive and resonant American cuisine. We stumbled along the way, however, in the second half of the nineteenth century, just when the range replaced the hearth at the center of our kitchens. That unsettling transition coincided with other major economic and social changes that exacerbated the uncertainty and produced serious conflicts in priorities.

Science, Technology, and Cereal

The Industrial Revolution transformed the whole world in the nineteenth and twentieth centuries, but its impact on food struck earlier and heavier in the United States than anywhere else. The nation's first railroad started hauling commercial goods in 1830, speeding the distribution of produce and meat among different areas. Americans began mechanizing agriculture later in that decade, when Cyrus McCormick introduced the reaper and John Deere crafted a steel plow that could turn the grass-matted sod of the plains. The era of refrigerated storage and transportation gained momentum in the same period with the invention of manufactured ice, which accelerated the spread of home iceboxes.

Commercial canning developed even earlier, but didn't take off big until after the Civil War, when the discovery of steam-packing methods boosted production potential. Up to that time, the American cook spent much of her workday processing foods—maintaining the kitchen garden, putting up vegetables and preserves, milking cows, churning butter, making cheese, baking bread, corning beef, and much more. She operated a home food factory, a responsibility that a burgeoning food industry began coveting in the last decades of the nineteenth century. Henry J. Heinz capitalized quickly on the new canning technology, and the Van Camp, Franco-American, and Campbell companies followed his lead shortly. The new manufacturers soon sold more canned goods in the United States than foreign counterparts produced in the rest of the world combined.

Other aspects of food processing moved just as quickly from the farm to the factory. Meatpackers took on butchering and sausage making, dairies bottled milk and packaged butter and cheese, and commercial bakeries made our daily bread. Sugar prices dropped substantially in the last decades of the nineteenth century, decreasing a reliance on molasses and homemade sorghum, stimulating a huge refining sector, and suckling America's sweet tooth. By 1900, the food-processing industry accounted for a remarkable 20 percent of the nation's manufacturing output, signaling its rapid emergence as one of the biggest of the country's big businesses.

The transition to an industrial, urban society distanced the population increasingly from the sources and true nature of food, and produced changes in work and lifestyle that affected cooks even more directly. Women found attractive new opportunities outside the home and began taking jobs far from the kitchen, rejoicing in their liberation from the conventions and tedium of nineteenth-century housekeeping. The automobile added horsepower to all the transformations taking place, accelerating both industrial distribution and the sense of personal independence.

The scientific knowledge that propelled the technological and social changes also influenced our mode of thinking about diet and nutrition. Before the Civil War, American writers who dealt with these subjects generally adopted a stern moralistic perspective, arguing that what we ate and drank reflected our ethical values and affected everything from our family happiness to our personal salvation. The most ardent crusader of the day, Sylvester Graham, condemned the use of any preparation method or seasoning that was intended to enhance the sensual pleasure of eating, denounced meat for encouraging sexual excess, and urged abstinence from all stimulants and "heating substances," including alcohol, coffee, tea, mustard, pepper, and peppermint. If we live to eat, he said, we "darken the moral sense, and blindly pursue a course which inevitably leads to the worst of evils."

After the Civil War, science replaced religion as the tool for analyzing diet and nutrition, though much of the old message survived the change in methodology. The early nutritionists—who first called themselves "domestic scientists" and then "home economists"—zealously attacked foods that were spicy, foreign, fried, or otherwise "indigestible." Their biological and chemical analyses seem

The use of condiments is unquestionably a strong auxiliary to the formation of a habit of using intoxicating drinks. . . . The false appetite aroused by the use of food that "burns and stings," craves something less insipid than pure cold water to keep up the fever the food has excited. . . . A more serious reason why high seasonings lead to intemperance, is in the perversion of the use of the sense of taste . . . [which] was given us to distinguish between wholesome and unwholesome foods, and cannot be used for merely sensuous gratification, without debasing and making of it a gross thing.

Ella Eaton Kellogg, Science in the Kitchen (1910)

naive and incomplete today—as those of our age may well seem in the future—but over time they made considerable headway in convincing the nation that it was sinfully unhealthy to choose food on the basis of taste rather than nutritional content. This was, and has remained, like our closely related experiment with Prohibition, a characteristically American way of thinking about eating and drinking.

> **One of the stupidest things in an earnest but stupid school of culinary thought is that each of the three daily meals should be "balanced." . . . A balanced diet in almost any well-meaning institution is a plan for meals which means that at each of the three daily feedings the patient is given a set amount of carbohydrates and protein and starch, and a certain amount of International Units, and a certain number of vitamins in correct ratio to the equally certain amount of minerals, and so on and so forth. . . . Of course, this sad rigmarole varies a little in every institution, but it can be considered either a proof of democracy or a shocking human blindness, that intrinsically it is the same at the Arizona Biltmore and your county hospital.**
>
> M.F.K. Fisher, *How to Cook a Wolf* (1942)

The developers of convenience foods and the professionally trained nutritionists joined forces by the early twentieth century, united by a desire to change the American diet. That strange but effective alliance—described in vivid detail by historian Harvey Levenstein in *Revolution at the Table* (1988) and *Paradox of Plenty* (1993)—achieved its first major success in the cereal business. A couple of brothers named Kellogg, and a rival named Post, totally transformed the American breakfast—formerly one of the two major meals of the day—through a combination of health hokum, convenience claims, clever packaging, and massive advertising.

The Kelloggs developed a version of granola and "Toasted Corn Flakes" originally for a Seventh-Day Adventist health retreat in Battle Creek, Michigan, which traced its roots in part to the teachings of Sylvester Graham. Charles W. Post, once a patient at the sanatorium, began his business with a health-food substitute for coffee that he called "Postum" and moved on to "Grape-Nuts," which he marketed as a "brain food" that just might cure consumption and malaria. The catchy brand names helped sales, as did vigorous competitive marketing, lessons quickly absorbed throughout the food industry. Other companies in the trade also took note when William Kellogg started pumping up his cereal with sugar, one of the earliest of many additives used over the years to make highly processed foods seem palatable.

The growing mass media learned quickly to cater to their advertisers, and government agencies found reasons of their own to support the interests of major manufacturers and agribusiness, building a powerful coalition in favor of a diet that paid scant attention to the pleasure of eating. In the circumstance, the American cook faced a formidable challenge in maintaining the integrity of her craft. The speed and ease of packaged foods seduced her, the health concerns frightened her, the advertising dollars swayed her, and everywhere she turned, someone presented a new reason not to care about traditional cooking. The amazing thing is not what we lost in this period, already well bemoaned by other writers, but what survived an onslaught on taste unprecedented on earth.

In every corner of the country, cooks refused to give up their most cherished regional and ethnic dishes. They may have reserved them for special occasions, or may have altered them in some ways for convenience or health purposes, but they kept the heritage alive for future generations. Beyond that act of willfulness, they even made impressive new contributions to the legacy, applying an American bent to some foods not broadly popular before, such as fish and seafood, sandwiches, and salads. Home cooking faltered in its sense of continuity and direction, but the cooking fires never died.

Turning Another Century

As the twentieth century came to a close, signs abounded that American cooking had weathered the turbulent changes of the post–Civil War era and had begun a rebound that could lead it to new heights. That remains an optimistic assessment at this point, but it comes from a ground-level familiarity with what's happening, from our experience as home cooks who grew up during the crest of the convenience craze and have witnessed a steady revival of real food. Statistics, surveys, and such may or may not support our hopeful view, but we know the promising transformations that have occurred and the resulting potentials simply because we're active cooks.

Convenience today no longer resides solely in the can, the box, the frozen dinner, and the fast-food take-out sack. The technology that first gave us the iron range and mass-produced food has now provided new tools that speed and ease authentic home cooking, from good, affordable cutlery to all kinds of electric gadgets. Just the food processor alone has taken considerable time and tedium out of hundreds of preparations. Outside the kitchen itself, we enjoy backyard cooking equipment that restores some of the potentials of the old hearth. Americans are now smoking food at home again with ease, and getting crusty, juicy outcomes from high-heat, open-air grilling that approximate the results from true roasting, albeit with smaller cuts of meat.

A similar but more sweeping change has expanded the ready availability of truly fresh and other superior ingredients. The railroad helped undermine the seasonality and regionality of ingredients, leading to a serious loss in freshness and flavor, but jet air transportation now allows us to take advantage of the original opportunity for a broader selection of food without suffering the undesirable consequences. Inland seafood markets sell live lobsters from Maine year-round and softshell crabs from Maryland in May. Anyone with a telephone and a credit card can mail-order earthy morels from Michigan in the spring, juicy figs from California in the summer, just-picked New Mexico green chiles in the fall, and ripe, heady Texas grapefruit in the winter—all delivered directly to the front door. Just as easily, anywhere we live, we can get stone-ground grits from the South, full-bodied maple syrup from New England, handcrafted Cheddar from Wisconsin, and Native-style smoked salmon from Alaska.

Equally important, a growing number of farmers' markets, and even some grocery stores, are restoring seasonality and regionality throughout the country. We no longer have to accept produce grown for durability, looks, and uniform shipping size rather than flavor, and we're even seeing a reversal of the long trend toward the reduction of varieties being cultivated. The good news today is old news—about heirloom seeds, kitchen gardens, and sustainable agriculture—not the more recent preoccupation with increased shelf life and cosmetic hybrids.

Home cooks owe a major debt to contemporary American restaurant chefs for stimulating and supporting these developments. Larry Forgione, Mark Miller, Paul Prudhomme, Stephan Pyles, Alice Waters, Jasper White, and many others—following up on the earlier lead of James Beard and Julia Child—have reminded us

Slowly, it seems, the experts are beginning to acknowledge that the relationship between nutrition and health may be modified by so many other factors—individual biological makeup in particular—that few rules are universally applicable. Hopefully, this will lead both to a rethinking of the role of government in telling people what to eat and—more important, for they are still the main source of nutritional information—more restrictions on food vendors' ability to alarm and deceive the public by distorting the health benefits of their products. . . . Modified ideas about what constitutes a healthy diet may take hold, allowing Americans to—in a variation of the old saw—have their good food and eat it too.

of the value of fresh and flavorful foods. Their emphasis on taste and texture provides a powerful counterbalance to the dual influences of the food-processing industry and the health authorities who insist we should cook and eat as their notions of nutrition dictate.

The nutrition advisers differ substantially among themselves anyway, presenting a Babel of opinions that would flummox the most determined ascetic. The vast majority of Americans, we're sure, applaud the fact that our nation has the highest level of nutritional awareness in the world, and most of us heed the guidance to varying degrees, but many also seem to feel, as we do, that life is invariably short no matter how long we live, and now is the time to celebrate it with family and friends. That means a meal, and one driven by joy rather than denial.

Jet travel abroad has encouraged that gustatory attitude, and car and plane travel within the states has broadened our appreciation of regional American foods. Until recently, few of us knew much about the culinary specialties of different regions, a fact that obscured our understanding of the depth and vitality of American cooking overall. Sheila Hibben addressed the subject in the budding years of the automobile age, in *The National Cookbook* (1932), but it wasn't until the 1970s and 1980s that we began to probe the field as fully as cookbook authors did more than a century earlier, between 1820 and 1860. Now we enjoy a wealth of resources on the many varied regional styles, just when all of us for the first time have ready access to the ingredients that make the local dishes of other areas special.

As we head into the fifth century of American cooking, we're starting to see a confluence of streams from the different regions, a recognition of the commonalities of experience that have produced a richly diverse culinary legacy. The question of whether there's an American cuisine may be an obtuse one, to be pondered with the number of angels who can stand on the tip of a toothpick, but the best of our home cooking compares favorably with the same from any other country. It's hearty, earthy cooking based on the bounty of the land, strong regional roots, and a lasting debt to early influences from Britain, France, Germany, Africa, and Mexico. It's a cooking that thrives in spite of convenience concerns, the busyness of our lives, and fears about food, that draws its strength from the same universal human hungers behind great Italian or Chinese cooking—a passion for crafting and sharing an enjoyable meal.

This would certainly represent a giant step toward resolving the paradox of a people surrounded by abundance who are unable to enjoy it. But then again, these are difficult times for optimists.

Harvey Levenstein,
Paradox of Plenty
(1993)

FLAPJACKS, GRITS, HASH, AND OTHER

Hearty Ways to Start the Day

AMERICANS USED TO YELP THROUGH BREAKFAST RATHER than yawn. They rose early to take care of everyday chores, and then came to the table ready to devour half of the farm. Depending on where they lived, they loaded up on corn cakes, buckwheats, hot biscuits, cornmeal mush, fried salt pork, sausage, scrapple, country ham, beefsteaks, buffalo tongue, fried fish, shrimp, frog legs and, to wash it down, everything from mint juleps to creamy, fresh milk. A big breakfast was more American than apple pie, partially because the pie constituted only one of the many traditional morning treats.

In sharp contrast with the present, the first meal of the day usually surpassed the last in both size and variety. Throughout most of our history, until the last decades of the nineteenth century, Americans ate their dinner in the early afternoon and kept their evening supper relatively light and simple. They woke hungry, eager to break the fast of the night and fuel themselves for a day of labor. When jobs started taking people away from the home in increasing numbers, and most occupations became less physically taxing, Americans switched the main meal to the end of the working day and reduced the sustenance needed in the morn.

The economic and metabolic changes coincided, to the great fortune of the food industry, with the arrival of the boxed breakfast. Promoted initially by a zany band of health faddists, commercial cereals zoomed into popularity at the turn of the twentieth century, offering speed and convenience along with putative powers to treat a range of ills, from sluggish brains to loose teeth. While some Americans refused to downsize breakfast to anything less than bacon and eggs, or a short stack of pancakes, a growing majority got a quick and meager fill from a package of processed grain, our modern equivalent of the "Continental" breakfast. When we yearned for a return to the big morning meals of the past, the occasion usually became a weekend brunch, often featuring fancy egg dishes and other frilly concoctions far removed from the hearty fare of our ancestors.

As we turn the next century, the resurgence of interest in flavorful food offers hope for the revival of a real American breakfast. Few of us in our sedentary age can handle the quantity of old, but we can learn to brighten our mornings with the invigorating, bracing tastes once enjoyed as the proper way to wake. Anyone raised on convenience breakfasts will find a new day dawning in these American home classics.

Georgia Bits and Grits Waffles

SERVES 4 TO 6

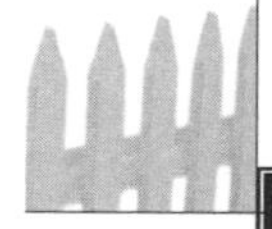

Not Waffling Around

When Katherine Hepburn starred opposite Spencer Tracy in the film *Woman of the Year,* her screen character tried to charm his by preparing waffles, with hilariously bad results. American audiences would have been sympathetic because waffles were widely viewed as a special-occasion offering, just difficult enough to require a little devoted effort.

The introduction of electric waffle irons around the turn of the twentieth century eased the challenges without erasing them. In some cases the new tool may just have spurred cooks to come up with more elaborate preparations. The first edition of Fannie Farmer's *The Boston Cooking-School Cook Book* (1896) provides three variations on the basic recipe, including one made with rice and another with a yeast batter that rises overnight. Several decades later, Irma Rombauer expanded the options substantially in early editions of the *Joy of Cooking,* suggesting additions such as raisins and chopped nuts, sliced bananas, orange juice, grated cheese, diced ham, and chocolate. Not to be outdone, Louis P. De Gouy in *The Gold Cook Book* (1947) blends in cooked chicken, chopped meat, and flaked codfish, accompanying these versions respectively with mushroom sauce, curry sauce, and scrambled eggs.

Made originally with long-handled fireplace waffle irons that date back to medieval Europe, waffles gained an early toehold in the New World primarily among Dutch settlers. Later, the dish secured a prominent place in southern cooking, as an accompaniment to fried and creamed chicken, ham, and even smothered catfish. This is a southern breakfast version, crunchy with grits and bacon bits. On a summer morning, accompany it with slices of juicy peaches with a drizzle of sweet cream. The rest of the year, we spoon on peach preserves.

2 cups unbleached all-purpose flour
2 tablespoons sugar
1¼ teaspoons baking powder
1 teaspoon salt
¾ cup stone-ground grits
¾ cup (1½ sticks) unsalted butter
4 large eggs, separated
1¼ cups milk
6 to 8 slices crisp cooked bacon, crumbled
Unsalted butter
Peach preserves, cane syrup, or real maple syrup

Sift together the flour, sugar, and baking powder and reserve.

Bring 4 cups of water to a boil in a medium saucepan over high heat. Stir in the salt and then the grits, whisking constantly until the mixture comes back to a boil. Reduce the heat to low and continue cooking, stirring occasionally, until very thick and creamy, about 30 minutes. Stir in the butter until melted and scrape the grits mixture into a large bowl.

Stir in the egg yolks, one at a time, mixing well after each addition. Add the flour mixture, mixing only until combined, followed by the milk. The batter should be thin. In another bowl, beat the egg whites with a mixer until stiff but still glossy.

Heat a greased waffle iron. Stir the bacon into the batter and fold in the egg whites. Cook the waffles, one at a time, following the directions of the waffle-iron manufacturer. They should be crisp and golden when done.

Hold the waffles in a warm oven until all are finished, or even tastier, serve them individually as they are ready. Accompany them with butter and preserves.

Narragansett Jonnycakes

Makes about 30 thin cakes, enough for 4 to 6 main-dish servings

The Narragansett people of Rhode Island—like other Native Americans—cooked a version of these basic corn cakes long before Roger Williams settled his flock in Providence. The English colonists everywhere adopted the notion because it fit comfortably in their own experience. Bakers made other types of unleavened hearth breads back in the mother country, and corn—however new and strange—bore some similarities to oats as a grain. The colonists even named the cake, apparently, after an oat-based bread from Lancashire called "jannock." The term transmuted into "johnny cake" or "journey cake" in other British colonies, but Rhode Island has always spelled it differently and remained passionate about the purest form of the cake, made with little more than great cornmeal and water. The state legislature has decreed that authentic jonnycakes must be based on the local White Cap flint corn, but other superior stone-ground meals also produce a tasty version of the thin, crunchy cakes. Butter enhances the rich corn flavor, though more than a dab of syrup will drown the forthright taste and texture.

1½ cups stone-ground cornmeal, preferably from White Cap flint corn (see Ingredient Tip)

1 teaspoon salt

1½ cups boiling water

¼ cup milk

Bacon drippings, sausage drippings, vegetable oil, or a combination for pan-frying

Unsalted butter, softened

Real maple syrup, optional

Preheat the oven to 325°F.

Pour the cornmeal into a heatproof medium bowl. (We use stainless steel with a spout for easy pouring of the batter later.) Stir in the salt. Place the bowl in the oven for 5 to 8 minutes, to warm the meal through and toast it lightly. Remove it from the oven as soon as it begins to deepen in color.

Pour the boiling water into the warm cornmeal, about ½ cup at a time. Be cautious of the hot bowl. Stir vigorously, eliminating any lumps. Mix in the milk, then continue stirring the batter for a couple of additional minutes. The batter will resemble an unappealingly thin gruel at this point.

Warm a griddle, preferably, or a large heavy skillet over medium heat. Well-seasoned cast-iron or a sturdy nonstick surface works best. Add the cooking fat to the griddle, just enough to coat the surface with a thin film. Pour the batter by

No Johnny-Come-Latelys

Hardly any corn-cake cook in Rhode Island dares dispute the Society for the Propagation of the Jonnycake Tradition about the importance of White Cap flint cornmeal, but people in the state do differ about other parts of the preparation. In 1957, locally born culinary authority Sidney Dean, in *Cooking American*, characterized the main camps as Eastern Shore and Western Shore. Westerners, he said, favored a thin batter like ours, while Easterners reduced the water and upped the cornmeal to create half-inch-thick cakes.

Outside of Rhode Island, johnnycakes often gained additional ingredients and went by a variety of names, from pone to hoecakes. The first published recipes, in Amelia Simmons's 1796 *American Cookery*, call for flour in one option and molasses and shortening in another in addition to "Indian meal," an old term for cornmeal. Well before then, in the rice lands of colonial South Carolina, cooks started mixing prepared rice into the cornmeal, and a century after Simmons, in Wisconsin, one enthusiastic cook developed a "wedding johnnycake" boasting sour cream, butter, baking soda, raisins, and citron, reputed to be affordable only "if one does not marry more than once in a lifetime." The most common enrichments everywhere became eggs, flour, leavening, and buttermilk, all of which began to twist the tradition and turned the earthy, unpretentious johnny into a puffed-up pancake.

tablespoonfuls onto the griddle, leaving several inches between the dollops. The batter will spread immediately into thin cakes about 3 inches in diameter. (The batter should bubble merrily. If it splatters menacingly instead, the griddle is too hot. Reduce the heat before continuing.) Cook the cakes until the batter appears quite firm, about 3 minutes. Turn carefully and cook the cakes on the other side until medium brown and crispy, 2 to 3 additional minutes. Repeat with the remaining batter, adding a bit more water to the batter if it thickens and more fat to the griddle as necessary. (While the cakes are best right from the griddle, you can keep them warm in a low oven on baking sheets while you finish making the entire batch of cakes. Don't stack the cakes until serving time.)

Serve the jonnycakes stacked on warm plates, topped with plenty of butter. Pass maple syrup separately to drizzle lightly over the cakes, if desired.

INGREDIENT TIP: Rhode Island's White Cap flint corn is a sturdy but low-yielding native variety distinctively different from the feed-corn and sweet-corn hybrids of the Midwest. You can order the flavorful meal by mail from a handful of Rhode Island mills, including Gray's Mill in Adamsville (508-636-6075). Keep stone-ground cornmeal in the freezer for longest life.

Buttermilk Flapjacks with Warm Fruit Sauce

Makes about sixteen 4-inch pancakes, enough to serve 4 or more

An ancient form of flatbread, originally as simple in ingredients as a johnnycake, pancakes crossed the Atlantic in various forms with settlers from all corners of Europe. Over time, American cooks put their own stamp on the dish, flavoring it with local products, fluffing it up with baking powder and other leavening agents, and eventually turning an all-occasion bread into the nation's signature breakfast specialty. The pancake's place in the culture, and its power to inspire the imagination, leap out in the names it acquired—flapjacks, slapjacks, flannel cakes, hot cakes, griddle cakes, flatcars, slappers, and heavenly hots, to mention a few. This classic version uses buttermilk for its light tang and browning abilities, and a little cornmeal for crunch. Rather than adding blueberries or other fruit to the batter, as is often done, we opt for an intense fruit sauce on the side, and always insist on pure maple syrup.

FRUIT SAUCE

3 cups blueberries, thin-sliced strawberries, or peaches, fresh or frozen

2 to 4 tablespoons sugar

Fresh lemon juice

PANCAKES

1½ cups unbleached all-purpose flour

¼ cup stone-ground cornmeal

1 teaspoon baking powder

½ teaspoon baking soda

½ teaspoon salt

1 tablespoon unsalted butter, melted

1 egg, separated, and the yolk lightly whisked

1¾ to 2 cups buttermilk

Vegetable oil for pan-frying

1 to 2 teaspoons bacon drippings, optional

Unsalted butter, softened

Real maple syrup, warmed

Prepare the sauce, combining the blueberries, 2 tablespoons of the sugar, and ¼ cup of water in a medium saucepan. Bring the mixture to a simmer over medium-high heat. Cook until the sugar melts into a syrup and the fruit is soft, 5 to 10 minutes. Taste the sauce and add an additional 1 to 2 tablespoons of sugar if needed to round out the fruit flavor. Dissolve any additional sugar into the sauce before removing it from the heat. Stir in a few drops of lemon juice, just enough to cut the sweetness and liven up the fruitiness. Keep the sauce warm.

Prepare the pancakes, first stirring together the flour, cornmeal, baking powder, baking soda, and salt in a medium bowl, preferably one with a spout for pouring. Scrape in the melted butter and stir the mixture until the butter disappears into the dry ingredients.

Bread I at first made of pure Indian meal and salt, genuine hoe-cakes, which I baked before my fire out of doors on a shingle or the end of a stick of timber sawed off in building my house; but it was wont to get smoked and to have a piny flavor. I tried flour also; but have at last found a mixture of rye and Indian meal most convenient and agreeable. In cold weather it was no little amusement to bake several small loaves of this in succession, tending and turning them as carefully as an Egyptian his hatching eggs. They were a real cereal fruit which I ripened, and they had to my senses a fragrance like that of other noble fruits, which I kept in as long as possible by wrapping them in cloths.

Henry David Thoreau, Walden (1854)

TECHNIQUE TIP:
If you have a bowl with a pouring spout, use it for mixing and pouring pancake batter, letting the batter stand just briefly after stirring it together. When you use baking powder or soda for leavening, avoid mixing the batter too thoroughly, leaving slight streaks of dry ingredients still visible. Cook the pancakes in the thinnest film of oil, and replenish it between batches. Pancakes should sizzle and hiss when they hit the griddle or skillet. For a pretest, flick a few drops of water over the hot cooking surface, adjusting the temperature until they sizzle and evaporate instantly. Never use chilled butter or syrup, and for optimum luxuriance, heat the syrup. While pancakes are quick and easy, make them when there's enough time to enjoy them. When we were kids, families had "pancake mornings," typically a Saturday or Sunday when everyone was home and Mom or Dad would leisurely cook up batch after batch of golden cakes. It's not a bad idea to resurrect, even if it's for Monday supper.

Pour the egg yolk and 1¾ cups of the buttermilk into the dry ingredients and mix until lightly combined. If the batter doesn't seem easily pourable, add up to the remaining ¼ cup of buttermilk. Beat the egg white until soft peaks form and fold the egg white into the batter.

Warm a griddle, preferably, or a large heavy skillet over medium heat. Pour a thin film of oil on the griddle. If you wish, add ¼ to ½ teaspoon of the bacon drippings to the oil for a heartier flavor. Pour or spoon out the batter onto the hot griddle, where it should sizzle and hiss. A generous 3 tablespoons of batter will make a 4-inch pancake. Make as many cakes at a time as you can fit on the surface without crowding.

Flip the pancakes just once, after 1 to 2 minutes when their top surface is covered with tiny bubbles but before all the bubbles pop. The pancakes are done when the second side is golden brown, an additional 1 to 2 minutes. Repeat with the remaining batter, adding a bit more oil and optional bacon drippings to the griddle as needed.

Serve immediately with butter and the fruit sauce. Maple syrup is the perfect addition, but use it judiciously to enhance rather than dominate the pancakes.

Rice and Cornmeal Griddle Cakes with Nutmeg Syrup

MAKES ABOUT SIXTEEN 4-INCH PANCAKES, ENOUGH TO SERVE 4 OR MORE

In the lowcountry of South Carolina, corn and rice got together early as a natural pair in pancakes and similar dishes, with both benefiting from the match. As rice cultivation spread west, so did the combination, finding a featured place as far from home as Milwaukee, where *"The Settlement" Cook Book* of 1903 recommended this American style of griddle cake to its audience of newly arrived immigrants. For optimum results, use a fragrant rice such as Texmati. Pumpkin Chip Preserves (294) and Skillet Asparagus (254) on the side fill out a big breakfast.

NUTMEG SYRUP

6 tablespoons (¾ stick) unsalted butter

1½ teaspoons ground nutmeg

2 cups light corn syrup

1 tablespoon white wine

Pinch of salt

GRIDDLE CAKES

½ cup stone-ground cornmeal

½ cup all-purpose unbleached flour

¾ teaspoon salt

½ teaspoon baking soda

⅛ teaspoon ground nutmeg

1½ cups cooked rice

2 tablespoons unsalted butter, melted

1 egg, separated

2 cups buttermilk

Vegetable oil for pan-frying

1 to 2 teaspoons bacon drippings, optional

Prepare the syrup, first melting the butter in a small saucepan over medium-low heat. Stir in the nutmeg, cooking just until fragrant. Mix in the corn syrup, wine, and salt, and heat through. Keep the syrup warm. (The syrup can be made a day or two in advance and refrigerated, covered. Reheat before proceeding.)

Prepare the pancakes, first stirring together the cornmeal, flour, salt, baking soda, and nutmeg in a medium bowl, preferably one with a spout for pouring. In another bowl, mash together the rice and the melted butter with a large fork to break up the rice a bit. Add the egg yolk to the rice and continue mashing until the rice grains are mostly broken but not smashed smooth.

Beat the egg white until soft peaks form and reserve it.

Pour the buttermilk into the dry ingredients and mix until well combined. Stir in the rice mixture, then fold the egg white into the batter.

Warm a griddle, preferably, or a large heavy skillet over medium heat. A sturdy nonstick surface or well-seasoned cast iron works best. Pour a thin film of oil on the griddle. If you wish, add ¼ to ½ teaspoon of the bacon drippings to the oil for a heartier flavor. Pour or spoon out the batter onto the hot griddle, where it should sizzle and hiss. A generous 3 tablespoons of batter will make a 4-inch pancake. Make as many cakes at a time as you can fit on the surface without crowding.

Flip the pancakes just once, after 1 to 2 minutes when their top surface is covered with tiny bubbles but before all of the bubbles pop. The pancakes are done when the second side is golden brown, an additional 1 to 2 minutes. Repeat with the remaining batter, adding a bit more oil and optional bacon drippings to the griddle as needed.

Serve immediately with the syrup.

Buckwheats

MAKES ABOUT TWELVE 4-INCH PANCAKES, ENOUGH TO SERVE 4 OR MORE

Probably brought to the colonies by Dutch settlers, buckwheats became the most popular of all breakfast cakes in nineteenth-century America and then vanished almost completely in the modern rush for convenience. They aren't complicated to make, but good ones demand slow, overnight fermentation of the batter, accomplished in the past with a sourdough starter that was used and freshened daily over a winter of robust eating. Starting the batter the night before rewards you with a gutsy and ethereal pancake, nutty, tangy, and toothsome. Buckwheats are often dressed with molasses, sorghum syrup, or buckwheat honey, but maple syrup and butter also work well. For added crunch, top them with spoonfuls of chopped walnuts.

"NIGHT BEFORE" INGREDIENTS

- 1¼ cups milk, heated to lukewarm
- 1 teaspoon active dry yeast, about ½ envelope
- 1 cup buckwheat flour
- ½ cup unbleached all-purpose flour
- 2 tablespoons stone-ground cornmeal
- 2 teaspoons brown sugar, optional
- ½ teaspoon salt

"MORNING" INGREDIENTS

- 1 egg, separated
- ½ teaspoon baking soda
- 1 tablespoon unsalted butter, melted

- Vegetable oil for pan-frying
- 1 to 2 teaspoons bacon or sausage drippings, optional
- Unsalted butter, softened
- Real maple syrup or sorghum syrup, or molasses, or honey, warmed

Begin the pancakes the night before you plan to serve them. Pour the milk into a medium bowl, preferably one with a spout for pouring. Stir in the yeast and set it aside briefly until it begins to bubble. Stir in both flours, cornmeal, brown sugar, if using, and salt. Cover the bowl with a towel and refrigerate it overnight.

In the morning, let the bowl sit at room temperature while you get the remaining ingredients together and set out plates and flatware. Beat the egg white until soft peaks form and reserve it.

Mix into the batter the egg yolk, baking soda, and enough water to make the batter pourable, about ¼ cup or a bit more. Scrape in the melted butter and stir the mixture until the butter disappears into the ingredients. Fold the egg white into the batter.

Warm a griddle, preferably, or a large heavy skillet over medium heat. Pour a thin film of oil on the griddle. If you wish, add ¼ to ½ teaspoon of the bacon or sausage drippings to the oil for a heartier flavor. Pour or spoon out the batter onto the hot

The American species [of pancake] is a good three whoops and a holler removed from the European variety. On the other side of the water, pancakes are either dessert or the main dish of luncheon. The American alone has discovered that the offspring of a happy marriage between a hot surface and a batch of batter is the proper adornment of the breakfast table. His uncanny insight into these spiritual truths may arise from the fact that maple syrup is a strictly American institution. Odd kinds of maple trees do grow in foreign parts, but the sugar maple, that graceful and yet businesslike vegetable, decided long ago to stick to that side of the Atlantic where the inhabitants would eventually have the sense to bore holes in its trunk.

GEORGE RECTOR,
DINE AT HOME WITH RECTOR
(1934)

griddle, where it should sizzle and hiss. Two to 3 tablespoons of batter will make a 3- to 4-inch pancake. Make as many cakes at a time as you can fit on the surface without crowding.

Flip the pancakes just once, after 1 to 2 minutes when their top surface is covered with bubbles but before all of the bubbles pop. (The bubbles will be fewer and larger for buckwheats than for wheat-flour pancakes, looking more like those of Swiss cheese.) The pancakes are done when the second side is golden brown, an additional 1 to 2 minutes. Repeat with the remaining batter, adding a bit more oil and optional drippings to the griddle as needed.

Serve immediately with butter and syrup.

Shirred Eggs with Indiana Farm Breakfast Sausage

Serves 4

Fried, scrambled, or turned into an omelet, eggs seem the essence of an American breakfast. They assumed that leading role, however, only toward the turn of the twentieth century, when they became more widely available. Before then, much of the limited supply of the barnyard went into baking. John Mariani, in *The Dictionary of American Food and Drink* (1994), says the term "shirred eggs" dates to 1883 and is a peculiarly American way of describing eggs cooked in a mold. We serve this simple but flavorful version with ground-pork breakfast sausage, a Midwest favorite with an English lineage.

FARM SAUSAGE

- 1½ tablespoons unsalted butter
- ¼ cup minced onion
- 1½ pounds pork shoulder, twice-ground by your butcher with all of its fat
- 1 tablespoon crumbled dried sage
- 1 teaspoon salt
- 1 teaspoon freshly milled black pepper
- ½ teaspoon dried thyme
- ½ teaspoon dried marjoram
- ½ teaspoon paprika
- ⅛ to ¼ teaspoon cayenne pepper

SHIRRED EGGS

- 2 tablespoons unsalted butter, softened
- 2 tablespoons dried bread crumbs
- 4 large eggs
- Hot pepper sauce, such as Tabasco, optional
- ¼ cup whipping cream or half-and-half
- Salt and freshly milled black pepper
- Paprika

At least 1 night, and up to several days before you plan to serve the dish, prepare the sausage. Melt the butter in a small skillet over medium-low heat. Add the onion and cover and sweat for about 5 minutes, until the onion is well softened. Scrape the butter-onion mixture into a large bowl. Add the remaining ingredients and mix together with your hands until well blended. Knead it thoroughly. (If you want to get an idea of the flavor and do any adjusting, cook a bit of the sausage, bearing in mind that the flavors will both strengthen and mellow at the same time while sitting overnight.) Roll the sausage into a cylinder about 2 inches in diameter, wrap it in plastic, and refrigerate it overnight.

Preheat the oven to 350°F.

Cut the chilled sausage into ½-inch-thick rounds. Fry the sausage rounds in a heavy skillet over medium heat, in batches if necessary. Cook until browned on the surface and well done throughout.

Breakfast in America always fascinates me. It is a unique repast that seems to have come into being naturally, born of the pioneer dishes and the indigenous foods. I can find no close resemblance to this morning meal in the European countries from which the settlers came; you couldn't say there was anything Dutch or German or Swedish or French or even English about it. I am not talking here about the convenience breakfast of frozen orange juice and packaged cereal, or the drugstore-hotel monotony of half a grapefruit with a maraschino cherry on top, with eggs and bacon, toast and coffee. I don't consider that kind of meal to have any national identity. To me the quintessential American country breakfast is the strange (to a European) and unforgettable mingling of sweet and meat—of syrup-saturated pancakes with sausage, waffles with bacon, ham and eggs with hot breads and sweet breads, all manner of coffee-cakes and muffins, doughnuts and even pie.

JOSÉ WILSON, AMERICAN COOKING: THE EASTERN HEARTLAND (1971)

Prepare the eggs, buttering the sides and the bottom of 4 individual ramekins. Leave the butter that remains in the bottom of each ramekin, smearing it around evenly. Sprinkle the crumbs equally into the ramekins and twirl each around so that crumbs stick to the side and bottom. Break an egg into each ramekin, being careful to keep the yolks unbroken. Add the shot of hot sauce to each if you wish, then pour the cream over. Season each with a bit of salt and pepper, and a healthy sprinkling of paprika. Bake the eggs for 8 to 12 minutes, depending on how firmly set you like your eggs. (They will continue to cook a bit after you remove them from the oven.) Serve piping hot with the sausage patties.

TECHNIQUE TIP: Plain fried eggs also go well with this farm sausage. In our preferred approach, we melt a generous portion of butter or bacon drippings in a heavy skillet or on a griddle over medium-high heat. We break the eggs onto a saucer or plate, and when the fat is hot, gently pour the eggs onto the sizzling surface. With a spatula, we scrape up some of the cooking fat and pour it over the whites so they cook faster than the yolks, leaving the latter creamy and runny.

If you want a substitute for the sausage rather than the eggs, consider the old Pennsylvania Dutch standard, scrapple. Brought from Germany in the late seventeenth century, but altered in the colonies with the addition of cornmeal, scrapple is a thick buckwheat porridge flavored with bits of pork and fried like sausage. Pork liver, kidneys, heart, or other scraps are simmered until very tender, then ground and returned to the original broth. Brought back to a simmer, buckwheat and cornmeal are stirred in, seasonings added, and the mixture cooked down to a thick mush. The scrapple is poured into pans and cooled, then later cut into slices and fried. Some folks eat it plain, others with molasses, maple syrup, or apple butter.

WeatherBerry Scramble

Serves 6

We went to Owensboro, Kentucky, a number of years ago for the sole purpose of eating the local specialty, barbecued mutton. We left in awe of an even better dish, these scrambled eggs that Susie and Bill Tyler serve at their stately 1840s-era WeatherBerry bed-and-breakfast. They go great with buttery grits.

- Five 4- to 5-ounce red waxy potatoes, scrubbed but unpeeled
- ¼ cup (½ stick) unsalted butter
- 2 large onions, halved and sliced very thin
- 1¼ cups julienned country ham or other well-smoked ham
- ¼ cup minced scallion greens, optional
- 5 large eggs, beaten
- 3¾ cups small-curd cottage cheese
- ½ cup plus 2 tablespoons herb-seasoned poultry-stuffing bread crumbs (Susie uses Pepperidge Farm)
- Salt and freshly milled black pepper
- Orange slices or red-ripe tomato wedges

Cut each potato in half, preferably lengthwise if they're oval enough in shape to have a lengthwise. Then slice the potatoes ⅛ inch thick.

Warm the butter in a large heavy skillet over medium heat. When melted, stir in the potatoes and onions and pat down into a thick layer. Fry the mixture until the potatoes are tender with brown edges, 10 to 15 minutes, scraping up from the bottom a couple of times and patting the mixture back down again. Stir in the ham and, if you wish, the scallion greens, our own addition for color. Pour in the eggs and continue cooking, stirring the eggs to cook evenly. As they begin to set, mix in the cottage cheese and stuffing crumbs. Add salt and pepper to taste and remove from the heat when the eggs have cooked into soft curds.

Serve immediately, garnished with oranges or tomatoes.

Tex-Mex Migas

Serves 4

Migas may have evolved from Mexican *chilaquiles,* but it became a scrambled egg dish only north of the border. The name derives from the Spanish word for crumbs, a reference to the tortilla chips that provide a distinctive flavor and texture. Serve the savory concoction with warm flour tortillas.

- 8 large eggs
- Salt and freshly milled black pepper
- 2 small red-ripe tomatoes, preferably Italian plum
- 1 fresh jalapeño chile
- 4 ounces Mexican-style chorizo or other spicy sausage
- ¾ cup chopped onion
- 2 to 2½ dozen tostada chips, broken into bite-size pieces
- 6 to 8 ounces mild Cheddar cheese, grated (1½ to 2 cups)
- 2 tablespoons minced cilantro

Whisk the eggs lightly in a small bowl with 2 tablespoons of water and sprinklings of salt and pepper. Set aside.

Roast the tomatoes and jalapeño. Either hold them on a fork directly over the flame of a gas-stove burner, or place them on a baking sheet under the broiler until browned all over and blackened in spots. The tomato skins, in particular, will probably split a bit. When cool enough to handle, chop the tomato and the charred skin fine, then seed the jalapeño and mince it.

Crumble or thinly slice the chorizo and fry it in a large heavy skillet over medium heat until brown around the edges. Add the onion and sauté until limp, then stir in the tomato and jalapeño and heat through. Pour in the eggs and stir them up from the bottom of the skillet as they cook to your desired doneness. About a minute before the eggs are done, add the chips, stirring them in well. Remove the eggs from the heat and stir in the cheese and cilantro. Serve the migas immediately.

Blue-Flower Featherbed

Serves 6

Delightfully named in an earlier time, this dish is better known today as a strata, a layered egg-and-bread casserole as deep and comforting as a featherbed when the winter wind howls. Like other people around the world, Americans mastered the use of stale bread in puddings both sweet and savory, and the strata was one of the best. Any type of strata makes for a hassle-free morning meal because the texture is creamiest if the ingredients are assembled the previous evening, which lends the concoction its more straightforward name of overnight casserole. Here a stale but stalwart loaf is layered with soft cheese and, if available, chives with their blue-lilac flowers intact. The flowers add their own delicate crunch, onionlike flavor, and lovely color to the strata, but the dish still shines without them.

1-pound loaf country or sourdough bread, crusts removed if thick
1¾ cups small-curd cottage cheese
1¼ cups Monterey Jack or Muenster cheese, grated
3 tablespoons minced chives
3 tablespoons chopped chive blossoms or additional minced chives
Whole chives, with blossoms if available
5 large eggs
1 cup milk
1 teaspoon dry mustard
½ teaspoon salt
Freshly milled black pepper

Oil or butter a deep 9- to 10-inch baking dish.

Slice the bread into 9 to 12 slices no more than ½ inch thick. Arrange the bread, cottage cheese, grated cheese, chives, and chive blossoms in three equal alternating layers. Lay a few whole chives decoratively over the top.

Whisk the eggs with the milk, mustard, salt, and pepper. Pour the custard over the bread mixture. Cover and refrigerate the strata for at least 1 hour or up to overnight. Remove the strata from the refrigerator 20 to 30 minutes before you plan to bake it.

Preheat the oven to 350°F. Bake the strata for 50 to 55 minutes, until puffed, golden brown, and slightly set in the center. Serve hot.

Bran-Date Muffins

MAKES 12 MUFFINS

Americans may have picked up the idea of hot breads for breakfast from the English toast tradition, but we carried the notion to dizzying new heights. Biscuits rank at the top of our contributions, but anything quick wins favor, particularly if it's also sweet, from banana bread to coffee cake, sticky buns to doughnuts. These popular contemporary muffins fit the mold, but take their taste from much more than sugar.

FILLING

4 ounces cream cheese, softened
1½ tablespoons granulated sugar
2 teaspoons unbleached all-purpose flour
¼ teaspoon pure vanilla extract

BATTER

1¼ cups unbleached all-purpose flour
½ cup granulated sugar
1¼ teaspoons baking soda
¾ teaspoon salt
¼ teaspoon ground nutmeg
¼ teaspoon ground allspice
1 cup buttermilk
1 egg
¼ cup vegetable oil
½ teaspoon pure vanilla extract
¼ cup packed brown sugar
1¾ cups raisin bran cereal
¼ cups oats, the "old-fashioned" noninstant variety
½ cup chopped dried dates

Preheat the oven to 400°F. Grease a muffin tin for 12 muffins.

Prepare the filling, mixing together the ingredients in a small bowl.

Prepare the batter, first sifting together in a medium bowl the flour, granulated sugar, baking soda, salt, nutmeg, and allspice. In another larger bowl, whisk together the buttermilk, egg, oil, and vanilla. Combine the brown sugar with the dry mixture, then stir in the cereal, oats, and dates. Pour the dry ingredients into the wet ingredients, and mix by hand with just enough strokes to combine.

Spoon out half the batter into the bottom of each muffin cup. Top each with 1 to 2 teaspoons of the cream cheese filling. Spoon the remaining batter equally over the muffins, covering the cream cheese completely. Bake the muffins for about 20 minutes, until brown and a toothpick inserted into a muffin comes out clean. Cool the muffins briefly, then turn out onto a baking rack. They can be eaten immediately or later at room temperature. Wrapped tightly, the muffins remain tasty for up to 2 days.

Buttermilk Biscuits with Country Ham and Red-eye Gravy

SERVES 4 HEARTY EATERS

People who don't enjoy this classic southern combo at least once a year ought to turn in their passports. Real biscuits cook quickly, are easy to prepare, and taste two miles higher on a heavenly scale than anything that starts out in the box or tin. The ham only needs heating, and what could be handier for making gravy than the cup of coffee you're clutching?

BUTTERMILK BISCUITS

- 2 cups low-gluten biscuit flour, preferably, or 1¾ cups unbleached all-purpose flour plus ¼ cup cake flour or, less desirably, 2 cups unbleached all-purpose flour
- 2 teaspoons baking powder
- ¾ teaspoon salt
- ½ teaspoon baking soda
- 3 tablespoons lard, well chilled
- 2 tablespoons unsalted butter, well chilled
- ¾ cup plus 2 tablespoons buttermilk, well chilled

HAM AND GRAVY

- 1 tablespoon bacon drippings or unsalted butter
- 4 slices moist country ham or other smoky ham, about ⅓ inch thick (see Ingredient Tip)
- 2 teaspoons unbleached all-purpose flour
- 1 cup fresh hot coffee
- Pinch of brown sugar
- Pinch of cayenne pepper
- Salt and freshly milled black pepper, optional

Sift the flour, baking powder, salt, and baking soda into a large bowl, preferably a shallow one. Cut the lard and butter into small chunks, and add them to the dry ingredients. Combine with a pastry blender just until a coarse meal forms. Make a well in the center and pour in the buttermilk. With your fingers and a few swift strokes, combine the dough just until it's a sticky mess. Turn out onto a lightly floured board or, better, a pastry cloth. Clean, dry, and flour your hands. Gently pat out the dough and fold it back over itself about a half-dozen times, just until smooth. (A dough scraper helps greatly with this.) Pat out again into a circle or oval about ½ inch in thickness. Cover the dough lightly and refrigerate it for about 20 minutes.

Preheat the oven to 475°F.

Meanwhile, prepare the ham and gravy, first melting the drippings in a large heavy skillet over medium-high heat. Slash the edges of the ham's exterior fat to keep the slices from curling while cooking. Fry the ham slices in batches until

Breakfasting in bed is an imported fashion, and to my notion, is not a clean practice. The tray brought to an unaired room, a tumbled bed and an unwashed body, looks well in French engravings, but is a solecism in an age of hygienic principles, much ventilation and matutinal baths.

MARION HARLAND, MARION HARLAND'S COMPLETE COOK BOOK (1906)

lightly browned in spots and a bit crispy on the edges, about 2 minutes per side. Arrange the ham slices on a platter as they are done. Keep the ham warm and reserve the pan drippings in the skillet.

Remove the biscuit dough from the refrigerator. Cut it with a biscuit cutter, trying to get as many biscuits as possible, since they toughen if the dough is rerolled. You should be able, with practice, to get about eight 3-inch biscuits or twelve to fourteen 2-inch biscuits from the dough. Make your biscuits with a quick, clean, straight-down push on the cutter. If you twist the cutter (as seems to be a natural motion for many people), it twists the dough, resulting in an uneven biscuit. Bake the biscuits in the center of the oven, turning the baking sheet around once halfway through the baking time. Bake 3-inch biscuits for 8 to 10 minutes total, and 2-inch biscuits for 7 to 9 minutes, until raised and golden brown.

While the biscuits cook, finish the gravy. Reheat the pan drippings over medium heat and whisk in the flour. Pour in the coffee and scrape up any browned bits from the bottom of the skillet. Add at least ¼ cup of hot water, more for a milder coffee jolt. Season with brown sugar and cayenne. Taste the gravy and add salt and pepper as needed. Serve the gravy immediately over the ham slices accompanied by the biscuits for soaking up all the plate juices. Put any thought of calories and cholesterol out of your mind for the moment, and sit down and savor a remarkable flavor and texture blend.

INGREDIENT TIP: Any good ham works in this dish, but the flavor peaks with smoked, aged country ham, drier and much saltier than most hams. When we want a few slices of a good country ham, rather than a whole hindquarter, we order from one of two mid-South sources, Gatton Farms in Kentucky (502-525-3437) for the earthiest, most complex meat, or the Loveless Café (615-646-0067) for a moister, less stout ham. Located just outside of Nashville, Tennessee, the café is humble but hardly loveless—a favorite spot for miles around for great home-cooked breakfasts and a fine mail-order source for fruity preserves as well as ham.

Traverse City Cherry French Toast

Serves 4

New Orleans *pain perdu* (literally "lost bread"), originally a dessert dish from France, seems the likely link between the American version of French toast and its European antecedents, which go back centuries. It's certain, at least, that the French wouldn't recognize the New World rendition, particularly on the breakfast table, and might well be mortified at our terminology for it. Here we slit and stuff the bread, using a cherry filling from the magnificent orchard country around Traverse City, Michigan. Local cooks favor tangy Montmorency cherries (also luscious in pies), but any tart variety works well. We always serve French toast with smoky bacon or sausage links, and maybe a glass of fresh-squeezed orange juice.

1-pound loaf of white bread, unsliced

FILLING

4 ounces cream cheese, softened

1 to 2 tablespoons sugar

¼ teaspoon almond extract, optional

1½ cups pitted tart cherries, fresh, frozen, or canned, mashed lightly

¾ cup whole milk

½ cup whipping cream or half-and-half, preferably, or additional whole milk

3 eggs

1 tablespoon sugar

1 teaspoon pure vanilla extract

Pinch of salt

Unsalted butter for pan frying

Vegetable oil for pan frying

Confectioners' sugar

Real maple syrup, warmed

Preheat the oven to 325°F. Butter a baking sheet. Cut the bread in 8 equal slices, about 1 inch thick.

Prepare the filling. Mash together in a medium bowl the cream cheese with the smaller amount of sugar and, if you wish, the almond extract. Stir in the cherries and add more sugar if the flavor is overly tart. The mixture should be thick and chunky.

In a shallow dish or bowl, whisk together the milk, cream, eggs, sugar, vanilla, and salt.

With a serrated knife, cut a pocket into the side of each piece of bread, carefully slicing into but not all the way through the bread. Spoon equal portions of the filling into each slice. Dunk the stuffed bread slices into the egg mixture and soak them several minutes, turning if needed to coat evenly, until saturated but short of falling apart.

Warm 1 tablespoon of butter and 1 tablespoon of oil together on a griddle or in a large heavy skillet over medium heat. Cook the French toast in batches briefly until golden brown and lightly crisp, turning once. Place the first slices on the baking sheet and keep them warm in the oven. Continue cooking the remaining slices, adding more butter and oil as needed. When all of the French toast is ready, dust it with confectioner's sugar, sprinkling it through a fine sieve. Serve immediately with maple syrup.

A Toast to the Bagel

Zelda Fitzgerald once said she always left the preparation of toast to trained servants because it burns so easily. Other Americans must have felt daunted as well, at least before the introduction of the electric toaster, because a number of older cookbooks devoted entire sections to the subject. They usually started with a detailed explanation of how to make plain toast and proceeded from there through French, cinnamon, and other versions.

Of all the different breads toasted today for breakfast in the U.S., the bagel is clearly the most cherished, ahead at least in overall enthusiasm if not in total bites consumed. Joan Nathan, in her *Jewish Cooking in America* (1994), traces the bagel from its Eastern European roots to its contemporary popularity, a relatively recent development. She says Jewish bakers became bagel specialists in Poland and Russia, brought the expertise to New York around the turn of the twentieth century, and then struggled for decades to win any acceptance for the roll with a hole. Even East Side Jews seldom ate bagels except on Sundays. A 1951 Broadway comedy, *Bagels and Yox,* brought national attention to the bread for the first time, and Lender's bakery began marketing frozen bagels across the country in the early 1960s. Within a single generation since then, some eight hundred bagel bakeries have sprouted in all corners of the land, carrying an old Eastern European tradition to a mainstream New World market. If Americans added anything along the way, it was the equally old British notion of toasting bread for a crisper flavor and texture.

Fried Cornmeal Mush with Sorghum Syrup

Serves 4 to 6

"Mush" doesn't ring well in contemporary ears, but it's a time-honored American name for a simple cornmeal porridge, also known in colonial days as hasty pudding or suppan. If you want a trendier term, call it polenta, but that obscures its deep Anglo-American roots. Often eaten in the past as a one-dish supper, it was sometimes served again the next morning fried like a breakfast cake. We drizzle the mush with sorghum syrup, a traditional accompaniment in parts of the South and Midwest. Sorghum came here from Africa, providing one of the numerous instances in which foods and foodways from that continent mingled in America with those from the other continent that's frequently spelled with a capital C.

MUSH

- 1 teaspoon salt
- 1½ cups coarse-ground cornmeal or grits
- 2 tablespoons unsalted butter
- Flour for dusting, optional
- Vegetable oil for pan-frying
- Unsalted butter, softened
- Sorghum syrup (see Ingredient Tip) or real maple syrup, warmed

Oil a loaf pan.

Heat 6 cups of water with the salt in a heavy saucepan over high heat. When the water reaches a rolling boil, scatter in the cornmeal a handful at a time, stirring constantly. When you have added all the cornmeal, reduce the heat to a bare simmer. Cook the cornmeal until creamy and very thick, 40 to 50 minutes, depending on its coarseness. Remove from the heat and stir in the butter. Spoon the mush into the loaf pan and set aside to cool to room temperature. Cover the pan and refrigerate for at least 4 hours and up to several days.

Turn the mush out of the pan and cut it into neat slices about ½ inch thick. If the slices seem fragile—some cornmeal sets up more thickly than others—dust them with flour.

Warm a lightly oiled griddle or large heavy skillet over medium heat. Fry the mush slices in batches, avoiding crowding, until golden brown and crusty on both sides, 8 to 10 minutes total. Add more oil to the griddle if the slices offer any resistance.

Serve the slices of mush hot with thick pats of butter. It's tasty as is, but a little sorghum syrup adds extra dash.

INGREDIENT TIP: Cheryl's dad, who grew up in southern Illinois in the 1930s, remembers when sorghum syrup was a seasonal treat, available in the fall just after the coarse stalks were crushed and the juice boiled down in a process similar to the production of molasses. As with maple syrup, much of the sorghum syrup on the market today has little of the real thing in it. Look for 100 percent sorghum syrup, sometimes called sorghum molasses, such as the one made by Arrowhead Mills and sold in natural foods stores. For a mail-order source, call Lee Brothers Boiled Peanuts Catalogue (843-720-8890), which carries a top-of-the-line syrup made for them in small batches in Benton County, Tennessee.

Red Flannel Hash

Serves 4 to 6

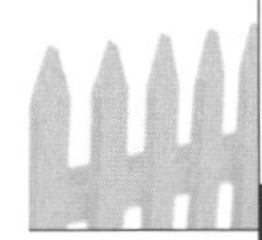

Let your breakfasts be of wholesome and substantial food. The system needs nourishment in the morning after the long, unbroken fast of the night. The practice of taking only a cup of tea or coffee with hot biscuit, and possibly pie or doughnuts, gives a very poor foundation for the morning's labor, which is and should be the hard labor of the day. Milk, coffee, or chocolate, mushes, fruits, potatoes or bread, meat, fish, or eggs, in some of their simple and digestible combinations should form the basis of the breakfast. The morning meal should be taken as soon as possible after rising. Any prolonged bodily exertion or exposure to the early morning air, before the stomach is fortified by food, is now condemned by the majority of physicians.

Mary J. Lincoln,
Mrs. Lincoln's Boston
Cook Book (1884)

The traditional New England Boiled Dinner (page 198) makes a fine meal in itself, but it's even better the next few mornings chopped into a hearty hash. This version includes the corned beef that's part of the full dinner, but the descendants of the Green Mountain Boys might lynch us for that in Vermont. For many purists, a true red flannel hash—named for the color contributed by the beets—contains only vegetables and bacon. We enjoy it that way, but to us the also-common beefed-up rendition is America's greatest contribution to the wide and wonderful world of hashes.

- ¼ cup (½ stick) plus 2 tablespoons unsalted butter
- ½ to 1 cup chopped cooked onion
- 2 to 3 cups chopped cooked red waxy potatoes
- ½ to 1 cup chopped cooked beets
- 1 to 1½ cups chopped cooked mixed additional vegetables, such as carrots, turnips, or cabbage
- 1 to 1½ pounds cooked corned beef, chilled and chopped fine
- ½ to 1 cup Boiled Dinner cooking liquid or salted beef stock (see Ingredient Tip)
- 2 teaspoons yellow mustard
- Freshly milled black pepper
- Prepared or freshly grated horseradish, optional

Warm ¼ cup of the butter in a heavy skillet, preferably 10 to 12 inches in diameter, over medium-high heat. Add the onion and cook for a minute; then add the potatoes, beets, and other vegetables. Cook for 5 minutes, stirring the mixture around, warming it through, and allowing some of the steam from the vegetables to escape.

Pat the mixture down and let it cook for 6 to 8 minutes, until it begins to brown richly. Scrape it up again with a sturdy spatula, getting up any browned bits, and add the remaining 2 tablespoons butter, allowing it to melt down through the hash. Pat it back down evenly again, add the corned beef and the cooking liquid, and cook for an additional 6 to 8 minutes. Stir in the mustard and pepper. Scrape the hash back up, again retrieving all the browned bits. You may need to adjust the temperature downward a little, but don't unless you're close to burning the mixture. You need enough heat to develop a rich brown crust. Cook until the hash is well browned and crisp and the vegetables and meat are still moist, an additional 6 to 8 minutes. Serve immediately, with optional horseradish on the side.

INGREDIENT TIP: Add the greater amount of liquid mentioned in the recipe if using less meat—it provides body and a heartier character to the dish. Also, it's important to the final flavor and texture of the hash to use about as many potatoes as the other vegetables combined, and to chop the meat and vegetables by hand. Always cook in a heavy skillet with plenty of surface area, and make a sport of energetically scraping up and patting down the mixture until it's as crusty as a seared steak.

South Carolina Shrimp and Grits

SERVES 4

In his *Hoppin' John's Lowcountry Cooking* (1992), John Martin Taylor says that no dish is more typical of coastal South Carolina than this sumptuous creation. Most locals just call it "breakfast shrimp," but the less common name of shrimp gravy puts the focus on the true essence, the sterling sauce that pulls together the grits and the seafood. You won't find a finer eye-opener in the whole of the country.

1½ pounds shrimp, peeled, halved lengthwise and, if you wish, deveined

Juice of 1 lemon

Hot pepper sauce, such as Tabasco

1½ teaspoons salt or more to taste

1½ cups stone-ground grits, not an instant or quick-cook variety (see Ingredient Tip)

6 bacon slices, chopped

1 small onion, finely chopped

¼ cup finely chopped green bell pepper

1 garlic clove, minced

½ cup thin-sliced scallion rings

2 tablespoons unbleached all-purpose flour

1 cup chicken stock

1 to 2 tablespoons unsalted butter

1 cup (4 ounces) medium to sharp Cheddar cheese, grated

Combine the shrimp with the lemon juice and a couple of generous splashes of hot pepper sauce. Let it sit while you begin the grits and gravy.

Make the grits in a large heavy saucepan, first bringing 6 cups of water and 1 teaspoon of the salt to a boil. Whisk in the grits a few handfuls at a time. (They will bubble up initially.) When you have added all the grits, reduce the heat to a very low simmer and cook over low heat for 35 to 40 minutes, stirring occasionally at first and more frequently toward the end.

While the grits simmer, get the gravy under way. Fry the bacon in a medium skillet over medium heat until brown but still limp. Stir in the onion, bell pepper, and garlic, and continue cooking until the onion and pepper are limp, about 5 minutes. Add the scallions, sprinkle the flour over the mixture, and continue sautéing for an additional 5 minutes. Stir in the stock and remaining ½ teaspoon salt, and cook for 5 minutes longer. Remove from the heat while you finish the grits.

When the grits are thick and creamy, stir in as much of the butter as you wish, followed by the cheese. Add a splash of hot pepper sauce and additional salt if you like. Cover the grits while you finish the gravy.

Return the gravy to medium heat and stir in the shrimp. Cook until the shrimp are opaque throughout, about 5 minutes. Serve immediately, mounding the grits in large shallow bowls or on plates and covering them with a similar-size portion of the shrimp and gravy.

Spring would bring our first and just about only fish—shad. It would always be served for breakfast, soaked in salt water for an hour or so, rolled in seasoned cornmeal, and fried carefully in home-rendered lard with a slice of smoked shoulder for added flavor. There were crispy fried white potatoes, fried onions, batter bread, any food left over from supper, blackberry jelly, delicious hot coffee, and cocoa for the children. And perhaps if a neighbor dropped in, dandelion wine was added.

EDNA LEWIS,
THE TASTE OF COUNTRY
COOKING (1977)

INGREDIENT TIP: The instant grits commonly available today lack real flavor and texture, even when gussied up with butter and salt. Happily, a handful of mills still produce the genuine article. John Martin Taylor sells one fine version through his Charleston culinary mail-order business, Hoppin' John's (800-828-4412).

Breakfast from the Sea and Stream

Apart from the deli delight of smoked salmon on bagels, most Americans today don't think of eating fish and seafood early in the day. We weren't so limited in our perspective in the past, when almost everything edible from the water seemed as appropriate at breakfast as any other meal.

Bostonians relished codfish balls on Sunday mornings, the same time typically reserved in Tidewater Virginia for fat roe herring caught during spring spawning. Clam hash thrived in Seattle, fried trout in the Rocky Mountains, fish "steam" in the Florida Keys, lobster scramble on Gay's Island in Maine, and oyster sausages everywhere from Beaufort, South Carolina, to Portland, Oregon. During the California Gold Rush of 1849, one rich miner reputedly paid a sack of gold for another oyster favorite, Hangtown fry. According to most accounts of the origin of the dish, which was named after the town's reputation for hangings, the prospector asked a restaurant for a meal worth his treasure and got an omelet bountiful with oysters and eggs, the most precious and pricy items in the kitchen.

French Quarter Veal Grillades

SERVES 4

Health-conscious cooking authorities have railed against fried foods since the mid-nineteenth century, even these lightly sautéed slices of veal finished with a piquant sauce. *The Picayune's Creole Cook Book* defended the honor of the New Orleans dish in 1901 like it was a southern lady slandered by a Yankee: "Our 'Grillades,' or Fried Meat à la Créole are famous, relishable and most digestible dishes, no matter what scientists say about the non-advisability of eating fried meat. The many octogenarians who walk our streets, and who have been practically raised on 'Grillades,' for it is a daily dish among the Créoles, are the best refutation of the outcry that is made in the North and West against fried meat." A single bite is the next best refutation. We like our forkfuls with a side of creamy grits, made in the same way as in the recipe on page 38, substituting milk or cream for the cheese.

4 veal top-round cutlets, about ¼ inch thick and 4 ounces each

Salt and freshly milled black pepper

Vegetable oil for pan-frying

2 tablespoons unbleached all-purpose flour

1 medium onion, chopped

1 small green bell pepper, chopped

¼ cup minced celery

1 plump garlic clove, minced

1 cup chicken stock

⅔ cup chopped canned tomatoes with juice

½ teaspoon dried thyme

Pinch of cayenne pepper

1 bay leaf

Sprinkle the cutlets with salt and pepper. Warm the oil in a large heavy skillet over medium-high heat. Brown the cutlets in the oil, turning once, then remove them from the skillet and keep them warm. Reduce the heat to medium-low and sprinkle the flour into the pan drippings, scraping up from the bottom to loosen any browned bits. Cook the mixture until it's a rich, deep brown, about 5 minutes. Watch it carefully and stir frequently, as it can go quickly from the desired shade to burned. Immediately mix in the onion, bell pepper, and celery, and cook until they begin to soften, about 5 minutes. Stir in the garlic and cook another minute.

Pour in the stock and tomatoes, add the thyme, cayenne, and bay leaf, and simmer the sauce for 5 minutes. Return the veal cutlets to the sauce, pushing them down into the mixture. Cook until the sauce is thick and the veal tender, about 10 minutes longer. Adjust the seasoning if you wish, adding just a bit more salt, pepper, or cayenne. Serve the cutlets warm beside mounds of creamy grits covered with the sauce.

Santa Fe Breakfast Burritos

Serves 4 generously

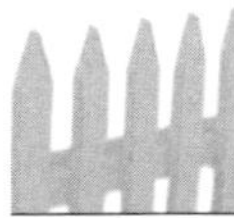

New Mexicans like to start their day with hefty burritos smothered in a red or green chile sauce. This potato and bacon combo is our favorite of several popular styles.

GREEN CHILE SAUCE

2 tablespoons vegetable oil

½ medium onion, minced

2 garlic cloves, minced

2 tablespoons unbleached all-purpose flour

2 cups chopped roasted mild green chiles, such as New Mexican, preferably fresh or frozen

2 cups chicken stock, preferably homemade

1 teaspoon salt

Hash Browns (page 268) or 3 to 4 cups other hash-brown potatoes, warm

4 thin to medium-thick flour tortillas, warmed

8 to 12 crisp cooked bacon slices

6 to 8 ounces mild Cheddar cheese, grated (1½ to 2 cups)

Prepare the green chile sauce, first warming the oil over medium heat. Add the onion and sauté until soft and translucent, about 5 minutes. Stir in the garlic and sauté for an additional minute, then add the flour and continue cooking for another minute. Mix in the chiles, stock, and salt. Bring the mixture to a boil. Reduce the heat to low, and simmer for 15 to 20 minutes, until thickened but still very pourable. Keep the sauce warm. (It can be made up to 5 days ahead, covered, and refrigerated, or kept frozen for longer. Reheat before proceeding.)

Preheat the oven to 400°F.

Spoon one-fourth of the potatoes onto a tortilla. Top the potatoes with 2 to 3 slices of bacon. Roll up into a loose cylinder, and place the burrito, seam side down, on a heatproof plate. A true Santa Fean would spoon one-fourth of the chile sauce over the burrito, but you may want to start with less, serving the remaining sauce on the side for chileheads. Sprinkle the burrito generously with cheese. Repeat with the remaining ingredients to prepare the rest of the burritos.

Bake the burritos until the cheese is melted and gooey, about 5 minutes. Serve immediately.

Baked Apples with Apple-Glazed Bacon

Serves 6

In one form or another, usually in English-style savory pies, apples found an early place on the American breakfast table. The morning pie became so common in New England by the nineteenth century that Ralph Waldo Emerson felt the need to ask, somewhat defensively, when else you might eat one. To cook apples on their own, in the days before modern oven baking, Americans sometimes roasted them at the hearth, which Mark Twain recalled as a childhood treat that made "old people's old tales and old jokes sound fresh and crisp and enchanting." Apple-glazed bacon doubles the joy.

- 3 cups apple cider or juice
- ½ teaspoon ground cinnamon
- 6 large baking apples, such as Granny Smith, Rome, or McIntosh
- ⅔ cup chopped pecans
- ¼ cup packed dark brown sugar
- 1½ teaspoons unbleached all-purpose flour
- ¼ cup (½ stick) plus 1 tablespoon unsalted butter, softened
- Pinch of salt
- 1½ tablespoons apple jelly or apple butter
- 1½ tablespoons yellow mustard
- 12 thick bacon slices (about ¾ pound) (see Ingredient Tip)
- 3 to 4 tablespoons whipping cream

Preheat the oven to 375°F. Butter a baking dish large enough to hold the apples upright with an inch or two between them.

Pour the cider into a saucepan, sprinkle in ¼ teaspoon of the cinnamon, and reduce by half over high heat.

While the cider cooks, scoop out the apple cores, leaving the bottoms intact. We find the small end of a melon baller works better than apple-coring gadgets. Slice a thin ribbon of peel from around the top of each apple cavity, which helps keep the peel from splitting while baking.

Blend together in a small bowl the pecans, brown sugar, flour, butter, salt, and remaining ½ teaspoon cinnamon. Stuff equal portions of the mixture into each apple cavity, mounding it over the top a bit if necessary. Pour 1¼ cups of the reduced apple cider into the dish, drizzling a little over each apple in the process. Cover the apples and place them in the oven.

Stir the jelly and mustard into the remaining ¼ cup of apple cider to make the glaze for the bacon.

Arrange the bacon in a single layer on a baking sheet. Place it in the oven along with the apples after they have baked for about 30 minutes. Uncover the apples. Bake the bacon for 10 to 12 minutes, until it begins to look opaque and its fat begins to render. Pour off any accumulated drippings.

Turn over the bacon and brush about half of the glaze on each slice. Return the bacon to the oven and cook for an additional 3 to 4 minutes. Remove the bacon from the oven and turn it over again. Brush it with the remaining glaze and return it to the oven for 3 to 5 additional minutes, until well browned and somewhat stiff. (With the glaze coating, the bacon gets nicely chewy with crunchy edges but stays short of crisp.) If you wish to drain the bacon, use a rack rather than paper towels to avoid wiping off the glaze.

Bake the apples for a total of 45 to 55 minutes (depending on their size and variety), until they can be pierced easily with a knife tip but still hold their shape.

Remove the apples and stir the cream into the pan juices. Arrange the apples in small bowls, pouring the enriched pan juices over them. Set the bowls on plates and arrange a pair of bacon slices beside each bowl. Serve warm.

INGREDIENT TIP: At least for special occasions, it's worth the extra cost to get bacon that's really cured and smoked rather than flavored to resemble those processes. We particularly like the Nueske's brand, from a northern Wisconsin family business nearly seventy years old. The bacon is distributed nationally in select supermarkets and meat markets, or it can be ordered directly at 800-382-2266. Other companies that sell high-quality mail-order hams typically sell fine bacon too.

Soothing the Sick

Until recent decades, American cookbooks frequently contained a chapter devoted to dishes appropriate for the sick. Ideas about convalescent eating remained remarkably consistent across the country for at least a century. Even books as completely different as Lydia Maria Child's *The American Frugal Housewife* (1832), a New England classic, and Lafcadio Hearn's *La Cuisine Créole* (1885), about New Orleans cooking, manage to agree on dishes for the ill. Both authors recommend gruel, beef tea, arrowroot pudding, tapioca, and stewed prunes, among their select options, and each encourages the use of wine in various preparations. Hearn also favors milk punches spiked with gin, rum, or brandy, a range of candies and custards, and baked apples, making his sickroom one of the most appetizing around.

Curiously, if only coincidentally, recipes for invalids started disappearing from cookbooks about the time of Prohibition. Even then the dishes were similar, though usually minus any spirits. Up in Grand Forks, North Dakota, in 1924, according to the local *Y.M.C.A. Cook Book,* recuperating patients could still count on most of the foods suggested in common by Child and Hearn, but only the tapioca would have a trace of wine now and a box of gelatin would be added to the juice of the stewed prunes.

Fresh Fruit Smoothie

Serves 2

On-the-go families of recent decades often opt for breakfast in a glass, putting together a rich but usually low-fat blend of fruit and dairy products that satisfies all ages. The suggested fruits are some of our favorites for a smoothie, but substitute freely according to what's in season.

- 1 generous cup chopped fruit, such as mango, cantaloupe, honeydew, or strawberries
- 1 small banana, chunked
- ½ cup plain yogurt
- ½ cup skim milk
- 6 ice cubes
- Sugar, optional
- Fresh fruit chunks and fresh mint sprigs, optional

Combine in a blender the chopped fruit, banana, yogurt, milk, and ice cubes. Purée until smooth. Add a little sugar if the drink is not as sweet as you like. Pour into tall glasses and drink up. On a leisurely morning, garnish the smoothie, if you wish, with fruit chunks on toothpicks and sprigs of mint for each glass.

In the memory of the passing generation, Nutmeggers, like other New Englanders, ate formidable breakfasts. They commenced a summer day with a light menu of broiled steak, or ham and boiled eggs, with wheat battercakes, or boiled or baked potatoes, graham or Boston brown bread, and baked apples or applesauce. The meal that broke the fast in winter was more heating—fried sausages and potatoes, and cold boiled tongue or other cold meat, fried "Indian" mush, buckwheat battercakes, and pickled cucumbers. . . .

Minnesota Breakfast Cereal of Wild Rice and Oatmeal

Serves 4

We first encountered the idea of wild rice as a breakfast food in one of the earliest coast-to-coast surveys of American regional cooking, Cora, Rose, and Bob Brown's *America Cooks* (1940). The book suggests eating wild rice with just sugar and cream, described as Minnesota style, but we like to add oats and dried fruit, hardly out of character with either the dish or the state. In the depths of December, we simmer up enough of this satisfying cereal for several chilly morns. It's guaranteed to take the edge off the iciest day.

- ¾ cup uncooked wild rice
- 1½ cups oats, the "old-fashioned" noninstant variety
- ½ cup dried cherries or raisins
- ¾ teaspoon salt
- ¼ cup milk
- Brown sugar, maple sugar, or real maple syrup

Steam the wild rice or boil it covered by 2 inches of water. It is ready when tender but pleasantly chewy, with many burst kernels, after about 45 minutes. Drain the rice. (The rice can be prepared up to several days ahead, covered, and refrigerated. Reheat it before proceeding.)

Combine the oats with the dried cherries, salt, and 3 cups of water in a saucepan. Cook over medium heat for about 5 minutes, until soft and thick. Stir in the wild rice and milk. Serve steaming hot in large bowls, topped lightly with sugar or syrup.

Those were the days that have been pared down to the meager living of New York commuters who rush out of their Connecticut homes of a summer morning sustained only by a glass of tomato juice and a cup of black coffee, and the rest of the time seem to subsist on canapés and cocktails.

Cora, Rose, and Bob Brown, *America Cooks* (1940)

PILED HIGH: The American Sandwich

THE CONTEMPORARY CUSTOM OF EATING MEAT BETWEEN bread supposedly goes back to a marathon card game in England in the middle of the eighteenth century, when the Earl of Sandwich ordered the combination brought to the gaming table so he wouldn't miss any of the action. The British failed to exploit the idea fully, seldom moving beyond a sliver of tongue or a dainty helping of watercress, but across the Atlantic, Americans went wild with the possibilities, coming up with more inventive and tempting pairings than the Kama Sutra can suggest for a different sort of natural mating.

The big breakthroughs took time, however. Prior to the Civil War, Americans remained as timid about their fixings as the British, and perhaps as a consequence, were also tepid about eating sandwiches except as an occasional supper dish or traveler's snack. The explosion of interest started in the decades following the war, ignited partially by the increasing availability of commercial products such as soft white bread, spreadable condiments, and canned meats like deviled ham.

By the mid-twentieth century, the sandwich had become an American institution and icon, the most popular type of food in the country and a symbol of both our ingenuity in the kitchen and our haste to get out of it. Some of the favorites today, especially fast-food concoctions, shame our robust culinary heritage, but the best creations stand taller than the State of Liberty in honoring the national spirit. A good home-style sandwich, made with superior ingredients and a deft hand, is spunk, spark, and simplicity—authentic signatures of American eating.

Peanut Butter

Native to South America, the peanut arrived in North America via Africa, brought by slaves who first learned about the nutlike legume from early Portuguese traders. By the eighteenth century, Southerners were growing peanuts, but the treat didn't spread across the country until after the Civil War, when George Washington Carver stimulated demand through his extensive research and promotion efforts at Alabama's Tuskegee Institute.

Around the turn of the twentieth century, a St. Louis physician came up with a "peanut butter" that promised a source of protein for people with weak or missing teeth. Home cooks of the same era made a "peanut paste" similar to the doctor's product, but his name prevailed after a concessionaire at the 1904 St. Louis World's Fair successfully marketed peanut butter as a health food.

Today, according to the Peanut Advisory Board, the average American child consumes 1,500 peanut butter and jelly sandwiches before high school graduation. Adults don't necessarily eat less of the jarred spread, but they generally move on to new combinations, everything from Meta Given's pairing with watercress to Michael McLaughlin's addition of bacon and hot pepper jelly. As Laurie Colwin claims in *Home Cooking* (1988), Americans may tell you they eat salad when they're home alone, but if you persist, they'll likely confess to a peanut butter sandwich.

Summer's Best BLT

SERVES 4

The bacon, lettuce, and tomato sandwich probably derives from its cousin, the club, one of the earliest restaurant sandwiches in the country. No one knows who dropped the chicken and the third tier from the older combo to make the first BLT, but we would lay our bet on a tomato grower. The sandwich reaches a peak of perfection at the height of tomato season, when garden-fresh slices of the juicy orbs marry magically with smoky bacon and crunchy lettuce. To further the harmony, we spread the bread with a simple version of a basil-scented mayonnaise. Add on the side, if you wish, handfuls of crisp potato chips, or ears of summer sweet corn, dripping with butter.

BASIL MAYONNAISE

½ cup mayonnaise

¼ cup minced fresh basil

Splash of hot pepper sauce, such as Tabasco

8 large slices good white sandwich bread

Crisp iceberg lettuce leaves or softer, but not limp, leaf- or butter-lettuce leaves

12 thick bacon slices, preferably a very smoky variety, fried crisp

8 thick slices large red-ripe beefsteak tomatoes

Salt

Prepare the basil mayonnaise, mixing together the ingredients.

Toast the bread until golden brown. Immediately spread each slice on one side with a full tablespoon of basil mayonnaise. Don't skimp! Arrange the lettuce on top of the mayonnaise on 4 bread slices, adding enough to show off a green fringe for each sandwich. Pile on equal portions of bacon and tomatoes for each sandwich, salting the tomatoes lightly, and add the remaining toast slices. Carefully slice each sandwich into halves and serve immediately.

Classic Backyard Burger

Serves 6

Of all the sandwiches concocted in the United States, the burger best illustrates the American knack for turning a favorite food into an even more beloved sandwich. German immigrants in the mid-nineteenth century introduced the country to the Hamburg steak, a chopped beef dish that became a pan-fried staple across the land by the end of the century. Accounts differ about who first put the meat on a bun, but the idea flourished at roadside stands with the advent of the automobile age. The hamburger finally replaced the original Hamburg steak in home cooking during the outdoor grilling revolution that began right after World War II. Grilling wasn't really a big advance over frying, but the open-air setting and the substitution of a bun for a washable plate quickly made the backyard burger into a hallmark American meal. For optimum flavor, grill burgers uncovered, as our dads used to do, and form the patties from freshly ground beef. Load up the sandwich with the conventional condiments—still better than most nouvelle dressings—and savor every drippy bite.

⅔ cup mayonnaise

2 tablespoons ketchup

2 to 2½ pounds freshly ground chuck (see Ingredient Tip)

1 teaspoon salt

¾ teaspoon freshly milled black pepper

6 large hamburger buns, preferably bakery-made sesame-seed buns

12 thin slices Cheddar, Monterey Jack, Colby, brick, or even American cheese, at room temperature, optional

6 thick slices large red-ripe tomatoes

6 thin slices red onion

Dill pickle slices, optional

Crisp iceberg lettuce leaves

Fire up your grill in a way that allows for cooking first over high heat (where you can hold your hand comfortably an inch or two above the cooking grate for only 1 to 2 seconds) and then over medium heat (about 4 to 5 seconds with the same hand test). With a charcoal grill, pile the charcoal about three coals deep on one side for the higher heat level, and spread it in a single layer on the opposite side for medium heat. With a gas grill, start on high and adjust the temperature later to medium.

Combine the mayonnaise and ketchup in a small bowl. Refrigerate it until serving time.

Mix together the ground chuck, salt, and pepper. Gently form the mixture into 6 patties about ¾ inch thick. The patties should hold together firmly, but don't compact them or handle them any longer than necessary.

I doubt if God has given us any refreshment which, taken in moderation, is unwholesome, except microbes. Yet there are people who strictly deprive themselves of each and every eatable, drinkable and smokeable which has in any way acquired a shady reputation. They pay this price for health. And health is all they get for it. How strange it is! It is like paying out your whole fortune for a cow that has gone dry.

MARK TWAIN, THE AUTOBIOGRAPHY OF MARK TWAIN (CHARLES NEIDER, EDITOR) (1961)

Grill the burgers uncovered over high heat for 1½ minutes per side. Move the burgers to medium heat and cook for 4 to 5 minutes per side for medium doneness, until crusty and richly brown (not charred) with a slight hint of pink at the center. Toast the buns at the edge of the grill if you wish. If you plan to make cheeseburgers, place 2 overlapping slices of cheese on the burgers a few minutes before you remove the meat from the grill.

Spoon the mayonnaise-ketchup mixture generously over both sides of a bun. Add the burger, tomato, onion, optional pickle, and lettuce, and repeat with the remaining burgers and ingredients. Eat the burgers hot, squeezing firmly to release and combine the juices.

INGREDIENT TIP: Freshly ground beef always enhances a burger. Many butchers, even in chain supermarkets, will grind the chuck for you on request, but you should be prepared to cook it within a few hours to retain the flavor advantage. The best approach is to grind the meat yourself at home right before you grill. Use a meat grinder or the grinding attachment on a mixer, but you can also use a food processor. Take the beef directly from the refrigerator and cut it into chunks or strips. In an average-size processor, grind the meat one burger at a time, pulsing it with the regular chopping blade. For superior taste and texture, we like a grind slightly coarser than the regular supermarket style.

Piedmont Country 'Q

MAKES 12 SANDWICHES

One of the glories of southern cooking, barbecued pork dates back to the early years of European settlement. Colonists learned the outdoor slow-smoking technique from Native Americans, who used it for fish and game, and then applied the cooking method to the hogs they brought from the Old World. Nineteenth-century cookbooks usually ignored the subject because the pork wasn't ordinary home fare prepared in the kitchen. Men generally did the cooking, and did it in the underground pits, for large family and communal feasts. A party is still the best occasion for the meat, and this twentieth-century sandwich, dressed in a North Carolina style, makes a festive way to enjoy it. Don't skimp on the quantity of pork you cook because people always eat more than you expect and it freezes well for future meals.

BARBECUE SAUCE

¼ cup (½ stick) unsalted butter
6 tablespoons minced onion
1⅓ cups cider vinegar
1⅓ cups ketchup
1 cup packed dark brown sugar
1 teaspoon Worchestershire sauce
¼ teaspoon cayenne pepper
Salt and freshly milled black pepper

CAROLINA DRY RUB

3 tablespoons coarsely ground black pepper
3 tablespoons packed dark brown sugar
3 tablespoons paprika
2 tablespoons kosher salt or other coarse salt
1 teaspoon cayenne pepper

2 untrimmed Boston pork butt sections, about 3 pounds each

SANDWICH COLESLAW

1 cup mayonnaise
6 tablespoons cider vinegar
6 tablespoons Barbecue Sauce (see above)
3 tablespoons granulated sugar
12 cups lightly packed shredded cabbage
Salt

BARBECUE MOP

1 cup cider vinegar
1 tablespoon Worcestershire sauce
1 tablespoon coarsely ground black pepper
1 tablespoon kosher salt or other coarse salt
2 teaspoons vegetable oil
½ teaspoon cayenne pepper

12 soft hamburger buns, warmed

Prepare the sauce, first melting the butter in a large saucepan over medium heat. Add the onion and sauté until soft and translucent, about 5 minutes. Stir in the remaining ingredients and bring the mixture to a boil, stirring occasionally. Reduce the heat to a low simmer, and cook until the sauce has reduced to approximately 2½ cups, about 15 minutes. Season with salt and pepper. Cool to room temperature. (The sauce can be used immediately or refrigerated, covered, for 1 week.)

Prepare the dry rub, combining the ingredients in a small bowl. (The rub, covered, can be made as much as a week ahead.)

Place the pork, fat side up, on a work surface. Cut each pork section in half lengthwise, forming a total of four long strips. Sprinkle the dry rub evenly over the pork sections, and massage them vigorously, covering them all with a generous coating of the spice mixture. Cover and chill for at least 2 hours and up to 8 hours.

While the pork marinates, prepare the coleslaw, first mixing together in a large bowl the mayonnaise, vinegar, barbecue sauce, and sugar. Stir in the cabbage and season with salt. Cover the coleslaw and refrigerate it until needed. (The slaw can be made up to 8 hours in advance.)

Make the barbecue mop or baste (see Technique Tip), combining the ingredients with ½ cup water in a small saucepan. Reserve until needed.

Fire up a smoker or covered grill to between 225°F and 250°F, following the manufacturer's instructions for smoking. Remove the pork from the refrigerator and let it sit covered at room temperature for 30 minutes.

Transfer the pork to the smoker and smoke covered for 3 to 3½ hours, until the pork reaches 165°F to 170°F. Open the smoker only when necessary, and cover as quickly as possible, to minimize the loss of heat and smoke. Turn the pork and brush it lightly with the barbecue mop each time the smoker is opened.

When cool enough to handle, shred the pork into bite-size pieces, discarding the fat. Mix the accumulated meat juices back in with the pork. Spoon the meat onto the bottom halves of the buns, add hearty drizzles of barbecue sauce and mounds of coleslaw, and top with the remaining bun halves. Serve immediately.

TECHNIQUE TIP: The manufacturers of some smokers do not recommend using liquid bastes such as our barbecue mop. Skip that step if yours is among those models.

Iowa Skinny

Serves 4

Anytime we're in Iowa, Illinois, or Indiana we start salivating for a pork "tenderloin" sandwich, often called a "skinny" in the "I" states. A platter-size piece of meat, pounded thin, dwarfs the bread it's served in, always a diminutive burger bun. It looks like a flying saucer when it lands on your plate, and it does deliver out-of-this-world flavor. Instead of a slender tenderloin, the sandwich actually starts with a chunky pork loin, hammered to a skinniness that further tenderizes the already succulent meat. Served at a café, tenderloins frequently come with just chips or fries, but for a fresh vegetable option at home try Summer Succotash (page 240) or Yellow Squash Casserole (page 249).

- Four 6- to 7-ounce boneless center-cut pork loin chops
- ½ cup stone-ground cornmeal, preferably yellow
- ¼ cup all-purpose unbleached flour
- 1½ teaspoons salt
- ½ teaspoon freshly milled black pepper
- Vegetable oil or shortening for pan-frying
- Soft hamburger buns
- Lettuce leaves
- Ketchup, mustard, or mayonnaise, or a combination
- Dill pickle slices

Place a pork chop between 2 sheets of wax paper and pound with a mallet to ¼-inch thickness or less. The chop should be large, round, and lacy-edged. You should be able to see through the pork in places. Repeat with the remaining chops.

Stir together on a plate the cornmeal, flour, salt, and pepper.

Pour ½ inch of oil into a heavy skillet and heat it to 365°F. Dredge the first pork chop heavily in the cornmeal-flour mixture and fry it until golden and crisp. about 2 minutes per side. The chop will shrink by a couple of inches while frying, but will remain large. Drain and repeat with the other pork chops, checking the temperature of the oil each time.

Serve hot on buns with lettuce, spreading the bread thickly with ketchup or other condiments and serving pickles on the side.

Dagwood

Makes a giant sandwich, adequate for 1 Dagwood or 4 to 6 other diners

Named long ago for its most experienced engineer, this hefty sandwich honors "Chic" Young's comic-strip everyman, Dagwood Bumstead. The first cartoon version of the sandwich, which appeared in the strip during the Great Depression, was more modest than it became over time with increased prosperity and Dagwood's growing appetite. In superior versions, the mix of ingredients varies with the eater's whims, but the components are always high-quality fresh meats, cheeses, and vegetables. Our Dagwood bulges out as well as up, making it a little easier to handle and even to share, if such a heretical notion strikes your fancy.

1 unsliced loaf of white or whole-wheat sandwich bread, about 12 inches in length

3 tablespoons unsalted butter, softened

3 tablespoons mayonnaise, Thousand Island, or Russian dressing

1½ pounds to 2 pounds mixed thin-sliced meats, such as smoked turkey, roast beef, ham, pepperoni, salami, mortadella, or even bologna if from a good source, such as Hebrew National

½ pound mixed sliced cheese, such as Cheddar, provolone, or Monterey Jack

1 medium to large red-ripe tomato, sliced thin

½ small onion, sliced thin

Crisp lettuce leaves

Green and ripe olives, pepperoncini, and dill or sweet pickle slices, as you wish

This sandwich-building technique results in a grand towering presentation, but it simplifies eating when your mouth is smaller than your monument. We basically put two sandwiches on top of each other, so that they can be broken down into manageable portions.

Carefully cut the loaf lengthwise with a serrated knife into 4 thick slices. Spread the inside of the top and bottom slices with butter. On the middle 2 slices, spread the sides facing the top and bottom with mayonnaise. Arrange the remaining ingredients between the top 2 and bottom 2 bread slices, dividing them by color, flavor, texture, or whatever else suits your fancy. (The sandwich can be made an hour or two ahead to this point, wrapped tightly, and refrigerated.)

Spear the loaf with extra-long toothpicks or bamboo kebab skewers. If you're feeling especially artistic, skewer the olives or other garnishes to crown the sandwich, or just arrange them to the side of this zeppelin. Dagwood would likely attack the sandwich whole, but you may wish to slice it into 4 to 6 sections first. When it's time to dig in, unskewer the sandwich sections, separating the top layer from the bottom, and eat each layer as a separate sandwich.

Po'Boys and Po'Wives

Dagwoods are strictly home fare, but the sandwich has plenty of cousins eaten both at home and out, including the hero, submarine, grinder, hoagie, and po'boy. Normally served in a small loaf of Italian or French bread, sliced lengthwise, each variation features a cornuçopia of hearty fillings. Italian Americans developed many of the best versions, which can boast anything from meatballs with ersatz marinara sauce to a heap of authentic *salume.* One of our personal favorites, the New Orleans muffaletta, contains ham, mortadella, salami, provolone and, most important, a garlicky green-olive salad—a combination that soars above the sum of its parts.

The muffaletta goes back to the first decade of the twentieth century, but the New Orleans oyster loaf, an ancestor of the po'boy, is even older. *The Picayune's Creole Cook Book* (1901) gives a home recipe that calls for broiled or creamed oysters in a sliced loaf of French bread, and goes on to explain the social background of the dish. "This is called the 'famous peacemaker' in New Orleans. Every husband, who is detained downtown, laughingly carries home an oyster loaf, or Médiatrice, to make 'peace' with his anxiously waiting wife. Right justifiably is the Oyster Loaf called the 'Peacemaker,' for, well made, it is enough to bring the smiles to the face of the most disheartened wife."

Miles Standish

SERVES 4

Whimsically named by an anonymous wit for the early leader in the Plymouth Colony, this sandwich combines ingredients commonly associated today with Thanksgiving. We plan for holiday leftovers intentionally just so we can concoct this creamy, cranberry-laced turkey treat, but it's easy enough to make anytime you want to celebrate a winter evening.

CRANBERRY-ORANGE RELISH

1 large orange

12 ounces (1 bag) cranberries, fresh or frozen

½ to ¾ cup sugar

6 ounces cream cheese, softened

8 slices soft white sandwich bread

Sprinkling of crumbled dried sage or a small handful of fresh sage leaves, optional

8 to 10 ounces thin-sliced roast or smoked turkey breast

Crisp lettuce leaves

Fresh sage sprigs, optional, for garnish

Zest the orange and place the peel in a food processor. Cut the white pith away from the orange with a small sharp knife, a simple but often ignored step that markedly improves the flavor of the sauce. Discard the pith and any seeds, and cut the orange into several chunks. Add the orange, cranberries, and ½ cup of the sugar to the processor, and chop coarsely. Taste and add more sugar if you wish, keeping in mind that the relish should remain refreshingly tart. (The relish, covered and refrigerated, keeps for at least a week. You will have more than necessary for these sandwiches, but the relish enhances multiple meats and sandwiches.)

Spread the cream cheese equally on 4 slices of bread. If you wish, arrange sage over the cheese. Divide the turkey among the sandwiches, and then spoon 2 to 3 tablespoons of cranberry relish onto each. Top with lettuce and the remaining bread, and serve, garnished with sage if desired.

TECHNIQUE TIP:
Hot turkey sandwiches tend to be a restaurant speciality, but some of the best are much easier to make at home today, now that decent sliced turkey started displacing horrid processed turkey rolls. Try a Louisville Hot Brown, created at the city's venerable Brown Hotel. Served open-face on toasted bread, it features sliced turkey or chicken breast topped generously with a cheesy rarebit sauce, bacon, and tomatoes. A less famous country cousin is the horseshoe, the pride of Springfield, Illinois, probably devised by a hotel cook who listed the Brown on his résumé. Contemporary versions consist of turkey or ham on toast, a spicy rarebit sauce, and a crowning ring of French fries arranged in a horseshoe shape. Light eaters opt for a pony shoe.

Oregon Hot Crab and Cheddar Sandwich

Serves 4

New Englanders make good crab rolls, and Marylanders excel with soft-shell crab variations, but Pacific Northwest cooks came up with the country's premier crab sandwich. At first glance, the hot, open-face sandwich doesn't seem too promising because of the cheese and seafood pairing, often unsuccessful, and the reliance on a white sauce, an overused binder that's normally bland at best. Here a good Cheddar, such as Oregon's medium or sharp Tillamook, gives bite to the sauce and also highlights the silky luxuriance of the crab. Local cooks would favor the sweet meat from the Pacific's Dungeness crabs, but any flavorful crabmeat works well.

CHEESE SAUCE

2 tablespoons unsalted butter

2 tablespoons all-purpose unbleached flour

½ teaspoon dry mustard

Pinch of cayenne pepper

¾ cup whole milk

¼ cup half-and-half

½ teaspoon Worcestershire sauce

6 ounces medium or sharp Cheddar cheese, grated (1½ cups)

Salt

2 tablespoons mayonnaise

1 teaspoon Worcestershire sauce

¼ teaspoon dry mustard

12 ounces cooked crabmeat, preferably lump crabmeat, picked over for shells and cartilage (see Ingredient Tip)

4 large slices sourdough bread, crusts trimmed if especially chewy, toasted

1½ tablespoons minced green olives, optional

Warm the butter in a heavy saucepan over medium heat. When melted, sprinkle in the flour, dry mustard, and cayenne, and whisk to combine. Pour in the milk, half-and-half, and Worcestershire sauce in a slow, steady stream, continuing to whisk as the mixture thickens. Bring to a simmer, reduce the heat to low, and continue cooking for about 3 minutes to eliminate the flour's pasty taste. Stir in the cheese, mixing until melted evenly, and salt to taste. Remove the sauce immediately from the heat and keep warm.

Stir together in a medium bowl the mayonnaise, Worcestershire sauce, and mustard. Gently combine the crab with the mayonnaise mixture.

Heat the broiler.

Arrange the bread slices on 4 heatproof plates. Spoon the crab mixture equally over the toast. Ladle the cheese sauce over the crab, letting some of it pool around the edges of the plates. Scatter olives over the cheese sauce if you wish. Place the plates under the broiler, in batches if necessary, and heat for 1 to 2 minutes, until the sandwiches are heated through and the cheese is bubbly. Serve the open-face sandwiches immediately.

INGREDIENT TIP: Given the average 3- to 4-pound size of a whole Dungeness crab, it's relatively easy to pick out the meat yourself as described on page 112. You may also find fresh prepicked lump crabmeat, which is sometimes worth the added expense for the time saved. Newman's Fish Market in Portland, Oregon (503-227-2700), sells both whole Dungeness crabs and their meat by mail order. Fresh crab should be eaten within a day of purchase. Frozen crab and canned pasteurized crabmeat, sold in the refrigerated section of a seafood department, are a step down from fresh in flavor, but still much better than the conventionally canned crab found alongside the tuna on a grocery shelf.

Alabama Fried Catfish Sandwich

SERVES 4

You wouldn't fry a catfish this way to eat alone, and you wouldn't serve this pungent dressing as a relish on the side. They meld majestically, however, inside a toasted roll, creating a southern sensation with overtones reminiscent of a distant cousin, the barbecued pork sandwich. Pair the sandwich with Fried Okra (page 262) or Pea Salad (page 263).

MUSTARD DRESSING

5 tablespoons yellow mustard

2 tablespoons ketchup

½ teaspoon hot pepper sauce, such as Tabasco

⅔ cup buttermilk

Hot pepper sauce, such as Tabasco

½ cup stone-ground cornmeal

¼ cup extra-fine cornmeal (sometimes called corn flour), preferably, or unbleached all-purpose flour (see Ingredient Tip)

¾ teaspoon salt

½ teaspoon freshly milled black pepper

4 large soft rolls, split

Vegetable oil for pan-frying

Two 10- to 12-ounce catfish fillets, halved

½ small onion, sliced thin

Crisp lettuce leaves, such as romaine or iceberg

Prepare the dressing, mixing together the ingredients in a small bowl.

Pour the buttermilk into a shallow bowl and add several healthy splashes of hot sauce to it. In another shallow bowl or on a plate, stir together both cornmeals, salt, and pepper.

Hollow out the rolls so that a thin but substantial bread "shell" remains. Toast the rolls.

Pour enough oil in a heavy skillet to come up about halfway on the sides of the catfish pieces. Heat the oil to 360°F.

Dip each catfish piece in buttermilk and then in the seasoned cornmeal. Arrange the fish in the hot oil, avoiding crowding. Fry for a total of about 5 minutes per each ½ inch of thickness, turning once. Drain the fish.

Slather the rolls with generous portions of the dressing. Top each with a fish piece, equal portions of the onions, and a lettuce leaf. Serve immediately.

INGREDIENT TIP: If extra-fine cornmeal isn't sold locally, you can make a substitute for it by grinding regular cornmeal in a blender or food processor. Better yet, you can mail-order the extra-fine meal from companies specializing in southern food products. We've been getting ours for years from the venerable Adams Milling Company in Midland City, Alabama (800-239-4233 or 334-983-3539).

Food imaginatively and lovingly prepared, and eaten in good company, warms the being with something more than the mere intake of calories. I cannot conceive of cooking for friends or family, under reasonable conditions, as being a chore. Food eaten in unpleasant circumstances is unblessed to our bodies' good—and so is a drug-store sandwich—or a raw duck. Some of my dishes, such as alligator-tail steak or Minorcan gopher stew, may horrify the delicate, who may consider them, too, unblessed. I have included nothing that is not extremely palatable, and the reader or student of culinary arts may either believe me or fall back in cowardly safety on a standard cook book.

MARJORIE KINNAN RAWLINGS, CROSS CREEK COOKERY (1942)

Great Lakes Smoked Whitefish Salad Sandwich

Serves 6

Whitefish from the chilly waters of the Great Lakes taste great smoked, as any deli connoisseur can testify. Unlike lox, which is cold-smoked in a commercial process, whitefish is usually hot-smoked, by both retailers and numerous home cooks throughout the upper Midwest. Doing your own smoking adds to the enjoyment of this sandwich, but you can also get smoked fish from the deli or market. The salad mixture features flavors that come from the Scandinavian heritage of the Lake Michigan shores.

WHITEFISH BRINE

½ cup kosher salt

¼ cup packed brown sugar

1 tablespoon plus 1 teaspoon minced fresh dill, or 2 teaspoons dried dill

2 teaspoons freshly milled black pepper

1½-pound chunk whitefish, sablefish, sea bass, or pike

SALAD

½ cup plus 2 tablespoons sour cream

5 tablespoons mayonnaise

2 small celery stalks, chopped fine

2 tablespoons minced red onion

2 tablespoons minced parsley

1 teaspoon minced fresh dill or ½ teaspoon dried dill

Freshly milled black pepper

12 large slices pumpernickel or soft white sandwich bread

Crisp lettuce leaves

Prepare the brine, first stirring together the ingredients in a medium bowl, then adding 1½ cups of water. Stir to dissolve. Place the whitefish in a zipperlock plastic bag and pour the brine over the fish. Refrigerate it for at least 2 hours and up to 8 hours. (The saltiness and sweetness will become more pronounced the longer the fish marinates in the brine.)

Drain the fish and let it sit at room temperature to air-dry for 15 to 30 minutes.

Fire up a smoker or covered grill to between 225°F and 250° F, following the manufacturer's instructions for smoking. Oil the cooking grate well. Place the fish on the cooking grate as far from the fire as possible.

Smoke covered for 30 to 40 minutes, until the fish flakes throughout. Open the smoker only when necessary, and cover as quickly as possible, to minimize the loss of heat and smoke.

When cool enough to handle, flake the fish into a bowl, discarding the skin and the many bones. Stir in the salad ingredients. (The salad can be made a day ahead if you wish, and kept covered and refrigerated.) Mound the fish mixture onto half of the bread slices and top with lettuce and the remaining bread slices.

Denver Sandwich

SERVES 2 GENEROUSLY OR 4 MORE DEMURE DINERS

Also called a "Western sandwich," the Denver is definitely a child of the frontier. Essentially a well-seasoned omelet nestled between two slabs of sourdough bread, it may date, according to one theory, to wagon-train days. Others, including James Beard, speculate that the sandwich comes from Chinese cooks in railroad and logging camps, and was perhaps inspired by egg foo yung. Whatever the origin, it's good enough, in the words of Cora, Rose, and Bob Brown, to make you want to "jig-down to the tune of 'Turkey in the Straw.' "

4 large slices sourdough bread

2 to 3 tablespoons unsalted butter, softened

FILLING

4 large eggs

Salt and freshly milled black pepper

Hot pepper sauce, such as Tabasco, optional

4 bacon slices, chopped

2 tablespoons unsalted butter

1 medium onion, chopped

1 small to medium green bell pepper, chopped

Generously butter both sides of each slice of bread. Cook the bread on a griddle over medium heat until lightly brown and crisp on both sides, about 8 minutes total. Keep the bread warm. (Once you become familiar with the preparation, it is easy to toast the bread while you are whisking eggs and cooking the filling ingredients.)

Briefly whisk together the eggs, salt, and pepper with 2 tablespoons of water. Add splashes of hot pepper sauce if you wish. Whisk just enough to combine the yolks and whites barely.

Warm a 7- to 8-inch omelet pan or skillet, preferably nonstick, over medium heat. Scatter half of the bacon in the pan and cook until brown and crisp. Remove the bacon with a slotted spoon and drain it. Add half of the butter to the pan, swirling it to coat the entire surface thoroughly. Stir in half of the onion and bell pepper, and sauté until softened and the onions are translucent, about 5 minutes.

Raise the heat to high. Add half of the egg mixture and swirl it to coat the entire pan. Let the pan sit directly over the heat a few seconds, until the eggs firm in the bottom of the pan. Sprinkle the cooked bacon evenly over the eggs. Tilt the pan so that uncooked egg can flow to the bottom of the pan. The eggs should cook just a touch longer than a traditional omelet, remaining moist but not wet at the center. Pull the pan sharply toward you several times, and then tilt the pan so that the back half of the omelet begins to roll over the front portion. Use a spatula to help fold over the eggs evenly. The omelet should be golden outside. Tip the omelet out onto one of the grilled bread slices, shaping it with the spatula if needed. Top with the other slice of grilled bread, halve if you wish, and serve the first sandwich. Wipe out the skillet and immediately repeat the process with the remaining bread and filling ingredients.

Fannie Farmer, 1857–1915

Perhaps the most influential cookbook author ever in the United States, Fannie Farmer took up cooking as a young lady to supplement her family's income. At the age of thirty, she enrolled in a course at the Boston Cooking School, stayed on as an assistant principal, and became the head of the institution in 1891. She remained at the school for eleven years, plenty of time for the bright, determined administrator to produce *The Boston Cooking-School Cook Book,* now in its thirteenth revised edition as *The Fannie Farmer Cookbook.*

The original 1896 publication owed much of its success to factors that make Farmer a little controversial today. She approached cooking as a scientific task, introducing level measurements and discussing food largely in terms of its chemical and nutritive properties. Other writers of the day leaned in a similar direction, but Farmer lunged in so deep that she often left little to relish in the cooking or eating.

Some people fault Farmer in other ways, particularly originality, but she also deserves credit for many things, including early promotion of the sandwich. Following up on Sarah Tyson Rorer's small 1894 book, *Sandwiches,* Farmer became the first author to devote a whole chapter to the subject in an important general cookbook. She provided directions for an egg salad sandwich as well as options based on chicken, ham, lobster, fried oysters, and a combination of jelly with chopped walnuts. With the fame of her book, and its timing, Farmer helped launch a lunchtime revolution.

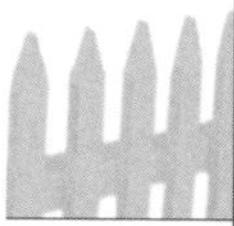

Shelby County Egg Salad Sandwich

Serves 4

Back in 1986, Jason Griffith of Center, Texas, entered the salad in this sandwich in the East Texas Poultry Festival and carried home the blue-ribbon prize. We gave his recipe originally in our *Texas Home Cooking* (1993), so we searched diligently while working on this book for a better egg salad from another corner of the country. We didn't find one. From our judge's perch, Mr. Griffith deserves the gold.

EGG SALAD

- 6 hard-boiled eggs, grated fine or sieved
- ¼ cup plus 2 tablespoons minced pimiento-stuffed green olives
- ¼ cup plus 1 tablespoon mayonnaise
- 2 tablespoons minced scallions
- 2 tablespoons minced parsley
- 1 tablespoon Dijon mustard
- Salt and freshly milled black pepper

- 8 slices soft white sandwich bread or soft whole-wheat bread
- Crisp lettuce leaves

Combine the salad ingredients in a bowl, mixing thoroughly. Refrigerate the salad, covered, for at least 30 minutes for the flavors to develop. (The salad can be made several days ahead if you wish.) Spread the salad equally on half of the bread slices, and top each with lettuce and the remaining bread. Halve the sandwiches before serving.

Golden Grilled Cheese

Serves 4

Both the English and the French make cheese sandwiches, but nothing from either nation combines simplicity and flavor in such a pleasant package as the American grilled cheese. At its best cooked on a griddle or skillet, rather than grilled or toasted, the sandwich also benefits from tasty but moderately soft bread and cheese. Served with a vegetable-rich soup, it's the quintessential "good hot lunch" Americans have long loved.

8 slices soft but not spongy white bread, cut no thicker than ½ inch

5 to 6 tablespoons unsalted butter, softened

8 to 10 ounces mild or medium Cheddar or Colby cheese, or other good melting cheese, such as Monterey Jack, sliced ¼ inch thick (see Ingredient Tip)

Generously butter one side of each slice of bread. Warm a griddle or large heavy skillet over medium heat.

Arrange half of the bread slices on the warm griddle, buttered side down. Top with cheese slices, covering the entire exposed surface of the bread slices. Top with the remaining slices of bread, buttered side up. Cook until the sandwiches are golden brown and crisp, 8 to 10 minutes, turning once.

INGREDIENT TIP: The oldest cheese factory in the United States makes our favorite cheese for this sandwich. A Vermont original, first created by Winfield Crowley more than a century ago, Crowley Cheese defies easy categorization. Technically a Colby, it offers the more robust flavor of Cheddar, providing an unusual combination of creamy melting quality and bold but nonacidic taste. Supply is limited, since the company produces only a few hundred pounds of cheese a day. To order by mail from Healdville, Vermont, call 800-683-2606.

Pimiento Cheese Sandwich

Makes 4 to 6 sandwiches

Technicolor to the core from its mix of mild red peppers and orange-hued Cheddar, pimiento cheese looks appalling to the uninitiated. Those of us who grew up on the homemade spread—always found in the refrigerator at Bill's childhood home in Texas—know differently. As Reynolds Price says in *The Great American Writers' Cookbook* (1981), for Southerners at least, "It's a sovereign nerve-salve."

- ¾ pound medium or sharp Cheddar cheese, grated (about 3 cups)
- ½ cup mayonnaise
- 3- to 4-ounce jar roasted red peppers or pimientos
- 1½ tablespoons minced onion
- 8 to 12 slices soft white sandwich bread

Purée the cheese, mayonnaise, peppers, and onion in a food processor. Refrigerate, covered, for at last 30 minutes and up to several days. Spread the mixture onto half of the bread slices. Top with the remaining bread, halve the sandwiches, and serve.

Louisville Benedictine

Serves 4

Ladies' tea parties featured light sandwiches over a century ago, but most of the creations are fortunately forgotten. This is an exception from the early sandwich days, conceived by Louisville hostess, caterer, and cookbook author Jennie Benedict. Peppery cress seasons the cream-cheese-and-vegetable spread and also tops our version of the sandwich, made heartier with the addition of crunchy bacon bits.

BENEDICTINE SPREAD

- 1 medium cucumber, peeled, seeded, and chunked
- 1 cup packed watercress, preferably, or spinach leaves
- 2 tablespoons minced onion
- 8 ounces cream cheese, softened
- 1 tablespoon Durkee's Famous Sauce or mayonnaise
- Hot pepper sauce, such as Tabasco

- 8 slices soft white sandwich bread or soft whole-wheat bread
- 6 crisp cooked bacon slices, crumbled
- Thin-sliced onion rings
- Watercress sprigs, preferably, or spinach leaves

Combine in a food processor the cucumber, watercress, and onion, and purée. Add the cream cheese, Durkee's sauce, and pepper sauce, and combine thoroughly. Refrigerate, covered, for at least 1 hour to allow the spread to firm up and develop full flavor.

Slather the spread equally on half of the bread, top each slice with bacon, onion rings, watercress, and the remaining bread. Halve the sandwiches and serve.

How to Cook a Husband

In selecting your husband you should not be guided by the silvery appearance, as in buying mackerel, nor the golden tint, as if you wanted salmon. Be sure to select him yourself, as tastes differ. Do not go to market for him, as the best are always brought to your door. It is far better to have none unless you will patiently learn how to cook him. A preserving kettle of the finest porcelain is best, but if you have nothing but an earthenware pipkin, it will do, with care. See that the linen in which you wrap him is nicely washed and mended, with the required number of buttons and strings nicely sewed on. Tie him in the kettle by a strong silk cord called comfort, as the one called duty is apt to be weak. They are apt to fly out of the kettle and be burned and crusty on the edges, since, like crabs and lobsters, you have to cook them while alive.

Make a clear, steady fire out of love, neatness, and cheerfulness. Set him as near this as seems to agree with him. If he sputters and fizzes, do not be anxious; some husbands do this until they are quite done.

Des Moines Missionary Sewing School, A Collection of Choice Recipes (1903) (and in other community cookbooks of the day)

LITTLE WHIMS

To Whet the Appetite

IN MOST HOME MEALS, TODAY AND IN THE PAST, Americans have felt little need to stimulate the appetite with predinner tidbits. We've usually come to the table ready to chow down on something substantial. If we served a first course, it was likely a hearty soup in previous centuries and, in more recent years, probably a green salad.

An exception to the routine was made mainly when we celebrated holidays or entertained guests. We brought out oysters or other seafood nibbles, and maybe for a ladies' luncheon, some canapés or other dainties. The types of appetizers didn't extend much further until Americans invented the cocktail party, one of the few lasting benefits of Prohibition. When we could no longer legally congregate at the neighborhood saloon, we began inviting friends home for a drink of bathtub gin, a form of entertaining that only grew in popularity as our booze improved in the following decade after repeal of the Eighteenth Amendment. Perhaps because our taverns had often served snacks, so did the American host and hostess, who developed a wide variety of finger foods meant to be eaten while standing, chatting, and drinking.

Those cocktail morsels included some of the worst favors friends have ever bestowed on one another, but also a select number that still ring bells of joy the next morning. We offer our choice of the best tidbits, plus a heaping handful of seafood and fish starters, most of which can be served either as a sit-down course or a stand-around nibble. Along with the soups and salads in later chapters, they warm up the taste buds with down-home sparkle.

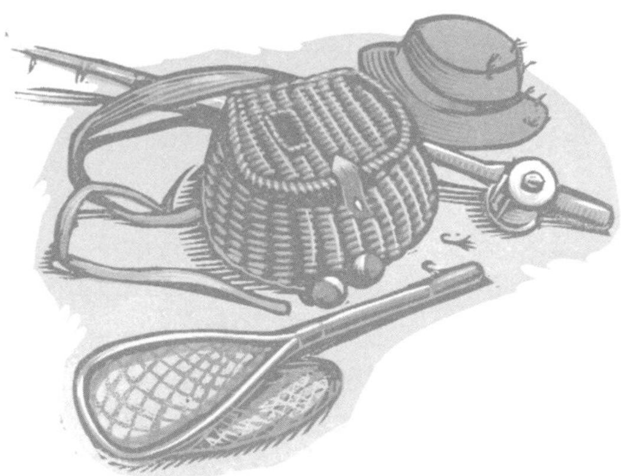

Mary Randolph, 1762–1828

Born into one of the most prominent families in Virginia, Mary Randolph grew up at Tuckahoe Plantation, taught from a young age to be the mistress-in-charge of a large southern household. Her father served in the colonial and state legislatures as well in as the revolutionary conventions of 1775 and 1776. Her brother Thomas wed Thomas Jefferson's daughter Martha, and eventually became governor of Virginia.

At the age of eighteen, "Molly" (as she was always known) married a cousin, David Randolph, then a captain of revolutionary troops. After the war, President George Washington appointed David a U.S. marshal, and the young couple moved to Richmond. They built a magnificent residence, Moldavia, where Mary quickly acquired a reputation for lavish hospitality. When Jefferson assumed the presidency, he removed David from office because of political differences, and the Randolphs had to sell their mansion and adapt to greatly reduced circumstances. Mary opened a fashionable boardinghouse, where she was called "the Queen," according to a contemporary chronicler, who also said that in her establishment, "wit, humor and good-fellowship prevailed, but excess rarely."

She published *The Virginia Housewife* in 1824, just a few years before her death. The book dominated southern thinking on the subject for generations. It was the first truly American cookbook, and perhaps in the end, the foremost of all our cookbooks.

Scalloped Oysters

Serves 4

An oyster hater in nineteenth-century America had little choice but to become a social recluse. Virtually every holiday and festive meal started with oysters in one form or another, sometimes raw on the half shell, but often cooked in a variety of ways. This baked style is a New Orleans elaboration of an old favorite that appeared in print as early as Mary Randolph's *The Virginia Housewife* (1824). A similar dish probably provided inspiration to Jules Alciatore—despite his claims of originality—when he added his rich Oysters Rockefeller to the menu at Antoine's restaurant in 1899. The chunks of artichoke bottom in the recipe come from Italian influences, which have been strong in New Orleans cooking since the late nineteenth century. Except for that addition, our version adheres closely to one featured in *The Picayune's Creole Cook Book* (1901).

- 2 dozen shucked oysters on the half shell
- 3 to 4 artichoke bottoms, fresh, frozen, or canned, halved and sliced thin
- ¼ cup minced fresh basil
- ¼ cup minced flat-leaf parsley
- ⅔ cup fresh bread crumbs
- 3 tablespoons unsalted butter, melted
- 2 to 3 tablespoons Herbsaint, Pernod, or other anise-flavored liqueur
- Kosher salt or other coarse salt, optional
- Fresh basil sprigs

Heat the broiler.

Arrange the oysters on a baking sheet or heatproof serving dish. Scatter with the artichoke slices. Sprinkle each with equal portions of basil, parsley, and bread crumbs. Drizzle the oysters with melted butter and liqueur. Pop them under the broiler just to heat the oysters through and brown the crumbs, 2 to 3 minutes. Watch them carefully.

If serving the oysters "help yourself" style, we usually arrange them on a bed of coarse salt, which keeps them in place. When offering individual portions, we typically just plate them for each guest. Sprigs of fresh basil brighten the presentation in either case. Serve the oysters hot.

Olympia Oyster-Stuffed Mushrooms

Makes 2 dozen

In the heyday of the cocktail party, after World War II, Americans liked to serve oysters tucked in mushrooms. On the Pacific shore, hints of Asian influences entered mainstream American cooking around the same time, most artfully in Helen Evans Brown's *West Coast Cook Book* (1952). In tribute to her and the small Olympia oysters she loved, we add a trace of soy sauce and rice vinegar to the basic ingredients, just enough to highlight the natural brininess of the fresh sea flavor. If the tasty Olympias don't reach your markets, use the freshest oysters you can find.

2 dozen shucked small to medium oysters
¼ cup (½ stick) unsalted butter
¼ cup soy sauce
3 tablespoons rice vinegar
2 dozen medium to large mushroom caps, stemmed
Minced scallion greens

Heat the broiler. Remove the oysters from the refrigerator to take the chill off them while you prepare the other ingredients.

Melt the butter in a small saucepan over medium heat. Stir in the soy sauce and vinegar and remove from the heat. Brush the mushrooms with about half to three-fourths of the butter mixture and arrange them, caps up, on a baking sheet. Broil the mushrooms for 2 to 3 minutes, just until softened. (The mushrooms can be prepared to this point an hour in advance and left at room temperature until ready to proceed.)

Reheat the butter mixture if it has solidified. Dip each oyster in the remaining butter mixture and tuck it in a mushroom cap. Return the stuffed mushrooms to the baking sheet and broil them just until the oysters are heated through and plumped, 1 to 2 minutes. Watch the stuffed mushrooms carefully to avoid overcooking and toughening the oysters. Sprinkle with scallion greens and serve.

The Great Century of the Oyster

Americans plucked down oysters in the nineteenth century as if they were candy. We ate them from the beginning, out of beds far more abundant than in Europe, but after the colonies won independence they came close to an addiction, a kind of badge of American prosperity and democracy. One English visitor remarked that one of the main social distinctions in the United States between the rich and poor was whether they washed down their oysters with champagne or beer.

Access seldom presented a problem, even far inland from the seaside sources. Suppliers packed barrels full of live oysters to ship across the country by canal, railroad, and stagecoach. Retailers kept them alive in saltwater tanks, and cooks did the same at home, following instructions such as those in Mrs. T. J. Crowen's *The American Lady's System of Cookery* (1852): "Put oysters in water and wash them with a broom until they are perfectly clean; then lay them, the largest shell downwards, in a tub; sprinkle well with flour or oat-meal; wet them with water: repeat this operation daily, and they will fatten."

In coastal cities, vendors sold them on the street from wagons and wheelbarrows, and oyster saloons proliferated, offering as many as you could eat for pennies. "Diamond Jim" Brady downed dozens raw a day, sometimes just as a snack, but at home Americans generally cooked their oysters. They put as many as two hundred in a stew, or stuffed them in a roasted bird, fried them, or encased them in a pie. The population as a whole never ate so well.

Shrimp Cocktail

SERVES 4 TO 6

When refrigerated transportation made shrimp more widely available across the country in the twentieth century, they gradually replaced oysters as the preferred first course at fancy meals. Shrimp cocktail became the prototypical starter, consumed so heavily a generation ago in both home and restaurants that it totally lost favor in fashionable circles. It remains a classic nonetheless, capable of bringing out the best in both the seafood and the ketchup-based sauce when the two are balanced with respect for each. We serve the shrimp with their tails on for a sit-down appetizer, but remove the tails if offered as a stand-up party dunker.

Surf and Turf Cocktails

Shrimp cocktail is a direct descendant of the oyster cocktail, made with a similar sauce and popular around the turn of the twentieth century. Lizzie Kander and the other Milwaukee ladies who wrote *The Way to a Man's Heart: "The Settlement" Cook Book* of 1903 prepared the sauce with ketchup, tarragon vinegar, Rhine wine, cayenne, salt, and lemon juice. They also suggested a comparable sweetbread cocktail as an alternative, with the meat cut into "pieces the size of small oysters." Cora, Rose, and Bob Brown, in *America Cooks* (1940), explain that the sweetbread cocktail "is better in any inland, oysterless spot than a phony cocktail of real oysters, that come flabby and tasteless out of cans." The Browns go on to predict that the sweetbread cocktail would take an esteemed place alongside the so-called "prairie oyster," a hangover cure that featured a raw egg yolk in a cocktail sauce, swallowed whole in one big gulp.

1 lemon, halved

2 bay leaves

1 tablespoon salt

½ teaspoon cayenne pepper

2 teaspoons liquid-concentrate seafood-boil seasoning or about 1½ tablespoons dry seafood-boil seasoning

1½ pounds large shrimp, shelled and, if you wish, deveined

COCKTAIL SAUCE

1 cup chili sauce (the ketchup-style condiment)

2 tablespoons prepared horseradish or more to taste

Minced zest and juice of 1 medium lemon

Minced zest and juice of ½ lime

Hot pepper sauce, such as Tabasco

Salt, optional

Pour 8 cups of water into a large saucepan. Squeeze the lemon into the water and then toss in the rinds. Add the rest of the seasonings and bring to a boil over high heat. Boil for 5 to 10 minutes to flavor the water. Stir in the shrimp and cook over high heat for just 2 minutes. (The water should just come back to a boil in this time.)

Immediately remove from the heat and pour off half the cooking liquid. Pour the remaining liquid and shrimp into a bowl, and add a half-dozen ice cubes. Place the bowl in the freezer, if you have space. (In midwinter, we set the bowl outside in the snow, watching carefully for curious cats.) Otherwise, place the bowl in the refrigerator. Cool the shrimp briefly until cold to your touch. Pour off the remaining liquid, cover, and refrigerate the shrimp for at least 1 hour and up to 12 hours.

Prepare the sauce while the shrimp chill. Combine the ingredients in a small bowl, adjusting the seasonings and optional salt until sassy in taste. Refrigerate the sauce for at least 30 minutes. (Leftover sauce can be kept for days, though the flavor begins to fade a bit. Spark it back up with a bit of horseradish and lime.)

To serve the cocktail, pile the shrimp into one serving bowl or into individual bowls or goblets, with the festive-colored sauce on the side. A large stemmed glass bowl can hold both the sauce and the shrimp, with the sauce filling the bowl and the shrimp hooked around the rim, tails down.

Shrimp Rémoulade

SERVES 6 AS AN APPETIZER

Rémoulade sauce waltzed into New Orleans from France, but soon started jumping to a different beat, a spicy tropical tempo from Africa. The creamy Gallic rendition, well seasoned but soothing, caught fire and, like the fabled phoenix, came back full of youth and beauty for a new life. Apart from the proper heat, the key to success is the mayonnaiselike emulsion that requires both room-temperature ingredients and a slow, steady drizzle of oil to form correctly.

> The colored cooks of the South are the only truly hereditary cooks of America, comparable to the great cooking families of France or Austria. In America the white cook, if a man, yearns to sell autos; if a woman, dreams of opening a beauty shop. This is swell for ambition, but hell on seasoning.
>
> GRACE AND BEVERLY SMITH AND CHARLES MORROW WILSON, THROUGH THE KITCHEN DOOR (1938)

RÉMOULADE SAUCE

- ½ cup thin-sliced scallions
- ⅓ cup chopped celery
- ⅓ cup chopped parsley
- 1 plump garlic clove, minced
- 1 tablespoon fresh lemon juice
- 1 tablespoon white-wine vinegar (tarragon-flavored is nice but not essential)
- 1 teaspoon paprika
- 1 teaspoon salt
- ½ teaspoon prepared horseradish
- ¼ teaspoon cayenne pepper
- Pinch of ground white pepper
- 2 large eggs, at room temperature (see Ingredient Tip)
- ⅔ cup vegetable oil
- ¼ cup Creole mustard
- 3 tablespoons ketchup

- 1½ pounds chilled large shrimp, prepared as for Shrimp Cocktail, page 69
- Watercress, optional

Mince in a food processor the scallions, celery, parsley, and garlic. Add the lemon juice, vinegar, paprika, salt, horseradish, cayenne, pepper, and eggs, and process again to combine. With the machine running, pour the oil in a slow, steady stream. When the oil is incorporated and the sauce is creamy and mayonnaiselike in consistency, stop the processor, add the mustard and ketchup, and pulse to combine. Chill the sauce for at least 30 minutes before serving. It keeps for up to several days, covered.

Use the sauce as a dip for the shrimp, or spoon it over them on individual plates. Garnish with watercress if you wish.

INGREDIENT TIP: If you're concerned about the safety of your raw eggs, make the rémoulade using three mashed hard-boiled egg yolks instead. The flavor and consistency will be a bit different, but you'll come close to the original.

Cajun Crawfish Balls

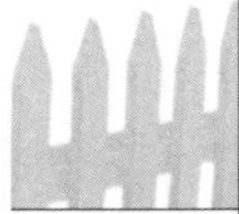

MAKES ABOUT 3 DOZEN BALLS

Anywhere Cajun influence extends along the Gulf coast, you find a fondness for crawfish fritters. If you start from whole crawfish, save the orange fat from the heads and mix it into the batter for extra richness.

3 cups packed fresh bread crumbs
½ cup (1 stick) unsalted butter
½ cup chopped onion
½ cup chopped celery
1 plump garlic clove, minced
1 tablespoon fresh lemon juice
2 teaspoons Worcestershire sauce
1 to 2 teaspoons hot pepper sauce, such as Cajun Chef or Tabasco
1 teaspoon cayenne pepper
1 teaspoon salt
¼ teaspoon freshly milled black pepper
Pinch of white pepper
1 egg, lightly beaten
1 pound blanched, peeled crawfish tails, chopped, plus any fat (see Ingredient Tip)
About ¼ cup unbleached all-purpose flour
Vegetable oil for deep-frying

When you have helped to raise the standard of cooking, you have helped to raise the only thing in the world that really matters anyhow. We only have one or two Wars a lifetime, but we have three meals a day.

WILL ROGERS, INTRODUCTION TO FASHIONS IN FOODS IN BEVERLY HILLS (1929)

Preheat the oven to 350°F. Scatter the bread crumbs on a baking sheet and bake 6 to 8 minutes, until dry and golden. Dump the crumbs into a large bowl.

Melt the butter in a small skillet over medium heat. Stir in the onion, celery, and garlic, and sauté briefly until soft. Stir in the lemon juice, Worcestershire sauce, hot pepper sauce, cayenne, salt, and both peppers, and remove from the heat. Scrape the mixture into the bread crumbs, add the egg and crawfish, and combine. Form the mixture into 1-inch balls and roll them in the flour. The balls will hold together a bit loosely. If the mixture gets too sticky or otherwise difficult to form into balls, refrigerate it for 5 to 10 minutes and then proceed.

Heat several inches of oil in a heavy saucepan or high-sided skillet to 350°F. Fry the balls in batches until golden brown, 1 to 2 minutes. Drain the balls and serve them immediately on a warm platter with additional hot sauce.

INGREDIENT TIP: Freshwater crustaceans related to lobsters, crawfish have a texture similar to shrimp but their own distinctive flavor. The meat is in the tails and the fat in the heads, with little in between. From November through early summer, try to find them alive and blanch them for 1 to 2 minutes before peeling. When starting from whole crustaceans, you'll need about 5 pounds of crawfish to equal the pound of tails called for in the recipe. Buying crawfish tails, already blanched and peeled, takes care of much of the work, but you may lose the succulent head fat. Some packagers are now bagging the fat with the tails, a good deal all around. Avoid blanched tails that are uncurled, an indication that the crawfish were already dead when cooked. Oh, and never call a crawfish a crayfish along the Gulf unless you're cultivating the image of a fool for a poker game.

Honolulu Poke

Serves 6

Because of heavy settlement by the Japanese, Hawaii discovered the delights of raw fish long before mainland America. In recent decades, sashimi evolved into a local dish called "poke" (pronounced *po-kay*), chunks of fresh fish, often ruby tuna, mixed sparingly but strikingly with Asian seasonings. We're forever indebted to Cyrus and Guy Tamashiro for introducing us to the varieties and subtleties of poke. We met them early one morning at the Honolulu fish market, where they were selecting the best of the day's catch for the thirty types of poke they make and sell at the family's Tamashiro Market. If you're ever in the city, visit them for a feast you'll never forget.

- 1¼ pounds sushi-quality fresh yellowfin or bluefin tuna
- 3 tablespoons Yamasa soy sauce or other good Japanese soy sauce
- 1½ teaspoons Asian sesame oil
- 3 tablespoons minced scallion greens
- ¼ to ½ teaspoon crushed dried hot red chiles
- ½ sheet nori (Japanese seaweed), optional (see Ingredient Tip)
- 1 tablespoon fine-chopped macadamia nuts, optional
- Pinches of sea salt

Cut the fish into ¾-inch cubes with a sharp knife and transfer them to a bowl. Mix the tuna gently with soy sauce and sesame oil, and mix in the scallion greens and chiles. If you use the nori, which we do, toast it first by passing it over a stove burner several times on each side until it crisps and deepens in color. With scissors, cut it into squares as tiny as your patience will allow, then use your fingers to crumble it. Add the macadamia nuts, too, if you wish. Taste and add salt by the smallest of pinches, enhancing the brininess but not overdoing it. Serve on a chilled platter and eat with chopsticks, preferably, in the local style.

INGREDIENT TIP: Hawaiians use nutrition-rich seaweed, known to them generically as *limu,* for seasoning fish and many other foods. *Ogo,* a red filament variety, is most common for making poke, but it's rarely found on the mainland. We suggest as a substitute the similarly briny nori, the paper-thin sea vegetable used to wrap sushi. Sold in sheets in many supermarkets, it's usually located in the Asian food section. You also find nori cut into strips about 3 inches long, already seasoned lightly. Six or so of the strips equal a half-sheet. We like the nori from Sound Sea Vegetables, available in some natural foods stores.

If food in Hawaii did not fit mainland stereotypes, neither was it like any food I had ever experienced. . . . Soon after I arrived, a local newspaper had a competition for the best grinds (food) in town: the categories were saimin, poke, sushi, Portuguese sausage, laulau, plate lunch, loco moco, kim chee, lumpia, french fries, ice cream, dim sum, manapua, mochi, shave ice, char siu, burgers, hot dogs, crack seed, mango chutney, muffins, and pizza. . . .

Gradually I figured out that what I had encountered was Local Food, as it is called in Hawaii. Locals (long-term residents of the island) eat Local Food—saimin, shave ice, manapua, and plate lunches of rice and terriyaki and macaroni salad. . . . All this adds up to a society with one of the richest culinary heritages in the United States.

Rachel Laudan, The Food of Paradise (1996)

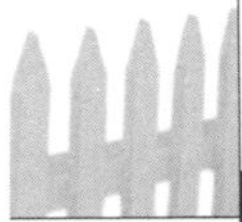

Marinated Salmon Bits

MAKES 3 TO 4 CUPS

Home pickling was a common means of preservation before refrigeration, but good cooks were seldom content with just keeping food, always looking for ways to turn the brining process into a flavoring method. This style of treating salmon comes from the Pacific Northwest and Alaska, but the idea of adding horseradish to the pickling mixture is from Lettice Bryan's *The Kentucky Housewife* (1839). As she describes her version, this is "a handsome and ready dish for any meal."

2-pound salmon fillet, skin removed, cut into neat ¾-inch squares

MARINADE

1½ cups rice vinegar or 1 cup white vinegar with ½ cup water

¾ cup seafood stock

½ medium onion, sliced into very thin half-rings

1 bay leaf, crumbled

1 teaspoon prepared horseradish

1 teaspoon yellow mustard seeds

1 teaspoon whole coriander seeds, bruised

1 teaspoon whole black peppercorns

1 teaspoon salt

1 teaspoon packed brown sugar

1 tablespoon extra-virgin olive oil

Watercress sprigs or other greens

Arrange the salmon in a single layer in a shallow nonreactive dish.

Prepare the marinade. Bring to a boil in a small saucepan the vinegar, stock, onion, bay leaf, horseradish, mustard seeds, coriander seeds, peppercorns, salt, and brown sugar. Reduce the heat to a bare simmer and cook for 10 minutes. Raise the temperature to high and bring the marinade to a rolling boil. Pour the hot marinade over the salmon and let it cool to room temperature. Drizzle the olive oil over the salmon. Put the salmon and marinade into a zipperlock plastic bag, and refrigerate for at least 4 hours and up to a couple of days. (While chilling, the salmon will become more firm in addition to absorbing the marinade.) To serve, drain the salmon squares, keeping a few onion rings and whole spices clinging to them, and serve with toothpicks on a bed of watercress or other greens.

Caveached Fish

Jews and Muslim Arabs share a number of historic dishes that probably evolved originally in the Middle East, including *escabeche.* Jewish immigrants brought the pickled-fish preparation to western Europe and the New World, and both here and in England, it came to be known as a Jewish dish. The idea appealed early to southern cooks, appearing as "caveached fish" in both Mary Randolph's *The Virginia Housewife* (1824) and Sarah Rutledge's *The Carolina Housewife* (1847). Randolph pronounces it "excellent" and Rutledge calls it "delicious."

Randolph also gives a recipe for pickled oysters, another old notion with British roots. Over time the two disparate traditions reinforced each other in southern cooking and ultimately helped inspire the modern regional favorite, pickled shrimp. The Junior League's classic *Charleston Receipts* (1950) provides two versions of the shrimp, one for putting away in airtight jars and another to serve, after a day of marinating, on a lettuce salad or as a cocktail party nibble.

Smoked Trout Spread

MAKES ABOUT 2 CUPS

From the old puréed shrimp paste of South Carolina to contemporary cream cheese concoctions, fish and shellfish spreads have a long (if not always venerable) history in the country. Of the many varieties around, this is our favorite, which we developed originally for one of our earlier books, *Smoke & Spice* (1994). If you don't want to smoke the trout yourself, use ½ pound of a good store-bought fish.

SMOKED TROUT

- 2 teaspoons fresh lemon juice
- ½ teaspoon prepared horseradish
- Salt and freshly milled black pepper to taste
- One 8- to 10-ounce trout, preferably brook trout, gutted (head on or off)

- 3 ounces cream cheese, softened
- 3 tablespoons minced onion
- 3 tablespoons pecan pieces, toasted
- 1 tablespoon fresh lemon juice
- 1½ teaspoons Creole mustard
- 1 teaspoon white-wine Worcestershire sauce
- Several drops of hot pepper sauce, such as Tabasco
- Crackers, zucchini rounds, or cucumber rounds

Prepare the trout for smoking. Stir together the lemon juice, horseradish, and a bit of salt and pepper. Rub the mixture inside the trout. Let the trout sit at room temperature for 20 to 30 minutes.

Fire up a smoker or covered grill to between 225°F and 250°F, following the manufacturer's instructions for smoking. Oil the cooking grate well. Place the fish on the cooking grate as far from the fire as possible.

Smoke the fish covered for 25 to 35 minutes, until the trout is opaque and flakes easily. Open the smoker only when necessary, and cover as quickly as possible, to minimize the loss of heat and smoke.

When cool enough to handle, flake the fish and place it in a food processor, discarding the skin and bones. Add the remaining ingredients, except for the crackers, and process until well mixed, but with a bit of texture to it. Pack the spread into a small serving bowl and refrigerate, covered, for at least 30 minutes.

Serve chilled with crackers or vegetables.

Chopped Chicken Liver

SERVES 8 TO 10

Eastern European Jews brought the basics of this spread from the Old World in the late nineteenth century, but the immigrants added different seasonings and turned it into a centerpiece of Jewish-American celebrations. Some people talk about it as a deli dish, but as early as 1912 in Portland, Oregon, Jewish home cooks included it in *The Neighborhood Cook Book,* published by the Oregon Council of Jewish Women. If you need a day off from cholesterol fear, you won't get better value for your vacation.

- ¼ cup plus 2 tablespoons melted chicken fat, butter, or margarine (see Ingredient Tip)
- 2 cups chopped yellow onion
- 1½ pounds chicken livers
- 3 hard-boiled eggs, quartered
- 1 teaspoon salt or more to taste
- ½ teaspoon freshly milled black pepper or more to taste
- Minced parsley
- Small rye bread slices or rye crackers

Warm the chicken fat in a skillet over medium-high heat. Stir in the onion and sauté until soft and beginning to brown in spots, about 5 minutes. Reduce the heat to medium, add the chicken livers, and continue sautéing until the livers become uniformly brown and firm, about 5 additional minutes. (Avoid overcooking the livers or they will become tough.)

Scrape the mixture into a food processor, and add the eggs, salt, and pepper. Pulse to chop the mixture evenly, stopping when you have fine pieces, not a purée. Chill the mixture for at least 1 hour and up to overnight, covered. Scoop the mixture into a serving dish and top with parsley. Serve, accompanied by rye bread.

INGREDIENT TIP: Chicken (or goose) fat, called schmaltz, has disappeared from most homes, though you still find it on the tables of some Jewish home-style restaurants such as Sammy's Roumanian in New York. It's certainly on the heavy side, but the taste is rich and remarkable. To render the fat yourself, buy a whole plump chicken and remove all of the skin and fat, saving the meat for cooking by some moist method. Wash and dry the skin and fat, and cut them into 1- to 2-inch pieces. Place the pieces in a heavy skillet with a couple of tablespoons or more of chopped onion, ¼ cup of water, and a little kosher salt. Cook uncovered over very low heat until the water has evaporated, the fat has melted completely, and the onion and skin have browned, about 30 minutes. Skim off the skin cracklings, called *gribenes,* saving them to top mashed potatoes or other dishes, or to nibble on as a killer snack. Strain the fat through a sieve or cheesecloth and reserve for cooking. It keeps, refrigerated, for weeks. You can use butter instead in the chopped chicken liver, or a kosher margarine substitute, but the flavor definitely pales.

The tidbits usually served at cocktail parties simply slay me. After looking at hundreds of silver platters and their ghastly contents for many years, I've reached the conclusion that someone must have offered an annual Pulitzer prize for the most deadly hors d'oeuvre. The competition for the ickiest appetizer seems to be pretty keen. Some of the stuff sensible women are dreaming up would make L. Borgia pack up her little black bag and go home.

TRADER VIC, TRADER VIC'S BOOK OF FOOD AND DRINK (1946)

Prairie Fire Dip

MAKES ABOUT 4 CUPS OF DIP

American bean dips likely evolved from the Mexican and southwestern habit of adding a few tortilla chips to refried beans as a handy scoop. Few of the dips actually grow notably beyond those roots, but this one is a real bloomer. Helen Corbitt, the maestro of modern Texas cooking, created the jalapeño-laced classic in the days when that chile was still new to the state. It seemed at the time as fiery as a raging range conflagration, hence the name. The dip spread as quickly as a prairie fire too, with recipes soon alighting in community cookbooks from Florida to Idaho.

- ¼ cup (½ stick) unsalted butter
- ½ medium onion, chopped fine
- 2 garlic cloves, minced
- 2 cups cooked pinto beans (canned are acceptable) plus ¼ cup cooking liquid or chicken stock
- 1 cup A Bowl of Red (page 214) or other chili con carne
- 8 ounces mild Cheddar, Monterey Jack, or asadero cheese, grated (about 2 cups)
- 2 to 3 pickled jalapeño chiles, chopped fine, plus liquid to taste
- Salt, optional
- Thin-sliced scallion greens
- ¼ cup chunky tomato salsa, such as Pico de Gallo (page 77), or sliced green or mild black olives, optional
- Tortilla chips

Melt the butter in a heavy skillet over medium heat. Add the onion and the garlic, and sauté briefly until the onion is soft and translucent, about 5 minutes. Pour in the beans and cooking liquid, and mash the beans with a potato masher or large fork while they warm through. Stir in the chili. When the beans and chili are heated, mix in the cheese and when melted, remove the skillet from the heat. Add the jalapeños and pickling liquid to the level of zip you prefer and salt if needed.

Pour into a bowl, sprinkle with scallion greens and, if you wish, garnish with salsa or olives mounded in the center of the dip. Serve immediately with tortilla chips or other corn chips for dunking. The dip is usually kept on a warming tray or over another heat source to keep the cheese from solidifying too soon.

James Beard, 1903–1985

Many fine American cooks grew up on monotonous food, and found their way into the kitchen in rebellion against their lot. James Beard came to cooking from the opposite direction, inspired by a childhood of hearty eating in Portland, Oregon, where his English mother, Mary, operated the Gladstone Hotel. She and her rakish husband instilled in the boy a love of European cuisine, and the hotel's Chinese chefs introduced him to Asian flavors, but ultimately Beard took the middle road geographically and became a promoter of American cooking.

He set out to sing opera professionally at first, then turned to acting, gaining theatrical experience that served him well in his culinary career. During the Great Depression, with acting jobs scarce, Beard opened a catering business in New York specializing in creative appetizers for upscale cocktail parties. Success in the enterprise led to his first book, *Hors d'Oeuvre and Canapés* (1940), and that in turn to the next, *Cook It Outdoors* (1942), the earliest of his extensive writings on the American passion for backyard cooking.

Beard attained fame a few years later as the nation's original television chef, hosting a show sponsored by the Borden Company and its Elsie the Cow. He returned to the small screen frequently after that, but also became an exceptional teacher, conducting classes in his home, and produced a prodigious array of books, including the monumental *James Beard's American Cookery* (1972). Better than anyone before him, Beard showed his generation the scope and caliber of our country's home cooking.

Pico de Gallo

MAKES APPROXIMATELY 2 CUPS

In Mexico, salsa is true to its name, which simply means "sauce." Different types accompany a wide range of dishes, including many meat, fish, and poultry main courses. In the United States, chile sauces play a similar role in some Southwestern specialties, but we usually reserve the term "salsa" for a table relish eaten before the meal as a dip. Called "pico de gallo" in Texas (literally, "beak of the rooster"), this is the favorite American style, full of fresh, uncooked vegetables.

- 1 pound Italian plum or other small red-ripe tomatoes, chopped
- 2 to 4 fresh jalapeño or serrano chiles, minced
- ¼ cup minced onion
- ¼ cup chopped cilantro
- Juice of ½ lime
- Salt

- Tortilla chips

In a small bowl, mix together the tomatoes, chiles, onion, and cilantro. Squeeze the lime juice over the mixture, add salt to taste, and stir again. Refrigerate for 30 minutes before serving, accompanied by tortilla chips.

TECHNIQUE TIP: For variety, roast the tomatoes under the broiler first and then purée them skin-on with the other ingredients for a smoother salsa. Soft fruits such as peaches and mangos often replace the tomatoes in contemporary versions.

In America since the repeal of the Prohibition Amendment there has developed a new and, at times, delightful form of hospitality—the cocktail party. . . . We have developed a most amazing variety of finger food to go with the cocktail and the glass of sherry, literally hundreds of variations, some of course borrowed from our European and Asiatic backgrounds and many that are distinctly our own. In many ways this is one of the most truly American contributions to the art of good living.

JAMES BEARD, HORS D'OEUVRE AND CANAPÉS (1940)

Bacon-Horseradish Dip

MAKES ABOUT 3 CUPS OF DIP

Home economists employed in the food-processing industry developed many of the most popular American dips, and helped make them a party staple soon after the end of World War II. The flavor combination in this recipe is much older and far more robust than usual.

- 2 cups sour cream
- ¾ pound crisp cooked bacon, crumbled
- ¼ cup minced red onion
- 2 tablespoons minced parsley
- ½ teaspoon Worcestershire sauce
- 1 to 2 tablespoons freshly-grated horseradish or 2 to 4 tablespoons prepared horseradish, or more to taste
- Salt, optional

Stir together the sour cream, bacon, onion, parsley, and Worcestershire sauce. Add the horseradish, starting with the smaller amount, then adding more until the mixture is pleasantly pungent. Add a bit of salt if you wish. Refrigerate the dip, covered, for at least 30 minutes before serving.

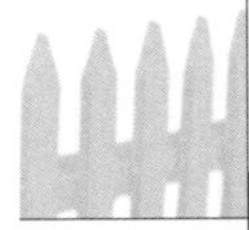

With a little experimentation, you'll soon develop a canapé repertoire equal to any occasion: from the cream-cheese-and-olive type that goes with sherry flips, chaperoned meetings and your "I-can't-think-of-you-as-an-undergraduate" line . . . to the pickled-herring-on-sea-biscuit type which supports your virile-bachelor, not-prepared-for-feminine-callers pose.

ESQUIRE'S HANDBOOK FOR HOSTS (1953)

Calcuttas

MAKES 2 DOZEN

The British brought bacon-wrapped tidbits to America under the name of "angels on horseback," and they've become a galloping success here in various heavenly guises. This appetizer is an old Virginia favorite, whimsically named for its chutney coating.

- 24 pitted prunes
- 1 small underripe banana, peeled and sliced into 24 rounds ¼ to ⅓ inch thick
- 12 thin bacon slices, halved
- ½ to ¾ cup mango chutney, any large chunks of fruit chopped or removed before measuring

Preheat the oven to 375°F.

Wrap a prune and a banana round snugly in a half-slice of bacon, securing with a toothpick. Place on an ungreased baking sheet. Repeat with the remaining prunes, banana rounds, and bacon.

Bake the tidbits for 18 to 20 minutes, until the bacon is browned. Remove from the oven and dip each in the chutney. Return to the oven and bake for an additional 4 to 6 minutes, until crisp. Serve hot.

Ham Biscuits

MAKES 3 DOZEN SMALL BISCUIT SNACKS

For centuries, a slow-cured country ham has been the southern host's secret to success, with which no impromptu party, snack, or meal is out of reach. Combined with a sweet and tangy fruit chutney and a hot, feather-light biscuit, it becomes the nearly addictive ham biscuit, a hallmark of southern hospitality.

PEACH CHUTNEY

1½ pounds ripe peaches, peeled and chopped

1 cup chopped red onion

½ cup golden raisins

¼ cup plus 2 tablespoons packed brown sugar

¼ cup plus 2 tablespoons granulated sugar

Scant 1 tablespoon minced fresh ginger

¼ teaspoon cayenne pepper

¾ cup cider vinegar

BUTTERMILK BENNE BISCUITS

4 cups low-gluten biscuit flour, preferably, or 3½ cups unbleached all-purpose flour plus ½ cup cake flour or, less desirably, 4 cups unbleached all-purpose flour (see Ingredient Tip)

1 tablespoon plus 1 teaspoon baking powder

1½ teaspoons salt

1 teaspoon baking soda

6 tablespoons lard, well chilled

3 tablespoons unsalted butter, well chilled

1 tablespoon Middle Eastern–style sesame oil

1¾ cups buttermilk, well chilled

2 to 3 tablespoons sesame seeds

Thin-sliced country ham

Brown mustard, optional

Freshly grated or prepared horseradish, optional

Prepare the chutney, first combining the ingredients and ½ cup of water in a heavy saucepan. Bring the mixture to a boil, then reduce the heat to low, and cook until the peaches are very tender and the chutney thick, 40 to 45 minutes. Chill the chutney, covered, for at least several hours and up to several weeks.

Prepare the biscuits, first preheating the oven to 475°F.

Sift the flour, baking powder, salt, and baking soda into a large bowl, preferably a shallow one. Cut the lard and butter into small chunks, and add them to the dry ingredients along with the sesame oil. Combine with a pastry blender just until a coarse meal forms. Make a well in the center and pour in the buttermilk. With your fingers and a few swift strokes, combine the dough just until it's a sticky mess. Turn out onto a lightly floured board or, better yet, a pastry cloth. Clean, dry, and flour your hands. Gently pat out the dough and fold it back over itself about a half-dozen times, just until smooth. (A dough scraper helps greatly with this.) Pat out again into a circle or oval about ½ inch in thickness. Cover the dough lightly and refrigerate for about 20 minutes.

Remove the biscuit dough from the refrigerator. Cut it with a small biscuit cutter, trying to get as many biscuits as possible, since they toughen if the dough is rerolled. You should be able, with practice, to get up to 3 dozen 2-inch biscuits from the dough. Make your biscuits with a quick, clean, straight-down push on the cutter. If you twist the cutter (as seems to be a natural motion for many people), it twists the dough, resulting in an uneven biscuit. Arrange the biscuits at least an inch apart on a baking sheet. (A dark metal sheet helps promote quick, even browning.) Sprinkle the biscuits with the sesame seeds. Bake the biscuits in the center of the oven, turning the baking sheet around once halfway through the baking time. Bake 2-inch biscuits for 7 to 9 minutes total, until raised and golden brown.

Split the biscuits and arrange a small ham slice or two on each. The quantity of ham should depend on its saltiness and flavor intensity. The venerable well-aged Virginia hams, such as Smithfield, are eaten as a single paper-thin slice, but you can add more meat if the flavor is less assertive. Add a dollop of chutney to each biscuit. We like to serve a small pot of mustard and one of horseradish on the side, for guests to garnish their biscuits as desired.

INGREDIENT TIP: The best southern biscuits require low-gluten flour for tender, flaky results. Knoxville, Tennessee's White Lily Flour, available at grocery stores throughout the South and by mail (423-546-5511), is probably the most popular among home bakers. Ground nearly to a powder from soft red winter wheat, it absorbs less liquid than hard-wheat varieties. Adding a portion of cake flour to all-purpose flour provides some of the desired effect, but real biscuit fans should stock up on soft-wheat flour. These particular biscuits are crunchy with sesame seeds, also known in the South by an African name, benne. We intensify the sesame flavor with a bit of the distinctively aromatic oil. Common in a slew of southern dishes, sesame seeds and their oil, peculiarly, are better known to many Americans from Middle Eastern and Asian foods than from our own.

TECHNIQUE TIP: The sesame seeds typically stick to the top of the moist biscuit dough. If you are concerned about them staying in place, simply brush each biscuit top with a bit of buttermilk before sprinkling on the seeds.

Deviled Eggs

Makes 2 dozen

As far back as 1886, in her *Philadelphia Cook Book,* Sarah Tyson Rorer suggested serving deviled eggs at garden parties, with the two halves pressed together and wrapped with fringed tissue paper, the "same as candies secrets." We forgo the packaging, but heartily second the notion of making the eggs for outdoor gatherings. Rorer used French mustard, and added olive oil and boiled ham or tongue, while other cooks have incorporated everything from ballpark mustard to chutney, capers, and pickle relish. Particularly hellish folks today might heat up the eggs with hot pepper sauce, but mustard is the old and honored way of making anything deviled.

12 large eggs

6 tablespoons mayonnaise, or 3 tablespoons mayonnaise and 3 tablespoons Durkee's Famous Sauce

1 tablespoon Dijon mustard

1½ to 2 teaspoons prepared horseradish

Salt

Paprika

Watercress sprigs or other greens

In a large saucepan, cover the eggs by an inch with cold water. Over medium heat, warm the eggs, bringing the water to the stage just before a full boil, when bubbles begin to break insistently around the water's edge. Gently stir the eggs a few times while heating, to help the yolks stay centered. Turn off the heat, cover the pan, and let it stand for 15 to 20 minutes. Pour off the water and cover the eggs with very cold water, letting them stand for a minute or two. Drain the water, and cover again with very cold water.

Drain the eggs and roll them around in the pan vigorously to crack them lightly. Peel them immediately. An egg is easiest to peel by further cracking its broader end, where there's usually an air pocket, and beginning to peel from there.

Slice the eggs in half lengthwise. Scoop out the yolks into a bowl and set the whites aside. Mash the yolks with a fork, and then mix in the mayonnaise, mustard, and enough of the horseradish to excite your tongue. Sprinkle in salt to taste. Another bit of horseradish probably won't hurt either. Season the eggs assertively to your palate because they will be served cold, which diminishes the flavor impact. Spoon or pipe the yolk mixture into the whites, mounding it attractively. Dust generously with paprika and chill for at least 30 minutes, covering the eggs if they will be refrigerated longer. Serve on a platter garnished with watercress or other greens.

American Cheeses

The English make a meal out of cheese, and the French finish one with it, but Americans are more likely to eat it beforehand as an appetizer. The Europeans have culinary logic on their side, but we can at least boast frontier abandon, a guileless appreciation for what's good whenever we want it.

American colonists started making cheese soon after they arrived, basing their products primarily on British counterparts, particularly Cheddar cheese. The craft flourished in Vermont and New York by the early nineteenth century, but got a big boost a few decades later when German, Swiss, and other European immigrants began settling in Wisconsin, our major dairy state. Anne Pickett opened Wisconsin's first small cheese factory in 1841, and other producers emerged so rapidly that the Dairymen's Association was marketing cheese nationally by the 1870s. Today, the state's two million cows yield an average of 14,000 pounds of milk each per year, 84 percent of which goes into making cheese.

Family factories produced Cheddar and Swiss early, but branched before long into a full array of Old World cheeses, including Edam, Gouda, Gorgonzola, Limburger, and Muenster. Wisconsin masters also created two new American varieties, brick and Colby, while a New York cheesemaker came up with Liederkranz. The United States is now the world's largest cheese producer and, at its best, its output is comparable in quality to that of any other country.

Cheese Straws

Makes 4 to 5 dozen wafers

A "straw" today often in name only, these crisp cheese-laced morsels commonly come as round wafers, a way of speeding the preparation for a treat that disappears as quickly as you can whisk the crackers warm from the oven. Of English lineage, though now thoroughly southern, cheese straws became acculturated with the zip of cayenne and the crunch of pecans. Mamie Davis Willoughby of Amite County, Mississippi, writing as Rose Budd Stevens, sums up the appeal in *From Rose Budd's Kitchen* (1988): "A cheese straw does to a meal what a brushing of rouge does to the tired housewife—perks her up, adds interest, and, above all, color appeal."

- ¾ cup chopped pecans, toasted
- 1½ cups unbleached all-purpose flour
- ½ cup (1 stick) plus 2 tablespoons unsalted butter, softened
- 8 ounces sharp Cheddar cheese, grated (about 2 cups)
- 1½ teaspoons Worcestershire sauce
- ½ teaspoon baking powder
- ½ teaspoon salt or more to taste
- ¼ teaspoon cayenne pepper plus additional for dusting
- Paprika
- Pecan halves, optional

In a food processor, process the pecan pieces with 1 tablespoon of the flour until they resemble coarse meal. Add the butter and process until it is smooth, then add the cheese and Worcestershire sauce, and process just until combined. Stir together the remaining flour with the baking powder, salt, and ¼ teaspoon cayenne, add the mixture to the processor, and pulse until a smooth dough forms. If the dough doesn't hold together easily when pinched with your fingers, add a few teaspoons of water and process the mixture again briefly. Remove the dough and shape it into 2 or more rolls of manageable length, about 1½ inches in diameter. Wrap each roll tightly and refrigerate for at least 1 hour before slicing into rounds about ¼ inch thick. For the roundest slices, rotate the rolls about a quarter turn after each cut. (You can form the dough into much wider rolls if you want large wafers. Keep the thickness about the same.) The dough will keep in the refrigerator for several weeks and in the freezer for several months, to be sliced off as desired.

Preheat the oven to 350°F.

Arrange the dough rounds ½ inch apart on ungreased cookie sheets. Dust with cayenne or paprika, and press a pecan half into the middle of each wafer if you wish. Bake for 7 to 9 minutes, until the edges of the wafers are lightly colored. Cool several minutes on the baking sheets, then transfer to baking racks. Serve warm or at room temperature.

Boiled Peanuts

Makes enough for you and several guests

They look like they've been drowned in a high tide, and don't sound appetizing either, but boiled peanuts are a special treat in scattered locales everywhere from the Old South to the new Hawaii. When treated like the legumes they are, peanuts show their true character, developing a distinctive bean flavor. Georgia food writer Damon Lee Fowler, author of *Classical Southern Cooking* (1995), introduced us to their proper preparation.

- 2 pounds whole unshelled unroasted peanuts, preferably young "green" peanuts
- 2 heaping tablespoons salt or more to taste

Rinse the peanuts, then dump them into a large pot. Pour in about 2 quarts of water, enough to cover them by a couple of inches. This isn't as easy as it sounds, since peanuts float. Push down as many as you can at a time, to gauge whether you have enough water.

Stir the salt into the water and bring the peanuts to a boil over high heat. Reduce the heat to a simmer and cook for 1½ to 2 hours, until the peanuts are fairly tender. Check them from time to time, popping the nuts from the shell to see if they're ready. We prefer them the way Damon does, when they still "fight back a little." The peanuts can be eaten immediately or allowed to sit in the brine at room temperature for up to another hour to develop a saltier flavor. When you're happy with the taste, drain the peanuts and serve them, accompanied by a bowl for the leftover shells. Your guests do the work, cracking the soft shells open and popping out nuts to their heart's delight.

Salted Green Soybeans

SERVES 4

In Illinois and Michigan, prime soybean turf, these are sometimes known as "salted peanuts," which they resemble in taste. The United States is the world's largest grower of soybeans, but most of the crop gets ground into meal, pressed into oil, or transformed into other soy products. Look for the whole young pods in the frozen-food section of Asian markets or supermarkets with a broad selection of Asian ingredients, where you may find them labeled by the Japanese name "edamame." They're worth a little sleuthing as a substitute for crudités and antipasto, the more common party vegetables of our day.

1 pound small, tender soybeans in the pod, fresh or frozen

3 tablespoons kosher salt, sea salt, or other coarse salt, or more to taste

Up to 2 hours before you plan to cook the soybeans, wash them well. Then soak them for a few minutes in ice water and drain them. Rub the soybeans with the salt and refrigerate them, covered, for up to 2 hours. (Sitting in salt allows the beans to absorb the flavor fully, but if you're rushed for time, skip this step and go on to the next, adding more salt before serving.)

Bring 2 quarts of water to a boil in a large saucepan over high heat. Stir in the soybeans and the salt and boil for 5 to 8 minutes, until the beans within the pods are tender but short of mushy. Drain the soybeans, refresh them in cold water, and drain them again.

The soybeans can be served immediately or within 1 to 2 hours at room temperature. Toss with additional salt if you wish. Serve the pods as you would peanuts in the shell. Arrange the whole pods in a shallow bowl or on a plate. Put a pod up to your lips and squeeze to pop the pealike beans into your mouth. Alternatively, put the pod into your mouth and pull it back out between your teeth, as you would with an artichoke leaf. Discard the pod and savor the beans.

Soup's On

Perhaps nothing says "home" as well as good soup. Food simmered in a pot forms the foundation for home cooking the world over, and in any corner of the globe, all you need is your nose to tell you where you are. As a mélange of what's at hand, soups and stews have developed around special local ingredients and usually retain strong local associations even today, when jet-age distribution provides access to everyone's larder.

Simmering food over a fire is an ancient way of cooking, practiced in both the Old and New Worlds long before Europeans arrived on our Atlantic shore. Early French and German immigrants, in particular, loved soups and contributed to their American evolution out of all proportion to their population numbers. The Pennsylvania Dutch spread their enthusiasm and expertise around the mid-Atlantic region originally and then, later, throughout the Midwest. A refugee from the French Revolution, who opened one of our country's first restaurants in Boston in 1794, gained a reputation as the "Prince of Soups," which helped to attract to his tables even the renowned French epicure Jean-Anthalme Brillat Savarin during a sojourn in the United States.

In the early centuries, Americans generally liked their soups hearty and full-bodied. Abraham Lincoln knew that predilection when he attacked Stephen Douglas's notion of popular sovereignty by likening it to "soup that was made by boiling the shadow of a pigeon that had starved to death." In a similar vein, cookbook author Eliza Leslie condemned "the flatulency of weak washy soups" and called for two "large fat fowls" and a couple of pounds of veal for a rich white soup.

Such prodigality had waned by 1897, the year Joseph Campbell introduced his canned soup. Instantly popular, particularly with children, the new product sold so well over the following decades that James Beard felt the need to remind Americans that can and soup are not synonymous. Today, real, made-from-scratch soups are enjoying a comeback, inspired in part by the increasing availability of key ingredients for some of America's best local and regional favorites. Maybe you can't ever go home again, as the pundits say, but you come close anytime you put the soup on.

Fishiest of all fishy places was the Try Pots, [an inn] which well deserved its name; for the pots there were always boiling chowders. Chowder for breakfast, and chowder for dinner, and chowder for supper, till you began to look for fish-bones coming through your clothes.

HERMAN MELVILLE,
MOBY DICK (1851)

New England Clam Chowder

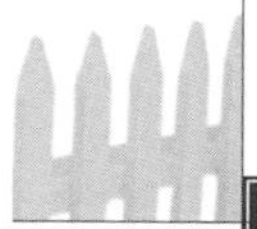

Serves 6

Americans seldom, if ever, put clams in chowder before the nineteenth century, but that's now become the traditional version of the soup. Aside from the fish favored originally in the dish, and the milk which was added later, the old basics of salt pork, potatoes, onions, and crackers have remained constants since colonial times. This is an elemental New England chowder, as simple and sumptuous as the version that Daniel Webster said would "make you no longer envy the gods." Thanks to Sandra Oliver for sharing her regional expertise on the nuances of making chowder.

- 1½ pounds russet or other baking potatoes, peeled
- 4 ounces salt pork, diced fine
- 2 bacon slices, chopped
- 1 medium onion, chopped
- 3 cups clams, chopped if larger than bite-size, with 3 to 3½ cups clam liquor or seafood stock (see Ingredient Tip)
- 1 bay leaf
- Salt and freshly milled black pepper
- 2 cups half-and-half
- 1 to 2 tablespoons unsalted butter, optional
- Split pilot, Boston, or Common crackers, or oyster crackers

Take a potato in hand and with a small paring knife, chip off irregular angular potato bits, large enough to be toothsome but small enough to blend in with the chopped clams. Repeat with the remaining potatoes, and reserve them.

In a large heavy saucepan, fry the salt pork and bacon over medium-low heat until the fat is rendered and the remaining pieces are brown and crisp. Increase the heat to medium, stir in the onion, and sauté until it is soft and translucent, about 5 minutes. Pour in the clam liquor, then add the potatoes, bay leaf, and a good pinch of salt and pepper. Simmer until the potatoes are very tender, about 15 minutes. Pour in the half-and-half and the clams, and heat through. Season with more salt and pepper if you wish. Turn off the heat and let the chowder sit for about 30 minutes. Reheat the chowder, just bringing it to a simmer, not to a boil. If you like, add the butter and stir to melt it, then remove from the heat. Serve with crackers on the side.

The Chowder Wars

The world of chowder is so diverse that Richard J. Hooker devoted a whole volume to the many permutations, *The Book of Chowder* (1978). Even if you overlook the fish, corn, chicken, potato, and bean variations—and forget entirely the peanut, cheese, and canned-tomato-soup version from a North Dakota community cookbook—you've got enough competing clam chowders north of the Brooklyn Bridge to warrant a United Nations peacekeeping mission.

Combatants battle over many fine points, but draw the major dividing line between milk and tomatoes, both shunned by the earliest chowder cooks. Fans of the creamy New England version consider the Manhattan clam chowder a heretical imposter, while tomato lovers swear the white soup pales thoroughly in comparison. The bickering gets so annoying at times that you want to pack your bags for the North Carolina coast, where the luscious local chowder gets its flavor from an abundance of clams and a clear, briny broth that speaks of the sea rather than pastures or gardens.

Landlubber's Cod Chowder

Serves 6

Before clams became common in chowder, New England cooks made the dish with fish, usually the copious cod. Fisherman's fare originally, made with the staples of a ship's galley and the catch of the day, chowder started out as a thick pottage containing only a little water and no milk. On land, it became soupier and evolved in multiple directions in the following centuries, showing how a popular, traditional dish can continue to take on new meaning with changes in tastes and ingredients. This is our favorite fish chowder today, mindful of heritage but contemporary in seasonings. To round out a meal, offer accompaniments such as Boston Brown Bread (page 346) or Multi-Grain Bread (page 344).

- 1 pound russet or other baking potatoes, peeled
- 1½ tablespoons bacon drippings or unsalted butter
- 1 medium onion, minced
- 1 garlic clove, minced
- 1 tablespoon Madeira, preferably, or brandy
- 2 cups clam liquor or seafood stock
- 1 cup chicken stock, preferably homemade
- 1 medium carrot, diced fine
- Salt and freshly milled black pepper
- 1 cup milk
- ½ cup whipping cream
- 1½ to 1¾ pounds cod fillets or other white fish fillets, such as haddock, flounder, petrale sole, mahi-mahi, or grouper, in bite-size chunks
- 2 egg yolks, lightly beaten
- Hot pepper sauce, such as Tabasco

Take a potato in hand and with a small paring knife, chip off irregular angular potato bits, large enough to be toothsome but small enough to blend in with the fish chunks. Repeat with the remaining potatoes, and reserve them.

In a large heavy saucepan, warm the drippings over medium heat. Stir in the onion and sauté until soft and translucent, about 5 minutes. Add the garlic and cook an additional minute. Pour in the Madeira, followed by the clam liquor and chicken stock. Add the potatoes, carrot, and a good pinch of salt and pepper. Simmer until the potatoes are very tender, about 15 minutes. Stir in the milk, cream, and fish, and heat through. Turn off the heat and let the chowder sit for about 30 minutes.

Reheat the chowder, just bringing it to a simmer, not to a boil. Whisk about ¼ cup of the stock into the egg yolks, then pour the mixture into the chowder, continuing to whisk until incorporated and thickened. Season with more hot pepper sauce and salt and pepper if you wish. Serve immediately.

The Sacred Cod

In 1784, the Massachusetts House of Representatives voted to hang a carving of the "Sacred Cod" in its chamber, "as a memorial of the importance of the Cod-Fishery to the welfare of this Commonwealth." Many of the legislators undoubtedly ate cod, as most New Englanders did, maybe once a week, but they weren't thinking about food in this tribute to the fish. Salted and dried aboard fishing vessels for preservation, then sold at home and abroad, the abundant and prolific cod of the North Atlantic became a critical article of commerce, a prime pillar in the New England economy that directly and indirectly provided much of the capital that ultimately fueled the Industrial Revolution.

Sadly, the fish and its traders also helped support slavery in the South. Salt cod, rum, and Spanish currency became the main goods exchanged in Africa for kidnapped people. New England ships carried the first two items to the African coast, brought slaves from there through the horrendous "Middle Passage" to the West Indies, and traded them for sugar and molasses, which they then sold to New England distillers to make more rum. Thomas Jefferson, a slaveholder himself, wanted to condemn this triangular trade in the Declaration of Independence, but a coalition of southern planters and northern "codfish aristocrats" overruled him. A few years later, the Massachusetts legislature hung its icon, still displayed today.

She-Crab Soup

SERVES 6

The mixed blessing of an American city's maintaining a cultural identity is expressed for me in the question of whether I would be willing to endure a lecture on the authenticity of detail in the historical renovation of Charleston south of Broad Street if I were allowed to eat Charleston she-crab soup while I listened.

CALVIN TRILLIN, ALICE, LET'S EAT (1978)

Crab is the most American of all shellfish, more abundant in our waters than anywhere else and cooked in a wider range of delightful ways. Of all the varieties caught in different areas, none is more beloved than the plump female blue crab, filled to bursting with neon-orange roe, and no preparation matches this Charleston classic.

- 8 to 10 female blue crabs, about 8 to 10 ounces each (see Ingredient Tip)
- 1 tablespoon plus 1 teaspoon dry seafood-boil seasoning
- 2 tablespoons unsalted butter
- 1 tablespoon unbleached all-purpose flour
- 3 cups milk
- 1 cup whipping cream
- 1 tablespoon fine-grated onion or onion juice
- 1 teaspoon minced lemon zest
- ½ teaspoon Worcestershire sauce
- Pinch of nutmeg
- Pinch of ground white pepper
- Pinch of cayenne pepper, optional
- Salt, optional
- 2 tablespoons dry sherry or more to taste

Pour 1 cup of water in the bottom of a steamer. Arrange the crabs in the steamer insert, layering them loosely and sprinkling each layer with seafood boil. Cover the crabs and steam them for about 20 minutes, until the crabs have all turned red. With tongs, remove the crabs from the steamer and set them aside to cool. Reserve the steaming liquid. When the crabs are cool enough to handle, crack them and pick from them their meat and the intensely orange roe found under the top shell, keeping the two separate. Then check the meat and roe again for any bits of shell or cartilage that you might have missed. You should have about 1 pound of crabmeat and ¼ pound of roe. Mash the roe a bit to crumble it.

Melt the butter in a large heavy saucepan over medium heat. Sprinkle in the flour, whisking it continually for 1 to 2 minutes. Slowly pour in the reserved steaming liquid, whisking continually, and then pour in the milk and cream. Mix in the onion, lemon zest, Worcestershire sauce, nutmeg, and white pepper. Stir in the crabmeat and heat the soup through but do not let it boil. Add cayenne if you wish, and salt to taste, keeping in mind that the seafood-boil seasoning normally adds plenty of both. Spoon 1 to 1½ tablespoons of the crab roe in each bowl and pour a teaspoon of the sherry over the roe. Stir any remaining roe into the soup and heat it through. Ladle the soup into the bowls and pass additional sherry if you wish.

INGREDIENT TIP: Female blue crabs cost more than their male counterparts, and it's always advisable to request them in advance to get a sufficient number. If you strike out locally, you can order the crabs by mail from the Bernard family's French Market Seafood Company in New Orleans (504-522-8911). Though many recipes suggest substituting egg yolk for the roe, the roe is essential to the soup's success.

She-Crab Soup

A soup to remember!
The feminine gender
Of crabs is expedient—
The secret ingredient.
The flavor is essential
Makes men reverential
Who taste this collation
And cry acclamation.

JUNIOR LEAGUE OF CHARLESTON, CHARLESTON RECEIPTS (1950)

Cioppino

SERVES 6

Two centuries after North Atlantic fishermen concocted chowder as a seafaring meal, a similar occupational situation led fishermen on the Pacific coast to develop their own, much different catch-of-the-day stew. The basic staples were Italian favorites in this case—olive oil, wine, tomatoes, and garlic—all already being grown and produced in California before the Gold Rush brought Ligurian fishermen to San Francisco. Just as today's chowder may owe a distant debt to an old Breton dish, cioppino gained its inspiration from a Genovese soup, but both landed firmly on an American shore and never set sail again.

> As a steady diet, plain water is inclined to make thin fare, and even saints, of which there are an unexpected number these days, will gladly agree that a few herbs and perhaps a carrot or two and maybe a bit of meager bone on feast days can mightily improve the somewhat monotonous flavor of the hot liquid. Soup, in other words, is good.
>
> M.F.K. FISHER, *HOW TO COOK A WOLF* (1942)

½ cup olive oil
1½ cups chopped onion
1 large green bell pepper, chopped
3 garlic cloves, minced
28- to 30-ounce can Italian plum tomatoes, mashed in bite-size pieces, with juice
3 cups seafood stock
3 cups dry red wine
3 bay leaves
1 tablespoon minced fresh basil or 1½ teaspoons dried basil
2 teaspoons minced fresh oregano or 1 teaspoon dried oregano
¼ teaspoon crumbled saffron threads
Salt and freshly milled black pepper
1 to 2 tablespoons tomato paste, optional
1 to 2 tablespoons red-wine vinegar, optional
1 dozen small to medium clams or mussels, or 2 dozen cockles (see Technique Tip)
1½ pounds firm-fleshed white fish fillets or steaks, such as sea bass, rockfish, halibut, shark, grouper, or mahi-mahi, in bite-size chunks
¾ pound crab claw meat, preferably, or lump crabmeat, Dungeness if available, picked over for shells and cartilage
½ pound medium shrimp, peeled and, if you wish, deveined
Minced flat-leaf parsley

Warm the olive oil in a stockpot over medium-low heat. Stir in the onion and bell pepper, cover them, and sweat them until very soft but not browned, about 10 minutes. Uncover the pot and stir in the garlic, cooking another minute. Pour in the tomatoes and juice, the stock, and wine. Add the bay leaves, basil, and oregano, and turn up the heat until the mixture comes to a boil. Reduce the heat to a low simmer and cook the mixture uncovered for 45 to 55 minutes. The mixture should be thickened but still souplike in consistency. Stir in the saffron and salt and pepper to taste. Cool the cioppino base and refrigerate it, covered, for at least a couple of hours and up to a couple of days.

Reheat the cioppino base. Depending on the acidity and sweetness of your tomatoes, wine, and stock, the liquid may now taste a little overly tart or sweet. Add a bit of the tomato paste or vinegar to balance the flavor if necessary. If the mixture seems thick after heating, add a few tablespoons or more of seafood stock or water.

Place the clams (or mussels or cockles), scrubbed well, into a saucepan. Pour in ¼ cup of water, cover, and steam the clams over high heat for several minutes until they open. Discard any that do not open within a couple of minutes of the rest. (If you wish, you can skip this step, and simply add the shellfish to the cioppino with the rest of the seafood. This step, however, allows you to make sure that all of the shells opened, rather than having to search around in the large cioppino pot.)

Bring the cioppino base to a strong simmer, stir in the fish, crab, and shrimp, and cover and cook for 3 to 5 minutes, until the seafood appears opaque rather than translucent. Stir in the clams and cooking liquid (strained of any grit) and heat them through. Taste again and add more salt or pepper if needed. Spoon up the cioppino in large bowls and sprinkle each with parsley before serving.

TECHNIQUE TIP: Cioppino and other seafood soups look appealingly bountiful when served with some of the shellfish still in the shell. Don't overdo the number of types of seafood with shells, though, because it makes the eating laborious, and with this tomato-based soup, downright messy too. We usually keep small bivalves like clams or mussels in the shell because they pop out easily. If you use whole Dungeness crabs instead of lump crabmeat, keep a few legs intact just to show them off, but crack them in a few spots to make the picking easier.

Seafood Gumbo

Serves 10 to 12

Gumbo takes its name from African words for okra and, as you might expect, gets much of its character from the same black cooks who gave it that tag. They likely added the spice and smoky meat savor, and certainly thickened the first gumbo with okra rather than filé powder, an alternative agent in common use by the mid-nineteenth century. This is a contemporary composite of three of the earliest printed New Orleans recipes for gumbo, all offered among other possibilities by Lafcadio Hearn in *La Cuisine Créole* (1885). In his day perhaps more than ours, Louisiana cooks used gumbo as a delicious and economical way of pulling together a variety of ingredients, depending on what was seasonal and what was left over from a previous dinner. That's still a fine approach, taking a recipe like this one only as a general guide.

- ¼ cup lard, bacon drippings, or vegetable oil
- ¼ cup unbleached all-purpose flour
- 4 medium leeks, white and light green parts, sliced thin
- ½ pound country ham, tasso, or other smoky ham, chopped
- 1 pound bone-in chicken thighs, breasts, or a combination
- 1½ cups chopped tomatoes, fresh or canned, with juice
- 1 teaspoon freshly milled black pepper
- ¼ teaspoon cayenne pepper or more to taste
- 1½ cups thin-sliced okra, fresh or frozen (see Ingredient Tip)
- 2 dozen shucked medium oysters, with their liquor (if there's not at least ½ cup liquor, add seafood stock to equal this amount)
- 1 pound peeled medium shrimp or crab claw meat, or a combination
- Salt
- ¼ cup minced flat-leaf parsley
- Cooked rice
- Hot pepper sauce, such as Tabasco

Soup comes into its own, poor-man style, as a main course. One small serving of a ravishing soup is infuriating. It is like seeing the Pearly Gates swing shut in one's face after one brief glimpse of Heaven.

Marjorie Kinnan Rawlings, Cross Creek Cookery (1942)

In a large heavy pot, warm the lard over medium-low heat. Sprinkle in the flour, stirring to combine. Stir the roux constantly until it turns a deep reddish brown, 15 to 20 minutes, being careful to avoid splashing yourself with the scalding mixture. Watch the color of the roux carefully, as it can go from just the right shade to burned in a few blinks of the eye. Turn off the heat and immediately add the leeks and ham, stirring until the sizzling subsides.

Add the chicken pieces to the pot and cover with 8 cups of hot water. Stir in the tomatoes, pepper, and cayenne, and bring the mixture just to a boil. Reduce the heat to a simmer, cover, and cook for about 1 hour. Remove the chicken from the pot and set it aside until cool enough to handle. Stir in the okra and simmer for another 50 to 60 minutes, until the okra is very soft. When the chicken is cool,

Lafcadio Hearn, 1850–1904

Lafcadio Hearn arrived in New Orleans hungry and almost broke in 1877, and left in little better shape a decade later, shortly after the publication of two books he wrote on the city. One of those works, *La Cuisine Créole,* shares with a local fund-raising publication the distinction of being the first New Orleans cookbook, but Hearn was more of an astute observer and writer than a cook. Scraping by on a journalist's low wages, he learned to feed himself well on small change, an experience that led him to open a restaurant featuring five-cent dishes and eventually to compile the cookbook. Neither project helped him much financially, but the book did better than the restaurant, which closed in a few weeks after his partner absconded with the cash and the cook.

Born on a Greek island, and educated in England, Hearn spent the last years of his life in Japan, continuing to write and ultimately earning a substantial literary reputation. He maintained a love for New Orleans—which he called "the most beautiful and picturesque old city in North America"—and now the city honors him as well with a classic Japanese garden dedicated to his memory. Polished cook or not, Hearn understood the prominence of Creole food in New Orleans life and hungered to make it central in his.

pull the meat from the bones, cut it into small bite-size chunks, and return it to the pot. (The gumbo can be made to this point a day in advance covered and refrigerated. Reheat it before proceeding.)

After the gumbo has cooked about 2 hours total, stir in the oysters, their liquor, and the shrimp, and simmer 5 to 10 minutes longer, until the seafood is cooked through. Season with salt and stir the parsley into the gumbo and remove from the heat. Serve piping hot over rice in bowls, passing hot sauce at the table.

INGREDIENT TIP: Lafcadio Hearn was ecumenical in the choice of thickening agents for gumbo, not especially concerned whether it was okra or filé powder. Ground dried sassafras leaves, filé enjoys an aura of mystique, promoted by local New Orleans writers who suggest, among other secrets, gathering it in the light of a full August moon. Employed in cooking originally by the Choctaw natives of the area, filé first found its way into gumbo when okra was out of season, and then later became a convenient substitute. If you want to use filé in this recipe, replace the okra with 1 tablespoon of the powder. Mix the powder first with a few spoonfuls of the gumbo liquid and then stir the mixture into the pot near the end of cooking. Avoid boiling the gumbo after you add the filé or the texture will become unpleasant.

Brown Oyster Stew with Benne

Serves 4

Milky oyster stews are an old American favorite for Christmas and New Year's celebrations. This is a Charleston variation with a sesame-seed (benne) base, adapted from recipes in Sarah Rutledge's *The Carolina Housewife* (1847) and the Junior League's *Charleston Receipts* (1950). Serve the stew with piping-hot cornbread.

- 6 tablespoons sesame seeds
- 4 bacon slices, chopped fine
- 1 medium onion, minced
- 2 tablespoons unbleached all-purpose flour
- 3 cups oyster liquor, seafood stock, bottled clam juice, or a combination (see Ingredient Tip)
- 1 cup chicken stock, preferably homemade
- Pinch of dried chervil or thyme
- Pinch of cayenne pepper
- 2 cups shucked oysters
- 3 tablespoons whipping cream
- Salt

Toast the sesame seeds briefly in a dry skillet over medium heat until they color deeply and become shiny with oil. Watch the seeds closely, as they can burn easily. Pour the seeds out of the skillet into a mortar, preferably, or a blender. Grind the seeds until they form a coarse paste and reserve them.

Place the bacon in a large heavy saucepan and fry it over medium heat. When it has begun to soften and release fat, stir in the onion and continue cooking until the onion is soft and translucent, about 5 minutes. Sprinkle the flour and the ground sesame seeds over the mixture, and cook 1 minute, stirring constantly. Whisk the oyster liquor and stock into the pan, then add the chervil and cayenne. Simmer the soup for about 15 minutes. (The soup can be made ahead to this point several hours in advance. Cool and refrigerate, covered. Reheat before proceeding.)

Stir in the oysters and cream, and simmer until the oysters have plumped and are heated through, about 5 additional minutes. Season with salt. Turn off the heat and let the soup sit for 10 to 20 minutes. Then reheat it quickly, bringing it just to a simmer. Ladle the soup into bowls and serve.

INGREDIENT TIP: Cookbooks often suggest bottled clam juice as a substitute for seafood stock, since there isn't a canned counterpart, as with chicken or beef stock. Avoid using it for all of the stock specified, especially when several cups are required, or you'll end up with a flat, one-dimensional flavor. We generally keep some on hand, preferably the Doxee brand, to add to stock in small amounts. If you lack your own supply of fish or shellfish stock, supermarkets often carry frozen seafood stock, and it's a fairly standard item at seafood markets, which often make it on the premises.

Stock Options

Much of traditional American cooking relies on stock for heartiness of flavor. Today we don't have the abundance of scraps for making it that cooks had in the past, but stock is still a key to many great dishes, including most soups.

Homemade stock always tastes best, and it's simple to fix and store. Keep trimmings and bones from raw or cooked poultry, beef, and seafood in separate plastic bags in the freezer, plus carrot peels, celery tops, and onion skins in another container to use in all the stocks. When you've got several pounds of ingredients, brown them in the oven to intensify the flavor, toss them in a large pot with garlic and peppercorns, cover them with double their volume in water, bring the water to a boil, lower the heat to a simmer, and cook, uncovered, until the liquid is reduced to about one-third of the original amount. Strain the stock and freeze it for use as needed.

If you're not home long enough at any one time to make your own stock, you're probably earning enough money to buy the frozen kinds found in supermarkets, the next best alternative. Even low-salt canned stocks work decently in many cases, particularly when cooked briefly with some aromatics. If any stock seems wimpy, enrich it with a little butter, or boil it down further and add a splash of wine, vinegar, lemon juice, brandy, or Worcestershire sauce. Do anything except let your stock options expire.

Gumbo Soup

SERVES 6 TO 8

Also known as ochra or okra soup in early American cookbooks, this is an old favorite in many areas rather than a Louisiana specialty. It turned into formula food in commercial soup factories as canned chicken gumbo, but home cooks seldom made it by a strict recipe, improvising instead with what was on hand. They might start with a beef shinbone or a tough old fowl, and add a variety of vegetables, from freshly shucked corn to potatoes. Okra and tomatoes remain the essentials, just as they were two centuries ago when African cooks first brought the savory combination to white tables.

2 tablespoons vegetable oil
1 large onion, chopped
⅓ cup minced country ham or other smoky ham
1 teaspoon dried thyme
1 teaspoon paprika
6 cups chicken stock
15-ounce can crushed tomatoes
1½ cups butter beans or baby limas, fresh or frozen
15-ounce can hominy
1 pound sliced small okra pods, fresh or frozen
Salt

Warm the oil in a large heavy saucepan. Stir in the onion and sauté just until it begins to soften, about 3 minutes. Add the ham, thyme, and paprika, and sauté another couple of minutes. When the mixture begins to seem dry, pour in the stock and tomatoes and simmer 10 minutes longer. Stir in the butter beans and simmer another 10 minutes. Add the hominy and okra, salt to taste, and cook for an additional 15 to 20 minutes, until the vegetables are tender and the soup lightly thickened. Ladle into bowls and serve.

Turtle Soup, a Shell of Its Former Self

Once a great favorite of American home cooks and restaurant chefs alike, turtle soup attracts little interest today. People used to make the soup from sea turtles, inland river turtles, and most of all, the famed diamondback terrapin that comes from the brackish waters along the Atlantic coast. You can still find the meat frozen and canned, but seldom fresh, one reason the enthusiasm waned. Also, cooks of the past started with a whole live turtle in making the soup, a daunting task few people want to face now. Harriet Ross Colquitt suggests in *The Savannah Cook Book* (1933) doing the beheading and eviscerating a few hours in advance of a party, to give you time to forget about it "if you can."

Vertamae Grosvenor has her own special take on terrapins, like many other things, in *Vibration Cooking* (1970). "Ain't nothing but swamp turtles. They used to be plentiful on the eastern seaboard. So plentiful that plantation owners gave them to their slaves. Now they are the rare discovery of so-called gore-mays. White folks always discovering something . . . after we give it up."

Lancaster County Chicken-Corn Soup

Serves 6

In almost any American home, regardless of ethnic background, chicken soup enjoys a reputation as a preeminent comfort food. Whether embellished with noodles, egg yolk, grain, dumplings, matzo balls, or a mélange of seasonal vegetables, it soothes body and soul. This Pennsylvania Dutch soup gives fresh appeal to the venerable idea, enticing us with the fragrance of saffron and indulging us with a bounty of quick homemade noodles and summer-sweet corn. Not as heavy as some German-American dishes, it's still hearty, easily capable of supporting an extra handful or two of limas, sliced green beans, chopped spinach, or other vegetables from the garden or fridge.

3- to 3½-pound chicken, cut in 6 to 8 pieces, or 3 to 3½ pounds chicken parts

1 large onion, chopped

1 garlic clove, minced

NOODLES

1 egg

1 tablespoon milk

¼ teaspoon salt

¾ to 1 cup unbleached all-purpose flour

2 to 3 cups corn kernels, fresh or frozen

2 celery stalks, minced, plus 1 tablespoon minced celery leaves

¼ teaspoon crumbled saffron threads

⅓ cup minced parsley

1 egg, beaten

Place the chicken in a large heavy saucepan or stockpot and cover it with 3 quarts of water. Add the onion and the garlic, then just bring to a boil over high heat. Reduce the heat to low and cook until very tender, about 1 hour. Skim foam and other impurities from the top as they surface.

While the chicken simmers, prepare the noodles. Whisk the egg with the milk and salt in a medium bowl. Stir in ¾ cup of the flour, about ¼ cup at a time. The dough should be no longer sticky and stiff but still pliable. Add more flour, if needed, by the spoonful until the texture is right. On a floured surface, roll the dough ⅛ inch thick. Cut into noodles ½ inch wide and several inches long. Let the noodles sit uncovered to dry briefly, about 30 minutes. If they need to sit longer, refrigerate them uncovered until ready to use.

When the chicken is ready, remove it from the pan and set it aside until cool enough to handle. If about one-third of the liquid has not evaporated during the simmering of the chicken, continue cooking a few more minutes to reduce the stock further. (The soup can be made to this point a day or two in advance, cooled,

Soup has always been a touchstone of what we eat, how we eat, and what we eat for. Because soup requires a heated vessel rather than a stick held over a fire to turn some raw bird or root into a cooked one, soup represents the first giant step from raw to cooked and the foundation, thereby, of cooking and culture. Soup demands a pot; a pot demands a potter. Civilization—the transformation of nature by art—begins with soup.

Betty Fussell, *Masters of American Cookery* (1983)

Enter the impish *Bucklich Mennli,* 'Little Humped-Back Man,' the eternal bane of the Pennsylvania Dutch kitchen, the designing elf who inhabits each and every Pennsylvania Dutch household. He is responsible for such mishaps as scorched toast, overturned wastepaper baskets, dumplings that fall apart, dripping faucets, chipped canning jars, and a host of other irritations, including his favorite: throwing ashes into soup.

The precautions that the Pennsylvania Dutch housewife undertook in order to create a perfect soup cannot be underestimated. Soup cookery was the centerpiece of her art.

WILLIAM WOYS WEAVER, PENNSYLVANIA DUTCH COUNTRY COOKING (1993)

and refrigerated, covered. Skim the fat from the stock if you wish.) When the chicken is cool enough to handle, shred it into bite-size chunks and reserve it, discarding the skin and bones.

Add the corn and celery to the soup. Stir a few spoonfuls of the stock into the saffron and pour the mixture back into the pan. Continue cooking an additional 15 minutes. Raise the heat to high. When the soup comes to a boil, stir in the noodles and parsley and cook until the noodles are tender, about 10 minutes. Whisk ½ cup of the soup liquid into the egg, then gradually whisk the mixture back into the soup to thicken it. Return the chicken to the soup and heat it through. Ladle into bowls and serve.

Wisconsin Cheese Soup

Serves 6

Often made with beer in British rarebit fashion, cheese soups pop up in most cheese-making areas, from Vermont to Oregon. A meal in itself, like many cream soups, this Wisconsin version gains depth from a generous splash of dry white wine and bits of crusty bread and vegetables. Use a good American-style Cheddar, not yet heavily aged but showing some gusto. For a satisfying supper, just add a green salad and follow with Chocolate Chip–Oatmeal Cookies (page 416).

CROUTONS

- 1 to 2 tablespoons unsalted butter
- 1½ cups day-old country or French bread, cut into ½-inch cubes

SOUP

- 2 tablespoons unsalted butter
- 1 large onion, chopped fine
- 2 tablespoons unbleached all-purpose flour
- ½ cup dry white wine
- 5 cups chicken stock, preferably homemade
- 1 bay leaf
- ½ teaspoon salt or more to taste
- Pinch of white pepper
- ½ cup diced carrots
- ½ cup tiny cauliflower florets
- ½ cup thin-sliced green beans
- ¼ cup whipping cream
- ¾ pound medium or sharp Cheddar cheese, grated (about 3 cups) (see Ingredient Tip)

Preheat the oven to 350°F.

Prepare the croutons, melting the butter in a large ovenproof skillet over medium-low heat. Stir in the bread cubes, tossing them to coat with the butter. Transfer the skillet to the oven and bake the croutons for 12 to 15 minutes, stirring occasionally, until golden brown and crisp. (The croutons can be made a day ahead, cooled, and wrapped airtight.)

Prepare the soup, melting the butter in a large saucepan over medium heat. Stir in the onion and sauté until soft and translucent, about 5 minutes. Sprinkle in the flour, stirring to combine, and cook an additional couple of minutes. Whisk in the wine, followed by the stock, and add the bay leaf, salt, and pepper. Simmer for 5 minutes, then stir in the carrots, cauliflower, and green beans, and cook just until the vegetables are tender, 8 to 10 additional minutes. Pour in the cream and then mix in the cheese until melted and heated through. Remove from the heat immediately and ladle into bowls. Scatter the croutons equally over the bowls and serve.

INGREDIENT TIP: Carr Valley, a family cheese factory in Sauk County, Wisconsin, makes an especially good Cheddar for this soup. Crafted in bantam batches by Sid Cook, a licensed cheesemaker since the age of sixteen, the cheeses are available outside southern Wisconsin only by mail order. We'd select their mild or medium Cheddar for this soup, but their sharper cheeses are splendid for eating on their own. To order, call 800-462-7258 or 608-986-2781.

Spanish Bean Soup

Serves 8

The Old World chickpea migrated to America with Spanish settlers, particularly in Florida and California, and found its way into New World variations on the Galician soup *caldo gallego.* This South Florida version features two southern favorites, a smoked ham hock and collard greens. It's similar to the bean soups found in Portuguese areas of New England, where linguiça sausage and kale complement the chickpeas, or even Great Northern or pea beans.

- ¼ pound Spanish chorizo, or Mexican chorizo for more spice, or other well-flavored pork sausage, sliced or crumbled
- 1 large onion, chopped fine
- 3 plump garlic cloves, minced
- 1 pound dried chickpeas, soaked at least 8 hours and drained (see Technique Tip)
- 2 cups chicken stock, preferably homemade
- 2 bay leaves
- 1- to 1¼-pound smoked ham hock
- ¾-pound russet or other baking potato, peeled and diced
- ½ pound tender collard greens or turnip greens, chopped
- 1 teaspoon salt or more to taste
- ½ teaspoon paprika
- ½ teaspoon freshly milled black pepper
- ¼ teaspoon crumbled saffron threads
- Minced red bell pepper, optional

Fry the chorizo in a large heavy saucepan or stockpot over medium heat until browned. Remove the chorizo with a slotted spoon, drain it, and refrigerate it. Stir the onion into the pan drippings, and sauté until soft and translucent, about 5 minutes. Add the garlic and cook an additional minute. Add the chickpeas, chicken stock, a quart of hot water, the bay leaves, and the ham hock. Bring the mixture just to a boil, reduce the heat to low, and cook about 1 hour, until the ham hock is very tender. Remove the hock and set it aside to cool. Continue cooking the beans until tender, adding more hot water as needed to keep the beans very soupy and stirring them up from the bottom occasionally.

When the beans are tender, stir in the potato, collard greens, 1 teaspoon of salt, paprika, and pepper. Mix a few spoonfuls of the liquid into the saffron, then pour into the pan. Continue cooking until the potato is very tender and somewhat crumbly, about 20 minutes. Add more water as necessary to make a thick soupy consistency. Finely shred or cube the meat from the ham hock, discarding the fat and bones. Add the ham and reserved chorizo to the soup, add more salt if you wish, and heat through. Ladle into bowls and serve hot, garnished with bell pepper if you wish.

TECHNIQUE TIP:
To soak or not to soak: the great bean controversy. To us, it depends on the density of the bean and the desired outcome. We prefer soaking extremely dense beans, such as chickpeas and black beans, to speed their time on the stove, pouring off the water before adding more in cooking. For a dish like Louisiana red beans and rice, where you want a creamy bean "gravy," we soak the beans but don't pour off the water. Not soaking southwestern pintos, which cook with relative ease, enhances both the flavor and texture.

Chilled Fresh Pea Soup with Mint

Serves 4 to 6

Fannie Farmer promoted cold soups in early editions of her *Boston Cooking-School Cook Book,* but they didn't catch on until electric refrigerators became common in American kitchens, a couple of decades later. When the trend hit high gear, soups based on spring and summer vegetables and herbs were those most often iced, in keeping with the weather. The combination of fresh peas and mint in soup may sound terribly *au courant,* but actually Mary Randolph suggested the idea in the 1820s in *The Virginia Housewife.*

- 1 tablespoon unsalted butter
- 3 to 4 scallions, chopped with all unwilted green parts
- ¾ pound sugar snap peas in the pod, tipped and stringed, or 2 cups shelled peas, fresh or frozen, or a combination
- 1 cup plain yogurt
- 2 tablespoons minced fresh mint

Melt the butter in a medium saucepan over medium heat. Stir in the scallions and sauté just until wilted, about 2 minutes. Add the peas and continue cooking until they just begin to wilt, a couple of additional minutes. Pour in 1½ cups of water, cover, and cook until the peas are tender, 5 to 10 additional minutes, depending on whether the peas are in the pod or shelled. Nibble on one to check doneness. Cool the mixture for about 5 minutes, then spoon it into a blender and add the yogurt and mint. Cover the blender firmly, because this is about as much warm liquid as a blender will purée without pushing the lid up. Purée until very smooth. Refrigerate the soup for at least 30 minutes and up to several hours, covered. (The soup remains tasty later but the verdant green color begins to fade.) Serve chilled, adding more cold water if the soup doesn't spoon easily.

Full of Beans

English colonists brought us the idea of pea-and-bacon soups, an ancient dish in the British isles. Americans exploited the possibilities with most of our common beans and peas, adopting and gradually adapting Old World preparations. Split-pea soup became a favorite in New England, then spread south and west from there. Contemporary versions without the meat appeared as early as the World War II era, when Genevieve Callahan offered a vegetable-and-herb version in *The New California Cook Book* (1955). Black-bean soup, sometimes associated today with the Southwest, actually has a much longer history on the eastern seaboard, where the local country ham often provided the salt-meat heft.

Lima and butter beans also went into soups, and in the homeland of the American lentil in the Pacific Northwest, the tiny legume starred in numerous preparations. Janie Hibler presents one version in her heritage-minded *Dungeness Crabs and Blackberry Cobbler* (1991), called a Skid Road Lentil Soup after the old logging roads built to slide timber down to the mill. At least a few Americans apparently made soups with just bean *vines* and bacon. Mrs. S. R. Lewis, a Cherokee, plugged the dish in the Depression-era *The Indian Cook Book* (1933), published by the Indian Women's Club of Tulsa, Oklahoma.

Tomato Soup

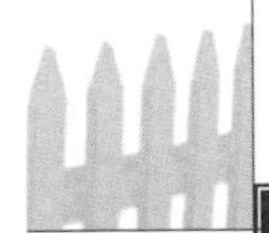

Serves 6

Like many Americans today, we grew up on canned tomato soup, never aware that a better version is hardly more complicated than popping the top from the tin container. We still use the old can opener for this rendition, but only on the tomatoes, to make a soup we can enjoy any time of the year. We like to sip it on a chilly winter day, between bites of a Golden Grilled Cheese sandwich (page 62).

I like to remember my mother's respect for her kitchen: it was a kind of holy place from which she ministered lavishly to her family via stove and sink and cupboards and flour bin. . . . She would have looked with smiling placidity, but inward scorn and despair for her sex, at today's housewives, who are helpless without packaged pie crust and canned potato salad and precooked rice and who deem it a chore to simmer daylong an honest soup, depriving themselves of its aromatic pleasure. Good cooking was a way of life and enjoyment. You did not save time but spent it recklessly, proudly, and with full reward inside these four spotless walls.

Edward Harris Heth, *Wisconsin Country Cookbook and Journal* (1979)

3 tablespoons unsalted butter
¼ cup minced onion
2 tablespoons unbleached all-purpose flour
Pinch of baking soda
1 cup vegetable or chicken stock
Two 15-ounce cans crushed tomatoes (preferably a variety labeled "with extra purée"), undrained
1 bay leaf
3 cups half-and-half
Salt
Pinch of sugar, optional

Warm the butter in a large saucepan over medium-low heat. Stir in the onion, cover the pan, and sweat the mixture for about 5 minutes, until the onion is quite limp. Stir in the flour and baking soda, and continue cooking uncovered for another minute. Add the stock, tomatoes, and bay leaf, and simmer for about 10 minutes longer. (If you wish, the mixture can be puréed in a blender at this point for a silky smooth texture. We've found, though, that we enjoy it with the little nubbins of tomato still intact.) Stir in the half-and-half and salt to taste. Add just the slightest bit of sugar, if you feel the tomato flavor needs to be brightened, and heat through. Remove the bay leaf and serve steaming in mugs or bowls.

Jerusalem Artichoke Soup

Serves 6

A sunflower tuber rather than a true artichoke, and from North America rather than Jerusalem, the Jerusalem artichoke suffers an understandable image problem. Native Americans cultivated and ate the root, but it never became a big favorite with immigrants. An appreciative minority did develop some tasty tuber dishes, however, including this subtly nutty soup, just different enough to excite but familiar enough to soothe. For a meatless meal, Cheese Straws (page 83) add crunch and "Red Turnip" Pickles (page 304) add color.

- 2 tablespoons unsalted butter
- 1 medium onion, chopped
- 4 cups veal, chicken, or vegetable stock
- 1 to 1¼ pounds Jerusalem artichokes, all but one small one peeled and chopped
- 1 small russet or other baking potato, about ½ pound, peeled
- ⅛ teaspoon dry mustard
- Salt and ground white pepper
- Scallions, sliced into thin rings

Melt the butter in a large heavy saucepan. Add the onion and sauté it until soft and translucent, about 5 minutes. Pour in the stock, the chopped artichokes, potato, and mustard, and cook until very soft, 30 to 35 minutes. Transfer the mixture to a blender in batches and purée it. The soup will be quite creamy.

Pour the soup back into the saucepan and season with salt and white pepper. Reheat, adding a little water if needed for your preferred consistency. While the soup warms, peel and julienne the remaining artichoke. Ladle the soup into bowls and garnish with equal portions of the julienned artichoke and a sprinkling of scallion rings.

In addition to the well-known salting and drying, our forebears relied on freezing to preserve food to an extent that would astonish many people today who think of food-freezing as a modern innovation. My own great-grandmother froze her soup as one way of stockpiling food for the winter. As soon as the weather was really cold she made a huge kettleful of meat and vegetable soup. When it had simmered down to the right concentration, the wide-mouthed kettle was set in a frigid back pantry, which was almost as cold as all outdoors. In the center of the kettle she stood upright a wooden paddle having a hole in the end of its handle.

When the soup had frozen to granite hardness, great-grandmother warmed the outside of the kettle just enough to slide the icy lump out intact. The frozen mass was hung by slipping the hole in the handle over a nail in a huge beam. When soup was needed, she merely chopped off a hunk with the hatchet and heated it with the requisite amount of water.

Beatrice Vaughan, Yankee Hill-Country Cooking (1963)

Summer Corn Chowder

SERVES 6 TO 8

By the time that chowder developed into a clam dish in New England, many Yankee farmers had pulled up their roots and moved along the Ohio Valley into the midwestern corn belt. They brought a love of chowder with them, but left clams and even saltwater fish far behind. Already used in some preparations in place of oysters, corn became a natural substitute for the seafood, producing an entirely different but equally delectable soup. For the essence of summer garden sweetness, scrape the kernels from a fresh ear of a fine corn variety such as Silver Queen. Among America's many creamy vegetable soups, this one will take the blue ribbon at any county fair.

3 bacon slices, chopped

1 large onion, minced

3 cups corn kernels, scraped (rather than sliced) from the cob, fresh or frozen

3 cups whole milk

1-pound russet or other baking potato, peeled and diced

1 teaspoon salt or more to taste

½ cup whipping cream

Hot pepper sauce, such as Tabasco

Freshly milled black pepper

Minced chives

Fry the bacon in a large saucepan over medium heat until brown and crisp. Remove the bacon with a slotted spoon and reserve it. Stir the onion into the bacon drippings and cook until the onion is soft and translucent, about 5 minutes. Purée 1 cup of the corn with 1 cup of the milk in a blender. Pour the mixture into the pan and add the remaining 2 cups corn and 2 cups milk along with the potato and 1 teaspoon of salt. Reduce the heat to medium-low and cook for 10 to 15 minutes, until the potato is tender. Stir in the cream and a few drops of hot pepper sauce. Add pepper and, if you wish, a bit more salt. Spoon into bowls, top with chives and the reserved bacon, and serve.

Tidewater Peanut Soup

Serves 6

You can trace the lineage of this soup from Africa to the West Indies and the American South, but it never found so hospitable a home as in the peanut farmlands of eastern Virginia. Don't frown at the idea if you've never tried it. This is a velvety rich soup with true tropical spark. It found favor as far away as San Francisco by 1904, when a version appeared in the Telegraph Hill Neighborhood Association cookbook, *High Living.*

2 tablespoons peanut oil
2 tablespoons unsalted butter
1 cup chopped onion
1 cup chopped celery plus 2 tablespoons minced celery leaves
1 garlic clove, minced
2 tablespoons unbleached all-purpose flour
Pinch of curry powder
1 teaspoon minced fresh chervil or thyme, or ½ teaspoon dried chervil or thyme
⅛ to ¼ teaspoon crushed dried hot red chiles
4 cups chicken stock, preferably homemade
1 cup creamy peanut butter
½ cup whipping cream
Salt
Chopped roasted peanuts, optional

In a large heavy saucepan, warm the oil and butter together over medium heat. Stir in the onion and celery, and sauté until the onion is soft and translucent, about 5 minutes. Add the garlic and cook 1 minute longer. Sprinkle in the flour, curry powder, chervil, and chiles, and cook an additional minute, stirring constantly. Pour in 2 cups of the stock and stir to combine. Pour the mixture into a blender, add the peanut butter, and purée. Pour the liquid back into the pan, add the remaining 2 cups stock, cream, and salt, and heat through. Ladle into bowls, garnish with peanuts if you wish, and serve.

Great-grandma had a farm, grandma had a garden, mother had a can opener. When it comes to soup, that pretty much sums up this century.

Jean Anderson,
The American Century
Cookbook (1997)

FROM SEA TO SHINING SEA,

The Catch of the Day

AMERICANS USUALLY TALK ABOUT THE HISTORY OF THE country from east to west, starting on the Atlantic seaboard and moving to the Pacific shores. In the case of seafood, at least, we should reverse directions. The Polynesian natives of Hawaii developed a sophisticated aquaculture system eons ago, trapping saltwater fish in oceanfront ponds and keeping them alive to serve fresh on the tables of royalty. By the time New England missionaries arrived in the islands in the early nineteenth century, the Hawaiians knew as much about the pleasures of seafood as anyone in the Americas, certainly more than the missionaries, who came bearing salt cod.

Native Americans on the mainland also enjoyed the bounty of the waters, but most early European immigrants preferred meat when they had a choice of vittles, seldom eating much from the sea except salt fish and oysters. Protestant settlers from Britain and the rest of northern Europe associated fish eating with poverty and Roman Catholicism, as Sandra Oliver points out in *Saltwater Foodways* (1995), but fish wasn't any more popular among the Spanish Catholics in the Southwest, even those close to coastal areas. Cooks worried about spoilage and small bones, issues ultimately addressed by the commercial canning of "fresh" fish in the late nineteenth century, and the marketing of fillets, which began in the United States in the 1920s. Fillets not only ended the bone problem, they also improved the appearance of the fish (causing them to look more like meat cuts than whole creatures), simplified cooking, and eventually paved the way for frozen fish.

While many Americans waited for these developments before wading very deep into the waters, coastal Southerners leaped in sooner, particularly in the Creole cities of Charleston and New Orleans. By the turn of the nineteenth century, Southerners ate fresh catfish, shad, sturgeon, rock fish, turtle, shrimp, crab, and more as well as the ubiquitous oysters and salt fish. Most of the preparations were simple and straightforward, but cooks soon began creating distinctive dishes utilizing other favorite ingredients, often with African flair.

When the rest of the country caught up in the twentieth century, encouraged largely by immigrants from southern Europe and Asia, fish and seafood cookery became one of the glories of the American home kitchen. We're still in a learning stage in some ways, but almost every region offers sterling dishes featuring the local catch, and because of the abundance and diversity of our waters, the variety matches that of any older cuisine on earth. For a full immersion in American flavors, dive in and catch the wave.

The good cook will, of course, be vain. But if she truly is a good cook, she will be no snob. She will not run on about being unable to cook without a certain growth of Tellichery pepper, but will make use of what materials (if they are honest ones) may come her way. Prejudices she will have, but prejudices that rise from the pit of the stomach are sound and just, and should by all means be respected. Moreover, what the taste-blind call prejudices is often only a decent right-mindedness, as witness my own dark intolerance of tea bags, and boned shad, and the ubiquitous fruit cup, and above all, of American bread.

Sheila Hibben,
A Kitchen Manual (1941)

Pan-Fried Soft-Shell Crabs

SERVES 4

France has its Belon oysters, England its Dover sole, and Italy the sweetest baby clams we've ever tasted, but no other country has crab like America. From the Pacific, we harvest the regally proportioned Alaskan king crab and the meaty Dungeness, and in the waters off Florida, we gather the exotically beautiful claws of the stone crab. The blue crab of the Atlantic and the Gulf of Mexico is the most common, however, and it rivals any other in taste. Blue crabs dress up seductively in cakes, but also taste just as good naked, when they shed their shells briefly during the spring to summer molting season. As long ago as the 1830s, Daniel Webster and other congressional leaders sought out the Chesapeake soft-shells in season for gracious Washington entertaining. A common treat today from Martha's Vineyard to South Padre Island, the crabs shine in this pan-fried preparation we learned several years ago from Mike and Paul Gaido, Galveston seafood sages who developed ways to combine Texas and Italian flair in their cooking.

> As for fish, both of fresh and salt water, of shellfish and others, no country can boast of more variety, greater plenty, or of better in their several kinds. . . .
>
> Those which I know of myself I remember by the names of herrings, rocks, sturgeons, shads, alewives, sheep's heads, black and red drums, trouts, taylors, greenfish, sunfish, bass, chub, plaice, flounders, whitings, fatbacks, maids, wives, small turtle, crabs, oysters, mussels, cockels, shrimps, needlefish, bream, carp, pike, jack, mullets, eels, conger eels, perch, and cats, etc.
>
> ROBERT BEVFRLY, THE HISTORY AND PRESENT STATE OF VIRGINIA (1705)

½ cup unbleached all-purpose flour
1¼ teaspoons dried oregano
¾ teaspoon freshly milled black pepper
½ teaspoon salt
½ cup whole milk
2 eggs
4 garlic cloves, minced
1½ cups (about 3 ounces) fine saltine cracker crumbs
Olive oil for pan-frying
8 fresh, cleaned medium soft-shell crabs
Lemon wedges

On a plate or in a shallow dish, stir together the flour, oregano, pepper, and a bit of salt. In another shallow dish, whisk together the milk, eggs, and garlic. Arrange the cracker crumbs on another plate or shallow dish.

Warm ¼ inch of oil in a large skillet over medium-high heat.

Dip each crab into the seasoned flour, then into the egg mixture, and then into the cracker crumbs. Gently shake to eliminate excess crumbs. Fry the crabs in batches until golden brown, 3 to 4 minutes per side. Drain the crabs and serve immediately, with lemon wedges. All of the crab is edible.

Chesapeake Bay Blue Crab Cakes

Serves 2 to 4

Blue crab is particularly luscious in preparations like these ethereal cakes from the Chesapeake Bay area. Our rendition takes its clues from the down-home version made by Nancy Faidley Devine, the third-generation proprietor of Faidley's, a Baltimore seafood merchant in the city's venerable Lexington Market. Like Nancy, we start with big chunks of lump crab and bind them loosely in a luscious, biscuit-size mound. Wash them down with zesty ginger beer, a Baltimore favorite with crab.

- 1 pound lump crabmeat, preferably blue crab (see Ingredient Tip)
- ½ cup saltine cracker crumbs
- 1 medium to large egg
- 2 tablespoons Dijon mustard
- 2 tablespoons mayonnaise
- ½ teaspoon celery seed (not celery salt)
- ¾ teaspoon Old Bay Seasoning, preferably, or other crab-boil seasoning (see Ingredient Tip), or a splash or two of Tabasco Sauce
- Vegetable oil for pan-frying
- Lemon wedges

Spread the crab out in a large shallow bowl, being careful to avoid breaking up the lumps. Sprinkle the cracker crumbs over the crab.

Whisk the egg in a small bowl just until foamy. Stir in the mustard and mayonnaise, then add the celery seed and Old Bay Seasoning. (If using a different brand of crab boil, start with half the amount, adding more to taste after you cook a test cake. Some brands have much more salt than Old Bay.) When well combined, spoon the seasoned mixture over the crab and gently mix the ingredients together. The mixture should remain chunky. Let the mixture sit for several minutes before forming it into cakes.

Form the crab lightly into 6 or 8 plump round mounds, about 1½ inches thick and wide. Press each cake together firmly so that the ingredients adhere, but avoid packing it down any more than necessary to hold it together. Cover the cakes and refrigerate for 1 hour or more before cooking.

Warm 1 inch of oil in a large saucepan or high-sided skillet to 350°F. Temperature precision is especially important here because higher heat may cause the cakes to disintegrate.

With a thin-bladed spatula, transfer the crab cakes one at a time to the oil, laying them into it gently. They may pop a bit just after they go into the oil. Fry until a deep golden brown, about 3 minutes per side. Drain on a rack and repeat with the remaining cakes. Garnish with lemon wedges and serve immediately.

INGREDIENT TIP: German-Jewish immigrant Gustav C. Brunn developed Old Bay Seasoning in Baltimore, Maryland, in 1939 specifically to flavor blue crabs. Supermarkets nationwide sell the spice mix today. If you want lump blue crabmeat shipped from Baltimore directly to your door, call Faidley's at 410-727-4898.

Cracked Dungeness Crab

SERVES 2 TO 4

Crab cracking and picking is a passion on many American shores, but the meat is never sweeter and easier to pluck than on the West Coast, where the crab of choice is a Dungeness. The crabs are usually cooked right after the catch, and many seafood markets will clean them for you, leaving little for you to do except feast. We serve Dungeness with a simple citrus vinaigrette, a dunk that looks and tastes like California sunshine in a bowl.

LEMON DRESSING

¾ cup extra-virgin olive oil

3 to 4 tablespoons fresh lemon juice

2 teaspoons Dijon mustard

1 large shallot, minced

¼ teaspoon Worcestershire sauce

Salt and freshly milled black pepper

2 large Dungeness crabs, 2½ to 3 pounds each, cooked, chilled, and cleaned (see Technique Tip)

Fresh lemon wedges

Whisk together the dressing ingredients in a small bowl. Arrange the crab claws, legs, and bodies on a platter. Garnish with lemons and serve with the dressing.

Crack open the crabs, piece by piece. Pick at them, suck them, whatever it takes to enjoy all the meat. Work your way, methodically and messily, through your entire treasure, dunking the meat into the vinaigrette as you go.

TECHNIQUE TIP: To clean a Dungeness crab yourself, use one hand to hold the legs down on one side of the body. With your other hand, pull up on the top shell and set it aside with any of the yellow fat for making stock later. Twist off the apron, or tail flap, from the bottom side, and then remove the gills just above the legs. Pull off the legs and claws and place them on a platter. Rinse out the body cavity, pulling out the mouth and white intestine and discarding them. Break the body in half, either with your hands or a cleaver. Add the body sections to the platter and you're ready to get cracking.

No One's Crabby Here

Alaskans often crack and pick the legs of the king crab in a similar fashion, maybe dunking the meat in a little drawn butter. The giant crab, up to six feet in length, regenerates lost legs. In the far Southeast of the country, the stone crab manages the same natural trick with its handsome, black-tipped claws. By law, fishermen can harvest only one claw from a stone crab, which is returned to the water to grow a replacement. Joe Weiss, the founder of Miami's legendary Joe's Stone Crab, popularized the typical crab-eating style, serving steamed and chilled cracked claws with a mustard-based sauce.

On the Chesapeake Bay, the equivalent ritual centers on whole blue crabs. Aficionados commonly boil or steam the crabs live over a mixture of flat beer, vinegar, and Old Bay Seasoning, and serve them casually on newspaper-covered tables with a mallet as the main utensil. New Orleans writer Lafcadio Hearn once taunted people who didn't like to cook blue crabs live, asking how else you would kill them since they have no head to cut off or blood to drain. Mimicking the street lingo of his city in the late nineteenth-century, he concluded: "You not can stick to dem troo de brain, for dat dey be same like you—dey not have of brain."

Oyster Pan Roast

SERVES 4

Called a pan roast, but akin to a quick stew, this dish pops up all across the country these days. Few things so simple offer such rich rewards. Serve it perhaps with equally quick sautéed spinach or Wilted Greens with Hot Bacon Dressing (page 256).

- ½ cup (1 stick) unsalted butter
- ¼ cup minced onion
- ¼ cup dry white wine
- ¾ cup whipping cream
- ¼ cup chili sauce (the ketchup-style condiment)
- 2 teaspoons Worcestershire sauce or more to taste
- 1 teaspoon celery salt or more to taste
- 2½ dozen shucked medium oysters, with their liquor (see Ingredient Tip)
- Toasted country bread
- Cayenne pepper or paprika

Melt the butter in a medium skillet over medium heat. Add the onion and sauté until soft and translucent, about 5 minutes. Pour in the wine and simmer for 1 minute. Mix in the cream, chili sauce, Worcestershire sauce, and celery salt, and heat through. Add the oysters and their liquor, and simmer several minutes longer to cook the oysters through. They are ready when just plump and lightly firm. Serve in broad shallow bowls over the bread or with it on the side. Dust with cayenne or paprika.

INGREDIENT TIP: For a pan roast, we like to use especially briny oysters, such as Kumamotos from Washington or Chincoteagues or Tangiers from the Chesapeake region. Even average oysters shine in the dish, though, because of the rich flavors in the sauce. As demand for oysters has revived in recent years, pasteurized preshucked varieties are becoming more common. They lack the intensely briny flavor of freshly shucked oysters, but work moderately well in this pan roast.

Fried Oysters

Serves 4

When old American recipes called for frying something, they often simply said to fry it like an oyster, assuming everyone knew how to do that. Today cooks take many different approaches, dipping oysters first in milk, eggs, or both, or even dill-pickle juice, and coating them with cornmeal, self-rising flour, bread or biscuit crumbs, Wheaties, *masa harina,* or a combination of the above and more. We follow the lead of master southern cook Edna Lewis, who in *The Taste of Country Cooking* (1977) adds a splash of peanut oil to an egg dip, uses cracker crumbs for the crust, and then fries the oysters in fresh, home-rendered lard. Realizing that most people won't want to make their own lard, we suggest additional peanut oil as a substitute in the frying. For extra punch, we sometimes serve the old favorite with a horseradish sauce, but apply it sparingly lest we lose the luster of the oyster.

HORSERADISH SAUCE OPTIONAL

½ cup sour cream

1 tablespoon prepared horseradish

2 teaspoons grated mild onion or onion juice

1 teaspoon Dijon mustard

Salt

4 eggs

2 tablespoons peanut oil (see Ingredient Tip)

1½ teaspoons salt

1½ teaspoons freshly milled black pepper

2 cups saltine cracker crumbs

1 quart drained shucked oysters

Peanut oil or home-rendered lard (see page 177) for pan-frying

Prepare the optional sauce, mixing together all the ingredients. Cover and refrigerate it until you're ready to serve. (The sauce can be made several days ahead if you wish.)

Lightly beat together in a shallow bowl the eggs with the oil, salt, and pepper. Pour the cracker crumbs on a square of wax paper. With a fork, pick up an oyster and dip it in the egg mixture. Transfer it to the cracker crumbs, laying it on them. Lift up one of the sides of the wax paper to shift the crumbs so that they coat the oyster. (This process keeps the crumbs from getting mashed down and wet.) Transfer the coated oysters to a platter. Repeat with the remaining oysters and place them uncovered in the refrigerator for 10 to 20 minutes.

Pour a scant ½ inch of oil into a high-sided skillet. Warm the oil until very hot, when it ripples and gives off shimmers of heat like a blistering sidewalk in summer, but isn't so hot that it begins to smoke. Cook the oysters a few at a time,

Though it originated in a culture of racism and sexism, Southern food has excelled and prevailed and finally transcended its origins. Blacks and women, once its slaves and vassals, are now its primary guardians, its insurance and assurance. Our cookery offers a striking parallel to jazz and the blues: Born out of misery, tempered and flavored by hard times, the food and music have soared to immortality. We properly condemn and despise the root causes of the misery, but we praise the food and the music for their excellence, and we celebrate the women and men who historically gave so much to them and got so little in return.

JOHN EGERTON,
SIDE ORDERS (1990)

avoiding crowding, until golden brown and crisp, about 1 minute per side. The oysters may pop a bit as they fry. Drain the oysters on a rack, keeping them in a single layer. Repeat with the remaining oysters until all are cooked. Serve immediately, with the sauce if you wish.

INGREDIENT TIP: Roasted peanut oil, which smells and tastes like fresh-roasted peanuts in the shell, works best in this and most recipes calling for peanut oil. Just a trace of the flavor lingers on the food, leaving an elusive but meaty quality behind. Our favorite brand is Loriva, found in many supermarkets and specialty stores. You can also order it direct by calling 800-94-LORIVA. Oysters and peanuts may sound like an odd combination, but in fact they have a natural affinity and were commonly paired in soup in the Old South.

Clams Posillipo

Serves 4 to 6

Unlike their English predecessors, Italian immigrants who settled in the Northeast quickly recognized the culinary value of the local clams, similar to ones from the Mediterranean shores of their homeland. They ate the Atlantic clams in traditional dishes they brought across the sea, such as *zuppa di vongole,* and also in new ones they devised after arriving, such as this robust preparation. We learned about clams posillipo from John Mariani, who notes in *The Dictionary of American Food and Drink* (1994) that the name and flavors certainly derive from Italy, but that Italian-American cooks devised the dish.

- 4 dozen littleneck clams, preferably, or cherrystones, or other small to medium hard-shell clams
- 6 tablespoons olive oil
- 1½ to 2 tablespoons minced garlic
- 2 small to medium dried hot red chiles, stemmed and seeded
- ½ cup dry white wine
- 3 cups chopped red-ripe Italian plum tomatoes, fresh or canned with juice
- ¼ cup minced flat-leaf parsley
- 1 tablespoon tomato paste
- 2 teaspoons dried oregano
- Salt

Rinse the clams well to eliminate any surface grit.

Pour the oil into a stockpot and warm it over medium-low heat. Stir in the garlic and chiles, and sauté for 2 minutes. Pour in the wine and cook until reduced by about half. Add the tomatoes, parsley, tomato paste, oregano, and salt to taste. Bring the sauce to a simmer, then cover and cook for 15 minutes. The mixture should remain somewhat soupy. Dump in the clams, cover again, and raise the heat to medium-high. Continue cooking for 8 to 12 additional minutes, until the clams have opened. Discard any clams that fail to open within a couple of minutes of the rest. The chiles can be fished out before serving, or left in the clams if you want more spiciness. Serve hot in broad shallow bowls with both a fork and spoon. Offer lots of good bread and a side of plainly dressed pasta if you like.

The Old-Fashioned Clambake

Newly fashionable again, and not as old as some people think, the clambake is such a revered institution that a mere mention of the name can bring up fond memories in people who've never even been to one. The country enjoys a wide range of outdoor seafood celebrations—from the oyster roasts of the South to the fish boils of Door County, Wisconsin—but none match the charisma of the clambake, where the clan gathers on the shore to feast on clams and other treats cooked in a rock pit on seaweed and wood embers.

The seaside setting is part of the allure, but much of the mystique comes from a long-held belief that the clambake is as traditional as Thanksgiving and even older in origin. Legends still current claim that the Native Americans of New England started the institution and bequeathed it to early British settlers. The clambake quickly became, in the words of one writer, "almost the only thing allowed to warm the cockles of a Puritan's heart." Actually, as Kathy Newstadt demonstrates in *Clambake* (1992), this story is a self-conscious fabrication intended to give cultural significance to a recreational pastime invented in the nineteenth century, long after most of the Native Americans had been eliminated.

The truth about its genesis doesn't diminish the fun of a clambake. Whether you keep the fare classic in Rhode Island style with just steamer clams, corn, and potatoes, or add everything from lobsters to champagne in the contemporary manner, it makes a magical and memorable meal.

California Fishermen's Mussels

Serves 4

Many of the early California fishermen came from the Mediterranean basin, and often seasoned their catch in simple ways that reflected that heritage, as with these mussels. Garlic bread is great for mopping up the sauce.

- 2 to 2½ pounds mussels, scrubbed and debearded
- 1 large leek, halved lengthwise, white and light green parts sliced into thin half-moons
- 2 tablespoons minced flat-leaf parsley plus additional for serving
- 2 garlic cloves, slivered
- 1 cup dry white wine
- 2 tablespoons extra-virgin olive oil

Dump the mussels into a Dutch oven or stockpot. Scatter the leek, 2 tablespoons parsley, and garlic over them, then pour the wine over all. Cover and place the mussels over medium-high heat. Cook 5 minutes, then check the mussels, removing those that have opened. Replace the cover, and steam any remaining mussels for a couple of additional minutes. Discard any mussels that fail to open with a minute or two of these. Scoop the mussels into shallow serving bowls, stir the oil into the pan liquid, and pour this sauce evenly over the mussels. Scatter minced parsley over the top and serve.

Steamed Maine Lobster

SERVES 2

"There are comparatively few who ever have anything to do with a lobster until after it has been boiled," says Massachusetts-born Maria Parloa in the 1877 edition of *Miss Parloa's Appledore Cook Book.* The popular writer went on to give instructions for boiling a live lobster "for the benefit of the few," suggesting an hour in the bubbling water. Nineteenth-century Americans often bought lobster precooked or even canned, and used it primarily in prepared dishes such as fricassees, stews, and salads. The pristine, whole lobster Americans prefer today comes out of the tradition of New England shore dinners—simple, festive meals where manners and messes mattered less than hearty eating. We like to serve steamed lobsters with similar summer fare, such as corn on the cob, fresh tomato slices, and another Maine treat, Down East Blueberry Toast and Butter Pudding (page 390).

Two live 1½-pound Maine lobsters or a single 3-pound Maine lobster (see Ingredient Tip)
Unsalted butter, melted
Fresh lemon juice
Lemon wedges

Refrigerate the lobsters until you're ready to cook them, best accomplished within a few hours of bringing them home. If the claws are banded, so much the better. Leave the bands in place until after the lobsters have been cooked.

Fill a lidded pot, large enough to hold the lobsters easily, with 2 inches of water, and have a pair of long-handled tongs nearby for retrieving them when they're cooked. Bring the water to a boil over high heat, plunge the lobsters headfirst into the pot, and immediately put on the lid. Reduce the heat to medium and steam the small lobsters for 8 to 10 minutes or the large lobster for 12 to 14 minutes. The lobster is ready when the tail meat temperature reaches 140°F, measured by sliding an instant-read thermometer between the body and tail joint. Continue steaming a couple of additional minutes if needed. Avoid overcooking by more than a few degrees or the lobster will toughen.

Place a hot lobster on a cutting board, topside up. Hold the lobster steady with a clean towel to protect your fingers. Remove the claw bands if necessary. With kitchen scissors or a chef's knife, poke a hole first into the shell's crosshatch spot, the only "plus sign" on its back side. (This is where water pools up inside the body, especially in a boiled lobster.) Use the scissors or knife to cut carefully down the top shell, cutting all the way to the head and the end of the tail from the initial hole. Slice down through the rest of the meat and bottom shell, dividing the lobster lengthwise into two parts. Remove the intestinal vein from the tail and stom-

Of all the sensuous experiences associated with the art of eating in America, few can equal the summer ritual of devouring a fresh lobster on the New England coast. . . . The grandest of lobster dinners are inevitably the simplest, and memories of them get tangled with the smell of spruce and wharves permeated with salt, or the sound of small boats knocking companionably at a dock.

JAMES VILLAS,
AMERICAN TASTE (1982)

ach. Tomalley, the tasty, gooey green substance near the head, should also be discarded, according to current health recommendations. Crack the claws and body lightly with a nutcracker, mallet, or clean hammer to make it easier to remove the meat at the table. Repeat with the second lobster if you cooked two.

Melt as much butter as you wish, then stir in lemon juice until just tangy. Plate the lobster halves, garnishing generously with lemon wedges. Serve immediately, accompanied by the butter for dunking. While the most meat will be found in the tail, nearly everything that's not shell is edible and delicious.

INGREDIENT TIP: We often select a single three-pounder for the two of us rather than a pair of smaller individual lobsters. It's easier to deal with one crawling creature than a duo, plus it's simpler to pry the meat from the larger shell, and to us at least, it seems there's generally more meat. Some people say the three-pounders are tougher, but we haven't found that to be the case. The main drawback is you have two less claws, a tasty part of the feast. Most stores that keep a tank of live lobsters can get you a three-pounder, but you may have to request it ahead. Whatever size you choose, save the shells to make a luscious stock.

Jacksboro Fried Shrimp

Serves 4 to 6

We've relished well-fried shrimp for decades, but didn't know just how good it could get until a recent trip to South Carolina. Charleston food lover and bookseller John Martin Taylor, author of *The Fearless Frying Cookbook* (1997), sent us to the lowcountry burg of Jacksboro to eat at the tables of Doris Cook and Zelma Hickman, sisters who ran the kitchen at the home-style Edisto Motel Café until their retirement in 1998. They took pride in searching out the best fresh local shrimp, and before they went out of season each year the cooks "put up," as they say, a big batch to ensure a tasty year-round supply for the three meals the café served each week. Most of us can't get truly fresh shrimp these days, but we can fry them in the manner perfected by Cook and Hickman, as easy as it is sublime.

- 2 pounds medium shrimp, shelled and, if you wish, deveined
- 2 large eggs
- ¾ cup whole milk
- 1 teaspoon salt or more to taste
- 1½ cups fine saltine cracker crumbs
- Peanut oil, preferably, or other vegetable oil for deep-frying
- Hot pepper sauce, such as Texas Pete or Tabasco
- Cocktail Sauce (page 69), optional

Place the shrimp in a medium bowl. Whisk together the eggs, milk, and salt, then pour the mixture over the shrimp. Toss together to coat all the shrimp, then drain the shrimp. Pour the cracker crumbs onto a plate.

Pour several inches of oil into a stockpot or Dutch oven. Warm the oil to 360°F. Dunk the shrimp in the cracker crumbs, and shake lightly to eliminate excess crumbs. Fry the shrimp in batches until golden brown, about 1½ minutes. Drain and serve immediately. Pass hot pepper sauce and, if you wish, cocktail sauce.

"Barbecued" Shrimp

Serves 4

Almost anywhere the Gulf of Mexico laps the American shore, you can find local variations on this tongue-tingling specialty. Neither grilled nor smoked, the shrimp take their name from a robust, outdoorsy marinade and sauce that turns them a warm mahogany color in the skillet. Ours reflects nuances shared by Ralph and Cindy Brennan of New Orleans. Serve the shrimp with bibs and lots of crusty bread for mopping up the juices that don't land on you and your guests.

MARINADE

- ½ cup Worcestershire sauce
- 1 tablespoon minced onion
- 3 plump garlic cloves, minced
- 1½ teaspoons freshly milled black pepper
- 1 teaspoon freshly cracked or coarse-ground black pepper
- 1 teaspoon salt
- 1 teaspoon paprika
- 1 teaspoon dried basil
- 1 teaspoon dried oregano
- ½ teaspoon dried thyme
- ¼ teaspoon cayenne pepper

- 1½ pounds large shrimp, preferably with heads on
- Juice of 1 lemon
- ¾ cup (1½ sticks) unsalted butter, cut into several chunks

Combine the marinade ingredients in a large bowl. Stir in the shrimp and let them soak in the mixture in the refrigerator for 30 minutes to 1 hour.

Select a 12-inch skillet or other skillet large enough to hold the shrimp in one layer. Warm the skillet over high heat. When very hot, pour the shrimp and marinade into the skillet, watching out for splatters. The liquid should bubble and hiss. Quickly rinse out the bowl that held the shrimp with ¼ cup of water and pour it into the skillet. Scrape the shrimp and sauce up from the bottom several times while the liquid reduces. When the sauce thickens and just begins to stick stubbornly, pour in the lemon juice and add the butter. Keep scraping until the butter melts and both it and the lemon juice are incorporated. Serve immediately.

Crawfish Étouffée

Serves 4

Like some other fine American creations, crawfish étouffée developed out of poverty-induced resourcefulness in dealing with cheap ingredients, and according to Cajun chef Alex Patout, it bore a badge of shame in the homes it came from until restaurants began touting the dish. Patout places the date of respectability in 1935, when a bar in Henderson, Louisiana, started serving the "smothered" specialty, but outside the bayous few other Americans learned about étouffée before the nationwide explosion in Cajun-style restaurants in the 1980s. In a full reversal of fortune, it's now even an off-the-menu option in New Orleans at Galatoire's, the bastion of traditional city Creole cooking. Despite the success in moving uptown, étouffée remains an earthy dish characterized by the bayou basics of a rich roux, bold seasonings with a touch of heat, and the vegetable trinity of onion, celery, and green bell pepper.

¼ cup vegetable oil
¼ cup unbleached all-purpose flour
1½ cups chopped onion
¾ cup chopped celery
½ cup chopped green bell pepper
2 plump garlic cloves, minced
¼ cup (½ stick) unsalted butter
1 large bay leaf
1 teaspoon salt
¼ teaspoon dried thyme
¼ teaspoon freshly milled black pepper
⅛ to ¼ teaspoon cayenne pepper
1 cup chicken stock, preferably homemade
1 pound blanched or cooked crawfish tails and any head fat (see Ingredient Tip)
2 scallions, sliced into thin rings
2 tablespoons minced parsley
Cooked rice

Prepare a roux, first warming the oil in a large heavy skillet or Dutch oven over high heat until very hot—close to but not smoking. Add the flour quickly, 1 tablespoon at a time, stirring constantly, and watching out for splatters. After all the flour is incorporated, continue cooking and stirring until the roux turns a medium reddish brown, 2 to 3 minutes. Make sure to get a rich color, but watch the roux carefully because it darkens very quickly. Immediately add the onion, celery, and bell pepper, and reduce the heat to medium-low. When the most insistent sizzling dies down, stir in the garlic, butter, bay leaf, salt, thyme, pepper, and cayenne, and continue cooking while the butter melts into the sauce. (The étouffée can be made ahead about an hour to this point and left on the stove. Reheat before proceeding.)

There are crawfish (or crayfish, or crawdads) all over the country, but outside of Louisiana they are all but ignored—lumps of clay lacking a sculptor. People outside of Louisiana, in fact, often scoff when they hear of people eating crawfish—the way an old farmer in Pennsylvania might scoff at the New York antique dealer who paid fourteen dollars for a quilt that must be at least a hundred years old and doesn't even look very warm. A New York crawfish craver who couldn't make it to the Atchafalaya Basin would have to settle for Paris, where crawfish are called *écrevisses,* except by people from Louisiana, who always call them inferior.

CALVIN TRILLIN,
AMERICAN FRIED (1974)

Simmer a couple of additional minutes, then raise the heat to medium and gradually stir in the stock. When the stock begins to bubble, add the crawfish and heat them through, stirring in the scallions and parsley just before removing from the heat. Serve immediately, ladled over rice.

INGREDIENT TIP: Farm-raised crawfish offer a decent alternative to their wild cousins. They generally come purged of the silt that gave them the nickname "mudbugs," a major plus. Whole frozen crawfish and tails (usually sold with the tasty head fat) are now relatively easy to find in well-stocked seafood departments, and fresh ones appear at least occasionally during their spring season. Five to 6 pounds of fresh crawfish will yield about 1 pound of tail meat. For special occasions, we get our crawfish direct from the Cajun part of southeast Texas, from Bill Yeager's Caddo Creek Crawfish Farm (903-876-4123). If you've got a problem serving mudbugs, substitute shrimp or lump crabmeat.

Old Sour Seafood Salad

Serves 6

We first learned about old sour on Harbour Island in the Bahamas, where we once bought a Bacardi bottle of the seafood seasoning, labeled by hand as "Patricia's." We've used it for years now, but we're novices with the concoction compared to the old-line "Conchs" in the Florida Keys, the native-born residents, who originally boasted a family link to Bahamians. Conchs made the elementary brew as a way to preserve the tangy juice of Key limes when the fruit went out of season. They would just add salt and often chile to the juice, and then store it in a used liquor bottle to keep as a table sauce for years to come. The locals would feature their namesake conch as the main seafood in this salad, but given its scarcity in most markets, we suggest scallops as a substitute. Another Atlantic delicacy rarely eaten until well into the nineteenth century, scallops taste similar to conch in some ways, but lack its gritty toughness, so prized in the Keys.

OLD SOUR

2 cups fresh Key lime juice, preferably, or other lime juice

1 tablespoon salt

1 or more small hot dried red chiles, optional

SEAFOOD SALAD

12 small clams, such as littlenecks or cherrystones

1 lime, halved

2 bay leaves

1 tablespoon salt

2 teaspoons freshly milled black pepper

1 to 2 small hot dried red chiles, or ½ teaspoon cayenne pepper

1¼ pounds large shrimp, shelled and, if you wish, deveined

10 to 12 sea scallops, halved or quartered if larger than bite-size, or ¾ pound conch, diced

¾ pound red snapper or other white fish fillets, cut in bite-size chunks

¼ cup finely chopped red bell pepper

¼ cup minced red onion

2 tablespoons vegetable oil

Several splashes of hot pepper sauce, such as Tabasco

2 tablespoons minced parsley

Paprika

Key limes, halved, or other limes, quartered lengthwise

Old sour is normally made ahead and stored for at least 4 to 6 weeks before serving. That kind of aging definitely benefits it, but if you're raring to toss together this refreshing seafood feast, even a day's aging will begin to develop the distinctive tang. Simply mix together the ingredients and pour into a small-necked bottle. With a rubber band or string, secure a small square of double-thickness cheesecloth over the top and leave the bottle uncapped. Store in a cool dark cabinet until ready to use. After the old sour has aged a month or more, remove the cheesecloth and cap or cork the bottle. It keeps indefinitely at room temperature.

Snail Salad

The Florida Conchs aren't the only conch lovers in the country. Italian Americans in New England cut the gastropod into paper-thin slices for the popular "snail" salad, named for the spiral shell of the conch. In the Federal Hill neighborhood of Providence, Rhode Island, where the salad is particularly popular, cooks serve the conch on a bed of lettuce with a pickled giardiniera mix of celery, peppers, black olives, and flakes of red chile.

To prepare the salad, cook the clams and shrimp separately for best taste and texture. First dump the clams, ½ to 1 inch of water, and 1 tablespoon of old sour in a large saucepan. Steam over high heat until the clams open, 5 to 8 minutes. Discard any clams that don't open within several minutes of the others. Chill the clams for at least 1 hour. Drain the pan and rinse it.

Pour 8 cups of water the pan and add 1 tablespoon of the old sour. Squeeze the lime into the water and then toss in the rinds. Add the bay leaves, salt, pepper, and chiles, and bring to a boil over high heat. Boil for 5 to 10 minutes to flavor the water. Stir in the shrimp and cook over high heat for just 2 minutes. (The water should just come back to a boil in this time.)

Immediately remove the pan from the heat and pour off half the cooking liquid. Pour the remaining liquid and shrimp into a bowl and add a half-dozen ice cubes. Place the bowl in the freezer, if you have space, or alternatively in the refrigerator. Cool the shrimp briefly until cold to your touch. Pour off the remaining liquid, cover, and refrigerate the shrimp for at least 1 hour.

While the clams and shrimp cool, mix together the scallops and fish in a large bowl with enough old sour to moisten the mixture, 4 to 6 tablespoons. Cover and refrigerate for at least 30 minutes to "cook" in the old sour. Gently stir in the clams and shrimp, along with the bell pepper, onion, oil, hot pepper sauce, and parsley. Serve in chilled stemmed glasses or clear glass bowls, if possible, to show the colors and shapes. Dust each portion with paprika and garnish with limes right before serving.

Seafood-Stuffed Eggplant

SERVES 4 AS A MAIN COURSE

Originally from the Orient, eggplant came to America via Africa. Blacks led the way in its early cultivation and cooking, with an assist later from Italian immigrants. This is a Louisiana preparation, traditionally called a "stuffed" dish but also similar to a casserole. By any name, it's a luscious seafood-and-vegetable combination. Offer Peach Ice Cream (page 391) for a cooling finish.

- 2 unpeeled medium purple globe eggplants, halved vertically
- ¼ cup (½ stick) unsalted butter
- 3 celery stalks, chopped fine
- 1 medium onion, chopped fine
- ½ cup dried bread crumbs
- 2 tablespoons freshly grated Parmesan cheese plus additional cheese for dusting the eggplant tops
- ¾ teaspoon salt
- ½ teaspoon freshly milled black pepper
- 1½ cups lump crabmeat (or crabmeat with any orange roe from female crabs)
- 8 ounces medium shrimp, peeled, deveined if you wish, and halved vertically

Preheat the oven to 350°F. Oil the eggplant halves and a baking dish large enough to hold them in a single layer.

Arrange the eggplants, cut side down, in the baking dish and bake for 35 to 40 minutes, until very soft.

While the eggplants bake, warm the butter in a medium skillet over medium heat. Stir in the celery and onion, and sauté until the onion is soft and translucent, about 5 minutes. Scrape the mixture into a medium bowl. Add the bread crumbs, Parmesan, salt, and pepper. Scoop the eggplant pulp out of the skins, reserving the "shells," and purée the eggplant pulp in a food processor. Mix the eggplant purée with the other ingredients in the bowl, combining it well. Stir in the crabmeat and shrimp gently, then spoon the mixture into the eggplant "shells." Dust the tops with additional Parmesan and bake until the tops have lightly browned, about 25 minutes. Serve hot.

TECHNIQUE TIP: This makes a great pot-luck or buffet dinner dish. If you prepare it for that purpose, since you probably won't know the number of servings needed, discard the eggplant "shells" and simply spoon the mixture into a large oiled baking dish for cooking.

Smoked Pacific Salmon

SERVES 6

The British smoked salmon long before England sent any settlers to the New World, and so did Native Americans in the Pacific Northwest long before any Europeans arrived in the area. Both peoples used a slow, cold-smoking technique for preserving the fish, but the Natives also cooked salmon during the spawning season for immediate consumption in ways similar to modern hot-smoking methods. We take the latter approach here, starting preferably with fresh wild salmon from Pacific waters rather than the milder, farm-raised Atlantic variety. The fish makes a regal feast, whether you use king salmon (also called chinook) or sockeye (a.k.a. red), both shipped mainly from Alaska these days.

- 1½-pound skin-on salmon fillet
- 2 teaspoons white-wine Worcestershire sauce
- 2 teaspoons packed brown sugar
- 1 teaspoon kosher salt
- 1 teaspoon freshly cracked black pepper or more to taste

Rub the flesh side of the salmon with the Worcestershire sauce. Sprinkle the brown sugar, salt, and pepper evenly over the salmon, and pat them into the surface. Cover and chill for 1 to 4 hours.

Fire up a smoker or covered grill to between 225°F and 250°F, following the manufacturer's instructions for smoking. Remove the salmon from the refrigerator and let it sit covered at room temperature for about 15 minutes.

Transfer the salmon to the smoker skin side down and smoke covered for 45 to 55 minutes, until the fish flakes easily. Open the smoker only when necessary, and cover as quickly as possible, to minimize the loss of heat and smoke. Have a large spatula and platter ready when you take the salmon from the smoker because it is fragile when cooked. Serve hot or chilled.

TECHNIQUE TIP: Another old way of cooking with wood, planking is enjoying a minor revival recently. Americans once did it regularly with a variety of fish, splaying their catch across a hardwood board and roasting it in front of a fire. They planked salmon in the Northwest, whitefish on Lake Michigan, and shad on the eastern seaboard, often turning the occasion into a large community party. Today people usually cook planked food in the oven, but the method still works best with a live flame, perhaps lakeside at a rock-rimmed fire pit or even indoors at a fireplace.

Salmon Poached in Hard Cider

SERVES 4

We got the idea for this dish from the Time-Life recipe collection in *American Cooking: The Northwest* (1970), but the basics of the preparation must date well before then. The British brought a taste for both cider and salmon to the colonies, and the two foods flourished side by side in New England and later in Oregon and Washington. Somewhere along the way, cooks combined the popular pair to savor them in tandem. For poaching, we prefer coho (or silver) salmon, a Pacific variety that's generally farm-raised today, even in places as far from its natural home as Nebraska.

4 thick bacon slices, diced
1 tablespoon unsalted butter
1 large onion, chopped
1 bay leaf
3 cups hard cider (see Ingredient Tip)
3 tablespoons cider vinegar
Salt and freshly milled black pepper
4 whole baby salmon, preferably baby cohos, about 1 pound each, gutted but with heads intact, or a 2-pound center or tail chunk of a larger salmon
Minced flat-leaf parsley or snipped chives

Fry the bacon in a fish poacher or large shallow pan until brown and crisp. Remove the bacon with a slotted spoon and reserve it. Stir the butter into the bacon drippings. Over medium heat, add the onion and bay leaf, and cook until the onion is soft and translucent, about 5 minutes. Pour in the hard cider and vinegar, and add salt and pepper generously. Simmer the liquid over medium heat for 5 minutes.

Reduce the heat to medium-low and arrange the salmon in the liquid, resting on the onions. Cover and poach gently for 10 to 15 minutes, just until the fish become opaque and flake. Remove the fish carefully and plate them. If you wish, spoon a little of the cooking liquid and onion in their cavities or over them. Sprinkle the bacon and parsley over them, and serve hot or chilled.

INGREDIENT TIP: A more popular drink than water in early America, fermented (i.e., hard or draft) cider is enjoying a nationwide resurgence today. The most common brand we've found cross-country, Woodchuck, comes from Vermont. It makes a fine mate for the salmon in this dish.

The more precious cookbooks, seeking to entice the housewife from her unimaginative culinary routine, revert to a crude medievalism in the richness and complexity of some of the sauces suggested for fish. . . . Here are some of the ingredients suggested in one of the "better" recipes for cooking a couple of pounds of sole: onion, parsley, thyme, celery, lemon, carrot, bay leaf, peppercorns, water, cooking wine, fish stock, milk, grated cheese, three tablespoons of flour, six tablespoons of cream, and a cup of butter. Doesn't that sound delicious? There is enough flour and butter to make a cream sauce for half the soles in the English Channel.

ANGELO PELLEGRINI,
THE UNPREJUDICED PALATE
(1948)

Creamy Cod Cakes

Serves 4

New Englanders built fortunes on cod fishing in the colonial period, shipping it dried and salted across much of the world. They ate their share of the fish too, often preparing it as a boiled dinner and then turning leftovers into breakfast cod cakes. We start with fresh cod rather than salted, preferring its creamier texture as a contrast to the crisply fried surface, but we also give instructions in the Technique Tip on using the original product.

- 1 pound cod fillets, roasted, baked, or broiled until just cooked through, flaked, or ½ pound salt cod, prepared as in the Technique Tip
- ½-pound russet or other baking potato, peeled, boiled, and mashed with 2 tablespoons unsalted butter
- ½ cup half-and-half
- 1 large egg
- ⅓ cup minced onion
- ¼ teaspoon salt, or more to taste
- ¼ teaspoon Worcestershire sauce
- Pinch of dried ginger
- Unbleached all-purpose flour or cracker crumbs, for dredging
- Bacon drippings or salt pork drippings, or a combination of butter and vegetable oil for pan-frying
- Lemon wedges

Combine the flaked cod and mashed potato in a medium bowl. Stir in the half-and-half, egg, onion, salt, Worcestershire sauce, and ginger. The mixture should be quite moist but not soupy. Refrigerate it briefly if it's too wet to hold together. Form into 12 patties about ½ inch thick, then dredge each lightly in flour. Refrigerate uncovered for 10 to 20 minutes.

Warm a thick film of the drippings in a large heavy skillet over medium heat. Fry the cod cakes in batches until medium-brown and crispy, 3 to 4 minutes per side. (Some cooks like to drop the cakes into the skillet from several inches above so that the plopped mixture will develop extra-crisp uneven edges or "whiskers." Be careful, if you try the technique, to avoid splashing cooking fat on the stove, bystanders, and yourself.) Serve the cakes immediately, garnished with lemon wedges.

TECHNIQUE TIP: To prepare cod cakes using salt cod, first rinse the salt from the surface of ½ pound of the fish. Cover the cod with cool water and let it soak for about 8 hours, or even up to 24 hours, changing the water a few times. Place the fish in a saucepan and cover with fresh cool water. Warm over medium heat, bringing the water just to a simmer, then adjust the heat as needed so that bubbles break only occasionally on the surface. Cook until soft and easily flaked, about 15 minutes, then drain again. When cool enough to handle, pull the cod into small shreds and proceed as for fresh cod. Salt the cakes more lightly, however, because the cod will retain some salinity.

Crunchy Catfish with Heavenly Hush Puppies

Serves 4 to 6

Southern cooks took to catfish early, but they didn't fry it frequently until vegetable oils came along. Among the six catfish recipes in Lettice Bryan's 1839 *The Kentucky Housewife,* only one gets fried "a handsome brown in boiling lard." Today most catfish are farm-raised, cleaning them of the muddy tendencies that sometimes marked them as poor folks' fare, while also making them milder in flavor than their river ancestors. The Mississippi Delta wetlands produce the bulk of the fish sold across the country, and one of the farm families from that area, Ed and Edna Scott and their six children, influenced the way we cook the cats and their hush puppy accompaniments. The touch of cayenne in the coating may sound contemporary, but Eliza Leslie suggested pairing it with the fish back before the Civil War. We like to accompany the "cats and dogs" with black-eyed peas and coleslaw.

HUSH PUPPIES

¾ cup stone-ground cornmeal

1½ teaspoons baking powder

½ teaspoon seasoned salt

½ teaspoon freshly milled black pepper

½ cup milk

1 egg, lightly beaten

½ cup minced onion

2 tablespoons minced scallion greens or chives, optional

CATFISH

1½ cups stone-ground cornmeal

½ cup extra-fine stone-ground cornmeal (sometimes called corn flour), preferably, or all-purpose flour

2 teaspoons seasoned salt

2 teaspoons onion powder

1 teaspoon freshly milled black pepper

1 teaspoon paprika

½ teaspoon cayenne pepper

2 pounds catfish fillets cut into 3- to 4-ounce sections

Peanut oil, preferably, or other vegetable oil for deep-frying

Hot pepper sauce, such as Texas Pete or Tabasco

Lemon wedges

Prepare the hush-puppy batter, first stirring together in a medium bowl the cornmeal, baking powder, salt, and pepper. Add the milk and egg, and stir vigorously until combined. Mix in the onion and, if you wish, the scallion greens. The batter should be nubbly and moderately thick in consistency.

A work on Cookery should be adapted to the meridian in which it is intended to circulate. It is needless to burden a country Cookery Book with receipts for dishes depending entirely upon seaboard markets, or which are suitable only to prepare food for the tables of city people, whose habits and customs differ so materially from those living in the country. Still further would the impropriety be carried were we to introduce into a work intended for the *American Public* such *English, French,* and *Italian* methods of rendering things indigestible. . . . Good *republican dishes* and garnishing, proper to fill an every day bill of fare, from the condition of the poorest to the richest individual, have been principally aimed at.

THE COOK NOT MAD OR RATIONAL COOKERY (1841)

Prepare the catfish coating, combining the cornmeals, salt, onion powder, pepper, paprika, and cayenne on a plate or in a shallow dish.

Pour several inches of oil into a Dutch oven or heavy high-sided skillet and heat to 350°F. Dunk the catfish in the cornmeal mixture, coating all sides well. Add about ½ cup of the remaining cornmeal mixture to the hush-puppy batter, a couple of tablespoons at a time. Mix in only until the batter is thick enough to spoon and hold its shape. Discard the remaining cornmeal mixture. Roll the batter or spoon it into 1-inch balls. (Avoid making the hush puppies any larger or they won't cook through properly before becoming too brown.)

Fry the catfish in batches until deep golden brown and crusty outside with flaky interiors, 6 to 8 minutes. Fry the hush puppies along with the fish, or just afterward, for 4 to 5 minutes, stirring them around to cook evenly. Serve the catfish and the hush puppies immediately with hot pepper sauce and lemon wedges.

No Fear of Frying

Catfish has never lacked company in the American frying pan. In addition to the fried fish and shellfish we feature in this book, cooks like to put the hot oil to bream, butterfish, cisco, croaker, eel, flounder, grouper, halibut cheeks, mackerel, mullet, perch, porgy, smelt, spot, and more. African Americans in the South developed such a passion for fried porgy that DuBose Heyward picked the name for his male protagonist in *Porgy and Bess.* The same kind of enthusiasm greets smelts each spring around the Great Lakes, when they head inland to spawn. Some people just scoop them from streams with a bucket and then pan-sizzle the fish whole, removing the bones with the head after cooking. Residents of southern Idaho and Utah go wild in the winter over the tiny Bonneville cisco, caught with dip nets in the freezing waters of local lakes and quickly deep-fried. In various areas, fish fries are major community fund-raising events, giving our love for the fare a truly charitable cast.

Rocky Mountain Pan-Fried Trout

SERVES 4

Ann Batchelder, a former editor of *Ladies' Home Journal,* said: "If you catch a trout and have no bacon, throw the trout back and wait until next year." That remains sound advice for cooking perfect trout, whether you're frying them streamside or at home. A Rocky Mountain region cookbook, *Buffet Dinners from the Española Valley* (1965), offers other good suggestions: add a little red chile for savor and serve the fish with watermelon-rind pickles.

8 smoky bacon slices
Vegetable oil
4 trout, about ¾ to 1 pound each, gutted but with heads intact
1 cup stone-ground cornmeal
1 teaspoon ground dried mild red chiles, such as New Mexican or ancho
1 teaspoon dried thyme
Salt and freshly milled black pepper
Lemon wedges

Fry the bacon in a large heavy skillet over medium heat until brown and crisp. Drain the bacon, reserving the drippings in the skillet. Add oil as necessary to measure a generous ¼ inch in the skillet.

Cut 2 moderately deep diagonal slashes into the sides of each fish. Stir together on a large plate the cornmeal, chiles, thyme, salt, and pepper. Roll each fish in the cornmeal mixture, pressing it into the cavities and slashes. Warm the bacon-dripping mixture over medium heat. Fry the fish, in batches if necessary, for 10 to 12 minutes, until lightly browned and flaky throughout, turning once. Serve the trout with bacon on the side and garnish the plate with lemon wedges.

Sweet-and-Sour Mahi-Mahi

SERVES 4

A Hawaiian dish, this is an authentic pan-Asian amalgam rather than a product of today's fusion fad. It blends traditional Japanese and Cantonese elements with a light, tropical version of sweet-and-sour sauce. Meaty but mild, mahi-mahi is often known on the mainland as dorado or dolphinfish. We like the dish with Mixed Vegetable Stir-fry (page 252).

SWEET-AND-SOUR SAUCE

- ⅓ cup sugar
- 1½ teaspoons cornstarch
- 2 tablespoons rice vinegar
- 2 tablespoons fresh lime juice
- 2 teaspoons Japanese soy sauce, such as Yamasa
- 1 teaspoon minced fresh ginger

- Juice of 1 large lime
- 2 teaspoons Japanese soy sauce, such as Yamasa
- 1½ pounds mahi-mahi fillets, cut into "fingers" about 3 inches in length
- About 1 cup dried bread crumbs
- Vegetable oil for pan-frying
- Hawaiian Chili Pepper Water (page 315), optional

Combine the sugar and cornstarch in a small saucepan. Whisk in ¼ cup of water. Add the remaining sauce ingredients and bring to a boil over medium heat. When the sauce thickens lightly, remove it from the heat. It can be used warm or at room temperature.

Drizzle the lime juice and soy sauce evenly over the fish pieces and let them sit for several minutes. Place the bread crumbs on a plate. Warm ¼ inch of oil in a large heavy skillet. When a few bits of bread crumbs sizzle merrily and brown quickly in the oil, drain each piece of fish and coat it with the bread crumbs. Sauté the fish on all sides until the bread crumbs are golden brown and the fish flakes, about 5 minutes total. Serve the mahi-mahi immediately with the sauce drizzled over it or on the side for dunking. Serve with Hawaiian Chili Pepper Water for more pizzazz.

Seared Tuna Steaks

SERVES 4

Most Americans didn't discover tuna until the early twentieth century, and even then it usually reached the plate only with the aid of a can opener. Japanese Americans in Hawaii in the same period knew the fish much more intimately as a fresh catch, and prepared it in a variety of tasty ways, from raw to broiled. In a dish called *tataki* (literally, "beating in the flavor"), cooks seared strips of tuna quickly, leaving the fish red inside, and then patted in seasonings with the broadside of a knife. Contemporary Hawaiian restaurant chefs adopted the searing idea, which soon surged ashore on the mainland with the force of a tsunami, usually awash in haute frills. This is our home version of the tuna, easy, fast, and wonderfully flavorful.

DIPPING SAUCE

½ cup Yamasa soy sauce or other good-quality Japanese soy sauce

1 tablespoon rice vinegar

¾ teaspoon Asian-style sesame oil

1 scallion, cut into thin rings

MARINADE

¼ cup Yamasa soy sauce or other good-quality Japanese soy sauce

¼ cup vegetable oil

1 tablespoon rice vinegar

2 teaspoons Asian-style sesame oil

1 tablespoon minced fresh ginger

1 garlic clove, minced

Two ¾- to 1-pound sushi-quality yellowfin tuna steaks, at least 1 inch thick

Salt and freshly cracked black pepper

Radish sprouts, broccoli sprouts, or other small delicate sprouts

Prepare the dipping sauce, mixing together the ingredients in a small bowl.

Prepare the marinade, combining the ingredients. Cut the tuna into four 1-inch-thick steaks. Rub the mixture over both sides of the fish steaks, cover, and let them sit at room temperature for 20 to 30 minutes. Drain the steaks, discarding the marinade.

Warm a wok or heavy skillet over very high heat. When quite hot, sprinkle salt and pepper over the tuna steaks and transfer them to the wok. Sizzle the steaks for about 45 seconds per side, until crusty. (When you turn the tuna, a little of the seasoning may be left behind, but the heat of the wok should prevent any additional sticking.) The centers will remain uncooked and red. Cool several minutes, then cut each steak across the grain into ¼- to ½-inch-thick slices. Arrange the slices over the sprouts and serve with the dipping sauce.

Black folks spend more money for food than white folks. White folks can take a can of tuna fish and feed multitudes. If we couldn't have meat we had greens and rice and we ate plenty of that but my mother never cooked none of that weird "tuna casserole."

VERTAMAE GROSVENOR, VIBRATION COOKING (1970)

New Orleans Court Bouillon

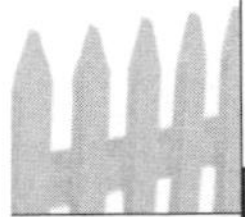

SERVES 4 TO 6

When Louisianans and other Americans talk about Creole food, they're invariably thinking about New Orleans. Actually, New Orleans is only one of many centers of fine Creole cooking in the Americas as a whole, and this popular local dish illustrates one of the links between them. The name refers to the well-known French poaching liquid court bouillon, but the result resembles nothing Gallic. Its closest cousin is another New World favorite, *huachinango a la veracruzana,* red snapper flavored with a spicy tomato sauce that comes from Veracruz, another Gulf city, which is the main fount of Creole cooking in Mexico.

- ⅓ cup vegetable oil
- 3 tablespoons unbleached all-purpose flour
- 1 cup chopped onion
- 1 cup chopped green bell pepper
- 2 plump garlic cloves, minced
- 2 cups chopped red-ripe tomatoes or 15-ounce can chopped tomatoes with juice
- 2 bay leaves
- 1½ teaspoons minced fresh thyme or ¾ teaspoon dried thyme
- Scant ¼ teaspoon ground allspice
- Tabasco sauce
- 1 cup fish or seafood stock, preferably homemade
- Salt and freshly milled black pepper
- 1½ pounds redfish, red drum, or red snapper fillets, cut into 4- to 6-ounce portions
- 2 tablespoons minced flat-leaf parsley
- Cooked rice

Prepare a roux, first warming the oil in a Dutch oven or large saucepan over high heat until very hot—close to but not smoking. Add the flour quickly, 1 tablespoon at a time, stirring constantly and watching out for splatters. After all the flour is incorporated, reduce the heat to medium-low and continue cooking for several minutes, stirring until the color of the roux is a rich medium tan. Add the onion and cook until it begins to soften, about 2 minutes. Stir in the bell pepper and garlic, and continue cooking until the vegetables are well softened but not browned, about 5 additional minutes.

Pour in the tomatoes and juice, and mix in the bay leaves, thyme, allspice, and several good splashes of Tabasco sauce. Simmer the sauce for about 15 minutes, stirring up from the bottom occasionally as the mixture thickens. Stir in stock, add salt and pepper to taste, and heat through. Arrange the fish in the sauce and sprinkle it with parsley. Cover the pan and continue cooking until the fish is cooked through and flaky, about 10 minutes. If the fish is cooking unevenly, stir it gently to avoid breaking the fish fillets. Serve the fish with generous spoonfuls of the sauce alongside or over rice.

TECHNIQUE TIP:
New Orleans cooks generally buy whole fish for this dish, saving the head and bones for stock. If you want to do the same, have the market fillet a 4- to 5-pound fish, or two of half that size, and give you the skin and bones for stock. Cover the trimmings with 5 to 6 cups of water, add onion, bay, celery, and garlic, and cook for 1 to 2 hours over low heat. Strain the stock, use what's required for this recipe, and refrigerate or freeze the rest.

Grilled Whole Pompano

SERVES 4

A land of promoters ever since Ponce de León landed, supposedly in search of the fountain of youth, Florida doesn't try to hide many of its glories from the rest of the nation. Pompano is a partial exception, still not widely known outside its natural turf in southeastern waters. It's the kind of thing that makes people possessive and a little secretive, described by Sheila Hibben in *The National Cookbook* (1932) as "the perfection of fish—and perhaps of all food." She recommended broiling pompano for peak flavor, but we think modern outdoor grilling works even better. Greens with a hint of bitterness are a nice foil to the fish, perhaps mustard greens, long-cooked in the traditional pot-liquor style found on page 260, or broccoli raab, quick-sautéed in a bit of olive oil.

- 4 whole pompano, 1 to 1¼ pounds each, or 2 whole pompano, 1¾ to 2 pounds each, gutted
- Vegetable oil or olive oil
- Zest and juice of 1 lemon
- 1 small onion, sliced very thin
- Salt and freshly milled black pepper
- Lemon wedges and fresh mint sprigs
- Chow-Chow (page 310), optional

Cut 2 or 3 moderately deep diagonal slashes into the sides of each fish. Rub each fish inside and out with a thin coat of oil. Sprinkle the cavities of each fish with lemon zest and juice, onion, salt, and pepper.

Fire up the grill, bringing the temperature to medium-high (where you can hold your hand comfortably an inch or two over the cooking grate for about 3 seconds). Oil the cooking grate. Transfer the fish to the grate with the tails arranged away from the hottest part of the fire. Grill the fish uncovered over medium-high heat for 9 to 10 minutes per inch of thickness, turning once, until opaque throughout. To turn the fish, roll each of them over gently rather than lifting them up and flipping them. If you feel any resistance when you turn the fish, re-oil the grate.

Brush the top side of each fish lightly with oil for a shinier appearance. Transfer the fish to a platter, garnish with lemon wedges and mint, and serve with chow-chow if you wish.

TECHNIQUE TIP:
Grilling is perhaps the best method overall for enhancing the innate flavor of many fish. Whole fish like this pompano should be under 2 or 3 pounds in size, and no thicker than 1½ inches at their most portly point. Using medium-high heat gets the right surface sear while allowing the center to cook through before the skin burns. Good candidates for the grill include sea bass or striped bass, bluefish, mackerel, snapper, and trout. In North Carolina in the fall, when the mullet are running, residents make a community event of grilling the fish whole over an open, outdoor wood fire.

With fillets and steaks, make sure they're freshly cut and preferably about an inch thick. Salmon, shark, and tuna grill well on a hot fire, but halibut, mahi-mahi, and swordfish do better on medium-high. Halibut steaks are one of our favorites, particularly fine after a long 2- to 3-day marinade in a Japanese-influenced West Coast blend of sake, mirin, and minced fresh ginger. When grilling any fish, make sure to keep the cooking grate clean and well oiled, to avoid leaving behind a chunk of your treasure.

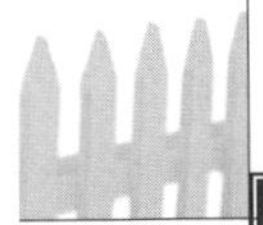

Broiled Petrale Fillets

Serves 4

Petrale sole (actually a flounder) has been a West Coast favorite for generations, particularly around the San Francisco Bay. A sweet, mild, flaky fish, it's best cooked simply and quickly on high heat. We add a nut crunch for a texture contrast.

- ¼ cup (½ stick) plus 1 tablespoon unsalted butter
- 6 tablespoons chopped filberts (hazelnuts)
- Juice of ½ lemon
- 1½ pounds petrale sole fillets, preferably 4 to 8 fillets of similar size and thickness
- Salt and freshly ground black pepper
- Fresh lemon slices

Heat the broiler.

Melt 1 tablespoon of the butter in a small skillet over medium-low heat. Stir in the filberts and cook briefly until toasted a bit and fragrant. Scrape the nuts out of the skillet onto a small plate or paper towel. Return the skillet to the stove and in it melt the remaining ¼ cup butter over medium heat. Remove from the heat and stir in the lemon juice. Brush each fillet on both sides with the lemon butter. Sprinkle lightly with salt and pepper.

Arrange the fillets on a baking sheet and broil them until cooked through and flaky, as little as 2 minutes with fillets of ¼- to ⅓-inch thickness. Check the fillets, cooking an additional minute or two as necessary. Watch them very carefully, as they can quickly dry out. Arrange the fillets on plates and then top with equal portions of the filberts. Serve immediately, garnished with lemon slices.

Odd Scraps for the Economical

That's the title Lydia Maria Child used in *The American Frugal Housewife* (1832) for her chapter on household hints. Most cookbooks of the nineteenth century, and many from even later, contained a section on home remedies, cleaning products, and housekeeping tips. The suggestions fulfilled a role much like recipes, keeping readers abreast of proven and new ways of doing things in the days before mass advertisers seized the initiative. Child's notions were typical in some respects, but she covered more ground than most writers and offered a few unusual ideas.

To drive off cockroaches, she recommended a mixture of molasses and boiled poke root, placed around the kitchen in bowls. Mindful of health and cleanliness, she advocated washing hair in New England rum to keep it free of both dirt and disease, and she also advised brushing teeth nightly in a mixture of honey and pulverized charcoal. We address the same needs today with different products, but after adding the cost of marketing, our solutions are hardly more economical.

FRYERS, ROASTERS, AND Wild Turkeys

THE SPANISH BROUGHT THE FIRST CHICKENS TO THE New World in the late fifteenth century. Soon afterward they reversed the voyage for the turkey, already domesticated in Mexico, and introduced it to Europe. Well before the English settled on our shores, they knew the turkey as a noble American bird, the kind of fowl they would expect to enjoy at a harvest Thanksgiving feast if they happened to be in Massachusetts. The early colonists ate chicken as well, but they prized the birds primarily for their eggs and seldom slaughtered them for meat until the end of their productive years.

With so many good game birds available for roasting, tough old chickens went into the stewpot instead of on the spit, putting them lower on the pecking order of dinner fare.

For that reason, ultimately, Americans developed more distinctive dishes for chicken than for turkey and other fowl. If a bird was tender enough for roasting, cooks lacked much incentive to develop other means of preparation, particularly during the long era when the hearth reigned in the kitchen and spit-roasting was truly a magnificent method of cooking. The flame of a wood fire, positioned behind and not under the food, brought out the innate flavor in a way that we can't quite duplicate in a modern home oven. Chicken required more ingenuity in the cooking and seasoning, a challenge that inspired a range of creative and delicious dishes.

Breeders began developing varieties of chicken specifically for meat in the nineteenth century, and that gradually changed the nature of the bird. Scrawny barnyard chickens that scratched their feed from the soil, and tasted of the earth, eventually gave way to the bland, factory-raised birds of today, still in need of an artful preparation but now for flavor instead of tenderness. Around 1950, during what one historian calls "the Golden Age of American food chemistry," scientists discovered ways to stimulate the growth of chickens and to pack them tightly together in batteries without causing the stress and contagious diseases that occur naturally in crowded, shut-in conditions. These developments helped breeders to bring plump, inexpensive chickens to market in a matter of weeks, though it certainly didn't taste like the meat of old.

A reaction to this regimen in recent decades has improved our choices today. Small-scale operations across the country raise chickens in traditional ways, with flavor as a goal, and similar efforts are returning the rich, wild tang to turkey and other fowl. You still have to search a bit for premier meat, and pay a little extra for it, but you won't regret the effort and cost for your favorite dishes. In our selections below, and in other popular preparations, standard supermarket poultry yields good results, but the flavor improves in direct relation to the integrity of the ingredients. Home cooks created these dishes, after all, to bring out the best in birds from the barnyard and the woods, and they shine their brightest the closer you stay to the original nest.

Chicken Fricassee over Cornbread Toast

SERVES 4 TO 6

Before most Americans had young chickens for frying, they often fricasseed old birds to tenderize them. An ancient European method, fricasseeing combines frying and simmering. America certainly has no exclusive claim on the dish, but neither does any other nation. Largely forgotten today, the fricassee deserves renewed respect, for both its legacy and its silky, soothing qualities. For a contrast in texture, we serve it on toasted slices of cornbread, but Georgia Bits and Grits Waffles (page 17) also make a good base.

INGREDIENT TIP: Whole chickens come in these categories today:

- Game hens weigh under 2 pounds and are less than a month old.
- Fryers or broilers gain a month in age and a pound or more in weight. The young chickens are tender and versatile, but not very flavorful.
- Roasters enjoy a few more weeks of life and weigh in at up to 5 to 6 pounds. Plumper and fuller in flavor than fryers, but still tender, they are our favorites for most dishes and for stock.
- Stewing hens, beyond their egg-laying prime, are older, larger, and tougher. They provide good flavor when cooked by moist methods such as poaching, but aren't as juicy as younger birds.

4-pound chicken, preferably a roaster, cut into 8 bone-in serving pieces, skin removed (see Ingredient Tip)

Salt and freshly milled black pepper

2 tablespoons unbleached all-purpose flour

½ cup (1 stick) unsalted butter

2 large shallots, chopped

6 ounces wild mushrooms, such as chicken-of-the-woods or oyster, preferably, or portobello or button mushrooms, sliced thin

¼ cup dry sherry

1½ cups chicken stock, preferably homemade

1 teaspoon minced fresh chervil or summer savory, or ½ teaspoon dried chervil or summer savory

Pinch of ground nutmeg

1 egg yolk

½ cup half-and-half

4 to 6 wedges Cast-Iron-Baked Buttermilk Cornbread (page 352) or other cornbread

Chervil or summer savory sprigs, optional

Sprinkle the chicken parts with salt and pepper, then dust them lightly with flour.

Melt the butter in a large heavy skillet over medium heat. Add the chicken parts and sauté them until golden brown on both sides and partially cooked through, about 10 minutes. Sprinkle the shallots and mushrooms around the chicken pieces, and cook about 2 minutes longer. Pour in the sherry and let it reduce by about half, an additional couple of minutes. Pour in the stock and sprinkle the chervil and nutmeg over it. Reduce the heat to a bare simmer, cover, and continue cooking for 20 to 25 additional minutes, until the chicken is quite tender. Remove the chicken from the skillet and place it on a plate.

Whisk the egg yolk and half-and-half together in a small bowl. Spoon a few tablespoons of the hot cooking liquid into the yolk mixture. Whisk the mixture into the skillet and cook several minutes until lightly thickened. Return the chicken pieces to the skillet, coating them with the sauce.

Split the cornbread and toast it. Place the toasted cornbread on each plate, then arrange the chicken beside it and spoon a portion of sauce over it. Garnish with herb sprigs, if you wish, and serve.

Buttermilk-Bathed Pan-Fried Chicken

Serves 4 to 6

Fried chicken rules the roost when it comes to American chicken specialties. Nothing is more popular, even in an age that is afraid of frying, and nothing is tastier when it is fried well. Mary Randolph provided the first recipe in *The Virginia Housewife* (1824), but as she knew, it worked well only with tender young chickens, which few people could afford to sacrifice from their egg-producing responsibilities. Fried chicken began its ascent into national prominence in the late nineteenth century, after the introduction of the range improved the control of frying temperatures, and gained icon status a few decades later when commercial chicken raised for meat became cheaper and more plentiful. As Laurie Colwin says about her recipe in *Home Cooking* (1988), everyone knows there is only one right way to fry chicken, but they happen to be wrong in thinking that it's their way. This is our approach, honed over many years of making and munching.

CHICKEN

Approximately 3 cups buttermilk

2 to 3 teaspoons hot pepper sauce, such as Texas Pete or Tabasco

2 to 3 teaspoons salt

3½- to 4-pound chicken, preferably a roaster, cut into 8 bone-in serving pieces

1½ teaspoons freshly milled black pepper

1 teaspoon dry mustard

2 cups unbleached all-purpose flour

Approximately 1½ pounds (3 cups) lard (see Technique Tip on page 177 if you'd like to render your own lard at least once) or 1½ pounds Crisco or other solid vegetable shortening plus 3 tablespoons bacon drippings

CREAM GRAVY

Pan drippings

3 tablespoons seasoned flour

12-ounce can evaporated milk

1 cup chicken stock, preferably homemade

3 tablespoons whipping cream or half-and-half

½ teaspoon freshly milled black pepper or more to taste

Salt

Mix the buttermilk, as much hot pepper sauce as you like, and 1 teaspoon of the salt in a shallow dish. Add the chicken parts, turning to coat them well. Cover and refrigerate for at least 2 hours and up to 12 hours, turning occasionally.

Combine the remaining 1 to 2 teaspoons salt, pepper, dry mustard, and flour in a large plastic bag or in the time-honored brown paper grocery sack. Place a wire rack for draining the chicken near the cooking area.

Melt the lard or shortening in a 12-inch to 14-inch cast-iron skillet over medium-high heat. If using shortening, then add the bacon drippings to the skillet. When the lard or shortening reaches 375°F, reduce the heat to medium and begin to prepare the chicken.

Starting with the dark meat and ending with the breasts, lift the chicken pieces, one by one, out of the marinade, letting excess liquid drain back into the dish. Drop each chicken piece into the seasoned flour and shake to coat it. Place each in the skillet, skin side down. The pieces should fit snugly together in a 12-inch skillet, although they shouldn't stick to each other. Quickly adjust the heat as needed to maintain a temperature of about 300°F (adding all of the chicken to the oil should have dropped the temperature to this degree already). Cover the skillet and fry for 16 minutes, resisting the urge to open the skillet. You should hear a constant ongoing bubbling and sizzling, neither urgent nor lackadaisical. After the allotted time, remove the lid and turn the chicken with tongs, using light pressure to avoid piercing the crust. Fry uncovered for 15 to 17 additional minutes, until the now crackling crust is a rich golden brown and the meat is cooked through but still juicy. Drain the chicken on the rack.

Prepare the gravy, pouring off the pan drippings through a strainer and leaving about ¼ cup of the drippings in the skillet. Return any brown cracklings from the strainer to the skillet and discard the remaining drippings.

Return the skillet to medium heat. Whisk in the flour, stirring to avoid lumps. Slowly add the evaporated milk, stock, and cream, whisking as you pour them in. Bring to a boil, then simmer until the gravy is thickened and the raw flour taste is gone, about 3 minutes. Stir the gravy up from the bottom frequently, scraping up the browned bits. Add pepper and salt to taste, keeping in mind that the pepper should be pronounced but pleasant on your tongue. Transfer the gravy to a gravy boat and the chicken to a platter. Serve immediately.

TECHNIQUE TIP: Don't bother with fried chicken unless you're committed to perfection in the pan. Start with the finest chicken you can find, avoiding ordinary supermarket poultry parts. Find a good meat market that takes pride in its chickens, and buy a whole bird, for the butcher or you to cut into parts. Soaking the chicken in buttermilk adds moisture as well as tang, so don't skimp on the time. Fry in a hefty cast-iron skillet, eschewing anything with an electric cord or a designer color. Never cook the chicken in more than ½ inch of oil or you will be deep-frying rather than pan-frying, and will lose the optimum balance between a crispy exterior and juicy interior. In the unlikely event of leftovers, eat fried chicken cold, which tastes much better than a reheated encore.

As in summer the rivers and creeks are filled with fish, so in winter they are in many places covered with fowl. There are such a multitude of swans, geese, brants, sheldrakes, ducks of several sorts, mallard, teal, bluewings, and many other kinds of waterfowl, that the plenty of them is incredible. . . . [On land there are] wild turkeys of an incredible bigness, pheasants, partridges, pigeons, and an infinity of small birds. . . .

ROBERT BEVERLY, THE HISTORY AND PRESENT STATE OF VIRGINIA (1705)

Chicken Pie

Serves 6

A seventeenth-century recipe manuscript that ended up in the hands of Martha Washington contained a variety of meat pies made with calf's foot, chicken, pigeon, pork, sheep's tongue, veal, and more. These came to America with the British, though other Europeans made similar pies, in their early forms essentially just stews or fricassees in crust. In this country the chicken version proved the most popular over the long term, evolving gradually into the beloved pot pie of today. All comfort-food restaurants offer it as a specialty, and some upscale establishments as well, but it's never better than in a basic home preparation.

CRUST

- ½ cup (1 stick) unsalted butter, well chilled
- 2½ cups unbleached all-purpose flour
- 1¼ teaspoons salt
- ½ cup plus 2 tablespoons vegetable shortening, well chilled
- 6 to 8 tablespoons chicken stock, well chilled, or ice water

FILLING

- 4 medium leeks
- ¼ cup (½ stick) unsalted butter
- 3 cups chicken stock
- 2 teaspoons minced fresh thyme or 1 teaspoon dried thyme
- ½ teaspoon freshly milled black pepper
- ½ teaspoon salt or more to taste
- 1¾ pounds bone-in chicken parts, such as breasts, thighs, or a combination
- ½ pound red waxy potatoes, peeled if you wish, and diced
- 1½ cups diced carrots
- 1 generous cup pearl onions, peeled, trimmed, and halved through the stem end
- 2 tablespoons unbleached all-purpose flour
- ¼ teaspoon dry mustard
- ½ cup half-and-half
- ½ cup peas, fresh or frozen
- 3 tablespoons minced parsley

- 1 egg white, lightly beaten

Prepare the crust, first cutting the butter into quarters lengthwise and then into small squares. Pulse the flour and salt together in a food processor. Scatter the pieces of butter over the mixture and quickly pulse several times just to submerge them in the flour. Scoop the shortening in small spoonfuls, scatter them over the flour-butter mixture, and pulse again quickly several more times until they disappear into the flour too. Dump the dough into a large bowl, sprinkle 4 tablespoons of the stock over it, and lightly combine with your fingers. Add more stock, 1 tablespoon at a time, rubbing it in with your fingers until the dough holds together when you press it together. Stop, it's ready. Divide the dough in half and lightly pat each half into a fat disk. Wrap in plastic and refrigerate for at least 30 minutes.

Prepare the filling, first cleaning the leeks well of any grit. Slice them in half vertically and then slice the white and light green parts into half-moons. You want about 3 generous cups.

Melt the butter in a Dutch oven or other large pot over medium heat. Add the leeks and sauté them until very soft, 5 to 7 minutes. Pour in the stock, add thyme, pepper, ½ teaspoon salt, and the chicken. Bring the stock just to a boil, reduce the heat to medium-low, and cover the pot. Cook covered for about 15 minutes, until the chicken is just cooked through. Remove the chicken with tongs and set it aside until cool enough to handle. Add to the stock the potatoes, carrots, and pearl onions. Cover again and continue cooking over medium-low heat for about 10 minutes, until the vegetables are just tender.

Roll out the pie dough into 2 thin crusts an inch or two larger than a 9-inch pie plate. Arrange the bottom crust in the pie pan and refrigerate it and the other crust for at least 15 additional minutes.

Preheat the oven to 400°F.

Meanwhile, slice the chicken into small cubes. In a small bowl, mix together the flour with the dry mustard and stir in the half-and-half until well combined. Pour the mixture into the vegetables and simmer uncovered briefly until thickened. Stir in the chicken, peas, parsley, and more salt if needed.

Pour the hot filling into the chilled crust, arrange the other crust over the filling, and crimp the edges neatly. Cut several steam vents in the top crust and brush with the egg white. Bake for 20 minutes, then reduce the heat to 350°F and continue baking for about 30 additional minutes, until the crust is golden brown and flaky. Let the pie sit for at least 10 minutes before slicing it into wedges.

Just lately I tilted with one of these modern, patent, machine-made chicken pies, pasted on a foil dish and the head welded on by the Bessemer process. . . . The chicken pie, like so much else, has been rudely reconciled to the ready-made, quick-style, slap-together category of the disposable container. . . . Instead, the chicken pie should be esteemed and respected, regarded as a work of art, and prepared with love and devotion over a decent period of time. If you want something self-contained and instant, eat a cold frankfurter.

JOHN GOULD,
MONSTROUS DEPRAVITY
(1963)

Chicken and Dumplings

SERVES 6

Another great combination of chicken meat and wheat, like Chicken Pie on page 144, this nationwide favorite may derive from Pennsylvania Dutch roots. Like other dishes from that tradition, it's a thrifty concoction that uses most of the bird, and it fills out the plate amply with a doughy mate. As an accompaniment, consider serving Green Beans with Country Ham and Peanuts (page 247).

4½- to 5-pound chicken, preferably a roaster, cut into 8 serving pieces, with back, wings, and giblets reserved

1 large onion, chopped

2 large carrots, chopped

1 teaspoon salt or more to taste

1 bay leaf

¼ teaspoon dried thyme

¼ cup minced parsley

¼ plus 2 tablespoons half-and-half

DUMPLINGS

1¾ cups unbleached all-purpose flour

Scant ½ teaspoon salt

2½ teaspoons baking powder

2 tablespoons minced parsley

¼ teaspoon dried thyme

¾ cup half-and-half

3 tablespoons unsalted butter

2 tablespoons unbleached all-purpose flour, kneaded together with 2 tablespoons softened unsalted butter

Chop the chicken back, thighs, and giblets into 1- or 2-inch pieces with a cleaver or chef's knife. They don't have to look good since you're only helping to coax the most flavor from the pieces. Transfer the chopped chicken parts to a Dutch oven or large deep skillet, and cook them (without oil) briefly over medium-high heat until they lose their raw look. Cover the pot, reduce the heat to low, and sweat the pieces for 20 minutes, stirring once. Uncover, turn up the heat to medium-high again, and pour in 6 cups of warm water. Bring the mixture to a simmer, and cook for about 30 minutes. Strain the stock, and return it to the pot.

Add the 8 chicken pieces, onion, and carrots to the pot. Stir in 1 teaspoon of salt, along with the bay leaf and thyme. Bring the pot just to a boil over medium-high heat. Reduce the heat to low and simmer the chicken partially covered until very tender, about 30 minutes. Remove the chicken and set it aside until cool enough to handle.

Pull the meat from the chicken in large sections. Discard the bones and skin. Shred the chicken into large bite-size chunks and reserve them. (The dish can be made ahead to this point a day in advance. Refrigerate the chicken and cooking liquid separately, covered.)

The Dutch Touch

The Inglenook Cook Book (1911), a popular Pennsylvania Dutch publication that collected recipes from scores of farmstead cooks, devoted an entire chapter to "Potpies, Dumplings, and Fritters." All these "rich dishes," as the editors called them, used dough to enhance and extend other foods, including chicken, beef, pork, mutton, sauerkraut, apples, and even asparagus. The contributors offered over a dozen ways to make chicken pies and chicken with dumplings, and gave them tags that ranged from "Virginia" to "Yankee."

The prototype for many of these dishes was the old Pennsylvania Dutch *Botboi,* a name that translates misleadingly as "pot pie." Rather than a crust, it contains large, flat noodles as the dough element. A simplified version of the Botboi became popular throughout the Midwest as "chicken and noodles," a combination many people know best today in a canned soup.

Add the parsley and half-and-half to the cooking liquid in the pot, and bring it back to a merry simmer while you mix up the dumpling batter. Stir together the dry ingredients in a small bowl. Heat together in a small saucepan the half-and-half and butter until small bubbles just break at the edge. Pour the warm liquid into the dry ingredients and stir quickly until the soft dough just holds together. Quickly form the dough into 16 balls, then drop them gently into the simmering liquid. Reduce the heat to low and cover the pot. Cook the dumplings for 12 to 15 minutes, until biscuitlike and tender. Remove the dumplings with a slotted spoon to a serving platter and discard the bay leaf.

Add more salt to the cooking liquid if needed. Whisk the flour-butter mixture into the liquid to thicken it slightly. Return the chicken to the sauce and simmer until heated through, about 5 minutes. Spoon the chicken and sauce over and around the dumplings and serve immediately.

Roast Chicken with Nut Sauce

Serves 4 to 6

While the modern oven doesn't roast as effectively as the old hearth, we have the advantage today of plump, tender chickens that are well suited to the cooking method. The approach here emulates the spit-roasting of the past, when "done to a turn" was a literal description, as Karen Hess points out in her copious notes on *Martha Washington's Booke of Cookery* (1981). An Eliza Leslie recipe for chestnut-stuffed roast chicken inspired our version. Peanuts also work well and are more easily found year-round. White rice or Mashed Idaho Russets (page 269) help soak up the sauce, while Spiced Acorn Squash (page 250) and steamed broccoli spears make it a Sunday feast.

4¾- to 5-pound chicken, preferably a roaster

2 to 3 tablespoons unsalted butter, softened

Salt and freshly milled black pepper

1 large bunch fresh thyme

1½ cups whole peeled chestnuts, fresh or canned, or 1¼ cups unsalted peanuts

1 medium onion, cut into 8 wedges

2 medium carrots, chunked

2½ cups chicken stock, preferably homemade

¼ cup dry white wine or additional chicken stock

Pinch of cayenne pepper

Preheat the oven to 450°F. Grease the rack of a heavy roasting pan just large enough to hold the chicken.

Slip your fingers under the chicken's skin and loosen it, being careful not to tear it. Rub the butter over and under the skin, then rub salt and pepper over, under, inside, and out. Arrange about half of the thyme sprigs under the skin, then add the rest to the chicken's cavity. Also insert about ½ cup of the nuts in the cavity. Truss the chicken if you wish. (It makes the bird a little easier to turn, and provides a prettier presentation at the table, but we often skip the step.) Let the chicken sit at room temperature for about 20 minutes.

Place the chicken on the rack in the roasting pan, breast side down. Rub the onion wedges and carrot chunks with a bit of butter and scatter them in the bottom of the pan. Plan on a total cooking time of about 1½ hours. Have a sturdy spatula and tongs handy to help turn the chicken. Roast for 15 minutes, then turn to one side (so that a leg and a wing are on top) and roast for 10 additional minutes. Turn to the other side, scatter the remaining 1 cup of nuts in the pan, and roast 10 more minutes. Turn the chicken breast side up and baste it with several tablespoons of the stock. Reduce the oven temperature to 325°F and cook the

No southern African-American main dish is as evocative as fried chicken. It turns up everywhere, from country suppers to breakfast. It helped hungry travelers on their way in the days of segregation, when no self-respecting African-Americans would hit the road without a shoebox full of fried chicken and deviled eggs to sustain them. It appears at church suppers and at after-hours joints, nourishing the Sunday "saved" and Saturday night "heathen" as well.

JESSICA HARRIS, THE WELCOME TABLE (1995)

chicken for 10 additional minutes. Repeat the basting two more times at 10-minute intervals. Continue cooking the chicken without further basting (so the skin can crisp) until the internal temperature at the inner thigh reaches 175°F to 180°F, 20 to 30 minutes longer. The chicken should be golden brown.

Place the chicken on a serving platter. Scoop the nuts and thyme from the chicken's cavity. Place them in a blender along with the pan juices, browned vegetables, and nuts from the roasting pan. Pour the remaining stock and wine into the blender, and purée. Add the cayenne to the sauce and season with more salt and pepper if you wish. Return the mixture to the roasting pan and simmer over medium heat for about 3 minutes, until thickened a bit more. Pour the sauce into a gravy boat. Carve the chicken and serve; pass the sauce on the side.

From Maryland to Molokai

There are probably more ways to make American fried chicken than there are cooks in Paris. Even the great French chef Escoffier had a version, which he identified as a Maryland rendition. He fried the chicken in clarified butter, covered it with a horseradish-laced béchamel sauce, and suggested a banana among the fitting accompaniments.

Back in the real Maryland, in Escoffier's day, lard usually filled the bottom of the skillet, cream gravy came poured on top of the chicken or served on the side, and if the plate contained anything yellow, it was corn. By the time the Hammond-Harwood House published its fund-raising cookbook, *Maryland's Way,* in 1963, some local cooks had switched to vegetable oil for frying and had dropped the gravy, but Mrs. Virgil Maxcy still used lard, flavoring it by frying parsley in it first.

Other ways to season fried chicken vary widely and wildly, from the tang of lemon to the heat of jalapeño, from a dunk in honey in Mississippi to a dip in an oyster sauce on the Hawaiian isle of Molokai. Accompaniments range from Southern "chicken biscuits" pan-cooked in the drippings to Pennsylvania Dutch "green apple pap," from the fried mush Mary Randolph liked on the side to the fried rice now served by Asian vendors in Baltimore's Lexington Market. American fried chicken is a world unto itself.

Chicken Long Rice

SERVES 4

A completely different take on the combination of chicken with dough or noodles, this is a Hawaiian favorite with a Cantonese ancestry. Boogie and Violet Luuwai, a seventh-generation Maui family, showed us how they make the dish one day when preparing a batch for a church supper. While the seasoning is subtle, the result shouldn't be bland or watery, as is often the case in commercial luau versions. The name comes from the Chinese bean-thread noodles, commonly called "long rice" in the islands.

- 1 ounce dried shiitake mushrooms or Chinese mushrooms, such as tree ears
- 2 ounces Chinese bean-thread noodles (cellophane noodles), or 1 "bundle" from a 3¾-ounce package of noodles
- 2 cups chicken stock, preferably homemade
- 1 tablespoon minced fresh ginger
- 2 teaspoons Japanese soy sauce, such as Yamasa, or more to taste
- 1 pound skinless, boneless chicken breasts, sliced into ½-inch by 2-inch strips
- 2 celery stalks, cut into 2-inch matchsticks
- 1 carrot, cut into 2-inch matchsticks
- 4 scallions, halved vertically and sliced on the diagonal into 2-inch matchsticks

Cover the mushrooms with boiling water and let them sit until soft, about 30 minutes. Cover the noodles with warm water and let them sit briefly until flexible. Drain the noodles and cut them into 3-inch lengths. Strain off the mushroom soaking liquid, carefully leaving any grit behind, and reserve the liquid. Slice the mushrooms into thin strips, discarding any woody stems.

Bring the stock and ginger to a boil in a large saucepan. Reduce the heat to medium and simmer for 5 minutes. Add the soy sauce, chicken, celery, carrot, and mushrooms and their soaking liquid. Simmer covered for 8 to 10 minutes, until the chicken is tender and the celery and carrot are softened but still have some crunch. Stir in the long rice and scallions, and continue to simmer until the stock is mostly absorbed but the mixture is still moist, about 5 additional minutes. If you feel the dish needs salt, add a bit more soy sauce, but it should only be used as a seasoning and should not overpower the more subtle flavors. Serve hot.

INGREDIENT TIP:
If you strike out locally getting premium chicken for this and other dishes, one good mail-order source is Pollo Real (505-838-0345). At their farm in Socorro, New Mexico, Tom Delehanty and Tracey Hamilton move their organically raised chickens daily through fields of alfalfa, oats, millet, wheatgrass, chicory, and brassicas, and supplement the birds' diet with corn, soybeans, buckwheat, and wheat from surrounding areas. They clean and dress the chickens on the farm and ship them out the same day.

Georgia Country Captain

Serves 6 to 8

Eliza Leslie provides the usual explanation for the origin and name of this wonderful dish in her *Miss Leslie's New Cookery Book* of 1857. She suggests that a British officer of native (i.e., "country") troops in India brought the dish to the West. Some Savannah, Georgia, residents dispute the story, claiming the idea came from a ship captain involved in the spice trade, a major link at the time between southern ports and the rest of the world. However the dish arrived, it developed a strong association with Georgia and became the most popular and refined of the various curried-chicken preparations found in southern cooking by the early nineteenth century. Serve country captain with fluffy white rice and a good ale.

If you like dishes made out
of a piece of lettuce and
ground-up peanuts and
a maraschino cherry
and marshmallow whip
and a banana
You will not get them in
Savannah,
But if you seek something
headier than nectar and
tastier than ambrosia
and more palatable than
manna,
Set your teeth, I beg you,
in one of these spécial-
ités de Savannah.
Everybody has the right to
think whose food is the
most gorgeous,
And I nominate Georgia's.

Ogden Nash, preface to Harriet Ross Colquitt, The Savannah Cook Book (1933)

- ⅓ cup unbleached all-purpose flour
- 1 teaspoon paprika
- 1 teaspoon salt or more to taste
- Pinch of ground allspice
- 4- to 4½-pound chicken, preferably a roaster, cut into 8 bone-in serving pieces
- 2 tablespoons peanut oil
- 2 thick bacon slices, chopped
- 2 medium onions, chopped
- 1 large green bell pepper, chopped
- 1 garlic clove, minced
- 1½ tablespoons curry powder
- 28-ounce can tomatoes, chopped and the juice reserved
- 1 cup chicken stock, preferably homemade
- 2 tablespoons mango chutney or other chutney
- ½ cup slivered almonds
- ⅓ cup dried currants

Combine the flour, paprika, 1 teaspoon of salt, and allspice on a plate. Dredge the chicken pieces lightly in the seasoned flour.

In a Dutch oven or other large heavy ovenproof pot, combine the peanut oil and bacon, and fry over medium heat until the bacon is brown and crisp. Remove the bacon with a slotted spoon and reserve it. Add a few pieces of the chicken to the drippings and brown over medium heat on all sides. Remove the chicken, then repeat with the rest. Stir in the onions, bell pepper, and garlic, cover, and sweat for 5 minutes until soft. Stir in the curry powder and cook an additional minute. Return the chicken to the pot, then add in the tomatoes and juice, stock, and chutney. Bring the mixture to a simmer, then reduce the heat to low. Cover and cook for 35 to 40 minutes, until the chicken is tender.

Mix in the almonds, currants, reserved bacon and, if you wish, more salt. Stir up from the bottom once or twice. Cook, uncovered, for about 10 additional minutes to meld the flavors. Serve hot.

King Ranch Chicken

Serves 6 or more

No one knows why this twentieth-century chicken casserole acquired an association with a famed Texas cattle ranch, but it may have something to do with Lone Star braggadocio. It's a big dish from a big state, just the kind of creation you might name for a legendary status symbol. As long as you stay away from the canned-soup shortcuts, which actually save little time, this is a Texas-size treat.

SAUCE

¼ cup (½ stick) unsalted butter

2 tablespoons unbleached all-purpose flour

1 to 1½ teaspoons chili powder

¼ teaspoon ground cumin

1 cup half-and-half

½ cup chicken stock

Salt

FILLING

2 tablespoons unsalted butter

1 medium onion, chopped

¾ cup chopped roasted mild green chiles, such as poblano or New Mexican, fresh or frozen

¼ pound button mushrooms, sliced thin

1 large red-ripe tomato, chopped, or 1 generous cup drained chopped canned tomatoes

1½ to 2 cups diced or shredded cooked chicken, preferably poached breasts, thighs, or a combination

2 to 4 tablespoons chicken stock

¼ cup sliced pimiento-stuffed green olives

Salt

About 12 corn tortillas

¼ cup thin-sliced scallion greens

1½ generous cups grated mild Cheddar cheese

Preheat the oven to 350°F. Oil a medium to large baking dish.

Prepare the sauce, first warming the butter in a saucepan over medium heat. Sprinkle in the flour, chili powder, and cumin, and whisk until smooth. Add the half-and-half and stock slowly, whisking to avoid lumps. Simmer the sauce for 3 to 5 minutes, until lightly thickened. Season with salt. (The sauce can be made a day or two ahead, cooled, and refrigerated, covered. Thin with a little milk if it seems overly thick.)

Prepare the filling, first warming the butter in a large skillet over medium heat. Stir in the onion, cover the skillet, and sweat for about 3 minutes to soften. Uncover and add the green chiles, mushrooms, and tomato. Sauté until the vegetables are well softened, about 10 minutes. Stir in the chicken, 2 tablespoons of the stock, olives, and salt to taste, and heat through. Stir in the remaining stock if the mixture seems at all dry. (The filling can be made a day ahead, cooled, and refrigerated, covered.)

When Blanche fried chicken, I always got a piece of crisply cooked gizzard or a chicken wing to stay my appetite until supper. And chicken we had—in pot pie, in stews, in soup, and mixed with other meats in main courses—and all for one simple reason. My father raised chickens in the backyard. Even when his brood was in short supply, we could always buy the chickens for pennies from one local farmer or another. They were depression food and if, throughout my career, I have printed more recipes for chicken than any other meat it is because it is the most versatile of viands.

CRAIG CLAIBORNE,
A FEAST MADE FOR LAUGHTER
(1982)

Layer half of the filling in the prepared dish. Top with several tortillas, enough to cover the filling thoroughly, overlapping them a bit. (It's okay to tear some of them if it makes them easier to arrange.) Spoon half of the sauce over the tortillas, then scatter half of the scallions and cheese on top. Add another layer of tortillas. Spoon the remaining filling over the tortillas, add another layer of tortillas, and repeat with the remaining sauce, scallions, and cheese. (The casserole can be made ahead to this point and refrigerated covered for several hours. Let it sit briefly at room temperature before continuing.) Bake for 25 to 30 minutes, until heated through and bubbly. Serve hot.

Mississippi Barbecued Chicken

Serves 4 or more

One of many writers employed by the WPA during the Great Depression, Eudora Welty spent some of her time collecting recipes from antebellum homes in Mississippi. She attested to the authenticity of each, and allowed as how even "Yankees are welcome to make these dishes." This tangy, wood-smoked chicken combines ideas from a couple of the barbecue recipes she found. To round out a fine backyard dinner, we would add Fried Green Tomatoes (page 246) or Fried Okra (page 262) and New Potatoes à la Diable (page 273).

BARBECUE SAUCE

¼ cup (½ stick) plus 2 tablespoons unsalted butter

⅔ cup ketchup

⅓ cup tomato-based barbecue sauce, preferably a not terribly sweet brand

¼ cup Worcestershire sauce

3 tablespoons fresh lemon juice

1 garlic clove, minced

½ teaspoon Tabasco sauce

½ teaspoon freshly milled black pepper

Salt

8 bone-in chicken parts—breasts, thighs, drumsticks—skin removed

Salt and freshly milled black pepper

Combine the sauce ingredients in a medium saucepan and simmer together for 15 minutes. (The sauce can be made several days ahead, cooled, and refrigerated, covered. Reheat before using.)

Fire up a smoker or covered grill to between 225°F and 250°F, following the manufacturer's instructions for smoking.

Season the chicken with salt and pepper and let it sit covered at room temperature for about 15 minutes.

Transfer the chicken to the smoker, starting with the thighs or drumsticks, which require 1 to 1¼ hours of cooking time. Baste them with the sauce, and smoke for 15 minutes. Add the breasts to the smoker and baste all the chicken with the sauce again. Continue smoking for 45 to 60 additional minutes, turning and basting about every 15 minutes. Open the smoker only when necessary, and cover as quickly as possible, to minimize the loss of heat and smoke. The chicken is done when its juices run clear. Serve hot, under magnolia trees for the full experience.

Willamette Valley Grilled Chicken with Blackberry Sauce

Serves 4 to 6

Unlike the antebellum art of slow-smoked barbecue, high-heat backyard grilling didn't start gaining momentum in the United States until the 1940s, with the West Coast providing the initial push. Around the same time Americans started buying more chicken parts than whole birds, a trend accelerated by the grilling revolution. In a merry mating of fruit and meat common in American cooking, we top these contemporary grilled breasts with a robust berry sauce from Oregon.

BLACKBERRY SAUCE

2 tablespoons unsalted butter

1 large shallot, minced

2 cups chicken stock, preferably homemade

2 cups blackberries or loganberries, fresh or frozen

½ teaspoon chopped fresh rosemary or ¼ teaspoon dried rosemary

½ teaspoon chopped fresh thyme or ¼ teaspoon dried thyme

Salt

Blackberry, loganberry, or raspberry jelly, preserves, or jam, optional

6 large boneless, skinless individual chicken breasts, pounded ½ to ¾ inch thick

1 teaspoon freshly milled black pepper

Salt

Vegetable oil spray

Fresh rosemary sprigs, optional, for garnish

Melt the butter in a medium saucepan over medium heat. Stir in the shallot and sauté until soft, about 3 minutes. Add the stock, berries, rosemary, and thyme, and bring to a boil. Reduce the heat to low and simmer until the berries have disintegrated, about 20 additional minutes. Strain the sauce into a bowl, pressing on the solids to extract from them as much liquid as possible. Return the sauce to the saucepan and season with salt. If the sauce tastes overly tart, stir in a bit of jelly, if you wish, to balance the flavor. Continue cooking the sauce until it has reduced to about 1½ cups. (The sauce can be prepared a day ahead to this point, cooled, and refrigerated, covered. Reheat before proceeding.)

Fire up the grill, bringing the temperature to medium (where you can hold your hand comfortably an inch or two above the cooking grate for 4 to 5 seconds).

Pepper the chicken and salt it lightly. Just before grilling, spritz the breasts with the oil.

Grill the chicken uncovered over medium heat for 5 to 6 minutes per side, until opaque but still juicy. Brush lightly with the sauce when you turn the cooked side of the chicken up, and coat the second side when it comes off the grill. Serve hot with the remaining sauce, garnished with rosemary if you wish.

Chicken Breasts Stuffed with Smithfield Ham

Serves 4

Most American cooks are more familiar with chicken cordon bleu or saltimbocca than this tasty southern twist on ham-flavored meat rolls. Use a long-aged, salty country ham in the dish and slice it as thinly as possible. Serve the stuffed breasts with Fresh Butter Beans (page 248) and Cream Biscuits (page 348), and offer a fruit cobbler for dessert.

- 4 boneless, skinless individual chicken breasts, about 6 to 7 ounces each, pounded thin
- Approximately 1½ tablespoons brown mustard or Dijon mustard
- Salt
- 3 ounces Smithfield ham or other well-aged country ham, sliced paper-thin, then chopped fine by hand
- 1 tablespoon unsalted butter, softened
- 2 teaspoons minced fresh sage or 1 teaspoon crumbled dried sage
- 1 cup dried bread crumbs
- Vegetable oil for pan-frying

Preheat the oven to 350°F. Grease a small baking dish.

Coat the chicken breasts lightly with mustard, rubbing them on both sides. Salt them lightly. Mix together the ham, butter, and sage, and spread the mixture evenly across the chicken breasts. From one of the long sides, roll a breast up, snug but not tight, and secure it with toothpicks or kitchen twine. Repeat with the remaining breasts. Place the bread crumbs on a plate and pat each chicken roll with the crumbs.

Warm ¼ inch of oil in a skillet over medium-high heat. Sear the chicken rolls quickly on all sides. (The oil may pop a bit.) Transfer the chicken to the prepared dish, cover, and bake for 20 minutes. Uncover and bake for about 5 additional minutes, until golden brown with clear juices. Let the rolls rest several minutes, then cut them into individual slices and fan them on plates. Serve immediately, with additional dollops of mustard if you wish.

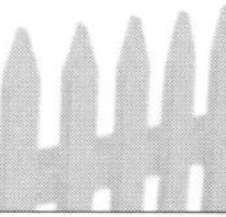

Charleston Benne Chicken

Serves 4

Still known in the South Carolina lowcountry by the African name of benne, sesame seeds make a tasty, nutty coating for a variety of foods. Charleston cooks put the ground seeds on catfish, oysters, and chicken, including this style of orange-scented breasts. It's easily the most memorable quick chicken sauté we've ever eaten.

- ¼ cup plus 2 tablespoons sesame seeds
- 2 tablespoons unbleached all-purpose flour
- Minced zest and juice of 1 large orange
- ¾ teaspoon salt
- ⅛ teaspoon cayenne pepper plus more for garnish
- Pinch of freshly milled black pepper
- 4 boneless, skinless individual chicken breasts, pounded evenly to no more than ½-inch thickness
- 1 tablespoon unsalted butter
- 1 tablespoon vegetable oil
- ¾ cup chicken stock
- 1½ tablespoons whipping cream
- Orange slices

Blend ¼ cup of the sesame seeds with the flour in a blender just until a coarse meal forms. Pour the mixture onto a plate and stir into it the orange zest, salt, cayenne, and pepper. Set aside 2 tablespoons of the sesame-flour mixture, then pat the chicken breasts with the rest.

Warm the butter and oil in a large skillet over medium heat. Sauté the chicken breasts for 4 to 6 minutes per side, until golden brown and just cooked through. Remove the chicken breasts and place them on a platter. Sprinkle the reserved sesame-flour mixture into the pan drippings, stirring to avoid lumps. Whisk in the stock slowly and bring the sauce to a boil. When lightly thickened, pour in the orange juice and cream and heat through.

Spoon the sauce over the chicken breasts. Sprinkle the remaining sesame seeds over the chicken and dust lightly with cayenne. Garnish with orange slices and serve warm.

Chicken Chop Suey

SERVES 4 TO 6

Chop suey probably debuted in the camp kitchens of the workers who built the Pacific railroad lines in the second half of the nineteenth century. The railroad companies often employed Chinese cooks, who sometimes simply tossed together the ingredients at hand to fix a quick meal. This approach owed a debt to Chinese culinary concepts, but the result was thoroughly American. The dish reached the mainstream public rather quickly, appearing in cookbooks across the country by the first decades of the twentieth century, when water chestnuts were still frequently called "Chinese potatoes." Chop suey doesn't really require a recipe, since the meat and vegetables can vary widely, so when you make it just focus on achieving a balance of flavors and textures. Serve it with rice, of course, and perhaps a dollop of Chinese chile paste as a condiment.

- 1 tablespoon cornstarch
- ¼ cup soy sauce
- ¼ cup chicken stock or water
- 1 tablespoon dry sherry
- 2 tablespoons peanut oil
- 12 ounces boneless, skinless individual chicken breasts, pounded evenly to no more than ½-inch thickness and cubed
- 1 to 2 celery stalks, sliced on the diagonal into ½-inch slices
- 2 to 4 scallions, sliced on the diagonal into ½-inch slices
- 3 cups mixed sliced vegetables, such as bamboo shoots, fresh or canned, button mushrooms, bok choy, spinach, or snow peas
- 1 cup sliced water chestnuts, fresh or canned (see Ingredient Tip)
- ½ cup to 1 cup bean sprouts or sunflower sprouts

In a small bowl, combine the cornstarch, soy sauce, chicken stock, and sherry.

Heat a wok or large skillet over high heat. When very hot, pour in the peanut oil and swirl it around to coat the wok. Quickly add the chicken and stir-fry 1 to 2 minutes, until it loses its raw look. Mix in the celery and scallions, and continue stir-frying another minute. Add the mixed vegetables, cook another minute, and add the water chestnuts. Give the cornstarch mixture a stir and pour it into the wok. Continue stir-frying another couple of minutes until the sauce has thickened and the vegetables are crisp-tender. Stir in the sprouts and remove from the heat. Serve immediately.

INGREDIENT TIP: With the proliferation of Asian markets in some of our smallest burgs, it's getting easier to find fresh water chestnuts and bamboo shoots. The canned products remain a lot more common, however, and work fine in chop suey if you blanch them first in boiling water to eliminate the tinny taste.

Chinese Cooking in America

Sylvia Lovegren makes a perceptive point in *Fashionable Food* (1995) when she compares the culinary influence of twentieth-century Chinese houseboys on the West Coast with that of African cooks in the South. Both groups changed the accepted notion of seasoning in the people they served by introducing different ways to flavor food and encouraging a fresh sense of taste.

The first Chinese immigrants came to California with dreams of striking it rich, but ran smack into fears of the "Yellow Peril." Racism and language barriers denied the men entry into many types of work, often forcing them to accept jobs usually relegated to women, who were scarce in the frontier West. They ran laundries and tailor shops, and took up cooking in both homes and restaurants. Like African Americans, they endured much and gave back more.

Chow-Chow Chicken Salad

Serves 4

Green salads probably existed before meat salads, but they didn't come first in the priorities of many Americans until recently. Chicken salad surfaced with increasing frequency after the Civil War, and judging by the number of fancy restaurant versions today, it may still be on an upward track in popularity. This simple mustard-pickle rendition is a local treasure in Tallahassee, Florida, where Crosse & Blackwell is the brand of choice for the chow-chow in the mixture. We learned about it from Jeanne Voltz, onetime food editor of *The Miami Herald* and author of several notable cookbooks, including *The Florida Cookbook* (1993). It may sound like an odd accompaniment, but fried oysters go great with the salad.

2 cups neatly chopped cooked boneless chicken, preferably poached breasts, thighs, or a combination

1 cup diced celery

¼ cup minced onion or more to taste

½ cup mayonnaise

½ cup mustard-based chow-chow pickle, such as Crosse & Blackwell, or more to taste

Hot pepper sauce, such as Datil Do It or other Dixie Datil chile sauce, or Tabasco

Celery salt to taste

Boston lettuce or other soft lettuce leaves

Combine the chicken, celery, and onion in a medium bowl. Mix in the mayonnaise, ½ cup of chow-chow, a splash of hot pepper sauce, and celery salt. Chill at least 1 hour. Taste, adding more chow-chow if you wish and otherwise adjusting the seasonings. Mound the salad on lettuce leaves and serve cold.

TECHNIQUE TIP: Unlike some chicken salads, this Tallahassee version keeps a focus on its main ingredients. The dish is so versatile and accepting of different flavors, it's easy to get carried away and lose both the chicken and the balance of seasoning in a grand presentation. In old and contemporary recipes alike you find everything from almonds to sweetbreads, chili sauce to cranberry jelly. In her Runnymede Salad, Fannie Farmer combined the chicken with potatoes, artichoke bottoms, and truffles, and then stuffed the mixture in hollowed-out cucumbers, arranging it all on lettuce leaves. In more recent years, Ida Bailey Allen in *Best Loved Recipes of the American People* (1973) suggested adding pineapple, pimiento, ginger, sour cream, and crab apples. Such salads may be tasty, at least to their authors, but somewhere on the way to the plate the chicken flew the coop.

Roasted Wild Turkey with Madeira Sauce

Serves 6 or more

Once abundant across the country, wild turkeys became such common food that hunters brought them to the verge of extinction in many areas. Conservation measures enacted after World War II have restored the population considerably, making them popular game birds once again. Farmers have started raising some of the tastier breeds as well, and it's now moderately easy to find fresh wild turkeys in November and December and frozen ones the rest of the year. They taste much different than their domesticated cousins, with a gamier flavor and darker, denser meat.

9- to 12-pound wild turkey, fresh or frozen, with giblets and neck

SEASONING BUTTER

¼ cup (½ stick) unsalted butter, softened

2 plump garlic cloves, minced

½ teaspoon salt

½ teaspoon freshly milled black pepper

AROMATICS

1 medium onion, quartered

1 dozen bruised juniper berries

5 thick bacon slices

SAUCE

Pan drippings

1 tablespoon unbleached all-purpose flour

¼ cup Madeira, preferably, or port, or more to taste

Remaining stock

Salt and freshly milled black pepper

Prepare a stock. Chop the turkey's giblets and neck with a cleaver or heavy chef's knife into 1- to 2-inch pieces. Place them in a stockpot or large saucepan and cook over high heat (without oil) until they lose their raw look and begin to brown in spots. Cover the pan, reduce the heat to medium-low, and sweat the meat for 20 minutes. Uncover, add 3 cups of water, bring to a simmer, and cook for about 30 minutes. Strain the stock and keep it warm. (The stock can be made a day ahead, cooled quickly, and refrigerated, covered, until needed. Reheat it before proceeding.)

Remove all but one baking rack from the oven and set it as low as possible. Preheat the oven to 450°F. Grease the rack of a heavy-duty roasting pan just larger than the turkey. (You will need a heavier roasting pan than the old-style blue speckled enamel versions once popular, and certainly sturdier than the lightweight—in all respects—disposable aluminum foil pans sold in supermarkets and discount stores.)

Slip your fingers under the turkey's skin and loosen it with your fingers, being careful not to tear it. In a small bowl, combine the butter, garlic, salt, and pepper.

TECHNIQUE TIP:

The conventional wisdom claims that wild turkey, because of its leanness, must be cooked at a low temperature to stay moist. However, we find the flavor better and the meat even juicier when we start cooking the bird over high heat and finish over low, as described in the recipe. Turning the meat breast side down for a portion of the cooking, and then barding it with bacon, combine to keep the especially vulnerable breast meat succulent. Turning the turkey by hand is a bit of bother, but for us the results seem worth the small effort. As a final consideration in maintaining moistness, don't overcook wild turkey; many recipes suggest much longer cooking times than are necessary or desirable.

A Thanksgiving Menu

Oysters on Half Shell.
Cream of Asparagus Soup.
Spanish Olives. Celery.
Mixed Pickles. Radishes.
Salted Almonds.
Baked Red Snapper à la
Créole. Mashed Potatoes.
Lamb Chops au Petits
Pois. Chicken Sauté aux
Champignons.
Cauliflower, Sauce
Blanche. Pineapple
Fritters au Rhum.
Pâtes de Foies Gras.
Stuffed Tomatoes.
Turkey Stuffed with
Chestnuts, Cranberry
Sauce. Endive Salad.
French Dressing.
Pababotte à la Créole.
Plum Pudding, Hard or
Brandy Sauce. Pumpkin
Pie. Lemon Sherbet.
Assorted Cakes.
Assorted Fruits.
Assorted Nuts. Raisins.
Neufchatel. Quince
Marmalade. Crackers.
Café Noir.

The Picayune's
Creole Cook Book (1901)

Rub the turkey inside and out with the butter, especially under the breast skin. Fill the turkey's cavity with the onion and juniper berries. Truss the turkey or tie its legs with kitchen string, which makes the bird a little easier to turn. Let the turkey sit covered at room temperature for about 30 minutes.

Place the bird on the rack in the roasting pan, breast side up. Plan on a total cooking time of a little under 2 hours. For a turkey of this size, we turn it twice early in the cooking to baste the bird naturally. (If you lack upper body strength, consult the Technique Tip on page 162 for more conventional roasting instructions.) To help turn the turkey, have ready a sturdy spatula and a goodly thickness of paper towels or oven mitts that you don't mind getting greasy.

Cook for 15 minutes. Remove the bird from the oven, turn it breast side down, return it to the oven quickly, and cook for another 15 minutes. Turn the heat down to 325°F and cook for another 15 minutes.

Remove the turkey from the oven and turn it breast side up again. Baste the turkey with a few tablespoons of stock and any accumulated pan juices. Lay the bacon strips over the breast. Place one strip running lengthwise down the protruding breastbone. Lay the other strips across the breast, from wing to wing, overlapping them slightly. Continue cooking for 6 to 7 additional minutes per pound, basting two more times at 20-minute intervals. During the last 30 minutes of cooking, stop basting the turkey, and remove and discard the bacon so that the turkey breast skin can brown and crisp all over. The turkey is ready when the internal temperature at the inner thigh reaches 170°F (this is a bit less than for domesticated birds).

Remove the turkey from the roasting pan to a large heavy-duty platter or cutting board. Let it sit for 15 to 20 minutes.

Meanwhile, prepare the sauce. (Degrease the pan drippings, if you wish. Pour the liquid out into a large cup, wait briefly for the fat to rise, then skim it off. Return the skimmed drippings to the pan.) Place the roasting pan over one or two stove burners on medium-high heat. Sprinkle in the flour and whisk it with the drippings. Pour the Madeira carefully into the pan drippings and cook it down by about half, scraping up any of the browned bits from the bottom of the pan. Add the remaining stock and bring the mixture to a boil. Reduce as needed to make a thin sauce for the turkey, cooking it at least long enough to eliminate any floury pastiness, about 5 minutes. Adjust the seasoning. Pour the sauce into a gravy boat or bowl.

Scrape the onion and juniper berries from the turkey's cavity and discard them. Carve the meat into very thin slices and serve accompanied by the warm sauce.

Classic Thanksgiving Turkey with Sage Dressing

SERVES 8 OR MORE

A remnant of the traditional English harvest feast, Thanksgiving has been a "Turkey Day" in America since the 1620s. Until Abraham Lincoln established Thanksgiving as a national holiday in 1863, individual colonies and states declared both fasts and thanksgivings (small "t") for religious reasons, and only Connecticut made the latter an annual occasion. Since the Puritans and many other early settlers treated Christmas as an ordinary working day, thanksgivings became the main time for rejoicing, a position the event maintained throughout most of the nineteenth century. The celebration centered on food from the beginning, and a roasted turkey almost always took the spotlight. Americans inherited an enthusiasm for stuffing birds from the English, and our proposed sage dressing bespeaks that same culinary tradition, even though we cook it separately instead of inside the turkey because of contemporary health concerns.

12-pound fresh turkey, with giblets and neck

1 pound miscellaneous chicken necks, backs, wings, or giblets

1 medium onion, chunked

2 celery stalks, chopped

SAGE DRESSING

10 cups ¾-inch cubes of country white bread or French bread (about 1 pound)

6 tablespoons (¾ stick) unsalted butter

3 cups thin-sliced leeks (white and light green parts)

1½ cups thin-sliced celery

4 to 6 ounces button or wild mushrooms, sliced thin

2 teaspoons crumbled dried sage or more to taste

1½ teaspoons dried thyme or dried marjoram, or a combination

1 teaspoon salt

½ teaspoon freshly milled black pepper

Several cups turkey stock

2 large eggs

½ teaspoon baking powder

SEASONING BUTTER

6 tablespoons (¾ stick) unsalted butter, softened

1 teaspoon salt

½ teaspoon freshly milled black pepper

½ teaspoon crumbled dried sage

½ teaspoon dried thyme or marjoram

GRAVY

Pan drippings

2 tablespoons unbleached all-purpose flour

Remaining turkey stock

Salt and freshly milled black pepper

Fresh sage sprigs, thyme sprigs, or other fresh herbs

TECHNIQUE TIP:

A turkey roasted just on high heat tastes great, but the technique can be dangerous in a less than scrupulously clean oven, and even then creates enough smoke to set off all the detectors in the house. It may also leave you with burned pan drippings, a real shame. The method of roasting we specify starts at moderately high heat and then drops the temperature a bit, a compromise that yields excellent results—still moist, tasty meat and beautifully brown, crisp skin. However, it does require careful turning of a hot bird. If that does not appeal to you, or your celebration requires a bird too big to turn, you can roast it in a more conventional way. Plan on a longer cooking time, 17 to 20 minutes per pound. Prepare the turkey for cooking in the same manner, but bring the oven temperature to only 325°F and maintain it there. Cover the turkey breast tightly (not loosely) with a small piece of foil and baste it while roasting at about 30-minute intervals. Raise the foil and baste under it too. Remove the foil in the last 30-minutes or so of roasting. If cooking a wild turkey in this way, use bacon to protect the breast instead of foil, and reduce the roasting time to about 12 minutes per pound.

Sarah Josepha Hale, 1788–1879

Though she is chiefly remembered today as the author of the nursery rhyme "Mary had a little lamb," Sarah Hale was one of the most influential American women of the nineteenth century. She enjoyed so much clout at the time of the Civil War that Abraham Lincoln declared Thanksgiving a national holiday almost solely, according to most accounts, on her urging.

Hale gained her standing as the editor of *Godey's Lady's Book,* by far the most successful woman's magazine of her day. After the early death of her husband, she devoted herself to writing and soon took a job with a different though similar journal, where she stayed for over a decade before *Godey's* started publishing in 1837. She ran the new magazine for the next forty years, making it the nation's leading authority on cooking, fashion, and manners. Circulation figures topped all existing records.

Despite the energy Hale devoted to her job, she also managed to write or participate in the writing of some fifty books, including *The Good Housekeeper* (1841) and several other cookbooks. She sought to combine thrift and taste in her cooking, taking a practical, businesslike approach to the kitchen. We may not remember her primarily as a cook, but it is worth remembering how well she fit that skill and appetite into an exceptionally busy and productive life.

Prepare a stock. Chop the turkey's giblets and neck, and the chicken parts, with a cleaver or heavy chef's knife into 1- to 2-inch pieces. Place them in a stockpot or large saucepan and cook (without oil) over high heat until they lose their raw look and begin to brown in spots. Cover the pan, reduce the heat to medium-low, and sweat the meat for 20 minutes, stirring once or twice and adding the onion and celery after about 10 minutes. Uncover, add 6 cups of water, bring to a simmer, and cook for about 30 minutes. Strain the stock and keep it warm. (The stock can be made a day ahead, cooled quickly, and refrigerated, covered, until needed. Reheat it before proceeding.)

Preheat the oven to 325°F. Toast the bread cubes on baking sheets for about 25 minutes, stirring once or twice, until lightly brown and crisp. Dump them into a large bowl. Leave the oven on. Remove all but one baking rack from the oven and set it as low as possible. Butter a 9-inch × 13-inch baking dish.

Start the dressing, first warming the butter in a large skillet over medium heat. Stir in the leeks, celery, and mushrooms, and sauté until very soft, about 7 minutes. Stir in the sage, thyme, salt, and pepper, and then scrape the vegetable and herb mixture into the bowl of toasted bread crumbs. Add the stock, 1 cup at a time, until the bread is very moist but not soupy. You will probably use 2 to 3 cups of the stock. Reserve the remaining stock. Cover and refrigerate the dressing until you are ready to proceed with it. (The dressing can be made to this point a day ahead. In this case, cover and refrigerate the remaining stock too.)

Slip your fingers under the turkey's skin and loosen it with your fingers, being careful not to tear it. Prepare the seasoning butter, combining the ingredients in a small bowl. Rub the turkey inside and out with the butter, especially under the breast skin. Truss the turkey or tie its legs together with kitchen string. (The turkey can be prepared to this point a day ahead.) Let the turkey sit covered at room temperature for about 30 minutes.

Turn the oven up to 425°F. Grease the rack of a heavy-duty roasting pan just larger than the turkey. Don't use a lightweight or disposable foil pan. Place the bird, breast side up, on the rack in the roasting pan. Plan on a total cooking time of about 2 hours. For a turkey of this size, we turn it twice early in the cooking to help baste the bird naturally. (If you lack upper body strength, or want to cook a larger bird, consult the Technique Tip.) To help turn the turkey, have ready a sturdy spatula and a goodly thickness of paper towels or oven mitts that you don't mind getting greasy.

Cook the turkey initially for 15 minutes. Take the turkey from the oven and turn it breast side down. Return it to the oven quickly and cook for another 15 minutes. Turn the heat down to 325°F and continue to cook for another 15 minutes.

CONTINUED

Take the turkey from the oven again and turn it breast side up. Baste generously with some of the remaining stock and any accumulated pan juices. Continue cooking for about 1¼ hours, basting with more stock and pan drippings two additional times at 20-minute intervals. Avoid basting in the last 30 minutes or so of cooking, so that the skin has time to crisp. The turkey is ready when the internal temperature at the inner thigh reaches 175°F to 180°F.

Finish preparing the dressing after the turkey has roasted for about 1½ hours. Taste and adjust the seasoning if you wish. Whisk the eggs and baking powder together and mix them into the dressing. Spoon the dressing into the baking dish and cover it. Place it in the oven with the turkey and bake for 25 minutes. Uncover and continue baking 15 to 20 additional minutes, until lightly browned and crusty on top. (The timing of these steps should allow the dressing to come to the table still hot from the oven.)

When the turkey is done, remove it from the roasting pan to a large heavy-duty platter or cutting board. Let it sit uncovered for 20 to 30 minutes.

Meanwhile, prepare the gravy. (Degrease the pan drippings, if you wish. Pour the liquid out into a large cup, wait briefly for the fat to rise, then skim it off. Return the skimmed drippings to the pan.) Place the roasting pan with the pan drippings over one or two stove burners on medium-high heat. Scrape up any browned bits from the bottom. Sprinkle in the flour and whisk it with the drippings. Pour in the remaining stock and bring the mixture to a boil. Reduce the liquid as needed to make a thin gravy, cooking at least long enough to remove any floury pastiness, about 5 minutes. Add salt and pepper to taste. Pour into a gravy boat or bowl.

Serve the turkey on a platter garnished with herb sprigs for the traditional dramatic presentation. Carve tableside, accompanied by the hot gravy and dressing.

Our Thanksgiving-dinner table is not furnished as our grandmothers loaded theirs in the olden time. . . . Begin the meal with a *good* soup. Either oyster or tomato soup is recommended. To this should succeed fish. . . .

Then, leading up to the main business of the hour, let the next offering be a nice *entrée* or made-dish—chicken-patés or croquettes, *in memoriam* of the ponderous chicken-pie which was a standing dish with our grandmothers. . . .

Then—the central theme, the point of clustering interests—the Thanksgiving turkey! . . . If you introduce game, let it succeed the turkey, and serve lettuce with it. . . . Crackers and cheese follow this course, and, if you like, olives. . . .

The pumpkin pie is the next consideration. The crust should be short and flaky, *not* friable and tasting like desiccated lard. . . .

C. H. Cushing and Mrs. B. Gray, The Kansas Home Cook-book (1886)

Smoked Turkey Breast

SERVES 6 TO 8, WITH SOME LEFTOVERS FOR MILES STANDISH SANDWICHES (PAGE 56)

Even people who won't touch traditional barbecue meats usually love the taste of smoked turkey. We generally cook the breast rather than the whole bird, since even that takes most of a day at a low smoking temperature. To keep the meat juicy, we inject it with an enhanced stock and wrap it in wet cheesecloth.

½ cup salted chicken or turkey stock

3 tablespoons unsalted butter, melted, or garlic-flavored vegetable oil

1 tablespoon Worcestershire sauce, optional

5- to 7-pound bone-in skin-on turkey breast

DRY RUB

1 tablespoon kosher salt or other coarse salt

1 tablespoon freshly cracked black pepper

2 teaspoons packed brown sugar

TECHNIQUE TIP: Many cookware and outdoor cooking equipment dealers carry kitchen syringes for injecting seasoned liquids into food, particularly poultry. Beyond helping to keep meat moist, the technique allows you to add flavor beneath the surface.

The night before you plan to smoke the turkey breast, combine the stock, butter, and optional Worcestershire sauce in a small bowl. With a kitchen syringe, inject the mixture deep into the turkey breast in a half-dozen places, moving the needle around in each spot to shoot the liquid in several directions.

Prepare the dry rub, combining the ingredients in another small bowl. Massage the mixture over the entire breast, rubbing over and under the skin. Wrap it in plastic and refrigerate overnight.

Cut a 3-foot length of cheesecloth and dampen it thoroughly with water (it should be wet but not dripping). Wrap the breast in the cheesecloth and tie the ends. Let it sit at room temperature for about 30 minutes.

Fire up a smoker or covered grill to between 225°F and 250°F, following the manufacturer's instructions for smoking.

Transfer the breast to the smoker skin side up (you should be able to feel it through the cheesecloth). Plan to cook the breast for 50 to 65 minutes per pound, until the internal temperature reaches 180°F. Wet the cheesecloth down at 1-hour intervals, if needed to keep the cloth moist, unless the manufacturer recommends against adding liquid while cooking. Open the smoker only when necessary, and cover as quickly as possible, to minimize the loss of heat and smoke. After the breast has cooked about 3 hours, remove the cheesecloth, snipping it with scissors and discarding it. Continue smoking the turkey until it is done. Allow it to sit covered for about 10 minutes before carving. Discard the skin, slice, and serve warm. Smoked turkey is also wonderful chilled.

Leelanau Peninsula Roast Duck with Cherry Sauce

Serves up to 4

Early American settlers marveled at the number and variety of wild ducks that filled the skies. They relished the flavor of the native canvasback in particular, but also enjoyed mallards, redheads, and others, all generally roasted. Domesticated ducks caught on slowly because of the natural plenitude, though they dominate American tables today. This is a traditional mating, flavored with a tart fruit sauce from the cherry-growing region on the shores of Lake Michigan.

5½-pound duckling
1 teaspoon ground ginger
Salt and freshly milled black pepper
2 large shallots, slivered

SAUCE

3 to 4 large shallots, minced (about ⅓ cup)
2 cups sour cherries, fresh, frozen or canned, with juice
3 tablespoons brandy
1 to 1½ tablespoons soy sauce
1 to 3 teaspoons red-wine vinegar
Real maple syrup or brown sugar, optional

Reserve the duck's neck and giblets, usually stuffed inside a supermarket duck. Pull or cut off the excess fat and skin from both ends of the duck's cavity and reserve both. Loosen the duck's skin and rub over and under it, and inside of the duck, with the ginger, salt, and pepper. Prick the skin with a fork, pushing all the way through the skin but not penetrating the flesh. Make sure to puncture in particular around where the legs join the body. Place the shallots in the duck's cavity. If you wish, tie the legs together with kitchen twine.

Place the duck, breast side down, on the rack of a roasting pan just larger than the duck. Pour a couple of inches of water into the roasting pan. It shouldn't touch the duck. Cover the pan tightly with foil or a lid, and place the roasting pan over two stove burners. Steam the duck over medium heat for 45 minutes to release much of its excess fat.

Preheat the oven to 425°F.

Uncover the duck, remove the rack with the duck, and pour off the greasy water from the pan. Turn the duck breast-side up on the rack and return the rack to the roasting pan. Oven roast for 35 to 40 minutes, until the duck's skin is well browned and crispy.

While the duck roasts, prepare the sauce. In a small saucepan over high heat, brown the duck neck and giblets (without oil) to begin a simple stock. When the parts are well browned, cover the pan, reduce the heat to medium, and sweat them for about 10 minutes. Pour 1½ cups of warm water into the pan and simmer until reduced to ½ cup of liquid. Reserve the stock.

Place the reserved duck fat and skin in a medium saucepan. Over medium heat, render the fat from the duck until you have about 2 tablespoons of fat. Discard the skin and fat pieces. Add the shallots to the rendered fat and cook 1 to 2 minutes, until soft. If using fresh cherries, add them to the shallots, cook briefly until the cherries have softened and released a good bit of juice, and then add the brandy and the smaller amount of soy sauce. If the cherries are frozen or canned, they will already have plenty of juice, so add the brandy and smaller amount of soy sauce at the same time. Stir in your duck stock and continue simmering until reduced by about one-fourth. Scrape the sauce into a blender and purée it. Return the sauce to the pan and taste, adding the remaining soy sauce for salt, vinegar for tang, and just a hint of maple syrup if needed for balance. Continue reducing the sauce to 1 to 1¼ cups.

When the duck is done, let it sit for 10 minutes before carving, including some of the crispy skin with each slice of meat. Serve the duck over small pools of the sauce on each plate.

Smothered Quail

Serves 4

From the bobwhites of the Southwest to the bobolinks of South Carolina, American quails frequently fly into the frying pan. They're the tastiest of our small game birds, even the farm-raised quails, particularly when smothered in rich brown gravy. Peach chutney makes a tangy counterpoint but is hardly essential.

- 1 cup unbleached all-purpose flour
- 3 tablespoons stone-ground cornmeal
- 2 teaspoons paprika
- 2 teaspoons chili powder
- ¾ teaspoon salt
- ½ teaspoon ground coriander
- Pinch of ground cinnamon
- 8 quail, split or semiboned, about 6 to 7 ounces each
- Vegetable oil for pan-frying
- 2½ to 3 cups chicken stock, preferably homemade
- Peach Chutney (page 80), optional

Combine the flour, cornmeal, paprika, chili powder, salt, coriander, and cinnamon in a shallow dish. Reserve ¼ cup of the seasoned flour and dredge the quail in the rest of it.

Pour 1 inch of oil into a large heavy skillet and heat the oil to 350°F. Fry the quail until golden and crisp, 3 to 4 minutes per side. Transfer the quail to a rimmed platter or shallow serving dish and keep them warm.

Pour off all but about ¼ cup of the cooking oil through a strainer, returning any cracklings from the strainer to the skillet. Warm the oil over medium heat and sprinkle in the reserved seasoned flour, stirring well to avoid lumps. Pour in the stock gradually, while continuing to stir. Simmer the mixture until it has thickened into a rich tan gravy, about 3 minutes. Adjust the seasoning if needed. Pour the gravy around the quail and serve immediately. Pass chutney on the side if you wish.

WE'VE ALWAYS GONE Whole Hog

NO OTHER FOOD, NOT EVEN CORN, HAS CONTRIBUTED AS much as the pig to the character of American cooking. It has lent its flavor to everything from New England baked beans to southern collard greens, and in the form of lard it stoked our initial love for fried foods and pies with flaky crusts. Cooked whole, the pig became our public celebration meat, starring in barbecues on the eastern seaboard and in luaus all the way west in Hawaii. We coddled its hind legs over many months to create country ham, and turned pork belly into our favorite breakfast meat, but we also pickled the feet, made the head into "cheese," and transformed the tough ribs into a meal that tickled and stuck to our own.

No one seems to know whether the English settlers or their pigs disembarked first in Jamestown in 1607, but we do know that the porkers adjusted to the new home more quickly and easily. While the colonists endured the "starving times" and even set out once to return to the mother country, their pigs enjoyed a hog heaven on Hog Island in the middle of the James River. Unlike cattle, which required more care, pigs could forage on their own for nuts, roots, and scraps, making them almost a free meat market on the loose.

Like moonshine whiskey, hogs also became a way to store and market corn that wasn't consumed in season. The happy symbiosis of pork and corn is associated with the South, but it achieved its greatest commercial success in the Midwest heartland, particularly in Indiana, Illinois, and Iowa. Four pounds of corn, easily grown in the vast farmlands of those states, yielded one pound of pork, making it abundant fare across the region and the country. We ate it in smaller quantities than beef throughout most of our history, according to recent archeological evidence, but pork appeared at more meals in one form or another.

The frequency of use, coupled with declining prices of beef ultimately undermined some of the appeal. We began thinking of pork as common and coarse, fit for poor folks but not a booming middle class. That's a view destined for the dustbin if traditional American cooking is to survive. As our ancestors knew, pork is our most versatile meat, offering us a parade of luscious hams, succulent chops and roasts, robust ribs and sausages, and salt-cured cuts for wonderful seasoning. No other food provides such a wealth of flavor.

The actual ham we were wolfing down, she assured me, was quite within the law, but the sort of country ham that local people traditionally bought from a farmer—a farmer who might kill three or four hogs a year, cure the hams to sell, and use the rest of the meat for his own table—could no longer be sold legally because such farmers were obviously not set up to meet modern government meat-inspection standards.

"You mean the country ham you cook at home has to be bought from a supermarket?" I asked.

"Well, it's sort of like bootleg whiskey," Mrs. Carter told me. . . . I suddenly had a vision of Tom and his aunt Daisie racing from their long-time supplier with three or four bootleg hams in the back seat, the Agriculture Department's version of revenuers in hot pursuit—Tom and Aunt Daisie tearing around curves, losing the law at last on the back roads they knew so well, and arriving home with the contraband they would cook secretly at night, hoping the succulent aroma would not draw the authorities to their door.

Calvin Trillin,
Alice, Let's Eat (1978)

Baked Ham and Cauliflower Casserole

American home cooks often pair ham with vegetables. Chard and kale are favorites for this role, but we particularly like the cauliflower combination in this casserole, adapted from a dish in Edward Harris Heth's *Wisconsin Country Cookbook and Journal* (1979). It'll raise a ruckus at any potluck supper from Florida to the Dakotas.

1 large head cauliflower (about 2¼ pounds), broken into small florets

BREAD CRUMBS

1 tablespoon unsalted butter

1 cup packed fresh bread crumbs

CHEESE SAUCE

6 tablespoons (¾ stick) unsalted butter

3 tablespoons unbleached all-purpose flour

6 tablespoons minced onion

2 cups whole milk

1 teaspoon prepared horseradish or more to taste

1 teaspoon salt or more to taste

Freshly milled black pepper

Pinch of nutmeg

8 ounces sharp Cheddar cheese, grated (about 2 cups)

12 ounces smoky ham, sliced thin, then cut in bite-size squares

Preheat the oven to 375°F. Butter a large baking dish.

Steam the cauliflower for 8 to 10 minutes, until lightly cooked but still with a little resistance to the bite.

Meanwhile, prepare the bread crumbs, melting the butter in a small skillet over medium heat. Stir in the bread crumbs and toast them until golden, stirring occasionally. Scrape out the bread crumbs from the skillet and reserve them.

Prepare the sauce, melting the butter in a large heavy saucepan over medium-low heat. Mix the flour into the butter gradually, stirring constantly. When the flour is incorporated, stir in the onion and keep stirring for 2 to 3 additional minutes. Raise the heat to medium-high and immediately begin to whisk in the milk. Bring the mixture to a boil and continue to stir it until lightly thickened, about 4 minutes. Reduce the heat to medium-low, mix in the horseradish, salt, pepper, and nutmeg and continue cooking another 5 to 7 minutes, stirring occasionally. Remove from the heat and immediately mix in the cheese, stirring until melted.

Spoon half of the cauliflower into the baking dish, cover with half of the ham, and pour half of the sauce over it. Repeat with the rest of the ingredients.

Sprinkle the bread crumbs over the casserole. Bake for 30 to 35 minutes, until heated through and golden brown and crunchy on top.

Virginia Country Ham

SERVES TWO DOZEN OF YOUR CLOSEST FRIENDS AND THEN SOME

In the early days, everyone who kept hogs, which used to be almost everyone, butchered some in the fall or early winter, as soon as the weather cooled enough to retard spoilage. The family enjoyed fresh pork for a short time, but they processed most of the meat for use over the year ahead, salt curing much of it for the pork barrel and turning the rest into sausage, lard, and other products. The ham was the cut that got the most attention, particularly in Virginia and states due west where many Virginians migrated. In Smithfield and other Tidewater communities, colonists developed the American country ham, dry curing the meat in salt, smoking it slowly, and then aging it for several months. The process bore similarities to English and other European methods, but the result was distinctively different, as densely flavored as a prosciutto, but drier, smokier, and saltier than most Old World hams. It takes advance planning, time, and a big pot to cook a Virginia-style ham properly, but it's a feast that keeps on giving, providing leftovers that can energize many a dish in even the smallest quantities. The best accompaniment is a tart and tangy condiment, like this variation on a popular pear relish.

14- to 17-pound dry-cured, smoked country ham, aged at least 6 months (see Ingredient Tip)

PEAR CHUTNEY

1½ pounds firm, somewhat underripe pears, peeled and chopped (about 3 cups)

1½ cups packed light brown sugar

1½ cups cider vinegar

1 cup golden raisins

1 cup chopped onion

⅓ cup chopped crystallized ginger

½ medium lemon, peeled and thinly sliced

2 teaspoons yellow mustard seeds

1 teaspoon cayenne pepper

½ teaspoon ground cinnamon

¼ teaspoon ground white pepper

Pinch of ground cloves

1 cup cider vinegar

GLAZE (OPTIONAL)

3 tablespoons packed brown sugar

2 teaspoons freshly cracked black pepper

1 tablespoon bourbon

Three days before you plan to serve the ham, begin its preparation. Make sure you have a pot large enough to hold the ham. In the South many cooks have two-burner "ham boilers," but we use a 40-quart pot otherwise designated for outdoor fish and turkey fries. If it looks like the shank will stick out of the pot more than an inch or so, hacksaw it off or take it to a butcher for help in trimming it.

INGREDIENT TIP:
In the past, small-scale farmers made country hams commercially at home, but modern meat-inspection requirements have driven most of them out of business. That's meant a serious loss in artisanal variety, but you can still find high quality in the market. The best-known versions today are Smithfield hams, which by law have to be processed in Smithfield, Virginia, by traditional methods. Gwaltney's (800-292-2773) makes many of these hams and sells them under the label of Genuine Smithfield, aged 6 months. Aficionados often choose a ham that's aged longer, such as the 9-month "Wigwam" from S. Wallace Edwards & Sons (800-222-4267) in Surry, Virginia, just up the James River from Smithfield. For the ultimate in aging, Gatton Farms in Kentucky (502-525-3437) produces a wonderfully complex ham that is hung for 15 months. Some Asian groceries, especially in urban Chinatowns, also carry slices of Smithfield or other country hams as a seasoning meat for Hunan dishes.

Handcrafted Ham

Every individual farmer made country ham a little differently than the neighbors, varying the salt treatment, length of smoking, aging process, and other factors. Cooks also differed in preparation methods, ranging from the simple approach we adopt to much more elaborate techniques. Colonial Virginia aristocrat William Byrd, according to Evan Jones in *American Food* (1974), considered the subject so serious that he kept his recipe in the flyleaf of his Bible, reminding himself to soak the ham for 36 hours in milk and water before simmering it. He also noted once that Virginians ate so much ham they got "extremely hoggish in their temper . . . and prone to grunt rather than speak."

Thomas Jefferson, among many others, liked his ham baked after it was cooked, stuck with cloves, covered with brown sugar, and basted with a good white wine. Southern Maryland epicures often preferred the meat stuffed with a mixture of greens and seasonings, such as minced kale and spinach with shallots and celery seed, recommended by Frederick Stieff in *Eat, Drink & Be Merry in Maryland* (1932). To hold in the stuffing, Stieff sewed cheesecloth around the ham, but some contemporary cooks simply wrap the package in an extra-large white cotton T-shirt.

Don't be shocked by the ham's initial grungy appearance. Scrape off exterior mold and anything else that looks unsavory with a stiff brush under running water. The mold is perfectly normal and the ham inside should be fine.

Plop the ham in the pot and place the pot where it will be near a sink but out of the way for a couple of days. Then cover the ham with water—but only after the pot is in place because it gets very heavy. Over 2 to 2½ days, change the water a minimum of twice and up to four times. Each time the water is changed, and the longer the ham soaks, you reduce the saltiness a bit.

Sometime while the ham is soaking, prepare the chutney. Place the pears in a saucepan and just cover them with water. Cook briefly over medium heat until the pears become somewhat soft but not quite tender. Pour off the cooking liquid into a small heavy saucepan, mix in the brown sugar, and bring to a boil over high heat. Cook the mixture down to a thick syrup, about 15 minutes. Stir the remaining ingredients into the pears, add the syrup, and continue cooking, stirring occasionally, until reduced to a thick consistency, about 30 more minutes. Cool the chutney, then cover and refrigerate it. (The chutney keeps well for several weeks.)

Now you're ready to cook the ham. Change the water one more time. This will be easier to do if you pour off the water and then move the pot with the ham to the stove before filling it with more water. Once the ham is covered with water, pour in the vinegar. Cook the ham at a bare simmer, with only occasional breaking bubbles on the surface, for 15 to 20 minutes per pound, until tender. Let the ham cool in the water for about 1 hour. Then remove the pot from the stove, a task for which you'll definitely want at least one muscular friend. Remove the ham from the water, placing it on a cutting board, broader, flatter side up. Discard the water.

Trim off the skin and all but ¼ to ½ inch of fat. Because the thickness of the fat can vary, it's best to work with a small knife and shave off small portions. No further preparation is necessary, and the ham can be eaten warm, but the texture is best after letting it cool to room temperature or chilling it. We don't normally glaze this type of ham because the taste gets lost when it is carved into paper-thin slices. However, if you will be presenting it whole at the table or on a buffet, the meat will look more attractive if you mix up the simple glaze (or any other favorite of yours) and smear it over the top of the ham. Bake the ham briefly in a 375°F oven about 20 minutes, just long enough to set the glaze.

Carve the ham by first cutting out a small V of meat from the top near the hock end. From that point, continue cutting at a 45-degree angle the thinnest slices you can manage. Because of the density of the meat, people will eat much smaller portions than with other moister hams. Country ham used to be left in a cool spot on the counter for anyone to help themselves. It's better, however, to refrigerate leftovers wrapped in foil. They will keep for weeks.

Cider-Baked City Ham

SERVES 12 TO 16

Many supermarket hams are a national embarrassment—injected with saline water, liquid smoke, and other stuff you don't want to read about—but good producers do make fine hams that aren't as dry, salty, and hard-to-handle as the country version. Sometimes called "city hams"—though they're actually a big favorite in the rural Midwest—they are typically smoked but not cured, giving them a hearty flavor with a moist, juicy texture. They usually come fully cooked and trimmed, ready to bake and maybe glaze. Out of respect for the venerable American combination of apples with ham, we do the baking in cider, and on our table, also add a side of chunky applesauce.

12- to 15-pound well-flavored, smoky, fully cooked bone-in ham (see Ingredient Tip)

Whole cloves, optional

2 cups apple cider or juice

3 bay leaves

1 tablespoon or more applejack or apple brandy, optional

SOME GLAZE OPTIONS

Apple cider and maple syrup

Applejack or apple brandy and brown sugar

Peach or apricot jam and mustard

Beer and molasses

Liquid from a jar of watermelon-rind pickles or pickled peaches

Bourbon and cane syrup or orange marmalade

Ginger preserves, pineapple juice or ginger ale, and dry mustard

Preheat the oven to 300°F.

Trim the rind from the ham if necessary. Trim the fat also, if needed, leaving ¼ to ½ inch of fat over the surface. Slice the top fat into the familiar crosshatch pattern, at about 1-inch intervals, cutting down to but not into the meat. Stud the surface with cloves if you wish. Place the ham in a large roasting pan, broad, fat-covered side up. Pour 1½ cups of water over the ham, then add the cider and bay leaves. Tent with foil, and bake for 10 to 11 minutes per pound, basting several times with the accumulated juices. The ham should be heated through and ready to serve unless you plan to glaze it.

If you wish to glaze the ham, raise the oven temperature to 400°F. Mix together one of the glaze combinations above or a favorite of your choosing, making the mixture somewhat thick. Brush or spoon the glaze over the ham and return it to the oven uncovered. Continue cooking for about 20 additional minutes. The ham is ready when the surface becomes a bit crusty and sticky.

A Farmyard Affinity

Ham and apple combinations are so good, and so common around the country, that some accomplished cooks don't bother much with other possibilities. Imogene Wolcott, in *The New England Yankee Cookbook* (1939), provides six ham recipes, four of which call for either cider or sliced apples. Her choices include two versions of ham baked in cider, one attributed to Vermont and the other called "colonial," plus ham fried with apple rings and a ham-apple pie, which she emphasizes is "an entrée, not a dessert."

The Pennsylvania Dutch gave us the most famous dish blending the ingredients, *schnitz und kneppe,* probably liked outside the original German circles as much for its name as its sweet, heavy character. Settlers imported the idea from the Old Country, where it's still known under a variety of monikers. Ham contributes an important saltiness to the dish, but the name refers to the other principal players, sliced, dried apples (*schnitz*) and dumplings cooked in the ham broth (*kneppe*).

The first hams of the season would be cooked about July and August in case an unexpected summer guest dropped in. Ham held the same rating as the basic black dress. If you had a ham in the meat house any situation could be faced. On short notice, it would be sliced and fried with special red gravy. Otherwise, it would be leisurely simmered, then defatted and browned.

EDNA LEWIS, THE TASTE OF COUNTRY COOKING (1977)

Skim the fat from the pan juices and strain the liquid. Pour it into a small saucepan and simmer until somewhat thickened, about 10 minutes. Add the applejack if you wish, adjust the seasoning, and pour into a gravy boat or small bowl. Carve the ham by first cutting out a small V of meat from the top near the hock end. From that point, continue cutting at a 45-degree angle into thin slices. Serve with the pan juices.

INGREDIENT TIP: Any serious butcher can secure a good version of this type of ham, though you may want to reserve it ahead at busy times like Christmas and Easter. A Richardson, Texas company, Ham I Am (800-742-6426 or 972-238-1776), offers a superlative Arkansas Ozarks version for mail-order sales. Equally tasty hams from the Missouri Ozarks can be acquired from Burgers' Smokehouse (800-624-5426 or 573-796-3134). Other worthy products include the younger hams from Gwaltney's and Edwards, mentioned on page 172 in the tip on country hams.

Chesapeake Bay Ham and Oyster Pie

Serves 6 to 8

Salty ham and briny oysters, both specialties of the Chesapeake Bay region, make natural mates in this lusty meat pie. Its richness begs for simple, cleanly flavored accompaniments, like a Mixed Salad of Greens, Nasturtiums, and Herbs (page 257) and Watermelon Ice (page 393).

LARD CRUST

2½ cups unbleached all-purpose flour

1¼ teaspoons salt

¼ cup (½ stick) unsalted butter, chilled

8 tablespoons lard, chilled (see Technique Tip)

4 tablespoons vegetable shortening, chilled

6 to 8 tablespoons ice water

2 cups shucked oysters, with their liquor, preferably Chincoteague or other Chesapeake oysters

Approximately 1 cup half-and-half

1¼ cups fine-chopped country ham or other smoky ham (see Ingredient Tip)

5 ounces Fontina or mild Swiss cheese, grated (1 generous cup)

3 tablespoons unsalted butter

3 tablespoons unbleached all-purpose flour

½ teaspoon Worcestershire sauce

Splash or two of hot pepper sauce, such as Texas Pete or Tabasco, optional

Pinch of ground mace or nutmeg

Oil a 10-inch pie pan or similar-size baking dish.

Prepare the pie crust, first placing the flour and salt in a food processor and pulsing to combine. Cut the butter into quarters lengthwise and then into small squares. Scatter the butter over the flour and quickly pulse several times, just to submerge the butter in the flour. Scoop the lard and shortening in small spoonfuls and scatter them over the flour-butter mixture. Pulse again quickly several more times until they too disappear into the flour. Sprinkle 4 tablespoons of the water over the mixture and pulse again until the water disappears. Dump the mixture into a large bowl or onto a pastry board. If needed, add more water, 1 tablespoon at a time, rubbing it in with your fingers. When the dough holds together when compacted with your fingers, stop. It's ready. Divide the dough in half and press each half into a fat disk. Wrap them both in plastic and refrigerate for at least 30 minutes. Roll out each disk on a floured board into a thin crust an inch or two larger than the pie pan. Arrange the bottom crust in the pan and refrigerate it and the other crust for at least 15 additional minutes.

Preheat the oven to 400°F.

Drain off the oyster liquor into a measuring cup for liquid. Add enough half-and-half to the liquor to measure 1¾ cups and reserve it.

Scatter the oysters and ham in the chilled crust and top evenly with the cheese.

Prepare the sauce for the pie, first melting the butter in a heavy saucepan over medium heat. Whisk in the flour and continue cooking for about a minute. Pour in the half-and-half mixture, whisking to avoid lumps. Add the Worcestershire sauce, hot pepper sauce, and mace and simmer the sauce until lightly thickened, about 3 minutes. Cool the sauce for about 5 minutes.

Pour the sauce over the other pie filling ingredients. Arrange the second crust over the filling and crimp the edges neatly. Cut several steam vents in the top crust. Bake for 20 minutes,then reduce the heat to 350°F and continue baking for about 30 additional minutes, until the crust is golden brown and flaky. Let the pie sit for about 30 minutes before slicing it into wedges. Refrigerate any leftovers, reheating them in a warm oven before serving again.

INGREDIENT TIP: On its home turf, this pie would always be made with a robust Smithfield or similar country ham. It's also good made with leftovers from our Cider-Baked City Ham (page 174), or another milder, moister ham. If you take this alternative route, add a good pinch of salt to the cream sauce before assembling the pie to complement the brininess of the oysters.

TECHNIQUE TIP: The medical profession now looks askance on lard, but along with bacon drippings and salt pork, it still provides the finest flavor to many of the country's favorite foods. Nothing else makes pastry so light and flaky, and no type of oil fries chicken or oysters so crisply. For the best version, render the lard at home, an easy process that people used to do regularly. Ask your butcher in advance to get you a couple of pounds of fresh, uncured pork fat, which will make about 3 cups of lard. Cut the fat into 1-inch squares. Place the squares in a heavy 10-inch or larger skillet and pour ½ cup of water over the fat. Cook over medium heat, stirring frequently, until the liquid comes to a simmer and the fat begins to melt. Reduce the heat to low and continue cooking for 3 hours, more or less, stirring occasionally and scraping up from the bottom. When the fat is completely liquid and all that remains of the original pieces is small golden-brown cracklings, it is ready. Away from the stove, carefully pour the lard through a fine-mesh strainer into a storage container. Cool to room temperature, cover, and then refrigerate. (It will remain softer and creamier than commercial versions.) The lard will keep for weeks, but the cracklings may last only minutes. The crunchy nuggets pack immense flavor, whether salted and eaten as a snack or added to cornbread or mashed potatoes.

Ham Loaf with Jezebel Glaze

SERVES 6 TO 8

You can do a lot of tasty things with leftover ham, but nothing beats a down-home loaf. A generation or two ago, moms fixed the loaf for dinner on Monday with the remains of Sunday's ham, and starting on Tuesday, used it as sandwich meat for the rest of the week. This is a brassy, come-hither rendition, flirtatious with a Jezebel glaze of fruit preserves and horseradish.

HAM LOAF

2 tablespoons unsalted butter
1 large onion, chopped
1 pound cooked smoky ham, ground by your butcher or in a food processor
1 pound ground pork
1 cup crushed saltine crackers
2 eggs, beaten lightly
1 cup milk
1 tablespoon yellow mustard
2 teaspoons prepared horseradish
2 teaspoons Worcestershire sauce
1 teaspoon freshly milled black pepper
¼ teaspoon ground cloves
Salt, optional

JEZEBEL GLAZE

¼ cup peach or apricot preserves or orange marmalade
2 tablespoons yellow mustard
1 tablespoon packed brown sugar
1 teaspoon prepared horseradish
¼ teaspoon freshly milled black pepper

Preheat the oven to 350°F.

Warm the butter in a skillet over medium heat. Add the onion and sauté briefly until soft and translucent, about 5 minutes. Combine the onion with the remaining ham loaf ingredients, adding a little salt if the ham itself is not especially salty. The mixture will be quite moist. Pack it into a loaf pan, mounding it up a bit in the center, and smooth the surface.

Bake the loaf for about 1 hour total. While it begins to cook, mix together the glaze ingredients. After 30 minutes, spoon half of the glaze over the loaf, spreading it evenly. After 15 minutes longer, cover the loaf with the remaining glaze. Continue baking until the exterior is crusty and the interior temperature, measured on an instant-read thermometer, reaches 165°F. Allow the loaf to stand for 10 minutes before cutting. Serve hot or chilled, in thick slices.

The most exquisite peak in culinary art is conquered when you do right by a ham, for a ham, in the very nature of the process it has undergone since last it walked on its own feet, combines in its flavor the tang of smoky autumnal woods, the maternal softness of earthy fields delivered of their crop children, the wineyness of a late sun, the intimate kiss of fertilizing rain, and the bite of fire.

W. B. COURTNEY, QUOTED IN *MARYLAND'S WAY* (1963)

Loin Roast with Cranberry Glaze

SERVES 8

When Americans cooked at the hearth, they usually roasted fresh pork, either a small, young pig or a large cut of the loin or leg from a freshly butchered hog. Today we tend to divide the succulent loin into smaller cuts, such as chops, but a roast remains a big treat. Here the meat is cooked with a cranberry glaze, another variation on the long-loved theme of pork and fruit.

3-pound boneless center-cut pork loin roast

GLAZE

12-ounce package cranberries, fresh or frozen

½ cup plus 2 tablespoons sugar

Minced zest and juice of 1 medium orange

2 tablespoons dry sherry

2 medium red onions, cut into 8 wedges each

2 tablespoons vegetable oil

Salt and freshly milled black pepper

Preheat the oven to 450°F. Let the pork roast sit covered at room temperature for about 20 minutes while you prepare the cranberry glaze and onions.

Prepare the glaze, first mixing together the cranberries, sugar, 1 cup of water, and orange zest in a medium saucepan. Bring the mixture to a boil over medium-high heat and continue boiling until the cranberries have popped open and the sauce is thick, 5 to 8 minutes. Stir in the orange juice and sherry and remove from the heat.

Rub the onion wedges with oil, season with salt and pepper, and reserve them.

Rub the pork roast with salt and pepper, then place it in a roasting pan, fat side down. Roast for 8 minutes, then turn it fat side up and roast for 8 additional minutes. Scatter the onion wedges around the meat, reduce the heat to 275°F, and continue cooking for 45 minutes. Brush thickly with about one-third of the cranberry glaze and cook 20 to 30 minutes longer, until the meat's internal temperature reaches 155°F to 160°F. The pork will still have a faintly pink center.

Let the pork roast sit at room temperature for about 10 minutes. Carve and serve on a platter with the onion wedges. Add a little water to the remaining glaze, if needed to make it easily spoonable, and serve it as a sauce on the side.

Sour Braised Loin with Cherries

Serves 6

Pennsylvania Dutch settlers ate as much or more pork than anyone in the country, and they also popularized the combination of sweet-and-sour flavors. We've adapted this somewhat unusual recipe from William Woys Weaver's tradition-minded *Pennsylvania Dutch Country Cooking* (1993). The moist-cooked roast offers a more refreshing tang than many sweet-sour dishes, with its tartness mellowed by a golden cheese crust. As with so many dishes of this heritage, broad egg noodles will help soak up the ruddy sauce.

SWEET-AND-SOUR CHERRIES

1 pound pitted sour cherries, frozen or canned

1 cup cider vinegar

¾ cup sugar

1-inch piece of cinnamon stick

2½-pound boneless pork roast, all surface fat removed

Salt and freshly milled black pepper

½ medium onion, chopped

3 to 4 tablespoons rye whiskey, preferably, or bourbon

4 ounces sapsago, Gruyère, or raclette cheese, grated (1 cup) (see Ingredient Tip)

Prepare the cherries, combining the ingredients in a nonreactive saucepan. Bring the mixture to a boil over high heat, then reduce to a simmer and cook for 3 minutes. Set the cherries aside to steep in the liquid. (The cherries can be made several days in advance, cooled, and refrigerated, covered. They improve with age.)

Preheat the oven to 350°F. Oil a roasting pan or other baking dish.

Rub the roast lightly with salt and pepper and lay it in the pan. Pour the cherries and liquid over the roast, sprinkle the onion around, and add the rye whiskey. Cover the dish and bake for 50 to 60 minutes, to an internal temperature of 140°F to 145°F. Raise the oven temperature to 400°F. Uncover the roast and sprinkle the cheese thickly and evenly over it. Return the roast to the oven and continue baking uncovered for about 10 additional minutes. The pork is ready when the meat's surface is lightly browned, the cheese is melting and golden, and the internal temperature reaches 155°F to 160°F. The pork will still have a faintly pink center. Remove the roast from the sauce and let it sit at room temperature for 10 minutes before carving it into thin slices. Remove the cinnamon stick from the cherries, spoon cherries and sauce over or alongside each portion, and serve.

INGREDIENT TIP: A version of sapsago cheese used to be made by some Pennsylvania Dutch families, but today any that is commercially available comes from eastern Switzerland. A skimmed cow's-milk cheese with a mellow earthy character and hints of fenugreek and wild clover, it's not easy to locate unless you live in an area of German or Swiss heritage, or near a well-stocked cheese shop. Gruyère and raclette make acceptable substitutes.

A regional cookery as complex as that of the Pennsylvania Dutch is a language of many changing textures, flavors, and smells. Yet above all else it is a cookery with a sense of place, a cuisine that recognizes the unchanging essence of *Bodegeschmack,* meaning that our food has in it the taste of the land. . . .

There are many components to our cookery other than *Bodegeschmack,* for it is only one interlinking element in the larger unity we call the "taste" of our culture. It is a taste created not by one or two famous chefs, or by a handful of certain "ethnic" ingredients, but by a vast orchestra of hands in kitchens down through the past three hundred years that pounded, shaped, rolled, kneaded, and molded the fruits of our landscape into a child of our genius.

William Woys Weaver,
Pennsylvania Dutch Country Cooking (1993)

Stuffed Pork Chops

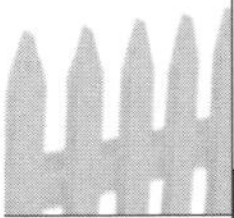

Serves 4 hearty eaters

Pork chops became a favorite in the late nineteenth and twentieth centuries, after stovetop and oven-range preparations replaced hearth roasting in popularity and practicality. Almost as soon as we took to chops, we began stuffing them, an idea probably inspired by the way that cooks in the past stuffed their roasts. For a rib-sticking winter dinner, serve the chops with Candied Sweet Potatoes (page 274), 'Simmon Biscuits (page 349), and Sour Cream–Raisin Pie (page 361).

- ¼ cup (½ stick) unsalted butter
- 1 small onion, chopped fine
- 2 celery stalks, chopped fine
- 1½ cups fresh cornbread crumbs
- ½ cup chopped dried fruit, such as cranberries, cherries, or quartered apricots
- 1 tablespoon minced flat-leaf parsley
- ½ teaspoon minced fresh thyme or ¼ teaspoon dried thyme
- Pinch of cayenne pepper
- Salt and freshly milled black pepper
- 1 tablespoon plus ½ teaspoon yellow mustard
- 1 cup chicken stock
- 4 double-thick bone-in center-cut pork chops, about 12 ounces each, with a large pocket cut to the bone in each
- Vegetable oil for pan-frying
- Unbleached all-purpose flour

Prepare the stuffing, first melting the butter in a small skillet over medium heat. Stir in the onion and celery, and sauté them until the onion is soft and translucent, about 5 minutes. Stir in the bread crumbs, fruit, parsley, thyme, cayenne, salt and pepper to taste, and ½ teaspoon of the mustard. The mixture should be moist but not soupy. If it is dry, add a tablespoon or two of the stock to the stuffing. Stuff equal portions of the mixture into each chop and then sprinkle each with a bit more salt.

Warm a thin film of oil in a large heavy skillet over medium heat. Rub the remaining tablespoon of mustard over the chops, salt and pepper them, and sprinkle them lightly but evenly with flour. Brown the chops well on both sides. Pour the remaining stock around the chops. Reduce the heat to medium-low, cover the skillet, and simmer the chops for about 25 minutes, until cooked through to an internal temperature of 160°F. The pan juices will have reduced to just a few tablespoons.

Serve the chops hot with the pan juices spooned over them.

Onion-Smothered Smoked Pork Chops

SERVES 4

This is classic midwestern farm fare, hearty and substantial. It starts with a popular regional cut, the smoked loin chop, which keeps the preparation time short since the meat is already cooked through. The idea had broad enough appeal to sneak into the covers of the *Nancy Drew Cookbook* (1973), where it kept company with Sleuth Soup, Ghostly Popcorn, and Captive Biscuits.

2 thick bacon slices, chopped

Four 1-inch-thick smoked pork loin chops (see Ingredient Tip)

2 medium onions, halved and sliced thin

1 medium red bell pepper, sliced into thin matchsticks

½ cup chicken stock

1 tablespoon Worcestershire sauce

½ teaspoon dried marjoram

Salt and freshly milled black pepper

Fry the bacon in a large heavy skillet over medium heat. Remove it with a slotted spoon, drain it, and reserve.

Brown the chops on both sides in the bacon drippings. Cover the chops with the onions and bell pepper, then add the stock, Worcestershire sauce, and marjoram. Add salt and pepper, starting a little on the light side since smoked pork chops can be seasoned with varying amounts of salt. Cover tightly, reduce the heat to medium-low, and cook for about 15 minutes, until the chops are heated through. Remove them to a platter and raise the heat to high under the skillet. Cook briefly until the remaining vegetables and stock have reduced to a thick tangle. Spoon the vegetables and sauce over the chops, sprinkle with bacon, and serve.

INGREDIENT TIP: Redolent of the great outdoors, presmoked pork loin chops can be found in many supermarkets and in most meat markets. They are a little denser than conventional pork chops, a bit closer to ham. They vary in flavor according to the level of smoke and salt, so you might want to sample different versions to find one that satisfies your tastes.

Edible, adj. Good to eat, and wholesome to digest, as a worm to a toad, a toad to a snake, a snake to a pig, a pig to a man, and a man to a worm.

AMBROSE BIERCE,
THE DEVIL'S DICTIONARY (1911)

Pork Chops Braised with Quinces

Serves 4

A late fall fruit, quinces used to be common in American cooking and seem to be making a rebound recently. They probably fell out of favor because they need to be long-cooked to bring out the distinctive apple-pear-berry flavor. That makes them a fine mate for shoulder pork chops, which also require low heat and slow cooking to be at their best. Derived from a recipe in Ronald Johnson's *The American Table* (1984), this dish makes a fine fall skillet supper. The chops go well with wild rice and a green salad.

- 1 tablespoon honey
- 2 medium quinces
- 4 pork shoulder chops, or from as near the shoulder as your butcher can provide (see Ingredient Tip)
- Salt
- 1 tablespoon vegetable oil
- 1 tablespoon unsalted butter
- 1 tablespoon fruit vinegar or cider vinegar
- 1 teaspoon minced fresh sage or ½ teaspoon dried sage
- ¼ teaspoon ground ginger or cardamom

Combine the honey and 2 cups of water in a small nonreactive saucepan and bring to a simmer over medium heat. While the honey heats, peel the first quince, slice it thin, and chop it. Cut quinces can turn brown quickly, so put the fruit into the simmering water as soon as it is chopped. Repeat with the remaining quince. Reduce the heat to low and simmer for 1 hour to parcook the mixture. It will still look coarse in texture and have little flavor.

Shortly before the quinces finish parcooking, sprinkle the chops with salt. Warm the oil and butter in a large nonreactive skillet over medium-high heat and brown the chops on both sides. Spoon the quince mixture over the chops, then add the vinegar, sage, and ginger. Pour in enough hot water to make the mixture soupy. Cover, reduce the heat to medium-low, and cook for about 1 hour, until the chops are very tender and the quinces cooked down and rosy. Check the dish once, about two-thirds of the way through the cooking time, scraping up from the bottom. Add a few tablespoons more hot water if the sauce seems dry.

When done, mash the quinces a bit to make them more like applesauce in texture. Adjust the seasoning if needed and serve the chops hot with the quince sauce.

INGREDIENT TIP: Shoulder chops start out a little tougher than their loin chop cousins, but they are richer in flavor, cheaper, and perfectly tender when braised low and slow just like the quinces. If you want to make the dish with uptown center-cut chops, increase the cooking time of the quinces in sauce by about 30 minutes, adding more water if the fruit appears dry, and cut the braising time of the chops with the quinces in half.

Grilled Pork Tenderloin with Sweet Potato–Apple Sauce

Serves 6

As a cooking method for meat, grilling serves as a modern replacement for hearth roasting, which applies a live fire to food to obtain a crusty surface and juicy interior. Both methods work best in elemental preparations, with much of the flavor coming from the fire rather than heavy sauces or other frills. The techniques do differ in important respects, of course, particularly in the size of the cuts of meat. Instead of roasting a large loin today, we grill the smaller butcher's cuts. Chops cook great on the grill, as they do in the skillet, but the tenderloin really thrives on fire, gaining widespread acceptance only recently with the upsurge in backyard grilling. Here we serve the succulent cut with an earthy sauce similar to a stuffing Irma Rombauer suggested for baked tenderloin in an early edition of the *Joy of Cooking.*

MUSTARD-BOURBON MARINADE

¼ cup brown or Dijon mustard

¼ cup plus 2 tablespoons bourbon

¼ cup Worcestershire sauce

2 tablespoons molasses

2 tablespoons soy sauce

Two 12-ounce to 14-ounce sections of pork tenderloin

SWEET POTATO–APPLE SAUCE

1¼ pounds sweet potatoes, peeled and cut into 1-inch chunks

2 tart apples, such as Granny Smith or Jonathan, peeled and cut into 1-inch chunks

¼ cup (½ stick) unsalted butter, softened

6 tablespoons apple cider or juice, boiled down to 3 tablespoons (see Ingredient Tip)

1 tablespoon bourbon, optional

1 teaspoon fresh minced sage

Pinch of ground nutmeg

Pinch of cayenne

Salt

Fresh sage sprigs, optional

At least 2½ hours and up to the night before you plan to grill the pork tenderloins, prepare the marinade, mixing the ingredients in a small bowl. Place the tenderloins in a plastic bag, pour the marinade over them, and refrigerate.

Meanwhile, prepare the sauce. Steam the sweet potatoes and apples until very tender, about 25 minutes. Mash or rice the sweet potatoes and apples together in a medium bowl. Stir in the butter, cider, optional bourbon, sage, nutmeg, cayenne, and salt to taste. The sauce should be somewhat thick but spoonable, resembling applesauce in consistency. If it seems too stiff, add a little hot water.

Irma Rombauer, 1877–1962

Christened Irma von Starkloff, the author of the *Joy of Cooking* alternated her childhood between her St. Louis home and Swiss boarding schools, where she became as fluent in French and German as in English. She was a worldly, beautiful bride when she married Edgar Rombauer at the age of twenty-two, talented in many fields except the culinary arts. Her husband gave her early lessons in cooking, and she gradually learned a great deal more as an energetic hostess.

Rombauer wrote the first edition of *Joy* to overcome her loneliness after Edgar's death. Her daughter Marion and son Edgar encouraged the effort to keep her occupied, and Marion assisted with production and recipe testing. Initially intended mainly for family and friends, the volume grew to five hundred recipes and Rombauer financed its publication as a book in 1931. It sold in St. Louis by word of mouth, and Bobbs-Merrill brought out the first commercial edition in 1936, expanded considerably in a 1943 revision that propelled *Joy* to the ranks of all-time cookbook best-sellers.

Rombauer defied the didactic, detached style common in many cookbooks of previous decades, offering an approach that was as comprehensive as Fannie Farmer's but more fun. Perky in personality instead of preoccupied with scientific exactitude, she chatted readers through recipes rather than prescribing rules for success.

Remove the tenderloins from the refrigerator, drain them, and blot any excess moisture from them. Let the pork sit covered at room temperature for 20 to 30 minutes.

Fire up your grill in a way that allows for cooking first over high heat (where you can hold your hand comfortably an inch or two above the cooking grate for only 1 to 2 seconds) and then over medium heat (about 4 to 5 seconds with the same hand test). With a charcoal grill, pile the charcoal about three coals deep on one side for the higher heat level, and spread it in a single layer on the opposite side for medium heat. With a gas grill, start on high and adjust the temperature later to medium.

Transfer the tenderloins to the grill, arranging them so that the thin end is angled away from the hottest part of the fire. Grill the tenderloins uncovered on high heat for 3 minutes, rolling them on all sides. Move the tenderloins to medium heat and estimate the rest of the cooking time according to the thickness of the meat. Thin tenderloins (about 1½ inches in diameter) need an additional 10 to 12 minutes on medium, and fat ones (about 2½ inches in diameter) require up to 25 minutes. Continue rolling the meat on all sides for even cooking. The pork is done when its internal temperature reaches 155°F to 160°F.

Reheat the sauce quickly if needed. Spoon it onto plates. Carve the pork into thin slices and arrange them partially overlapping the sauce. Garnish with sage, if you wish, and serve.

INGREDIENT TIP: In some apple-growing regions you can find syrupy "boiled cider" in stores, already cooked down by approximately one-half. The boiling deepens the flavor of the juice and any dish containing it—from apple pie to these tenderloins.

Kansas City Sugar-and-Spice Spareribs

Serves 6 generously

In most early barbecues, Americans cooked whole animals, including hogs, an experience that taught them the toughest, fattiest meats benefited the most from slow smoking. In the case of pork, ribs took top honors, along with cuts from the shoulder that today are often made into a sandwich (page 52). African-American pitmasters first perfected the art of barbecuing the ribs separately, usually saucing them heavily near the end of the cooking. Among the many styles of sauce, the tangy, tomato-based version from Kansas City mates the most magically with the meat.

DRY RUB

¾ cup packed brown sugar

½ cup paprika

2½ tablespoons freshly milled black pepper

2½ tablespoons salt

1½ tablespoons chili powder

1½ tablespoons onion powder

1 teaspoon cayenne pepper

3 full slabs of pork spareribs, "St. Louis cut" (trimmed of the chine bone and brisket flap), preferably 3 pounds or less each

SUGAR-AND-SPICE BBQ SAUCE

12-ounce bottle chili sauce (the ketchup-style condiment)

¼ cup plus 2 tablespoons ketchup

3 tablespoons packed brown sugar

3 tablespoons molasses

2 tablespoons Worcestershire sauce

2 tablespoons yellow mustard

2 tablespoons cider vinegar

½ teaspoon ground ginger

½ teaspoon freshly milled black pepper

¼ teaspoon hot pepper sauce, such as Tabasco, or more to taste

1 teaspoon pure liquid hickory smoke or more to taste, optional

The night before you plan to barbecue, combine the rub ingredients in a bowl. Apply about one-third of the rub evenly to the ribs, reserving the rest of the spice mixture. Transfer the ribs to a plastic bag and refrigerate them overnight.

Prepare the sauce, combining the ingredients (including the optional liquid hickory smoke) in a saucepan and cooking over medium heat for about 10 minutes until thickened a bit. Use warm or chilled. If the sauce becomes too thick for easy pouring, stir in a little water. (The sauce keeps, covered and refrigerated, for several weeks.)

Before you begin to barbecue, take the ribs from the refrigerator. Sprinkle them with another one-third of the rub, reserving the rest of the mixture. Let the ribs sit at room temperature for about 30 minutes.

It is the basic secret of all fine New England cookery of the old-fashioned kind. . . . Salt pork. That's it. Chunks of white meat from a barrel sparkling with salt crystals. The lowly pig, living on what the cows had left over and we had left over, was the keystone that held us all together as a happy family. His meat, current in every month of the year in the brine barrel, was the substructure for baked beans, eggs, all meats, all vegetables. . . . He united the animal kingdom, the vegetable, and all kingdoms between, into a new order of harmony.

Robert P. Tristram Coffin, *Mainstays of Maine* (1945)

Meanwhile, fire up a smoker or covered grill to between 225°F and 250°F, following the manufacturer's instructions for smoking.

Transfer the ribs to the smoker. Cook covered for about 4 hours, turning and sprinkling both sides with additional rub about halfway through the cooking time. Open the smoker only when necessary, and cover as quickly as possible, to minimize the loss of heat and smoke. In the last 45 minutes of cooking, slather the ribs twice with the sauce. When ready, the meat will bend easily between the ribs and the sauce will be gooey and sticky. Allow the slabs to sit for 10 minutes before slicing them into individual ribs. Serve with the remaining sauce on the side and plenty of napkins.

Pork Cutlets with Clam and Garlic Sauce

Serves 4 to 6

Portuguese settlers influenced American cooking in areas as far flung as New England and Hawaii. A seafaring people for centuries, they appreciate the bounty of the waters, and love pork as well, combining the two in this Massachusetts surf-and-turf specialty. Quick and scrumptious, the dish will spring a surprise on your taste buds.

- 2 dozen littleneck clams
- 6-ounce bottle clam juice
- 3 tablespoons olive oil
- 1¼-pound boneless center-cut pork loin, cut into ⅓-inch-thick slices and pounded thin
- Unbleached all-purpose flour
- 2 garlic cloves, minced
- 1 tablespoon Madeira

Dump the clams into a Dutch oven or stockpot. Add about ½ inch of water and steam the clams over high heat until they pop open, about 8 minutes. Discard any clams that don't open within a couple of minutes of the rest of the batch. Pull the clams from their shells, halve them if larger than small bite size, and reserve the clams and any accumulated juice. Strain the cooking liquid through a fine sieve or coffee filter into a measuring cup. You will need 1½ cups of liquid. Pour off any extra, or add bottled clam juice to equal that amount, and reserve it.

Warm the olive oil in a large skillet over medium-high heat. Dust the pork slices with flour and fry them in the oil, in batches if necessary, until lightly browned and just cooked through, 1 to 2 minutes per side. Remove the pork slices and keep them warm.

Reduce the heat to medium-low, stir in the garlic, and sauté for 1 minute. Pour in the Madeira, being cautious of the rising steam. Pour in the reserved clam liquid and stir briefly until the sauce thickens slightly. Return the pork to the sauce, cook another minute, add the clams and juice, and heat through. Arrange the pork on plates, topping it equally with the clams and sauce. Serve hot.

Chimayó Carne Adovada

Serves 6 to 8

Spanish colonists in New Mexico used chiles as a preservation agent for meat *(carne)*, fostering a taste for the melding of the two flavors. The notion evolved over time into this robust local favorite, substantially different from other dishes with similar names elsewhere. It represents the essence of traditional New Mexican cooking, always plain in preparation but potent in the mouth.

3 pounds pork shoulder, trimmed of fat and cut into 1-inch cubes

SAUCE

8 ounces (20 to 25) whole dried red New Mexican chiles, preferably Chimayó, stemmed, seeded, and rinsed (see Technique Tip)

2 cups chicken stock or beef stock, preferably homemade

1 medium onion, chunked

4 garlic cloves

2 teaspoons sherry or cider vinegar

2 teaspoons dried oregano, preferably Mexican

1 teaspoon ground coriander

1 teaspoon salt or more to taste

Shredded lettuce and chopped tomato, optional, for garnish

Preheat the oven to 300°F. Oil a large, covered baking dish. Place the pork in the baking dish.

To prepare the sauce, first arrange the damp chiles in one layer on a baking sheet and roast them in the oven for about 5 minutes. Watch the pods carefully to keep them from burning. The chiles can have a little remaining moisture. Remove them from the oven and let them cool. Break each chile into 2 or 3 pieces.

In a blender, purée half of the pods with 1 cup of the stock. You still will be able to see tiny pieces of chile pulp, but they should be bound in a smooth, thick liquid. Pour the mixture into the baking dish. Repeat with the remaining pods and stock, adding the rest of the sauce ingredients to the blender. Pour this mixture into the baking dish and stir the sauce together with the pork. (If you like, the pork can be prepared to this point and refrigerated overnight, covered. Bring the mixture back to cool room temperature before proceeding.)

Cover the dish and bake at 300°F until the meat is quite tender and the sauce has cooked down, about 3 hours. If the sauce seems watery, return the dish to the oven uncovered and bake for an additional 15 to 30 minutes. Serve hot, garnished if you wish with lettuce and tomato. Reheated, the leftovers are outstanding.

TECHNIQUE TIP: Farmers in the northern New Mexico village of Chimayó grow the state's finest red chiles, beautifully balanced between earthy sweetness and heat, but any New Mexican red pod will work in carne adovada. If you can't find the chiles in your area, order them from the Santa Fe School of Cooking (800-982-4688 or 505-983-4511). The school also usually carries the preground pods in a range of heat intensities, from mild on up. The hot variety meets anyone's truth-in-labeling requirements. Substitute ½ to ⅔ cup of ground chiles for the whole pods. If you buy ground chiles for carne adovada at a supermarket, make sure it has a bracing aroma and a strong red hue.

Arizona Chile Verde

Serves 6

Despite being southwestern neighbors with Spanish colonial roots, Arizona and New Mexico don't share a common sense of seasoning. Like carne adovada, this Arizona stew combines pork and chiles, and is just as characteristic of the local cooking, but it tastes considerably different, with a gentler, more mannered kick.

- 2 pounds Boston pork butt, trimmed of fat and cut into ¾-inch cubes
- 1 medium onion, chopped
- 4 garlic cloves, minced
- 1 cup chicken stock, preferably homemade
- 2 cups chopped roasted mild green chiles, preferably New Mexican or Anaheim, fresh or frozen
- 14½-ounce can Mexican-style stewed tomatoes, undrained
- 14½-ounce can chopped tomatoes, undrained
- 1 teaspoon dried oregano, preferably Mexican
- 1 teaspoon salt
- ¼ teaspoon ground cumin
- Grated Monterey Jack cheese, optional

Place the pork in a large heavy saucepan. Cook over medium heat, stirring often, until the meat is brown, about 10 minutes. Add the onion and garlic, and continue cooking until the onion is soft and translucent, about 5 additional minutes. Pour in the stock and scrape up any browned bits sticking to the bottom of the pan.

Stir in the green chiles, both kinds of tomatoes, oregano, salt, and cumin. Reduce the heat to a simmer and cover the pan. Cook for about 2 hours, stirring occasionally, until the meat is quite tender. The chile can be served immediately, but the flavor improves with at least a few hours' refrigeration and reheating. Serve steaming hot in bowls, topped with sprinklings of cheese if you wish.

A novelist, in consulting references on any given subject, is usually forced to discard the majority as inaccurate, biased, unreliable or untruthful. . . .

Books on diet ought to be different; for most of them are written by medical experts who have studied for years to find out exactly what happens to seven cents' worth of liver when it meets a Welch's bacillus in the upper colon of a sedentary worker aged forty-five.

Diet books ought indeed to be different; yet when I looked into some of them, I found myself entertaining grave doubts.

From each book, for example, I learned that all diets except the one advocated by the author of that particular book, are either based on the erroneous ideas of a faddist, or are downright dangerous. . . .

I further discovered that although a person may consider himself in perfect health, and may feel comfortable and happy, he is—unless he is eating foods that the diet books say he ought to eat—as effectively poisoned as though nurtured for years on poison-ivy salads with bichloride of mercury dressing.

Kenneth Roberts in Marjorie Mosser's *Good Maine Food* (1939)

Chaurice with Tomato Gravy

Serves 8

The charcuterie tradition came to American shores from myriad directions, and our sausages contain everything from pork and beef to wild boar, venison, oysters, and rice. South Louisiana produces some of the best blends, including boudin, andouille, and chaurice, the latter described by Natalie Scott in *200 Years of New Orleans Cooking* (1931) as "an old French Market specialty; . . . a very highly seasoned sausage." It evolved from Spanish chorizo, but went through some fanciful mutations along the way. You can stuff chaurice in sheep's casings for the most authentic effect, but it's much simpler to form the mixture into patties. We serve the sausage with nutty Texmati rice and, for dessert, New Orleans Bread Pudding (page 389).

CHAURICE

- 2 pounds Boston pork butt, ground with all of its fat by your butcher or with a meat grinder at home
- ½ cup minced onion
- 1 garlic clove, minced
- ¼ cup minced parsley
- 2 teaspoons minced fresh thyme or 1 teaspoon dried thyme
- 1 tablespoon ground dried mild red chiles, such as New Mexican or ancho
- 1½ teaspoons salt or more to taste
- 1 teaspoon cayenne pepper or more to taste
- ½ teaspoon freshly cracked black pepper, coarsely ground
- ¼ teaspoon ground allspice
- 1 bay leaf, crumbled very fine (or ground in a spice mill)

- ½ medium onion, minced
- 1 celery stalk, minced
- 1 garlic clove, minced
- 2 cups canned crushed tomatoes, preferably with purée or with extra purée
- ½ cup chicken stock
- Salt and freshly milled black pepper

Prepare the sausage, mixing together all the ingredients in a large bowl. Cover and refrigerate for at least 24 hours. (It keeps, uncooked and refrigerated, at least a week and freezes well.) Form it into 8 patties. Fry the patties in a large skillet over medium heat until richly browned and a bit crusty, about 4 minutes per side. Remove the chaurice from the pan and keep it warm.

Pour off all but 1 tablespoon of the pan drippings. Stir the onion, celery, and garlic into the pan drippings, and sauté the mixture until the onion is soft and translucent, about 5 minutes. Stir the tomatoes and stock into the vegetables, and simmer until reduced to a thick gravy, 10 to 15 minutes. Season with salt and pepper. Serve the chaurice patties on pools of the tomato gravy or with the gravy poured over them.

TECHNIQUE TIP:
The best way to test the sausage seasoning is to cook a small amount. We usually do this after the sausage has been refrigerated for 8 to 12 hours. That's long enough for the seasonings to mingle and mellow a bit, but also leaves ample time for any new additional flavors to work their way in fully before we cook the sausage.

Country Sausage and Wild Rice Bake

SERVES 6

A robust combo of upper Midwest favorites, this casserole blends homey appeal with sophisticated taste. It likely developed from a marriage of Swedish meatballs with "Up North" products, but became much more appetizing during its transformation. We got the idea from Kate Tremper, a fine cook in Santa Fe, who picked it up years ago from an employee of her former catering business.

1½ pounds uncooked Indiana Farm Breakfast Sausage (page 26) or other country-style bulk pork sausage

½ pound ground pork

2 teaspoons dried sage

Salt and freshly milled black pepper

1 tablespoon unsalted butter

2 cups chopped celery

1 large red or green bell pepper, chopped

1 cup hickory nut, walnut, or pecan pieces

1 plump garlic clove, minced

2 cups cooked wild rice

WHITE SAUCE

3 tablespoons unsalted butter

3 tablespoons unbleached all-purpose flour

1 cup whole milk

1 cup chicken stock, preferably homemade

Salt

Fresh sage sprigs, optional

Preheat the oven to 350°F. Grease a large baking dish.

Mix together the sausage, ground pork, sage, salt, and pepper. Form the mixture into approximately 3 to 3½ dozen meatballs, about 1 inch in diameter. Fry the meatballs in a nonstick skillet over medium heat until brown, about 5 minutes. Remove the meatballs with a slotted spoon and set them aside. Pour out all but 1 tablespoon of the pan drippings and add the butter to the remaining drippings in the skillet. Add the celery and bell pepper, and sauté until crisp-tender, about 5 minutes. Stir in the nuts and garlic, and continue cooking for about 2 additional minutes. Mix in the wild rice and spoon the mixture into the baking dish. Arrange the meatballs over the wild rice mixture.

Prepare the sauce, first melting the butter in a medium saucepan over medium heat. Whisk in the flour and cook for 1 minute, then slowly whisk in the milk and stock. Cook until the mixture comes to a boil and thickens, 3 to 5 additional minutes. Season with salt. Pour the sauce evenly over the wild rice mixture. Cover the casserole and bake for about 30 minutes, then uncover and bake for 10 minutes longer. Serve warm, with sage sprigs if you wish.

A World of Sausage

Many Americans don't even realize they can make sausage at home, though people have done it for thousands of years. As soon as any society acquired a surplus of meat, domesticated or wild, the members found ways to preserve it in sausage form. Native Americans made pemmican with buffalo or venison, fat, and berries, and virtually every group of settlers that came to this country brought a local style of their own.

The English gave us the basics for our ubiquitous breakfast sausage—ground pork, pepper, and sage—and baloney—only vaguely similar to its mortadella model from Bologna, Italy, but closer to the original than Pennsylvania Dutch sweet bologna, which is actually a German summer sausage. Germans also imported the frankfurter, bratwurst, and many more sausage varieties, and their neighbors from Austria, Hungary, Poland, and Switzerland brought along their regional favorites. The Portuguese contributed *linguiça* and the Chinese *lop cheong*. Swedish Americans still make sausages with potatoes in Minnesota and Wisconsin, and Japanese Americans on the West Coast still stuff mushrooms in sausage casings. If our country can't claim any of these or many other specialties as our own, it's largely because the world laid at our door as much sausage as we could eat.

Beefy Passions

The American colonists brought a fondness for beef with them from Britain, but they couldn't haul along the luxuriant English pastures that originally nurtured the attachment. The woodlands of the eastern coast, so welcoming to the pig, provided little forage for cattle. Many settlers kept a cow for milk, butter, and cheese, and always hoped for calves to slaughter for meat, but beef remained a special occasion meal at first, a love inflamed by longing.

As livestock levels grew over time, the colonists enjoyed beef more frequently, eventually consuming it in greater quantities than any other meat. A scarcity of good grazing land continued to be a constraint, however, until Americans settled the Great Plains. The native grass of the frontier West provided excellent feed for cattle, capable of supporting large herds year-round even in drought and harsh winter conditions. A relative of the cow with similar meat, the American bison thrived on the "buffalo grass," as it was commonly called, reaching a population of many million on the plains before the Civil War.

The cattle industry boomed right after the war, when Texas Longhorns first reached burgeoning eastern markets through a combination of fabled cattle drives and mundane railroad shipments. In some of the shrewdest wheeling and dealing ever seen in the state, Texas ranchers rounded up wild cattle that had escaped from earlier Spanish herds, raised them on free grass, and then marched the steers through open range to the nearest railhead. The country got ample affordable beef and the lowly paid cowhand who did the grunt work became the most legendary of all American heroes.

Our enthusiasm for beef produced many fine ways of cooking it, some indebted to British and other European traditions and some novel. Steak assumed an early primacy in our appetites, but originally we ate almost any cut, from the brains to the hooves, and applied the cooking fire in every conceivable way, from boiling to broiling. Over time, cooks culled the best from the rest, leaving us a beefy legacy worthy of our long-faithful love.

Pan-Fried Rib Eye

SERVES 2 OR MORE

Mark Twain loved a big, pan-fried American steak but thought Europeans incompetent with the meat. He complained about the cuts used, the smallness of the portions, and a tendency toward overcooking, concluding that the foreign version "rouses no enthusiasm." Confronted by such an "inert thing" on a trip to Europe, he imagined "an angel suddenly sweeping down out of a better land" with "a mighty porter-house steak an inch and a half thick, hot and sputtering from the griddle." We sizzle rib eyes the same way, and agree with Twain on a mushroom accompaniment, though we stop short of his craving for mounds of hot biscuits and buckwheat cakes on the side.

Coming Home

Mark Twain complained about his food experiences in Europe in the 1870s in *A Tramp Abroad.* He disdained all the offerings, from the bread to the butter, and compiled "a little bill of fare" that he looked forward to eating as soon as he got home. The list comprised over seventy-five dishes, not including generic items such as "fresh American fruits of all sorts."

Twain yearned for fried oysters and chicken, broiled Virginia bacon and steamed San Francisco mussels, black bass from the Mississippi River and brook trout from the Sierra Nevadas. He wanted apples baked with cream, and also in pie, dumplings, fritters, and puffs. Vegetable longings included hominy, succotash, butter beans, string beans, corn on the cob, and southern-style greens with bacon. Twain didn't eventually eat all these things at one meal, as he fantasized, but he worked his way through the menu many times in the decades ahead.

Two 1-pound boneless rib eye steaks, at least choice grade and preferably prime (see Ingredient Tip)

Salt and freshly cracked black pepper, coarsely ground

2 to 3 plump skin-on garlic cloves

3 tablespoons unsalted butter, softened

Sprinkle the steaks with salt and pepper. Let them sit at room temperature for about 20 minutes.

Warm a large cast-iron skillet over medium heat. Add the garlic cloves to the dry skillet and roast them until soft with lightly browned spots on the skin, 5 to 8 minutes. Squeeze the garlic from the skins, mash it, and mix it with the butter.

Return the skillet to high heat. When the skillet is very hot, place the steaks in it. Cook the steaks to your desired doneness, 4 to 5 minutes per side for medium-rare. Plate the steaks and top each one with a spoonful of the garlic butter. The butter will mingle deliciously with the steak's juices. Serve immediately.

INGREDIENT TIP: When you want the finest steak possible, the quality of meat is critical. Check with a good meat market about getting prime-grade, dry-aged steaks, but be open to a choice-grade cut if it's recommended by a knowledgeable butcher. For mail-order shopping, Prime Access (800-314-2875) and Balducci's (800-225-3822) provide premier meat, and Omaha Steaks International (800-228-9055) offers solid service and value.

Grilled T-bone with Horseradish Butter

Serves 4 or more

Modern outdoor grilling didn't become a major American cooking method until after World War II. Long before then, however, our ancestors did grill steaks inside, in their kitchen hearths. Among the many nineteenth-century cookbook authors who explained the "broiling" process, Eliza Leslie spoke the most clearly and surely in her 1837 *Directions for Cookery,* providing advice that's still a step above the usual: "Have ready on your hearth a fine bed of clear bright coals, entirely free from smoke and ashes. Set the gridiron [cooking grate] over the coals in a slanting direction, that the meat may not be smoked by the fat dropping into the fire directly under it. When the gridiron is quite hot, rub the bars with suet, . . . and lay on the steaks." In case of a flare-up, she said, move the meat away from the fire briefly to prevent its burning. Flavoring a steak with butter and horseradish is an equally venerable technique, with one or the other recommended by writers who preceded Leslie. We like to serve this T-bone with Essence of Tomato Salad (page 243) or just some sliced red-ripe tomatoes.

- Four 1- to 1¼-pound T-bone steaks, 1 to 1¼ inches thick
- 1 tablespoon kosher salt or other coarse salt
- 1 tablespoon freshly cracked black pepper, coarsely ground

HORSERADISH BUTTER

- 6 tablespoons (¾ stick) unsalted butter, softened
- 1½ teaspoons Worcestershire sauce
- Several generous teaspoons freshly grated horseradish root, preferably, or prepared horseradish

Generously sprinkle the steaks with the salt and pepper, and let them sit covered at room temperature for about 30 minutes.

Fire up a grill for a two-level fire capable of cooking first on high heat (where you can hold your hand an inch or two above the cooking grate for only 1 to 2 seconds) and then on medium heat (4 to 5 seconds with the same hand test). With a charcoal grill, pile the charcoal about three coals deep on one side for the higher heat level, and spread it in a single layer on the opposite side for medium heat. With a gas grill, start on high and adjust the temperature later to medium.

Meanwhile, prepare the horseradish butter, mixing together the ingredients in a small bowl. Add horseradish until its pungency is pleasantly tingling. The flavor should be sharp but not overwhelming to your tongue. The fresh root will be more pungent than the prepared variety. The butter can be chilled if you wish, but let it soften briefly before applying it to the steaks.

Eliza Leslie, 1787–1858

One of the first cookbook authors in the United States, Eliza Leslie still wins wide recognition as the best the country has produced. She cared passionately about the importance of fine ingredients—insisting, for example, in one famous instance that catfish caught in the middle of the river taste better than those taken near the shore—and she never skipped a step in the preparation of a dish, however inconvenient, that enhanced the flavor. Leslie's first cookbook, *Seventy-five Receipts for Pastry, Cakes, and Sweetmeats* (1828), went through many editions, and her more comprehensive *Directions for Cookery* (1837) became one of the most respected cookbooks of the nineteenth century. Though she also wrote a novel and numerous short stories, she focused on food throughout most of her life, publishing *Miss Leslie's New Cookery Book* (1857) just a year before her death.

A lifelong resident of Philadelphia, except for a childhood sojourn in Europe, Leslie took a cosmopolitan approach to American cooking. While her peers dealt primarily with foods from their region of the country, she embraced a national perspective, providing recipes for everything from Carolina punch to Yankee pumpkin pudding, Italian pork to Spanish buns. While her peers often used their cookbooks as a platform for lectures on a woman's moral responsibilities as a housekeeper, wife, and mother, Leslie concerned herself with taste and texture, the product rather than the preaching. For the breadth of her view and the depth of her wisdom, she remains a cook for all seasons.

When grilling T-bones, it's important to keep the smaller, more tender section of the steak angled away from the hottest part of the fire. Grill the steaks uncovered over high heat for 2½ to 3 minutes per side. Move the steaks to medium heat, turning them again, and continue grilling for 2½ to 3 minutes per side for medium-rare doneness. The steaks should be turned a minimum of three times, more often if juice begins to form on the surface. Transfer the steaks to plates and top each with a portion of the butter. Serve immediately.

TECHNIQUE TIP: The most common mistake in backyard grilling is failing to measure and monitor the cooking temperature of the fire. Many meats grill best on a two-level fire, where you start at a higher heat to sear the surface and then finish at a lower temperature to cook the food through without burning it. With thick steaks and a number of other meats, the desired levels are hot and medium, which we measure with the trusty old hand test that cooks have employed for centuries, particularly in baking. Simply place your hand right over the cooking grate and count the seconds before the fire forces you to move it. One second is a very hot fire, good for starting steaks, and 4 to 5 seconds indicates medium heat, usually as low as you want to go in grilling meat.

New England Boiled Dinner

SERVES 4 AMPLY AS A MAIN COURSE WITH PLENTIFUL LEFTOVERS FOR RED FLANNEL HASH (PAGE 37)

Unlike pork, which takes well to the heavy salting required for long-term preservation, beef tastes better when it's held for shorter periods with a lighter coating of salt. Americans adopted a British term for the process, "corning," which refers to the grainy texture of the surface rather than any use of corn. This slowly simmered one-pot dish became a common way to cook corned beef, closely related to French *pot au feu,* Italian *bollito misto,* and British variations on the same theme, but different in final complexion. In the first New England cookbook, *The American Frugal Housewife* (1832), Lydia Maria Child suggested salting your own beef for economy, and some cooks still do that for a personal touch. Others spread the preparation over two days, simmering the meat one day and saving the vegetables for the next. However you approach it, this is hearty, flavorful fare, much better than the old name and current reputation imply.

> The primary requisite for writing well about food is a good appetite. Without this, it is impossible to accumulate, within the allotted span, enough experience of eating to have anything worth setting down. Each day brings only two opportunities for field work, and they are not to be wasted minimizing the intake of cholesterol. They are indispensable, like a prize-fighter's hours on the road.
>
> A. J. LIEBLING, BETWEEN MEALS (1959)

- 3½- to 4-pound uncooked corned beef brisket section
- 2 bay leaves
- 1 teaspoon yellow mustard seeds
- 1 teaspoon whole peppercorns
- 6 medium beets
- 12 small waxy potatoes, such as Green Mountain or Red Bliss, peeled if you wish
- 3 to 4 carrots, cut into 2-inch lengths
- 2 large onions, cut through the root ends into 8 wedges each
- 1 large turnip or 2 medium turnips, cut into 1-inch chunks
- 1 large rutabaga or 2 medium rutabagas, cut into 1-inch chunks
- 2 parsnips, cut into 2-inch lengths, optional
- 1 medium cabbage head, about 1½ pounds, cut through the core end into 8 wedges
- Prepared or freshly grated horseradish and coarse-ground mustard

Arrange the corned beef, fat side up, in a large heavy Dutch oven or stockpot. Pour in enough water to cover it by about 1 inch. Stir in the bay leaves, mustard seeds, and peppercorns, and bring the mixture just to a boil, skimming the liquid of the impurities that rise to the surface. Immediately reduce the heat so that the liquid simmers gently, with just occasional bubbles breaking on the surface. Cover and cook for approximately 3 hours, checking occasionally to make sure the water level still covers the meat amply. The corned beef is ready when very tender, though short of beginning to fall apart.

Cook the beets separate from the other vegetables. Place them in a saucepan and cover with water. Simmer over medium heat until tender, 25 to 30 minutes. Drain them, and when cool enough to handle, strip off the skins and slice the beets.

To keep health and beauty, or to restore it when lost, it is necessary to observe the laws of health, discarding quackery and panaceas of all kinds as superstitions, and inventions of the devil. . . .

Leanness is caused generally by lack of power in the digestive organs to digest and assimilate the fat-producing elements of food. First restore digestion, take plenty of sleep, drink all the water the stomach will bear in the morning on rising, take moderate exercise in the open air, eat oat-meal, cracked wheat, Graham mush, baked sweet apples, roasted and broiled beef, cultivate jolly people, and bathe daily.

Buckeye Cookery and Practical Housekeeping (1880)

Remove the meat from the cooking liquid and cover it to keep it warm. Skim the fat from the cooking liquid if you wish and increase the heat to medium. Add the potatoes and carrots, and cook covered for 10 minutes. Add the onions, turnip, rutabaga, and optional parsnip to the other vegetables, and cook covered for an additional 15 minutes. Gently add the cabbage wedges and continue cooking covered for 5 to 10 minutes longer, until all the vegetables are quite tender (not al dente but not mush either). Drain the vegetables and arrange them neatly on a platter surrounding the meat. Serve warm with horseradish and mustard.

Glazed Corned Beef

Serves 6 or more

Similar to a boiled dinner in the initial simmering, this way of cooking corned brisket yields an entirely different result. It developed as a Jewish-American substitute for glazed ham and is just as tasty. Kosher cooks use margarine in the glaze, rather than butter, because of the prohibition against eating meat and dairy products together, but switch to the real thing if you wish.

4- to 5-pound uncooked corned beef brisket section

2 large onions, sliced thin

2 celery stalks with leaves, chopped

2 bay leaves

2 plump garlic cloves, slivered

1 heaping teaspoon whole peppercorns

1 heaping teaspoon whole coriander seeds

1 heaping teaspoon yellow mustard seed

1 teaspoon dried rosemary

Whole cloves

GLAZE

1 tablespoon margarine

3 tablespoons packed brown sugar

1½ tablespoons yellow mustard

1½ tablespoons ketchup

Place the brisket in a Dutch oven or other large heavy pot. Scatter the onions, celery, bay leaves, garlic, peppercorns, coriander and mustard seeds, and rosemary over and around the meat. Pour in enough water to cover the ingredients by about 1 inch. Bring just to a boil over high heat, then reduce the heat to low. Cover and simmer for 3½ to 4 hours, until quite tender.

Preheat the oven to 350°F.

Drain the meat, discarding the cooking liquid. Slice off any remaining exterior fat. Oil a roasting pan just a bit larger than the brisket. Place the brisket in the pan with its more attractive side up. Stud it with cloves.

Combine the glaze ingredients in a small pan and warm together over medium heat. Bring the mixture just to a boil, then spoon it evenly over the meat. Bake the brisket uncovered for 30 to 40 minutes, until the glaze is nicely baked onto the meat with some crisp and some chewy sections. Cool the brisket for at least 15 minutes, then cut it against the grain into thin slices right before serving. Serve warm or chilled.

Perhaps the most valuable piece of advice Mrs. Appleyard can give you is about carving: never let a man less than sixty years old do it unless he has a diploma from a certified carving school embossed on his shirt front. Youth is a wonderful thing but an ability to carve is not one of its attributes.

Louise Andrews Kent and Elizabeth Kent Gray, *Mrs. Appleyard's Summer Kitchen* (1957)

Pot Roast with Root Vegetables

SERVES 6 OR MORE

Americans call this a roast, but the meat is actually braised, an old European technique for tenderizing thick, tough cuts. True roasting requires naturally tender meat, and with beef in particular it isn't an optimum cooking method in either a brick or modern oven. Early cooks knew that, and the fact was reinforced for them during the transition period when the range began replacing the hearth. Cookbooks of those years distinguished between roasted and baked beef, the former done on a spit in front of a live flame and always considered superior. Eliza Leslie called oven-baked beef "a family dish," meaning a little ordinary, and Mary Cornelius in *The Young Houskeeper's Friend* (1856) suggested it was also a trickier preparation, more susceptible to burning. By 1886, when few people still had hearths, Sarah Tyson Rorer in the *Philadelphia Cook Book* maintained the distinction, but went on to recommend a pot roast for oven cooking. We agree, because the braising produces a delectable, fall-apart "roast."

3- to 3½-pound beef chuck roast
3 tablespoons unbleached all-purpose flour
1 teaspoon salt
½ teaspoon freshly milled black pepper
Lard or vegetable oil for pan-frying
1 cup beef stock
1 teaspoon brown mustard
1 teaspoon dried thyme or marjoram
12 small boiling onions (not pearl onions) or 2 large onions, cut into 6 wedges each
8 small red waxy potatoes, about 2 ounces each, peeled
4 to 6 medium carrots, halved horizontally
1 tablespoon unsalted butter, softened
1 tablespoon unbleached all-purpose flour

Preheat the oven to 300°F.

Sprinkle the meat well with the flour, salt, and pepper. Warm a ¼-inch piece of lard in a Dutch oven or heavy pot over high heat on the stove. Quickly brown the meat on all sides. Add the stock, mustard, and thyme to the meat, cover tightly, and place in the oven. Cook for 1 hour, then add the onions, potatoes, and carrots, and continue cooking for at least 2 to 2½ hours longer, until the meat and vegetables are very tender.

Arrange the meat and vegetables on a platter. Knead together the butter and flour, then whisk the mixture into the pan drippings and simmer on the stove for about 5 minutes to eliminate the raw flour taste. Serve the sauce alongside the pot roast.

Texas Barbecued Brisket

Serves 12 to 18

Some of the strongest barbecue traditions in the country developed in areas settled by German immigrants. The pattern appears in the Carolinas, where pork is the meat of choice, and certainly in central Texas, where beef brisket emerged as the king of the local 'Q about a century ago. This recipe works best in a log-burning, offset-firebox pit, the kind used originally, but we suggest an alternative approach for other types of smokers in the Technique Tip on page 203. Smoke with oak, hickory, fruitwood, or another hardwood, not mesquite, which leaves a bitter taste after long cooking despite its mythological association with Texas and barbecue. Never serve brisket with sauce on the top, only on the side if you insist on it at all, and always offer cold beer, hot beans, and maybe a gooey peach cobbler as a finale.

DRY RUB

¾ cup paprika
¼ cup freshly milled black pepper
¼ cup kosher salt or other coarse salt
¼ cup sugar
2 tablespoons chili powder
2 tablespoons garlic powder or onion powder
2 teaspoons cayenne pepper

8-pound to 10-pound packer-trimmed brisket (see Ingredient Tip)

BEER MOP

12 ounces beer
½ cup cider vinegar
¼ cup vegetable oil
½ medium onion, chopped
2 garlic cloves, minced
1 tablespoon Worcestershire sauce

BANDERA BARBECUE SAUCE, OPTIONAL

1 tablespoon vegetable oil
2 medium onions, chopped fine
6 garlic cloves, minced
1 to 2 chopped jalapeño or serrano chiles, minced
1 cup chili sauce (the ketchup-style condiment)
¾ cup Worcestershire sauce
¾ cup strong black coffee
½ cup dark molasses
¼ cup cider vinegar
2 tablespoons brown or yellow mustard
2 tablespoons chili powder
1 teaspoon ground cumin
1 teaspoon ground ginger
1 teaspoon salt or more to taste

The night before you plan to barbecue, combine the rub ingredients in a bowl. Reserve 1 tablespoon of the rub, then apply the rest evenly to the brisket, massaging it in thoroughly. Transfer the brisket to a plastic bag and refrigerate it overnight.

INGREDIENT TIP: Be sure to start with a packer-trimmed brisket, the whole cut with a thick layer of fat on one side. You may need to contact your butcher a few days ahead to get what you want. Don't trim away the fat until after the meat is cooked because it serves as a natural basting agent, helping keep the meat moist and flavorful. Much of the fat melts away during the cooking process and more can be cut off before serving.

Before you begin to barbecue, take the brisket from the refrigerator. Let it sit at room temperature for about 45 minutes.

Meanwhile, fire up a wood-burning smoker to between 200°F and 225°F, following the manufacturer's instructions.

Prepare the baste, mixing together the beer mop ingredients, ½ cup of water, and the reserved dry rub. Warm the mixture over low heat.

Transfer the brisket to the smoker, fat side up, so the juices will help baste the meat. Cook covered until well done, 1 to 1¼ hours per pound, basting every hour or so with the mop. Replenish the wood as needed.

While the brisket smokes, prepare the barbecue sauce if you wish. Warm the oil in a medium saucepan over medium heat. Stir in the onions, garlic, and chiles, and sauté until the onions are soft and translucent, about 5 minutes. Dump in the remaining ingredients and ½ cup water, give the sauce a good stir, and bring the sauce to a simmer. Cover and cook for 30 minutes, then uncover and continue cooking for about 15 additional minutes, until the sauce is reduced a bit and thickened to your liking. The sauce can be used warm or chilled.

Continue basting the brisket, adding more warm water to the mop when it evaporates. After several hours the brisket will look like an ominous black hulk. Don't worry about it; just keep the smoker's temperature in the proper range. When the meat has cooked the appropriate length of time, remove it from the smoker and let it sit at room temperature for 20 minutes. Then cut the fatty top section away from the leaner bottom portion. An easily identifiable layer of fat separates the two areas. Trim the excess fat from both portions and then slice thinly against the grain. Take care as you slice the meat because the grain changes directions. Serve the brisket hot, with barbecue sauce on the side if you wish.

TECHNIQUE TIP: The best barbecued brisket is heavily smoked and significantly shrinks during the cooking process. The only way to succeed completely is with a wood-burning pit or similar homemade smoker. If you want to smoke brisket on the more common water smokers or a covered grill, you can still get some of the old-timey barbecued taste with a modified approach. Start with a fully trimmed 4-pound brisket section, sometimes called the "flat cut," and don't use the mop if the smoker manufacturer recommends against it. In the dry rub, substitute ground dried chipotle chiles for the chili powder, to give a smokier taste. After 3 hours in the smoker or covered grill, wrap the brisket in foil, first adding some onion slices, several good splashes of Worcestershire sauce, or maybe a few ounces of beer. Return the foil-wrapped brisket to the smoker or covered grill, or a 225°F oven, and continue cooking for about 2 additional hours, until well done and very tender.

Boliche

SERVES 8

One of the mainstays of Spanish and Cuban cooking in Florida, boliche comes from the same European roots that inspired beef daubes and à la modes. Boliche outshines the other preparations, we think, because of its heady stuffing of chorizo, ham, vegetables, and seasonings.

3½-pound beef eye-of-round
3 ounces cooked smoky ham
3 ounces uncooked Mexican or Spanish chorizo, or well-seasoned breakfast sausage, crumbled
½ cup chopped onion
⅓ cup chopped green bell pepper
¼ cup thin-sliced pimiento-stuffed green olives
2 plump garlic cloves, minced
Salt and freshly milled black pepper
3 tablespoons olive oil, or bacon or ham drippings, or a combination
1 cup beef stock
8-ounce can tomato sauce
2 bay leaves
Two 6.5-ounce jars marinated artichoke hearts, drained, optional
Juice of 1 to 2 limes

Cut a pocket with a sharp knife from one end of the roast almost through to the other end. Hollow out enough of the meat to leave a 1- to 2-inch core. Place the beef scraps removed from the hollow in a food processor and pulse to grind coarsely. Add the ham and chorizo to the processor, and grind together finely. Spoon the mixture into a bowl and stir in the onion, bell pepper, and olives.

Rub some of the minced garlic over the inside and outside of the hollowed-out roast, then mix the rest into the stuffing. Sprinkle the roast lightly inside and out with salt and pepper. Pack as much stuffing into the cavity as will fit. The meat will balloon up a bit. Close the end with toothpicks if you wish.

In a Dutch oven or other heavy pot, warm the olive oil over medium-high heat. Brown the roast thoroughly on all sides. Crumble into the pan any remaining stuffing. Pour the stock and tomato sauce over the roast and add the bay leaves. Reduce the heat to low, cover, and simmer for about 3 hours, until very tender. Turn the meat over once about halfway through the cooking. Remove the boliche from the pan and let it cool for at least 20 minutes to firm up a bit.

If you wish to include the artichokes, add them to the pan juices now. (They aren't traditional, but complement the other flavors.) Bring the pan juices to a boil and reduce by about one-fourth. The liquid should still be thin, but have a little body to it. Discard the bay leaves from the pan juices, degrease if you wish, and stir in enough lime juice to give a tangy kick. Pour the pan juices into a gravy boat, or a shallow bowl if the artichokes are included, and adjust the seasoning. Slice the roast crosswise into thin rounds. Serve the boliche warm or chilled, with pan juices to pour over the slices.

Beef Before the Cowboy

The main braised beef dishes in early America, before boliche and even pot roast as we know it today, beef daube and à la mode (or alamode) flourished as ways of tenderizing tough meat. In both preparations, which overlap considerably and sometimes confusingly, cooks generally larded the meat and then simmered it slowly in an acid such as vinegar or wine. They were "made dishes," unlike roasted meat or a broiled steak, and that partially explains the French names, which connoted elegance. Often but not always, an à la mode contained a forcemeat or bread stuffing, and a daube came with a gelled gravy. Virtually every nineteenth-century cookbook offered a recipe for one, the other, or both.

Swiss Steak

Serves 4

Americans used to smother fine pan-fried steaks in onions, but knew that tougher cuts like round steak benefit from the addition of other juicy vegetables to create a braising liquid. Neither American nor Swiss cooks invented the technique, though it found a lasting home in the Midwest farm belt settled by many Central Europeans. This is how Cheryl's mother, Betty Alters, prepares the dish in Galesburg, Illinois, a way our families have relished for several generations. We accompany the steak with Scalloped Potatoes (page 271) or Twice-Baked Potatoes (page 272), and during the summer, fresh corn on the cob.

In Indiana the act of smothering anything with onions is not considered criminal as it is in some snooty circles in the effete East. Being Midwesterners ourselves, we never will forget the first time we suffocated a steak in New York to regale some notables from Washington, D.C. They sniffed, went pale, politely pushed the onions off and toyed with tiny bites of T-bone, as though they were eating skunk.

Cora, Rose, and Bob Brown, *America Cooks* (1940)

- 1½ pounds round steak, ¾ to 1 inch thick
- 2 tablespoons unbleached all-purpose flour
- Salt and freshly milled black pepper
- Olive oil or vegetable oil for pan-frying
- 1 large onion, sliced into thin wedges
- 1 green bell pepper, sliced into thick strips
- 1 garlic clove, minced
- 15-ounce can chopped tomatoes with juice
- 1 to 2 tablespoons tomato paste
- 1 teaspoon dried thyme, basil, or marjoram, optional

Rub the steak with flour, salt, and pepper. With a mallet, pound the flour and seasonings into the steak until the meat is an inch or two larger in diameter. Cut the steak into 4 equal pieces.

Heat ¼ inch of oil in a heavy skillet over high heat. Brown the steak sections quickly, in batches if necessary. Return all the steak to the skillet.

Scatter the onion, bell pepper, and garlic over the steak, then pour the tomatoes and 1 tablespoon of the tomato paste over all, sprinkling in one of the herbs if you wish. Reduce the heat to medium-low and simmer 1 to 1¼ hours, until the steak is pull-apart tender. If the sauce lacks body, add another spoonful of tomato paste and simmer a few additional minutes.

Chimichanga

SERVES 4

Another regional favorite —like Boliche—with a Hispanic heritage, the chimichanga is the pride of southern Arizona, in the heart of the southwestern cattle country that has produced some of our most distinctive beef dishes. Deep-fried and decked out with toppings, it's a souped-up burrito chock-full of chuck, vegetables, and mild chile. For a colorful fiesta spread, serve chimichangas with Mexican Rice (page 325), Watermelon Ice (page 393), and Orange Sangaree (page 429).

FILLING

3-pound boneless shoulder chuck roast

Salt and freshly milled black pepper

¼ cup bacon drippings or vegetable oil

1 medium onion, chopped

2 garlic cloves, minced

1 cup beef stock

2 small tomatoes, preferably Italian plum, chopped

½ cup chopped roasted mild green chiles, such as New Mexican, preferably fresh or frozen, seeded

4 thin 10- to 12-inch flour tortillas, warmed

Vegetable oil for deep-frying

Grated Monterey Jack, asadero, or mild Cheddar cheese, or a combination

Sour cream, chopped tomato, and sliced scallions

Pico de Gallo (page 77) or other favorite salsa

Rub the roast with salt and pepper.

Warm 2 tablespoons of the bacon drippings in a Dutch oven or other large heavy pot over medium-high heat. Brown the roast on all sides. Reduce the heat to low, scatter half of the onion and half of the garlic over and around the meat. Pour the beef stock over it. Cover and simmer for 1¼ to 1½ hours, until the roast is very tender. Let the meat sit in the cooking liquid until cool enough to handle. Drain the meat, reserving the cooking liquid. Shred the meat into bite-size pieces with your fingers or in several small batches in a food processor.

Warm the remaining 2 tablespoons bacon drippings in a heavy skillet over medium heat. Sauté the remaining onion and garlic in the fat until the onion softens. Add the meat and sauté until well browned, about 10 minutes. Scrape the meat up from the bottom every few minutes, getting it crusty in some spots. Pour the reserved cooking liquid into the pan and add the tomatoes and chiles. Cook for about 15 minutes, until most of the liquid has evaporated. The meat should remain moist but not juicy. Adjust the seasoning if you wish. (The meat can be made ahead to this point and refrigerated, covered, for up to several days. Warm the meat before proceeding.)

You'll need about 5 cups of the shredded meat mixture for the chimichangas. Spoon it evenly over the tortillas. Roll up each tortilla, tucking in the ends to make a secure fat tube that resembles an overgrown Chinese egg roll. Secure the rolls with toothpicks.

Shortly before you plan to eat the chimichangas, warm at least 4 inches of oil in a Dutch oven or other large heavy pan to 375°F. Fry the chimichangas one or two at a time until golden brown, about 3 minutes. Turn the chimis to fry them evenly. Drain them and arrange on serving plates. Top with cheese, sour cream, tomato, scallions, and salsa. Serve immediately.

Chicken-Fried Steak

Serves 4

When Harriet Bell, our New York book editor, saw this on our proposed list of dishes, she blanched a shade milkier than the cream gravy that covers this cowhand treat, named for its manner of frying. She returned to rosy after trying a steak, but hasn't mustered the courage yet to serve them on her home turf for a big dinner, once a common occurrence in the cattle lands of the Great Plains. Mrs. C. C. Burt of Overton, Nebraska, even devised a way to cook the steak for a Sunday noontime dinner *while* she attended religious services, a feat she described with undue modesty in her church's 1954 *Priscilla Cook Book.* We introduced our Texas grandson to the dish when he was only ten days old, not to taste of course, but just to glimpse the glories of life after weaning.

1¾ to 2 pounds round steak, sliced ½ inch thick and twice-tenderized by the butcher

2 cups unbleached all-purpose flour

2 teaspoons baking powder

1 teaspoon baking soda

1 teaspoon freshly milled black pepper

¾ teaspoon salt

1½ cups buttermilk

1 tablespoon Tabasco Sauce

1 egg

1 plump garlic clove, minced

Approximately 1½ pounds vegetable shortening, preferably Crisco, for deep-frying

CREAM GRAVY

3 tablespoons unbleached all-purpose flour

2 cups evaporated milk

¾ cup beef stock, preferably homemade

3 tablespoons whipping cream

½ teaspoon freshly milled black pepper or more to taste

Salt

Cut the steak into 4 equal portions. Pound the portions until each is about ¼ inch thick. Sprinkle the flour on a plate. Stir together in a large shallow bowl the baking powder, baking soda, pepper, and salt, and mix in the buttermilk, Tabasco, egg, and garlic. The mixture will be thin.

Add enough shortening to a deep cast-iron skillet to deep-fry the steaks in at least 4 inches of shortening. Heat the shortening to 325°F.

Dredge each steak first in flour and then in the batter. Dunk the steaks back into the flour, patting in the flour until the surface of the meat is dry.

Fry the steaks, pushing them down under the fat or turning them over as they bob to the surface, until a deep golden brown, 7 to 8 minutes. Drain the steaks and transfer them to a platter. Keep them warm while you prepare the gravy.

I shall never forget . . . one marvelous mid-day meal on an oil-well platform off the Texas coast—a lonely speck in the blue water, first stop for shrimp boats coming in from the Gulf of Mexico. The cook had lowered buckets into one of the boats and pulled them up brimming with freshly caught shrimp. . . . For the extra-hungry oil workers or the few who did not care for shrimp (and there are such melancholy people), there were also steaks pounded thin, dipped in a batter of egg and flour mixed with cornmeal, and fried crisp. I had heard of this Texas delicacy, the famous "chicken-fried steak," and had deplored it in advance—but those steaks were delicious.

JONATHAN NORTON LEONARD, AMERICAN COOKING: THE GREAT WEST (1971)

Pour off the fat from the pan through a strainer, leaving ¼ cup of pan drippings in the bottom of the skillet. Return any browned cracklings from the strainer to the skillet.

Warm the drippings over medium heat. Sprinkle in the flour, stirring to avoid lumps. Pour in the evaporated milk, stock, and whipping cream. Simmer until the liquid is thickened and the raw flour taste is gone, about 3 minutes. Stir the gravy up from the bottom frequently, scraping up the browned bits. Add the pepper and salt. Cream gravy should taste of more than a suspicion of pepper, so add more if necessary. Pour the gravy over the steaks or on the side and serve immediately.

Vaquero Fajitas

SERVES 6 GENEROUSLY

In various true and faux forms, fajitas have swept the country in recent decades, quickly leaping from ranch rations for workers into fashionable party fare. Mexican cowboys, or *vaqueros,* cooking on wood fires on the vast northern cattle ranges of their country, mastered the art of grilling the naturally tough but flavorful skirt steak, which they called *arracheras.* Immigrants brought the idea to the Southwest, where it evolved from a simple meat cookout to a sizzling spread of beef, vegetables, and salsa.

MARINADE

Juice of 4 limes

¼ cup Worcestershire sauce

2 tablespoons vegetable oil

2 to 3 pickled jalapeño chiles, minced, plus ¼ cup pickling liquid

6 garlic cloves, minced

1 teaspoon ground cumin

2 skirt steaks, 1 to 1¼ pounds each, trimmed of membrane and fat (see Ingredient Tip)

1 to 2 medium onions, sliced thick

1 whole green bell pepper

1 whole red bell pepper

1 whole fresh mild green chile, such as New Mexican or poblano

Vegetable oil

Salt

Flour tortillas, preferably thick, warmed

Avocado slices

Pico de Gallo (page 77) or other favorite salsa

At least 2½ hours and up to the night before you plan to grill the fajitas, prepare the marinade, combining the ingredients in a medium bowl. Place the skirt steaks in a plastic bag, pour the marinade over them, and refrigerate.

Coat the onion slices, the bell peppers, and chile with oil. Remove the meat from the refrigerator and drain it, blotting the surface of moisture. Salt the meat lightly. Let the steaks sit at room temperature for about 30 minutes.

Fire up the grill for a two-level fire capable of cooking on high heat (where you can hold your hand an inch or two above the cooking grate for only 1 to 2 seconds) and on medium heat (4 to 5 seconds with the same hand test). With a charcoal grill, pile the charcoal about three coals deep on one side for the higher heat level, and spread it in a single layer on the opposite side for medium heat. With a gas grill, start on high and adjust the temperature later to medium.

Place the skirt steaks over high heat and the onions, peppers, and chile over medium heat. Grill the steaks uncovered for 4 to 5 minutes per side to medium-rare, turning them more than once if juice begins to form on the surface. The total cooking time for the onions, peppers, and chile will be 8 to 18 minutes, until the onions are soft and the peppers and chile are soft with some charred skins.

Turn the onion slices at least once and the peppers and chile several times, to cook on all sides evenly. While the vegetables finish cooking, cut the meat across the grain and diagonally into thin finger-length strips. Pull the charred skin off the peppers and chile and slice them into strips.

To serve, pile a platter high with the meat, onions, peppers, and chile. Accompany with tortillas, avocado slices, and salsa. Let everyone help themselves by filling the tortillas with some of the meat strips, vegetables, and garnishes.

INGREDIENT TIP: Once a giveaway cut at the butcher, skirt steak or diaphragm muscle is no longer cheap, though it's still a good value. Readily available in the Southwest, it may need to be requested ahead in other areas of the country. Substitute flank steak if you can't locate it, but don't invite any real *vaqueros* to dinner that night.

Beef Stew with Savory Popovers

Serves 8

Trying to elevate the image of stew in *Jennie June's American Cookery Book* (1866), Mrs. J. C. Croly advised middle-class housekeepers to "make it of good meat and savory with sweet herbs, and the most fastidious will not object to it." A century later, *Esquire's Handbook for Hosts* (1953) went further in battling a "much maligned" reputation, declaring stew "second only to steak in its standing as a Man's Dish." If stew suffers from an esteem problem in your home, try this robust rendition, a composite of popular approaches old and new. We enjoy it for a fireside supper in winter with airy popovers that resemble—and may derive from—English Yorkshire pudding.

STEW

4 bacon slices, chopped

2 cups chopped onion

2½ pounds beef chuck, trimmed of surface fat and cut into 1-inch cubes (see Ingredient Tip)

3 tablespoons unbleached all-purpose flour

1 teaspoon salt or more to taste

½ teaspoon freshly milled black pepper

3 cups beef stock, preferably homemade

12 ounces beer

2 tablespoons tomato paste

2 teaspoons brown or yellow mustard

2 teaspoons fresh minced summer savory or marjoram, or 1 teaspoon dried summer savory or marjoram

Cayenne pepper

1½ cups pearl onions, peeled

6 medium carrots, cut into thick chunks

4 small red waxy potatoes, peeled and cut into chunks

3 parsnips or small turnips, cut into chunks

POPOVERS

1 to 2 tablespoons fine-grated fresh Parmesan or dry Jack cheese

1 cup unbleached all-purpose flour

¾ teaspoon salt

2 large eggs

1 cup whole milk

2 teaspoons fresh minced summer savory or marjoram, or 1 teaspoon dried summer savory or marjoram

1 tablespoon unsalted butter, melted

To prepare the stew, first fry the bacon in a Dutch oven or other large heavy pot over medium heat until brown and crisp. Remove the bacon with a slotted spoon, drain it, and reserve it. Stir the onion into the bacon drippings and sauté until soft and translucent, about 5 minutes. Toss the meat cubes with the flour, salt, and pepper, then brown about half the cubes in the bacon drippings over medium-high heat. When the meat cubes have given off liquid and lost their raw color, add the remaining cubes and cook briefly until all are well browned.

Pour in the stock and beer, the tomato paste, mustard, savory, and a pinch or two of cayenne. Simmer the stew covered for 1 hour, then add the pearl onions, carrots, potatoes, and parsnips. Simmer the stew uncovered for 1 to 1¼ additional hours, until the meat and vegetables are very tender and the liquid is thick. Skim the fat from the stew if you wish. (The stew can be made a day or two before serving. Cool it, then cover and refrigerate. Reheat before proceeding.)

To prepare the popovers, first preheat the oven to 450°F. Grease 8 ramekins or a popover pan or muffin tin with at least 8 cups. Dust each cup lightly with cheese. Stir together the flour and salt in a medium bowl. In another bowl, whisk together the eggs with the milk and savory. Whisk the egg mixture gradually into the dry ingredients, stirring well but only until combined. Add the butter and give the batter another stir or two. Pour the batter into the prepared cups. Bake for 15 minutes. Reduce the oven temperature to 350°F and bake for an additional 12 to 15 minutes, until the popovers are golden brown, crusty, and well puffed. Avoid opening the oven door anytime before what you estimate will be the last 2 to 3 minutes of cooking. Unmold the popovers, slit each with a knife to release the steam, and arrange each popover on a plate.

Stir the bacon into the stew and add more salt if needed. Ladle the stew on the plates, partially over the popovers, and serve immediately.

INGREDIENT TIP: Always avoid buying anything labeled "stew meat" to make stew. These meat scraps aren't the bargain they may seem because the package typically contains a mix of various parts. The cubes don't cook at the same rate or have the same texture when done.

TECHNIQUE TIP: Popovers are a steam-powered quick bread, rising tall from the high proportion of liquid in their batter. Advice about their preparation varies wildly. At the turn of the twentieth century, cookbook author Marion Harland beat her popovers for exactly 4 minutes. A skilled successor, Ann Batchelder, suggested in 1941 giving them "a good beating with the egg beater for as long as you can stand it." The 1997 update of the *Joy of Cooking* favors mixing the batter only until combined. Marion Cunningham, current author of *The Fannie Farmer Cookbook,* starts popovers in a cold oven. Lady Bird Johnson, a first-rate popover cook, begins not only in a hot oven, but preheats the pan to sizzling as well. It's an intimidating range of guidance, at least to us, but our recipe describes the method that has worked best in our experience.

Marion Harland, 1830–1922

Marion Harland liked a beefy breakfast. Her morning meat recommendations included beef stew, chili, Chateaubriand, Hamburg steaks, liver stew, and stewed tripe.

Christened Mary Virginia Hawes, she took the pen name of Marion Harland at the age of twenty-three when she entered a literary contest and claimed the fifty-dollar first prize. A precocious child raised in Virginia, she began writing essays and stories in her teens and didn't stop publishing until her eighty-ninth year. In that span of time, from the decades before the Civil War to the beginning of Prohibition, Harland produced two dozen books on cooking and household affairs, a similar number of novels, and a variety of other works on travel, biography, and colonial history.

After she married Edward Payson Terhune in 1856, she taught herself the skills of cooking and homemaking, summarizing the lessons for others in 1871 in *Common Sense in the Household,* her first work of nonfiction. A best-seller that was translated into French, German, and Arabic, the book brought her fame in the culinary field, which she continued to till for many years in ladies' magazines, syndicated newspaper columns, and other major tomes that included *The Dinner Year-Book* (1878), *Breakfast, Dinner and Supper* (1889), *Marion Harland's Complete Cook Book* (1903), and *The National Cookbook* (1896), the latter co-authored with her daughter, Christine Terhune Herrick.

A Bowl of Red

Serves 8

Will Rogers called chili con carne a "bowl of blessedness," but Dallas journalist Frank X. Tolbert trumped him for an endearing name in his cult classic, *A Bowl of Red* (1953). Originally a makeshift frontier stew, probably made most often with dried beef, the dish started growing in popularity after the flirtatious "chili queens" of San Antonio began hawking it from stands on a downtown plaza around 1880. Tolbert's book kicked up the fervor substantially, helping to ignite the current chili cookoff craze, one of the zaniest food fads in American history. If you want any respect in Texas, cook chili as a meat dish, not a soup, and remember that beans go on the side, never inside.

4 bacon slices, chopped

1 large onion, chopped

4 plump garlic cloves, minced

4-pound chuck roast, trimmed of surface fat and cut into ½-inch cubes

½ cup good-quality chili powder, such as Gebhardt's

1 tablespoon cumin seeds, toasted in a dry skillet and ground

1 tablespoon *molé* paste (see Ingredient Tip)

2 teaspoons crumbled dried oregano, preferably Mexican

2 teaspoons salt or more to taste

2 teaspoons cider vinegar

¼ teaspoon cayenne pepper or more to taste

Approximately 2 cups beef stock, preferably homemade

1 to 2 tablespoons *masa harina*

Chopped onions, minced fresh or pickled jalapeños, and saltine crackers, optional garnishes

Fry the bacon in a Dutch oven or other large heavy pot over medium heat until brown and crisp. Remove the bacon from the drippings with a slotted spoon and reserve it. Add the onion to the drippings and sauté briefly until softened. Mix in the garlic and sauté until the onion is translucent. Stir in the beef and sauté it until it loses its raw color. Add the reserved bacon, and the chili powder, cumin, *molé* paste, oregano, salt, vinegar, and cayenne. Pour in just enough stock to cover. Reduce the heat to very low and cook uncovered for about 3 hours, stirring about every 30 minutes. Add more stock as needed to keep the mixture from getting dry and sticking. In the last 30 minutes of cooking, stir in the *masa harina,* a couple of teaspoons at a time, to thicken or "tighten" the chili. Serve the chili immediately or let it cool, cover and refrigerate overnight, and reheat. Serve the chili steaming hot in bowls, with garnishes as you wish.

INGREDIENT TIP: Everyone has a secret ingredient for chili con carne, and *molé* paste is ours. Deep reddish brown, almost inky, the paste is a ground mixture of chocolate, toasted chiles and seeds, and seasonings, used to flavor black *molé,* the dark sauce often served with chicken or turkey in Mexico. Common in the Southwest and in Mexican markets elsewhere, its quality can vary. We particularly favor a version made in small batches in Oaxaca, Mexico, by American expatriate Susana Trilling and imported into the U.S. by Williams-Sonoma (800-541-1262).

Springfield Chilli

SERVES 6 TO 8

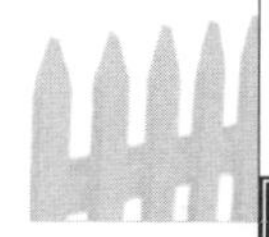

The midwestern version of chili, often spelled with an extra "l" in Illinois, derives from the Texas stew, but now outdistances the parent in popularity. This is the familiar version made with ground beef, tomatoes, and beans, all anathema to diehard fans south of the Red River. It's a different kettle of beef, to be sure, but also a classic.

- 2 bacon slices, chopped fine
- 1 large onion, chopped
- 2 plump garlic cloves, minced
- 1½ pounds ground beef
- 3 tablespoons chili powder
- 14- to 16-ounce can tomatoes with juice
- 8-ounce can tomato sauce
- 1 cup beer
- 1 teaspoon Worcestershire sauce
- 16-ounce can chili beans, undrained
- Salt
- Grated mild Cheddar cheese, chopped onions, and oyster crackers, optional

Sauté the bacon in a large saucepan or skillet over medium heat until brown but not yet crisp. Stir in the onion, cover the pan, and let the onion sweat for about 3 minutes, until translucent and just tender. Uncover the pan and mix in the garlic, cooking another minute.

Raise the heat to medium-high and add the ground beef. Cook until it loses its raw color, about 5 minutes. Stir in the chili powder, then pour in the tomatoes and juice, tomato sauce, beer, and Worcestershire sauce, and reduce the heat to medium-low. Cook the chilli until thickened but still soupy, about 30 minutes. Stir in the beans and salt to taste, and cook an additional 10 minutes. Serve the chilli immediately, or let it cool and refrigerate it, covered, for reheating a day or two later. Let guests customize their bowls of chilli with cheese, onion, and crackers as they wish.

The aroma of good chili should generate rapture akin to a lover's kiss.

JOE COOPER, WITH OR WITHOUT BEANS (1952)

No Longhorns Here

Chili wasn't quite its old self when it made a big national debut in several major cookbooks published right after the turn of the twentieth century. Fannie Farmer didn't include it in her original *Boston Cooking-School Cook Book,* published in 1896, but she added "chili con carni" to the second, 1906 edition, making it with "two young chickens" and "red peppers" or "canned pimientos." Sarah Tyson Rorer, in *Mrs. Rorer's New Cook Book* (1902), also used chicken instead of beef in her "chili con-cana," but she was clear on the need for chiles. Marion Harland suggested two different "chilli con carni" dishes as breakfast meals in *Marion Harland's Complete Cook Book* (1906). She built both on beef, though one also contained rice. Needless to say, none of these ladies flew a Lone Star flag over their front porch.

Meat Loaf

Serves 6

Maybe the most embellished meal in all of America, meat loaf, like love, is a many-splendored thing that can be tailored to any taste. We start here on home base with a solid though simple version that reflects the origin of the appeal. Adorn it as you wish, but don't let an excess of passion destroy the one you love.

¼ cup (½ stick) unsalted butter

2 cups chopped onion (about 2 medium onions)

1 medium green or red bell pepper, chopped

2 garlic cloves, minced

1 pound ground beef

½ pound ground veal

½ pound ground pork

¾ cup saltine cracker crumbs (½ bag from a "four-pack" box of crackers)

2 eggs, lightly beaten

5 tablespoons ketchup

1 tablespoon Worcestershire sauce

1½ teaspoons salt

1 teaspoon hot pepper sauce, such as Tabasco

4 bacon slices, cut in half crosswise

Preheat the oven to 350°F.

Melt the butter in a medium skillet over medium heat. Add the onion, bell pepper, and garlic, and sauté until soft, about 5 minutes. Scrape the mixture into a large bowl and let it cool briefly. Mix in the beef, veal, and pork, then the cracker crumbs, eggs, 3 tablespoons of the ketchup, the Worcestershire sauce, salt, and hot pepper sauce. Mix well.

Pack the meat mixture into a loaf pan, mounding a bit in the center, and smear the remaining 2 tablespoons ketchup over the loaf. Lay the bacon slices over the top side by side, overlapping if necessary, and tuck the ends down into the sides of the loaf.

Bake 1¼ to 1½ hours, until the loaf is brown and crisp on top with an internal temperature of 160°F. Pour off the accumulated grease and let the loaf sit at least 10 minutes before cutting into thick slices and serving. The meat loaf is outstanding made a day in advance and reheated or used cold in sandwiches.

Serious Loafers

Michael McLaughlin wrote a whole book on meat loaf variations, a little gem called *Fifty-two Meat Loaves* (1993). His "Good Old American" versions include New England Corned Beef Loaf, Pineapple Luau Loaf, Little Italy Pepperoni-Mushroom Pizza Loaf, Germantown Meat Loaf with Sauerkraut, Horse-radish and Dill, and two toothsome renditions from his grandmothers.

Other cookbooks provide plenty of alternative approaches, such as meat loaf with meringue over the top, and upside-down creations baked with a fruit sauce on the bottom. We've come across small individual loaves cooked in muffin tins, and large rolls laced with slices of ham and mozzarella to give a pinwheel look to each serving. Americans cooks are, as McLaughlin says, in constant search of new ways to loaf in the kitchen.

LOVE ME TENDER:

Game, Lamb, and Veal

IN THE SPAN OF FOUR CENTURIES, GAME WENT FROM a forbidden pleasure to a forgotten treasure, which in effect amounts to the same thing. In England at the time of colonization, the landed gentry controlled hunting preserves and kept the limited game for their personal tables. When the colonists arrived in the Americas, they found a New World indeed, teeming with an astonishing array of wild meat animals bearing no private brands.

We ate so avidly that supplies were depleted almost to earlier European levels, returning us eventually to where we started, sidelined from the only game in town.

The scarcity situation prevailed through much of the twentieth century, though it began to improve steadily by the 1980s. The increase in supply resulted from significant growth in the amount of farm-raised and ranch-harvested game, a trend that is still building. Whether or not we hunt, we can once more enjoy the depth and diversity of the country's natural bounty.

This is also an opportune time to renew our old love for lamb and veal, two other wonderful meats that lost favor in the mass-food climate of our era. It was actually mutton, rather than lamb, that we ate most frequently in the days of hearth cooking, but the younger, more succulent lamb is the version of the meat best suited to the contemporary kitchen. Veal usually lagged behind mutton in consumption, but appealed to plenty of people, particularly in areas with heavy German and Italian populations.

Lean as well as tender and tasty, game, lamb, and veal satisfy contemporary appetites, even those honed on other meats. They seem destined for a major comeback in the years ahead, a restoration of their proper place on a brimming American table.

Silver Dollar Venison Medallions

SERVES 4

Native Americans feasted frequently on venison before Europeans arrived, eating deer in the eastern woods, elk in the Southwest and California, moose farther north, and caribou in Alaska. The English, on the other hand, at the time of the earliest settlement, often tried to make beef taste like venison, a meat so prized in the mother country that it was a royal prerogative. The colonists quickly adapted to the real thing, preparing it in pies, puddings, hashes, hams, steaks, and stews. The name for these backstrap medallions comes from their size, not much larger than a silver dollar. The same method of cooking also works with thin venison scallops, typically cut from the upper hind leg, though they look more like a dollar bill. A crunchy nut conserve enlivens the result, regardless of the cut.

- 1½ pounds venison backstrap medallions, cut about ⅓ inch thick, or 1½ pounds venison scallops
- Salt and freshly milled black pepper
- 1 tablespoon vegetable oil
- Ozarks Black Walnut Conserve (page 295), warmed or at room temperature

> Let the stoics say what they please, we do not eat for the good of living, but because the meat is savory and the appetite is keen.
>
> RALPH WALDO EMERSON, *ESSAYS: SECOND SERIES* (1844)

Sprinkle the venison lightly with salt and pepper. Warm a large heavy skillet over high heat. When very hot, add the oil and let it heat for about 1 minute, until nearly smoking. Add the venison and fry quickly, in a stir-fry motion, for a minute or two, just long enough to sear all the surfaces. Avoid overcooking. Serve the backstrap medallions *immediately* accompanied by the conserve.

INGREDIENT TIP: If you don't hunt or have generous friends who do, you may need to get venison by mail order. Our favorite supplier is Mike Hughes's Broken Arrow Ranch (800-962-4263 or 830-367-5875), near Ingram, Texas, the largest game ranch in the United States. The venison comes from nonnative "exotics," such as the diminutive axis deer and the Nilgai antelope, both brought here years ago from Asia and now thriving in the Texas Hill Country. The animals roam free on Hughes's property and other ranch lands, where skilled harvesters field-dress them in the wild.

TECHNIQUE TIP: If you start with frozen venison, thaw it in inexpensive red wine or buttermilk, to help keep the lean meat moist. Either works well in this recipe, with the wine imparting a subtle flavor and the buttermilk leaving behind an elusive tang. In other recipes, use the one most compatible with the preparation, blotting the meat dry before cooking it in any dry-heat method that calls for a surface sear.

Grilled Elk Backstrap with Spiced Plum Sauce

Serves 4

Nineteenth-century American cookbooks usually specified venison steaks cut from the haunch or neck, but today most game aficionados prefer medallions from the backstrap, or tenderloin. However you slice the meat, take some cues from Abby Fisher, the earliest known African-American cookbook author. In *What Mrs. Fisher Knows About Old Southern Cooking* (1881), she suggests grilling venison steaks (i.e., "broiling" over hot coals on a gridiron), and provides the original version of the accompanying "game sauce," which she describes with no false modesty as "the best sauce in the world."

SPICED PLUM SAUCE

⅓ cup minced onion

½ cup cider vinegar

1 pound ripe plums, pitted and quartered, with their juice

½ cup plus 2 tablespoons sugar

1-inch piece of cinnamon stick

¼ teaspoon salt or more to taste

¼ teaspoon freshly milled black pepper

Scant ¼ teaspoon cayenne pepper

8 elk or other venison backstrap medallions, 4 to 5 ounces each, cut 1 to 1¼ inches thick (see Technique Tip)

Salt and freshly milled black pepper

Vegetable oil

1 large red onion, cut into ⅓-inch-thick slices

1 to 2 tablespoons unsalted butter, cut into small chunks, softened

Prepare the plum sauce, first combining the onion and vinegar in a nonreactive saucepan and cooking over low heat until quite soft, about 15 minutes. Add the remaining ingredients, raise the heat to medium-low, stir occasionally, and continue cooking until thick and reduced to jam consistency, about 1 hour. (The sauce can be made several days ahead, refrigerated, and served chilled or reheated. If it is too thick for easy spooning, mix in a bit of water.)

Fire up your grill in a way that allows for cooking first over high heat (where you can hold your hand comfortably an inch or two above the cooking grate for only 1 to 2 seconds) and then over medium heat (about 4 to 5 seconds with the same hand test). With a charcoal grill, pile the charcoal about three coals deep on one side for the higher heat level, and spread it in a single layer on the opposite side for medium heat. With a gas grill, start on high and adjust the temperature later to medium.

Sprinkle the backstrap medallions with salt and pepper. Wrap them tightly in plastic and let them sit at room temperature for about 20 minutes. Oil the onion slices and salt and pepper them too.

Abby Fisher

Mrs. Fisher knew a great deal about traditional southern cooking, but no one today knows much about her. She tells us that friends and patrons in San Francisco encouraged her to write a cookbook, and implies that some of them helped her to transcribe it since, as she says, she couldn't read or write. The rest of our current information on her comes largely from culinary historian Karen Hess, who researched and wrote background notes for a 1995 facsimile reprint of Fisher's book.

Hess found out through census records and city directories that Abby Fisher was born in South Carolina around 1832 as the mulatto child of a local mother and a French father. She married Alexander Fisher of Mobile, Alabama, and later moved to San Francisco, where she ran a pickle and preserve business out of her home. The scant evidence suggests she grew up as a slave and learned to cook in a plantation kitchen. Hess concludes, on the basis of her research and the strength of the cookbook, that Fisher was "a remarkably resourceful woman."

Plan on a total cooking time for the venison of 9 to 11 minutes, and for the onions, closer to 15 minutes. Place the onions on the grill first over medium heat and grill them uncovered for 6 to 8 minutes. Turn the onions and place the venison on the grill over high heat. Grill the venison uncovered over high heat for 1 to 1½ minutes per side. Move the medallions to medium heat, turning them again. Cook for 2 to 3 minutes per side, turning once, for rare to medium-rare doneness. Take off the onions and venison as each is done, arranging them on a platter and dotting them with a bit of butter. Keep the platter covered while everything finishes cooking. Serve the venison immediately with spoonfuls of the plum sauce.

TECHNIQUE TIP: Venison backstrap is sometimes cut into thin slices or scallops when being processed, especially if from deer or caribou, which are smaller than elk. If working with scallops, modify the grilling technique slightly. Cook the red onion slices over the medium-heat side of the grill first. Then cook the venison scallops just over high heat and for only 1 to 1½ minutes per side.

Venison Pot Roast with Kitchen Pepper

Serves 6

Custom blends of dry spices may seem like a contemporary seasoning idea, but they are a lot older than that hot chef downtown would like you to believe. Eliza Leslie gave her favorite mixture as early as 1837 in *Directions for Cookery,* combining white and black pepper, ginger, cinnamon, and other spices to make Kitchen Pepper. In this homey preparation, we use the blend like a barbecue dry rub, massaging it into the venison to marinate overnight. Like beef pot roast, this is really a braised dish. Enjoy it with Sweet Potato–Chestnut Purée (page 275) and Pickled Peaches (page 298).

KITCHEN PEPPER

- 1 teaspoon freshly milled black pepper
- 1 teaspoon ground ginger
- ½ teaspoon ground white pepper
- ½ teaspoon ground cinnamon
- ¼ teaspoon ground nutmeg or mace
- ¼ teaspoon ground cloves

- 3-pound venison chuck roast
- 2 tablespoons unbleached all-purpose flour
- ½ teaspoon salt
- 1 tablespoon vegetable oil
- ½ cup dry red wine
- 2 cups venison, beef, or chicken stock
- 1 tablespoon Worcestershire sauce
- 2 teaspoons brown mustard or Dijon mustard
- 1 large onion, cut into thin wedges

The night before you plan to cook the pot roast, prepare the kitchen pepper. Combine the ingredients in a small bowl. Rub the spice mixture evenly over the roast, coating it heavily. Wrap the roast in plastic and refrigerate overnight.

Preheat the oven to 300°F.

Blot the venison to eliminate surface moisture. Stir together the flour and salt, then pat the mixture over the roast. Warm the oil in a Dutch oven or other large heavy pot over medium-high heat and brown the roast in it. Pour in the wine and let it reduce by about half. Add the remaining ingredients to the pot and cover it tightly.

Bake the roast for 4½ to 5 hours, until quite tender. If the meat doesn't yet pull apart with a fork, keep cooking a bit longer. Serve hot with the pan juices.

It was a heavenly place for a boy, that farm of my uncle John's. The house was a double log one, with a spacious floor (roofed in) connecting it with the kitchen. In the summer the table was set in the middle of that shady and breezy floor, and the sumptuous meals—well, it makes me cry to think of them. Fried chicken, roast pig, wild and tame turkeys, ducks and geese; venison just killed; squirrels, rabbits, pheasants, partridges, prairie-chickens; biscuits, hot batter cakes, hot buckwheat cakes, hot "wheat bread," hot rolls, hot corn pone; fresh corn boiled on the ear, succotash, butter beans, string beans, tomatoes, peas, Irish potatoes, sweet potatoes; buttermilk, sweet milk, "clabber"; watermelons, musk-melons, cantaloupes—all fresh from the garden; apple pie, peach pie, pumpkin pie, apple dumplings, peach cobbler—I can't remember the rest.

MARK TWAIN, THE AUTOBIOGRAPHY OF MARK TWAIN (CHARLES NEIDER, EDITOR) (1961)

Venison Chili

Serves 8

One result [of women's liberation] is the notorious villainousness of American cookery—a villainousness so painful to a cultured uvula that a French hack-driver, if his wife set its masterpieces before him, would brain her with his linoleum hat. To encounter a decent meal in an American home of the middle class, simple, sensibly chosen and competently cooked, becomes almost as startling as to meet a Y.M.C.A. secretary in a bordello, and a great deal rarer.

H. L. Mencken,
In Defense of Women (1918)

In the frontier West, as elsewhere, game often ended up in stews, a tradition revived today by many chili cook-off champions. Strongly flavored meats, such as pronghorn, work particularly well in this chili, though any ground venison produces a delicious result. The native pronghorn, abundant across the West when Lewis and Clark explored the territory, resembles a small antelope but runs like a cheetah, the only animal on earth that can beat it in a race. Strictly a hunter's venison, it's worth chasing a taste any chance you have.

- 1 tablespoon vegetable oil
- ½ pound spicy pork sausage
- 1 large onion, chopped
- 3 garlic cloves, minced
- 3 pounds ground venison
- 6 tablespoons chili powder
- 1 tablespoon ground dried chipotle chile
- ½ teaspoon ground cumin
- 1½ cups venison, beef, or chicken stock
- 3 tablespoons tomato paste
- 2 cups corn kernels, fresh or frozen
- Salt
- Chopped onions and saltine crackers, optional

Warm the oil in a Dutch oven or other large heavy pot over medium heat. Add the sausage and fry until it loses its raw color. Add the onion to the drippings and sauté until soft and translucent, about 5 minutes. Mix in the garlic and sauté an additional minute. Stir in the venison and sauté until it loses its raw color. Add the chili powder, chile, and cumin. Pour in the stock, 1½ cups water, and the tomato paste. Reduce the heat to very low and cook covered for about 45 minutes. Stir in the corn, salt to taste, and continue cooking for 15 to 20 additional minutes, until the venison is very tender and the chili thick. Serve the chili immediately or even better, cool, refrigerate overnight, covered, and reheat. Serve the chili steaming hot in bowls, with onions and crackers as you wish.

Hunter's Game Sausage

Serves 6

Another strong, noncommercial meat, like pronghorn, javelina (or peccary) blends robustly with venison in sausage. If you're fresh out of javelina, the only wild pig native to the New World, substitute pork shoulder or wild boar. Make the sausage at least a day before you plan to cook it and then enjoy it for breakfast with eggs or grits, at lunch nestled in a roll, or at dinner in a mixed grill.

- 1½ pounds ground venison
- 1½ pounds ground javelina, wild boar, or pork shoulder
- ½ cup beer
- ¼ cup (½ stick) unsalted butter, softened
- 3 to 4 plump garlic cloves, minced
- 1 tablespoon freshly milled black pepper, coarsely ground
- 2 teaspoons salt
- 2 teaspoons cracked yellow mustard seeds
- 1 to 2 teaspoons crushed dried hot red chiles
- Approximately 2 yards of hog sausage casings (see Ingredient Tip)
- Vegetable oil

In a large bowl, mix together the venison, javelina, beer, and butter. With your fingers, mix in the garlic, pepper, salt, mustard seeds, and chiles. Cover and refrigerate overnight and up to several days.

Prepare the casings, soaking them in several changes of water over an hour or so. Run some water through each casing too, to eliminate any remaining salt from the inside.

Leave the sausage mixture in the refrigerator until just before you plan to stuff it into the casings. Using the stuffing attachment of a meat grinder or stand mixer, work quickly to keep the fat from softening, which makes the meat harder to grind consistently. Stuff the meat into the casings, making approximately a dozen sausages about 1 inch in diameter and 5 inches in length. With your fingers, twist the casings and then tie off the individual sausages with kitchen twine. Cut between them. Prick any air bubbles with a needle. The sausage can be pan-cooked or grilled, or smoked as described here.

Fire up a smoker or covered grill to between 225°F and 250°F, following the manufacturer's instructions for smoking. Coat the sausages lightly with oil.

Transfer the sausages to the smoker and smoke covered for 1¼ to 1½ hours, until the casings look ready to burst. Open the smoker only when necessary, and cover as quickly as possible, to minimize the loss of heat and smoke. Cut into one of the sausages to make sure it is cooked through before eating them. Serve the sausages hot.

INGREDIENT TIP: Sausage casings are the cleaned intestines of various farm animals. For this sausage, you want hog casings, which will yield plump links about an inch or more in thickness. Inexpensive and close to indestructible, the casings usually come packed in brine and require soaking to eliminate the salty taste. No matter how many feet of casings you need, it's easiest to work with them in lengths of no more than a yard or so. Any good meat market can round up as much as you want.

Grilled Buffalo Steak

SERVES 4

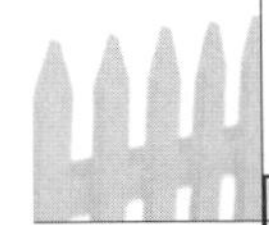

After its wretched slaughter in the nineteenth century, the American bison has rebounded from near extinction to become a mythic symbol of rugged endurance. According to Janie Hibler in *Wild About Game* (1998), farm-raised herds now exist in every state, with Native American ranchers taking the lead in restoring the vigor of the breed. Buffalo meat tastes similar to beef, and comes in the same cuts, but it's much leaner. If the price of the steaks today take a toll on your wallet, blame the western pioneers who considered the meat too cheap to care about.

- 2 tablespoons yellow mustard
- 2 teaspoons freshly milled black pepper, coarsely ground
- 2 teaspoons Worcestershire sauce
- 1 teaspoon dried sage or more to taste
- Four 8- to 10-ounce strip, rib eye, or sirloin buffalo steaks, about 1 inch thick (see Ingredient Tip)
- Salt

Mix together the mustard, pepper, Worcestershire sauce, and sage in a small bowl. Rub the mixture over the buffalo steaks. Generously sprinkle the steaks with salt and let them sit covered at room temperature for 20 to 30 minutes.

Fire up a grill for a two-level fire capable of cooking first on high heat (where you can hold your hand an inch or two above the cooking grate for only 1 to 2 seconds) and then on medium heat (4 to 5 seconds with the same hand test). With a charcoal grill, pile the charcoal about three coals deep on one side for the higher heat level, and spread it in a single layer on the opposite side for medium heat. With a gas grill, start on high and adjust the temperature later to medium.

Grill the steaks uncovered over high heat for 2 to 2½ minutes per side. Move the steaks to medium heat, turning them again, and continue grilling for 2 to 2½ minutes per side for medium-rare doneness. The steaks should be turned a minimum of three times, more often if juice begins to form on the surface. Serve immediately.

INGREDIENT TIP: We order our buffalo steaks from the Denver Buffalo Company (800-289-2833), which sells naturally raised and USDA-inspected meat. Because of the leanness, be especially vigilant to avoid overcooking.

A Strange Episode in Carnivore History

Abilene, Kansas, 1867. The first Longhorns arrive on hoof from Texas and leave on railroad cars bound ultimately for urban markets in the East. Not far away, at least as miles are measured on the Great Plains, cattle ranchers and railroad executives are paying hunters to slaughter American bison, sometimes skinning them for their hides and taking the tongue for food, but generally leaving the carcass to rot. In exactly the same time frame and place, while striving to satisfy a national craving for red meat, we virtually eliminated the greatest aggregation of wild meat animals ever gathered on earth.

We did this despite the fact that bison require less feed than cattle to produce meat that's not only similar to beef but superior in some respects. Ranchers wanted to end competition for grazing grass, the railroads felt the wild herds had no respect for their right-of-way, and frontier settlers saw the slaughter as a way to dispossess Native Americans, who relied on the bison for food and many other daily needs. We could perhaps have won the West in other ways, but we came to conquer.

Fried Rabbit Quarters

Serves 4

Native to both the New and Old Worlds, wild rabbits became America's most common small game animal, eaten across the country in many of the same preparations as chicken. During World War I, rabbit even claimed flag-waving rights, being recommended in the official cookbook of the *Patriotic Food Show* (1918) as a substitute for the beef, pork, and mutton needed to feed the troops overseas. Cooks often fried young, tender rabbits, as we do here in a variation on a dish we enjoyed at Colonial Williamsburg. Sides of greens and mashed potatoes with cream gravy fill out a plate sumptuously.

- 1½ cups buttermilk
- 3 tablespoons honey mustard
- 1½ teaspoons salt
- 1¾ pounds skinned rabbit hindquarters, preferably from a fryer (see Ingredient Tip)
- ½ cup salted roasted peanuts
- 1 cup unbleached all-purpose flour
- ¾ teaspoon freshly milled black pepper
- ¼ teaspoon cayenne pepper
- 2 cups peanut oil, 1 pound vegetable shortening, or a combination
- 4 thin slices country ham or other smoky ham, optional

Combine the buttermilk, mustard, and 1 teaspoon of the salt. Place the rabbit in a plastic bag and pour the buttermilk mixture over it. Refrigerate the rabbit for 1 to several hours, then drain it.

Place the peanuts in a food processor with about 2 tablespoons of the flour and grind the nuts fine. Pour the mixture out onto a plate and add to it the remaining ½ teaspoon salt, flour, pepper, and cayenne. Place a wire rack for draining the rabbit near the cooking area.

Lift the rabbit pieces, one by one, from the marinade, letting excess liquid drain back into the dish. Coat the rabbit with the seasoned flour.

Warm the oil in a 10- to 12-inch heavy skillet over high heat. When small bubbles form on the surface, reduce the heat to medium. Add the rabbit and fry covered for 12 minutes until a rich medium brown. You should hear a constant ongoing bubbling and sizzling, neither urgent nor lackadaisical. After the allotted time, remove the lid and turn the rabbit with tongs, using light pressure to avoid piercing the crust. Fry uncovered for about 12 additional minutes, until the crust is a rich golden brown and the meat is cooked through but still juicy. Drain the rabbit on the rack. If you wish, serve each rabbit piece over a slice of ham. Serve hot.

INGREDIENT TIP: Like chicken, farm-raised rabbit comes in categories of fryers (the youngest) and roasters, though actual labeling in stores is less common than with chicken. A good mail-order source is Geoff Latham's company, Nicky USA (800-469-4162 or 503-234-GAME), which also sells venison, buffalo, and other game.

California Conejo

Serves 6

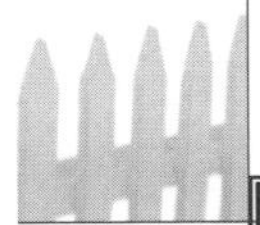

In the early days, American cooks generally braised or stewed older, tougher rabbits, developing some tantalizing flavor combinations that still shine with the farm-raised meat of today. This California dish features ingredients and tastes introduced by the early Spanish settlers of the state, and probably reflects their era, in concept at least. We like it with saffron rice.

Central heating, French rubber goods, and cookbooks are three amazing proofs of man's ingenuity in transforming necessity into art, and, of these, cookbooks are perhaps most lastingly delightful. Many an old belly has been warmed by the reading of them, and for one secret from them, steaming ruddy brown on plate, how many youthful pleasures have been counted well lost!

M. F. K. Fisher, Serve It Forth (1937)

3 tablespoons olive oil

½ medium onion, chopped

¾ pound button mushrooms, halved or if large, quartered

Two 2- to 2½-pound rabbits, cut into 4 to 6 serving pieces each, or 6 rabbit hindquarters, about 6 ounces each

2 cups dry red wine

1½ cups chicken stock, preferably homemade

1 tablespoon minced fresh oregano

1 teaspoon minced fresh rosemary

1 teaspoon ground dried mild red chiles, such as ancho or New Mexican, or more to taste

Salt

½ cup sliced ripe olives, the mild canned variety

Fresh oregano or rosemary sprigs, optional

Warm the oil in a Dutch oven or other heavy pot over medium heat. Stir in the onion and mushrooms, and cook until the onion is soft and translucent and the mushrooms are limp, about 5 minutes. Raise the heat to medium-high, add the rabbit pieces, and brown them lightly. Pour in the wine and reduce it by half, then add the stock, oregano, rosemary, chiles, and salt to taste. Reduce the heat to medium-low, cover, and simmer until the rabbit is cooked through and very tender, about 45 minutes. If the liquid is very soupy, remove the rabbit with tongs, raise the heat to high, reduce the liquid a bit, and then return the rabbit to the sauce. Stir in the olives and heat them through. Garnish, if you wish, with herb sprigs and serve.

Brunswick Stew with Rabbit

Serves 8 to 10

"The unchallenged aristocrat of American stews," in the words of James Villas, originated as a squirrel dish, perhaps in Brunswick County, Virginia, or Brunswick County, North Carolina, or Brunswick, Georgia. Today most people make the stew with chicken, which tastes fine, but rabbit probably comes even closer to approximating the celebrated maiden version. For a spirited southern supper, start with Cheese Straws (page 83), accompany the stew with Wilted Greens with Hot Bacon Dressing (page 256), and finish with Sweet Potato Pie (page 376).

- ¼ pound bacon, chopped fine
- ¼ pound salt pork, chopped fine
- 2 large onions, chopped
- 2½- to 3-pound rabbit, preferably a roaster, or a similar-size chicken or chicken parts
- 1¼- to 1½-pound veal shank
- 2½ to 3 cups fresh lima beans or butter beans, or two 10-ounce packages frozen lima beans
- 3 cups corn kernels, fresh or frozen
- 28-ounce can crushed tomatoes
- 6 ounces fresh green beans, sliced into ¾-inch lengths
- 2½ tablespoons Worcestershire sauce
- 1½ tablespoons yellow mustard
- 1 tablespoon freshly milled black pepper or more to taste
- 1 tablespoon salt or more to taste
- 1 teaspoon cayenne pepper or more to taste
- 3 large russets or other baking potatoes, peeled, boiled, and mashed

Warm the bacon and salt pork in a Dutch oven or stockpot over medium heat. When the fat is well rendered and the meat is partially brown and still limp, stir in the onions and cook until soft and translucent, about 5 additional minutes. Add the rabbit and the veal shank, and cover with 10 cups of water. Cook uncovered for about 1¼ hours, until both the rabbit and the veal are very tender. Remove the rabbit and veal from the pot and set aside until they are cool enough to handle. Stir in the lima beans, corn, tomatoes, green beans, Worcestershire sauce, mustard, pepper, salt, and cayenne, and continue simmering 30 additional minutes. Shred the rabbit and veal into bite-size pieces and return them to the pot along with the mashed potatoes. Continue to simmer until the meat and vegetables are quite soft and meld together into a thick stew, another 30 to 45 minutes, stirring up from the bottom occasionally. Add more water if needed to keep the stew from drying out. The stew can be dished up by the hearty bowlful immediately, but it improves with cooling and reheating.

The Taming of the Stew

Raymond Sokolov tells the most common story about the origin of Brunswick stew in *Fading Feast* (1983). According to the account, a Virginia slave named "Uncle Jimmy" Matthews created the concoction in 1828 for Dr. Creed Haskins and friends, using squirrels he shot in the woods of Brunswick County. Descendants of Haskins claimed that the original recipe contained nothing except squirrel, bacon, butter, onions, stale bread, and salt and pepper to taste, making it a meaty ragout.

Cooks began adding other vegetables within a few decades, and around the same time started considering chicken as a viable substitute for squirrel. In *Common Sense in the Household* (1871), Marion Harland, who grew up in Virginia, said you could use either meat, but gave a preference for squirrel (two large gray ones or three smaller critters). She also put potatoes, tomatoes, butter beans, and corn in the pot. Other popular cookbook authors of the same period dropped the squirrel entirely and threw in extra vegetables. Sarah Tyson Rorer, from Pennsylvania, called for chicken, ham, and limas, and Massachusetts native Maria Parloa went with leftover mutton, carrots, turnips, and parsnips, turning a sunny southern stew into a wintry northern hodgepodge.

Pan-Seared Lamb Chops with Wilted Dandelion Greens

SERVES 4

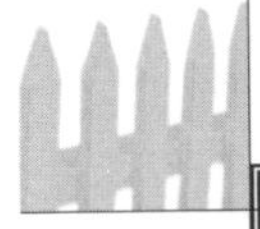

Among the early English settlers, mutton and lamb ranked close to beef as meats of choice. Cooks thought mutton best from the late summer into the early winter, and they generally ate lamb in the spring, a half-year after fall births. Lamb is no longer seasonal, but still tastes great with other spring treats, such as young dandelion greens. Rhubarb Brown Betty (page 384) offers a sweet seasonal finish.

Personally, I'd be happy eating or serving a hearty stew five nights out of the week—with hardly a second thought given to quick meat sautés, undergrilled poultry and vegetables, tasteless steamed fish, listless pastas, and all that other trendy stuff that makes a mockery of real American cookery.

JAMES VILLAS,
STEWS, BOGS & BURGOOS (1997)

- 8 rib lamb chops
- 1 to 2 garlic cloves, halved
- Salt and freshly milled black pepper
- Olive oil for pan-frying
- ¾ pound to 1 pound tender dandelion greens or other young, slightly bitter greens
- Pepper vinegar

Rub each lamb chop well with the cut side of a garlic clove. Sprinkle with salt and pepper.

Warm a large heavy skillet over high heat until very hot. Pour in enough oil just to coat the bottom of the skillet. Add the lamb chops and fry for 2 to 3 minutes per side for rare to medium-rare. Remove the chops and arrange them on a platter. Add the greens to the skillet, turn off the heat, and cover. The residual heat from the skillet will wilt the greens within a couple of minutes. Stir once if needed to wilt evenly. Give the greens a good splash or two of pepper vinegar, and spoon it around the chops. Serve immediately, with a cruet of pepper vinegar on the side.

Leg of Lamb with Mint Julep Sauce

SERVES 8

The English practice of serving lamb with mint jelly went tipsy in Kentucky, the home of bourbon. Try this grilled, butterflied leg with fresh green beans, perhaps the Kentucky Wonder variety in keeping with the theme.

4½-pound to 5-pound leg of lamb, boned, butterflied, and pounded to uniform thickness, about 1½ inches

Salt and freshly milled black pepper

MINT JULEP SAUCE

2 cups fresh mint leaves, chopped fine

⅔ cup raspberry vinegar or other fruit vinegar

⅓ cup sugar

3 tablespoons bourbon or other American whiskey or more to taste

Fresh mint sprigs, optional garnish

Generously sprinkle the lamb with the salt and pepper and let it sit covered at room temperature for about 30 minutes.

Prepare the sauce, combining the ingredients in a small bowl. Stir until the sugar dissolves.

Fire up a grill for a two-level fire capable of cooking first on high heat (where you can hold your hand an inch or two above the cooking grate for only 1 to 2 seconds) and then on medium heat (4 to 5 seconds with the same hand test). With a charcoal grill, pile the charcoal about three coals deep on one side for the higher heat level, and spread it in a single layer on the opposite side for medium heat. With a gas grill, start on high and adjust the temperature later to medium.

Grill the lamb uncovered over high heat for 2½ to 3 minutes per side. Move the lamb to medium heat, turning it again. Continue grilling for 12 to 16 minutes for rare to medium-rare doneness, turning at least two more times. Turn the lamb more often if juice begins to form on the surface. Let the lamb sit for about 5 minutes, then carve it into thin slices. Serve, passing the sauce on the side.

INGREDIENT TIP: When we want the finest lamb available, we mail order it from Jamison Farm near Latrobe, Pennsylvania (800-237-5262). John and Sukey Jamison (no relation to us) raise their lamb naturally and pasture-graze it on native bluegrass and wild clover. They process the meat themselves and then dry-age it. The delicate but well-flavored lamb is the most tender we've encountered, whether in chops, leg, or other cuts.

Food is the only element in our culture that reaches our consciousness through all five of the senses. We can feel its smooth or rough texture, see its diverse colors and shapes, hear it boil or sizzle in preparation for the table, smell its sweet or pungent aroma, and finally taste its wonders—and savor every moment of the experience.

JOHN EGERTON,
SOUTHERN FOOD (1987)

Pueblo Lamb Stew with Green Chile and Posole

Serves 6

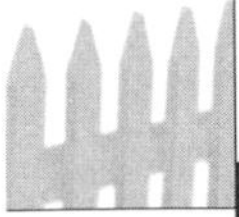

Spanish explorer Francisco Coronado brought sheep into the Southwest in 1540 and they have remained a major part of life in the region ever since, particularly among the Pueblos and Navajos. Both Native peoples make a stew similar to this one, though traditionally they use mutton rather than lamb. Pueblo cooks often serve the stew on the annual Feast Day of their village, a time of communal celebration and eating.

- 2 tablespoons lard or vegetable oil
- 1 large onion, chopped
- ⅔ cup chopped wild celery or regular celery stalks with leaves
- 1½ to 1¾ pounds boneless lamb shoulder, trimmed of surface fat, and cut into ¾- to 1-inch cubes
- Salt and freshly milled black pepper
- ½ to 1 cup chopped roasted mild green chiles, such as New Mexican, preferably fresh or frozen
- 1 teaspoon dried crumbled oregano, preferably Mexican, or more to taste
- 4 to 6 juniper berries, crushed
- 2 cups cooked posole (see Ingredient Tip) or hominy

Warm the lard in a Dutch oven or large saucepan over medium heat. Stir in the onion and celery, and cook until the onion is soft and translucent, about 5 minutes. Toss the lamb cubes with salt and pepper to taste, add them to the pot, and brown them. Pour in 2 cups of water, scraping up browned bits from the bottom. Stir in the chiles, oregano, and juniper berries. Bring the stew to a boil, reduce the heat to low, cover, and simmer for about 1½ hours. (Add more water if the mixture gets dry.) Stir in the posole and continue cooking uncovered until the meat is very tender and the stew thick and reduced, about 30 minutes longer. Degrease the stew if you wish. Adjust the seasoning and serve hot, ladled into bowls.

INGREDIENT TIP: A southwestern style of hominy, posole is always the local choice for this lamb stew. The Santa Fe School of Cooking (800-982-4688 or 505-983-4511) sells it by mail order.

Oven-Braised Lamb Shanks

Serves 4 or more

The inspiration for this dish comes from a recipe attributed to the Shaker community in Hancock, Massachusetts, one of over a dozen villages founded by the religious group in the late eighteenth and early nineteenth centuries. Known for their cooking, though less inventive than sometimes claimed, the Shakers raised flocks of sheep for both wool and meat. Our version of the shanks is a little lustier than the one developed by the celibate sisters, featured in *The Best of Shaker Cooking* (1985) by Amy Bess Miller and Persis Fuller.

- 2 tablespoons bacon drippings or vegetable oil
- 4 lamb shanks, cut by the butcher in 2 sections each
- 1 medium onion, chopped
- 2½ cups chicken or veal stock
- ½ cup halved prunes
- ½ cup halved dried apricots
- 1 cinnamon stick
- ½ teaspoon ground allspice
- ¼ teaspoon ground cloves
- Salt
- ¼ cup minced fresh parsley
- ¼ cup minced fresh mint
- Buttered or olive-oil dressed noodles

Preheat the oven to 350°F.

Warm the drippings in a Dutch oven or other large ovenproof pot over medium-high heat. Add the lamb shanks and brown them well. Reduce the heat to medium-low, stir in the onion, cover the pan, and sweat the onion for 5 minutes, until soft. Add the stock, prunes, apricots, cinnamon, allspice, cloves, and salt to taste. Cover and bake the shanks for about 2 hours, until very tender.

Stir 2 tablespoons each of the parsley and mint into the meat's pan juices. Plate the shanks and their rich juices over noodles. Garnish with the remaining 2 tablespoons parsley and mint and serve.

Two elements enter into successful and happy gatherings at table. The food, whether simple or elaborate, must be carefully prepared; willingly prepared; imaginatively prepared. And the guests—friends, family or strangers—must be conscious of their welcome. Formal dinners of ill-assorted folk invited for the sole purpose of repaying social obligations, are an abomination. The breaking together of bread, the sharing of salt, is too ancient a symbol of friendliness to be profaned.

Marjorie Kinnan Rawlings, Cross Creek Cookery (1942)

Veal Francese

Serves 4

Preparations similar to this one appear in some of the earliest American cookbooks, though this dish acquired an Italian name that suggests a French origin. An Italian-American cook may have developed *francese,* or someone may have given it the European tag to connote elegance, but it's not from another country. The white wine always present in the recipe, and the artichokes that we've added accentuate the delicate taste of the veal, often drowned in the best-known Italian-American preparation of the meat, veal Parmesan.

- 4 veal cutlets, about 3 to 4 ounces each, pounded thin
- 1 egg, lightly beaten
- Salt
- 6 tablespoons unbleached all-purpose flour
- 3 tablespoons unsalted butter
- 1 tablespoon olive oil
- 1½ cups artichoke hearts, halved, or artichoke bottoms, sliced, fresh, frozen, or canned
- ½ cup dry white wine
- Minced flat-leaf parsley

Dip each veal scallop in the egg. Sprinkle each lightly with salt to taste and then with flour. Warm the butter and oil in a large skillet over medium heat. Add 2 of the veal scallops to the skillet, and half of the artichokes, and sauté briefly until the veal is golden brown on each side. Remove the veal and artichokes and place them on a platter. Repeat with the remaining veal and artichokes. When the veal is cooked, pour the wine into the skillet and scrape up the browned bits from the bottom of the skillet. Pour the pan juices over the veal, sprinkle with parsley, and serve.

Veal and Peppers

SERVES 6

Tasting like a cross between Swiss steak and *osso bucco,* this is a slow-simmered Italian-American ragù of veal shoulder with peppers and tomatoes. We got tips on how to make it from Joe DeGiulio, longtime proprietor of Joe's Acorn Market in the Federal Hill neighborhood of Providence, Rhode Island. For accompaniments, consider vinaigrette-tossed greens garnished with Pickled Peppers (page 309) and orzo pasta mixed with olive oil and fresh-grated Parmesan.

2 pounds veal shoulder, top round, or chuck, cut into ¾-inch to 1-inch cubes

2 tablespoons unbleached all-purpose flour

3 tablespoons olive oil

2 large green bell peppers, cut into strips

1 large red bell pepper, cut into strips

1 medium onion, sliced into matchsticks

1 to 2 garlic cloves, sliced thin, optional

⅓ cup dry white wine

2 cups canned crushed tomatoes

½ teaspoon dried basil

½ teaspoon dried crumbled oregano or marjoram

Salt

Toss the veal with the flour.

Warm the olive oil in a Dutch oven or other large heavy pan over medium heat. Add the green and red bell peppers and onion to the oil, and sauté until the vegetables become a bit limp, about 3 minutes. Add the garlic, if you wish, and cook an additional minute. Stir half of the veal into the mixture, and when it loses its raw look, add the remaining veal. When the veal is lightly browned, pour in the wine and let it reduce by half. Add the tomatoes, basil, oregano, and salt to taste. Reduce the heat to medium-low, cover, and simmer for about 2 hours, stirring occasionally, until the veal is quite tender. If the mixture is still very soupy, uncover and cook until the liquid thickens a bit. Serve warm. As with many stew-like dishes, it tastes great after being reheated.

The Act of Toleration, passed by the General Assembly in 1649 with the hearty concurrence of Lord Baltimore, provided for the unrestricted freedom of conscience in Maryland.

By virtue of this Act (extended and revised), the users of this book are encouraged to employ such utensils, materials, methods and devices as may be designed to save them time and patience. It is understood, however, that such usage should in no way interfere with the preparation of a dish to perfection, or otherwise injure or impair the three hundred year old tradition of open door and abundant table to which the Marylander is somewhat consciously devoted.

MARYLAND'S WAY (1963)

Sautéed Sweetbreads on Country Ham

Serves 6

Undoubtedly the most neglected of fine meats in the United States today, veal sweetbreads used to be broadly popular. Virtually every cook had a cherished recipe, commonly a creamed version. This is our favorite in that style, a variation on a dish from Maryland and Virginia.

- 2 pounds veal sweetbreads
- ¼ cup Madeira or dry sherry
- 3 tablespoons unsalted butter
- 3 medium shallots, sliced thin
- 1½ cups sliced wild mushrooms
- 1 cup whipping cream
- ½ cup chicken stock or veal stock, or additional whipping cream
- Pinch of nutmeg
- Pinch of salt
- 6 thin but large slices of Smithfield ham or other salty, smoky ham, warmed
- Minced fresh chervil or flat-leaf parsley

Dunk the sweetbreads in several changes of ice water over about 1 hour. Change the ice water again and refrigerate the sweetbreads covered for at least 2 hours and up to overnight.

Drain the sweetbreads and transfer them to a saucepan. Add water to cover and bring them to a boil over high heat. Reduce the heat to medium-low and simmer the sweetbreads for 8 minutes to parboil them. (Longer cooking at this stage will toughen them.) Drain the sweetbreads again and plunge them into more ice water. They should be very white after these preparation steps.

When cool, peel off as much of the outer membrane as possible and gently pull off any tubes or fat, taking care to keep the sweetbread lobes intact. Transfer the sweetbreads to a shallow nonreactive dish, then sprinkle 2 tablespoons of the Madeira over them. Cover the sweetbreads with plastic, place a plate on top, and weight them down with a couple of heavy cans. Refrigerate for at least 2 hours and up to overnight.

Drain the sweetbreads and slice them with a sharp, thin knife crosswise into medallions about ⅓ inch thick. Melt the butter in a large skillet over medium heat. Stir in the shallots and sauté them just until softened, about 2 minutes. Raise the heat to medium-high, stir in the sweetbreads, and sauté them briefly just until lightly colored with a few crisp edges. Remove the sweetbreads from the skillet with a slotted spoon and tent them with foil. Working quickly, add the mushrooms to the pan and cook until they are limp. Pour in the remaining 2 tablespoons of Madeira, which will quickly cook down by half, and then stir in the cream and chicken stock. Season with nutmeg and only a hint of salt, since the ham is already salty. Cook just until thickened a bit. Arrange the sweetbreads over the ham slices, pour the sauce over the sweetbreads, garnish with chervil, and serve.

Swimming in Sweetbreads

Many American cooks in the past had more than one favorite way of preparing sweetbreads. Mary Lincoln, in *Mrs. Lincoln's Boston Cook Book* (1884), gave as many variations on the meat as on all other veal cuts combined. She sautéed sweetbreads, deep-fried them, baked them larded and in a rich cream sauce, broiled them with butter, stuck them on skewers, and turned them into fritters and croquettes.

Far away in New Orleans, *The Picayune's Creole Cook Book* (1901) provided close to a dozen different recipes for sweetbreads, and raved at length about the glories of the meat. The editors singled out for particular praise Sweetbreads Larded with Mushrooms, Sweetbreads with Green Peas, and Sweetbreads with Truffles, saying these preparations "are in a very distinct manner peculiar to New Orleans, and are elegant entrées at the most distinguished feasts."

FRESH FROM

The Garden

A PERSISTENT MYTH PLACES AMERICANS SOMEWHERE beneath barbarians when it comes to eating our vegetables. Historians tell us we hardly ever ate any raw vegetables in the past, only ones boiled to mush, culinary purists complain about a heavy hand in seasoning, dietitians lob grenades at the choices in our food "pyramid," and nutritionists now actually scold us for not living like Mediterranean peasants. Even our mothers get into the act, or did in the last generation at least, enticing us with pie if we would just finish the peas.

What mother wouldn't admit, and what the other cajolers and critics sometimes forget, is that those peas, freshly harvested from a can, tasted liked tin. American attitudes toward vegetables have often reflected the state of the supply. When we've had fresh, flavorful produce, such as Thomas Jefferson enjoyed from his immense garden, we've usually eaten our vegetables avidly. When we've lacked the soil, skill, or other resources to reap that kind of bounty, or had to rely on the mediocre offerings of supermarkets, we've pushed vegetables to the edge of the plate or resorted to odd ways of making them seem more palatable.

Many people in the past did cook vegetables longer than they do today, a practice conditioned partially by some of the produce they commonly grew—squashes, cabbages, and root vegetables sturdy enough to endure a winter of storage. Plenty of cooks treated tender ingredients more gently and, contrary to some accounts, a lot of them also served raw greens in salads. Most of the earliest American cookbooks contained basic instructions for salads, recommending the use of lettuce, cress, chervil, wild greens, celery, radishes, green onions, herbs, and more. The authors knew to pick greens fresh on the day of the meal for the best results, and often suggested doing it in the early morning while, as one said, "the dew is on."

You have to be a gardener to heed that advice today, but even those of us dependent on farm produce are much closer to the possibility than we've been in generations. Rapidly expanding farmers' markets, roadside farmstands, and stores selling locally raised products all offer sterling opportunities to graze in the national garden. Cooks are taking advantage of the goodness too, serving more vegetables and putting the premium back on freshness. We may be doing it to some extent in self-defense, to fortify those pointy pyramids, but we're eating our vegetables with renewed passion mainly because they taste so much better than tin.

New Mexico Calabacitas

Serves 6 to 8

In both the American Southwest and Mexico, corn and squash were cultivated centuries before European colonization. The Aztecs and their predecessors also raised chiles, and that plant migrated to the Southwest at least by the time of early Spanish settlement in New Mexico. From Guatemala to Taos Pueblo, cooks combined these principal crops in diverse ways, including many variations on calabacitas. Though the Spanish name refers to squash, corn remains an equal partner in the dish in New Mexico, the original corn capital of the country.

One farmer says to me, "You cannot live on vegetable food solely, for it furnishes nothing to make bones with;" and so he religiously devotes a part of his day to supplying his system with the raw material of bones; walking all the while he talks behind his oxen, which, with vegetable-made bones, jerk him and his lumbering plow along in spite of every obstacle.

Henry David Thoreau, Walden (1854)

2 tablespoons vegetable oil
2 tablespoons unsalted butter
5 cups (about 2 pounds) mixed yellow summer squash, zucchini, or light-green skinned calabacita squash
1 medium onion, chopped
1½ cups corn kernels, fresh or frozen
½ to 1 cup chopped roasted mild green chiles, such as New Mexican, fresh or frozen
½ teaspoon salt or more to taste
2 to 4 ounces creamy fresh goat cheese or cream cheese, cut into small bits, optional
Hulled pumpkin seeds (*pepitas*) or hulled sunflower seeds, optional

Warm the oil and butter in a large skillet over medium heat. Add the squash and onion, and sauté for about 10 minutes, until well softened. Add the corn, chiles, and salt, cover, and reduce the heat to medium-low. Cook until very tender, about 10 additional minutes. About halfway through the cooking time, add a few tablespoons of water if the mixture seems dry. Stir in the cheese, if you wish, before removing from the stove, letting it melt into the vegetables. For a contrasting crunch, sprinkle with optional pumpkin or sunflower seeds before serving.

Summer Succotash

SERVES 4

Another Native American dish in origin, succotash may be even older than calabacitas, but it's also possible that people accord it more historic respect just because of the eastern seaboard, English-oriented presentation of our history. Cooks prepared succotash year-round, with dried beans and corn in the winter, but it shines most brightly in the summer when made with fresh vegetables. For peak flavor, use a variety of corn that's not too sweet, such as Golden Bantam, and include the milky scrapings from the cob.

1½ cups baby limas or butter beans, fresh or frozen

Salt and freshly milled black pepper

3 tablespoons unsalted butter

2 ounces fresh green beans, cut into ⅓-inch pieces

4 ears of fresh sweet corn, kernels and scrapings (2 generous cups) removed and kept separate (see Technique Tip)

Cider vinegar

Paprika, optional

Cover the lima beans with water, add salt and pepper to taste, and cook until tender, as little as 5 minutes for small fresh beans or up to 20 minutes for larger frozen beans. Drain the beans, reserving them and the cooking liquid.

Melt the butter in the same saucepan over medium heat. Stir in the green beans and corn kernels, season with salt and pepper, and cook for a couple of minutes, just until limp. Add the reserved cooking liquid, cover the mixture, and simmer for about 10 minutes, until the green beans are tender. Stir in the corn scrapings and lima beans, reduce the heat to low, and cook uncovered for a few minutes longer until piping hot with little remaining liquid. Add just a spot of vinegar to balance the corn's sweetness—not so much that you really taste it. Spoon into a dish, dust with paprika, if you wish, and serve.

TECHNIQUE TIP:
One of Cheryl's great-grandmothers made what she called "corn off the cob," which always tasted remarkably creamy. Her secret, like that of many cooks before her, was to skim a portion of the kernels off the ears, then scrape the cobs to release all the custardy milk. For succotash or other dishes, stand ears of corn upright for handling. With a medium knife, slide down the ear, slicing off the top half of the kernels. Rotate the ear and repeat the motion until you've given the entire ear a trim. Turn the knife over on its dull top side and scrape down the ear again, pressing against the cob to release the thick, semiliquid cream.

Nantucket Corn Pudding

SERVES 6

Fresh corn pudding may owe its inspiration to the popular colonial dish known as Indian or hasty pudding, which was itself a cornmeal adaptation of a flour-based English porridge. The earlier pudding used corn as a grain, while today's version treats it as a vegetable. This simple rendition comes from a Helen Witty recipe in a *Cuisine* magazine article, a recipe so tasty we've saved and savored it for nearly twenty years.

- 2 large eggs
- 1 cup half-and-half
- ¾ teaspoon salt or more to taste
- ⅛ teaspoon ground white pepper
- Pinch of nutmeg
- 8 to 10 ears of fresh sweet corn, kernels and scrapings (4½ to 5 cups) removed as in the Technique Tip, page 240
- ¾ cup crushed pilot crackers, hardtack, Nabisco Uneeda biscuits, or oyster crackers
- 3 tablespoons unsalted butter, melted
- 2 to 3 ounces sharp Cheddar cheese, grated (¼ to ⅓ cup)
- Paprika

Preheat the oven to 350°F. Grease a medium baking dish.

Whisk the eggs and half-and-half together in a large bowl along with the salt, white pepper, and nutmeg. Mix in the corn kernels and scrapings, ½ cup of the crackers, and 2 tablespoons of the melted butter. Spoon the pudding into the prepared baking dish and scatter the cheese over it. In a small bowl, mix together the remaining ¼ cup of crackers and 1 tablespoon of butter, and sprinkle them over the cheese. Dust with paprika for a bit of extra color.

Bake the pudding for 45 to 50 minutes, until puffed and golden brown. The edges should be a bit crusty, but the center should remain a little soft. Serve the pudding hot.

Maque Choux

Serves 4 to 6

Many things can go into a maque choux in Louisiana, but fresh corn is the essential ingredient. Many cooks make the dish a center-of-the-plate preparation, with the addition of crawfish, chicken, or the local ham known as tasso. We like to serve it on the side with "Barbecued" Shrimp (page 121) or Fried Rabbit Quarters (page 226).

- 2 tablespoons unsalted butter
- 2 tablespoons unrefined corn oil, preferably, or additional unsalted butter
- 1 medium yellow onion, chopped fine
- ½ medium red or orange bell pepper, diced
- ½ medium green bell pepper, diced
- 6 ears of fresh sweet corn, kernels and scrapings (about 4 cups) removed as in the Technique Tip, page 240
- ½ teaspoon ground white pepper
- Pinch or two of cayenne pepper
- Salt
- 1 to 3 tablespoons milk, optional

Warm together the butter and oil in a medium saucepan over medium heat. Stir in the onion and bell peppers, and sauté until soft, about 5 minutes. Add the corn kernels and sauté for several additional minutes. Stir in the corn scrapings, white pepper, cayenne, and a generous bit of salt. Cover and simmer for 10 additional minutes, stirring up from the bottom once or twice. The mixture should be thick, but add some or all of the milk if it becomes dry. Serve warm.

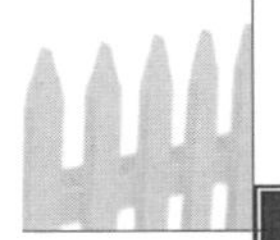

Essence of Tomato Salad

Serves you or a group of friends on a hot summer night

According to Andrew Smith in *Food History News,* Sandra Oliver's fascinating newsletter, Spanish settlers introduced tomatoes in the South around the turn of the eighteenth century, and African Americans who came up from the Caribbean soon incorporated them into southern cooking. Though tomatoes are native to the New World, perhaps originally Peru, Northerners didn't eat them until more than a century after Southerners—not because they thought them poisonous, an old myth, but because they didn't suit the climate or cuisine. Tomatoes thus became an early dividing line between the food of the two regions, linking southern cooking more closely to other New World styles. This recipe is the simplest of all preparations for the juicy orb, more representative today of California than either the South or the North.

Juicy-ripe tomatoes, as many varieties, shapes, and colors as you can find

Sweet onion, sliced paper-thin, optional

Extra-virgin olive oil

Salt and freshly milled black pepper

Minced fresh mint or basil, or both

Cut large tomatoes, such as Brandywine, Big and Better Boys, Striped German, and Cherokee Purple into medium-thick slices. Medium tomatoes, such as Jubilee and Green Zebra, can be sliced or cut into wedges. Halve small tomatoes, such as Green Grape, cherry, and yellow pear, and leave whole the tiniest tomatoes, like currant and Sweet 100.

Arrange the tomatoes on a big platter, starting with the largest, alternating colors and shapes, and interspersing them occasionally with onion if you wish. Drizzle the completed arrangement with the barest amount of oil, just enough to make it all glisten, then sprinkle salt and pepper and scatter herbs lightly over all. Serve and savor the very best the Americas offer.

Short List of Simple American Favorites, No Recipe Needed

- Avocado slices with a splash of vinaigrette
- Pole beans long-simmered with a chunk of fatback
- Steamed broccoli with a squeeze of lemon
- Carrot-stick and celery-stalk snacks
- Boiled or grilled corn on the cob dripping with warm butter
- Cold cucumber slices with vinegar and sugar
- Sautéed spring fiddleheads
- Steamed sugar snap peas
- Baked russet potatoes (preferably without the silly foil)
- Cherry tomatoes right from the vine
- Baked whole tomatoes
- Roasted sweet potatoes with honey butter
- Crisp, chilled watercress

Pensacola Gazpachee

Serves 6 to 8

People reading Mary Randolph's *The Virginia Housewife* (1824) for the first time are likely to drop the book, not to mention their jaw, when they come to the recipe for "Gaspacho—Spanish." It's not the cold tomato soup you expect, but something of a cross between it and a European-style bread salad. Today, Pensacola, Florida, boasts the strongest association with that preparation, an exuberant and luscious layering of red-ripe tomatoes, cucumbers, seasonings, and hardtack biscuits.

- About 8 ounces hardtack or Nabisco Uneeda biscuits, preferably, or dried French or Italian bread cubes
- ⅔ cup mayonnaise
- ¼ cup minced fresh basil
- 1 tablespoon minced fresh oregano
- 2 garlic cloves, minced
- ½ to 1 teaspoon Dijon mustard, optional
- 3 large red-ripe tomatoes, chopped
- 2 large cucumbers, peeled, seeded, and diced
- 1 medium onion, diced fine
- 1 large green bell pepper, diced fine
- Salt and freshly milled black pepper
- Paprika
- Basil leaves, leaf lettuce, or thin-sliced romaine ribbons

Soak the hardtack biscuits in water for at least several hours and up to overnight. (If using Uneeda biscuits or bread, soak them just briefly until very soft.)

Stir together the mayonnaise, basil, oregano, garlic, and optional mustard. Chill until needed.

Squeeze as much moisture as possible from the now-sodden hardtack biscuits and arrange half of them in the bottom of a salad bowl, preferably a broad shallow one. Scatter half of the tomatoes, cucumbers, onion, and bell pepper over the bread. Season lightly with salt and pepper, and spread half of the mayonnaise over the vegetables. Repeat with the remaining ingredients. Refrigerate the salad for at least an hour and up to 6 hours. The salad should be moist but not watery.

Dust with paprika before serving and garnish with basil or lettuce.

Stewed Tomatoes

Serves 4

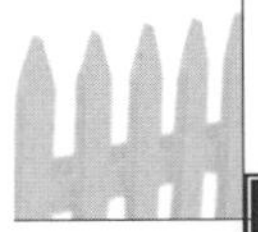

An old American favorite recently robbed of a big audience by steam-table and school-cafeteria travesties, stewed tomatoes deserve another chance. Here we cook them more lightly than some people do, and add crunchy bread cubes for a contrast in texture. Serve them on the side with grilled chicken or fish.

A bit of tomato skin was once as much out of place at a dinner table as a bowie knife. The discovery that tomato skins contain highly valued vitamins makes them *salonfaehig,* so whether to serve tomatoes skinned or unskinned rests with the hostess' sense of delicacy or her desire for health.

Irma Rombauer,
Joy of Cooking (1943)

- 2 thick bacon slices, chopped
- 1 slice good white bread, crusts trimmed
- 1 celery stalk, chopped fine
- 2 tablespoons minced onion
- 1½ pounds very ripe tomatoes, cut into wedges
- 1 to 2 teaspoons packed brown sugar
- 1 teaspoon paprika
- ¾ teaspoon salt
- ½ teaspoon freshly milled black pepper

Fry the bacon in a skillet over medium heat until brown and crisp. Remove the bacon from the rendered drippings with a slotted spoon, drain it, and reserve. Cut the bread into bite-size cubes, stir them into the hot drippings, and cook until lightly toasted. Remove the bread cubes with a slotted spoon and reserve them.

Stir the celery and onion into the remaining drippings (there won't be much left), then cover and sweat the vegetables for about 3 minutes until soft. Add the tomatoes and the remaining seasonings, cover again, and continue cooking for about 15 additional minutes, until the tomatoes are juicy and tender. If they are downright soupy, uncover and cook over high heat briefly to eliminate some of the liquid. Just before serving, mix in the reserved bread cubes and bacon.

Fried Green Tomatoes

Serves 4 to 6

Americans fry red tomatoes too, and used to do it all over the country, not just in the South. Green tomatoes hit the skillet more often than their ripe mates simply because frying's a fine way to finish off an immature crop before the frost bites.

- 1 to 1½ cups stone-ground cornmeal
- 1½ teaspoons salt
- ¾ teaspoon freshly milled black pepper
- ¼ teaspoon cayenne pepper
- Pinch of sugar, optional
- 4 to 6 medium firm green tomatoes, sliced ¼ to ⅓ inch thick
- Bacon drippings, vegetable oil, or olive oil for pan-frying

Mix together the cornmeal, salt, pepper, and cayenne on a plate. If the tomatoes seem especially acidic, add the sugar. Dredge the tomato slices in the mixture. Warm enough drippings in a large skillet over medium heat to cover the skillet generously. Fry the tomatoes about 2 minutes per side, until golden. Serve hot.

TECHNIQUE TIP: A slice of fried green tomato with some bacon and lettuce on toasted sourdough bread makes a great BLT or, with a piece of mild Cheddar or mozzarella, a BCLT. When we've got a gang to cook for, instead of frying individual slices of tomatoes we bake them gratin style. Layer tomato slices of the same size in a shallow dish, tuck paper-thin onion slices in around them, and top with crisp crumbled bacon, salt, pepper, cayenne, grated mild cheese, and buttered cornbread crumbs. Bake in a 375°F oven for about 20 minutes, until the topping is crisp and the tomatoes are creamy and heated through.

If you would fry
tomatoes right,
Select large fresh ones,
clean and bright;
Slice them as thick as
are your thumbs,
And roll them well in
cracker crumbs;
Add salt and
pepper to the taste,
A little sugar too in haste;
Then with a fire hot
and bright,
Heat well your pan and
do not slight
The lard and butter,
lest it burn.
When brown on one
side over-turn;
And when at last, both
sides are done,
Hot from the spider,
give us one.

From an unnamed New Hampshire cookbook quoted in Cora, Rose, and Bob Brown's *America Cooks* (1940)

Green Beans with Country Ham and Peanuts

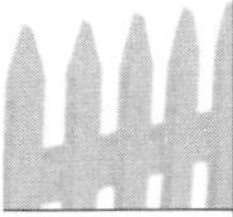

Serves 6

This is a contemporary take on the old notion of cooking beans with salted or smoked pork, a practice common across the country with different beans. We've found a number of green bean dishes with ham, nuts, or both, but have adapted this particular combination from a recipe given by John Shields in *Chesapeake Bay Cooking* (1998).

- 1½ to 1¾ pounds fresh thin green beans
- ¼ cup plus 2 tablespoons unsalted butter
- ⅔ cup roasted salted peanuts
- 1 cup julienned country ham or other salty, smoky ham
- 1½ tablespoons brown mustard

Bring several inches of lightly salted water to a boil in a large saucepan over high heat. Plunge the beans into the water and reduce the heat to medium. Cook until tender, with no raw taste, 7 to 10 minutes. Drain the beans, then cover them with ice water to retain the deep green color. When cool, drain the beans again.

Shortly before you plan to serve the beans, melt the butter in a large skillet. Stir in the peanuts and sauté them for several minutes, just long enough to deepen their color and crunch. Stir in the ham and mustard, and heat the ham through. Add the green beans and toss to coat them. Arrange them in a serving bowl, laid out as best you can, with the beans and ham running the same direction. Serve immediately.

Fresh Butter Beans

SERVES 4

Butter beans is the southern term for small baby limas, as tender and creamy as the name implies. Limas themselves also come honestly by their appellation, a reference to the capital of Peru, where the beans originated eons ago. They traveled ancient trade routes through Mesoamerica into the Southwest, but like several New World crops, they arrived in the English colonies via Europe, a product of Spanish dissemination.

- 2 ounces salt pork, diced, or 2 teaspoons peanut oil
- 1 medium onion, chopped fine
- 1 teaspoon minced fresh thyme or ½ teaspoon dried thyme
- 1 to 2 small dried hot red chiles
- ½ teaspoon salt or more to taste
- 4 cups butter beans or baby limas, fresh or frozen
- Fresh thyme sprigs, optional

Fry the salt pork in a large saucepan over medium heat until the fat has rendered, about 10 minutes. Remove the pork with a slotted spoon and discard it. Add the onion to the drippings, cover, and sweat for about 5 minutes, until soft. Pour in 2 cups of water, then add the thyme, chiles, and salt. Bring the liquid to a boil uncovered, then add the beans. Cover again and cook over medium-low heat for 25 to 30 minutes, until tender. If the beans begin to get dry, add more water to keep them soupy. Remove the chiles, and serve the beans garnished, if you wish, with thyme sprigs.

On a summer evening some years ago, two of the South's most celebrated writers, William Faulkner and Katherine Anne Porter, were dining together at a plush restaurant in Paris. Everything had been laid on to perfection; a splendid meal had been consumed, a bottle of fine Burgundy emptied, and thimble-size glasses of an expensive liqueur drained. The maître d' and an entourage of waiters hovered close by, ready to satisfy any final whim. "Back home the butter beans are in," said Faulkner, peering into the distance, "the speckled ones." Miss Porter fiddled with her glass and stared into space. "Blackberries," she said, wistfully.

EUGENE WALTER,
AMERICAN COOKING:
SOUTHERN STYLE (1971)

Yellow Squash Casserole

SERVES 6

Famed eighteenth-century naturalist John Bartram once pronounced a dish of boiled squash "poor entertainment." Some preparations still merit that memorable epitaph, but this soufflélike casserole of summer squash can take an Oscar on any stage. The common crookneck variety suggested in the recipe is one of our oldest domesticated squashes, probably native to New Jersey, according to William Woys Weaver in *Heirloom Vegetable Gardening* (1997).

- 1¾ pounds crookneck yellow squash or other yellow summer squash
- ¼ pound zucchini or additional yellow summer squash
- ½ cup coarse-chopped carrots
- ¼ cup (½ stick) unsalted butter
- 1 large onion, preferably yellow, chopped
- 1 plump garlic clove, minced
- 1¼ cups saltine or Ritz cracker crumbs
- ½ cup grated mild to medium Cheddar cheese
- Hot pepper sauce, such as Tabasco
- Salt and freshly milled black pepper
- 2 eggs, lightly beaten

Preheat the oven to 350°F. Butter a medium baking dish.

Slice the yellow squash and zucchini lengthwise into quarters, then cut into ½-inch-thick wedges. Place the yellow squash, zucchini, and carrots in a saucepan, barely cover with water, and salt well. Bring to a boil, reduce the heat to medium, and cover. Cook about 20 minutes, until the vegetables are very soft.

Meanwhile, warm 3 tablespoons of the butter in a medium skillet over medium-low heat. Stir in the onion and cook slowly until very soft and translucent, 6 to 8 minutes. Add the garlic and cook an additional minute. Scrape the mixture into a mixing bowl. Wipe out the skillet, return it to medium-low heat, and add to it the remaining tablespoon of butter. Stir in ½ cup of the cracker crumbs and cook briefly until the crumbs are golden. Scrape them onto a small plate and reserve them.

Drain the squash mixture, mashing the vegetables just a bit. Spoon it into the mixing bowl. Stir in the remaining ¾ cup of cracker crumbs, cheese, and a good splash or two of the pepper sauce. Salt and pepper generously to taste. Stir in the eggs and spoon the mixture into the prepared baking dish. Scatter the toasted cracker crumbs over the top. Bake uncovered for about 30 minutes, until golden brown and lightly firm in the center. Serve hot.

Spiced Acorn Squash

Serves 4

Americans often pair winter squash with something sweet, such as maple syrup, molasses, cranberries, or apples. We like the approach of Vertamae Grosvenor in *Vibration Cooking* (1970), combining honey with crunchy sesame seeds. Halves of acorn squash make good individual portions, but other types of winter squash also work, cut if necessary into manageable chunks.

2 acorn squash, halved
4 tablespoons honey
Pinch of ground mace or nutmeg per squash half
Salt and freshly milled black pepper
Approximately ¼ cup (½ stick) unsalted butter
1 to 2 tablespoons sesame seeds

Preheat the oven to 375°F. Oil a baking dish.

Remove and discard the membranes and seeds from the squash. Set the squash halves, cut side up, in a shallow baking dish. Drizzle each squash cavity with about 1 tablespoon of honey. Sprinkle with mace, salt and pepper to taste, and dot with butter. Cover with foil and bake for about 40 minutes, until very tender. Remove the foil, sprinkle on the sesame seeds, and bake for 5 to 10 minutes longer, until the seeds turn golden. If you want a more burnished, caramel-like surface, omit the uncovered baking. Instead, follow Vertamae's lead and "stick under the broiler for a hot minute," being careful not to burn the sesame seeds. Serve warm.

Jailed Salads

Made much like glue from the glutinous material in animal bones and tissue, gelatin seems an unlikely candidate for elegance. It played that role, however, in ornate molded desserts on aristocratic tables in Europe, and came to the colonies as a symbol of refined luxury, used in blancmange and jellies at special meals. Most Americans made the gelatin from calves' feet in a laborious process that few people without kitchen help would attempt.

The rise of the food-processing industry in the late nineteenth century changed everything dramatically. Boxed sheets of gelatin appeared first, and then in the 1890s, easy-to-use powdered gelatin and Jell-O. Middle-class cooks leaped at the opportunity to enjoy the food of the wealthy, and Jell-O pushed the upscale image actively in its advertising, showing fashionable ladies serving the quivery concoction in champagne glasses.

Salads had a similar association with upper-class dining at the time, and prospered in many cases in direct proportion to their sweetness, leading to a quick mating with commercial gelatin. Charles Knox, a pioneer in the business, turned the idea into an institution by the widespread promotion of "perfection salad." A kind of imprisoned coleslaw, with cabbage, celery, and bell peppers captured in a gelled mold, the salad inspired thousands of others. The dish was so influential that Laura Shapiro, in a study of turn-of-the-century cooking, characterized the period with the name *Perfection Salad* (1986). The national craze didn't start subsiding until the 1960s and 1970s, and even today, versions of congealed salads still show up on many a potluck table.

The Gardener's Wife Salad

Serves 6 to 8

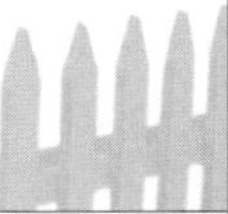

The Picayune's Creole Cook Book (1901) provided the name and inspiration for this mixed vegetable platter, composed as a gardener's wife (or husband) might from the freshest seasonal ingredients. The book was among the first to focus extensively on vegetable salads, relegating mayonnaise-bound meat and fish mixtures to a secondary role for light meals or teas. The editors explained that the Creoles of New Orleans served salads "for breakfast, luncheon and dinners," always dressed in fine oil and vinegar, the typical treatment elsewhere as well. Residents liked them partially, the book suggests, because of health considerations, believing that an abundance of oil prevented headaches and lettuce acted as a sedative for nervous people. Today we've got different reasons for feeling self-assured about the health benefits, but the salad's enduring virtue, we think, is the lively harmony of textures, colors, and flavors.

- ¾ cup extra-virgin olive oil
- 3 tablespoons red-wine vinegar or more to taste
- Salt
- 3 medium carrots, shredded
- 2 large cooked beets (a combination of red and gold beets is nice), shredded
- 2 medium cucumbers, peeled, halved lengthwise, seeded, and cut into thin matchsticks
- 1 medium celery root (celeriac), peeled and cut into thin matchsticks, or 1 medium fennel bulb, cut into thin matchsticks, optional
- Lettuce leaves or watercress
- Big handful of slim baby green beans, blanched, or fresh peas or pea shoots, optional
- Small handful of thin sweet onion or red onion slices, or scallion rings
- Freshly milled black pepper

Whisk together the oil and vinegar with a big pinch of salt in a small bowl. Toss each type of shredded or sliced vegetable with just enough dressing to coat lightly. Arrange them on a platter, tucking them into or around the lettuce. If you are using green beans, toss them in enough dressing to make them glisten. Scatter the beans or peas and onion slices over the other vegetables as you wish. Season with a generous grinding of pepper. Serve the salad immediately or chill for up to several hours.

TECHNIQUE TIP: This salad benefits from long, lovely strands of the various vegetables. Shred them with the julienne disk of a food processor, on a box grater, or with a mandoline, even an inexpensive plastic one. For optimum results with a food processor, take an extra moment to cut the vegetables to just the right length for the feed tube and stack them evenly in the tube. With a box grater, you can create longer strands by rolling the vegetables about a quarter-turn while you slide them down the side. The technique lengthens the exposed surface.

Mixed Vegetable Stir-fry

Serves 4 to 6

If Chinese cooks had brought a wok to colonial America and stir-fried vegetables, they might have been suspected of sorcery. The idea of cooking small bits of food over high heat until crisp-tender, so foreign to accepted European traditions, needed almost a century to make headway in home kitchens, even after Americans began eating Chinese-style dishes. Given its English name of stir-frying in Buwei Yang Chao's *How to Cook and Eat in Chinese* (1945), the method went mainstream in the 1970s and quickly established a place in our cooking repertory. Stir-frying is about technique, not exact ingredients, so use this recipe as a guideline, varying the vegetables and amounts as you wish and changing or omitting the sauce if you prefer.

SAUCE
- 1 teaspoon cornstarch
- 3 tablespoons oyster sauce
- 3 tablespoons soy sauce
- 1 tablespoon dry sherry or rice wine
- 1 teaspoon sugar
- 1 teaspoon Asian sesame oil, optional

- 1 tablespoon vegetable oil
- 1 tablespoon minced fresh ginger
- 2 teaspoons minced garlic or more to taste
- ½ teaspoon Chinese chili paste or more to taste, or crushed dried hot red chiles to taste
- 2 cups snow peas, tipped and stringed
- 1 cup sliced water chestnuts
- Handful of thin red bell pepper strips or carrot strips, optional
- 2 cups bite-size broccoli florets and tender stems, or halved baby bok choy, blanched

Combine the sauce ingredients in a small bowl with ¼ cup of water and mix well.

Heat a wok or large skillet over highest heat. When very hot, pour in the oil and swirl it around to coat the wok. Quickly stir in the ginger, garlic, and chili paste. Cook for about 10 seconds, then stir in the snow peas, water chestnuts, and any other uncooked vegetables. Stir-fry for about 1 additional minute, then pour in the sauce, stirring continuously to avoid lumps. When combined, add the broccoli, stir again, and heat through. Serve immediately.

Artichokes New Orleans

Serves 4

Imported from its Mediterranean homeland in colonial times, the artichoke attracted few devoted fans in the United States until Italian immigrants began reaching the country in significant numbers in the late nineteenth century. Even today, artichokes remain most popular in areas where Italians settled, including New Orleans and California, the garden state that raises the country's entire commercial crop. This is a contemporary version of a classic New Orleans preparation, baked at the end with a crunchy bread crumb stuffing.

- 2 medium to large artichokes
- 1 lemon, halved
- 3 to 4 tablespoons Louisiana crab-boil seasoning, such as Zatarain's, or Cajun seasoning blend
- 2 garlic cloves, slivered
- 1½ cups packed fresh bread crumbs
- 2 tablespoons olive oil plus more to drizzle
- ¼ cup freshly grated Parmesan cheese
- ¼ cup sliced briny green olives
- 2 tablespoons minced flat-leaf parsley

With scissors, cut the thorny ends from the outer leaves of the artichokes. Slice off the top one-third of each and trim the stems. As you work, rub the lemon halves over the cut surfaces to avoid discoloration.

Place the artichokes in a large nonreactive saucepan and cover them by about 1 inch with water. Squeeze the lemon halves into the water and then toss in the remaining lemon "shells." Stir in the crab boil and garlic, and bring the artichokes to a boil over high heat. Reduce the heat to a simmer, cover, and cook the artichokes until tender, 15 to 20 minutes depending on size. When done, the leaves should release easily if tugged. Dunk the artichokes in cold water. Drain upside down.

When cool enough to handle, reach inside and pull out the center cone of inner leaves from the first artichoke, using a quick twist of the wrist. With a small spoon, scrape out the fuzzy choke, which should now be visible. Repeat with the remaining artichoke, then halve both of them.

Preheat the oven to 375° F. Oil a baking dish large enough to hold the artichokes cut side up.

Stir together the bread crumbs and olive oil in a medium bowl. Mix in the cheese, olives, and parsley. Pack equal portions of the mixture into each artichoke. Drizzle a little oil over the top of each. Bake 20 to 25 minutes, until the artichokes and filling are heated through and the top is crusty. Serve hot or at room temperature.

Skillet Asparagus

SERVES 4 TO 6

Americans raised asparagus in kitchen gardens from an early period. They often boiled the delicate vegetable to a very tender state, and then served it English-style on toast or "ambushed" inside a roll with a cream sauce. We prefer an approach, suggested by Edna Lewis in *The Taste of Country Cooking* (1977), that not only concentrates the flavor of asparagus that isn't freshly picked (the usual situation), but respects the innate taste of any just gathered from the garden or the wild. You can add a touch of vinaigrette to the spears, though the best need no embellishment.

1½ pounds fresh asparagus spears, tough ends trimmed or peeled

2 tablespoons unsalted butter

Salt and freshly milled black pepper

Rinse the asparagus in water and shake it, leaving the water that clings to it. Warm the butter in a 10-inch or 12-inch skillet over medium-high heat. When the butter is foaming, add the asparagus in a shallow layer running in a single direction. Cover and cook for 3 minutes. Roll the spears to their other side, season with salt and pepper, and continue cooking until tender with a few browned spots, 3 to 5 additional minutes. Serve immediately.

Broccoli-Rice Casserole

SERVES 6 TO 8

A perennial potluck favorite, with or without the rice, for much of the twentieth century, this and other vegetable casseroles often gained favor as a way of cooking flavorless canned or frozen ingredients. Casseroles became doubly appealing as a quick and economical dish after the Campbell company convinced cooks that its soups made a good substitute for sauces. This trend gathered momentum with the introduction in 1934 of cream-of-mushroom soup, which quickly usurped the role played previously by the bland but ubiquitous white sauce. The surprise is how tasty this casserole can be when made with fresh broccoli and a genuine, though simple, sauce.

- 1¼ pounds fresh broccoli florets and tender stems, chopped
- ½ cup chopped onion
- ¼ cup (½ stick) unsalted butter
- ¾ cup minced button mushrooms
- 1 tablespoon unbleached all-purpose flour
- 12-ounce can evaporated milk
- ½ teaspoon salt or more to taste
- ⅛ teaspoon ground white pepper or more to taste
- 2 cups sharp Cheddar cheese, grated
- 1½ cups cooked rice

Preheat the oven to 350° F. Butter a medium baking dish.

Steam the broccoli and onion together for 7 to 10 minutes, until very tender.

Meanwhile, melt the butter in a skillet over medium heat. Stir in the mushrooms and cook until well softened, 5 to 8 minutes. Sprinkle the flour over the mushrooms and stir to combine. Continue cooking for another couple of minutes to eliminate the flour's raw taste. Stir in the milk, ½ teaspoon of salt, and the white pepper, and continue cooking until lightly thickened, about 3 additional minutes. Add all but about ⅓ cup of the cheese to the sauce, stir to melt it, and remove the skillet from the heat.

Salt the broccoli lightly if you wish. Layer one-third of it in the prepared dish. Top with one-third of the rice and cheese sauce. Repeat two more times with the remaining ingredients. Sprinkle the rest of the cheese over the casserole. Cover and bake for about 25 minutes, until heated through and bubbly at the edges. Serve hot.

Never question the contents of your neighbor's compost heap or casserole.

LOUISE ANDREWS KENT AND ELIZABETH KENT GAY, *MRS. APPLEYARD'S SUMMER KITCHEN* (1957)

Wilted Greens with Hot Bacon Dressing

SERVES 4 TO 6

Hot bacon drippings can flavor a salad even better than the edible flowers in the following recipe, but the dressing is on the opposite, downhill course currently in fashionable tastes. It gained favor originally with rural and poor families who lacked access to olive or other vegetable oils, and had to be used hot so that the fat didn't congeal. Today the dressing makes a rich, lively change of pace, worth sneaking in occasionally when you're not having any doctors to dinner. We especially like it on Black-Seeded Simpson lettuce, an old favorite in American gardens, but it adds a smoky lustiness to any tender, leafy greens. Some Southerners call this a "killed salad," and just north of the Mason-Dixon line, cooks may refer to it as "Dutched," after the Pennsylvania Dutch.

- 12 cups torn leaf lettuce, dandelion greens, baby spinach, or other tender greens (see Ingredient Tip)
- 6 ounces sliced smoky bacon
- 2 to 3 scallions, trimmed of any limp ends and sliced into thin rings
- 1 garlic clove, minced
- 1 tablespoon honey
- 3 tablespoons cider vinegar
- Thin-sliced radishes, optional
- Salt and freshly milled black pepper

Arrange the greens in a large salad bowl.

Fry the bacon in a skillet over medium heat until brown and crisp. Remove the bacon from the drippings, crumble it, and reserve it. Add to the drippings the scallions and garlic, and sauté 1 minute. Add the honey and vinegar and heat through, stirring until the honey dissolves. Immediately pour the hot dressing over the greens and toss lightly. Like cooked spinach, the greens will reduce substantially in volume. Sprinkle the bacon over the salad, along with the radishes if you wish. Season with salt and pepper, and serve hot or at room temperature.

INGREDIENT TIP: Tender young spinach works well in this recipe, but we take a modified approach with more mature leaves, such as crinkly savoy spinach. After frying and reserving the bacon, we stir orange juice, red-wine vinegar, curry powder, and a hint of brown sugar into the drippings. When the mixture is merely warm, not hot, we pour it over the spinach and toss to combine, seeking to relax the greens rather than wilt them. We then sprinkle the salad generously with salt and pepper, toss again, and top it with thin slices of red onion, quartered hard-boiled eggs, and the bacon.

TECHNIQUE TIP: If a doctor drops by unexpectedly at dinnertime, blend the bacon drippings with some olive oil, and say that it's a fabulous new brand of oil you discovered on vacation in Tuscany. Cut the amount of bacon to 3 or 4 slices, and top off the drippings with the oil to measure ½ cup total. Gently warm through and continue as in the recipe. Even with the lighter lubrication, you retain much of the original bacon flavor.

I shudder wholeheartedly and without either affectation or regret at what and how we ate [at college in the late 1920s].

We would buy ginger ale, rolls, cream cheese, anchovy paste, bottled "French" dressing, and at least six heads of the most beautiful expensive lettuce we could find in that little town where only snobs ate anything but cabbage, turnips, and parsnips for the winter months.

We would lock the door, and mix the cheese and anchovy together and open the ginger ale. Then we would toast ourselves solemnly in our toothbrush mugs, loosen the belts on our woolen bathrobes, and tear into that crisp cool delightful lettuce like three starved rabbits.

Now and then one or another of us would get up, go to a window and open it, bare her little breasts to the cold sweep of air, and intone dramatically, 'Pneu-mo-*o-o-onia!*' Then we would all burst into completely helpless giggles, until we had laughed enough to hold a little more lettuce. Yes, that was the best part of the year.

M.F.K. FISHER,
THE GASTRONOMICAL ME (1943)

Mixed Salad of Greens, Nasturtiums, and Herbs

SERVES 6

A mixture of herbs, edible flowers, and greens may look chic on a contemporary restaurant menu, but it's actually rather old-fashioned. Nasturtium blossoms and leaves, which Americans imported originally from the West Indies, became prized additions to salads by the nineteenth century, joining different flowers eaten in various ways in earlier times. Substitute other edible blossoms if you wish, and tailor the herbs to your taste, striving for a blend of distinct yet harmonizing flavors and textures.

SIMPLE GARLIC VINAIGRETTE

½ cup plus 1 tablespoon extra-virgin olive oil

1 plump garlic clove, minced

1 teaspoon Dijon mustard

Salt

2 to 3 tablespoons tarragon vinegar or white-wine vinegar

4 large handfuls tender salad greens, preferably a mix of leaf and soft-head lettuces, such as butter, Bibb, oakleaf, baby romaine, and Lollo Rossa

2 large handfuls of nasturtium leaves or peppery greens, such as arugula

1 large handful of mixed herbs (avoid any with odd textures like spiky rosemary and fuzzy borage leaves)

1 dozen nasturtium blossoms, 6 shredded into individual petals and 6 whole (see Ingredient Tip)

Freshly milled black pepper

Prepare the dressing, combining the oil, garlic, mustard, and salt in a small bowl. Let the dressing sit for about 15 minutes so that the garlic flavor fully infuses the oil. Whisk in the vinegar, adjusting the seasoning a bit if necessary, and reserve.

Toss the greens, nasturtium leaves, herbs, and shredded nasturtium blossoms together in a salad bowl, preferably one that is broad and shallow. Give the dressing another good whisk and drizzle about two-thirds of it over the greens. Toss again, adding more dressing if needed. Add a bit more salt as needed and a good grinding of pepper. Arrange a mounded tangle of salad on chilled individual salad plates. Garnish each with a whole nasturtium blossom and serve.

INGREDIENT TIP: An increasing number of supermarkets sell edible flowers, but most are inexpensive, simple, and compact to grow at home, allowing you to pluck them at your pleasure for a salad. Consider raising nasturtiums, calendulas, roses, Johnny-jump-ups, bee balm, borage, and chives. Nasturtiums and chives have particularly fetching flavors, while other pretty faces, such as roses and calendulas, taste a little flatter. Scatter flowers in a salad with a light hand. A single whole blossom can be a refreshing touch, but a big bowlful may make guests feel like grazing goats.

TECHNIQUE TIP: A few tablespoons of vinaigrette should dress about two large handfuls of greens. Dressings should just cling to the greens, not puddle in the bottom of the salad bowl. We work with the general but oft-broken rule of 4 parts oil to 1 part acid in our salads, always adding vinegar or lemon juice in dribbles in case their strength threatens to overcome a fine oil sooner than anticipated. Also bear in mind that the more tender and delicate the greens, the less vinegar you'll need. Leftover dressing can be refrigerated for another day, but avoid making large batches in advance because refrigeration can damage the delicate flavor of olive oil.

Iceberg Wedge with Maytag Blue Dressing

Serves 6

Gulp as you might at this unregenerate suggestion, the salad is luscious when you use crisp, glacier-cold lettuce and an exuberantly cheesy dressing. In recent decades, iceberg lettuce has become a well-flogged symbol of all that is wrong with American food, ridiculed as an agribusiness specialty raised for its indestructible shipping and storing qualities rather than flavor, and dismissed as fast-food fodder at best. The critics score many appropriate hits, but sometimes forget that iceberg lettuce is an American heirloom variety, with a progenitor dating back to the early nineteenth century, and that it shines in the right preparation, like any other vegetable. Iceberg needs a hefty dressing, and its tremendous commercial success in the twentieth century helped spawn many varieties, including Thousand Island and ranch. We like a wedge of the lettuce best with a blue cheese dressing, made with an assertive cheese such as Iowa's Maytag Blue.

DRESSING

- ¾ cup mayonnaise
- ½ cup sour cream
- 1 tablespoon fresh lemon juice
- 1 tablespoon white vinegar
- 1 tablespoon minced parsley
- 1 plump garlic clove, minced
- ¾ cup crumbled blue cheese, preferably Maytag or other American blue cheese
- Salt

- 1 medium head iceberg lettuce, well chilled
- Freshly milled black pepper, coarsely ground

Prepare the dressing, first combining the mayonnaise and sour cream in a small bowl. Mix in the remaining ingredients and refrigerate until needed. (The dressing can be made a day ahead if you wish.) Let the dressing sit at room temperature for about 10 minutes before serving.

Just before serving, cut the cold lettuce through its stem end into 6 wedges. Remove any loose, limp leaves and discard them. Arrange the wedges on well-chilled salad plates, spoon dressing over each, add sprinklings of pepper, and serve immediately.

Sarah Tyson Rorer, 1849–1937

Sarah Tyson Rorer once berated people like us who "are still in the palate stage of existence. Strive to reach a higher plane of thought—eat to live," she implored. "It has been fifteen years since I published my first book; during this time I have seen the art progress from 'fancy cookery' to the highest type of Domestic Science."

Despite these words, Rorer often cooked heartily and appetizingly in both the initial 1886 *Philadelphia Cook Book* and the work quoted from above, *Mrs. Rorer's New Cook Book.* A spirited and striking woman, she embraced a range of contemporary ideas and activities without paying too much attention to potential conflicts and contradictions, gaining widespread recognition in the field of dietetics, for example, while writing advertising pamphlets for food-processing companies.

She succeeded both as an entrepreneur and an editor, founding the Philadelphia Cooking School and also playing formative roles at *Ladies' Home Journal* and *Good Housekeeping.* A prolific writer and active lecturer, called "the life of the party" when she attended a convention at age eighty-five, Rorer reached many people in many different ways. We don't follow all of her advice, but we enjoy listening.

Agreeable seasonings to be kept at hand for salad making: Garlic, mushroom catsup, tomato catsup, Worcestershire sauce, soy, tabasco oil, tarragon vinegar, mint sauce, capers and celery seed. All these can be purchased for one dollar and fifty cents and will last a year.

SARAH TYSON RORER, *MRS. RORER'S NEW COOK BOOK* (1902)

INGREDIENT TIP: If you want to grow iceberg lettuce, you can get the seeds from Burpee's Heirlooms catalog (800-888-1447). Thomas Jefferson grew an even older type of head lettuce at Monticello called "tennisball," still thriving in the mansion's garden today. The Thomas Jefferson Center for Historic Plants (804-984-9821) sells the seeds. Other good sources for heirloom seeds include Johnny's Selected Seeds in Albion, Maine (207-437-4301), Heirloom Seed Project at Landis Valley Museum in Lancaster, Pennsylvania (717-569-0401), and Native Seeds/SEARCH in Tucson (520-622-5561), specializing in plants of the arid Southwest.

Greens with Pot Liquor

SERVES 4 TO 6

The way to a Junior Leaguer's heart, says southern food authority John Egerton, is to serve a steaming bowl of pot "likker" under the name of consommé. A delicious blend of juices from slowly simmered greens and seasoning pork, it shouldn't need a false label on anybody's table. We use readily available bacon in the cooking, but smoked shoulder, hog jowl, ham hocks, and other pork cuts can add extra flavors, and some people even substitute peanut oil successfully. Serve the greens in their liquor with cornbread to sop up the juice, and maybe pinto beans on the side.

- 4 to 6 bacon slices, chopped
- 2 medium onions, chopped
- 3 plump garlic cloves, minced
- ½ teaspoon crushed dried hot red chiles
- 4 pounds collard greens, mustard greens, turnip greens, or a combination, stems and tough ribs discarded (see Ingredient Tip)
- 4 cups chicken stock, preferably, or water
- 1 tablespoon cider vinegar
- Salt and freshly milled black pepper

Fry the bacon in a stockpot or other large pot over medium heat until the fat is rendered and the bacon has begun to color. Stir in the onions and cook until soft and translucent, about 5 minutes. Stir in the garlic and chiles, and cook an additional minute. Dump in about half of the greens and toss until somewhat wilted. Add the rest of the greens and toss again. Pour in the stock and vinegar, and season with salt and pepper. Cover and simmer the greens until very tender, 25 to 30 minutes. Serve the greens and pot liquor in a big bowl, hot and soupy.

INGREDIENT TIP: Wash the greens well in several changes of cool water to eliminate all grit. The greens can be added to the pot with the washing water still clinging to them. You can cut the greens into smaller pieces prior to cooking, but that's just extra work since they cook down considerably anyway.

According to my mother, I did discredit the race when I cooked collard greens on TV. . . . I decided to go with a traditional "Soul Food" menu, but I'd prepare the dishes in a nontraditional way. For example, the collard greens: Instead of ham hocks, I would use a seasoning of peanut oil and bouillon cubes.

I figured that would take care of the Muslims and the vegetarians. I didn't even think about my mother. I had no idea of the embarrassment she would suffer.

It seems that some of her church sisters saw the show.

"Mrs. Smart's daughter was on coast-to-coast TV and cooked naked greens! . . ."

"Where do you think she picked that up?"

"Maybe she was raised like that."

"Umhuh, uumm, ummumm!"

"It's a shame before the living justice, 'naked' greens."

VERTAMAE GROSVENOR, *VIBRATION COOKING* (1970)

Sugar Creek Fried Morels

Serves a few lucky souls

Early American settlers found thousands of different mushroom varieties growing wild, including the divine morel, a forager's delight sometimes sold in stores. This is a common and tasty midwestern preparation, named for Gertrude Meyer's Illinois farm, where her granddaughter Cheryl spent many a spring day hunting and eating morels.

- Fresh morel mushrooms, as many as you can find or afford (see Ingredient Tip)
- Salt
- Eggs
- Saltine cracker crumbs
- Unsalted butter

Halve the mushrooms vertically and place them in a good-size bowl. Pour very hot water over them, then add about a tablespoon of salt per quart of water. Swish the mushrooms around to dislodge dirt or any little visitors that might hide in the spongy tops, then quickly drain the mushrooms. They should be moist, not completely dry.

Whisk one or more eggs, enough to coat all the mushrooms lightly. After dipping the mushrooms in egg, dunk them in cracker crumbs. Pan-fry them in the butter over medium heat for several minutes until golden and crunchy. Serve the mushrooms immediately.

INGREDIENT TIP: If you're not a skilled forager living in the upper Midwest or Pacific Northwest, morels can get expensive and difficult to find. Usually available in late April and early May, quantities vary with the whims of the weather. Check with specialty markets or greengrocers, or ask around at farmers' markets. American Spoon Foods in Petoskey, Michigan (800-222-5886 or 616-347-9030), often gets in a small supply, but call well ahead of the season for a reasonable spot on the waiting list. A cautionary note: never eat morels raw.

Fried Okra

SERVES ABOUT 4

The mucilaginous quality of okra makes it great for thickening gumbo and stews, but less appealing to most people on its own. Frying okra in cornmeal disguises that gluey characteristic, yielding a delectably crunchy vegetable with a creamy center. The texture contrasts brightly with a mess of Greens with Pot Liquor (page 260) or Macaroni and Wisconsin Cheese Sauce (page 335).

- 1 pound small perky-looking okra, sliced into ¼-inch-thick rings
- 1¼ cups stone-ground cornmeal
- 1 teaspoon salt
- ½ teaspoon freshly milled black pepper
- Pinch or two of cayenne pepper
- Peanut oil or vegetable oil for pan-frying
- Hot pepper sauce, such as Texas Pete or Tabasco

Cover the okra with lightly salted ice water and refrigerate for 15 to 30 minutes. Drain the okra. Combine the cornmeal, salt, pepper, and cayenne on a plate, and dredge the okra with the mixture.

Heat ½ inch of oil in a large skillet until it ripples. Place batches of okra in a strainer and shake lightly to knock off excess cornmeal. Fry the okra in the oil in batches just until golden, 1 to 2 minutes, stirring occasionally to fry evenly. Drain the okra and serve it hot, accompanied by hot sauce.

Pea Salad

SERVES 6

Used mostly as a binder for fish and meat salads in earlier times, mayonnaise started appearing frequently in fruit and vegetable salads after the introduction of bottled versions in the early twentieth century. It showed up in every kind of salad, from the famous Waldorf to the notorious "candlestick," an upright banana on a pineapple-ring base with a pimiento flame and a blob of mayo meant to represent dripping wax. Few of the concoctions brought on the giggles as much as the anatomically suggestive candlestick, but we eventually laughed off the table most of the overly creamy, cloying concoctions. This heartland salad is a long-term survivor, particularly when made with fresh spring peas, though it won't last long at a picnic.

½ cup mayonnaise
¼ cup plus 2 tablespoons sour cream
¼ cup minced (really minced) onion
½ to 1 teaspoon sugar
Salt
4 cups fresh baby peas, or two 10-ounce packages frozen baby peas, thawed but uncooked
6 ounces medium to sharp Cheddar cheese, cut into tiny cubes
4 to 5 crisp cooked bacon slices, crumbled

Whisk together the mayonnaise and sour cream in a small bowl. Add the onion, the smaller amount of sugar, and salt to taste. Stir together the peas, cheese, and bacon in a large bowl. Spoon on the mayonnaise mixture and toss lightly just until combined. Add more sugar or salt if you wish. Refrigerate for at least 30 minutes and up to 12 hours before serving.

Oscar and His Famous Salad

Restaurants created some of the country's most renowned salads, with California establishments leading the way. The Brown Derby in Los Angeles gave us the Cobb in the 1920s, and just across the border in Tijuana in the same decade, Caesar Cardini concocted the Caesar, propelled to stardom by fans in Hollywood. In San Francisco, the Palace Hotel developed the Green Goddess and the Palace Court salads, and the St. Francis contributed Celery Victor. The restaurant salad bar debuted in Chicago in 1971, a product of the imagination of Rich Melman and Jerry Orzoff.

New York maître d' Oscar Tschirky, who liked to be called "Oscar of the Waldorf," claimed the biggest success of all, the widely known apple, celery, and mayonnaise combination named after the Manhattan hotel where he presided in the late nineteenth and early twentieth centuries. The haughty headwaiter published the first recipe for a Waldorf, minus the now common walnuts, in a 1896 cookbook, and has won widespread recognition for it. Home cooks quickly adopted the glamorous name for the dish, but needed no introduction to the elements or their mixture. Both celery and apples were conventional salad components at the time and often ended up together or with walnuts, usually topped with a boiled dressing, easier to make at home than mayonnaise. Oscar put an aristocratic face on the humble notion and regally accepted all the credit.

Creamy Jalapeño Spinach

SERVES 6 TO 8

We developed a slightly different version of this dish originally for our *Texas Home Cooking* (1993), adapting it from a canned-soup, processed-cheese dish that appeared in the 1976 *Dallas Junior League Cookbook*. It's a staple on our table for special holiday meals, and always wins many raves.

- 3 pounds fresh spinach, preferably the crinkly savoy variety
- ½ cup half-and-half
- ¼ cup (½ stick) unsalted butter
- ½ cup minced onion
- ½ cup chopped celery
- 2 tablespoons unbleached all-purpose flour
- 1 cup whipping cream
- ¾ cup grated mild to medium Cheddar cheese
- 2 to 3 tablespoons minced pickled jalapeño plus 1 or more tablespoons jalapeño pickling liquid to taste
- Salt and freshly milled black pepper

CRACKER CRUMBS

- 1 tablespoon unsalted butter
- ¾ cup saltine cracker crumbs

Preheat the oven to 375° F. Butter a medium baking dish.

Wash the spinach leaves thoroughly in a large bowl or sinkful of cold water to remove every bit of grit. Repeat the process if necessary to clean the leaves thoroughly. Place the spinach, with the water that clings to it, in a large heavy pan. Cover the pan and wilt the spinach over medium heat, stirring it around once or twice. Wilting should take about 5 minutes. When the spinach is cool enough to handle, squeeze out any excess moisture, rinse it in ice water, and drain again. (The spinach can be prepared to this point earlier in the day, wrapped tightly, and refrigerated.)

Purée about one-third of the spinach with the half-and-half in a blender or food processor. Finely chop the remaining spinach.

Melt the butter in a large saucepan over medium heat. Add the onion and celery, and sauté until the vegetables are soft, about 5 minutes. Sprinkle the flour over the vegetables, then cook for another couple of minutes, stirring frequently. Pour in the cream and bring the mixture to a boil. Reduce the heat to a simmer and cook briefly until the mixture is lightly thickened. Remove from the heat and immediately stir in the cheese. When the cheese is melted, stir in the puréed spinach and the chopped spinach. Add as much jalapeño and pickling liquid as you wish for zip, but keep it balanced with the other flavors. Season with salt and pepper. Spoon into the prepared dish.

Prepare the cracker crumbs, melting the butter in a small skillet over medium heat. Stir in the crumbs and sauté until just golden. Scatter the crumbs over the spinach mixture. Bake for 20 to 25 minutes, until lightly brown and bubbly. Serve warm.

One November, at a literary festival in Dallas, Texas, I and the other participants were fed a delicious meal in a beautiful house. The side dish was creamed spinach with jalapeño peppers and it was so good it made me want to sit up and beg like a dog.

LAURIE COLWIN,
HOME COOKING (1988)

POTATOES, DRIED BEANS, AND Other Keepers

IF THE EXPERTS DEFINED CUISINES BY THE MOST prominent source of the calories, they would label Americans a potato people. More than meat or even sweets, we load up on spuds, eating them at breakfast, lunch, or dinner, at home or out. A potato blight would devastate the national diet. Deprived of hash browns in the morning, home fries, French fries, and chips at all hours, and mashed and baked potatoes with our meat, half the country would emigrate to Ireland.

Our lust for potatoes grew slowly, peaking only in the twentieth century, but it derives from a long dependence on vegetables and grains that store well over the winter. Before the industrialization of the food supply, "keepers" of this kind provided valuable sustenance for several months of the year, and as a result, became the basis of some of our most comforting dishes.

Dried beans, cabbage, onions, and other root vegetables preceded potatoes in popularity, and each retains its appeal in many of the traditional preparations. Slow to spoil and lose flavor, these foods sometimes were associated with coarseness and poverty in the past, but their staying power earned them a place in all kitchens. From the depths of the winter root cellar, and the tables of the working class, they rose over time into broadly cherished, year-round vegetables. For a potato people, even one increasingly devoted to freshness, they'll always be keepers.

I remember once going to a picnic given by other people where canned beans of a famous make . . . were served. I thought they were very chic and told my mother her beans were old-fashioned. At the next picnic of ours, Mother brought a huge mess of canned beans and insisted that I eat them instead of hers. I never complained again, nor have I ever again wanted another canned baked bean.

James Beard, *Delights and Prejudices* (1964)

Home Fries

SERVES 2 GENEROUSLY AS A MAIN DISH, 4 AS A SIDE DISH

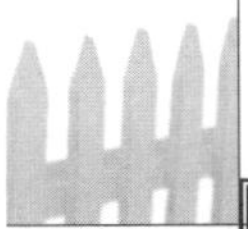

Though native to South America, potatoes probably didn't reach North America until the eighteenth century. By the time of the Civil War, it became clear, both here and abroad, that potatoes have a natural affinity for hot oil, and American cooks began frying them at home in this straightforward style. The best versions, we think, start with chunks of raw potatoes rather than leftovers, and therefore require slow cooking to achieve a proper balance of internal creaminess and outside crunch. When we eat the fries as a main course, we often sprinkle a handful of grated Cheddar over the top before serving, but we forgo the cheese when cooking them as a side dish.

2 tablespoons unsalted butter or rendered duck fat

1½ to 1¾ pounds russets or other baking potatoes, peeled and cut into ¾-inch cubes

Salt and freshly milled black pepper

½ cup chopped green or red bell pepper, or a combination

2 tablespoons minced parsley, chives, rosemary, or a combination

Plan on a total cooking time of about 70 minutes. (You have to check the potatoes occasionally, so you should stay in the vicinity, but they don't require constant attention. We read the Sunday paper or catch up on magazines while they cook.) First, warm the butter in a 10- to 12-inch cast-iron skillet over medium-low heat. Stir in the potatoes and when they're coated with a bit of fat, season them with salt and pepper and cover the skillet. Cook for 20 minutes, during which time you should hear only a faint cooking noise.

Uncover the potatoes and cook for about 30 minutes longer, turning them at 10-minute intervals and patting them back down. When you turn them the first time, stir in the bell pepper. As the potatoes soften, pat them down again lightly, bringing as much of their surface in contact with the skillet as possible without squashing them.

Cook the potatoes for about 20 additional minutes, turning them at 5-minute intervals. During the last 10 minutes, bring the heat up to medium, add the herbs and, if you wish, more salt and pepper. The home fries are ready when the potato cubes are richly browned and wonderfully crisp, with tender, melting centers. To double the recipe, use two skillets.

A plate of fried potatoes—eaten with a small bowl each of cottage cheese and homemade bread-and-butter pickles, or perhaps a salad of bitter greens and a piece or two of bacon on the side—makes a fine supper for two consenting adults, who know that pan-fried potatoes have, ounce for ounce, fewer calories than unbuttered bread, and that frying is a synonym not for damnation but for satisfaction.

JOHN THORNE, SERIOUS PIG (1996)

Hash Browns

Serves 4

Like home fries, hash browns appear on many restaurant menus, but seldom excel in that setting because they must be cooked in small, family-size batches to reach their potential. For hash browns, we use precooked potatoes—never the frozen variety—and we fry them in an ample amount of fat and cream, both of which contribute to the texture and flavor. Keep their name in mind as you cook them, thoroughly browning the surface as you would with a hearty hash.

- ¼ cup (½ stick) unsalted butter
- ¼ cup bacon drippings or additional butter
- ¼ cup plus 2 tablespoons minced onion
- 4 baked russets or other baking potatoes, equaling 2 to 2½ pounds, cooked, peeled, and chopped
- ¼ cup whipping cream
- Salt and freshly milled black pepper

Melt the butter and bacon drippings together in a heavy 12-inch skillet over medium heat. Stir in the onion and sauté it for a couple of minutes, only until limp. Add the potatoes and pat them down in a solid mass. Plan to cook the potatoes for a total of 15 to 20 minutes, scraping them up, turning them over, and patting them back down just three times. As you make the second turn, drizzle with the cream and add salt and pepper to taste. When done, the potatoes should be richly brown and crusty.

Potato Pancakes

American hash browns are closely related to potato pancakes, which immigrants brought to the United States from virtually every country between Ireland and Russia. The pancakes typically contain flour, and mashed or finely grated potatoes rather than chunks, but some thin, crisp versions veer so near hash browns that they could confuse a good short-order cook.

One of the oldest forms of the pancake, Jewish *latkes* probably even antedate the introduction of potatoes in Europe, likely originating as a buckwheat fritter, according to Joan Nathan in *Jewish Cooking in America* (1994). While potatoes constitute the core of a traditional *latke* today, the essential ingredient is the cooking oil, symbolizing the sacred oil the Maccabees used to rededicate the Temple in Jerusalem after defeating the Syrians, the event commemorated at Hanukkah. Potatoes carry no religious significance, but fried in pancakes or hash browns, they certainly taste divine.

Mashed Idaho Russets

Serves 6 or more

Before potatoes became the country's dominant root vegetable, cooks often mashed parsnips and turnips like we do spuds today. After the potato gained ascendancy, Idaho claimed the vegetable as its own, to such an extent that a U.S. senator from that state put spuds in a chocolate cake recipe submitted for *The Congressional Cook Book* of 1933. We'll stick with the old mashing approach, still favored by most Idaho cooks.

- 3 pounds russets or other large baking potatoes, peeled
- 1½ tablespoons salt or more to taste
- 1¼ cups whole milk
- ¾ cup sour cream
- 6 to 10 tablespoons unsalted butter, softened
- Freshly milled black pepper

Combine the potatoes in a large pan with 1½ tablespoons of salt and enough water to cover by at least 1 inch. Bring to a boil over high heat, then reduce the heat to medium and cook until quite tender, 20 to 30 minutes, depending on the size of the potatoes. When done, the exteriors of the potatoes should be crumbly, almost dissolving in spots.

While the potatoes cook, warm the milk over low heat in a small pan deep enough to prevent the milk from bubbling over as it heats. When the milk is hot, remove it from the heat and stir in the sour cream.

When the potatoes are ready, drain them and then put them back in the hot pan. Cover them with a clean, folded dishtowel and place the lid back on the pan. The towel will absorb steam, making the potatoes drier. Let the potatoes sit covered for about 5 minutes. Remove them from the pan and while they're still very hot, mash or rice them back into the pan.

Stir the warm milk mixture into the potatoes, then add butter a few tablespoons at a time as your conscience allows. Season with pepper and, if you wish, with extra salt. Serve piping hot.

Red Bliss Potato Salad

Serves 6 to 8

If you had to draw a single conclusion from American cookbooks of the last century and a half, the clearest inference would be that no one can have too many recipes for potato salad. Hot or cold, mashed or chunked, cloying or creamy, different versions of the salad fill picnic baskets from Hoboken to Honolulu, and hardly a one is bad. Our choice—inspired by the traditions of northern European immigrants in Wisconsin—varies from the most common American styles in having no mayonnaise, eggs, or sweet accents. We make it with waxy red potatoes because they don't crumble under the heft of the thick, savory dressing.

- 2½ pounds red waxy medium potatoes, such as Red Bliss, peeled if you wish
- Salt
- 1 cup sour cream
- 2 tablespoons fresh lemon juice
- 1½ tablespoons minced fresh dill
- 1½ teaspoons Dijon mustard
- 1 teaspoon prepared horseradish
- ⅛ teaspoon ground white pepper
- 1 cup fine-chopped celery
- 1 cup thin-sliced scallions, including the greens

Place the potatoes in a saucepan with water to cover and add about 1 teaspoon of salt. Bring to a boil over high heat, then reduce the heat to a simmer and cook the potatoes until tender when pierced with a fork, 20 to 25 minutes. Drain the potatoes and let them sit until cool enough to handle.

In a large bowl, mix together the sour cream, lemon juice, dill, mustard, horseradish, and pepper.

Cut the potatoes into bite-size pieces, and combine them with the sour cream mixture. Sprinkle with the celery and scallions, add salt as desired, and toss together gently but thoroughly. The salad can be served immediately or covered and refrigerated for several hours.

Super Markets

Nowadays most Americans shop for food at large supermarkets, a twentieth-century institution developed to cater to our penchants for automobile transportation and marketing-based buying. Before we had cars and clever packaging, people shopped differently, often in sprawling urban markets divided into numerous stalls selling everything from live fish to imported spices. The next time you're stuck in a checkout line, daydream about how much more fun the old way was.

A visitor to the Philadelphia market in 1818 marveled at the vegetables and fruits, speculating that no other place in the world offered as much selection. The market stretched for a mile around the Delaware River, with goods brought in by boat, ship, and wagon. Even in an inland city like Cincinnati, vendors sold fresh fish from Lake Erie and oysters from Baltimore. In Charleston, shoppers could pick up cabbages from northern states, oranges from Florida, and pineapples from Cuba. In New Orleans, the French Market stunned out-of-towners with its breadth and vitality.

"All races and nationalities are buying and selling all imaginable wares," said one journalist of the French Market, who concluded that "the scene in its fullness is simply indescribable." A visitor to the New York market, quoted by Richard Hooker in *Food and Drink in America* (1981), resorted to verse:

All sects and colors mingle there,
Long folks and short, black folks and grey,
With common bawds and folks that pray. . . .

Twice-Baked Potatoes

SERVES 6

Once through the oven doesn't do it for us. Millions of Americans love baked potatoes, but we think they're twice as good when you bake them a second time. Known in some earlier cookbooks as potatoes on the half shell or stuffed potatoes, they probably developed as a way to use leftovers, but they're too good to relegate to that role. For a manly meal on Father's Day or any other day, lead off with Shrimp Cocktail (page 69), then serve the potatoes with Pan-Fried Rib Eye (page 195), corn in some form, and Door County Sour Cherry Pie (page 364).

6 small or 3 large russets or other baking potatoes

Vegetable oil

2 to 3 bacon slices

¼ cup (½ stick) unsalted butter

¾ cup sliced scallions

⅓ to ½ cup whole milk

1 tablespoon sour cream

¾ teaspoon salt or more to taste

⅛ teaspoon ground white pepper

4 ounces mild to medium Cheddar cheese, grated (1 cup)

1 egg yolk, lightly beaten, optional

Paprika

Preheat the oven to 375°F. Coat the potatoes with oil and prick them in several spots with a fork, so that steam can escape. Bake the potatoes for about 1 hour, until soft to the touch. Remove the potatoes, leaving the oven on.

In a small skillet, fry the bacon over medium heat until brown and crisp. Remove the bacon from the skillet and drain the bacon. Add the butter to the pan drippings. When the butter is melted, add the scallions and sauté briefly until soft.

If using 6 potatoes, cut off a thin slice from a long side of each potato. If using 3 potatoes, cut them in half lengthwise. Scoop out the potato "shells," leaving a thin layer of potato around the inside so they hold their shape. Rice or mash the scooped-out potatoes, adding ⅓ cup of the milk and mixing well. Scrape in the scallion mixture and add the sour cream, salt, pepper, and three-fourths of the cheese. If you like the potatoes extra-rich, add the egg yolk. Stir in the remaining milk if the mixture doesn't spoon very easily.

Mound the potato filling into the "shells." (The potatoes can be made ahead to this point and refrigerated, covered, but allow a few extra minutes of baking time.) Sprinkle the remaining cheese over the potatoes and dust with paprika. Arrange in a baking dish. Return the potatoes to the oven for about 15 minutes, until heated through and lightly browned and bubbly.

Scalloped Potatoes

Serves 6 to 8

Another luscious way of baking potatoes, related to French gratin dishes, this is an all-round keeper because it can be cooked in advance and held for hours without suffering. That made it into a potluck-supper specialty, and the communal meals in turn spread its celebrity across the country. Some versions rely on little more than milk to give the potatoes their silky sheen, while many midwestern cooks add chunks of ham or pork chops to create a one-dish meal. With or without the meat, it's a filling treat, a sort of spud lovers' mac and cheese.

- 1 tablespoon unsalted butter
- ¾ cup fresh bread crumbs
- 2 tablespoons unbleached all-purpose flour
- 1½ teaspoons dried thyme
- 1½ teaspoons salt
- 1 teaspoon freshly milled black pepper
- 2½ to 2¾ pounds russets or other baking potatoes, peeled and sliced thin
- ½ small onion, sliced very thin and divided into half-rings
- 1½ cups chicken stock
- ¾ cup whipping cream
- 1 tablespoon Dijon mustard

Butter a 9-inch × 13-inch baking dish. Preheat the oven to 400°F.

Melt the butter in a small skillet. Stir in the bread crumbs, sauté until just golden, and reserve them.

Mix together the flour, thyme, salt, and pepper. Layer one-third of the potatoes, add one-third of the seasoned flour, and top with one-half of the onions. Repeat, then top with the remaining potatoes and seasonings.

Whisk together the stock, cream, and mustard, and pour the mixture evenly over the potatoes. Bake for 25 minutes, then scatter the bread crumbs over the potatoes. Continue baking for 50 to 60 minutes longer, until the potatoes are crusty and medium brown on top with a tender, creamy center. The liquid should be mostly absorbed but the potatoes still moist. Serve warm.

New Potatoes à la Diable

Serves 4

Potato Temptress

Our favorite variation on traditional scalloped potatoes is the dish known as Jansson's Temptation. It's made in much the same way, though the addition of anchovies and extra onions yields a different dimension in flavor. You find it more often today in Sweden and Norway than the United States, but many people say that it's American in origin.

The name comes from an old story—disputed by local historians—about the gluttony of Eric Jansson, a Swedish religious reformer who founded the village of Bishop Hill in west central Illinois in 1846. Jansson demanded an austere asceticism from his followers, in diet as in all other matters. One day a devoted believer discovered the leader feasting excitedly on a creamed potato-and-anchovy concoction, suggesting his piety was only pretense. For a taste of his Temptation, according to the tale, Jansson gave up his kingdom on earth, if not in heaven.

New Orleans tradition, as related in *The Picayune's Creole Cook Book* (1901), claims revenge as the origin of this spicy dish. Madame Jean Marie asked her worthless husband—a "no-count Creole what love one good game of card, one good story, and one good glass wine . . . more better than work"—to fetch her some new potatoes from the French Market. Resenting the intrusion on his leisure, he cried out, "Pommes de terre aux diable!" Madame replied that no man said "to the devil" at her, and decided to burn his tongue with a cayenne-and-mustard dressing on the potatoes. Sadly for her, the scoundrel loved it, and so will anyone with a hellish bent.

- 1¾ to 2 pounds unpeeled new red waxy potatoes or fingerlings, preferably, or other small potatoes, halved if larger than bite-size
- 3 tablespoons unsalted butter
- 2 to 3 teaspoons Creole mustard
- Pinch of cayenne pepper or more to taste
- Salt and freshly milled black pepper
- 1 tablespoon minced parsley

Steam the potatoes for 10 to 15 minutes, until tender.

Melt the butter in a large skillet over medium heat, then mix in the mustard. Stir in the potatoes and toss to coat them. Add at least a healthy pinch of cayenne and salt and pepper to taste. Sprinkle with parsley and serve warm.

Candied Sweet Potatoes

Serves 8

A lot of linguistic confusion surrounds the sweet potato, one of Christopher Columbus's early "discoveries" in the West Indies. It isn't related to the white potato in any way, and differs significantly from the yam, a tuber rarely found in the United States. African slaves had eaten yams in their homeland, and in the New World they substituted sweet potatoes for them, giving rise to our practice of using the names interchangeably. Southern cooks pioneered the first colonial preparations of the vegetable and contributed heavily to the development of later dishes, including the candied form that became popular near the end of the nineteenth century. Our rendition, with the potatoes sliced rather than mashed, leaves out the marshmallows common in many versions, but if sweet memories compel you, feel free to add them.

3 pounds (about 4 medium to large) sweet potatoes
2 tablespoons molasses
2 tablespoons honey
Zest and juice of 1 large orange
¼ cup (½ stick) unsalted butter
½ teaspoon pure vanilla extract
¾ teaspoon salt or more to taste
2 teaspoons cornstarch
½ cup chopped black walnuts or pecans, optional
Paprika or cayenne pepper

Preheat the oven to 375°F. Butter a medium baking dish.

Peel the sweet potatoes, halve them lengthwise (quarter especially pudgy ones), and slice them ¼ inch thick. Bring a large pot of lightly salted water to a boil, then add the sweet potatoes and boil until nearly tender, about 4 minutes. You should be able to pierce them easily. Drain the potatoes and arrange half of them in the prepared dish.

In a medium saucepan, warm together the molasses, honey, orange zest and juice, butter, vanilla, and salt. Stir occasionally to mix the syrup evenly as the butter melts. Stir together the cornstarch with 1 tablespoon of water and add it to the syrup. Remove from the heat and pour half of the syrup over the sweet potatoes. Repeat with the remaining sweet potatoes and syrup. If you like nuts, scatter them over the sweet potatoes. Dust the top with paprika or, for a little kick, cayenne.

Cover the dish and bake for 45 minutes. Uncover and continue baking for 15 to 20 minutes longer, until the sweet potatoes are very tender and nicely glazed. Serve hot.

At home we'd bake [sweet potatoes] in the hot coals of the fireplace, had carried them cold to school for lunch; munched them secretly, squeezing the sweet pulp from the soft peel. . . . Yes, and we'd loved them candied, or baked in a cobbler, deep-fat fried in a pocket of dough, or roasted with pork and glazed with the well-browned fat; had chewed them raw—yams and years ago.

Ralph Ellison, *Invisible Man* (1952)

Sweet Potato–Chestnut Purée

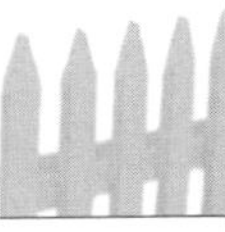

Serves 8

Sweetly spiced rather than sugary, this mashed dish is from the same era as candied sweet potatoes, but isn't as easily snubbed in trendy circles today. Some cooks at the turn of the twentieth century made this kind of chestnut-flavored mixture into croquettes; others added bread crumbs and used it as a turkey stuffing. Our approach is closer to June Platt's New England version in *The June Platt Cook Book* (1958), though our seasonings hint more at the tropical roots of the sweet potato. Serve the purée with Roasted Wild Turkey with Madeira Sauce (page 160), pork Loin Roast with Cranberry Glaze (page 179), or simply grilled pork chops.

- 3 pounds whole unpeeled sweet potatoes
- 6 to 8 tablespoons (¾ to 1 stick) unsalted butter
- 15- to 16-ounce can chestnut purée
- 2 tablespoons dark rum or more to taste
- 1½ teaspoons salt
- ¼ teaspoon ground allspice
- ¼ teaspoon ground cardamom
- ¼ teaspoon ground cinnamon
- 2 tablespoons packed brown sugar

TOPPING

- 2 tablespoons packed brown sugar
- ¼ teaspoon ground cinnamon

Preheat the oven to 400°F. Pierce the sweet potatoes in several places with a fork, then bake them directly on an oven rack for 50 to 60 minutes, until very tender. Remove and reduce the oven temperature to 375°F. Butter a large shallow baking dish.

When cool enough to handle, scoop the potatoes from their skins and mash or rice them in a large bowl. Mix in the butter, and when it's well combined, add the chestnut purée (rice or mash it if it doesn't stir easily), rum, salt, spices, and brown sugar. Spoon into the prepared dish. (The purée can be made to this point a day ahead, then refrigerated, covered. Let it return to room temperature before proceeding.)

Stir together the topping ingredients and sprinkle evenly over the sweet potato mixture. Bake uncovered for about 30 minutes, until heated through and bubbly. Serve hot.

Boston Baked Beans

Serves 8 or more

In one of the staunchest traditions in American cooking, New Englanders used to bake beans in a special bean pot every Saturday night. Over time the practice grew into a ritual and the dish became a regional icon that migrating New Englanders took across the country. Few people today have a narrow-neck, earthen pot for baking the beans, or an equally venerable brick oven, but we can get a reasonable approximation of the old flavor using modern equipment. Our recipe hews closely to the seasonings fancied since the late nineteenth century, emphasizing the old trinity of salt pork, molasses, and mustard.

- 1 pound dried pea (navy) beans, yellow-eye beans, or Jacob's cattle beans
- 1 large onion, sliced into thin wedges
- Salt
- 3 tablespoons molasses
- 2 teaspoons dry mustard
- ½ teaspoon freshly milled black pepper
- 2 tablespoons dark rum, optional
- 6 ounces salt pork, quartered so that each piece contains some of the rind

Cover the beans by several inches with water and add the onion. Bring the beans to a boil. Reduce the heat to a bare simmer and cook the beans for about 2 hours, until tender but not beginning to burst. Salt them as soon as they have started to soften. Add more hot water to the beans as necessary to keep them from becoming dry. When cooked, drain off some of the water if there is more than an inch of it topping the beans.

Preheat the oven to 300°F. Grease a bean pot or baking dish large enough to hold the beans. Pour the beans and liquid into the pot, and stir in the molasses, mustard, pepper, and optional rum. Score the rind of each piece of salt pork and partially submerge them in the beans so that just the rind is exposed.

Bake the beans, covering them loosely with a lid or foil if you are not using a narrow-necked bean pot. Bake the beans for 8 hours, adding hot water if they begin to get dry. If you're rushed, so to speak, 6 to 7 hours of cooking will yield good results too.

A Barrelful of Pork and Beans

Boston baked beans are sometimes known simply as "pork and beans," but they are only one of many American dishes that feature the delicious combination. We're partial to black beans with sausage, pintos with bacon, Great Northerns with pig knuckles and, perhaps most of all, the Kentucky pairing of large dried limas or other white beans with a meaty bone from a country ham. Some cooks go a step further and add greens to the mixture. Tommy Lasorda, of Los Angeles Dodgers fame, grew up in Rochester, New York, during the Great Depression eating a dish of cannellini beans, pepperoni, and dandelion greens freshly picked from nearby fields. His Italian-American mother seasoned the blend with garlic and olive oil, and she taught young Tommy how to make it for himself, which he still does.

Red Beans and Rice

Serves 6

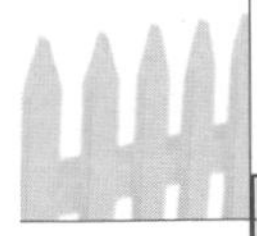

Mary Lincoln, 1844–1921

"In spite of the slurs against 'Boston Baked Beans,' " Mary Lincoln said, "it is often remarked that strangers enjoy them as much as natives; and many a New England bean-pot has been carried to the extreme South and West, that people there might have 'baked beans' in perfection." Lincoln provided a model recipe for the dish, seasoned simply with little more than salt pork, mustard, and molasses, and baked for eight hours in the all-important bean pot.

Lincoln excelled in teaching basics and principles, a talent she discovered after her husband's ill health forced her to earn most of their joint income. Her big break came in 1879, when the newly founded Boston Cooking School hired her as a teacher on a trial basis. She stayed at the school for over five years, getting it well established financially and well known nationally.

Lincoln published the first and most influential of her several cookbooks in 1884. Titled *Mrs. Lincoln's Boston Cook Book: What to Do and What Not to Do in Cooking,* it's a broad, clearly written compendium of nineteenth-century cooking, particularly as practiced in New England. Lincoln later became a magazine editor, author of numerous commercial pamphlets for food companies, and a leader of the early home economics movement, but she speaks to us today most forcefully as a culinary educator dedicated to the traditions of her native region.

This New Orleans classic—traditionally simmered most of Monday with leftovers from a Sunday ham while the cook did the week's laundry—probably derives from the Hoppin' John (page 319) of South Carolina. The evolution worked in a curious way, turning a rice dish with beans into a bean dish with rice. Some of the best New Orleans cooks, including many in Ella Brennan's famous family, prefer to use the local pickled pork for the meat flavor in the beans, but since it's hard to find outside of Louisiana, we substitute a ham hock, equally popular on the home turf.

- 1 pound dried red beans or small kidney beans (see Ingredient Tip)
- 1½ pounds smoked ham hocks, cut into 1-inch-thick slices by your butcher
- 2 medium onions, chopped
- 1 large green bell pepper, chopped
- ¾ cup chopped celery
- 2 to 4 garlic cloves, minced
- 2 bay leaves
- 2 to 3 teaspoons salt
- 1 teaspoon fresh milled black pepper
- ½ to 1 teaspoon cayenne pepper
- 2 cups uncooked rice
- Louisiana hot pepper sauce, such as Crystal or Tabasco (see Ingredient Tip)

The night before you plan to cook the beans, cover them with water and soak them overnight. When ready to cook them, don't pour off the liquid; instead dump it with the beans into a large heavy pot. Add the ham hocks, onions, bell pepper, celery, garlic, bay leaves, salt, pepper, and cayenne, and bring the mixture to a boil over high heat. Reduce the heat to a bare simmer and cook the beans, stirring them often, until the ham hocks are very tender, about 1 hour. Remove the ham hocks and set them aside. Continue cooking the beans, occasionally stirring them, until very tender, somewhat mushy, and beginning to break apart, about 45 additional minutes. Add more hot water whenever the beans begin to get dry. There should be plenty of creamy, almost gravylike thick liquid. Pull the meat off the ham hocks in bite-size pieces and return the meat to the pot. Continue cooking another few minutes. The beans are even better if you make them far enough in advance to cool, refrigerate, covered, and later reheat.

Shortly before you plan to serve the beans, cook the rice according to your own favorite method or as in our technique described on page 321. Spoon rice onto each plate or in shallow bowls, then top each with a generous ladle of beans. Serve piping hot, accompanied by hot pepper sauce.

INGREDIENT TIP: Both Camellia red beans, the local Louisiana standard, and Crystal hot sauce are distributed nationally. If you can't find them in your area, you can mail-order them from the New Orleans School of Cooking (800-237-4841 or 504-525-2665). If you want to try pickled pork in the beans, it can be ordered in 1-pound packages from the French Market Seafood Company (504-522-8911).

Picante Pintos

SERVES 6, WITH ENOUGH SALSA FOR ANOTHER HELPING

We first enjoyed these wonderful beans in Pilot Point, Texas, in the home of Jim and Sandy Neale, the parents of our son-in-law, J. B. Neale. Sandy's secret lies partially in the slow simmering of the pintos, but she gets most of her flavor from the addition of a cooked salsa made with ingredients from her garden. Sandy cans the salsa in large batches, but we typically prepare just double the amount needed for the recipe, storing the rest in the refrigerator for up to 2 weeks for use in a second batch of beans or another dish. The pintos go great with Jalapeño Cornbread (page 353).

SANDY'S COOKED SALSA

1 quart peeled and chopped red-ripe tomatoes

1 cup chopped onion

1 cup mixed red and green peppers, bells and mild chiles, chopped

2 to 3 fresh jalapeño chiles, minced

2 garlic cloves, minced

3 tablespoons tomato paste

2 to 3 teaspoons salt or more to taste

½ teaspoon sugar

¼ teaspoon cumin

¾ cup cider vinegar

Minced cilantro

1 pound dried pinto beans

1 tablespoon minced garlic

1½ teaspoons freshly milled black pepper

1½ teaspoons Cajun seasoning blend

Salt

Prepare the salsa at least a day before you plan to serve the beans. In a large nonreactive pan, combine the tomatoes, onion, mixed peppers, jalapeños, garlic, tomato paste, salt, sugar, and cumin. Bring the mixture to a boil over high heat, then reduce the heat to a simmer and cook for 15 to 20 minutes. Pour in the vinegar and simmer about 15 minutes longer, stirring occasionally, until thick. Add cilantro to taste and cook for 5 additional minutes. Cool the salsa and refrigerate it.

Cover the beans by a couple of inches with water. Bring the beans to a boil with the garlic, pepper, and Cajun seasoning. Reduce the heat to low and cook the beans at a bare simmer for about 2½ hours, stirring up from the bottom frequently. Add hot water to the beans as necessary to keep the liquid thick. When the beans are very tender, but before they begin to break up, add about half of the salsa, salt to taste, and continue cooking for 30 additional minutes. Serve the beans hot.

TECHNIQUE TIP: When tomatoes overrun Sandy's garden, she simply freezes the extras whole in heavyweight plastic bags for later use. It's remarkably simple if you have the extra freezer space. The tomatoes lose a bit in texture, but work fine in any cooked dish such as the salsa.

Scientists in general agree that animal proteids yield more easily to the digestive apparatus of man than vegetable proteids. . . . We in this generation find it difficult to digest the leguminous vegetables (peas, beans and lentils) which contain the proteid materials useful in the building of muscles and tissues; hence the increased demand for meat. Primitive man found no difficulty whatever in building muscle, brain and nerve from these coarse vegetable foods; but it must be borne in mind that his mental activity was far less than ours.

SARAH TYSON RORER,
MRS. RORER'S NEW COOK BOOK (1902)

Stewed Black-eyed Peas

SERVES 6

African field peas—including such close cousins as black-eyed peas, cowpeas, and crowders—reached the South by the eighteenth century through the West Indies and became a staple of regional cooking, particularly among African Americans. Creamier and less starchy than most dried beans, black-eyed peas stewed simply with ham and seasonings make a fine supper served with greens of any kind.

1 tablespoon bacon drippings or vegetable oil
1 large yellow onion, chopped
1 celery stalk, minced
2 garlic cloves, minced
6 cups chicken stock
1 pound dried black-eyed peas
2 bay leaves
½ teaspoon dried thyme
4- to 6-ounce slab or chunk of country ham or other smoky ham
Hot pepper sauce, such as Tabasco, optional
Salt, optional

Melt the bacon drippings in a large saucepan over medium heat. Add the onion, celery, and garlic, and sauté until soft, about 5 minutes. Pour in the stock, then stir in the peas, bay leaves, thyme, and ham. Add a few splashes of hot sauce, if you wish, or just serve it as an accompaniment at the table. Bring the stock to a boil, reduce the heat to low, and cook the peas at a bare simmer.

When the ham is very tender, in about 30 to 40 minutes, remove it. When it's cool enough to handle, shred or dice the meat. Continue cooking the peas until they are very tender but not mushy, 1½ to 1¾ hours longer. If the peas begin to get dry, add hot water to them as necessary. They should remain somewhat soupy. Return the ham to the pot and cook for another 10 to 15 minutes, adding a little salt if the ham itself hasn't provided enough. Remove the bay leaves and serve warm.

Our southern meals were always rich with vegetables—fresh in season, canned or dried for winter meals—all cooked with side meat from hogs raised, killed, and processed on the farm. . . . A typical summer meal would be fried chicken, cut corn, sliced tomatoes, field peas (stewed in their own juice), new Irish potatoes, hot biscuit, corn bread, and a stack cake, cobbler, or two-crusted fruit pie—with pouring cream, of course! If the ice truck came by, iced tea was a special treat.

ROSE BUDD STEVENS, FROM *ROSE BUDD'S KITCHEN* (1988)

Texas Caviar

Serves 6

Texas farmers grow a lot of black-eyed peas, particularly around Athens, and Lone Star cooks make many a fanciful dish out of the legume. Among the treasures trotted out at Athens's annual harvest festival, you might find Gazpeacho, Jeepers Pea-pers, or Jala-Pea-No-Pie, and, off the grounds, maybe a pitcher of Marpeanis with a pea replacing the olive in the gin-vermouth mixture. This is easily the best of the Texas creations, a pickled and chilled dish popularized around the state decades ago by Helen Corbitt.

- 1 pound dried black-eyed peas
- 6 cups chicken stock
- 1 bay leaf
- ¾ cup corn oil, preferably unrefined (see Ingredient Tip)
- ¼ cup cider vinegar
- 1 small green bell pepper, diced
- ½ cup diced sweet onion, such as Texas 1015 or Vidalia, or mild red onion
- 1 fresh or pickled jalapeño or serrano chile, minced
- 2 plump garlic cloves, roasted and peeled
- 1 teaspoon freshly cracked black pepper
- ¼ teaspoon ground cumin
- ½ teaspoon salt or more to taste

Combine the peas, stock, and bay leaf in a large saucepan, and bring them to a boil over high heat. Reduce the heat to low and simmer the peas until tender, about 1½ hours. Add more hot water to the peas if they begin to seem dry. Stir only occasionally and avoid mashing the peas. When soft but not mushy, drain the peas.

Transfer the peas to a large bowl and toss gently with the remaining ingredients. Refrigerate for at least 2 hours and preferably overnight. Serve the peas as a salad or, if you wish, as an appetizer with tortilla chips for scoops.

INGREDIENT TIP: Unrefined vegetable and nut oils are fragrant with the aroma of their ingredients and deeper in color than their refined cousins. Refined corn oil, the common supermarket variety, works best in cooking because of its higher smoke point, but the unrefined oil gives more earthy character to a salad. Spectrum Naturals and Arrowhead Mills both make good unrefined corn oil, sold widely in natural foods stores.

Stewed Cabbage

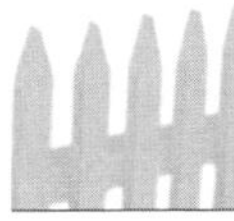

Serves 4 to 6

Most Europeans who settled in the United States brought along a taste for cabbage. It had a reputation as a coarse vegetable, but since it grew easily and kept well, cooks stuffed it, cut it up for coleslaw, paired it with corned beef, and even prepared it as a "Ladies" dish, heavily creamed so that it couldn't offend the most delicate appetite. Most people simply boiled or stewed cabbage, an excellent approach if handled well. For a tasty, old-fashioned vegetable plate, combine this with Yellow Squash Casserole (page 249) and Hoppin' John (page 319), serving Dinner Rolls (page 350) on the side with Blackberry Jam (page 291) or Tomato Chutney (page 296).

Cabbage, n. A familiar kitchen-garden vegetable about as large and wise as a man's head.

Ambrose Bierce, The Devil's Dictionary (1911)

- 1½ tablespoons rendered chicken fat (see page 75), duck fat, or unsalted butter
- ½ medium green bell pepper, cut into matchsticks
- 1 small onion, cut into matchsticks
- 1 plump garlic clove, minced
- 1 small to medium cabbage head (about 1¼ pounds), sliced into thin ribbons
- 1 tablespoon tomato paste
- ¼ teaspoon freshly milled black pepper
- Pinch of sugar
- Salt

Melt the fat in a large saucepan over medium heat. Stir in the bell pepper and onion, cover, and sweat them for about 5 minutes, just until soft. Add the garlic and cook uncovered another minute. Stir in the cabbage, 1½ cups water, tomato paste, pepper, and sugar, and cover again. Reduce the heat to medium-low and cook for 20 to 25 minutes, until the cabbage is very tender but not washed out. Add salt to taste. If the liquid is still soupy, uncover and cook over high heat briefly until lightly reduced and coating the cabbage leaves. Serve hot.

Coleslaw

SERVES 8

An old term for cabbage salad, coleslaw found an early home in Dutch and German settlements, and spread into other communities in the nineteenth century. Anglo-Americans often misunderstood the name and called their versions "cold slaw," encouraging inventive cooks to develop numerous variations on "hot slaw." Lettice Bryan offered renditions of each as early as 1839 in *The Kentucky Housewife,* coating both with a vinegar dressing instead of the more common boiled dressing, which eventually gave way to commercial mayonnaise. Bryan understood clearly how to cut cabbage for a salad, instructing her readers, "Take a very sharp knife, shave off the cabbage roundwise, cutting it very smoothly and evenly, and at a rate no more than a quarter of an inch in width." We follow her lead on that, but only for a cold slaw.

1 medium to large cabbage head, about 1½ pounds, halved and cored

2 carrots

DRESSING

1 cup sour cream

¾ cup mayonnaise

¼ cup cider vinegar

¼ cup sugar

1½ teaspoons celery seeds

1 teaspoon salt or more to taste

As Lettice Bryan recommended, slice the cabbage rather than grate it, keeping the shreds about ¼ inch thick. Grate the carrots on the large holes of a grater and combine them with the cabbage in a large bowl.

Whisk together the dressing ingredients in a small bowl. Pour the dressing over the vegetables and mix well. For the best flavor, refrigerate the slaw for at least 30 minutes before serving. It keeps well for several days.

The TV Chefs

In 1984, *Cuisine* magazine skewered TV cooking shows, calling them "menu-tainment." "What's next?" the respected magazine asked. "Two years ago no one would have predicted the success of rock videos on MTV. Maybe CTV is just around the corner. Or would it be FTV?" A decade later it was indeed the TV Food Network, and its most popular chef-host bounded onto his nightly stage to the accompaniment of live music from a house band.

However corny the antics get, the best TV cooking shows have substantially raised American awareness of good food, and the best have always been entertaining as well as instructional and supportive. When James Beard went on the air in 1946 as one of the medium's earliest chefs, the trained actor rejoiced at the opportunity to combine theater and cooking. Other hosts, from Graham Kerr to Emeril Lagasse, displayed similar showmanship, either natural or learned.

The Emmy goes, of course, to Julia Child. Shortly after her debut on public television in the early 1960s as "The French Chef," *The New York Times* hailed her series as "campier than 'Batman,' farther-out than 'Lost in Space,' and more penetrating than 'Meet the Press' as it probes the question: Can a Society Be Great if its Bread Tastes Like Kleenex?" Even the *Cuisine* article cut Child some slack, praising her clarity and practicality, wry wit, and wonderful recipes. All so true, plus her down-to-earth relish for cooking that lights up any screen.

Rutabaga–Colby Cheese Casserole

SERVES 6

Lynne Nelsen, a college roommate of Cheryl's, introduced her years ago to a number of root vegetables that she hadn't eaten as a child. Like many immigrants of Norwegian descent, the Nelsens settled in Wisconsin, where Scandinavian staples such as rutabagas grow well. Cooks learned to prepare the tuber with other local ingredients, including the state's own Colby cheese, named for its town of origin. In tandem, the two Wisconsin favorites produce a creamy but earthy casserole.

- 2 pounds rutabagas, peeled and cut into ¾-inch cubes
- 2 tablespoons unsalted butter
- 3 ounces Colby cheese, grated (¾ cup)
- Salt and freshly milled black pepper
- Pinch of ground nutmeg, optional

BREAD CRUMBS

- 1 tablespoon unsalted butter
- ¾ cup fresh bread crumbs

Preheat the oven to 375° F. Grease an 8-inch square baking dish or other small baking dish.

Place the rutabagas in a saucepan with enough salted water to cover them. Bring them to a boil, then simmer until very tender, about 20 minutes. Drain the rutabagas of all but about 1 tablespoon of the cooking liquid. Transfer the rutabagas and liquid to a food processor, and add the butter and cheese. Purée the mixture. Season with salt, pepper, and optional nutmeg, and pulse to combine. Spoon the mixture into the prepared dish.

Prepare the bread crumbs, first melting the butter in a small skillet over medium heat. Stir in the bread crumbs and toast them until golden, stirring occasionally. Scrape the bread crumbs out of the skillet and sprinkle them over the rutabaga mixture.

Bake for about 25 minutes, until heated through and golden brown and crunchy on top. Serve hot.

Baked Vidalia Onions

Serves 4

Farmers raise sweet onions in several areas of the country, but none are better known and more widely available today than the mild-mannered Vidalias from southeastern Georgia. Unlike most onions, Vidalias are technically not keepers because of their high sugar and water content, but few contemporary cooks care about the distinction. Some people eat Vidalias, Walla Wallas, Mauis, Texas 1015s, and other sweet onions raw, as they would an apple. We like them baked with a little butter and a crunchy nut topping, an approach approved in Georgia.

- 4 medium to large whole Vidalia onions or other sweet onions, outer skins removed
- ¼ cup (½ stick) plus 1 tablespoon unsalted butter, softened
- Salt
- 2 tablespoons chopped pecans

Preheat the oven to 375° F. Grease a baking dish large enough to hold the onions comfortably.

Trim the root end of an onion, without cutting into it, then slice off a thin piece across the onion's stem end. With a melon baller or small spoon, scoop out a little hollow in this side of the onion, just large enough to hold a tablespoon of butter. Repeat with the remaining onions. Using 1 tablespoon of the butter, coat the outsides of all the onions. Arrange them in the baking dish with the cavity up, fill the hollow of each with 1 tablespoon of butter, and sprinkle the onions lightly with salt.

Bake the onions for 45 minutes until nearly tender, basting twice with the pan juices. Sprinkle with the pecans and continue baking for 15 to 20 additional minutes, until quite tender with some brown edges. Serve the onions with the pan juices in shallow bowls.

INGREDIENT TIP: To store Vidalias for more than a few days at home, tie them in old panty hose with a knot between each one, creating a real conversation starter when someone pops into your pantry. The air circulation helps prolong their lives. A good mail-order source for the onions is Bland Farms (800-VIDALIA), still a family operation some fifty years after newlyweds Raymond and Rubye Jean Bland founded the business. The company also sells small "cookers," inexpensive dishes that are sized for baking and serving individual onions.

TECHNIQUE TIP: If the idea of serving a whole baseball-size sweet onion per person seems excessive, you probably didn't grow up in Georgia. To split the portions in half, slice the onions through their middles, scoop out a shallow hollow in the cut surface of each section, and fill the cavities with equal portions of the butter. Continue with the preparation as presented, but reduce the cooking time by a few minutes.

Onion and Olive Enchiladas

Serves 6

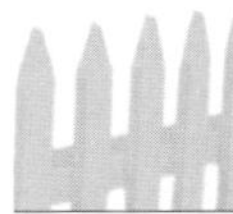

Jacqueline Higuera McMahan, a descendant of the original Spanish settlers in California, grew up eating these unusual enchiladas at family barbecues and breakfasts alike. She recalls them in *California Rancho Cooking* (1988) as "a favorite of *las comidas del pais* (the native foods)," and a single serving will show you why.

ENCHILADA SAUCE

2 tablespoons vegetable oil

2 tablespoons fine dried bread crumbs or unbleached all-purpose flour

2 garlic cloves, minced

1 teaspoon dried oregano, preferably Mexican

¼ cup plus 2 tablespoons ground dried mild red chiles, such as ancho or New Mexican

1 tablespoon cider vinegar

1 teaspoon salt

3 tablespoons olive oil

4 cups diced onions

12 large thin flour tortillas

¾ pound medium to sharp Cheddar cheese, grated (about 3 cups)

¾ cup sliced pitted water-packed black olives

> There are many ways to love a vegetable. The most sensible is to love it well-treated. Then you can eat it with the comfortable knowledge that you will be a better man for it, in your spirit and your body too, and will never have to worry about your own love being vegetable.
>
> M.F.K. Fisher, *How to Cook a Wolf* (1942)

Prepare the sauce, first warming the oil in a large heavy saucepan over medium heat. Sprinkle in the bread crumbs and brown briefly. Add the garlic, oregano, and chiles. Slowly pour in 4 cups of water, stirring to avoid lumps, and then add the vinegar and salt. Bring the sauce to a boil, reduce the heat to a simmer, and cook until somewhat thickened and reduced, 20 to 25 minutes. (The sauce can be made up to several days in advance and refrigerated, covered, or frozen for up to several months. Reheat before proceeding.)

Preheat the oven to 350° F. Oil a large baking dish, one that is at least as wide as your tortillas.

Warm the olive oil in a large heavy skillet over medium-low heat. Add the onions and sauté them for 30 minutes, stirring occasionally. The onions should become translucent and very soft, but not brown. Reduce the heat if needed.

Dip a tortilla into the chile sauce and place it on a plate. Sprinkle about 3 tablespoons of the cheese and 2 tablespoons of the onions down the center of the tortilla. Scatter a couple of teaspoons of olive slices over the onions. Instead of rolling up the tortilla, just fold the tortilla in half. With a spatula, transfer the enchilada to the baking dish. Repeat with the remaining tortillas and filling ingredients, placing each enchilada so that it overlaps the previous one. Spoon the remaining sauce over the top of the enchiladas. Sprinkle with any remaining cheese or olives.

Bake the enchiladas for 20 minutes until the cheese is melted and bubbly. (Some tortillas may balloon up a bit as they cook.) Serve the enchiladas immediately.

SWEETS AND SOURS for the Pantry

USING SUCH TERMS AS "WINTERING IN" AND "PUTTING up," early American cooks always preserved as much as possible of their harvest of fruits and vegetables to supply and refresh the winter table. The old preservation methods of drying, salting, brining, and smoking go back centuries before European settlement of the New World, and colonists used them all. They also made jellies, jams, marmalades, and preserves by cooking fruit with sugar, storing these sweetmeats in stoneware jars sealed with brandy-soaked parchment paper. The various foods helped keep bellies full on frigid days and, even more important over time, succored the appetite any time of the year with marvelous flavors.

Some settlers preferred fruity, sweet tastes, while the Pennsylvania Dutch in particular enjoyed a tart, vinegary tang as a complement to their pork and dough dishes. The flavors merged early in some relishes, particularly pickles of Asian origin such as chutney, a dish imported through the trade routes of the British empire. In other cases, the two tastes remained distinct, but became increasingly linked as contrasting styles in home-canned condiments. The Pennsylvania Dutch earned renown for their "seven sweets and seven sours" by the end of the nineteenth century, but other American tables also brimmed with pickles and preserves in the same period.

Modern home-canning technology developed earlier in the nineteenth century, stimulated initially by Napoleon Bonaparte's quest for a better way to feed his French armies. When the emperor offered a reward for the most effective solution, a Paris confectioner named Nicolas Appert won the prize with a sanitized bottling and canning process that ensured a long, unspoiled life for army rations. Napoleon tried to keep the method a military secret, but it soon spread to other countries, including the United States. A few decades later, John Landis Mason of Brooklyn patented the glass jar that bears his name, an easy-to-use airtight container for home preparations based on Appert's procedure.

The improvements in technology and tools helped maintain enthusiasm for home canning during and after the period when new commercial products eliminated the preservation need. Now prized as tasty accents for any season, our sweets and sours remain home-crafted treasures, full of flavors refined over many harvests past.

Home Canning Basics

When the need for preservation drove home canning in the past, the process could be both a chore and a challenge. Cooks often dealt with massive quantities of produce, much of it ready for wintering-in at about the same time, a situation that required many long, hot days of preparation. Sanitation, sealing, gelling, and the purity of ingredients all loomed as major spoilage concerns.

Today it's much easier and safer to can foods. Just bear in mind a few basics:

- Keep your work area and yourself scrupulously clean. Sterilize all jars, canning funnels, and other equipment before starting. This is easily accomplished by running everything through the dishwasher and leaving it there until needed.
- Always start with new metal lids for your canning jars, and check to see that the jars are free of cracks and chips.
- If you use a boiling-water bath to create long-lasting shelf-stable items, check the vacuum seal on all completed jars. If the seal is not tight after the jar cools, the food is still good, but should be refrigerated immediately and used within a couple of weeks.
- Use common sense. If preserved food doesn't look or smell right, discard it without tasting it.
- The Ball Blue Book, republished regularly with updated canning and preserving advice, remains a good and inexpensive source for basic information. Order through the company's canning hot line, 800-240-3340, which can also answer questions.

Apple Butter

Makes about 3 half-pints

The most venerable "sweet" on the Pennsylvania Dutch table, apple butter probably derives from a German plum spread made in a similar way. Putting up a supply for the winter and the rest of the year ahead became an annual harvest ritual, typically done over an outdoor fire in a huge kettle with enormous quantities of peeled apples and cider. Three generations of a family might participate in the preparation, cooking the apples slowly over many hours into a thick, intensely flavored butter, much richer and more concentrated than applesauce. Use two or more different apples if possible for this spread, preferably hearty varieties with a full fruit taste.

2 quarts apple cider
4 pounds apples, peeled and cored
½ teaspoon ground cinnamon
¼ teaspoon ground coriander
Several tablespoons of packed light brown sugar, optional

Prepare 3 half-pint jars or freezer containers.

Pour the cider into a large heavy pan and bring to a boil over high heat. Cook the cider down by about one-third. While the cider reduces, slice the apples in a food processor, using the thinnest slicing blade. (This can be done by hand too, but it takes a good bit more time.)

When the cider is ready, add the apples, reduce the heat to medium, and cook until the apples begin to disintegrate, about 1 hour. Reduce the heat to low and continue cooking until very thick, spreadable, and nearly smooth, 3½ to 4 additional hours. Stir the apple butter every 10 to 15 minutes during the last 1½ hours of cooking. Add the spices and then some brown sugar if you feel the apple butter needs more sweetness. Start with a tablespoon of brown sugar and add more as necessary. (Many recipes load up on the sugar by the cupful, which makes the spread softer and more syrupy but less redolent of apples.) Spoon into the jars, leaving at least ¼ inch of headspace.

For long shelf life, the apple butter can be processed in a boiling water bath according to the jar manufacturer's directions. Given the small yield, we typically freeze it or just refrigerate it to eat within a couple of months.

Apples Aplenty

In her *Pennsylvania Dutch Cookbook* (1990), Betty Groff recalls the childhood delight of making and eating apple butter. Each year her father and uncle started the outdoor fire early on an October morning, and the women and girls spent the day peeling apples for the copper kettles and constantly stirring the butter with a big wood paddle. The "family experts" selected a mixture of tart Stayman and Smokehouse apples to mix with *schnitz* (dried apples), sugar, and spices. The cooked-down spread stayed on the table the rest of the year, Groff recalls, to put on bread and in half-moon pies, and to eat with ham, scrapple, wild game, and even the Thanksgiving turkey, in place of cranberry sauce.

Organic farmer Glenn Brendle, one of Groff's "English" schoolmates—"English" meaning non-Dutch in local parlance—likes apple butter based on *schnitz* and grainy, early-season varieties of the fruit. Other people add quinces to the kettle, or make a similar butter of them alone. Popular in the past for jellies and marmalades in particular, and making a comeback today, quinces fell out of favor in the early twentieth century, probably because they require long cooking to bring out their distinctively delicious flavor. Anglo-Americans used to call the fruit butter "quince honey," because of its rich thickness, while Spanish Americans in the Southwest knew it as *cajeta*, after the goat-milk caramel that resembles honey in consistency.

Scarlet Pepper Jelly

Makes 6 to 7 half-pints

You might guess that pepper jellies and jams come from California or Texas, but one of the earliest and most influential recipes appeared in the landmark 1950 *Charleston Receipts,* published by the city's Junior League. Mrs. Johnson Hagood's version in the book featured red bell peppers, suggesting a leap from more common fresh pepper relishes. Other cooks heated up the jelly considerably by the next decade, adding a range of chiles. We mix bells and jalapeños, preferably red ones for a scarlet sheen. Mrs. Hagood served her preserve over cream cheese, still a popular approach, but it also makes a great glaze for pork chops or tenderloin and it really zips up a peanut butter sandwich.

- 6 medium red bell peppers, chopped
- 6 to 8 jalapeño chiles, preferably red, seeded and chopped
- 6½ cups sugar
- 1 cup white vinegar
- ½ cup fresh lemon juice
- ½ teaspoon unsalted butter
- 6 ounces liquid pectin, such as Certo

Prepare 7 half-pint canning jars according to the manufacturer's directions.

Combine the bell peppers, jalapeños, sugar, vinegar, and lemon juice in a large saucepan, and bring to a boil over high heat. Boil until the pepper mixture is tender, about 15 minutes. If it threatens to overflow the pan at any time, reduce the heat a bit. Pour the mixture into a food mill or through a coarse sieve and press the liquid through. Discard the remaining solids. Rinse the pan, return the liquid to it, add the butter, and bring the liquid back to a rolling boil over high heat. Pour in the pectin, stir well, and continue boiling for 1 minute or however long the pectin manufacturer specifies. Skim off any foam with a clean spoon, though the butter should decrease its formation. Pour the jelly into the prepared jars, leaving at least ¼ inch of headspace.

Process the jars in a boiling-water bath according to the manufacturer's directions, generally about 10 minutes. The jelly may require several hours to set. Refrigerate it after opening.

Receipt vs. Recipe

Throughout this book,
as you will see,
We never mention
recipe,—
The reason being that
we felt,
(Though well aware how
it is spelt!)
That it is modern and
not meet
To use in place of old
receipt
To designate time-
honored dishes
According to ancestral
wishes.

Junior League of Charleston, Charleston Receipts (1950)

Blackberry Jam

MAKES 3 HALF-PINTS

Fruit jams are America's favorite sweet condiment, found in commercial versions in almost all home pantries and on every restaurant breakfast table in the country. At first, fruits were so abundant in the wild, we hardly cultivated any for our home canning needs, just picking and putting them up as needed. That produced a wealth of local specialties, mostly forgotten today since every eating establishment from Alaska to Florida offers, in ubiquitous single-serving jars, exactly the same kinds of jam. One of the choices, invariably, is strawberry, perhaps the all-time favorite. Commercial strawberry jams taste of little more than sugar, but it's hard to get much better fruit flavor in home canning unless you grow your own berries. For a premium jam you need fresh delicate strawberries bursting with juice, a kind rarely found in markets because they are too fragile for packing and shipping. As an alternative for a homemade jam, we opt for blackberries, the fruit Walt Whitman said "would adorn the parlors of heaven."

TECHNIQUE TIP: Experienced jam makers typically eyeball the boiling fruit mixture and know when it has gelled sufficiently by the way it looks on a spoon. This method always made us nervous when we were novices until we discovered a more precise technique. To make sure that a jam or jelly mixture gels, know the exact temperature at which your water boils before you begin cooking. The widely accepted temperature of 212° F is correct at sea level, but the vast majority of us live at a somewhat different altitude. Stick a reliable candy or deep-fry thermometer in a pot of water, bring the heat to high, and check the temperature when the water first reaches a full rolling boil. Add 8 degrees to that figure to get the correct temperature for gelling. If you find that your water boils at 210° F, for example, cook a jam or jelly to 218° F.

- 4 cups wild or domestic blackberries, preferably mixed half and half with loganberries
- 2 cups sugar
- 2 tablespoons fresh lemon juice

Prepare 3 half-pint canning jars according to the manufacturer's directions.

Place the berries in a heavy saucepan. Mash the berries lightly with a pastry blender or large fork. Stir in the sugar and let the berries sit from 1 to several hours.

Add the lemon juice and bring the mixture to a boil over medium-high heat. Cook for about 10 minutes, until thick and somewhat gelled-looking on a clean spoon. Remove from the heat and skim off any foam with another clean spoon. Pour the jam into the prepared jars, leaving at least ¼ inch of headspace.

Process the jars in a boiling-water bath according to the manufacturer's directions, generally about 10 minutes. The jam may require several hours to set. Refrigerate the jam after opening.

Beach Plum Jam

Makes 7 to 8 half-pints

Colonists from New England to Virginia learned to love the wild beach plums they found growing on the sandy shores of the Atlantic coast. Too tart to eat out of hand, unlike European plums, they make great jellies and jams. In inland areas, substitute other tart plums, such as damsons, or even wild grapes with a similar tang.

- 3½ pounds beach plums or other tart plums, or wild grapes, preferably a combination of very ripe fruit plus about one-fourth underripe
- Approximately 3½ cups sugar
- 3 tablespoons light rum, optional

Prepare 8 half-pint canning jars according to the manufacturer's directions.

Combine the beach plums in a large saucepan with 1 cup of water and bring to a boil over high heat. Boil until the plums are very tender, about 10 minutes. Pour the mixture into a food mill or through a coarse sieve and press it through. Discard the remaining solids. Measure the liquid and pulpy fruit and return it to the pan. (There should be approximately 4 cups total.) For every 2 cups of fruity liquid, add 1¾ cups of sugar. Bring the mixture back to a boil over high heat, stirring as needed to keep it from boiling over. Cook for about 10 minutes, until thick and somewhat gelled. Skim off any foam with a clean spoon. Remove from the heat and immediately stir in the rum if you wish. Spoon the jam into the prepared jars, leaving at least ¼ inch of headspace.

Process the jars in a boiling-water bath according to the manufacturer's directions, generally about 10 minutes. The jam may require several hours to set. Refrigerate the jam after opening.

It is a thrill to possess shelves well stocked with home-canned food. In fact, you will find their inspection (often surreptitious), and the pleasure of serving the fruits of your labors, comparable only to a clear conscience or a very becoming hat.

Irma Rombauer,
Joy of Cooking (1943)

Fig Preserves

Makes about 3 half-pints

Most early American recipes for preserves call for whole fruit, packed simply in syrup to be served as a separate dish. As preserves evolved into more of a seasoning condiment and spread, cooks began to cut the fruit into chunks. Fig preserves caught on early in mild climes favorable to the fruit, which the Spanish introduced in the New World in the sixteenth century. As a child, Bill loved his Grandmother Cleveland's version, made with figs picked from her trees in Buda, Texas. Our rendition rekindles that flame, but reduces the sugar content and dispenses with the canning.

2 pounds ripe figs, preferably Missions, stemmed and halved

¼ cup sugar

Zest of 1 lemon, minced

1 tablespoon lemon juice or a little more to taste

TECHNIQUE TIP:
For shelf-stable food safety, authorities recommend preserving low-acid food in a boiling-water bath or by pressure canning. Sometimes we forgo long-shelf life, opting for quick consumption from the refrigerator or midrange storage in the freezer. Typically we do this when working with small batches of a scarce or pricey food—or when the key ingredient is so common that we can make the condiment easily whenever the urge strikes.

Prepare 3 half-pint jars or freezer containers.

Combine the figs, sugar, and lemon zest with ½ cup of water in a heavy saucepan. Cook 25 to 35 minutes over low heat, stirring occasionally, until the figs and other ingredients have cooked down into a thick fragrant mass. Remove the preserves from the heat and stir in the lemon juice. Spoon into jars or freezer containers, leaving at least ¼ inch of headspace. Cover and refrigerate for up to several weeks (though they never last that long at our house) or freeze for several months.

Pumpkin Chip Preserves

MAKES 4 TO 5 HALF-PINTS

Preserves made with peach or pumpkin chips are an old favorite, found in many early cookbooks. Get a true cooking pumpkin for the preserves, not one grown for jack-o'-lantern looks, and try to start the preparation a day before you plan to can the preserves. If you want to taste a good commercial version before making your own, call 843-720-8890 for a copy of The Lee Bros. Boiled Peanuts Catalogue, a sterling source for other traditional condiments as well.

- 5- to 5½-pound pumpkin, preferably a cheese or pie pumpkin
- 5 cups sugar
- Juice and minced zest of 2 large lemons
- 1 medium to large lemon, sliced thin

Prepare 5 half-pint canning jars according to the manufacturer's directions.

Cut the pumpkin into large chunks, discarding the stem, seeds, and the stringy innards attached to them. Pare the skin from the chunks. Slice each chunk into pieces about ½ to ¾ inch square, as evenly as your patience allows. Stir to combine the pumpkin pieces in a large bowl with sugar, lemon juice and zest, and ½ cup water. Cover and let the mixture sit overnight, or a few hours longer, at room temperature. It will give off a good bit of liquid.

Spoon the pumpkin mixture into a large heavy saucepan and bring it to a boil over medium-high heat. Reduce the heat to a bare simmer and cook covered until the pumpkin pieces are quite tender, but still hold their shape and have become somewhat translucent in a glaze of thick syrup, about 30 minutes. While the chips cook, blanch the lemon slices in a small saucepan of boiling water, just enough to soften them, and drain them. Stir the lemon slices into the chips just before removing the preserves from the heat. Spoon the chips into the prepared jars, leaving at least ¼ inch of headspace.

Process the jars in a boiling-water bath according to the manufacturer's directions, generally about 10 minutes. Refrigerate the preserves after opening.

Ozarks Black Walnut Conserve

MAKES 4 TO 5 HALF-PINTS

Americans have often pickled nuts and sometimes made them into jams. This approach is adapted from Billy Joe Tatum's *Wild Foods Cookbook & Field Guide* (1976), a work still as fresh as the ingredients she foraged in the Ozarks two decades ago. The country's native black walnuts, widely cherished in the past, virtually disappeared from commercial circulation at one time, but can be found again today in specialty stores. If they aren't available, substitute hickory nuts or pecans rather than the mild English walnuts.

- 1½ cups packed dark brown sugar
- ½ cup honey
- 1 cup cider vinegar
- Zest of 1 lemon, minced
- ¾ teaspoon curry powder
- ½ teaspoon ground allspice
- ½ teaspoon ground ginger
- ½ teaspoon yellow mustard seeds
- ½ teaspoon salt or more to taste
- ¼ teaspoon ground cloves
- 3 cups black walnut pieces, toasted (see Ingredient Tip)
- ¼ cup plus 2 tablespoons bourbon or other American whiskey

Prepare 5 half-pint canning jars according to the manufacturer's directions.

Combine in a large heavy saucepan the brown sugar, honey, vinegar, lemon zest, curry powder, allspice, ginger, mustard seeds, salt, and cloves. Add 2 cups of water and bring the mixture to a boil over high heat. Reduce the heat to a simmer and cook for 5 minutes. Add the walnut pieces and cook until thick and syrupy, 5 to 10 additional minutes. Remove from the heat and stir in the bourbon. Spoon the conserve into the prepared jars, leaving at least ¼ inch of headspace.

Process the jars in a boiling-water bath according to the manufacturer's directions, generally about 10 minutes. Let the conserve sit for at least a week before serving. Refrigerate the jars after opening.

INGREDIENT TIP: Black walnuts are prized on their home turf, from the Carolinas to the Ozarks, for their rich, slightly bitter pungency. The shells are extremely hard to crack, so if you're buying them, as opposed to collecting them in the wild, you'll typically find them shelled. Store them in the freezer to keep their flavorful oil from going rancid. Black walnut pieces can be ordered by mail from Sunnyland Farms in Albany, Georgia (800-999-2488).

Let the young woman with wasp-like waist, who lives on candies, salads, hot bread, pastry, and pickles, whose listless brain and idle hands seek no profitable occupation, whose life is given to folly, remember that to her ignorance and folly may yet be traced the downfall of a nation.

BUCKEYE COOKERY AND PRACTICAL HOUSEKEEPING (1880)

Tomato Chutney

MAKES ABOUT 3 HALF-PINTS

Technically fruits rather than vegetables, tomatoes make wonderful chutneys. Sweet and tangy, this recipe goes great alongside Hoppin' John (page 319) or Spoonbread (page 329). We call for red tomatoes, but pert ripe yellow ones work well too.

- 2 pounds red-ripe tomatoes, peeled and chopped (see Ingredient Tip)
- 1 cup chopped onion
- ½ cup dried currants
- ¼ cup plus 2 tablespoons sugar
- ¼ cup plus 2 tablespoons cider vinegar
- 2 teaspoons yellow mustard seeds
- 1 teaspoon salt
- ¼ teaspoon ground allspice
- ¼ teaspoon ground cinnamon
- ⅛ to ¼ teaspoon cayenne pepper

Prepare 3 half-pint jars or freezer containers.

Combine the ingredients in a large heavy saucepan and bring the mixture to a boil over high heat. Reduce the heat to medium-low and cook until thick, about 1 hour. Stir frequently toward the end of the cooking. Cool the chutney, then spoon it into the prepared jars, leaving at least ¼ inch of headspace. The chutney can be refrigerated for at least several weeks and frozen for several months. It's best served after the flavors have had a chance to mingle for at least a day.

INGREDIENT TIP: A credible version of the chutney can be made out of season with good canned tomatoes, such as the Muir Glen brand. Start with a bit less salt, adding more later in the cooking if needed.

Dried Fruit

Another method of preserving fruit for the winter, as common as canning, drying offered some major advantages. The cook didn't need sugar, fire, water, or special jars with tight seals. She spread the fruit in the sun, or strung pieces together and suspended them from rafters inside or out, or sometimes used low heat in an oven to dehydrate the pickings. Drying worked with virtually all fruits, and some became local specialties, including the *schnitz* of the Pennsylvania Dutch and the red chiles of the New Mexico Spanish.

In *The Way We Ate* (1996), Jacqueline B. Williams tells about the enthusiasm in the Pacific Northwest for "tomato figs." Pioneers dried ripe tomatoes in sugar to create what one newspaper called "an article fully equal to the best fig." Williams says the idea came west from the mid-Atlantic states, where a Washington, D.C. cook actually tried to patent it in the 1840s. The authorities denied her application, but the attempt shows a dedication to home-drying methods that are almost completely forgotten today.

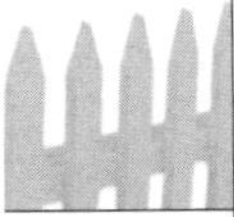

Baked Cranberry Sauce

MAKES ABOUT 2½ CUPS

One of the country's most distinctive native fruits, cranberries grow in bogs in a number of northern states, mainly Massachusetts, New Jersey, Wisconsin, and Oregon. Native Americans ate them prepared in various ways, and they may have brought them to the first Thanksgiving feast in Plymouth in 1621. Today the berries are intimately associated with the holiday, usually appearing in a sauce similar to this, though most versions are boiled instead of baked. The sauce keeps for several weeks in the refrigerator, ready to dress quail or duck as well as turkey.

12-ounce bag cranberries, fresh or frozen

1 to 1¼ cups sugar

¼ teaspoon ground cinnamon

Pinch of nutmeg

3 to 4 tablespoons bourbon (our favorite), brandy, or light rum

Preheat the oven to 350°F.

Combine the cranberries, sugar, cinnamon, and nutmeg in a small baking dish, and cover the mixture. Bake for 55 minutes, uncover, and stir to melt undissolved sugar, and return to the oven for 5 to 10 additional minutes. The cranberries are ready when soft with a syrupy sauce. Remove from the oven and immediately stir in the bourbon. Let the sauce cool to room temperature, then chill it for at least an hour before serving. If the sauce becomes too thick to spoon easily, stir in a small amount of water. The sauce keeps for several weeks.

INGREDIENT TIP: Never pass up a chance to visit a cranberry bog in summer or fall. In Wisconsin, where we once toured some fields, farmers grow the berries in three- to five-acre tracts surrounded by dikes. The bushes blossom in early summer with light pink flowers, and rented bees take care of the pollination. The amount of sunshine shapes the size of the berry, but the vibrancy of their color comes from the cool nights as autumn approaches. At harvest time, workers flood the plants and the berries float to the surface in a crimson wave for picking.

Pickled Peaches

MAKES 2 QUARTS

Early Spanish explorers brought peaches to the New World and they thrived throughout much of the area that became the United States. Native Americans adopted the fruit first, but European colonists didn't lag far behind, particularly in the prime growing regions of the South. By the first half of the nineteenth century, cooks had developed dozens of ways to pickle and preserve peaches, including a style similar to this one.

- 2½ dozen unblemished small ripe but firm peaches (about 4 pounds)
- 3 cups granulated sugar
- 3 cups cider vinegar
- ½ cup packed light brown sugar
- 1 tablespoon whole allspice
- 2 teaspoons whole cloves
- 2 ounces fresh ginger, diced fine
- 2 cinnamon sticks

Prepare 2 quart canning jars according to the manufacturer's directions.

Bring a saucepan of water to a boil over high heat. Dunk the peaches in the water, a few at a time, for about 1 minute. The skin should now be loose and easy to peel off in strips with your fingers. Peel each peach carefully, since any gouges mar the beauty of the finished jars of peaches.

In a pan large enough to hold all of the ingredients, combine the granulated sugar, vinegar, and brown sugar with 2 cups of water. Tie the allspice and cloves in a small section of cheesecloth and add it, the ginger, and the cinnamon sticks to the pan. Bring the mixture to a boil over high heat, then reduce to a simmer and cook for 10 minutes, long enough for the syrup to reduce a bit and for the spices to begin to release their flavors. Gently spoon the peaches into the syrup and continue simmering for about 8 minutes, until you can easily pierce a peach with a toothpick. Remove the cheesecloth bag and discard it.

Pack the peaches into the prepared jars, distributing a cinnamon stick and about half of the ginger to each jar. Cover the peaches completely with the syrup, leaving at least ½ inch of headspace.

Process the jars in a boiling-water bath according to the manufacturer's directions, generally about 15 minutes. Let the peaches sit for at least several weeks before serving. Refrigerate the jars after opening.

When the peach orchard "hit" it meant joy to the plantation. Peaches had so many charms—and there were so many ways of stretching the charms on through winter scarcity. . . .

August peaches were for drying—in September, early, came the Heaths, for preserves, brandy fruit, and so on. October peaches, nearly all clear-seed, made the finest peach butter.

MARTHA McCULLOCH-WILLIAMS, *DISHES AND BEVERAGES OF THE OLD SOUTH* (1913)

Spiced Crabapples

Makes 5 to 6 pints

We inherited spiced fruit from the British, but picked up crabapples from the wild. A staple on midwestern relish trays, the small, crisp, tart apples make superlative jellies and pickles. Start preparing these a day before you plan to can them. After letting them sit a spell, serve the crabapples with grilled venison or roast duck.

- 2¾ to 3 pounds firm, unblemished crabapples with stems intact, about 1 inch in diameter
- 3½ cups sugar
- 3 cups cranberry juice
- 2 cups cider vinegar
- 1 cup red-wine vinegar
- 3 cinnamon sticks, broken in several pieces each
- 2 teaspoons whole allspice
- 2 teaspoons whole cloves

Prick each crabapple's skin with a straight pin in about a dozen spots, to help keep the skins from splitting while cooking.

Combine the sugar, cranberry juice, and vinegars in a large heavy saucepan. Tie the cinnamon sticks, allspice, and cloves in a small piece of cheesecloth and add the bag to the liquid. Bring the mixture to a boil over high heat, then reduce the heat to a simmer and cook for 5 minutes. Cool the liquid for at least 10 minutes, then gently spoon in the crabapples. Cook the crabapples over low heat just until tender, about 15 minutes. Stir occasionally. Don't be tempted to raise the heat to speed up the process because it can cause the crabapple skins to split. Only the barest of bubbles should break on the surface. Remove the pan from the heat and let it cool. Cover the pan with a clean dishtowel and let it sit at room temperature for 12 to 24 hours.

Prepare 6 pint canning jars according to the manufacturer's directions. We prefer wide-mouthed jars because they are easier to fill with crabapples.

With a slotted spoon, arrange the crabapples in the prepared jars, nudging them in gently but not squashing them. Return the liquid to a boil over high heat and cook for 5 to 10 minutes, reducing it by about half, until it drizzles from a spoon like syrup. Remove and discard the bag of spices. Pour the syrup evenly over the crabapples, covering them completely, but leaving at least ¼ inch of headspace.

Process the jars in a boiling-water bath according to the manufacturer's directions, generally about 10 minutes. Let the crabapples sit for at least several weeks before serving. Refrigerate the jars after opening.

TECHNIQUE TIP:
In spite of your best efforts, a few crabapples will likely split their skins during the pickling process. You may want to add a few extra apples at the beginning, just in case, or choose not to worry about it. The crabapples may look less attractive, but they'll taste the same. We simply segregate the ones with split skins to a jar we keep for ourselves and serve the prettier ones to guests.

California Brandied Dates

Makes 2 pints

The hot, dry Coachella Valley surrounding Palm Springs, California, provides a welcoming climate for date palms, imported from the Middle East about a century ago. Brandy preserves dates, as it does with other fruit, but it also balances the concentrated, cloying sweetness. We work with plump, moist versions of dried dates, but if you're lucky enough to find fresh dates in season, they can be used instead. Elena Zelayeta, whose recipe in *Elena's Favorite Foods California Style* (1967) inspired ours, liked to serve the fruit with ice cream or custard. We add frozen vanilla yogurt to the desserts they enhance, or serve them as a relish with roasted leg of lamb or grilled lamb chops.

- 1½ pounds dried dates, preferably Medjools
- 1 cup packed brown sugar
- 1½ cups brandy
- Heaping ½ teaspoon whole coriander seeds per jar
- ½ cinnamon stick per jar
- 2 strips orange or lemon zest per jar

Prepare 2 pint canning jars according to the manufacturer's directions.

Place the dates in a saucepan and cover them with water. Bring to a boil, then reduce the heat to a simmer and cook for 2 to 3 minutes, just until the skins begin to separate from the dates. Drain the dates and when cool enough to handle, pull the loose skins from them. Using a paring knife, slit down one side of each date and remove the large pit. With your fingers, re-form each date into its original shape.

Rinse out the saucepan, then combine in it the brown sugar and 1 cup of water. Bring the liquid to a boil over high heat. Reduce the heat to a simmer, add the dates, and simmer for 2 to 3 minutes. Remove the pan from the heat and stir in the brandy.

Spoon coriander seeds into each prepared jar. Spoon the dates and syrup into the jars, covering the dates completely with the syrup. Add the cinnamon sticks and orange zest to each jar, sliding them down an outer side of the jar. When cool, refrigerate the dates for at least a week before serving.

INGREDIENT TIP: Beautiful fresh California dates are available in the early winter from Melissa's (800-588-0151).

We have been too spoiled by a craze for food out of season; for peaches from South Africa and strawberries picked green and shipped too far. Refrigeration and good canning mean progress, but before now, in many fields, progress has upset the apple-cart of permanent and enduring standards.

Sheila Hibben, *The National Cookbook* (1932)

Gingered Cantaloupe Pickles

MAKES 7 TO 8 HALF-PINTS

Spiced cantaloupe pickles sit side by side with watermelon-rind pickles (following recipe) on many tables, and appear together in many Pennsylvania Dutch and southern cookbooks. They share some of the same sweet-sour flavors, though in this recipe the fruit itself is pickled rather than the rind. For the best results, use underripe cantaloupe, the kind found most commonly in supermarkets.

3½ pounds cantaloupe (about 1 large or 2 small underripe melons), cut in bite-size chunks
Pickling salt or kosher salt
5 cups sugar
3 cups white vinegar
⅓ cup minced crystallized ginger
Cinnamon sticks

Arrange the cantaloupe chunks in a large nonreactive shallow bowl. Cover the surface of the fruit completely with ice cubes. Over the ice, sprinkle a thin layer of salt, enough to cover it with the coarse granules. Set the bowl aside at room temperature while the ice begins to melt. When about half of the ice has melted and the remaining ice looks very brittle and crackled, like a shattered windshield, rinse and drain the cantaloupe. (The melting time will vary depending on the heat of the kitchen. We allow 45 minutes to 1 hour.)

Return the fruit to the bowl and add the sugar, vinegar, and ginger. Stir to dissolve the sugar. Weight the fruit with a plate, cover the bowl with a clean dishtowel, and let it stand 12 to 24 hours.

Pour the cantaloupe, syrup, and ½ cup of water into a large saucepan and bring the mixture to a boil over high heat. Reduce the heat to a simmer and cook until the liquid is reduced by about half and the cantaloupe becomes transparent, about 1 hour.

Prepare 8 half-pint canning jars according to the manufacturer's directions.

Spoon the cantaloupe and syrup into the prepared jars, dividing the ginger and cinnamon sticks more or less evenly among the jars and leaving ¼ inch of headspace.

Process the jars in a boiling-water bath according to the manufacturer's directions, generally about 10 minutes. Let the pickles sit for at least several weeks before serving. Refrigerate the jars after opening.

Watermelon-Rind Pickles

MAKES 7 TO 8 PINTS

In the first cookbook written by an American, Amelia Simmons made preserves out of a whole watermelon ("seeds excepted"), and also pickled the rind of green melons. By the time Sidney Dean, a fellow Yankee, wrote *Cooking American* in 1957, watermelon-rind pickles had carved a special, almost emblematic niche in our food culture. As he said, "This is perhaps the richest and most luscious of all fruit pickles, really a conserve. To me it is incomparable, and my mother made it every year. It is certainly cooking American; what could be more American than our national favorite, the watermelon?"

- Rind of 1 large watermelon (see Ingredient Tip)
- ¾ cup pickling salt or ¾ heaping cup kosher salt
- 6 cups granulated sugar
- 2 cups packed light brown sugar
- 4 cups cider vinegar
- 4 cinnamon sticks, halved
- 1 tablespoon whole cloves
- 1 tablespoon whole allspice
- ¼ teaspoon yellow mustard seeds
- 2 lemons, sliced thin

Cut the watermelon rind into manageable chunks. Scrape away any remaining melon meat from the rind, then pare off the hard green skin from the outside. This is the only laborious part of the process, so persevere. Cut the rind into bite-size cubes or small strips or, if you have lots of rind and more patience than we do, into decorative shapes. You should end up with 14 to 15 cups of lightly packed chunks.

Combine the salt and 1 gallon of water in a large bowl. When dissolved, add the watermelon rind and top it with a plate to keep it submerged. Soak the rind for at least 8 hours and up to 24 hours. Drain the rind, rinse it well, and drain it again.

Combine the granulated sugar, brown sugar, vinegar, and cinnamon sticks in a large saucepan, and add 1 cup of water. Tie the cloves, allspice, and mustard seeds in a small section of cheesecloth and add to the pan. Bring the mixture to a boil over high heat, then reduce the heat to a simmer and cook for 5 minutes. Remove the syrup from the heat and stir in the watermelon rind and lemon slices. Cover the pan with a clean dishtowel and let the mixture sit at room temperature for 12 to 24 hours.

Prepare 8 pint canning jars according to the manufacturer's instructions.

The home preserving calendar in New England once ran roughly like this: first rhubarb, red, white, and black currants, and strawberries; then cherries; next the wild berries of summer—blueberries and huckleberries and three kinds of raspberries, red, white (really a pale yellow), and blackcaps or thimbleberries; then, overlapping the raspberries, honey-sweet high bush blackberries, gooseberries (these cultivated), and beach plums; last, the wild and cultivated grapes and other fruits of late summer and early autumn, to say nothing of tomatoes and watermelon.

SIDNEY DEAN,
COOKING AMERICAN
(1957)

Return the watermelon mixture to the heat, bringing it to a boil over high heat. Reduce the heat to a simmer and cook until the rind turns somewhat translucent, 5 to 10 minutes. Discard the bag of spices. Spoon into the prepared jars, dividing lemon slices and cinnamon sticks more or less evenly among the jars and leaving ¼ inch of headspace.

Process the jars in a boiling-water bath according to the manufacturer's directions, generally about 10 minutes. Let the pickles sit for at least several weeks before serving. Refrigerate the jars after opening.

INGREDIENT TIP: Many watermelons today have thin rinds compared with those that our grandparents grew. If you have any choice in the matter, choose a melon with a thick rind, such as a Dixie Lee variety.

"Red Turnip" Pickles

Makes 3 to 4 cups

The early Pennsylvania Dutch often referred to all root vegetables as variations on turnips, calling carrots "yellow turnips," for example, and beets "red turnips." Local cooks brought the custom of pickling beets from Europe, and used raspberry vinegar regularly long before its contemporary revival, but we combine the old ideas here in an untraditional way. The year-round availability of beets today makes them a good candidate for an uncanned, overnight pickle that is more sprightly seasoned than the usual varieties. Serve the beets alongside a pork roast or grilled sausages, or use them to garnish a salad of zesty watercress and some American blue cheese.

2 pounds whole beets, trimmed of greens (see Ingredient Tip)
2 tablespoons packed brown sugar
Pinch of salt
⅔ cup raspberry vinegar or other fruit vinegar
½ to 1 teaspoon grated fresh horseradish or 1 to 2 teaspoons prepared horseradish, optional

Steam the beets until tender but not mushy, 30 to 40 minutes, depending on size. Plunge the beets into cold water, and when cool enough to handle, peel them. Slice the beets into small wedges, no thicker than ½ inch at their widest edge. Place the beets in a nonreactive bowl (avoid plastic, since the beets will stain it). Sprinkle the brown sugar and salt over the beets, then add the vinegar, optional horseradish, and ⅓ cup of water. Cover and refrigerate the mixture overnight or up to several days, stirring occasionally. Drain the beets with a slotted spoon and serve chilled or at room temperature. The beets will keep well for a week or longer.

INGREDIENT TIP: A mix of red beets with golden or chioggia beets dresses up a platter of the pickles in a tantalizing way. Just make sure to segregate each variety during preparation, combining them only when you're ready to serve. Chioggias will be most attractive sliced in rounds to show off their concentric circles of color. Look for beets of these varieties at farmers' markets if not available in your local supermarket.

Betty Crocker, c. 1922–present

Betty Crocker, a fictional representative of a milling company that became part of General Mills, began signing advice letters to flour users in the early 1920s. The advertising department christened her "Crocker" after a popular corporate director and gave her the first name of "Betty" because it sounded all-American. She instantly reached the age of thirty-two and hasn't grown a day older in eight decades.

Her unchanging youth and adaptable appearance kept Betty Crocker in touch with consumers of General Mills products. From the time she debuted as a live voice on national radio in 1927, and started appearing in portrait form in 1936, she served as a sympathetic counterpart to the matronly cooking authorities common at the time. As traditional family networks ceased to be viable sources of cooking guidance, modern, mobile homemakers turned increasingly to outside advisers, none of whom rivaled Betty until the age of television.

Crocker was actually a team of female marketing professionals at General Mills, led for thirty years by Marjorie Child Husted. The company sometimes encouraged Husted to call herself Crocker, but generally preferred to keep Betty a mythical figure needing no real salary or status. Husted eventually resigned, never fully acknowledged for her success and seldom given credit under her own name.

Bread-and-Butter Pickles

Makes 2 pints

Bred on the bread-and-butter pickles of our grandmothers, we also cut our pickling teeth on them many years ago when we started canning at home. Our first yellowed recipe from a newspaper is still pasted in a cooking notebook, but it's evolved over time into these personal favorites. We don't process the pickles in a water bath any longer because we make them in small batches for a rather short shelf life in the refrigerator. If you want to keep them longer, use standard pickling procedures.

- 2 pounds unpeeled plump pickling cucumbers, 4 to 5 inches long, sliced in ¼-inch rounds
- 1 sweet onion, or mild onion, sliced into ¼-inch rings and separated
- 1 medium red bell pepper, sliced into ¼-inch rings
- 2 tablespoons pickling salt or 2 heaping tablespoons kosher salt
- 1½ cups packed brown sugar
- 1 cup cider vinegar
- 2 garlic cloves, minced
- 2 small dried hot red chiles
- 1½ teaspoons yellow mustard seeds
- 1 teaspoon whole black peppercorns
- 1 teaspoon ground turmeric
- 1 teaspoon celery seed

Prepare 2 pint jars.

Combine the cucumbers with the onion and bell-pepper slices in a large nonreactive bowl. Toss with ½ dozen ice cubes. Scatter the salt over the mixture and toss it again lightly. Set aside at room temperature for 3 hours. The cucumbers will release a good bit of water during this time.

Drain the cucumber mixture and rinse well with cold water.

Combine the brown sugar, vinegar, garlic, and remaining spices in a large heavy pan, and bring the liquid to a boil over high heat. Spoon the cucumber mixture into the liquid and bring back to a full boil. Immediately remove the pan from the heat. Ladle the pickles into each jar, covering them in syrup and dividing the spices more or less evenly. Leave ¼ inch of headspace. Refrigerate the pickles for at least a week before eating. The pickles keep for several months.

> Nothing is so effective in keeping one young and full of lust as a discriminating palate thoroughly satisfied at least once a day.
>
> Angelo Pellegrini, *The Unprejudiced Palate* (1948)

Dill Crock Pickles

MAKES 2 QUARTS

Cucumbers pickled in an old-fashioned dill crock come out both more subtle and complex than their ordinary peers, and as a bonus, they almost make themselves, with no cooking or canning required. "Everyone *needs* a dill crock," Edward Harris Heth wrote in his *Wisconsin Country Cookbook and Journal* (1979). Aunt Dell, Heth's Wisconsin neighbor, introduced him to the marvel during his first year in the state, and it became "as integral a part of summer as fireflies or shooting stars." Try it, and you'll share his rhapsody over the dill crock as "a safeguard against life's inconstancies, a reminder that some good things endure."

- Handful of sour cherry or grape leaves, optional
- 4 pounds small plump pickling cucumbers, about 2 to 3 inches, halved lengthwise
- 4 fresh dill heads, with seeds, plus a few additional fronds
- 2 teaspoons yellow mustard seeds
- 2 small dried hot red chiles
- 6 tablespoons pickling salt or 6 heaping tablespoons kosher salt
- ½ cup white vinegar
- A few more fresh dill heads, yellow mustard seeds, and chiles, optional

Arrange half of the leaves at the bottom of a crock, large jar, or nonreactive bowl. (It will be easiest to work with a straight-sided wide-mouthed container.) Add the cucumbers, interspersed with dill, mustard seeds, and chiles.

Mix together the salt and vinegar with ½ gallon of water until the salt is dissolved. Pour this brine over the cucumbers and top with the remaining leaves. Place a heavy plate or large plastic zipperlock bag of water over the pickles to keep them submerged. Cover the crock with a clean dishtowel or cheesecloth. Set the mixture aside in a cool (not cold), out-of-the-way spot to ferment.

Check the pickles after a couple of days and skim off any white scum that has formed. Do not stir the pickles. You should see small bubbles, within the next day or so. Each day, as convenient, skim any additional scum, wash the plate, and return it to the crock. (It is important that the pickles stay completely submerged in brine. You can add more brine, using the same proportions as in the original recipe, should it be necessary.) After about 2 weeks, or maybe a little longer, the bubbling will stop and the pickles will be ready for their final preparation. They will now look like pickles, deeply olive colored, and taste pleasantly sour.

Skim the brine once more, then drain the brine from the pickles through a strainer into a nonreactive saucepan. Discard the dill heads and other residue left from the brine. Bring the brine to a boil over high heat, boil it for 3 minutes, and then let it cool to room temperature. It will remain somewhat cloudy due to the previous fermentation process. While the brine cools, rinse the pickles well in two changes of cold water, discarding any that have become soft or mushy. The pickles can be returned to the container in which they fermented (after washing it), or placed in 2 quart jars. Add fresh dill heads, mustard seeds, and chiles if you wish. Cover with the brine and refrigerate. The pickles can be eaten as soon as they are chilled through, but will keep for at least 6 months.

TECHNIQUE TIP: Writers remembering the pickle barrels of yesteryear frequently mention people sticking a hand into the brine and pulling out a pickle. Forget it! Use a fork, spoon, or other clean utensil for plucking home-preserved goods from the jar. Dallas friends Deborah and Richard West even found us a "pickle plucker," one of the strangest little gadgets we've ever seen. Resembling something that James Bond might carry in his pocket, the plucker has a plunger, which pushes out several predatory, needlelike protrusions to grasp the quarry.

Pickled Okra

Makes 6 to 7 pints

Given the depth of affection for pickled okra in the South, we had always assumed that it was an old, long-honored dish. Actually, it appears to be a twentieth-century invention, with few if any printed recipes dating back before World War II. If you're wary of okra, this is the place to retrain your taste buds, as this pickle offers more tasty snap and crunch than you ever thought possible from the vegetable.

- 3 pounds small fresh okra pods
- 1 garlic clove per jar
- 1 small dried hot red chile per jar
- 1 bay leaf per jar
- ½ teaspoon yellow mustard seeds per jar
- 1 quart white vinegar
- ½ cup pickling salt or ½ heaping cup kosher salt

Prepare 7 pint canning jars according to the manufacturer's instructions.

With clean fingers, arrange okra pods vertically in as many jars as you need to hold them. Alternate them with the stem end or tip end up so that they fit as snugly as possible. Wedge in each jar in a visible spot a garlic clove, chile, and bay leaf. Sprinkle mustard seeds over each jar.

Combine the vinegar, salt, and 1 cup of water in a large saucepan, and bring the liquid to a boil over high heat. Boil for several minutes, then pour the liquid over the okra into each jar, leaving at least ¼ inch of headspace. Process the jars in a boiling-water bath according to the manufacturer's directions, generally about 10 minutes. Let the pickled okra sit for several weeks before serving. Refrigerate the jars after opening.

Pickled Peppers

MAKES 2 PINTS

Southern Italians were among the few major immigrant groups who didn't bring a strong pickling tradition with them to the United States. The balmy climate at home allowed them to raise peppers, tomatoes, and other favorites much of the year, eliminating the need for extensive preservation. Boston, New York, and other widely chosen destinations weren't so kind, and early immigrants refused to resort to commercially canned food, which they regarded with suspicion. Some took up pickling as a solution, particularly for their beloved peppers. Serve these peppers as part of an antipasto, drizzled with olive oil and topped with a sprinkling of herbs, or on a sandwich with mozzarella and tomatoes.

- 4 large plump red bell peppers
- 1 large yellow or orange bell pepper
- 1 or 2 small onions, ends trimmed, then halved vertically
- 2 garlic cloves
- Several sprigs of fresh thyme or oregano, or 2 bay leaves
- 2 cups white-wine vinegar
- 2 teaspoons pickling salt or 2 heaping teaspoons kosher salt

Slice the red and yellow peppers into ¾-inch-wide strips, discarding the seeds and cores. Arrange the pepper strips, onions, garlic, and the herbs attractively in 2 sterilized pint jars. Combine the vinegar and salt with 1 cup of water, dissolve the salt, and pour the mixture over the peppers. Cover and refrigerate the peppers for at least 5 to 6 days. The peppers keep well for months.

Chow-Chow

Makes 4 to 5 pints

A mixed vegetable pickle, chopped fine and assertively spiced, chow-chow provides punch for the palate and puzzles for the mind. The name dates to the early period of Chinese settlement in the country, but the dish existed under other handles at least a century before. John Egerton found a South Carolina recipe from 1770 called Ats Jaar, which indicates, according to William Woys Weaver, an origin in India, like chutney. The concoction seems to have been thoroughly acculturated by 1880, when Miss T. S. Shute in *The American Housewife Cook Book* labeled it Old Virginia Chow-Chow. Eat it alongside Virginia Country Ham (page 172) or with a simple cheese sandwich.

- 3 pounds green tomatoes or a combination of green tomatoes and peeled, seeded cucumbers
- ½ pound green cabbage
- ½ pound cauliflower or additional cabbage
- 2 medium to large sweet or mild onions
- 1 large green bell pepper
- 1 large red bell pepper
- 1 to 2 jalapeño chiles, optional
- 3 tablespoons pickling salt or 3 heaping tablespoons kosher salt
- 1½ cups sugar
- 1½ cups cider vinegar
- 3 broken cinnamon sticks
- 2 teaspoons celery seeds
- 2 teaspoons yellow mustard seeds
- 1 teaspoon ground turmeric
- 1 teaspoon crushed dried hot red chiles
- ½ teaspoon ground ginger

Chop the tomatoes, cabbage, cauliflower, onions, bell peppers, and optional jalapeños in a food processor in batches, chopping only as much as easily fits in your processor each time. Stop short of puréeing the vegetables. Combine the vegetables in a large nonreactive bowl and sprinkle with the salt. Set the mixture aside for 3 to 4 hours. The vegetables will release a good bit of liquid during this time.

Prepare 5 pint canning jars according to the manufacturer's instructions.

Pour the sugar into a large heavy saucepan or stockpot and caramelize it over medium-low heat. There is no need to stir the sugar unless it is melting unevenly. When it turns a deep red-gold brown, remove it from the heat and immediately pour in the vinegar, standing back from the pan to avoid the pungent steam. The sugar will harden somewhat. Return it to the heat and continue cooking until it melts back into a syrup. Stir in the cinnamon sticks and remaining spices, and cook for 10 minutes on low heat. While the syrup simmers, drain the vegetables and rinse them.

Stir the vegetables into the simmering syrup and cook for 10 additional minutes. Spoon the chow-chow into the prepared jars, leaving at least ¼ inch of headspace. Process the jars in a boiling-water bath according to the manufacturer's directions, generally about 10 minutes. Store for at least a week before serving. Refrigerate the relish after opening.

TECHNIQUE TIP: The idea of caramelizing the sugar for the chow-chow was inspired by Abby Fisher's Napoleon Sauce, a mixed vegetable relish. In *What Mrs. Fisher Knows about Old Southern Cooking* (1881) she took brown sugar "and put it in a frying pan on the fire, and let it bake thoroughly—just next to burning." Caramelization gives the sugar a deeper, richer complexity that we find appealing with the tart green tomatoes and hint of mustard.

Pickled Lily

Mary Emma Showalter collected hundreds of old recipes and tales in putting together the *Mennonite Community Cookbook* (1950). On the importance of the "seven sours," she cited the story of Tillie the Mennonite maid, who rejected advice that vinegar would drain the color from her cheeks by saying, "Who wants pink cheeks at the expense of pickles?" The many sours recipes the author found included one for Pickled Lily, usually known as piccalilli, a kissing cousin of chow-chow. It's hard in fact to specify a consistent difference between the two dishes, though many pickle lovers, including Showalter, come up with different versions of each. In her case, both preparations contain mustard, sometimes regarded as the distinguishing ingredient, appropriate only for chow-chow. Personally, we love the ring of both names and use them indiscriminately.

Calico Corn Relish

Makes 5 to 6 pints

Found today among the pickle entries at every state fair in the country, corn relish derives ultimately from the same sweet-sour seasoning inspiration as chow-chow. It's clearly an American creation, featuring our native corn, but it shows the lingering strength of old international influences from the colonial period. The tangy flavor goes well with grilled or roasted chicken, and we also like to mix the relish with rice for a summery salad.

- 2 cups chopped sweet or mild onions
- 1 large red bell pepper, diced fine
- 1 large green bell pepper, diced fine
- ⅔ cup chopped celery
- ¼ cup minced jalapeño chiles or other moderately hot fresh green chiles
- 2 tablespoons fine-chopped garlic
- 1 quart cider vinegar
- 1 cup packed light brown sugar
- 2 tablespoons yellow mustard seeds
- 1 tablespoon plus 1 teaspoon pickling salt, or 1½ tablespoons kosher salt
- 1 teaspoon celery seeds
- 6 cups fresh whole corn kernels

Prepare 5 to 6 pint canning jars according to the manufacturer's directions.

Combine in a large heavy pan the onions, bell peppers, celery, jalapeños, garlic, vinegar, brown sugar, mustard seeds, salt, and celery seeds. Bring the mixture to a boil over high heat, then reduce the heat to a simmer and cook for 10 minutes. Stir in the corn and cook for an additional 10 minutes until the mixture is cooked down and somewhat thick. Spoon the relish into the prepared jars, leaving at least ¼ inch of headspace.

Process the jars in a boiling-water bath according to the manufacturer's directions, generally about 15 minutes. Store for at least a week before serving. Refrigerate the relish after opening.

The writer has no apology to offer for this cheap little book of economical hints, except her deep conviction that such a book is needed. In this case, renown is out of the question, and ridicule is a matter of indifference.

Lydia Maria Child, *The American Frugal Housewife* (1832)

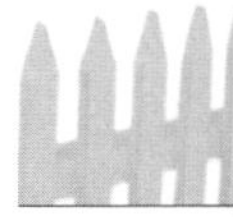

Jerusalem Artichoke Relish

Makes about 5 pints

Pickling enlivens Jerusalem artichokes, slightly sweet by nature. Some cooks pickle them whole or in slices, but we prefer them chopped fine with onions and bell peppers. Even in small bits, the artichokes deliver a lot of crunch, much like a water chestnut. The relish mates smartly with grilled pork chops or shrimp.

- 2¼ pounds Jerusalem artichokes, scraped of loose skin, pared of any brown spots, and chopped fine
- 2 cups yellow onions, chopped fine
- 2 cups red bell peppers, chopped fine
- 1 cup pickling salt or 1 heaping cup kosher salt
- 3 cups white vinegar
- 1½ cups sugar
- 1 tablespoon yellow mustard seeds
- 1 tablespoon ground turmeric
- ½ teaspoon ground ginger
- ¼ teaspoon cayenne pepper

Prepare 5 pint canning jars according to the manufacturer's directions.

Combine the Jerusalem artichokes, onions, and bell peppers in a large nonreactive bowl. Sprinkle the salt over them, then cover with about 1 gallon of cold water. Let the mixture sit for at least 4 hours and up to overnight.

Drain the vegetables and rinse them in cold water. Drain again, then pour the mixture out onto a clean dishtowel or similar-size double thickness of cheesecloth. Wring out all remaining moisture from the vegetables. Rinse the bowl well and return the vegetables to it.

Bring the vinegar, sugar, mustard seeds, turmeric, ginger, and cayenne to a rolling boil over high heat and boil for 1 minute. Pour the mixture over the vegetables and, with a clean spoon, stir to combine. Spoon the relish into the prepared jars, leaving at least ¼ inch of headspace.

Process the jars in a boiling-water bath according to the manufacturer's directions, generally about 10 minutes. Store for at least a week before serving. Refrigerate the relish after opening.

TECHNIQUE TIP:
This is a case where the food processor makes preserving much simpler. In many versions of artichoke relish, the tubers and accompanying vegetables are chopped so fine they're almost ground, a result accomplished in the processor with much less effort than cutting by hand.

Tomato Ketchup

MAKES ABOUT 1 QUART

The English brought the idea of ketchup from Asia and carried it with them to the colonies. Both here and in the mother country, cooks made it originally with mushroom, oyster, and walnut bases. Southerners probably introduced a tomato version by the late eighteenth century, though the first published recipe didn't appear until the 1820s, in Mary Randolph's *The Virginia Housewife.* From then until now, good home renditions offer far greater tomato character and tasty complexity than any of the sweet commercial imitations. After one batch of your own, you'll wonder why you ever bought a bottle of candy ketchup.

- ½ gallon homemade tomato juice, preferably, or a 46- to 48-ounce can tomato juice
- ¾ cup inexpensive red-wine vinegar
- ¼ cup plus 2 tablespoons sugar
- 1 tablespoon salt
- 1 teaspoon paprika
- 1 teaspoon ground cinnamon
- ½ teaspoon dry mustard
- ¼ teaspoon cayenne pepper
- ½ teaspoon freshly milled black pepper
- 1 tablespoon mixed pickling spice
- ½ teaspoon whole cloves
- 1 medium onion, quartered
- ½ red or green bell pepper, cut in several chunks

Combine in a large heavy pan the tomato juice, vinegar, sugar, salt, paprika, cinnamon, mustard, cayenne, and pepper. Tie the pickling spice, cloves, and onion and bell pepper chunks in a section of cheesecloth and add them to the pan. Bring the mixture to a boil over high heat, then reduce the heat to a simmer and cook for 1 to 1¼ hours, reducing the juice by about half. Stir up from the bottom frequently during the last few minutes of cooking.

Remove and discard the cheesecloth bag. The ketchup can be processed in a boiling-water bath according to the manufacturer's directions, for a long-term preservation. We prefer to spoon it into a sterilized jar and refrigerate it, for use over a couple of months.

"DOWN CELLAR"

See the rows and rows
of berries

Peaches, plums, and
bright red cherries,

Pickles sour and pickles
sweet,

Piles of apples—good to
eat—

Catsup, jam and
marmalade. . . .

Makes me glad there's
food for all

In rows around the cellar
wall.

FAVORITE RECIPES OF COLFAX COUNTY CLUB WOMEN (1945)

Hawaiian Chili Pepper Water

MAKES ABOUT 1 PINT

The American fascination with hot and spicy foods, widely regarded as a recent phenomenon, emerged as early as the eighteenth century, particularly in cosmopolitan cities such as Philadelphia. Decades before Louisiana Tabasco sauce reached the market in 1868, worldly importers introduced adventuresome eaters to West Indian hot pepper vinegars, and some cooks even began making their own at home. Of all the current home options, we're partial to this Hawaiian table seasoning, used in the islands to flavor everything from fish to noodles.

- 4 to 8 small dried hot red chiles
- 2 teaspoons rice vinegar
- 2 quarter-size slices of fresh ginger, bruised
- 1 garlic clove, slivered
- 1 teaspoon salt

Combine the ingredients in a clean pint bottle or jar. Pour in about 2 cups of hot water and let the mixture steep at room temperature overnight. The chili pepper water is ready to use, but will gain potency over time. While it contains ample preservatives, and many people keep it out on the table like salt and pepper, it is safest to refrigerate the liquid spice between uses.

AMBER Waves of Grain

EXCEPT FOR BREAD, AMERICANS DON'T GENERALLY EAT grains in great amounts, at least in comparison with many Asian and Mediterranean peoples. We've grown more fond of pasta recently, and like a dab of rice on the side with some entrées, but a big meal has usually meant meat and potatoes, a preference inherited from our northern European forebears. Given that bent, it's surprising that American grain dishes rank among the best in the world and constitute some of our most compelling foods. The nutritionists who berate us for not adopting foreign diets should turn their forks, like their pitches, homeward.

We sometimes forget that our native corn is first and foremost a grain, rather than a vegetable, and plays that role not only in cornbreads but in many breakfast specialties and a heaping handful of dinner accompaniments. Even more often and regretfully, we overlook the significance of rice in several of our most vibrant regional cuisines, particularly those from the South Carolina lowcountry, southern Louisiana, and areas of the Pacific states with a heavy Asian influence. We're aware of the wheat in our breads, but maybe not of our long history of eating it in noodles and pasta.

Experts quibble about calling many of these dishes American because they usually have foreign antecedents in some form. Grains are such an ancient food the world over, so thoroughly explored and exploited in distant times, no modern society can claim much in pure originality. Our ancestors left us plenty of room to tinker and tailor, however, and American cooks took the opportunity to do so with imaginative flair. They added new, indigenous ingredients to the pot, treated old ideas with resourceful irreverence and, most important, blended flavors from the disparate cultures that mingled in our home kitchens. In the same way that they put their signature on many other foods, American cooks made grain dishes their own by making them their own way.

"Tell me. Is it just us who call this hopping-john? Or is it known by that name through all the country? It seems a strange name somehow."

"Well, I have heard it called various things," said Berenice.

"What?"

"Well, I have heard it called peas and rice. Or rice and peas and pot-liquor. Or hopping-john. You can vary and take your pick."

"But I'm not talking about this town," F. Jasmine said. "I mean in other places. I mean through all the world. I wonder what the French call it."

CARSON McCULLERS,
THE MEMBER OF THE WEDDING
(1946)

Hoppin' John

SERVES 4 AS A MAIN DISH, 6 AS A SIDE DISH

Give southern storytellers a name like hoppin' John and they'll spin yarns about it until hogs howl at the moon. The truth seems more prosaic than all the colorful tales, probably being a substitution of similar-sounding English words for a generic, foreign name for the dish, not a reference to a street vendor with a limp, or a description of children dancing one-footed around the dinner table on New Year's Day. Beyond any doubt, black slaves introduced the famous "pea" pilau on the rice plantations of the South Carolina lowcountry, and it's closely related to common African and West Indian concoctions. Carolina cooks put their stamp on hoppin' John through local ingredients, particularly the field peas, seasonings, and pork. Many people treat it as a side dish, but we like it on the center of the plate, accompanied by a summer salad or winter soup, and we keep the preparation simple to focus on the earthy elegance of the combination.

TECHNIQUE TIP: Cooks fine-tune hoppin' John in multiple ways, using salt pork instead of a ham hock, replacing the water with chicken stock, or adding aromatics such as garlic, bay, or mint. When they trade the field peas for okra, another African vegetable, and substitute bacon for other kinds of pork fat, the pilau becomes a lesser-known cousin called "limpin' Susan." Anyone avaricious for knowledge about hoppin' John and other lowcountry pilaus should check out *The Carolina Rice Kitchen* (1992) by culinary historian Karen Hess, who covers the subject in doctoral-dissertation detail. John Thorne also writes extensively (and much more readably) about hoppin' John in "Rice & Beans; The Itinerary of a Dish," a pamphlet he reprinted in *Serious Pig* (1996). The two authors don't always agree, but both know their beans.

- 1 cup dried black-eyed peas, red field peas, or other small dried peas
- 1 medium onion, chopped fine
- 1 small smoked ham hock, sliced in chunks by the butcher
- 1 small dried hot red chile or pinch or two of cayenne pepper
- 1 teaspoon salt
- Freshly milled black pepper
- Sprig of fresh thyme or ¼ to ½ teaspoon dried thyme, optional
- 1 cup uncooked rice (see Ingredient Tip)
- Hot pepper sauce, such as Tabasco, or hot pepper vinegar

Combine the black-eyed peas with 6 cups of water in a large saucepan. Add the onion, ham hock, chile, salt, a good grinding of pepper and, if you wish, the thyme. Bring to a boil over high heat, reduce the heat to a simmer, and cook until the peas are soft but not mushy, about 1½ hours.

Drain the cooking liquid from the peas into a large measuring cup. You will need 2 cups of liquid to cook the rice. Discard any extra liquid or, if necessary, add hot water to equal 2 cups.

Pour the liquid back into the peas. Add the rice to the pot, give it a quick stir, then cover and cook over low heat for 20 minutes. Without lifting the lid, set the hoppin' John aside to steam for 10 to 15 additional minutes. Fluff the mixture and serve immediately with hot pepper sauce or pepper vinegar.

INGREDIENT TIP: Traditional hoppin' John recipes always call for long-grain rice, the type grown originally in the lowcountry. We generally use nutty-scented Texmati rice (also marketed as wild pecan rice or popcorn rice because of its aroma), though many southern cooks prefer Indian basmati rice. If you buy rice in bulk at a natural foods market, as we do, make sure the proprietors store it properly and replace it frequently. If the rice lacks fragrance, shop for it elsewhere.

Shrimp Pilau

SERVES 6 AS A MAIN DISH

John Egerton in *Southern Food* (1987) gives sixteen alternative spellings for pilau—ranging from plaw to perloo—used somewhere in the region at one time or another. The variations testify to the widespread popularity of this particular pilau, a rice entrée usually accented with shrimp or chicken. Like hoppin' John, it can be traced ultimately to Persia, but sank American roots in the area around Charleston and spread from there across the South. French Huguenots from Provence probably brought the basics of the dish to the city, and African cooks undoubtedly contributed to the sense of seasoning.

- 1 pound medium shrimp, peeled, deveined if you wish, and sliced in half lengthwise
- 4 thick smoky bacon slices, chopped
- 2 medium onions, chopped
- 2 cups uncooked rice
- 1¼ pounds fresh tomatoes, chopped, or 2½ cups diced canned tomatoes
- 2 teaspoons Worcestershire sauce
- ½ to 1 teaspoon crushed dried hot red chiles
- 1 teaspoon salt
- 1 bay leaf
- 3 cups shrimp stock or chicken stock, or a combination, preferably homemade
- Minced parsley or scallion greens, for garnish

Set the shrimp out at room temperature to remove their chill while you go about early steps in the preparation.

Fry the bacon in a Dutch oven or other large pan over medium heat until brown and crisp. Remove the bacon with a slotted spoon and set it aside. Stir the onions into the pan drippings and cook them over medium heat until soft and translucent, about 5 minutes.

Add the rice and stir just until the individual grains glisten with fat. Mix in the tomatoes, Worcestershire sauce, chiles, salt, and bay leaf, and cook for several additional minutes, scraping up from the bottom.

Pour in the stock and raise the heat to bring the stock to a boil. Cover the rice, reduce the heat again to medium-low, and cook for 20 minutes. Immediately add the shrimp to the pan and quickly cover it again.

Remove the pan from the heat and let the pilau steam undisturbed for about 10 minutes. Fluff the mixture, spoon it into a serving dish, and scatter the parsley and reserved bacon over the top. Serve piping hot.

> The woman who leads her family to imagine that a full stomach is the aim of a meal is doing a disservice not only to her family but to the community; careless eating is as anti-social as careless cooking, and a child should no more be encouraged to be indifferent to the flavor of his food than to sing off tune.
>
> SHEILA HIBBEN, A KITCHEN MANUAL (1941)

TECHNIQUE TIP: In Carolina rice cooking, the goal is always to keep every grain separate, dry, and nonsticky. When cooking rice by itself, we get the desired result through a combination of boiling and steaming. Combine 1 part rice to just under two parts cold water with a pinch of salt in a heavy saucepan, and bring the water to a boil over high heat. As soon as the water bubbles all around the edges, cover the pan and reduce the heat to medium-low. Cook for 13 minutes—some cooks swear by 12½, to the second—then set the pan aside to steam undisturbed for 15 minutes. Never remove the cover while the rice cooks or steams—you have to go on faith here. The steaming provides time for the moisture to be absorbed to the center of each grain and for excess liquid to evaporate. Fluff the rice and serve.

The Rice Called Carolina Gold

The name came from the radiant hue of the rice in the Carolina coastal fields, but it also foretold the economic impact of the area's main product. Carolina Gold gained an aristocratic reputation around the world for the purity of its whiteness and its sumptuous texture, bringing wealth to the planters and the port city of Charleston. The golden glow lasted for over a century and a half, and almost everyone in the lowcountry benefited except the African slaves, who not only did the backbreaking work but also created the local system of rice cultivation.

The early English settlers didn't even know how to cook rice, much less grow it. The grain seed probably came from Africa and certainly the agricultural expertise did. Rice farming originated in ancient India, and traveled from there through Persia to the shores of the Mediterranean and the African West Coast, where people mastered the intricate techniques of manual cultivation long before any colonists arrived in Carolina. Lowcountry planters deliberately sought out slaves captured in this region, and delegated to them the design as well as the operation of their farms.

The rice plantations were so dependent on the African workers that Carolina Gold gradually lost its luster and ultimately vanished after the abolition of slavery. A hurricane hastened the end of production, and so did the efficiency of mechanized rice raising in Arkansas, Louisiana, and Texas, but the collapse of one of the country's most successful and notable crops resulted mainly from freed blacks fleeing the fields of their servitude. Richard and Patricia Schulze grow small quantities of the rice today on an old lowcountry plantation, dedicating profits to charity, but that's the last of the Gold in Carolina.

Duck and Sausage Jambalaya

SERVES 8 AS A MAIN DISH

Some people suggest that Louisiana jambalaya derives from Spanish paella; others see a French connection from the word *jambon,* meaning ham; and Irma Rombauer evidently had Italy in mind when she called it "a fine rice dish in spaghetti sauce." The flexibility of the ingredients supports the range of interpretations, but Karen Hess's recent research indicates that jambalaya developed hand in hand with American pilaus from the same Arabic, Provençal, and African roots. Basic versions, containing just a little sausage or shrimp, taste great, but we dress up the dish here with duck for a special-occasion meal.

- 3½- to 4-pound duck
- 1½ cups chopped onions
- 4 ounces tasso, country ham, or other smoky ham, minced
- 4 ounces andouille sausage, preferably, or other smoked pork sausage such as kielbasa, chopped
- 1½ cups minced celery
- 1 large green bell pepper, minced
- 2 plump garlic cloves, minced
- 2 cups uncooked rice
- 3 bay leaves
- 1 teaspoon dry mustard
- 1½ teaspoons salt
- ¾ teaspoon dried thyme
- ¼ to ½ teaspoon cayenne pepper
- ½ teaspoon freshly milled black pepper

Cut the skin away from the duck and reserve it. Cut the meat away from the bones and chop it into neat ½-inch pieces, then cover and refrigerate it until needed. Transfer the bones and all scraps to a large saucepan and cover with 2 quarts of cold water. Bring to a boil over high heat, reduce the heat to a bare simmer, and cook for about 2 hours.

While the stock simmers, cut the duck skin into pieces about 1 to 2 inches square. Place the skin in a heavy saucepan or deep skillet with ½ cup of water. Warm over low heat to render the fat from the skin. It may take up to 2 hours for the fat to render completely, leaving behind dark, crispy cracklings. Remove the cracklings with a slotted spoon, drain them, and reserve them. Measure out 3 tablespoons of duck fat, saving the rest for flavoring other dishes. (The duck fat keeps for weeks, tightly covered and refrigerated. Use the duck fat as a replacement for butter or oil in other rice or potato dishes.)

When the stock has cooked down, strain and skim it. You will need 3 cups of liquid. Measure the stock, adding a little water, if necessary, or reserving any extra for another recipe. (The jambalaya can be made a day ahead to this point. Cool the stock, cover it, and refrigerate.)

Warm the 3 tablespoons of duck fat in a large heavy skillet over high heat. Mix in the onions, tasso, and andouille, and sauté until the onions are well browned but not burned, 8 to 10 minutes. Add the duck meat, celery, bell pepper, and garlic, reduce the heat to medium, and continue cooking until the vegetables are softened, about 5 additional minutes. Stir in the rice and cook for about 3 minutes longer, until the grains are translucent. Pour in the stock and add the remaining seasonings. Cook until the rice is tender and the liquid is absorbed, 18 to 20 minutes, stirring up from the bottom once about halfway through the cooking. Remove the jambalaya from the heat and let it sit covered for 10 minutes. It should remain moist but not soupy. Spoon it into a large bowl or onto plates, garnish with the cracklings, and serve.

TECHNIQUE TIP: For a quicker jamabalaya, simply skip the duck. Sausage and tasso will give plenty of flavor. Use 3 tablespoons of vegetable oil instead of rendered duck fat, and replace the homemade duck stock with 3 cups of chicken stock. You'll lack cracklings for garnishment, but you'll have a hearty one-dish supper on the table with minimal effort.

Such a poor wretch as a rice hater I have never met.

M.F.K. FISHER, WITH BOLD KNIFE AND FORK (1968)

Fried Rice

SERVES 4 TO 6 AS A MAIN DISH

Early Chinese immigrants to Hawaii, the first imported plantation workers, refused to substitute poi for rice, and began turning irrigated taro fields into rice paddies by the mid-nineteenth century. Planted even on the shores of Waikiki, the crop grew into the second largest in the islands, after sugar, until mechanized competition from the United States mainland undercut demand. The Chinese brought the idea of fried rice with them from the homeland, but it evolved in Hawaii and other Pacific states from a versatile way to use leftovers into a distinct dish, with a new emphasis on soy flavor. Keep the original utility in mind when you make fried rice, varying the vegetables and meat with what's on hand to get a tantalizing blend of tastes and textures.

- 5 cups cold cooked rice
- 2 tablespoons peanut oil
- 2 medium celery stalks, sliced thin on the diagonal
- 3 to 4 scallions, sliced thin on the diagonal
- ¾ to 1 cup julienned ham, 1 to 1½ cups julienned roast pork or roast chicken, or other cooked pork or chicken
- 3 tablespoons soy sauce
- 2 eggs, lightly beaten
- ½ teaspoon Asian sesame oil, optional

Dump the rice out onto a baking sheet. Using a fork, break the rice apart so that it no longer clumps.

Place a wok or large heavy skillet over very high heat. When quite hot, pour in the oil and swirl it around to coat the pan. Add the celery, give it a good stir, and add the scallions. Stir in the rice, followed by the meat, soy sauce, eggs, and optional sesame oil, continuing to stir until well combined and heated through. The whole cooking process should take just 3 to 4 minutes. Serve hot.

Food is perhaps the greatest barometer to America of today and tomorrow. . . . We are dubbed as a horsepower nation; as begetters and livers of a mechanical civilization. But I believe the nation is more accurately measurable by food than by horsepower, by gadgets, or by the tallies of a presidential election. American food is us—good, bad, indifferent. American culture stalks in and out of the kitchen door.

GRACE AND BEVERLY SMITH AND CHARLES MORROW WILSON, THROUGH THE KITCHEN DOOR (1938)

Mexican Rice

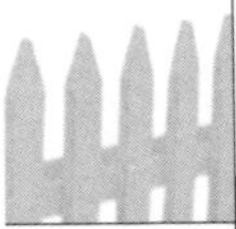

SERVES 4 AS A SIDE DISH

"Spanish" rice— actually Mexican in origin and seasonings—became one of the first dishes of its heritage to win broad acceptance across the United States, appearing in major national cookbooks by the turn of the twentieth century. Southern California led the way in popularizing Mexican foods, and also produced many of the heartiest versions. Our rendition of the rice takes its cues from a recipe attributed to silent-movie star Ramon Novarro, the original cinematic Ben Hur, in a 1929 cookbook published by the Beverly Hills Woman's Club. We've cut the level of meat and fat in Novarro's recipe, but retain his inspired notion of using chorizo to spice the rice.

4 to 6 ounces chorizo, preferably a variety that crumbles rather than slices

1 cup uncooked rice

1 cup tomato juice

Salt and freshly milled black pepper

Chopped parsley, cilantro, marjoram, or basil, or a combination

Crumble the chorizo in a heavy saucepan and fry it over medium heat until well browned, 5 to 8 minutes. Remove the chorizo with a slotted spoon and reserve it. Pour off all but about 1 tablespoon of the drippings. Stir in the rice and sauté it until translucent, about 5 minutes. Pour in the tomato juice and 1 cup of water. Season with salt and pepper. Bring to a boil over high heat, then cover, reduce the heat to medium-low, and cook for 15 additional minutes. Remove from the heat, toss in a small handful of herbs without stirring, and immediately cover the rice. Let the rice steam for about 10 minutes. Fluff it with a fork, then stir in the chorizo and serve.

Red Rice

Serves 6 to 8 as a side dish

Essentially a tomato pilau, this Carolina classic should be cooked on top of the stove in that manner rather than baked, as is often done. Many people add green bell peppers, but we prefer to use red ones to subtly amplify the sweetness of the tomatoes, and we purée the vegetables together to blend the flavors. We like red rice with steamed blue crabs, Roast Chicken with Nut Sauce (page 148) or Jacksboro Fried Shrimp (page 120).

14- to 15-ounce can diced tomatoes with juice

4-ounce jar roasted red bell peppers or pimientos, undrained

4 bacon slices, chopped

½ large onion, chopped

2 cups uncooked rice

1½ teaspoons salt

1 teaspoon dried thyme

Pinch of crushed dried hot red chiles

2¾ cups chicken stock

1 tablespoon tomato paste

Purée the tomatoes and bell peppers and their juices in a blender and reserve them.

Fry the bacon in a large heavy saucepan over medium heat until brown and crisp. Remove the bacon from the drippings with a slotted spoon and reserve it. Add the onion to the drippings and continue cooking just until the onion becomes translucent, about 3 minutes. Stir in the rice and cook briefly until it becomes translucent. Pour in the tomato–bell pepper mixture and stir it in with the salt, thyme, and a bold pinch of the dried chiles. Cook uncovered until the tomato mixture begins to dry out, about 5 minutes. Stir up from the bottom a couple of times.

Pour in the stock, add the tomato paste, stir again, and cover the pan. Reduce the heat to medium-low and simmer for about 18 minutes, until the liquid is absorbed. If a steady stream of steam is still escaping from the pan after 18 minutes, cook an additional couple of minutes without peeking. Take the pan off the heat, remove the lid, and quickly arrange a folded dishtowel over the pan. Cover the towel with the pan lid and let the rice steam for at least 10 minutes. Fluff the rice and stir in the bacon just before serving.

In this work are to be found nearly a hundred dishes in which rice or corn form a part of the ingredients.

Sarah Rutledge,
The Carolina Housewife
(1847)

Pilau with Pistachios and Pine Nuts

SERVES 4 TO 6 AS A SIDE DISH

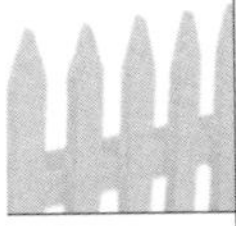

Thomas Jefferson reportedly loved this unpretentious pilau, and it's easy to see why it would appeal to his classic tastes. Sautéing the nuts separately from the rice keeps them crunchy, providing a finely proportioned contrast to the softer rice. We can eat a plateful for a simple supper, but we mainly serve it as a side dish with grilled fish, especially Grilled Whole Pompano (page 136).

- 1 cup uncooked rice
- 1¾ cups plus 2 tablespoons chicken stock, preferably homemade
- ¾ teaspoon salt or more to taste
- 3 tablespoons unsalted butter
- ½ cup unsalted pistachio nuts
- ½ cup unsalted pine nuts
- Scant ¼ teaspoon ground mace, preferably, or ground nutmeg

Combine the rice, stock, salt, and 1 tablespoon of the butter in a large saucepan. Bring the rice to a boil over high heat, cover, reduce the heat to medium-low, and cook for 18 minutes.

While the rice cooks, melt the remaining 2 tablespoons of butter in a large skillet over medium heat. Add both types of nuts and mace, and sauté briefly until the nuts are golden. Remove from the heat.

When the rice has cooked, remove it from the heat and set it aside to steam for 10 minutes. Fluff the rice with a fork and scoop it out into the skillet. Toss well with the nuts and butter and serve.

Cheese Grits

SERVES 6 AS A SIDE DISH

Marjorie Kinnan Rawlings provided one of the first published recipes for cheese grits in her *Cross Creek Cookery* (1942), calling them "a major contribution to good Southern eating" with a likely home in Baskin, Alabama. Forty years later, Mississippi native Craig Claiborne said his recipe for the dish ranked among the top one hundred (out of eight thousand) printed in *The New York Times* during his quarter-century tenure as the newspaper's food editor. We cook cheese grits a little differently than either of them, but the result is as tasty as they claim.

- ¾ teaspoon salt
- 1 cup stone-ground grits (see Ingredient Tip)
- 6 ounces mild Cheddar cheese, grated (1½ cups)
- 2 tablespoons unsalted butter
- 1 garlic clove, minced
- 2 eggs, lightly beaten
- Hot pepper sauce, such as Texas Pete or Tabasco

Preheat the oven to 325°F. Oil or butter an 8- to 9-inch baking dish.

Bring 4 cups of water and the salt to a boil in a large heavy saucepan over high heat. Whisk in the grits, a handful at a time. Reduce the heat to a bare simmer and cook the grits until thick and soft, about 30 minutes. Give the grits a stir occasionally as they cook, more frequently toward the end, to avoid scorching. Scrape them up from the bottom each time. Properly cooked grits should never be gritty in texture.

Remove the grits from the heat and stir in the cheese and butter, mixing until they disappear into the grits. Stir in the garlic, eggs, and several generous splashes of hot pepper sauce. Scrape the mixture into the prepared pan. Bake for 50 to 55 minutes, until slightly brown and lightly set. Let the grits sit at room temperature for 5 to 10 minutes before cutting into soft-textured squares or wedges.

INGREDIENT TIP: Avoid "instant grits," on a par with instant coffee. If you're really in a rush, the "quick" 5- to 10-minute grits work tolerably in this recipe, with the cooking time reduced accordingly. For maximum flavor and texture, get the genuine article, available by mail from Hoppin' John's in Charleston (800-828-4412).

Spoonbread

Serves 6 as a side dish

More of a savory custard than a bread, this dish may be cornmeal's highest destiny. A venerable southern specialty, spoonbread is as soothing on the side of the plate as clotted cream on a scone. Our version owes a big debt to the way Nita Dixon prepares the dish at her home-style, namesake café in downtown Savannah, Georgia.

- 1 teaspoon salt
- 1 cup stone-ground cornmeal, preferably fine-ground (sometimes called corn flour)
- 2 tablespoons unsalted butter
- 4 ounces mild to medium Cheddar cheese, grated (1 cup)
- 1 cup whole milk or half-and-half
- 1 teaspoon baking powder
- Pinch or 2 of cayenne pepper
- Pinch of ground white pepper
- 1 cup finely sliced fresh spinach leaves
- 3 eggs, separated

Preheat the oven to 350°F. Butter a 9- to 10-inch cast-iron skillet or similar baking dish.

Bring 2 cups of water and the salt to a boil in a large heavy saucepan over high heat. Stir in the cornmeal gradually and cook for about 3 minutes, stirring constantly and eliminating any lumps. Add the butter, cheese, milk, baking powder, cayenne, white pepper, and spinach, and remove from the heat.

Beat the egg yolks together until they are light and frothy, then mix them into the cornmeal mixture. With a clean whisk or beaters, beat the egg whites until soft peaks form. Fold the whites gently into the cornmeal mixture. Pour into the prepared skillet. Bake for 45 to 50 minutes, until just set at the center. Serve spooned from the skillet.

Corn has bestowed on our cuisine not only countless wonderful dishes but a poetic food language of great beauty and vitality: hush puppies, pot dodgers, spoonbread, cornpone, Awendaw bread, cornmeal mush, hog and hominy, Indian pudding, spider cornbread, succotash, and on and on.

John Thorne,
Serious Pig (1996)

Chicos

SERVES 6 TO 8 AS A SIDE DISH

J. George Frederick talks ecstatically about "Shaker dried corn" in *The Pennsylvania Dutch Cook Book* (1935). He says the oven-dried sweet corn is better than any right off the cob, and that it makes canned corn "seem fit only for pigs." He's absolutely right about the concentrated flavor, though we think the hard corn nuggets are best not in a Pennsylvania dish but in a New Mexican stew based on chicos, a nearly identical product toasted in an adobe *horno* rather than a brick oven. Curiously, no one else in the country dried sweet corn in the same way as these two disparate communities, so far apart culturally and geographically.

- 2 tablespoons vegetable oil
- 2 medium onions, chopped fine
- 4 to 5 plump garlic cloves, minced
- 2 cups chicos (see Ingredient Tip)
- 6 cups chicken stock, preferably homemade
- 1 teaspoon salt or more to taste
- 1 bay leaf
- ½ to ¾ cup chopped roasted mild green chiles, such as New Mexican, preferably fresh or frozen

Warm the oil in a large saucepan or Dutch oven over medium heat. Stir in the onions and garlic, and sauté until the onions are soft and translucent, about 5 minutes. Add the chicos and stock, then the salt and bay leaf. Bring the mixture to a boil, reduce the heat to a simmer, and cook uncovered until the chicos are tender but still a bit chewy, about 1½ hours. Add more hot water if the chicos begin to dry out before they are done. Stir in the green chiles and continue cooking for about 15 minutes longer. The chicos should remain somewhat soupy. Serve them warm, spooned into bowls with some of the cooking liquid.

INGREDIENT TIP: The Santa Fe School of Cooking (800-982-4688 or 505-983-4511) is a good mail-order source for chicos. Cooked by themselves, the small corn kernels make a tasty addition to a pot of pinto or black beans, or they can be added to a vegetable soup to pump up the intensity. Simply simmer them in salted water until tender but still a bit chewy, about 1½ hours.

Down-Home Hominy

New Mexicans also dry field corn as the first step in making posole, a local style of hominy. As with any hominy, cooks remove the hulls from dried kernels by treating them with a wood-ash or mineral solution, a technique developed by Native Americans that releases valuable nutrients for human consumption. New Mexicans prepare posole with pork and chiles as a side dish, making it a different kettle of corn than the hearty Mexican stew known as *pozole.*

Americans in all regions used to eat hominy with some frequency, but over time it developed a strong association with the South, probably because it's often ground for grits. We like to bake whole (a.k.a. big) hominy with diced canned tomatoes and their juice, or sauté it in a little butter with minced pickled jalapeños for a crosscultural treat.

Spelt Salad with Corn

SERVES 4 AS A MAIN DISH, 6 AS A SIDE DISH

A masterful mix of corn and saffron with whole-wheat kernels of spelt, this is a toothsome grain salad of Pennsylvania Dutch heritage. It makes a lively but light lunch or, in smaller portions, a good accompaniment to a Shelby County Egg Salad Sandwich (page 61).

- 1½ cups spelt berries (see Ingredient Tip)
- Salt
- 3 cups corn kernels, fresh or frozen
- 2 garlic cloves, minced
- ½ teaspoon crumbled saffron threads
- ½ cup plus 1 tablespoon sunflower oil or corn oil, preferably unrefined
- 3 tablespoons cider vinegar
- 1 teaspoon ground cumin
- ½ teaspoon freshly milled black pepper
- 1 medium red bell pepper, diced
- 6 to 8 scallions, sliced into thin rings
- ¼ cup minced fresh lovage, celery leaves, parsley, or a combination

Soak the spelt for several hours or up to overnight. Drain and cover it with several inches of fresh water in a large heavy saucepan. Bring the spelt to a boil over high heat, then simmer until tender but still a bit chewy. Plan on a cooking time of 1 to 1½ hours, adding more hot water if the spelt begins to seem dry before being done. Stir in salt to taste after the kernels have softened. When ready, pour off any remaining liquid and immediately add the corn, garlic, and saffron (mixed with a tablespoon of warm water) to the spelt. Cover, cook over low heat for 5 minutes, remove from the heat, and let the mixture sit until cool.

Spoon the spelt-corn mixture into a large bowl and toss with the oil, vinegar, cumin, and pepper. Mix in the bell pepper, scallions, and half of the lovage. Scatter the remaining lovage over the salad. Chill for at least 1 hour, or up to a day, before serving.

INGREDIENT TIP: Spelt is a variety of wheat, softer when ground than the hard winter wheat favored for bread flour. Whole spelt wheat berries, sometimes called "groats," are the full kernel of the wheat with the bran and germ intact. Spelt is available in natural foods stores, and a growing number of other groceries and markets. You can also make a similar grain salad by substituting 4½ cups of cooked rice for the spelt.

Wild Rice Medley

SERVES 6 AS A SIDE DISH

Native Americans harvested wild rice on Minnesota lakes long before the Europeans arrived, calling it by such names as "good berry." The seed of an aquatic grass rather than a true rice, it remained a local treasure little known elsewhere until well into the twentieth century. Cooks frequently combine wild rice with mushrooms, as we do here, and we also add a second grain, such as brown rice, to highlight the differences in nutty flavor.

- ¼ cup (½ stick) unsalted butter or olive oil
- 2 heaping tablespoons minced onion
- 2 heaping tablespoons minced celery plus 1 tablespoon minced celery leaves
- 1 garlic clove, minced
- 1 cup uncooked wild rice (see Ingredient Tip)
- 1 cup uncooked brown rice
- 6 cups chicken stock, preferably homemade
- 1½ teaspoons salt or more to taste
- 1½ cups lightly packed thin-sliced mushrooms, such as button, cremini, chicken-of-the-woods, or porcini

Warm 2 tablespoons of the butter in a large heavy saucepan over medium heat. Add the onion, celery, and garlic, and sauté until the onion is soft and translucent, about 5 minutes. Stir in the wild rice and the brown rice, and sauté briefly until they glisten with fat and look lightly toasted. Add the stock and salt and bring to a boil. Cover, reduce the heat to medium-low, and cook about 55 minutes, until most of the wild rice kernels split open to reveal their white centers, and both it and the brown rice are tender. Remove the mixture from the heat and let it steam covered for about 10 minutes.

While it steams, warm the remaining 2 tablespoons of butter in a small skillet over medium-high heat. Add the mushrooms and sauté them just until they begin to color. Reduce the heat to medium-low and continue to cook for several minutes until tender. When the wild rice is ready, scrape the mushrooms into it and toss together. Serve hot.

INGREDIENT TIP: Most of the wild rice found in stores today is farm-raised in Minnesota and California rather than hand-harvested from the wild in the traditional manner. Both types taste wonderful, but the hand-harvested variety is typically lighter in color and texture, and fluffier too, differences that stand out in simple preparations like this recipe. Indian Harvest in Bemidji, Minnesota (800-294-2433), offers the original product, picked by the Ojibwa people from canoes. The firm also sells cultivated wild rices and wild rice blends, so be sure to specify what you want.

There are numerous instances of worthy merchants and mechanics, whose efforts are paralyzed, and their hopes chilled by the total failure of the wife in her sphere of duty; and who seek solace under their disappointment in the wine-party, or the late convivial supper. Many a day-laborer, on his return at evening from hard toil, is repelled by the sight of a disorderly house, and a comfortless supper; and perhaps is met by a cold eye instead of "the thriftie wifie's smile;" and he makes his escape to the grog-shop, or the under-ground gambling-room.

MARY CORNELIUS,
THE YOUNG HOUSEKEEPER'S FRIEND (1856)

Pennsylvania Dutch Noodles with Corn and Tomatoes

SERVES 2 OR MORE AS A MAIN DISH, 4 OR MORE AS A SIDE DISH

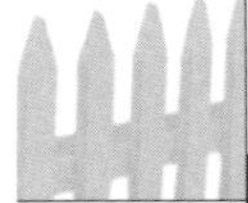

This bright tangle of egg noodles with late-summer vegetables satisfies big appetites but lacks the heaviness of some Pennsylvania Dutch dishes. It makes a bountiful supper with fresh fruit and a little cheese for dessert.

- 4 cups chicken stock, preferably homemade
- Salt
- ¾ pound broad egg noodles, store-bought or homemade (see Technique Tip)
- 2 cups corn kernels, fresh or frozen
- 1 medium red-ripe tomato, chopped
- 2 small ripe yellow tomatoes or another medium red-ripe tomato, chopped
- ⅓ cup thin-sliced scallions
- ⅓ cup minced parsley
- Freshly milled black pepper

Pour the stock into a large pot and bring it to a boil with a bit of salt over high heat. Stir in the noodles and cook until tender, 8 to 15 minutes, depending on the noodles. (As the noodles cook, the stock will reduce.) When the noodles are just tender, add the corn and cook for several additional minutes. The mixture should remain a bit soupy. Remove the mixture from the heat and pour it onto a rimmed platter or into a shallow bowl. Top with the tomatoes and any of their juice, the scallions, and parsley. Sprinkle a bit of pepper over the top and serve.

TECHNIQUE TIP: Making your own noodles for the dish is relatively easy and adds to both the texture and the freshness. Start by whisking together 2 eggs, 2 tablespoons of milk, and ½ teaspoon of salt in a large bowl. Stir in 1½ cups of flour, about ½ cup at a time, then knead briefly. If the dough remains sticky, knead in a few more tablespoons of flour. Roll the dough out ⅛ inch thick on a floured board, then cut it into noodles about ½ inch wide and several inches long. Let the noodles dry briefly, about 30 minutes. They can be kept for several hours if you wish, refrigerated but left uncovered. A pinch of saffron is a nice touch too, soaked first in the milk to distribute its color evenly.

Saimin

SERVES 4

Hawaii's version of an Asian noodle soup, saimin is the supreme comfort food of the islands, eaten any time of the day for a light meal or snack. Rachel Laudan in *The Food of Paradise* (1996) suggests it may have been the original "local food," as Hawaiians call their homey specialities, appearing in community cookbooks since the 1930s. She says Japanese immigrants consider saimin to be Chinese, and the Chinese claim it's Japanese, but everyone makes it, even McDonald's. Beyond the broth and noodles, all the ingredients serve as toppings, and vary with individual tastes, like the condiments for hot dogs. We recommend some typical options, but as Laudan advises, use a combination of imagination and restraint.

8-ounce package thin Chinese egg noodles (mein), preferably, or other thin Asian wheat-flour noodles

4- to 6-inch strip kombu (a dried sea vegetable) or other dried kelp

2 to 3 tablespoons dried shrimp (minced), several teaspoons bonito flakes, or Japanese dashi seasoning

"Thumb"-size piece of fresh ginger, sliced into thin matchsticks

Japanese soy sauce (not a light variety), such as Yamasa

2 to 3 scallions, sliced thin on the diagonal

Thin matchsticks of char siu (Chinese roast pork available in many Asian groceries or from Chinese take-out restaurants), or cooked chicken breast, or slices of Asian fish cake

Fresh spinach leaves, tiny cubes of firm tofu, thin-sliced fresh mushrooms, or a combination

Additional scallion slices, optional

Bring several cups of hot water to a rolling boil in a large saucepan. Add the noodles and cook them briefly until soft, just a few minutes for dried noodles, even less with fresh noodles. While the noodles cook, pull them apart with chopsticks or two forks as they soften in the pot. Rinse the noodles and reserve them.

Place the kombu, dried shrimp, and ginger in another large saucepan, and add 3 cups of water. Bring to a boil over high heat, then reduce the heat to a simmer and cook for about 5 minutes. Add several splashes of soy sauce, tasting as you go, giving the broth body and a slight saltiness. Stir in the noodles and other toppings and heat through. You will end up with a large proportion of noodles relative to broth. Serve hot in bowls, sprinkled, if you wish, with additional sliced scallions. Saimin is best eaten with spoons—the Chinese ceramic variety are especially nice—and chopsticks. Slurping is encouraged—and nearly inevitable.

INGREDIENT TIP: In Hawaii and on much of the West Coast, you can pick up the ingredients for saimin about as easily as you can buy a bag of potato chips. Elsewhere, a natural foods store or Asian market can supply the more exotic elements suggested.

Macaroni and Wisconsin Cheese Sauce

Serves 4 to 6 as a main dish, 6 to 8 as a side dish

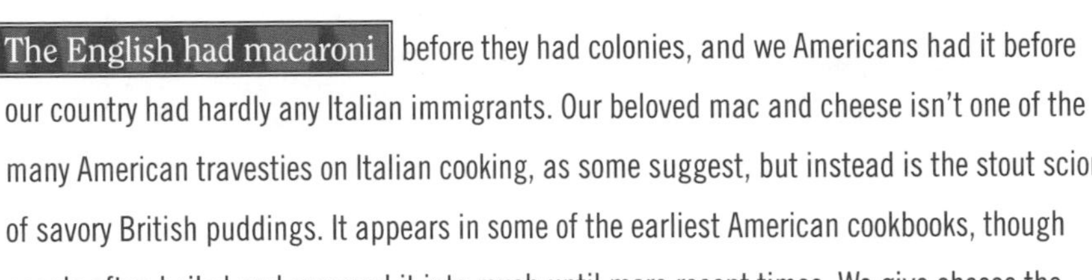

The English had macaroni before they had colonies, and we Americans had it before our country had hardly any Italian immigrants. Our beloved mac and cheese isn't one of the many American travesties on Italian cooking, as some suggest, but instead is the stout scion of savory British puddings. It appears in some of the earliest American cookbooks, though people often boiled and creamed it into mush until more recent times. We give cheese the spotlight it deserves in the dish and use nothing less than a good, sharp Cheddar.

BREAD CRUMBS

1 tablespoon unsalted butter

1 cup packed fresh bread crumbs

CHEESE SAUCE

6 tablespoons (¾ stick) unsalted butter

3 tablespoons unbleached all-purpose flour

1 to 2 tablespoons minced onion

1¾ cups whole milk

½ cup buttermilk, preferably, or additional milk

¼ teaspoon hot pepper sauce, such as Tabasco

¾ teaspoon salt or more to taste

Freshly milled black pepper

Pinch of nutmeg

¾ pound sharp Cheddar cheese, grated (about 3 cups)

¾ pound elbow macaroni, cooked according to package directions and tossed with 1 tablespoon butter

Preheat the oven to 375°F. Butter a medium to large baking dish.

Prepare the bread crumbs, first melting the butter in a small skillet over medium heat. Stir in the bread crumbs and toast them until golden, stirring occasionally. Scrape the bread crumbs out of the skillet and reserve them.

Prepare the sauce, first melting the butter in a large heavy saucepan over medium-low heat. Stir the flour into the butter gradually. When the flour is incorporated, mix in the onion and cook for 2 to 3 minutes, stirring frequently. Raise the heat to medium-high and gradually whisk in the milk and buttermilk. Bring the mixture to a boil and continue to stir it until lightly thickened, about 4 minutes. Reduce the heat to medium-low, mix in the hot pepper sauce, salt, pepper, and nutmeg, and continue cooking for about 5 additional minutes, stirring occasionally. Remove from the heat and immediately mix in the cheese, stirring until melted. Toss the macaroni with the cheese sauce and spoon it into the prepared baking dish.

Scatter the bread crumbs over the macaroni and cheese sauce. Bake for about 30 minutes, until heated through and golden brown and crunchy on top.

Mac Pudding and Pie

The English roots of mac and cheese surface clearly in the first published American recipe, Mary Randolph's version in *The Virginia Housewife* (1824). Calling the dish "maccaroni pudding," she combines a half-pound of the cooked pasta with five egg yolks and two whites, a half-pint of cream, minced poultry and ham, and a little grated cheese. Randolph finishes the preparation by steaming the mixture in a mold for an hour and serves it with a rich gravy.

Many modern cooks still use eggs in the dish, which creates a compact macaroni pie that holds together on the plate. Cheryl's grandmother Mayme perfected a midwestern rendition we still love, presented in our *Smoke & Spice* (1994). Damon Lee Fowler's southern grandfather made another tasty-sounding version, similar to one the Savannah author gives in *Classical Southern Cooking* (1995). Pudding, pie, or hodgepodge, made-from-scratch mac and cheese remains a sturdy and serendipitous link to our British heritage.

Pasta Primavera

SERVES 8 AS A MAIN DISH

Home cooks appropriated most of the dishes in this chapter through adaptation. This one they simply stole. Manhattan's Le Cirque restaurant created pasta primavera in the mid-1970s, offering it mainly as a homey, off-the-menu item for regular customers. It gained instant cachet, and the kitchen happily provided recipes that began to appear everywhere. Within a decade, it became the most stylish home-pasta dish in the country, elegant but easy, and finely balanced between healthy, seasonal vegetables and an indulgently rich sauce. While *primavera* means spring in Italian, the combination has no specific Roman roots, and may be best in the early fall, when most local produce peaks.

2½ pounds trimmed, mixed seasonal vegetables, such as small broccoli florets; thick matchsticks of zucchini or yellow squash; sugar snap-pea pods or snow peas; green beans sliced lengthwise, if thick; and pencil-thin asparagus, cut into 2- to 3-inch lengths

¼ cup olive oil

1 small leek, cut into thin matchsticks

1 plump garlic clove, minced

6 ounces button mushrooms, sliced thin (see Ingredient Tip)

1 cup crème fraîche

8 ounces (1 cup) mascarpone cheese, preferably, or cream cheese

1 pound fettuccine (a mix of plain fettuccine with either a spinach or tomato variety adds even more color)

Salt

1 cup shelled peas, fresh or frozen

½ cup freshly grated Parmesan cheese

3 tablespoons minced fresh basil

3 tablespoons minced flat-leaf parsley

1 medium to large red-ripe tomato, chopped

½ cup pine nuts

Prepare a large bowl about half full of icy cold water and reserve it.

Over boiling water steam each of the mixed vegetables separately just until tender. Each will cook only briefly, but the cooking times will vary a bit. When cooked, plunge each vegetable into the bowl of cold water and let it sit, adding a handful of ice cubes each time you add a new vegetable. When all vegetables have been steamed and chilled, drain them and set them aside at room temperature. (These steps can be taken earlier in the day that you plan to serve the pasta, refrigerating the vegetables in the meantime. Let them return to room temperature before proceeding.)

Warm the oil in a large saucepan over medium heat. Add the leek and sauté until soft, about 5 minutes. Stir in the garlic and mushrooms, and cook until the mushrooms are limp, about 5 additional minutes. Stir in the crème fraîche and

To be unable to cook, it seems to me, is as revelatory of a person's upbringing as would be the inability to read good books. . . . If I were a high-up dispenser of world-important jobs—senatorships, say, or United Nations delegates, or admirals, or generals, or tax officials—my first question to each would be, "Can you make a decent cup of coffee and coddle an egg?" If he was unable to prove that he could do so, he wouldn't get the job. The world would be better off without him.

KENNETH ROBERTS, INTRODUCTION TO MARJORIE MOSSER'S *FOODS OF OLD NEW ENGLAND* (1957)

mascarpone, and when they're melted into a smooth sauce, remove the pan from the heat. (The sauce can be made ahead, covered, and refrigerated. Reheat before proceeding.)

Cook the pasta in boiling salted water according to the package directions. Drain it and immediately toss it together in a large bowl with the sauce. When the pasta is well coated, mix it with the steamed vegetables and the shelled peas (which will cook lightly from the residual heat). Spoon the pasta onto a large platter or into a shallow bowl, and scatter the Parmesan, basil, parsley, tomato, and pine nuts over it. Serve warm.

California Fettuccine with Artichokes and Garlic

Serves 4 as a main dish

Italian immigrants to the United States retained a strong attachment to the culinary culture of their homeland. Over time, however Italian-American cooking took on more of the characteristics of the different areas where immigrants settled. This happened in New England, New Orleans, and perhaps most distinctively in northern California, where an abundance of fresh ingredients encouraged creative combinations of beloved Old Country flavors.

- ¼ cup plus 2 tablespoons extra-virgin olive oil
- 6 to 8 garlic cloves, sliced thin
- 2 cups sliced artichoke hearts or bottoms, fresh, frozen, or canned
- Zest and juice of 1 large lemon
- ¾ pound linguine or fettuccine, cooked according to package directions
- Salt and freshly milled black pepper
- ⅓ cup freshly grated Parmesan cheese
- ¼ cup minced flat-leaf parsley

Warm the oil in a large sauté pan or skillet over medium-low heat. Add the garlic and cook until it reaches a nutty light-golden stage, several minutes. Remove the garlic slices with a slotted spoon and reserve them. Add the artichokes and lemon zest to the oil, and continue sautéing briefly until the artichokes are soft. Stir in the lemon juice. Add the pasta to the sauce, toss it to coat evenly, and add salt and pepper to taste. Turn the pasta out onto a rimmed bowl or platter. Top with the Parmesan and parsley and serve.

Italian Cooking in America

Even before the upsurge in Italian immigration in the late nineteenth century, other Americans knew a little about Italian cooking—just enough to be proverbially dangerous. Early recipes attributed to Italy usually missed their mark by as much as a continent, a situation that often persisted into the twentieth century. Even the educated staff at the Minneapolis Public Library, the compilers of the 1928 *Library Ann's Cook Book,* thought that "Italian Raviola" was a long-simmered stew of steak, peppers, and noodles that should be served with steamed rice.

Maria Gentile's *The Italian Cook Book* (1919), one of the first American books on the subject, furthered our understanding considerably, though Gentile had her odd moments as well, as when she touted the copious use of an ordinary American-style white sauce. Beginning around the same time, Italian-American restaurants taught us lessons both bad and good—from the use of pregrated Parmesan to properly cooked pasta. In more recent decades, we've begun to get it right, propelled ahead by a barrage of fine cookbooks and a new generation of chefs. For a solid look at Italian cooking on this side of the Atlantic, get a copy of Nancy Verde Barr's *We Called It Macaroni* (1990), a story of triumph over travesty.

"THE MORE PERFECT THE BREAD, the More Noble the Lady"

SARAH JOSEPHA HALE'S VIEW OF THE RELATIONSHIP between bread and ladies, pithily expressed in 1857, represented a common opinion of her day. Bread making stood in a league of its own among all the responsibilities of a housewife. The skill sustained life on the most practical level, but it also exemplified the peak of achievement in the culinary arts, and for the many moralists of the era, it demonstrated fidelity to duty and home. If you couldn't do better than sliced bread, you might as well turn in your apron and abandon your family.

Though some writers embellished grandly on the theme, the core idea about the importance of bread making simply reflected reality throughout most of American history. A cook couldn't run to the local market for a loaf if her own failed, and success in the effort required seasoned diligence. She produced and maintained her own yeast cultures for wheat breads, and baked in brick ovens without temperature controls or steady heat. When the bread came out well, it approached the perfection that Sarah Hale sought, offering flavor and texture difficult to replicate today in a modern oven. The job and the results warranted all the respect they received.

Home bread making began to decline seriously in the second half of the nineteenth century, booted along by the baking limitations of new ranges and the increasing availability of commercial bread. Within a couple of generations, American bread lost even a claim to the name, deteriorating in its most common form to spongy, sliced cake. Our bread became a symbol again, no longer of excellence and nobility, but of stunted tastes and the shameful state of American food.

We've recovered enormously in recent years from that low point, though it's still a vivid memory to most of us. Bakers in homes and at small commercial operations are rapidly reclaiming their craft from the sponge factories. We're rediscovering coarse, flavorful grains, and relearning the life cycle of bread that lives instead of stores. Few yearn to return home bread making to its former eminence, but that's not practical anyway with our contemporary kitchens and hardly necessary with the good bread available today in most communities. Like many American home cooks, we specialize in selected breads, a baker's dozen or so, that we enjoy too much to leave to someone else. That's perfection aplenty, we figure, whether noble or not.

Crusty San Francisco Sourdough

MAKES ENOUGH FOR TWO 1½-POUND LOAVES PLUS EXTRA STARTER FOR FUTURE BREADS OR OTHER SOURDOUGH PRODUCTS

Everyone should make at least one loaf of sourdough in their lives to experience the ancient process of working with natural yeast. Before commercial yeast and baking powder appeared in the mid-nineteenth century, most Americans knew the sourdough technique and practiced it to varying degrees, though many considered the results unrefined. It became associated with western pioneers because, lacking ready access to new leavening products, they continued using the method longer than other people. Gold prospectors in California and Alaska took such pride in their breads that people called the miners "sourdoughs," a term eventually extended to all Alaskans. Partially because of a hospitable climate for yeast cultures, San Francisco developed superior versions of the bread, emulated here. We explain first how to create a sourdough starter, a homey treasure you can keep and "refresh" for years, and then how to turn it into a tasty loaf of bread.

SOURDOUGH STARTER

About 2 cups unbleached bread flour

A few unwashed organic grapes or a dribble of honey, optional

TECHNIQUE TIP:
Remember that sourdough starter is alive and needs to be fed and exercised every couple of weeks if you don't use it. Take the starter from the refrigerator, add to it a tablespoon or two of flour and warm water, stir, and let the starter sit out at room temperature overnight. Scoop it out and knead it a bit before returning it to the refrigerator. Every few times you exercise it, replace half the starter with a similar amount of flour and water to give it plenty of nourishment. It can corrode metal, so store the starter in a glass jar or small ceramic container.

To prepare the starter, begin at least a week before you plan to make your first loaves of bread. It may not take that long to develop the starter, but you want to make sure that it has plenty of time if necessary. Think of this phase as similar to growing a plant from seed, taking pleasure in its daily changes.

Spoon ⅓ cup of the flour onto a work surface. Pour 1 tablespoon of water over the flour and work it in. Mix in 2 more tablespoons of water, or a bit more, as necessary to form into a simple cohesive dough. (If you overdo the water, just add a bit more flour.) Knead this little mass for about 5 minutes. It should look like putty and be lightly springy and just a bit sticky. This is all that's necessary to gather your yeast, but adding a grape or two or a little honey will encourage the process. Place the starter in a small bowl and cover it with a clean, damp dishtowel or damp cheesecloth. Set the starter in a warm (not hot), out-of-the-way spot, and dampen the cloth once or twice each day as needed. By the third or fourth day, the starter should have developed a mild but not unpleasant sour aroma. It should have grown a tiny bit and look wrinkled. Give it another day or so, if needed, to reach this stage. If you used grapes in the starter, remove their solid remnants now.

CONTINUED

When the starter is ready, place it back on a work surface, scraping off or pulling off any hard crust. Sprinkle over the starter ⅔ cup of the flour and then 2 tablespoons of water. Work the starter and new ingredients together into a soft cohesive dough, again adding a few more tablespoons of water if dry, then knead for about 5 minutes. Rinse the bowl if it is crusty and return the starter to the bowl. Cover as before and leave it for another couple of days until it looks a bit softer, with a touch more puffiness and spring to it. Remember to keep the cloth damp, and if you live in a particularly dry climate, you may want to wipe the surface with just a bit of water to make sure the starter itself stays moist.

Repeat the process again, this time adding 1 cup of flour and ¼ cup of water. After kneading, let the starter rise for about 12 hours, give or take a few hours. The starter should now look like a lightly raised dough, and if you poke it, the mark from your finger will remain. The starter is ready to be used. Divide it into 2 blobs and put one half in a lidded container and refrigerate, to save for future use. The other half can now be used to start the sourdough bread, or placed in a lidded container and refrigerated for later use. Always return ½ to 1 cup of dough to the starter jar before proceeding, to have it ready for the next batch of bread.

THE BREAD

½ to 1 cup sourdough starter
4 to 5 cups unbleached bread flour
1 tablespoon kosher salt

The bread is made in stages, or refreshments, as professional bakers call them. It's a slow process, but one that allows natural fermentation to work at its best, slowly developing a distinctive though pleasant tang.

Place the starter in a heavy-duty electric mixer with a dough hook. Pour in ¾ cup of lukewarm water and begin to mix slowly. The starter should dissolve partially, becoming soupy. This mixture will only fill the very bottom of the mixer bowl, so you may need to stop and stir it up from the bottom by hand. Pour in 1 cup of the flour gradually while mixing, then increase the speed to medium. Add the salt. Mix for about 5 minutes, adding another ¼ to ½ cup of flour after several minutes as needed to get a very wet, stretchy, sticky dough. (You can get similar results by mixing the dough by hand, kneading it for about 10 minutes.)

Remove the dough from the mixer bowl, wash the bowl, and dry it. Grease the bowl with oil, then return the dough to the bowl and turn it to coat it evenly with oil. Cover the bowl with a damp cloth and let the dough rise in a warm, draft-free spot until doubled in size, 4 to 6 hours. Alternatively, refrigerate the dough for up to a day, then let it return to room temperature before proceeding. Place the bowl back on the mixer, pour in ¾ cup of lukewarm water, and begin to mix slowly. Pour in 2½ cups of flour gradually while mixing, then increase the speed to medium. Mix about 5 minutes, adding another ¼ to ½ cup of flour after several minutes as needed to get a very soft, elastic dough. It should be just slightly sticky

How often do we see the happiness of a husband abridged by the absence of skill, neatness, and economy in the wife! . . . However improbable it may seem, the health of many a professional man is undermined, and his usefulness curtailed, if not sacrificed, because he habitually eats *bad bread*.

MARY CORNELIUS, THE YOUNG HOUSEKEEPER'S FRIEND (1856)

Dough Gods

Sourdough starter is virtually a perpetual-motion bread machine. It's not as quick and convenient as the contemporary gadget sold under that label, but it's much cheaper and adds wonderful tang to food. Many cooks make pancakes and waffles from the starter, but real "sourdoughs" go further. In her *Alaskan Cookbook* (1960), Bess Cleveland uses it as the leavening in angel food and fruit cakes.

Cowboys in the old West judged chuck-wagon cooks by the quality of their sourdough biscuits, which they baked on the range over an open fire in a Dutch oven covered on top with burning coals. To make the "dough gods," as they were known, mix a cup of low-gluten biscuit flour with a cup of starter and a little salt. Knead the dough lightly a few times, pinch off pieces the size of an egg, and let them rise overnight or at least a couple of hours. Melt bacon drippings in a cast-iron skillet, dip one side of each biscuit in the fat, and put it in the skillet with the greased side up. Bake the biscuits for fifteen minutes and holler, "Come and get it."

to the touch, but no longer clinging forcefully to the bowl or your hands. (You can get similar results by mixing the dough by hand, kneading it for about 10 minutes.)

Remove the dough from the mixer bowl and again wash the bowl and dry it. Grease the bowl with oil, then return the dough to the bowl and turn it to coat it evenly with oil. Cover the bowl with a damp cloth and let the dough rise in a warm, draft-free spot until doubled in size, 4 to 6 hours. Alternatively, refrigerate the dough for up to a day, then let it return to room temperature before proceeding.

Punch the dough down, divide it in half, and form it into 2 free-form oblong or round loaves. Place them on a floured cookie sheet, cover with large inverted bowls, and let them rise in a warm, draft-free spot until larger by half, about 2 hours. You're almost there.

Near the end of the rising time, preheat the oven to 425°F. Place an empty heavy skillet on the lowest rack of the oven and, for the best results, place a baking stone on the middle shelf. Transfer the bread to the oven, using a large spatula to place it directly on the heated baking stone if you are using one. Otherwise leave the bread on the cookie sheet and place it on the middle shelf. Before closing the oven, pour ½ cup of water into the skillet to create steam in the oven. Close the oven immediately.

Bake for 35 to 40 minutes, until the bread is deeply brown on top and sounds hollow when thumped. If it thuds rather dully, it's not yet ready. Cool the loaves to room temperature on a baking rack. Eat within several hours for the best flavor, though the bread keeps at room temperature for several days, making great toast after it loses the first blush of freshness.

Multi-Grain Bread

MAKES 1 LARGE LOAF

The "thirded" and brown breads of the past, after being eclipsed for years by pale white bread, have enjoyed a revival of interest in recent decades and have helped to inspire contemporary whole-grain breads. Our rendition, filled with crunch from the grains and sunflower kernels, is dense but not heavy, stout but not tasting of cardboard. Pair it with Summer Corn Chowder (page 105) and The Gardener's Wife Salad (page 251), or when the snow falls, with steaming bowls of Wisconsin Cheese Soup (page 100).

- 1 envelope active dry yeast (see Ingredient Tip)
- 2 tablespoons honey
- 1 cup buttermilk
- 1 cup Grape-Nuts or other corn–barley nugget cereal
- 1 cup whole-wheat flour
- ½ cup stone-ground cornmeal
- 2 teaspoons salt
- 2 tablespoons sunflower oil, preferably, or corn oil
- ½ cup hulled salted sunflower seeds (sunflower kernels)
- Approximately 2 cups unbleached bread flour, preferably, or unbleached all-purpose flour

Combine the yeast with the honey and 1 cup of lukewarm water in a small bowl. Set aside until foamy. Heat the buttermilk to lukewarm in a small pan. Remove from the heat and stir in the Grape-Nuts.

In an electric mixer with a dough hook, mix together on medium speed the whole-wheat flour, cornmeal, and salt. Add the yeast mixture and the Grape-Nuts mixture, followed by the oil and sunflower seeds. Mix in about 1¾ cups of the bread flour. Beat for several minutes, adding an additional ¼ cup or more of flour as needed if the dough remains hopelessly sticky. Beat for 5 more minutes until the dough becomes smooth and supple but is still a little tacky. Pat the dough into a fat disk, transfer it to an oiled bowl, and turn it to coat it with oil. Cover the bowl and set it aside in a warm, draft-free spot until the dough doubles in bulk, 1 to 1½ hours.

Punch down the dough, kneading it a few turns. Pat it back into a fat disk and return it to the bowl. Cover and let it rise until doubled again, another 1 to 1½ hours. Shape the dough into a loaf. Grease an 8½-inch x 4½-inch loaf pan and place the bread in it. Let it rise until doubled again, 45 to 60 additional minutes.

Near the end of the rising time, preheat the oven to 375°F. Place an empty heavy skillet on the lowest rack of the oven. Slash the top of the bread with a sharp knife. Transfer the bread to the middle shelf of the oven. Before closing the oven, pour ½ cup of water into the skillet to create steam in the oven. Close the oven immediately.

Wheat, n. A cereal from which a tolerably good whiskey can with some difficulty be made, and which is used also for bread. The French are said to eat more bread *per capita* of population than any other people, which is natural, for only they know how to make the stuff palatable.

AMBROSE BIERCE,
THE DEVIL'S DICTIONARY
(1911)

Bake for about 50 minutes, until the bread is deeply brown on top and sounds hollow when thumped. If it thuds rather dully, it's not yet ready. Cool the loaf to room temperature on a baking rack. Eat within several hours for the best flavor, though the bread keeps at room temperature for days, making great toast.

INGREDIENT TIP: Today's packaged yeast is highly dependable as long as it's used by the specified expiration date. Just make sure you dissolve it in lukewarm water, not hot, because yeast dies at 138°F. Though you can't speed yeast up except by using a rapid-rise variety, you can slow the rising action. Stash the dough in the refrigerator between steps if you have errands to run, then bring it back to room temperature and continue with the steps. Before you set aside yeast dough to rise, rub it with oil—not butter, which will harden—to keep it from drying out.

Boston Brown Bread

MAKES ONE 1-POUND "LOAF"

This New England classic developed out of popular "thirded" breads, which contain the same trinity of primary ingredients—cornmeal, rye flour, and wheat flour. Brown bread differs primarily in being steamed rather than baked and in substituting a quick, baking-soda leavening for yeast. Mildly sweet and a bit reminiscent of a simple bran muffin, it goes great with baked beans, the traditional Boston pairing, and also makes a stalwart grilled cheese sandwich.

- ½ cup stone-ground cornmeal
- ½ cup whole-wheat flour
- ½ cup rye flour
- ¾ teaspoon baking soda
- ½ teaspoon salt
- 6 tablespoons vegetable oil
- ¼ cup molasses
- 1 cup buttermilk
- 1 egg, lightly beaten
- ½ cup dark raisins

Preheat the oven to 375°F. Grease a clean 1-pound coffee can.

In a large bowl, combine the cornmeal, wheat flour, rye flour, baking soda, and salt. Stir in the oil and molasses, just to combine. Add the buttermilk and egg, and mix with just enough strokes to combine. Stir in the raisins.

Spoon into the prepared can. There should be about 1½ inches of clearance for the bread to rise. Cover the top of the can tightly with greased foil. Place the can in a large saucepan and pour in enough hot water to come halfway up the can. Bring the water to a bare simmer, then cover and steam for 1½ to 1¾ hours, until a toothpick inserted in the top (with the foil removed) comes out clean. Replenish the water if needed while steaming. Cool on a baking rack for at least 10 minutes, then unmold. Slice the bread into thick rounds and serve warm, preferably, or at room temperature. Store any leftover bread in the refrigerator for up to several days.

Catharine Beecher, 1800–1878

Sarah Hale, Mary Cornelius, and a number of other cookbook writers of the antebellum era liked to talk about wifely duty, often in relation to bread, but no one matched the preaching of Catharine Beecher on such subjects. Her strident moralizing came naturally, shared with her famous father, evangelical minister Lyman Beecher, and seven younger brothers who joined the clergy. Her siblings included Henry Ward Beecher, the foremost pulpit orator of the nineteenth century, and Harriet Beecher Stowe, author of *Uncle Tom's Cabin.*

Catharine assumed major household responsibilities at a young age, learning how a woman influences the values and beliefs of her family through ministering to them as a cook and housekeeper. She contended throughout the rest of her life that this was a woman's profession, tending the home in a way that implanted "durable and holy impressions" on the people under her care.

She wrote extensively on her ideas, most notably in *A Treatise on Domestic Economy* (1841) and *Miss Beecher's Domestic Receipt Book* (1846). Described by biographer Barbara Cross as "didactic, homilectic, and emphatic," the two books foreshadowed the home economics movement, and provided inspiration to some of its early leaders. Both tomes went through many editions, finding an eager audience not only in New England, Beecher's base, but also among Yankee pioneers heading west. Her pronouncements on plain cooking and mundane practicalities may not rally many women today, but Beecher crusaded passionately in her own way on behalf of her sex.

Flour Tortillas

Makes about 8 tortillas, approximately 7 to 8 inches in diameter

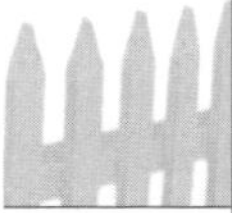

Whenever we feel an urge for plain, sliced white bread, say for a sandwich or a plate mop, we usually substitute a flour tortilla. Individually browned in spots during the quick, high-heat cooking, they simply taste better than an equally basic loaf. Flour tortillas probably originated in the Mexican state of Sonora, but they're far more popular in the United States than south of the border, where corn tortillas generally reign. Southwestern cooks developed their own home version, chunkier and chewier than Sonoran or commercial styles. We learned this preparation from the family of Carlos, Patsy, Lenore, Lasandra, and Lori Tapia, long-term natives of Santa Fe, a city where many people make the tortillas regularly.

- 2 cups low-gluten pastry or biscuit flour, preferably, or unbleached all-purpose flour
- 1½ teaspoons baking powder
- 1 teaspoon salt
- 1½ teaspoons vegetable oil
- ¾ cup lukewarm water
- Unsalted butter, Pico de Gallo (page 77), or your favorite salsa

Sift together into a large bowl the flour, baking powder, and salt. Pour in the oil and work it into the dry ingredients lightly with your fingers. Add the water, working it quickly until a sticky dough forms.

Knead the dough vigorously on a floured board for 1 minute. The mixture should no longer be sticky. Pinch your earlobe. If the dough is the same softness as your lobe, you can stop kneading. If the dough remains more firm, knead it a few more strokes until it's "earlobe" soft. Cover the dough with a damp, clean dishtowel, and let it rest for about 15 minutes.

Divide the dough into 8 equal pieces and form them into balls. Cover the balls again with the damp towel and let them rest for another 15 to 30 minutes. (The dough can be refrigerated at this stage and held for up to 4 hours. Bring the dough back to room temperature before proceeding.)

Roll out each dough ball on a floured surface into a circle approximately ¼ inch thick. Roll out from the center and turn the dough about a quarter-turn between rolls. With experience, it gets easier to make the tortillas round, but in the meantime you can trim off any ragged edges and discard them. To avoid toughening the dough, don't roll over the same spot more than a couple of times.

Warm a dry griddle or large cast-iron skillet over high heat. Cook the tortillas 30 seconds on each side until the dough looks dry, slightly leathery, and has brown speckles in a few spots. Serve the tortillas warm in a napkin-lined basket, with butter or salsa, or reserve them for another use.

TECHNIQUE TIP:
You can use a rolling pin to spread the tortilla dough, but the best tool is an inexpensive tortilla roller, which looks like (and sometimes is) a short section of broomstick. Mexican markets usually carry them, and the Santa Fe School of Cooking (800-982-4688 or 505-983-4511) sells them by mail order.

Cream Biscuits

MAKES ABOUT EIGHT 3-INCH BISCUITS OR TWELVE TO FOURTEEN 2-INCH BISCUITS, SERVING 4 TO 6

In *The Savannah Cook Book* (1933), Harriet Ross Colquitt tells about a northern visitor to the South who was asked about what impressed him the most about the area. He said it was the advice offered by the hostess in every home: "Take two, and butter them while they're hot." Americans started making biscuits in the early nineteenth century, soon after finely milled flour became available, preparing them in a variety of styles, from beaten to buttermilk (page 32), for different meals. Colquitt describes cream biscuits as the ones to serve "for state occasions," though we've sneaked them into ordinary dinners as well.

- 2 cups low-gluten biscuit or pastry flour, preferably, or 1¾ cups all-purpose flour plus ¼ cup cake flour or, less desirably, 2 cups unbleached all-purpose flour
- 2½ teaspoons baking powder
- ¾ teaspoon salt
- 3 tablespoons unsalted butter, well chilled
- 2 tablespoons lard, well chilled
- ¾ cup plus 2 tablespoons whipping cream, well chilled

Preheat the oven to 475°F.

Sift the flour, baking powder, and salt into a large bowl, preferably a shallow one. Cut the butter and lard into small chunks, and add them to the dry ingredients. Combine with a pastry blender just until a coarse meal forms. Make a well in the center and pour in the cream. With your fingers and a few swift strokes, combine the dough just until it's a sticky mess. Turn out onto a lightly floured board or, better, a pastry cloth. Clean, dry, and flour your hands. Gently pat out the dough and fold it back over itself about a half-dozen times, just until smooth. (A dough scraper helps greatly with this.) Pat out again into a circle or oval about ½-inch in thickness. Cover the dough lightly and refrigerate it for about 20 minutes.

After removing the dough from the refrigerator, cut it with a biscuit cutter, trying to get as many biscuits as possible, since the dough toughens if it's rerolled. You should be able, with practice, to get about eight 3-inch biscuits or twelve to fourteen 2-inch biscuits from the dough. Make your biscuits with a quick, clean, straight-down push on the cutter. If you twist the cutter, as seems to be a natural motion for many people, it twists the dough, resulting in an uneven biscuit. Bake the biscuits in the center of the oven, turning the baking sheet around once halfway through the baking time. Bake 3-inch biscuits for 8 to 10 minutes total, and 2-inch biscuits for 7 to 9 minutes, until raised and golden brown. Serve piping hot.

Biscuits High and Low

The American biscuit evolved from the quite different British biscuit, a thin, crisp cracker or cookie. Of all our many types of biscuits today, the unleavened beaten biscuit comes closest to the English model, and even takes its name from the old European technique of pounding the dough with a heavy mallet for a half hour or longer. The few people who make the biscuits now generally use a food processor for the beating, work that was once performed by slaves on southern plantations.

At the opposite extreme in fluffiness, the acme of the American style, the angel biscuit rises as high and heavenly as the term implies. The cook accomplishes the feat by using a combination of leavenings—typically dry yeast and baking powder or soda—that ensure the dough will rise, even for an inexperienced baker. The dual-action guarantee inspired the alternative name for the bread, "bride's biscuits."

'Simmon Biscuits

MAKES TWELVE TO FOURTEEN 2-INCH BISCUITS, SERVING 4 TO 6

That innocent and new-born crispness when you break a hot biscuit, the savory, steaming substance of its two halves between the teeth, those are experiences as soul-stirring as falling in love, and can be indulged in much oftener without serious consequences.

GEORGE RECTOR, *DINE AT HOME WITH RECTOR* (1934)

The brightest harbinger of winter in much of the Midwest, wild orange-red persimmons ripen in the late fall on bare-branched trees. Native Americans and early settlers loved the indigenous fruit, using it in beer and breads both, but an easier-to-cultivate Asian variety ultimately pushed the local persimmon out of the commercial market. The more intensely flavored wild fruit adds spark to these midwestern biscuits, though other persimmons or even apricots make a good rendition.

- ½ pound ripe persimmons (see Ingredient Tip)
- ⅓ cup milk
- 1½ cups low-gluten biscuit or pastry flour, preferably, or 1¼ cups plus 1 tablespoon unbleached all-purpose flour mixed with 3 tablespoons cake flour or, less desirably, 1½ cups unbleached all-purpose flour
- 1 tablespoon sugar
- 2 teaspoons baking powder
- ¾ teaspoon salt
- ¼ teaspoon ground mace or nutmeg
- 2 tablespoons unsalted butter, well chilled
- 2 tablespoons lard or vegetable shortening, well chilled

Preheat the oven to 450°F. Grease a baking sheet.

Halve the persimmons, remove the seeds, and scoop the pulp away from the skin. You will need ½ cup of persimmon pulp. Purée the persimmon pulp in a food processor or blender with the milk.

Sift the flour, sugar, baking powder, salt, and mace together into a mixing bowl, preferably a shallow one. Cut the butter and lard into small chunks, and add them to the dry ingredients. Combine with a pastry blender just until a coarse meal forms. Make a well in the center and pour in the persimmon-milk mixture. With your fingers and a few swift strokes, combine the dough just until it's a sticky mess. Turn out onto a lightly floured board or, better, a pastry cloth. Clean, dry, and flour your hands. Gently pat out the dough and fold it back over itself about a half-dozen times, just until smooth. (A dough scraper helps greatly with this.) Pat out again into a circle or oval about ½ inch in thickness. Cover the dough lightly and refrigerate it for about 20 minutes.

After removing the dough from the refrigerator, cut it with a biscuit cutter, trying to get as many biscuits as possible, since the dough toughens if it's rerolled. You should be able, with practice, to get about twelve to fourteen 2-inch biscuits from the dough. Make your biscuits with a quick, clean, straight-down push on the cutter, without twisting it. Bake the biscuits in the center of the oven, turning the baking sheet around once halfway through the baking time. Bake the biscuits for 8 to 10 minutes, until raised and lightly brown. (These biscuits rise less than plain biscuits and remain a bit denser.) Serve hot.

INGREDIENT TIP: Persimmons must be fully ripe to taste right, which is easily accomplished by letting them sit out at room temperature until very soft. They freeze well, either left whole and wrapped or seeded and puréed first.

Dinner Rolls

Makes 12 rolls

In many rural areas of the country, no Sunday or holiday meal seems complete without warm, soft rolls enriched with butter and eggs. The rolls boast a British pedigree, but American cooks changed more than the appearance when they shaped the bread in cloverleaf, crescent, and Parker House styles.

- ½ cup whole milk
- 2 tablespoons unsalted butter
- 1 package dry yeast
- 3 to 3¼ cups unbleached bread flour, preferably, or unbleached all-purpose flour
- 2 tablespoons sugar
- 1 teaspoon salt
- 1 egg, lightly beaten
- Approximately 3 tablespoons unsalted butter, melted

Warm the milk and 2 tablespoons butter together in a small saucepan over medium heat just until the butter melts. Remove from the heat and let the mixture stand until lukewarm.

Mix the yeast with ½ cup of lukewarm water and let it dissolve.

Combine 3 cups of the flour with the sugar and salt in a heavy-duty electric mixer with a dough hook. Mix on low speed until lightly combined. Slowly pour in the milk-butter mixture and the yeast mixture, then beat in the egg. Increase the mixer speed to medium and beat for 5 to 7 minutes, until the dough is smooth and elastic, adding some or all of the remaining flour if needed to make it nonsticky. Remove the dough from the mixer and knead it a few times with your hands, just to form the dough into a ball. Transfer the dough to a lightly oiled bowl, turning the dough to coat it evenly with oil. Cover the bowl with a clean dishtowel and set it in a warm, draft-free spot. Let the dough rise until doubled in size, 1 to 1½ hours. Punch the dough down, form it back into a ball, and cover it again. Let it rest for 10 to 15 minutes and then shape the dough in one of the following fashions.

For cloverleaf rolls: Grease a 12-cup muffin tin. Pinch the dough off in 1-inch pieces, rolling each into a ball. Arrange 3 balls so that they touch in each muffin cup. Drizzle melted butter generously over each roll.

For Parker House rolls: Grease a baking sheet. Roll out the dough ½ inch thick with a rolling pin on a floured board. Use a biscuit cutter to cut rounds 2½ to 3 inches in diameter. Using a chopstick or clean pencil, press an indention across each round, in a way that bisects the round into 2 sections, one twice as large as the other. Brush each round generously with melted butter. Fold the smaller section of each round over the larger section. Using your thumb, press down in the middle of the outside edge to lightly secure top to bottom. Transfer the rolls to the baking sheet, each slightly overlapping an edge of the previous roll.

For crescent rolls: Grease a baking sheet. Divide the dough into 2 balls. Roll out 1 ball into a 12-inch circle on a floured board, then cut it into 6 pielike wedges. Brush with half of the melted butter. Roll up each section loosely from its large end. Transfer the rolls to the baking sheet, arranging them at least 1 inch apart with the tip of each dough wedge tucked underneath. Repeat with the remaining dough.

Let the rolls rest in a warm, draft-free spot until doubled in size, about 45 minutes. (You can slow down the rising, if you wish, by placing the rolls in the refrigerator, then bringing them back to room temperature before baking.) Preheat the oven to 400°F while the rolls are rising.

Bake the rolls for 14 to 18 minutes, turning the baking sheet around once halfway through the baking time. When done, the rolls will be a deep golden brown and lightly puffed. Serve warm in a napkin-lined basket.

Cast-Iron-Baked Buttermilk Cornbread

SERVES 6 OR MORE

The original unleavened cornbreads, such as Narragansett Jonnycakes (page 18), provoke numerous controversies despite an utter simplicity in ingredients. The leavened types, better known today, ignite even deeper disputes, the kind you want to avoid with anyone clutching a cast-iron skillet. One school frames the debate in Civil War terms, claiming all Yankees make cornbread with yellow cornmeal and sugar, while every Southerner knows you save sugar for iced tea and use white cornmeal in bread. Various good cooks swear by additions of broccoli, buckwheat, corn kernels, cracklings, squash, sausage, sweet potatoes, or sour cream. We come down on the side of buttermilk against sweet milk, and then add a little sugar, but we only get really hardheaded about starting with stone-ground cornmeal and cooking in cast-iron.

> **The North thinks it knows how to make corn bread but this is gross superstition. Perhaps no bread in the world is quite so good as Southern corn bread and perhaps no bread in the world is quite so bad as the Northern imitation of it.**
>
> MARK TWAIN, THE AUTOBIOGRAPHY OF MARK TWAIN (CHARLES NEIDER, EDITOR), (1961)

- 1 tablespoon bacon drippings or vegetable oil
- 1½ cups stone-ground yellow or white cornmeal (see Ingredient Tip)
- ½ cup unbleached all-purpose flour
- 2 tablespoons sugar
- 2 teaspoons baking soda
- ½ teaspoon baking powder
- 1 teaspoon salt
- Pinch of cayenne
- 3 eggs
- 1½ cups buttermilk
- 3 tablespoons unsalted butter, melted

Preheat the oven to 400°F. After all of the ingredients are assembled, place the drippings in a 9- to 10-inch cast-iron skillet and put the skillet in the oven.

In a large bowl, stir together the cornmeal, flour, sugar, baking soda, baking powder, salt, and cayenne. In another smaller bowl, whisk the eggs together, then mix in the buttermilk. Pour the liquid ingredients into the dry ingredients and stir until barely combined, with a few dry steaks remaining. Pour in the butter, then mix just to incorporate. Take the hot skillet from the oven and spoon the batter into it. You should get a good sizzle when the batter hits the skillet. Smooth the batter and return the skillet to the oven. Bake for about 18 minutes, until lightly browned and a toothpick inserted in the center comes out clean.

The cornbread is scrumptious served piping hot right from the skillet. If you plan to serve it at room temperature, let it cool in the skillet for about 10 minutes before turning it out onto a baking rack, where its surface will stay crisper. Cut it into wedges just before serving.

INGREDIENT TIP: Good sources of stone-ground cornmeal for cornbread (and other milled grains) include War Eagle Mill in Arkansas (501-789-5343) and the Old Mill at Guilford in North Carolina (336-643-4783).

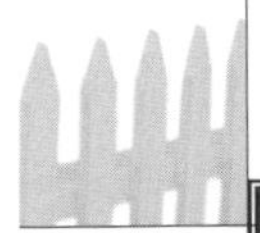

Piki Bread

The original southwestern cornbreads were tortillas and paper-thin sheets of piki. The Hopi and Zuni in particular ate lots of piki in centuries past and continue to make it today in a similar way. A cook grinds roasted corn, adds water to it to make a gruel, and spreads the batter thinly over a smooth stone griddle heated by a fire underneath. As the batter dries and curls at the edges, the cook peels it from the stone and wraps two or more sheets together to form a loose roll. Hopis and Zunis never put jalapeños in the bread, but they did mix in herbs and vegetable dyes, and varied the color of the corn to create as many kinds of piki as our types of cornbread.

Jalapeño Cornbread

SERVES 8 OR MORE

Texans added jalapeños to cornbread sometime around LBJ's tenure as president, and cornbread fans everywhere quickly took up the hot idea. Here we adapt the approach to what is sometimes called a custard cornbread, a creamier, sweeter version that accommodates the chile soothingly. We enjoy the cornbread with other Lone Star favorites, such as a bowl of chili or pinto beans, but it also goes great with something as distant from the source as Steamed Maine Lobster (page 118).

- 1¼ cups stone-ground cornmeal
- ¾ cup unbleached all-purpose flour
- 2 teaspoons baking powder
- 1 teaspoon salt
- ¾ cup (1½ sticks) unsalted butter, softened
- ⅓ cup sugar
- 4 eggs
- 2 tablespoons milk
- 14- to 15-ounce can creamed corn
- 2 to 3 jalapeño chiles, minced
- ¼ cup minced red bell pepper
- 8 ounces mild or medium Cheddar cheese, grated (about 2 cups)

Preheat the oven to 325°F. Butter a 9-inch × 13-inch baking dish.

In a small bowl, stir together the cornmeal, flour, baking powder, and salt. Cream together the butter and sugar with an electric mixer. Beat in the eggs, one at a time, then the milk, corn, jalapeños, bell pepper, and cheese. Add the dry ingredients to the wet ingredients, beating just a few strokes until the dry ingredients are incorporated.

Pour the batter into the prepared dish. Bake for 35 to 40 minutes, until a toothpick inserted in the center comes out clean. Let the cornbread sit for 15 minutes before cutting it into squares. Serve warm or at room temperature.

Rice Bread

MAKES 1 LARGE ROUND LOAF, ABOUT 12 INCHES IN DIAMETER

When rice grew tall in the Carolina lowcountry, and wheat not at all, rice bread was the everyday staff of life, so prized that Sarah Rutledge led off her 1847 *The Carolina Housewife* with thirty different recipes for it. The end of rice cultivation and the decline in home baking took a big toll on the popularity of this bread, but it's ripe for a renaissance, deliciously dense and moist with a crunchy crust. We're indebted to John Martin Taylor's instructions for making it in a modern oven in his *Hoppin' John's Lowcountry Cooking* (1992).

1 cup uncooked rice
1½ tablespoons kosher salt
1½ quarts bottled spring water
Two packages active dry yeast
2 pounds unbleached bread flour (about 7 cups)
Vegetable oil

Bring the rice, salt, and water to a boil in a large saucepan, then reduce the heat to medium-low. Simmer uncovered until the rice is very soft and the water has been absorbed, about 20 to 30 minutes. The rice should remain moist, not dried out. (Resist any urge to taste what will be a very salty mixture.) Spoon the rice into a large bowl and set aside for a few minutes until lukewarm. Sprinkle the yeast onto the rice and mix it in thoroughly. Work in about 5 cups of the flour, about a cup at a time. When the mixture begins to get stiff and lumpy, and you can't believe it's ever going to form bread dough, dump it out on a floured surface for easier working. Knead the dough for 10 to 15 minutes, incorporating some or all of the remaining 2 cups of flour if you think the dough can absorb it. When ready, the dough will be transformed into a smooth, elastic mass. Coat the bread lightly with oil and return it to the bowl. Cover the bowl with a clean dishtowel and let the dough sit in a warm, draft-free spot to rise until doubled in size, about 2 hours.

Punch the dough back down and knead it lightly for a minute or two, forming it into a fat round risk while you work. Arrange the bread on a greased cookie sheet. Cover the bread again with a towel and set it in a warm, draft-free spot to rise until expanded by half in size, about 1 hour.

Near the end of the rising time, preheat the oven to 450°F. If you have a baking stone, which results in a crisper crust, place it in the oven when you start heating. If using a baking stone, slide the bread off the cookie sheet and onto the stone in the oven when the oven is ready. Otherwise, bake the bread on the cookie sheet.

It is better to be plump than to live on baker's bread. We call it "light bread" at the Creek, and a friend from the Big Scrub goes an intelligent step farther and calls it "wasp-nest bread.". . . We serve baker's bread only to our enemies, trusting they will never impose on our hospitality again.

MARJORIE KINNAN RAWLINGS, CROSS CREEK COOKERY (1942)

Short List of Favorite American Fried Breads

- Aebelskiver
- Beignet
- Cala
- Cruller
- Dough Boy
- Doughnut
- Fastnacht
- Funnel Cake
- Malasada
- Navajo and Pueblo Fry Bread
- Sopaipilla
- Utah Scone

Bake for 15 minutes, then reduce the temperature to 400°F and bake 15 minutes longer. If you used a cookie sheet under the bread, remove it now and return the bread to the oven, placing it directly on the oven rack. If you used a baking stone, leave it in place but turn the bread over onto its top side. Continue baking for 10 to 15 additional minutes, until the bread is golden brown and sounds hollow when thumped. If it thuds rather dully, it's not yet ready. If the bread appears to be getting too dark, reduce the oven temperature to 350°F during the last stage of baking. Cool the loaf to room temperature on a baking rack. The crusty loaf yields beautiful slices for eating as is or for toasting later.

Caramel Pecan Sticky Buns

Makes 1 dozen large rolls

American sticky buns and cinnamon rolls probably derive from the German *kuchen* tradition of sweetened yeast breads, though there are British precedents as well. German and Dutch settlers used to serve similar coffee cakes when entertaining neighbors informally, in afternoon-tea fashion, and we think the gooey buns still make a better snack than a breakfast bread, side dish, or dessert.

STICKY BUNS

- ¾ cup milk
- ½ cup (1 stick) unsalted butter
- 1 package active dry yeast
- 2¾ to 3¼ cups unbleached all-purpose flour
- ¼ cup granulated sugar
- 1 teaspoon salt
- 2 eggs
- ½ teaspoon pure vanilla extract
- ⅓ cup packed light brown sugar

CARAMEL PECAN GLAZE

- ¾ cup packed light brown sugar
- 1 cup pecan pieces
- ½ cup (1 stick) unsalted butter, cut into tablespoons
- 6 tablespoons light corn syrup
- ½ teaspoon pure vanilla extract

Prepare the buns, first warming the milk and ¼ cup (½ stick) of the butter together in a small saucepan just until the butter melts. Remove the mixture from the heat and let sit briefly until it cools to lukewarm. Sprinkle in the yeast and let it dissolve.

In a heavy-duty electric mixer with a dough hook, blend together on low speed 2¾ cups of the flour, the granulated sugar, and the salt. Raise the speed to medium and beat in the eggs and vanilla, then the milk-butter mixture. Continue beating for a minute. If the dough remains a sticky mass, add the remaining flour, a few tablespoons at a time, and beat until the dough becomes smooth and satiny but still soft, up to another minute. Remove the dough from the mixer and knead a few times on a floured board into a ball. Lightly oil a medium bowl. Transfer the dough to the bowl and turn it to coat the dough with oil. Cover with a clean dishtowel and set in a warm, draft-free spot until doubled in size, about 1½ hours.

Punch down the dough, return it to the bowl, and let it rise until doubled again, about another hour. (As an alternative, the dough can be refrigerated overnight or up to 12 hours, to give you more flexibility about when you bake and serve the buns. Return it to room temperature before proceeding.)

Preheat the oven to 350°F.

Roll the dough out on a floured board into a rectangle about 10 inches by 12 inches. Melt the remaining ¼ cup (½ stick) butter and brush it over the dough.

Sprinkle the brown sugar evenly over the butter. Roll up the dough from one of the rectangle's longer sides.

Prepare the glaze, scattering the brown sugar, pecans, and butter in a 9-inch × 13-inch baking pan. If you have a choice, a light-colored shiny metal pan is preferable to one that is dark because the rolls and topping will more easily stay a pretty golden brown. Drizzle the corn syrup and vanilla evenly over the other ingredients. Set the baking pan over a low burner for several minutes, just long enough for the butter to melt and the ingredients to get gooey.

Slice the dough into rounds about 1 inch thick. Arrange the dough rounds evenly in the baking dish over the topping, with a spiral-cut side up. Cover the pan with the dishtowel again, and let the rolls rise for about 30 minutes, until they are puffed up and have risen to the top edge of the baking dish.

Bake the rolls for 25 to 30 minutes, until golden brown on top. Let the buns sit on a baking rack for just 5 minutes. Run a knife around the inside edge of the pan and invert the rolls onto a foil-lined baking sheet. The topping will ooze down and around the buns. When cool enough to handle, pull the rolls apart and serve still warm.

Maui Mango Bread

Makes 1 large loaf, serving 8 or more

Virtually every cook in Hawaii has a favorite recipe for mango bread, as common in the islands as zucchini bread is on the mainland. Both quick breads, made without yeast, thrive for the same reason: an abundance of late-season produce that rots unless it's used in some way. Many of the mango bread recipes go overboard with sugar and other seasonings, such as coconut, cinnamon, and vanilla, all of which can mask the allure of the vibrant fruit. We keep our bread simple to let the mango flavor shine as gloriously as its color.

2 cups unbleached all-purpose flour
1 cup sugar
2 teaspoons baking soda
½ teaspoon salt
½ teaspoon ground cinnamon
3 large eggs
½ cup vegetable oil or ¼ cup vegetable oil and ¼ cup macadamia nut oil
2 teaspoons fresh lemon juice
2 cups chopped fresh ripe mango (about 2 medium mangos)
½ cup macadamia nuts, halved

Preheat the oven to 350°F. Grease a 9-inch × 5-inch loaf pan.

In a large mixing bowl, stir together the flour, sugar, baking soda, salt,and cinnamon. Make a well in the center of the ingredients. Whisk together in a small bowl the eggs, oil, and lemon juice, and pour the mixture into the well in the dry ingredients. Lightly combine, then stir in the mango and nuts. Do not overmix. Scrape the batter into the prepared pan. Bake for 65 to 70 minutes, until a toothpick inserted in the center comes out clean. Cool in the pan for 10 minutes, then turn out onto a rack covered with a clean dishtowel, to avoid indentations. Let the bread cool for at least 10 additional minutes before slicing. The bread can be served warm or at room temperature, enhanced perhaps with a bit of butter. The bread keeps well for several days and makes good toast too.

All the countryside folk and half the city folk once counted hot breadstuffs twice a day as part of the pattern of living, and if you could have persuaded the beneficiaries of that usage that a day was at hand when all the hot bread would come out of a toaster, they would have thought you were describing a world gone to pot.

Sidney Dean, *Cooking American* (1957)

PEERLESS PIES, Crisps, Cobblers, and Creams

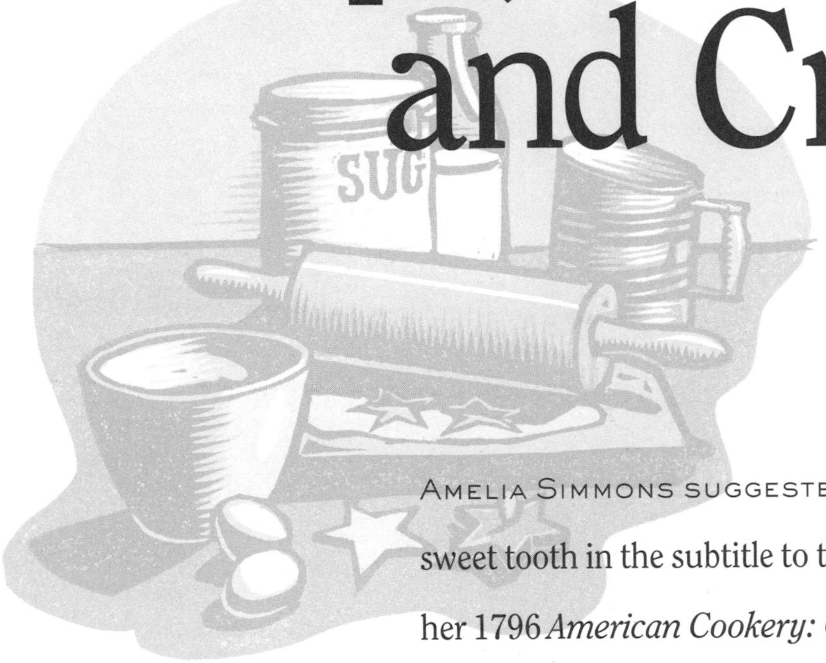

AMELIA SIMMONS SUGGESTED THE SIZE OF THE NATION'S sweet tooth in the subtitle to the first American cookbook, her 1796 *American Cookery: Or, the Art of Dressing Viands, Fish, Poultry and Vegetables, and The Best Modes of Making Puff-Pastes, Pies, Tarts, Puddings, Custards and Preserves, and All Kinds of Cakes, From the Imperial Plumb to Plain Cake.* Sweet treats comprised about half the recipes in the short work, a pattern repeated frequently in cookbooks for more than a century afterward. In the immensely popular *Boston Cooking-School Cook Book* (1896), for example, Fannie Farmer offered eleven separate chapters on desserts. Given the intensity of our sugar rush, it's no wonder we were a country on the move.

Americans inherited their love of sweets from the British, who also provided early direction for the form of our desserts. With few regional deviations, colonists relished trifles, tarts, puddings, elaborate cakes, dumplings, and molded jellies, all traditional in England. Pie came from the mother country too, stuffed originally with meat more often than fruit, but Americans gradually reversed the choice of fillings. As pie moved from the middle to the end of a meal, other pastry and fruit desserts gained increasing favor as well, displacing in many cases, or at least transforming, the older British favorites.

Sugar still reigns in American tastes, though today, as in the past, many of the best home cooks put the spotlight on the other ingredients in a dessert. In the dishes featured in this chapter, fruit takes top billing, with pastry accents and dairy products playing strong supporting roles. Rather than an abundance of recipes, in the manner of many old cookbooks, we strive in our selections for a diversity of flavors—keen, clean favors not masked by an excess of sugar. We're not sour on sweets, but we are sweet on desserts that offer more.

Sour Cream–Raisin Pie

Serves 8

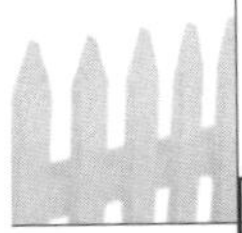

We once drove a couple of hundred miles out of our way, and added a day to a trip, just to eat a slice of this pie for dinner that night and then again for breakfast the next morning. Our destination was the Norske Nook café in Osseo, Wisconsin, as close as you get to a pie heaven in the United States. Helen Myhre, a fine farm cook, developed an extensive repertory of pies years ago, and the kitchen still makes them her way even though she's retired. Her meringue-topped version of this pie is a dairyland delight, probably created as a way to use cream that soured naturally in the days before refrigeration.

Buttery Single Pie Crust, prepared and parbaked as on page 370

FILLING AND MERINGUE

4 large eggs, separated

2 cups sour cream

½ cup plus 2 tablespoons granulated sugar

¼ cup unbleached all-purpose flour

1¼ cups dark raisins

¼ to ½ teaspoon fresh lemon juice, optional

Pinch of cream of tartar

Pinch of salt

3 to 4 tablespoons confectioners' sugar

Preheat the oven to 350°F.

Prepare the filling, first combining the egg yolks, sour cream, granulated sugar, and flour in a heavy saucepan. Stir together well, then mix in the raisins. The mixture will be thick at first, but thins when you begin to heat it. Cook over medium-low heat until it again gets quite thick, glossy, and puddinglike, with full, plumped raisins, about 15 minutes. Remove from the heat and taste the filling. If you feel the tang of the sour cream could be heightened by adding some or all of the lemon juice, stir it in now. The object isn't to taste the lemon, but to have the sour flavor nicely balanced with the sweet.

Pour the filling into the prepared pie shell.

Prepare the meringue, preferably in a copper bowl. Beat the egg whites until frothy, then add the cream of tartar and salt. Gradually beat in the confectioners' sugar and continue beating until the egg whites hold their shape but are still glossy.

Top the filling with the meringue, heaping it high in the center and making sure that it touches the crust all the way around the edge. Bake for 15 to 18 minutes, until the meringue is golden. Let the pie cool for at least 1 hour before slicing it into wedges and serving. Leftovers are best refrigerated, though the texture of the meringue suffers a bit.

I can't remember Mother cautioning us not to overeat, but I do remember her telling us a story of a very hungry man who passed by a farmhouse while the farm wife was making pies and asked for one. She began to taste them to see which one was the best and ended up eating them all, whereupon she turned into a woodpecker. When you see a woodpecker, notice its front. That is the pie lady, still wearing her white apron.

EDNA LEWIS, THE TASTE OF COUNTRY COOKING (1977)

Apple-Cranberry Pie

SERVES 6 TO 8

When something is "as American as apple pie," it's a national passion but not necessarily a native product. Both the fruit and the pastry wrap came from Europe, particularly England, but Americans made the pie their own by the place they gave it on their tables. J. Hector St. John de Crèvecoeur, the eighteenth-century author of *Letters from an American Farmer* (1782), said that supper for half the year on his New York homestead consisted of apple pie and milk. Amelia Simmons provided three recipes for the pie—as many as for any dish—with one modified in New England fashion with the addition of cranberries, a solid suggestion. We also flavor the crust with sharp Cheddar cheese, another felicitous twist tuned to an American appetite.

CHEDDAR CRUST

2¾ cups unbleached all-purpose flour

1 tablespoon confectioners' sugar

¾ teaspoon salt

6 ounces flavorful sharp Cheddar cheese, preferably white, grated fine (1½ cups)

4 tablespoons (½ stick) unsalted butter, cut in small cubes, well chilled

¼ cup vegetable shortening, well chilled

¼ cup lard, well chilled

4 to 6 tablespoons ice water

FILLING

2¼ pounds apples, preferably a combination of tart and sweet, peeled and sliced thin

1½ cups cranberries, fresh or frozen, or 1 cup dried cranberries

¼ cup plus 2 tablespoons granulated sugar

2 tablespoons cornstarch

¼ cup packed light brown sugar

¼ to ¾ teaspoon ground cinnamon

¼ teaspoon ground nutmeg

¼ teaspoon salt

Juice of ½ lemon, optional

2 tablespoons unsalted butter, cut in small bits

GARNISH

2 tablespoons milk or 1 egg white, beaten lightly

Turbinado sugar or other coarse granulated sugar, preferably, or regular granulated sugar

Grease a 9-inch pie pan.

Prepare the pie crust, first pulsing together the flour, sugar, and salt in a food processor. Scatter the cheese and butter over the mixture, and quickly pulse several times just to submerge them in the flour. Scoop the shortening and lard into small spoonfuls and scatter them over the mixture; pulse again quickly several more times until they disappear into the flour too. Sprinkle in 4 tablespoons of the ice water and pulse again quickly, just until the water disappears.

Do not suppose that we limit the apple-pie to the kinds and methods enumerated. Its capacity in variation is endless, and every diversity discovers some new charm or flavor. It will accept almost every flavor of every spice. And yet nothing is so fatal to the rare and higher graces of apple-pie as inconsiderate, vulgar spicing. It is not meant to be a mere vehicle for the exhibition of these spices in their own natures; it is a glorious unity in which sugar gives up its nature as sugar, and butter ceases to be butter, and each flavorsome spice gladly vanishes from its own full nature, that all of them, by a common death, may rise into the new life of apple-pie.

HENRY WARD BEECHER, QUOTED IN CORA, ROSE, AND BOB BROWN, AMERICA COOKS (1940)

It became our preeminent national dish because in the isolated, primitive farmhouses of colonial America, apple pie was much more than dessert. Ideally suited to the rugged climate and the low technology of the farms where most settlers lived, the apple pie was a basic means of survival: appetizer, entrée, and dessert at winter meal after winter meal in the dawn of the Republic.

Raymond Sokolov,
Fading Feast (1983)

Dump the mixture into a large bowl or onto a pastry board. Lightly rub the dough with your fingers, adding more water, 1 tablespoon at a time, as needed. When the dough holds together if compacted with your fingers, stop. It's ready. Divide the dough in half and press each half into a fat disk. Wrap the dough in plastic and refrigerate for at least 30 minutes.

Preheat the oven to 425°F. Form a drip pan for the lower shelf of the oven, turning up the sides of a large piece of foil.

Roll out each disk on a floured surface into a thin round an inch or two larger than the pie pan. Arrange the bottom crust in the pie pan, avoiding stretching it. Even out any ragged edges, leaving about ¾ to 1 inch of crust overhanging the pan. Refrigerate both crusts for about 15 additional minutes.

Prepare the filling, first placing the apples and cranberries in a medium bowl. Combine the granulated sugar and cornstarch, and spoon half of the mixture into the bottom pie crust. Stir the rest of the sugar-cornstarch mixture into the fruit and mix with the brown sugar, cinnamon to taste, nutmeg, and salt. Add the lemon juice if the apples are mostly sweet rather than tart or if you are using dried cranberries in the filling. Spoon the filling into the crust and dot with butter. Top with the second crust and crimp the edge neatly. Cut several vent holes. Embellish the top crust with any remaining pieces of dough cut decoratively if you wish. Brush the top with milk, then sprinkle lightly with sugar. Cover the edge of the pie with a strip of foil.

Bake the pie for 10 minutes, then reduce the temperature to 350°F. Continue baking for 45 to 50 additional minutes, removing the foil strip when about 20 minutes of baking time remain. The pie is done when the crust is golden brown and flaky. Let the pie cool for at least 1 hour, to allow the juices to be reabsorbed. Slice into wedges and serve.

Door County Sour Cherry Pie

SERVES 6 TO 8

Parson Weems, an itinerant bookseller and biographer, invented the fable of George Washington and the cherry tree, curiously promoting the value of truthfulness through a deliberate fabrication. The real Washington probably got as earnest about pies as about lies, though he preferred beef inside them rather than cherries or other fruit. French colonists planted sour cherries on the shores of Lake Michigan before the country even had a president, and residents of the region still specialize in pies made with the tangy orbs, especially in Door County, Wisconsin. The use of a lattice crust, which we scent with almonds, allows some of the fruit juice to evaporate and concentrate in flavor. If you want to pay homage to Washington with the pie, top it with ice cream, one of his true cravings.

ALMOND PIE CRUST

¾ cup sliced almonds (2.25-ounce bag)

2¾ cups unbleached all-purpose flour

3 tablespoons confectioners' sugar

1 teaspoon salt

¾ cup (1½ sticks) unsalted butter, cut in small cubes, well chilled

6 tablespoons vegetable shortening, well chilled

6 tablespoons lard, well chilled

5 to 7 tablespoons ice water

FILLING

2 pounds pitted sour cherries, fresh, frozen, or canned, with juice

1 teaspoon fresh lemon juice

Scant ¼ teaspoon almond extract

1 tablespoon instant tapioca

Dash of red food coloring, optional

¾ cup granulated sugar, plus another tablespoon or two if the cherries are quite tart

2 tablespoons cornstarch

Grease a 9-inch pie pan.

Prepare the crust in a food processor, first chopping the almonds fine with ¾ cup of the flour. Add the rest of the flour, the confectioners' sugar, and salt, and pulse to combine. Scatter the butter over it and pulse quickly until it disappears into the flour, then mix in the shortening and lard just until combined. Sprinkle in 4 tablespoons of the ice water and pulse again quickly, just until it disappears.

Dump the mixture into a large bowl or onto a pastry board. Lightly rub the dough with your fingers, adding more water, 1 tablespoon at a time, as needed. When the dough holds together if compacted with your fingers, stop. It's ready. Divide the dough in half and press each half into a fat disk. Wrap in plastic and refrigerate for at least 30 minutes.

Prepare the filling, first mixing the cherries in a bowl with the lemon juice, almond extract, tapioca, and optional food coloring. (Use only the tiniest bit of coloring. Pie filling shouldn't be the color of fire engines.) Let the mixture sit for 10 minutes.

Preheat the oven to 400°F. Form a drip pan for the lower shelf of the oven, turning up the sides of a large piece of foil.

Roll out each disk on a floured surface into a thin round an inch or two larger than the pie pan. Arrange the bottom crust in the pie pan, avoiding stretching it. Even out any ragged edges, leaving about ¾ to 1 inch of crust overhanging the pan. Cut the top crust into inch-wide strips, preferably with a decorative pastry cutter, and lay the strips side by side on greased wax paper. Refrigerate the crust and the lattice strips for about 15 additional minutes.

Combine the granulated sugar and cornstarch, and spoon half of the mixture into the bottom pie crust. Stir the rest of the sugar-cornstarch mixture into the cherries and pour the filling into the crust. Lay several of the lattice strips over the cherries, in opposite directions, leaving inch-wide gaps of filling exposed. Weave the strips over and under to create an open diamond pattern over the pie. Crimp the edge neatly, making it rather high to help keep the juices from bubbling over. Cover the edge of the pie with a strip of foil.

Bake the pie for 40 minutes, then remove the foil strip. Continue cooking for about 10 additional minutes, until the crust is golden brown and flaky. Let the pie cool for at least 1 hour, to allow the juices to be reabsorbed. Slice into wedges and serve.

Catahoula Sweet-Dough Pies

MAKES 12 TO 14 INDIVIDUAL TURNOVERS

We first learned about these Catahoula, Louisiana, pies in Marcelle Bienvenu's *Who's Your Mama, Are You Catholic, and Can You Make a Roux?* (1991), published in the Cajun city of Lafayette. The crust intrigued us, being a cross between a French *pâte sucrée* and an American sugar cookie. We found Catahoula on a map, called around the area, and finally located a delightful piemaster named Emma Lou Bourque, who calls herself Miss Emma Lou. She told us that sweet-dough pies, usually filled with blackberries, are a Good Friday tradition that goes back at least as far as her grandmother's day. Miss Emma Lou and other ladies of the local church bake some 350 large pies, providing a hefty slice for all their 1,700 neighbors. For herself, the spry octogenarian also makes a smaller turnover version, which we emulate here.

SWEET-DOUGH CRUST

2 cups unbleached all-purpose flour
2 teaspoons baking powder
½ teaspoon salt
¼ cup (½ stick) unsalted butter, softened
2 tablespoons vegetable shortening
¼ cup plus 2 tablespoons sugar
1 egg
¼ cup whole milk or half-and-half
½ teaspoon pure vanilla extract

FILLING

3 cups blackberries, fresh or frozen
2 to 3 tablespoons sugar
1 to 2 teaspoons fresh lemon juice

1 to 2 tablespoons whole milk or half-and-half
Turbinado sugar, preferably, or granulated sugar

Prepare the dough, first stirring together the flour, baking powder, and salt.

Cream the butter, shortening, and sugar together, beating until fluffy and light, about 5 minutes with an electric mixer at high speed. Beat in the egg, milk, and vanilla, and then add about half the flour mixture, beating it in before adding the rest. Stop as needed to scrape down the sides of the bowl. Scrape the dough from the bowl and pat it out into an inch-thick disk. Wrap in plastic and refrigerate for at least 20 minutes. (The dough can be made ahead and refrigerated for up to several days. Let it sit briefly at room temperature before proceeding.)

While the dough chills, prepare the filling. Combine in a small heavy saucepan two cups of the blackberries with the sugar and lemon juice. Bring to a simmer over medium-high heat and cook until the berries have broken down and become

Now you talk about something that's fun, that's Pie Day. We hold it every Good Friday. Back in the old days, Cajuns were so isolated they didn't have their own priests. They knew they were supposed to do something on Good Friday—fast or feast—but they didn't know which, so they decided to do both. So they'd have coffee-milk, then they'd fast in the morning. But all the while they'd be busy making pies—crawfish pies, tuna pies, chicken pies, mince pies, sweet dough pies, all kinds of pies. Then everyone would get together and eat nothing but pie.

Louisiana cook "Tootie" Guirard, quoted in Jean Anderson, The Grass Roots Cookbook (1974)

very thick and jamlike in consistency, 15 to 25 minutes, depending on the juiciness of the berries. Stir in the remaining 1 cup of berries and remove from the heat. (The filling can be made up to several days ahead, covered, and refrigerated.)

Preheat the oven to 350°F.

Roll out the dough on a floured surface to a generous ¼-inch thickness. Cut the dough into squares or circles about 4 inches across. Spoon 1 tablespoon of filling in the middle of each section of dough, then fold one side of the dough over the other and pinch to make a tight seal. (A few crackles in the dough's surface are common, but if it cracks badly when forming the turnovers, reroll the dough just a bit thicker.) Crimp neatly with your fingers or the tines of a fork. Move the pies with a dough scraper or spatula to avoid tearing the dough. Brush each turnover lightly across the top with milk, then sprinkle with sugar.

Arrange the turnovers at least ½ inch apart on an ungreased cookie sheet. Bake for 13 to 15 minutes, until set and just slightly colored. Cool the turnovers on the cookie sheet for several minutes, then finish cooling them on baking racks. Serve warm or at room temperature.

Slip-Skin Concord Grape Pie

Serves 6 to 8

Right before the Civil War, Ephraim Bull of Concord, Massachusetts, a friend and neighbor of Thoreau and Hawthorne, developed the hybrid grape named for his town. Almost immediately a prohibitionist named Thomas Welch put the grape into "Dr. Welch's Unfermented Wine," now known as grape juice, but cooks with a different agenda preferred it in a pie. The "slip-skin" tag comes from the process of separating the grapes from their peel, worth the labor involved for the flavor returned.

BUTTERY DOUBLE PIE CRUST

2½ cups unbleached all-purpose flour

1¼ teaspoons salt

½ cup (1 stick) unsalted butter, cut in small cubes, well chilled

½ cup plus 2 tablespoons vegetable shortening, well chilled

6 to 8 tablespoons ice water

FILLING

3½ pounds Concord grapes (about 6 to 6½ cups, stemmed)

Approximately ¾ cup sugar

Minced zest of 1 lemon

1½ tablespoons fresh lemon juice

1½ tablespoons instant tapioca

Grease a 9-inch pie pan.

Prepare the pie crust. In a food processor, pulse together the flour and salt, then scatter the butter over the flour and quickly pulse several times just to submerge the butter. Scoop the shortening into small spoonfuls and scatter them over the flour-butter mixture; pulse again quickly several more times until they disappear into the flour too. Sprinkle in 4 tablespoons of the ice water and pulse again quickly, just until the water disappears.

Dump the mixture into a large bowl or onto a pastry board. Lightly rub the dough with your fingers, adding more water, 1 tablespoon at a time, as needed. When the dough holds together if compacted with your fingers, stop. It's ready. Divide the dough in half and press each half into a fat disk. Wrap in plastic and refrigerate for at least 30 minutes.

Roll out each disk on a floured surface into a thin round an inch or two larger than the pie pan. Arrange the bottom crust in the pie pan and refrigerate it and the other crust for at least 15 additional minutes.

Prepare the pie filling. First, slip the grapes from their skins, pinching each near its bottom end and squeezing gently but firmly. Place the skins in a medium bowl and the skinned grapes in a heavy medium saucepan. Add ½ cup of the sugar to the grapes and cook over medium heat for 5 to 10 minutes, until the grapes separate from their seeds. Using a food mill or coarse strainer, separate the pulp from the seeds and discard the seeds. Combine the pulp with the skins and add as much of the remaining ¼ cup sugar as necessary to leave the mixture just a bit tangy but not sour. Stir in the lemon zest, juice, and tapioca, and reserve. (The filling can be made a day ahead and refrigerated, covered, if you like. Return to room temperature before proceeding.)

Preheat the oven to 425°F. Form a drip pan for the lower shelf of the oven, turning up the sides of a large piece of foil.

Pour the filling into the bottom crust and then arrange the top crust over and crimp the edge neatly. Cut several vent holes. Embellish the top crust with any remaining pieces of dough cut decoratively if you wish. Cover the edge of the pie with a strip of foil.

Bake for 15 minutes, then reduce the oven temperature to 375°F. Continue baking for about 35 additional minutes, removing the foil when about 20 minutes of baking time remains. The pie is done when the crust is golden brown and flaky. Let the pie cool for at least 1 hour, to allow the juices to be reabsorbed. Slice into wedges and serve.

Rhubarb Custard Pie

Serves 6 to 8

French immigrant Pierre Blot, in his *Hand-Book of Practical Cookery* (1867), suggested savoring rhubarb in some form "at least every other day." By the late nineteenth century, many other Americans agreed, wrapping chunks of the tangy, rosy-red stems so often in pastry that it acquired the nickname of "pieplant." This particular pie, like many others, probably comes from the Pennsylvania Dutch heritage.

BUTTERY SINGLE PIE CRUST

1¼ cups unbleached all-purpose flour

¾ teaspoon salt

¼ cup (½ stick) unsalted butter, cut in small cubes, well chilled

¼ cup plus 1 tablespoon vegetable shortening, well chilled

3 to 4 tablespoons ice water

FILLING

¾ pound fresh rhubarb, cut into ⅓-inch dice (about 2 cups)

¾ cup sugar

2 teaspoons cornstarch

2 eggs

¾ cup half-and-half

½ teaspoon pure vanilla extract

Grease a 9-inch pie pan.

Prepare the pie crust, first pulsing together in a food processor the flour and salt. Scatter the butter over the flour and quickly pulse several times just to submerge the butter. Scoop the shortening into small spoonfuls and scatter them over the flour-butter mixture; pulse again quickly several more times until they disappear into the flour too. Sprinkle in 2 tablespoons of the ice water and pulse again quickly, just until the water disappears.

Dump the mixture into a large bowl or onto a pastry board. Lightly rub the dough with your fingers, adding more ice water, 1 tablespoon at a time, as needed. When the dough holds together if compacted with your fingers, stop. It's ready. Pat the dough into a fat disk. Wrap in plastic and refrigerate for at least 30 minutes. Roll out the dough on a floured surface into a thin round an inch or two larger than the pie pan. Arrange the crust in the pie pan, crimping the edge neatly, then refrigerate it for at least 15 additional minutes.

Preheat the oven to 400°F. Form a drip pan for the lower shelf of the oven, turning up the sides of a large piece of foil.

Line the pie crust with greased foil, then fill with pie weights or dried beans. Parbake the pie crust for 15 minutes, then remove the weights and foil, and bake for 5 to 8 minutes longer, until set and no longer raw-looking. Set the pie crust aside to cool. Reduce the oven temperature to 325°F.

[Eating pie only twice a week, as suggested, is] utterly insufficient . . . as anyone who knows the secret of our strength as a nation and the foundation of our industrial supremacy must admit. Pie is the American synonym of prosperity, and its varying contents the calendar of the changing seasons. Pie is the food of the heroic. No pie-eating people can ever be permanently vanquished.

THE NEW YORK TIMES, 1902, QUOTED IN JOSEPH AMENDOLA AND DONALD E. LUNDBERG, UNDERSTANDING BAKING (1970)

Prepare the filling. Place the rhubarb in a heatproof bowl and pour about 3 cups of boiling water over it. In a separate bowl, stir together the sugar and cornstarch. With an electric mixer, beat together the eggs and sugar until the mixture falls from the beater in light yellow ribbons, about 2 minutes. Mix in the half-and-half and vanilla until well incorporated. Drain the rhubarb, then scatter it in the cooled pie crust. Pour the custard mixture over it evenly. Bake in the middle of the oven for about 40 minutes, until the custard is just lightly firm. You may have to jiggle the pan a bit to tell. Cool the pie for at least 1 hour before slicing into wedges and serving.

TECHNIQUE TIP: When a custard pie is ready to be taken from the oven, an inch-wide area in the center should still jiggle, but not seem like a lake. The pie will continue to bake as it cools. Don't overcook a custard pie, or try to rush it by raising the baking temperature, or the filling will come out tough and will leak liquid when cut.

Bourbon-and-Butter Pecan Pie

SERVES 8

This is the pie that's more American than apple, featuring an indigenous nut virtually unknown in the rest of the world. Both George Washington and Thomas Jefferson grew pecans, Abraham Lincoln relished a molasses version of this pie, and Eleanor Roosevelt served a modern rendition at White House holiday dinners, giving it as much presidential stature as any dish in the country. Its roots go back to chess pie, a simple egg, butter, and sugar dessert long beloved in the South. After the introduction of Karo corn syrup in 1902, pecan pie began displacing its predecessor in popularity. We prefer sugar-cane syrup in the filling, but so many people use corn syrup that we've seen this called "Karo nut pie" in Arkansas.

SUPERBLY FLAKY SINGLE PIE CRUST

1¼ cups unbleached all-purpose flour

¾ teaspoon salt

2 tablespoons unsalted butter, cut in small cubes, well chilled

4 tablespoons lard, well chilled

2 tablespoons vegetable shortening, well chilled

3 to 4 tablespoons ice water

FILLING

1 cup packed dark brown sugar

⅔ cup cane syrup, preferably, or ⅓ cup light corn syrup and ⅓ cup molasses (see Ingredient Tip)

¼ cup (½ stick) unsalted butter

½ teaspoon salt

3 tablespoons bourbon or other American whiskey

½ teaspoon pure vanilla extract

4 eggs

3 tablespoons half-and-half

2 generous cups pecan pieces

24 pecan halves

Grease a 9-inch pie pan.

Prepare the pie crust. In a food processor, pulse together the flour and salt, then scatter the butter over the flour and quickly pulse several times just to submerge the butter. Scoop the lard and shortening into small spoonfuls and scatter them over the flour-butter mixture; pulse again quickly several more times until they disappear into the flour too. Sprinkle in 2 tablespoons of the ice water and pulse again quickly, just until the water disappears.

Dump the mixture into a large bowl or onto a pastry board. Lightly rub the dough with your fingers, adding more water, 1 tablespoon at a time, as needed. When the dough holds together if compacted with your fingers, stop. It's ready. Pat the dough into a fat disk. Wrap in plastic and refrigerate for at least 30 minutes.

Shoo, Fly!

The heavy, molasses-based shoo-fly pie can be made "wet bottomed," an extra-gooey way, or "dry bottomed," with flour in the filling. Both attract sugar-loving creatures, from people to flies. Montgomery pie, a related Pennsylvania Dutch specialty, is a step down in sweetness. Local maestro Betty Groff makes her version with a lemony bottom layer and a white cakey top, poured on top of each other in a pie crust. She says some neighbors reverse the layers, but they still remain friends.

A nation with its heart in the right place would long since have erected a monument as tall as the Statue of Liberty to the unknown heroine who baked the first American pie—its unworthy ancestors abroad can be disregarded. The pedestal should be round and divided into six pieces and the figure should be holding up a pie the size of those in Paul Bunyan's lumber camps. . . . On the pedestal should be inscribed what might be a quotation from Walt Whitman: "O Pieoneers!"

George Rector,
Dine at Home with Rector
(1934)

Roll out the dough on a floured surface into a thin round an inch or two larger than the pie pan. Arrange the crust in a pie pan, avoiding stretching it. Crimp the edge decoratively, then refrigerate it for at least 15 additional minutes.

Preheat the oven to 375°F. Form a drip pan for the lower shelf of the oven, turning up the sides of a large piece of foil.

Prepare the filling, first combining the brown sugar, cane syrup, butter, and salt in a large heavy saucepan. Bring the mixture to a boil over high heat and leave it at a rolling boil for exactly 1 minute, stirring constantly. Remove the pan from the heat, stir in the bourbon and vanilla, and let the mixture cool to warm room temperature.

Whisk the eggs with the half-and-half, then whisk them into the cooled syrup mixture. Stir in the pecan pieces. Pour the filling into the pie crust. Top with a layer of pecan halves, covering the entire surface neatly. Cover the edge of the pie with a strip of foil.

Bake the pie for 10 minutes, then reduce the oven temperature to 350°F. Cook for 30 to 35 additional minutes, removing the foil when about 20 minutes of baking time remains. The pie is done when a toothpick inserted into the center comes out clean. Let the pie sit for at least 1 hour before slicing into wedges and serving.

INGREDIENT TIP: Cane syrup looks like a light molasses and tastes a bit like it too, though not as heavily flavored. We think it gives greater dimension to the filling than molasses paired with the flatter-tasting corn syrup. The long-popular Steen's brand can be found in many supermarkets or ordered by mail from the New Orleans School of Cooking (800-237-4841 or 504-525-2665).

Lemon Meringue Pie

SERVES 6 TO 8

Cooks started putting meringue on top of lemon pudding tarts in the second half of the nineteenth century, often calling the concoction "frosted lemon pie." The meringue used up the egg whites left over after the yolks went into the filling and, as the old name implies, did serve the traditional role of a dressy, white frosting for a baked dessert. Any way you label it, as long as you keep the pie creamy rather than starchy, this is a sunburst of goodness.

- Buttery Single Pie Crust, prepared and parbaked as on page 370
- Minced zest and juice of 4 large lemons (about 2 tablespoons zest and ¾ cup juice)
- 1¼ cups sugar
- Salt
- 4 large eggs, separated, plus 3 large eggs
- 6 to 8 tablespoons unsalted butter
- ½ teaspoon pure vanilla extract
- ¼ teaspoon cream of tartar
- 3 to 4 tablespoons confectioners' sugar

Preheat the oven to 350°F.

Prepare the filling. Whisk together the lemon zest and juice, sugar, 2 pinches of salt, the separated egg yolks, and whole eggs in a heavy saucepan over medium-low heat. Add 3 tablespoons of the butter. Cook the filling until it thickens enough to coat a spoon heavily, about 15 minutes. Whisk in 3 more tablespoons of butter, a tablespoon at a time. Taste a small spoonful of the filling; if it tastes overly acidic, add 1 to 2 more tablespoons of butter. Remove the filling from the heat and cool for 5 to 10 minutes while you prepare the meringue, stirring the filling a couple of times to release some steam.

Prepare the meringue, preferably in a copper bowl. Beat the egg whites with the vanilla until foamy. Add the cream of tartar and a pinch of salt. Stir in the confectioners' sugar gradually, continuing to beat until the egg whites hold their shape but are still glossy.

Pour the warm filling into the pie crust. Swirl the meringue over the filling, mounding it high in the center. Make sure the meringue is spread so that it touches the crust all the way around the edge. Bake the pie for 15 to 18 minutes, until the meringue is golden. Let the pie cool uncovered for at least 1 hour before slicing into wedges and serving. Leftovers are best refrigerated, though the texture of the meringue suffers a bit.

After a long period abroad nothing could make me more homesick or emotional than an American magazine ad of a luscious layer cake, except one, and that was a pictured lemon pie.

IRMA ROMBAUER,
JOY OF COOKING (1943)

TECHNIQUE TIP:
Lemon meringue pies frequently come out with a starchy runny filling or a weepy meringue. We avoid the former by not using cornstarch or other thickeners in the filling—just a full complement of eggs, butter, and lemon juice that provide the proper consistency. The acidity of the lemon juice keeps the eggs from curdling when the mixture is cooked over moderate but direct heat. We prevent the meringue from weeping by sweetening it with confectioners' sugar, which contains a little cornstarch, a tip we learned from Helen Myhre, whose meringue-topped sour cream–raisin pie inspired ours earlier in this chapter. Spooning the meringue over a warm filling also helps to curtail weeping, as does baking the pie in a moderate oven instead of a high oven.

Key Lime Pie

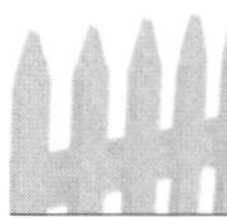

SERVES 8

The Florida Keys got lime trees and condensed milk about the same time, the middle of the nineteenth century, and it didn't take long for a clever cook to put the two together in a pie. A hurricane blew away most of the local trees in 1926, and trucks began delivering fresh milk around then too, but residents refused to give up the pie, even when they had to make it with common supermarket limes. Superior versions still use the small, tart Key limes, now imported from the Caribbean and Mexico, the original source of Florida's lime trees.

GRAHAM CRACKER CRUST

1¼ cups graham cracker crumbs (about 16 crackers)

2 tablespoons granulated sugar

3 tablespoons unsalted butter, melted

FILLING AND MERINGUE

4 eggs, separated

1 tablespoon minced lime zest

14-ounce can sweetened condensed milk

½ cup plus 1 tablespoon Key lime juice (see Ingredient Tip)

Pinch of cream of tartar

Pinch of salt

3 to 4 tablespoons confectioners' sugar

Preheat the oven to 350°F. Grease a 9-inch pie pan.

Prepare the crust, combining the graham cracker crumbs and granulated sugar in a large bowl, then stirring in the butter. Press the crust into the pie pan and bake for 10 minutes, until lightly colored and set. Cool to room temperature.

Prepare the filling, first combining the egg yolks and lime zest in a medium bowl. Whisk the yolks with the zest, which will cause the eggs to turn peculiarly green. This is the effect that you want, as it helps color the filling a deeper green naturally. Whisk in the milk and lime juice. Pour into the crust, and bake for 15 minutes.

Prepare the meringue, preferably in a copper bowl. Beat the egg whites until foamy, then add the cream of tartar and salt. Beat in the confectioners' sugar gradually. Continue beating until the egg whites hold their shape but are still glossy.

Remove the pie from the oven and let it sit at room temperature for about 10 minutes. While still warm, swirl the meringue over the filling, mounding it high in the center. Make sure to spread the meringue so that it touches the crust all the way around the edge. Bake the pie for 15 to 18 minutes, until the meringue is golden.

Let the pie cool uncovered for at least 1 hour before slicing into wedges and serving. Leftovers are best refrigerated, though the texture of the meringue suffers a bit.

INGREDIENT TIP: Key limes are increasingly available across the country, especially in midwinter, but can also be mail-ordered from Melissa's (800-588-0151).

Sweet Potato Pie

SERVES 6 TO 8

Pumpkin and sweet potato fillings, both puddings originally, play similar roles in late-fall pies. This celebratory sweet potato version comes from Virginia, where it's traditional at fish fries as well as at Thanksgiving and Christmas. Peanuts, a local crop, flavor the crust, and the delicacy of the tuber, compared to pumpkin, lets you go lighter on the spicing and sweetening.

PEANUT SINGLE PIE CRUST

- ⅓ cup salted peanuts
- 1¼ cups plus 2 tablespoons unbleached all-purpose flour
- 2 teaspoons confectioners' sugar
- ½ teaspoon salt
- 4 tablespoons (½ stick) unsalted butter, cut in small cubes, well chilled
- 3 tablespoons vegetable shortening, well chilled
- 3 tablespoons lard, well chilled
- 3 to 4 tablespoons ice water

FILLING

- 1½ pounds sweet potatoes, peeled and cut into 1-inch cubes
- ½ cup granulated sugar
- ¼ cup packed light brown sugar
- 2 eggs
- 1 cup half-and-half
- 2 tablespoons light rum or 1¼ teaspoons pure vanilla extract
- ¾ teaspoon ground ginger
- ¼ teaspoon ground cinnamon

Chopped honey-roasted peanuts

Grease a 9-inch pie pan.

Prepare the crust in a food processor, first chopping the peanuts fine with 2 tablespoons of the flour. Add the rest of the flour, the confectioners' sugar, and salt, and pulse to combine. Add the butter and pulse until it disappears into the flour. Mix in the shortening and lard just until combined. Sprinkle in 2 tablespoons of the ice water and pulse again quickly, just until the water disappears.

Dump the mixture into a large bowl or onto a pastry board. Lightly combine with your fingers, adding more water, 1 tablespoon at a time, as needed. When the dough holds together if compacted with your fingers, stop. It's ready. Pat the dough into a fat disk. Wrap in plastic and refrigerate for at least 30 minutes.

Roll out the dough on a floured surface into a thin round an inch or two larger than the pie pan. Arrange the crust in the pie pan, avoiding stretching it. Crimp the edge decoratively, then refrigerate it for at least 15 additional minutes.

Preheat the oven to 425°F. Form a drip pan for the lower shelf of the oven, turning up the sides of a large piece of foil.

Long-haired preachers
come out every night,
Try to tell you what's
wrong and what's right;
But when asked about
something to eat,
They will answer in
voices so sweet:
Chorus:
You will eat bye and bye,
In that glorious land
above the sky;
Work and pray, live on hay,
You'll get pie in the sky
when you die.

JOE HILL, LYRICS FROM THE LABOR SONG "PIE IN THE SKY"

Steam the sweet potato chunks for 20 to 25 minutes, until very soft. Mash or rice the potatoes into a mixing bowl. With a mixer, beat in the remaining filling ingredients until well combined. Pour the filling into the prepared pie crust. Cover the edge of the crust with a strip of foil. Before baking, sprinkle the chopped peanuts over the top.

Bake for 10 minutes, then reduce the baking temperature to 350°F. Bake for 35 to 40 additional minutes, removing the foil when about 20 minutes of baking time remains. The pie is done when a knife inserted into the center of the filling comes out clean but the filling still quivers a bit. Let the pie cool uncovered for at least 1 hour before slicing into wedges and serving.

Peach Cobbler

Serves 8

Lettice Bryan suggests the origin of fruit cobblers in *The Kentucky Housewife* (1839), where she gives "peach pot-pie" as an alternative name for this one. She also says that "although it is not a fashionable pie for company, it is very excellent for family use, with cold sweet milk." Typically lacking the thickeners added to fruit fillings in standard pies, cobblers tend to be juicy and runny, less enticing on the plate than on the palate. We use an upside-down batter for the crust, which rises through the fruit and is both cakey and crunchy. A handful of fresh raspberries or blueberries makes a good addition to the peaches in the filling.

FILLING

3 to 3¼ pounds ripe juicy peaches (about 12 medium), peeled, pitted, and sliced thickly (see Ingredient Tip)

¼ cup plus 2 tablespoons sugar

1 tablespoon fresh lemon juice

½ teaspoon ground ginger

½ teaspoon ground nutmeg

Pinch of salt

BATTER

½ cup (1 stick) unsalted butter

1¼ cups unbleached all-purpose flour

¾ cup sugar

½ teaspoon baking powder

½ teaspoon baking soda

Pinch of salt

1 cup buttermilk

1 teaspoon pure vanilla extract

Nutmeg Syrup (page 22), optional

Vanilla ice cream or softly whipped cream, optional

Preheat the oven to 350°F.

Prepare the filling, stirring together the ingredients in a large bowl.

Prepare the batter, first melting the butter in a 9-inch × 13-inch baking dish, either in the oven or on the stove over low heat. In a medium bowl, stir together the flour, sugar, baking powder, baking soda, and salt. Mix in the buttermilk and vanilla, and pour the batter over the butter in the baking dish. Pour it throughout the dish, but don't worry if you have a few holes or a bit of unevenness. (Don't stir the batter, which would reduce its ability to form the desirable crunchy edges.) Spoon the peach filling over the batter.

Bake the cobbler for about 45 minutes, until the crust has oozed up through the fruit and is golden brown, lightly raised, and still moist. Serve the cobbler warm, accompanied by nutmeg syrup or ice cream if you wish, though it's plenty scrumptious without a thing on top.

INGREDIENT TIP: Lettice Bryan specified clingstone peaches for her cobbler, but we prefer freestone peaches in baked dishes. Clingstones generally ripen first, making them tempting after doing without fresh peaches for months, but they are best for pickling and canning. While today most of the commercial peach crop is shipped cross-country from California, look for picked-ripe local fruit for peak flavor. Many areas of the country produce superior peaches, including Colorado's Western Slope, Utah's Brigham City, the Texas Hill Country, south-central Illinois, and the great state of Georgia.

Blackberry Cobbler

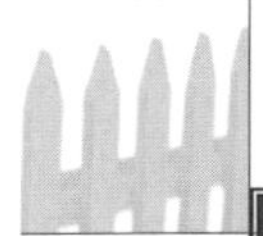

SERVES 6

Plump fresh blackberries give off loads of purple juice, making them even better for a cobbler than a regular pie. For the same reason, they're also perfectly suited to this thick, dropped-batter topping, which absorbs the liquid lusciously. Janie Hibler, an authority on the foods of the Pacific Northwest, convinced us that the best cobblers combine two types of blackberries or blackberry hybrids, such as gloriously sweet marionberries and the more tart loganberries. If you're limited to one choice, however, you'll still be berry blithe.

Provided brothers and sisters go together, and are not allowed to go with bad children, it is a great deal better for the boys and girls on a farm to be picking blackberries at six cents a quart, than to be wearing out their clothes in useless play. They enjoy themselves just as well; and they are earning something to buy clothes, at the same time they are tearing them.

LYDIA MARIA CHILD,
THE AMERICAN FRUGAL
HOUSEWIFE (1832)

4 cups fresh blackberries, marionberries, loganberries, boysenberries, tayberries, or black raspberries, preferably a combination of two varieties

¾ cup granulated sugar or a bit more to taste

Ground nutmeg

Salt

1 to 2 teaspoons fresh lemon juice, optional

2 tablespoons packed light brown sugar

1½ cups unbleached all-purpose flour

2 teaspoons baking powder

6 tablespoons (¾ stick) unsalted butter, cut into 6 chunks

1 cup half-and-half

Whipping cream or more half-and-half, optional

Preheat the oven to 325°F. Butter a 10-inch deep-dish pie plate or similar-size shallow baking dish.

Stir the berries together in the pie plate with ½ cup of the granulated sugar and pinches of nutmeg and salt. If the berries are not at the height of flavor, add another tablespoon or so of sugar and enough lemon juice to perk up the taste. Combine in a food processor the remaining ¼ cup granulated sugar, the brown sugar, flour, baking powder, and more pinches of nutmeg and salt. Pulse until the dry ingredients are mixed. Add the butter and pulse again until mealy-looking. Pour in the half-and-half and mix just until the batter forms.

Drop the batter in spoonfuls over the berries, leaving the topping a bit uneven and some of the berries uncovered in spots. Bake the cobbler for about 35 minutes, until golden brown and lightly raised. Serve the cobbler warm, with a drizzle of cream if you wish.

Apple Crisp

SERVES 6 TO 8

Irma Rombauer called this "the best dessert imaginable when made with good cooking apples." It's a stalwart midwestern favorite featuring a German-inspired streusel topping. Few after-dinner treats are both so quick and memorable.

- 3 pounds tart apples, such as Jonathan or Granny Smith
- 1 cup unbleached all-purpose flour
- 1 cup packed light brown sugar
- 1 teaspoon ground cinnamon
- ½ teaspoon salt
- ½ cup (1 stick) unsalted butter, cut into small chunks, well chilled

Preheat the oven to 375°F. Butter an 8-inch baking dish.

Peel, core, and slice the apples into small chunks. Pile them into the prepared dish. Mix about 2 teaspoons of the flour with the apples.

Combine the remaining flour, brown sugar, cinnamon, and salt in a food processor, and pulse to combine. Add the butter and pulse until the mixture becomes a crumbly meal. Spoon it over the apples evenly, packing it down lightly. Bake the crisp for about 30 minutes, until the topping is crunchy and the apples tender. Serve warm.

Filling Up

Pies, cobblers, crisps, pandowdies, and brown Bettys—all represented in these pages—are just a slender slice of the many ways that American cooks have combined fruit and pastry. Other favorites include:

- Dumplings: fruit wrapped in a pielike pastry and then boiled or baked
- Roly-polys: similar to dumplings but usually with a biscuit dough
- Fritters: fruit bound in batter and then deep-fried
- Fried pies: pan-fried, half-moon pies especially popular in the mid-South
- Turnovers: baked pie or puff pastry with a jamlike filling
- Crumbles: similar to crisps but with a crumbly topping
- Slumps: stovetop-cooked fruit with a dropped dumpling or biscuit topping
- Grunts: same as slumps except in name
- Buckles: fruit baked into a cakey batter with a crisp topping

Pear Crisp

SERVES 8 TO 10

Other fruits besides apples work well in crisps, too, particularly pears. The new edition of *Joy of Cooking* (1997), the successor to Irma Rombauer's 1943 work, lacks the original's sense of personal enthusiasm for crisps, but expands the offerings to include a pear and mango medley. In our version, pears tango with bourbon instead, and the topping gets extra crunch from oats and nuts.

FILLING

3 pounds pears (about 7 to 8 medium), such as Bosc or Bartlett

3 tablespoons bourbon

1 teaspoon pure vanilla extract

⅓ cup packed light brown sugar

⅓ cup granulated sugar

1 tablespoon unbleached all-purpose flour

¼ teaspoon ground nutmeg

Pinch of salt

1 tablespoon unsalted butter, cut into small bits

TOPPING

1 cup oats (not the quick-cooking variety)

1 cup chopped pecans

1 cup packed light brown sugar

1½ cups unbleached all-purpose flour

Pinch of salt

¾ cup (1½ sticks) unsalted butter, chunked

Preheat the oven to 375°F. Butter a 9-inch × 13-inch baking dish.

Prepare the filling, first peeling, coring, and cutting the pears into small chunks. Pile the pieces into the prepared dish. Mix the remaining filling ingredients into the pears.

Prepare the topping, combining the oats, pecans, brown sugar, flour, and salt in a food processor. Add the butter and pulse until the mixture becomes a crumbly meal. (There will be quite a bit of topping.) Spoon it over the pears evenly, packing it down lightly. Bake the crisp for 40 to 45 minutes, until the topping is crunchy and the pears are tender. Serve warm.

Apple Pandowdy

Serves 8

Apple pandowdy is both venerable and variable, honored in New England in particular, but prepared in many places in a confusing diversity of ways. For us, it's a dish where the fruit is cooked down under a pie or biscuit crust that, late in the baking, is broken in pieces and pushed into the filling to absorb juices. Crunchy in spots and gooey in others, it's a cross between an apple pie and an apple crisp, but it boasts bragging rights of its own. Here's an old-fashioned version with a lard crust and a little salt pork in the filling, which result in an illusive flavor that complements the apples and balances the sweetness of the maple syrup.

FILLING

2¼ to 2½ pounds tart apples, such as Granny Smith or Jonathan

1 tablespoon fresh lemon juice

½ teaspoon ground cinnamon

¼ teaspoon freshly ground black pepper

Pinch or two of ground cloves

1 tablespoon unbleached all-purpose flour, optional

⅓ cup real maple syrup

3 tablespoons minced salt pork, preferably, or 2 tablespoons unsalted butter

Superbly Flaky Single Pie Crust, prepared as on page 372, rolled into a 10-inch square and reserved, to top the pandowdy

Whipping cream

Real maple syrup

Preheat the oven to 400°F. Butter a 9-inch square baking dish.

Place the apples in the baking dish and sprinkle over them the lemon juice, cinnamon, pepper, and cloves. If the apples are especially juicy, stir in the flour too. Drizzle the maple syrup evenly over the apples and dot with the salt pork.

Cover with the prepared crust, tucking it in and down around the sides. Bake for about 45 minutes, until lightly brown and flaky. Remove from the oven, and with a spoon, break up the crust into pieces of varying size. Crunch it up all over but don't turn it to crumbs. Push some of the pieces back down into the apple juices. Return to the oven for 10 to 15 additional minutes, until the pandowdy is nicely brown and crisp in spots. Serve warm with a drizzle of cream sweetened to taste with more maple syrup.

Cooking Charitably

Lizzie Kander's *"The Settlement" Cook Book* (1901), discussed on page 385, was the most successful charitable cookbook ever published in the country, but similar fund-raising endeavors have flourished across the land. Each year, home cooks put together hundreds of books to benefit a community cause of one kind or another, from churches to schools, garden clubs to libraries. The results provide a snapshot of American life in various times and places, showing us much more about local dynamics than just what people prepare for dinner.

Charitable cookbooks are occasionally published in other countries, but the phenomenon started in the United States and remains almost exclusively American. According to Janice and Daniel Longone in *American Cookbooks and Wine Books, 1797–1950* (1984), the first entry in the field was published at the beginning of the Civil War to help volunteers care for Union troops, particularly the wounded. Women's organizations soon came out with additional works to aid victims of the war, including the families of the men who were killed, and then after Appomattox, they turned their cooking and writing skills to other causes.

Margaret Cook amassed a collection of charitable cookbooks—now at Texas Woman's University in Denton—and compiled a bibliography of those written before 1915. She found that three thousand had been published by that year, covering every state and most every conceivable charitable concern. Since then the numbers of books have grown steadily each year, giving us a vivid and constantly changing portrait of American food. The magnitude of talent and energy represented in the books overall is a monumental testament to the generosity of American home cooks.

Rhubarb Brown Betty

SERVES 8

In the cooking classes that Lizzie Kander and other ladies taught to Milwaukee Jewish immigrants at "The Settlement," the first lesson in the early years focused on measuring ingredients, setting the table, washing dishes, building a fire, fixing coffee, and making an apple version of this dish. Kander called it "scalloped apples," and suggested the same approach with rhubarb, the route we take here. In both cases, slices of fruit are layered with buttered bread crumbs to produce a brown beauty who somehow acquired the name of Betty.

¼ cup (½ stick) unsalted butter
4 cups packed fresh bread crumbs
1¾ cups sugar
Scant ½ teaspoon ground cinnamon
Scant ½ teaspoon ground nutmeg
Minced zest of 2 medium oranges plus the juice of 1 orange
2 pounds rhubarb, cut into ½-inch slices (about 6 cups)

Preheat the oven to 375°F. Grease a 9-inch × 13-inch baking dish.

Melt the butter in a medium skillet. Stir in the bread crumbs and cook until lightly brown and crisp, about 5 minutes. Scrape the crumbs into a small bowl and reserve them. Mix together the sugar, cinnamon, nutmeg, and orange zest in a medium bowl.

Sprinkle one-third of the bread crumbs over the bottom of the pan. Spoon half of the rhubarb over it evenly, topped by half of the sugar mixture. Repeat with the crumbs, rhubarb, and sugar mixture. Pour the orange juice and ¼ cup of water evenly over the sugar mixture, then top with the last one-third of the bread crumbs. Cover and bake for 30 minutes. Uncover and continue baking for about 15 minutes longer, until the rhubarb mixture is tender and the top crumbs are medium brown. Serve warm.

Lizzie Black Kander, 1858–1940

Sometimes called the Jane Addams of Milwaukee because of her devotion to social service in the city, Lizzie Kander got up at five o'clock in the morning so she could complete her housework early and spend the rest of the day on charitable activities. Raised in a Jewish pioneer family, she became interested at the age of twenty in the problems of new Jewish immigrants, then flooding American cities, and stayed involved in their cause for the next sixty years.

For most of the time, the focus of her efforts was "The Settlement," an organization that sponsored, among other programs, night classes in English and United States history, vocational training, and cooking demonstrations oriented to American ingredients and kitchens. In 1901, as an aid to the cooking lessons, Kander put together the first edition of *The Way to a Man's Heart: "The Settlement" Cook Book.* After Settlement trustees refused to finance the text, she sold advertising and extra copies of the book. It turned out to be immensely popular—a major boost to the organization's resources rather than a drain—and has remained in print in various revisions ever since.

Kander said the success of the book came from its homey roots. She and the other volunteer instructors at "The Settlement" taught from practical experience, and when they and others contributed recipes, Kander herself tested them all in her own kitchen. There may have been other ways to a man's heart in turn-of-the-century Milwaukee, but this one came proven to work.

Strawberry Shortcake

SERVES 6 TO 8

Good, fresh berries certainly contribute to the success of this dessert, but what most people get wrong is the shortcake. The biscuit pastry should rise high and crumble gracefully into a medley of tastes with the strawberries and cream. For us, sponge cake doesn't wash. The all-American combination seems to date from the mid-nineteenth century, but it rose in popularity in tandem with the use of baking powder.

BERRIES

5 cups halved strawberries, or 3 cups halved strawberries with 2 cups raspberries, blueberries, or blackberries

3 tablespoons sugar or more to taste

SHORTCAKES

2¾ cups unbleached all-purpose flour

2 tablespoons sugar

1½ teaspoons baking powder

1 teaspoon salt

¼ cup vegetable shortening, well chilled

2 tablespoons unsalted butter, well chilled

1 cup buttermilk

1 teaspoon pure vanilla extract

WHIPPED CREAM TOPPING

1½ cups whipping cream, well chilled

2 teaspoons pure vanilla extract

2 tablespoons sugar or more to taste

Stir together the strawberries with the sugar, mashing them very lightly with a fork to help release the juice. If you are using a portion of the other berries, keep them separate for now. They are best added to the strawberries shortly before serving so that they will hold their shapes. Let the berries sit at room temperature while you prepare the shortcakes and whipped cream topping.

Preheat the oven to 450°F.

Sift the flour, sugar, baking powder, and salt into a large bowl, preferably a shallow one. Cut the shortening and butter into small chunks, and add them to the dry ingredients. Combine with a pastry blender just until a coarse meal forms. Make a well in the center and pour in the buttermilk and vanilla. With your fingers and a few swift strokes, combine the dough just until it's a sticky mess. Turn out onto a lightly floured board or, better, a pastry cloth. Clean, dry, and flour your hands. Gently pat out the dough and fold it back over itself about a half-dozen times, just until smooth. (A dough scraper helps greatly with this.) Pat out again into a circle or oval about ¾ inch in thickness. Cover the dough lightly and refrigerate it for about 20 minutes.

Cut the dough with a biscuit cutter, trying to get as many shortcakes as possible, since the dough toughens if it's rerolled. You should be able, with practice, to get about eight 3-inch biscuits or six 3½-inch biscuits from the dough. Make your

The biscuits, hot as a poker, were split the instant they came from the oven and simply baptized in butter. Then the strawberries, taken from the cold room—and were they cold! Cut or lightly mashed, sugared and clapped between those steaming hot biscuit halves, then more berries and juice all around—oh my! And cream. Not whipped cream. Cream from a jug, a very fat jug with a nozzle just meant to spill and not retard cream from joining those shortcakes in an indissoluble union which should not fade from memory while memory remains! That, my dears, is a breakfast dish.

Sidney Dean, Cooking American (1957)

shortcakes with a quick, clean, straight-down push on the cutter. If you twist the cutter, as seems to be a natural motion for many people, it twists the dough, resulting in an uneven shortcake. Bake the shortcakes in the center of the oven, turning the baking sheet around once halfway through the baking time. Bake 3-inch shortcakes for 10 to 12 minutes total and larger shortcakes for 12 to 15 minutes, until raised and golden brown.

Prepare the topping, beating together the cream with the vanilla and sugar with a whisk or in a chilled mixing bowl with chilled beaters over medium-high speed. Beat the cream only until soft peaks form.

If you are using another variety of berries with the strawberries, gently stir them into the strawberries now.

Split a shortcake in half and place the bottom portion in a broad shallow bowl or on a dessert plate. Spoon several tablespoons of fruit and juice over it. Spoon on a dollop of whipped cream. Place the shortcake top over the cream and add another layer of berries and whipped cream. Repeat with the remaining shortcakes, berries, and cream, and serve immediately.

Banana Pudding

SERVES 8 TO 10

When bananas began arriving in the United States from the West Indies in the nineteenth century, southern cooks used them to turn an English trifle into an American classic. They started originally with a base of stale cake, reviving it with milk custard and flavoring it with the mild creaminess of bananas. The Nabisco company convinced most people to switch from cake to its vanilla wafers, but other similar options work just as well. The meringue topping is another relatively recent addition, providing a complementary way to use the remaining egg whites.

1 cup sugar
2 tablespoons cornstarch
Salt
6 eggs, separated
1½ cups whole milk
1 cup half-and-half
2 teaspoons pure vanilla extract
12-ounce box vanilla wafer cookies, or similar amount of gingersnaps, shortbread, or other compatibly flavored crisp, thin cookies (see Ingredient Tip)
5 to 6 bananas
⅛ teaspoon cream of tartar
3 to 4 tablespoons confectioners' sugar

Stir together the sugar, cornstarch, and a pinch of salt in the top of a double boiler. Whisk in the egg yolks, followed by the milk and half-and-half. Place the pan over a simmering water bath. Cook the pudding over medium-low heat, stirring frequently, until thickened so that it coats a spoon, then slides off it slowly. Expect the process to take about 20 minutes. Remove the pudding from the heat and stir in the vanilla.

Preheat the oven to 350°F. Butter a 9-inch × 13-inch baking dish.

Arrange a layer of cookies in the prepared dish. Slice the bananas thin and arrange half of them over the cookies. Spoon half of the warm pudding over the banana slices. Repeat with more cookies, the remaining banana slices, and the rest of the pudding. Tuck more cookies around the sides of the dish too. We use about two-thirds of the cookies, but other cooks—and probably the Nabisco folks—figure out how to use them all.

Prepare the meringue, preferably in a copper bowl. Beat the egg whites until frothy, then add the cream of tartar and a pinch of salt. Gradually beat in the confectioners' sugar and continue beating until the whites hold their shape but are still glossy.

Top the pudding with the meringue, heaping it gloriously high in the center. Make sure the meringue is spread so that it touches the cookies all the way around the edge. Bake for 15 to 18 minutes, until the meringue is golden. Let the pudding cool for at least 30 minutes before serving.

INGREDIENT TIP:
For an interesting change of pace, replace the cookies with their predecessor, leftover cake. Try this approach using Cornmeal Pound Cake (page 397) or any other mildly flavored, dense cake.

New Orleans Bread Pudding

Serves 8

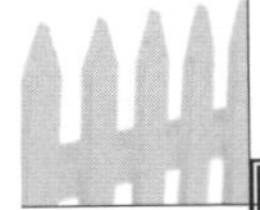

Joe Cahn, the founder of the New Orleans School of Cooking, used to start his classes by emphasizing the importance of food in local life, making his point by showing that the city telephone directory included, along with emergency numbers, a recipe for bread pudding. Most cuisines around the world have variations on bread pudding—some sweet, some savory—developed as a way of using leftovers. Among Americans at least, few cooks elevated the idea as artfully as the New Orleans Creoles.

Bread pudding and other custard dishes were popular in the early spring because of new calves and new green grass producing extra pails of milk. . . . I can still remember entering the kitchen, which was detached from the main house, and there, cooling on a table near the door, would be a big pan of delicious-looking bread pudding, filling the air with the rich smell of butter and nutmeg rising from the layers of bread that were submerged in a custard of rich milk, fresh country eggs, and plump raisins.

Edna Lewis, The Taste of Country Cooking (1977)

½ cup dark raisins

⅓ cup Irish whiskey or bourbon

6 to 7 cups lightly packed bite-size cubes of day-old French or Italian bread

½ cup chopped pecans

3 eggs

1¼ cups whole milk

1¼ cups half-and-half

1 cup granulated sugar

¼ cup (½ stick) unsalted butter, melted

1 tablespoon pure vanilla extract

½ teaspoon ground cinnamon

¼ teaspoon ground nutmeg

WHISKEY SAUCE

½ cup (1 stick) unsalted butter

1½ cups confectioners' sugar

2 egg yolks, lightly whisked

¼ cup plus 2 tablespoons Irish whiskey or bourbon

Combine the raisins and whiskey in a small bowl. Preheat the oven to 350°F. Butter a medium baking dish.

Arrange the bread in the baking dish and scatter the pecans over it. When the raisins have absorbed most of the whiskey, scatter them and any remaining whiskey over the bread. Whisk together the eggs, milk, half-and-half, granulated sugar, butter, vanilla, cinnamon, and nutmeg, and pour the custard mixture evenly over the bread. Lightly pat the bread down into the custard. Let the mixture sit at room temperature for about 15 minutes, then stir and pat back down again. A bit of the bread should remain just above the custard. Bake the pudding for 50 to 55 minutes, until the pudding is slightly puffed and golden brown, with a few crunchy spots on top.

While the pudding bakes, prepare the sauce. Combine the butter and confectioners' sugar in a medium saucepan, and warm over medium heat until the butter and sugar melt together. Stir 2 tablespoons of the butter-sugar mixture into the egg yolks, then pour it back into the rest of the butter-sugar mixture and whisk until combined, about another minute. Remove from the heat and immediately whisk in the whiskey. The sauce will be somewhat thin, but it thickens as it cools.

Serve the pudding warm, spooned onto individual plates, with a few tablespoons of the sauce poured over each. Pass the remaining sauce separately.

Down East Blueberry Toast and Butter Pudding

SERVES 6

Robert Frost rhapsodized about New England's wild blueberries, like "jewels, a vision for thieves." In Maine and Massachusetts, in particular, the tiny berries often go into a bread pudding that is quite different from the New Orleans version. Even in the home region, today most cooks have to rely on cultivated hybrid berries, larger and sweeter than the native variety but less complex in taste. If you have access to Frost's jewels, you may want to bump up the amount of sugar slightly.

- 1½ pints (3 cups) blueberries, fresh or frozen
- 1 teaspoon fresh lemon juice
- Several pinches of ground cinnamon
- Several pinches of salt
- ⅓ cup sugar or more to taste
- 1 egg
- 1 cup whole milk
- 4 to 6 slices good white bread, sliced ½ inch thick and halved
- 2 to 3 tablespoons unsalted butter
- Approximately 1 tablespoon confectioners' sugar
- Whipping cream or half-and-half
- Fresh mint sprigs, optional

Butter an 8-inch square baking dish or other small shallow baking dish.

Simmer the blueberries in a saucepan over medium heat with the lemon juice, a pinch or two of cinnamon and salt, and ⅓ cup of sugar. Add a bit more sugar if the mixture doesn't taste sweet enough to you. Simmer for about 10 minutes, until the mixture is thick and saucy. Spoon the blueberries into the prepared baking dish. Set aside to cool.

Whisk together in a shallow dish the egg and milk with pinches of cinnamon and salt. You'll need enough bread to completely cover the top of the berries. Dunk the bread into the egg-milk mixture a few slices at a time, allowing them a minute or so to absorb the liquid. Turn them if needed to coat evenly. Melt 2 tablespoons of the butter in a large skillet over medium heat. Fry the coated bread pieces like French toast until just golden, about 2 minutes per side. Repeat with the remaining bread and egg-milk mixture, adding the remaining tablespoon of butter to the skillet if necessary. Arrange the bread over the berries. (The pudding can be prepared to this stage before you sit down to eat the rest of your meal. Complete just before serving.)

Heat the broiler. Dust the pudding generously with confectioners' sugar, sprinkled through a fine sieve. Place the pudding under the broiler until nicely browned with melted sugar. Spoon it into bowls with some of the berries and juice over the toast topping. Drizzle cream over the pudding, garnish with mint sprigs if you wish, and serve hot.

Peach Ice Cream

MAKES 1 QUART

Americans get passionate about ripe peaches, particularly when it comes to ice cream. Listen to Virginia's Mary Randolph on this old treat: "Get fine soft peaches perfectly ripe, peel them, take out the stones, and put them in a China bowl: sprinkle some sugar on, and chop them very small with a silver spoon—if the peaches be sufficiently ripe, they will become a smooth pulp; add as much cream or rich milk as you have peaches; put more sugar, and freeze it." Marion Harland, a later Virginian, got so fixated on the ripeness of the peaches that she specified a day for making the ice cream, on Sunday of the second week in July. We don't see anything wrong with Saturday or Monday, but the dish does excel when made with tree-ripened local peaches, fruit that's too fragile to ship.

2 to 2¼ pounds ripe juicy peaches, peeled, pitted, and sliced thickly
2 teaspoons fresh lemon juice
½ cup sugar
3 large eggs
1 cup half-and-half
¼ teaspoon pure vanilla extract
Several drops of almond extract

Mash half of the peaches well or purée them in a food processor or blender. Combine the mashed peaches with the sliced peaches in a large bowl, and toss them with the lemon juice and 1 tablespoon of the sugar.

Whisk together the remaining sugar and eggs in a heavy saucepan. Gradually whisk in the half-and-half, then the vanilla and almond extracts. Place over medium-low heat and cook, stirring frequently, until small bubbles form at the edge of the pan. Do not let the mixture actually come to a boil. Pour it over the peaches and refrigerate until chilled, at least 1 hour and up to a day.

Freeze the ice cream in an ice cream maker according to the manufacturer's directions. Served directly from the ice cream maker, the ice cream will be a bit soft. If you like it firmer, place it in the freezer for several hours. The flavor is best within the first couple of days.

TECHNIQUE TIP: The Donvier ice cream maker has become one of our favorite kitchen aids. You keep the metal core in the freezer until you're ready to make ice cream, pop it in the casing frozen, turn the handle just occasionally, and you're dishing out dessert in under 20 minutes. The handy little device is widely available in cookware stores.

Many More Than 31 Flavors

Mary Randolph's *The Virginia Housewife* (1824) offered over a dozen variations on ice cream, including the first printed American recipes for chocolate and vanilla versions. For the latter, she boiled a vanilla bean in a quart of rich milk "until it has imparted the flavor sufficiently," added eight eggs and sugar, and put the mixture into a pewter container, which she immersed in a tub of salted ice, stirring the cream with a silver spoon until it froze. We're certain Randolph got a wonderful result in that case, but we're a little dubious about her oyster ice cream, made with oyster soup.

After the invention of hand-crank ice cream makers in the 1840s, cooks branched out to other flavors. We've come across macaroon in Milwaukee, rice in eastern Arkansas, avocado in California's Imperial Valley, sweet potato in Atlanta, and brown bread in Philadelphia. We've considered Sarah Tyson Rorer's comment that if you lack cream or condensed milk, you can make a "fair" ice cream by adding olive oil to regular milk, and we didn't totally dodge Miss T. S. Shute's suggestion of deepening the green tint of pistachio ice cream with spinach juice. Somewhere, someone can make decent ice cream from anything.

Lemon Cream Sherbet

MAKES ABOUT 1 QUART

Mary Randolph also liked ice cream made with lemons, a once-popular flavor for frozen desserts that deserves greater attention today. We put the lemon tang in a creamy sherbet that has a high proportion of fruit juice and plenty of cream as well. It's an elegant, silky, and full-bodied way to finish a meal.

- Zest and juice of 4 medium to large lemons (measuring at least ½ cup of juice)
- 3 cups whipping cream
- 1 cup sugar
- 1 cup milk

Warm the lemon zest in a small saucepan with the cream over medium-low heat. Slowly heat the cream to the point where small bubbles just begin to break at the edges. Remove from the heat and let the mixture steep for about 20 minutes. Strain the cream into a medium bowl.

In a small bowl, combine the sugar and lemon juice, stirring until the sugar is completely saturated and partially dissolved. Whisk this gradually into the cream, then whisk in the milk in a slow but constant stream. (These steps keep the mixture from curdling.) Refrigerate until chilled, at least 1 hour and up to a day.

Freeze the cream sherbet in an ice cream maker according to the manufacturer's directions. Served directly from the ice cream maker, the cream sherbet will be a bit soft. If you like it firmer, place it in the freezer for several hours. The flavor is best within the first couple of days.

Watermelon Ice

Makes 1 quart

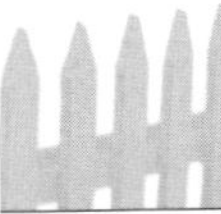

Mark Twain called watermelon the king of all fruits, fit for angels. From his day to ours, a watermelon cooled in a stream or iced-down in a tub has been the sure cure for heat and humidity. Turning the watermelon pulp into an ice captures that essence, simplifies storage, and eliminates the temptation to spit seeds. For a contemporary touch, we sometimes stir in several tablespoons of silver tequila before freezing the purée.

- 4 heaping cups chopped, seeded, red-ripe watermelon
- 2 to 3 tablespoons sugar
- 1 tablespoon fresh lemon or lime juice

Place the watermelon, in batches if necessary, in a food processor or blender. Add the sugar and lemon juice, and purée. Refrigerate until chilled, at least 1 hour and up to a day.

Freeze the purée in an ice cream maker according to the manufacturer's directions. Served directly from the ice cream maker, the ice will be a bit soft. If you like it firmer, place it in the freezer for several hours. The flavor is best within the first couple of days.

COOKING TO EXCESS WITH

Cakes, Cookies, and Candies

COLONIAL COOKS CALLED THEM "GREAT CAKES," "wedding cakes," and "black cakes," among other names, but the creations differed more in terminology than in taste. All were highly flavored yeast breads from the British heritage, moderately sweetened and scented with spices and fruit. Cooks reserved the cakes for special occasions, unlike pies, and usually put substantial effort into their production.

We maintain the old traditions in some ways today, still serving fancy cakes at weddings and birthday parties and eating holiday fruit cakes, a direct descendant of the great cakes. Baking changed considerably, however, with the development of modern leavenings and the transition to ovens with steady, regulated heat, and cakes changed apace. By the mid-nineteenth century, the country began acquiring cakes the way Rockefeller accumulated oil, turning a tested but low-yield field into a gusher of opportunities.

We came up with ribbon cakes that alternated the colors of batters, with domino cakes decorated like the game tiles, and a Picayune cake from New Orleans, which you supposedly never tired of, like the news in the local paper of the same name. There was a cake called "Wacky" and another named "Mississippi Mud." California cooks gave us an artichoke cake, German Americans contributed a sauerkraut cake, and the Campbell company tried to sell us a tomato-soup cake. We didn't strike it as rich as Rockefeller, but we keep on prospecting and speculating.

As baseball wags say of the Chicago Cubs, any team can have a bad century. American cooks won a few along the way and added those successes to our repertory, but a weak batting average with zany cakes, cookies, and candies eventually tempered our wild swinging. We'll always like a little excess, a little extravagance, but now we're moving back toward a more centered, classic approach, a proven path to a championship season.

Cornmeal Pound Cake

SERVES 12 OR MORE

When you think [the pound cake] is done, run the blade of a knife down through the middle of it, and if upon drawing out, you find it is entirely clean, you may safely calculate it is done. . . . Another way to tell it is done, is to take it from the oven, touch it to your face, and if it is thoroughly done, it will not burn in the least.

LETTICE BRYAN, THE KENTUCKY HOUSEWIFE (1839)

A sturdy cake with British roots and a colonial pedigree, pound cake takes its name from the weight of the principal ingredients. No one needed a written recipe, simply measuring out one pound each of butter, sugar, flour, and eggs. Eliza Leslie liked to substitute cornmeal for some of the flour, which we think improves the texture. Small portions of the dense, rich cake satisfy big appetites, particularly when served with a seasonal fruit compote.

2 cups unbleached all-purpose flour
1 cup stone-ground yellow cornmeal
¼ teaspoon salt
¾ teaspoon ground coriander, optional
2 cups (4 sticks) unsalted butter, softened
2 cups sugar
⅔ cup sour cream or plain yogurt
2 teaspoons pure vanilla extract
¼ teaspoon almond extract
5 large eggs
Confectioners' sugar, optional

Preheat the oven to 350°F. Grease and flour a 10-inch Bundt cake pan or 9-inch × 5-inch loaf pan.

Sift together the flour, cornmeal, salt and, if you wish, the coriander.

Cream the butter and sugar together, beating until fluffy and light, 5 to 7 minutes, with an electric mixer at high speed. Reduce the mixer speed to medium, then mix in the sour cream and the vanilla and almond extracts. Beat in the eggs, one at a time, alternating them with equal portions of the flour-cornmeal mixture. Stop as needed to scrape down the sides of the bowl. Mix each time just until combined.

Spoon the batter into the prepared pan. Bake for about 1 hour, until the cake is deep golden and a toothpick inserted in the center comes out clean. (Late in the baking, some of the butter may foam a bit around the cake's edges, but it will reabsorb into the cake perfectly as it cools.) Transfer the cake to a baking rack and let it cool for 10 minutes. Then run a knife around the edges, invert it, and remove from the pan. Finish cooling, top side up, on a baking rack. Cool the cake for at least 10 additional minutes. If you wish, dust the whole cake, or individual slices, with confectioners' sugar, sprinkled through a fine sieve. Serve warm or at room temperature.

Hartford Election Cake

SERVES 12

In the early Republic, Election Day in New England used to be a time for celebrating and feasting. Voters gathered in towns like Hartford and Salem, both associated with this cake, and stayed with family and friends for up to a week, particularly when they had to travel some distance to exercise their democratic rights. Cooks made the yeasted cake in huge loaves that would provide a generous slice to anyone who stopped by for a visit. Despite the patriotic overtones, the cake came from the vanquished British, being one of the surviving great cakes of the colonial era. In light of its distinguished heritage and the time involved in the preparation, we make a double loaf, freezing one for later if we're not feeding a crowd. The cake continues to delight because of its moist richness, still worthy of a vote in Hartford or anywhere else.

- 1 cup raisins, preferably half light and half dark
- 3 tablespoons dark rum
- 1 package active dry yeast
- 1½ cups lukewarm milk
- 1¼ cups packed light brown sugar
- 3½ cups unbleached all-purpose flour
- ¾ cup (1½ sticks) unsalted butter, softened
- 2 large eggs
- 1 tablespoon orange-flower water (see Ingredient Tip)
- 1 teaspoon ground cinnamon
- 1 teaspoon ground coriander
- ¾ teaspoon ground allspice
- ½ teaspoon salt
- 1 tablespoon minced orange or lemon zest
- 1½ cups chopped walnuts

SUGAR CRACKLE TOPPING

- 3 tablespoons unsalted butter, melted
- 6 tablespoons sugar

Butter and flour two 8-inch × 4-inch loaf pans. Combine the raisins and rum in a small bowl.

Dissolve the yeast in the warm milk in a large mixing bowl. With an electric mixer, beat in the brown sugar, 1¾ cup of the flour, and then the butter, eggs, and orange-flower water. When combined, mix in the remaining 1¾ cup of flour and beat for 3 minutes. Cover the bowl with a clean dishtowel and set it in a warm, draft-free spot until doubled in size, about 1½ hours. The batter will be sticky, with the consistency of a soft, moist dough.

When doubled in size, stir down the batter. Mix into it the spices and salt, followed by the zest, walnuts, and raisins with any remaining rum. Divide the batter between the two pans, smoothing it so that it is mounded on the top. Cover the

Election Cake

Thirty quarts flour, 10 pound butter, 14 pound sugar, 12 pound raisins, 3 doz eggs, one pint wine, one quart brandy, 4 ounces cinnamon, 4 ounces fine colander seed, 3 ounces ground alspice; wet the flour with milk to the consistence of bread over night, adding one quart yeast; the next morning work the butter and sugar together for half an hour, which will render the cake much lighter and whiter.

Amelia Simmons, American Cookery (1796)

pans and let the batter rest again in a warm, draft-free spot until risen to the top of the pans, about 1 additional hour. Near the end of the rising time, preheat the oven to 350°F.

Top the cakes with the sugar crackle. Pour the butter evenly over the dough and sprinkle it thickly with sugar.

Bake the cakes in the center of the oven. Cook for 50 to 55 minutes, until the tops are golden and a toothpick inserted in the center of each comes out clean. Cool the cakes in the pans for 10 minutes, then unmold and cool for at least 15 additional minutes. Serve warm or at room temperature. Leftovers can be toasted and slathered with sweet butter.

INGREDIENT TIP: Our common use of vanilla extract to flavor baked goods is largely a twentieth-century development. Before then, cooks scented their dishes with lemon and perfumy distillations of orange and rose blossoms. Look for fragrant rose water and orange-flower water in large grocery stores and Middle Eastern or Asian markets. In election cake, orange-flower water gives a lighter, more flowery complexity than vanilla.

Lady Baltimore Cake with Seven-Minute Frosting

SERVES 8 OR MORE

Once American cooks started using baking powder in the second half of the nineteenth century, fluffy layer cakes replaced the old great cakes at festive meals. Charleston bakers excelled quickly in the new art, reaching an apogee with this creation. In *200 Years of Charleston Cooking* (1930), Blanche Rhett says, "Each year at Christmas time hundreds of white boxes go out of Charleston to all parts of the country bearing the round, the tall, the light, the fragile, the ineffable Lady Baltimore cakes." One of the recipes she provides comes from Alicia Rhett Mayberry, who often gets credit for conceiving the cake, which author Owen Wister popularized nationally in his romantic novel *Lady Baltimore* (1906). Since the cake is already over-the-top, we add a frosting to match, a billowy crown for the Lady.

CAKE

3¼ cups sifted cake flour
1 tablespoon baking powder
½ teaspoon salt
1 cup milk
1 teaspoon pure vanilla extract
¼ teaspoon almond extract
1¼ cups (2½ sticks) unsalted butter, softened
2 cups sugar
6 large egg whites, at room temperature

GLAZE

¾ cup sugar
1 teaspoon pure vanilla extract
1 teaspoon almond extract

SEVEN-MINUTE FROSTING AND FILLING

1½ cups sugar
2 large egg whites
2 teaspoons light corn syrup
¼ teaspoon cream of tartar
½ teaspoon pure vanilla extract
2 to 3 drops of almond extract
¾ cup coarse-chopped walnuts
⅓ cup coarse-chopped dried figs
⅓ cup dark raisins

Preheat the oven to 350°F. Grease and flour two 9-inch round cake pans. Cover the pan bottoms with wax paper or parchment cut in circles to fit the pans, and grease and flour the paper.

Sift together twice (to lighten the mixture) the flour, baking powder, and salt. Stir together the milk, vanilla, and almond extract. Reserve both mixtures.

Cream together the butter and sugar until fluffy and light, 5 to 7 minutes, with an electric mixer at high speed. Reduce the mixer speed to medium. Mix in the flour mixture and the milk mixture in thirds, alternating the two, and stopping as needed to scrape down the sides of the bowl. Mix each time just until combined.

TECHNIQUE TIP: When frosting a cake, first let it cool completely. Otherwise the cake may tear or its heat could melt the frosting. Cakes generally look best when their flatter bottom side is turned up, especially for the top layer. Applying frosting is easiest with a slim cake spatula, especially made for the job. Brush off crumbs from the cake and if any stick to the spatula, wipe them off before dipping the spatula back into the frosting bowl. Most bakers find it easiest to cover the surface first with a thin layer of frosting, to keep the crumbs in check, then add the rest for decoration.

Edwardian Extravagance

In *Biscuits, Spoonbread, and Sweet Potato Pie* (1990), Bill Neal presents a cogent perspective on the country's lavish Edwardian cakes, including the Lady Baltimore. "Cooks were smitten with the airy and fine crumbled qualities of the baking powder layers," he says, "but did not want to lose the richness of the old English-style cakes. The fruits and nuts went into dense fillings between the layers instead of into the batter."

A friend in Savannah, Jim King, remembers another of these southern creations, the Lane Cake, as a favorite Christmas treat of his Alabama childhood. The filling in this cake usually consists of a passel of egg yolks flavored with bourbon, pecans, coconut, raisins, and more. Perhaps the oddest of all these cakes, at least in name, is the Japanese Fruitcake, which isn't remotely Japanese or a true fruitcake. One or more of the layers contain some fruit and nuts, and a coconut filling separates them, but otherwise it's a plain yellow cake.

In another bowl, with clean beaters, beat the egg whites at high speed until soft, glossy peaks form. By hand, fold the egg whites into the batter just until combined. Divide the batter between the prepared pans.

Bake for 30 to 35 minutes, until the layers are just lightly browned and a toothpick inserted in the center of each comes out clean. Cool the layers in their pans for about 10 minutes.

While the layers cool, prepare the glaze. In a small pan, combine the sugar with 6 tablespoons of water and cook over medium heat, stirring until the sugar dissolves. Continue cooking without stirring until the mixture reaches 230°F to 234°F, the "thread" stage. Remove from the heat and cool, again without stirring, until the mixture reaches 110°F. Stir in the vanilla and almond extracts. Run a knife around the edges of the cake layers, invert them, and remove them from their pans. Spread half of the glaze over each layer. Finish cooling the layers on cake racks. The glaze will firm and turn from clear to translucent white as it dries.

To prepare the frosting, combine the sugar, egg whites, corn syrup, and cream of tartar with ¼ cup plus 1 tablespoon of water in the top of a double boiler. Place the pan over its already simmering water bath, and beat with a hand mixer on low while the mixture cooks for 4 minutes. Raise the mixer speed to high and continue beating over the heat for another 3 minutes, totaling the seven minutes of the frosting's name. The mixture will be opaque, thick, and glossy, like melted marshmallows. Remove from the heat. Now add the vanilla and almond extracts, and continue beating until the frosting partially cools and forms soft, meringue-like peaks, 3 to 5 additional minutes. Mix one-fourth of the frosting with the walnuts, figs, and raisins to use as the filling.

Fill and frost the cake immediately. Arrange the first cake layer on a platter and spread the nut-and-fruit filling over it. Top with the second layer. Spread the frosting over the top and sides of the cake, swirling it decoratively. Let the cake stand for at least 30 minutes before slicing it.

Angel Food Cake with Boiled Custard

MAKES A 10-INCH TUBE CAKE, SERVING 8 TO 10

Airy and angelic from its abundance of egg whites, this cake ascended to the highest spheres of American comfort foods after ovens offered well-regulated baking temperatures. Pennsylvania Dutch cooks, who used plenty of egg yolks in other dishes, probably developed the cake. We serve it with what Americans misname "boiled custard," which is neither but does complement the lightness of the angel food cake.

BOILED CUSTARD SAUCE

1 cup sugar

1 tablespoon cornstarch

2 whole large eggs plus 3 yolks

1 quart whole milk

1 tablespoon pure vanilla extract

CAKE

1¼ cups plus 2 tablespoons cake flour, sifted

1¾ cups sugar

1¾ cups egg whites (from 13 to 14 large eggs), chilled

1½ teaspoons cream of tartar

1 teaspoon pure vanilla extract

1 teaspoon fresh lemon juice

½ teaspoon almond extract

½ teaspoon salt

Prepare the sauce, first stirring together the sugar and cornstarch in the top of a double boiler. Whisk in the whole eggs and yolks, and place the pan over gently simmering water. Whisk in the milk gradually, and once it is incorporated, stir the mixture continually but gently. (Stirring a stovetop egg-based cream is what keeps it from setting like a baked custard, but if the mixture is stirred vigorously it stays too thin.) The sauce should thicken slowly, taking about 20 minutes, to the point where it coats a spoon lightly and offers the most gentle resistance to your stirring. Lower the heat if the mixture gets close to a boil. Stir in the vanilla and remove from the heat. Cool the sauce to room temperature and then chill it, covered, for later use. Boiled custard will look like thin vanilla pudding, with a silky consistency, perfect for a sauce.

Preheat the oven to 325°F.

Prepare the cake, first sifting together the flour with ¾ cup of the sugar. Using an electric mixer at medium speed, beat the egg whites in a metal or glass bowl with the cream of tartar, vanilla, lemon juice, and almond extract. When just uniformly foamy, beat in the salt and gradually add the remaining 1 cup of sugar, about ¼ cup at a time. Continue beating until soft, barely sturdy peaks form. The egg whites should remain moist, glossy, and pourable.

General directions for Making Cake

Tie up your hair so that none can fall, put on a long-sleeved apron, have the kitchen put in order, and then arrange all the articles and utensils you will have occasion to use. If you are a systematic and thrifty housekeeper, you will have your sugar pounded, all your spices ready prepared in boxes, or bottles, your saleratus sifted, your currants washed and dried, your ginger sifted, and your weights, measures, and utensils all in their place and in order.

Catharine Beecher, Miss Beecher's Domestic Receipt Book (1849)

By hand, fold the flour mixture into the egg-white mixture, about ¼ cup at a time. Pour the batter into an ungreased 10-inch tube pan with a removable bottom. Run a knife through the batter to eliminate large air bubbles. Smooth the top of the batter by tilting the pan rather than using a spatula, which would compact the mixture.

Bake the cake for 45 to 50 minutes, until pale brown and springy to the touch. There are likely to be some cracks in the surface, but if the batter was properly mixed, there should be no gaping canyons. Immediately invert the cake pan, placing it over a long-necked bottle (such as a wine or soft-drink bottle) if your pan lacks "feet" that elevate it. Cool the cake upside down for at least 1 hour, to set its high, light structure. Invert the cake and run a knife around its inside and outside edges to loosen it. Transfer the cake to a serving plate, top side up. Cut the cake with an angel cake "comb" or a serrated knife, sawing through it gently. Spoon boiled custard over the slices and serve.

TECHNIQUE TIP: When you whisk or beat egg whites for meringues, you want them to be at room temperature, which allows them to reach their greatest volume, and you beat them until they are stiff. For angel food, you'll get better results by starting with chilled egg whites and beating them only to the point where they barely form peaks. Make sure that everything that touches the egg whites—bowl, beaters, spatula—is grease-free or you'll have trouble getting any volume at all.

Ginger Pear Upside-Down Cake

Serves 8

In *The American Century Cookbook* (1997), Jean Anderson relates a fascinating story about how pineapple upside-down cake zoomed to popularity during the glamorous age of the Hawaiian beach boy and steamship travel to the islands. She cites a couple of mentions of the cake in 1924–1925, and then describes a 1926 recipe contest sponsored by the Hawaiian Pineapple Company, founded by James Dole, who had already turned the island of Lanai into his personal pineapple farm. Cooks sent in 60,000 recipes using the fruit—including 2,500 for upside-down cake. A homey cake, often cooked and served in a skillet, it has retained its reputation much better than the multitiered extravaganzas typical of the time. We use pears instead of pineapple to cut the sweetness, and canned fruit unless we can get particularly ripe and luscious fresh pears.

TOPPING

- 6 tablespoons (¾ stick) unsalted butter
- ¾ cup packed dark brown sugar
- ½ teaspoon ground ginger
- 5 juicy-ripe medium pears, peeled, halved, and cored, or a 28- to 29-ounce can plus an 8- to 9-ounce can pear halves, drained
- Approximately ⅓ cup pecan halves

CAKE

- 1½ cups sifted cake flour
- ¾ teaspoon ground ginger
- ¾ teaspoon baking powder
- ¼ teaspoon baking soda
- ½ teaspoon salt
- 3 large egg yolks
- ½ cup sour cream
- 1 teaspoon pure vanilla extract
- ½ cup (1 stick) plus 1 tablespoon unsalted butter, softened
- ¾ cup granulated sugar

Preheat the oven to 350°F.

Prepare the topping. Melt the butter in a heavy 8- to 9-inch skillet, preferably cast iron, over medium heat. Stir in the brown sugar and ginger, and remove the pan from the heat. Arrange the pear halves, cut side up, in the skillet. Fit them snugly in concentric circles or in another pattern that pleases you. Tuck pecans in spaces between the pears.

Prepare the cake batter, first sifting together the flour, ginger, baking powder, baking soda, and salt. In a small bowl, lightly whisk the egg yolks with the sour cream and vanilla. Cream together the butter and granulated sugar with an electric mixer at medium-high speed until light and fluffy, about 5 minutes. Mix in the egg mixture and flour mixture in thirds, alternating the two. Mix for about 20 seconds following each addition, stopping to scrape down the sides of the bowl as necessary. Spoon the batter over the topping in the skillet, smoothing the surface. Bake for about 50 minutes, until nicely brown and a toothpick inserted in the center comes out clean.

Immediately run a knife around the sides of the cake and invert the skillet onto a serving plate. Leave the skillet in place over the cake for a couple of minutes, then carefully remove the skillet. This gives time for the caramelized topping to release fully from the skillet, but if any clings stubbornly, scrape it out and smooth it onto the cake. Cool for at least 10 additional minutes before slicing into wedges. Serve warm or at room temperature.

Devil's Food Cake with Chocolate Butter Frosting

MAKES A THREE-LAYER CAKE, SERVING ABOUT 10

Cookbook author Maria Parloa, in the last few decades of the nineteenth century, became the first American champion of chocolate cake, teaming up with the Baker's company to promote the strange idea of using a beverage-and-candy ingredient in home baking. Devil's food cake, perhaps the most popular style, appeared around the turn of the twentieth century, taking its name possibly from a contrast to angel's food cake. Our used copy of the 1903 *Good Housekeeping Everyday Cook Book* contains a recipe calling for only a little chocolate, but a former owner of the book in 1920 penned in a lustier version. Our moist, finely textured rendition is deeply devilish in chocolate flavor.

CAKE

- 1 cup unsweetened cocoa, such as Hershey's or Ghirardelli (not Dutch process or alkylized cocoa)
- 3½ cups sifted cake flour
- 1 teaspoon baking soda
- ¾ teaspoon salt
- ¾ cup (1½ sticks) unsalted butter, softened
- 2¼ cups sugar
- 1 tablespoon pure vanilla extract
- 4 large eggs, at room temperature, lightly beaten

FROSTING

- 12 ounces bittersweet or semisweet chocolate, chopped
- 9 ounces milk chocolate (six 1.5-ounce Hershey's chocolate bars), chopped
- 1½ cups (3 sticks) unsalted butter, softened

Preheat the oven to 350°F. Grease and flour the bottom and sides of three 9-inch round cake pans. Cover the pan bottoms with wax paper or parchment, and grease the paper.

Pour 1½ cups of boiling water over the cocoa in a small bowl and stir until smooth. Set the mixture aside to cool to room temperature, giving the mixture a couple of additional stirs as you prepare the other ingredients.

Sift together the flour, baking soda, and salt.

Cream together the butter and sugar until light and fluffy, 5 to 7 minutes, with an electric mixer at high speed. Reduce the mixer speed to medium, beat in the vanilla and then the eggs, drizzling the eggs in steadily. Add the cocoa mixture, beating just until incorporated. Mix in the flour mixture about one-third at a time,

Maria Parloa, 1843–1909

Fannie Farmer and Mary Lincoln made their reputations initially at the Boston Cooking School, but it was Maria Parloa who initially made the reputation of the school. The group of women who founded the institution in 1879 asked Parloa, already an established author and teacher, to serve as principal. She declined, but agreed to lecture every other Saturday.

Orphaned and self-supporting at an early age, the young Parloa worked as a cook in private homes and as a pastry chef in several New Hampshire summer resorts, including the Appledore House on the Isles of Shoals. That experience inspired *Miss Parloa's Appledore Cook Book,* which she published in 1872, and its success led to a variety of other culinary works large and small. *Miss Parloa's New Cook Book and Marketing Guide* (1880) offers guidance on shopping as well as cooking, and *Miss Parloa's Kitchen Companion* (1887) focuses more fully than any previous American cookbook on kitchen equipment and design.

In the latter tome she says that she decided to endorse some "manufactured products" only "after much consideration," though the choice seems to have flowed naturally from her entrepreneurial spirit. Likewise, her active involvement in the early home economics movement grew out of her earnest dedication to teaching. Parloa exemplified her era in many respects, but her priorities came largely from within.

stopping as needed to scrape down the sides of the bowl. Mix after each addition just until combined. Divide the batter among the prepared pans.

Bake for about 25 minutes, until a toothpick inserted in the center of each comes out clean. Cool the layers in their pans for about 10 minutes. Then run a knife around their edges, invert them, and remove them from the pans. Finish cooling the layers on greased baking racks.

Prepare the frosting, first melting the chocolates together in a heavy medium saucepan over low heat. Stir frequently and remove the chocolate from the heat while a few lumps remain. Continue to stir, letting the residual heat of the pan finish the melting. Set the chocolate aside to cool. Beat the butter with an electric mixer until fluffy, then spoon in the chocolate and continue beating until the frosting stands up in cloudlike swirls. The color of the frosting will lighten considerably.

To assemble the cake, invert the first layer onto a serving plate. Spread frosting over the top of the first cake layer. Repeat with the second and third layers, placing each bottom side up. Finish spreading the frosting over the sides of the cake, swirling it decoratively. Let the cake sit at least 30 minutes before slicing.

TECHNIQUE TIP: Despite the abundance of chocolate, a devil's food cake remains a classic butter cake, where butter and sugar are creamed together as the first step. It's important to start with softened but not melted butter. The creamed mixture becomes much lighter in color as it is beaten with the mixer, and it gains substantial fluffiness. The texture typically stays a little grainy, but the sugar dissolves partially and becomes evenly distributed through the batter. Proper execution of this step is essential to the texture and height of this and other butter cakes.

German Chocolate Cake

MAKES A THREE-LAYER CAKE, SERVING ABOUT 10

This chocolate cake, a favorite in our family, has nothing to do with Germany. The name comes from the distinguishing ingredient, Baker's German's Sweet Chocolate, christened after Samuel German, an early confectioner at the Baker's company. The cake gained fame quickly after Julie Bennell, the longtime food editor of *The Dallas Morning News,* printed a reader's recipe for it in 1957. That caused a run on German's chocolate in north Texas, which led the manufacturer to feature the cake on the wrapper. General Foods bought Baker's, and Kraft took over General Foods, but the recipe is still there on every box of the chocolate sold.

CAKE

2 cups cake flour, sifted
1 teaspoon baking soda
¼ teaspoon salt
4 ounces Baker's German's Sweet Chocolate
1 cup (2 sticks) unsalted butter, softened
2 cups sugar
4 eggs, separated
1½ teaspoons pure vanilla extract
1 cup buttermilk

COCONUT-PECAN FROSTING

1½ cups evaporated milk
1⅓ cups sugar
¾ cup (1½ sticks) unsalted butter
4 egg yolks, lightly beaten
2 teaspoons pure vanilla extract
Pinch of salt
2 cups shredded coconut
1¾ cups chopped pecans, toasted

Preheat the oven to 350°F. Grease and flour the bottom and sides of three 9-inch round cake pans. Add wax paper or parchment cut in circles to fit the pans, and grease and flour the paper.

Sift together the flour, baking soda, and salt.

Melt the chocolate with ½ cup of water in a small saucepan over low heat. Stir frequently and remove the chocolate from the heat while a few lumps remain. Continue to stir, finishing the melting with the residual heat of the pan. Keep the mixture warm.

With an electric mixer, cream together the butter and sugar, beating until fluffy and light. Add the egg yolks, chocolate mixture, and vanilla, beating well after each addition. Mix in the sifted dry ingredients and buttermilk in thirds, alternating the two. Combine well.

TECHNIQUE TIP:
Keep these steps in mind for fine layer cakes:

- Take the chill off butter, eggs, and other refrigerated ingredients before starting
- Follow all recipe suggestions on greasing, flouring, and lining the baking pan
- Alternate wet and dry ingredients, or add them gradually, to keep the batter from collapsing
- Avoid overbeating dry ingredients, once combined with the liquid, mixing only until fully combined
- Bake cakes near the center of the oven, cooking only until a toothpick inserted in the center comes out clean.

Anyone who spends any time in the kitchen eventually comes to realize that what she or he is looking for is the perfect chocolate cake.

LAURIE COLWIN,
GOURMET, MAY 1990

Beat the egg whites in another bowl, with clean beaters, until sturdy but not-quite-stiff peaks form. Fold the whites gently into the batter by hand. Divide the batter equally among the prepared pans. Bake for 25 to 30 minutes, until a toothpick inserted in the center comes out clean.

Cool the layers in their pans for about 5 minutes. Run a knife around their edges, invert them onto greased baking racks, and remove them from the pans. Let them cool.

Prepare the frosting while the cake cools. Combine the milk, sugar, butter, egg yolks, vanilla, and salt in a large heavy saucepan. Cook over medium-low heat, stirring constantly, until the mixture thickens to the consistency of thin pudding, 12 to 15 minutes. Remove the pan from the heat, and stir in the coconut and pecans. Cool, stirring occasionally, until firm enough to spread thickly.

To assemble the cake, invert the first layer onto a serving plate. Only the tops of the layers will be frosted. Spread one-third of the frosting over the top of the first cake layer. Repeat with the second and third layers, placing each bottom side up. Let the cake sit for at least 30 minutes before slicing.

Carrot Cake

MAKES A TWO-LAYER CAKE, SERVING 12 OR MORE

America's grande dame of desserts, Maida Heatter, once exclaimed she'd never met a carrot cake that she didn't like. We agreed so fervently in the same year, 1985, that we chose a four-tiered version for our wedding cake. The use of carrots in breads and sweets goes back for centuries in Central Europe, but didn't catch on here until recent decades. Some American fans thought the addition of a vegetable made the cake healthy, without really considering whether carrots displaced any of the fatty and calorie-laden ingredients. A dreamy dessert indeed.

2 cups unbleached all-purpose flour
1 tablespoon ground cinnamon
1½ teaspoons baking soda
½ teaspoon ground allspice
½ teaspoon salt
3 eggs
1 cup granulated sugar
1 cup packed brown sugar
¾ cup buttermilk
¾ cup vegetable oil
1 tablespoon pure vanilla extract
3 cups shredded carrots
8-ounce can crushed pineapple in juice, drained but juice reserved
1 cup chopped walnuts or pecans

GLAZE

¼ cup (½ stick) unsalted butter
¼ cup buttermilk
3 tablespoons granulated sugar
1 tablespoon light corn syrup
½ teaspoon pure vanilla extract

FROSTING

8 ounces cream cheese, softened
2 tablespoons unsalted butter, softened
1 teaspoon pure vanilla extract
1 to 2 tablespoons drained pineapple juice
3¼ to 3¾ cups confectioners' sugar

Preheat the oven to 350°F. Grease and flour the bottom and sides of two 9-inch round cake pans. Add wax paper or parchment cut in circles to fit the pans, and grease and flour the paper.

Sift together the flour, cinnamon, baking soda, allspice, and salt. With an electric mixer, beat together the eggs, both sugars, buttermilk, oil, and vanilla. When the sugar is dissolved and the ingredients are well combined, mix in the dry ingredients gradually, about ½ cup at a time, stopping to scrape down the sides as necessary. Mix in the carrots, pineapple, and nuts just to combine. Spoon the batter into the prepared pans. Bake for 35 to 40 minutes, until medium brown and a toothpick inserted in the center of each layer comes out clean. Cool about 10 minutes on greased baking racks.

Prepare the glaze, first combining the butter, buttermilk, sugar, corn syrup, and vanilla in a medium saucepan. Simmer over medium heat for 5 minutes and remove from the heat. Slowly pour the hot glaze over the still-warm cake layers, then let them cool thoroughly.

Loosen the layers by running a knife around the inside edges. Without removing the layers from the pan, place the pans on top of each other, glazed sides together. Remove the pan from the top layer. Invert the cake onto a platter and then remove the second pan. Press the layers gently together.

Prepare the frosting, combining the cream cheese, butter, vanilla, and the smaller amounts of pineapple juice and sugar in a mixer or food processor. Combine until smooth. Check the texture for easy spreading consistency, adding more juice to thin, or sugar to thicken, if necessary. Frost the top and sides of the cake. (The frosting has a fine consistency for decorative piped-frosting treatments, such as a basket-weave pattern.) Refrigerate the cake for at least 30 minutes to set the frosting, then cover it if you don't plan to serve it shortly. Let the cake sit at room temperature for about 20 minutes before serving.

Okracoke Fig Cake

SERVES 8 OR MORE

Connected to the mainland only by ferries, Okracoke Island on North Carolina's Outer Banks remains a serene refuge from the hubbub of contemporary life—unless you make the mistake of trying to tell a local cook how to make a fig cake. Residents insist on the importance of figs from their own trees, of course, and some favor double layers and a cream cheese frosting, all of which we ignore but never dispute out loud on a moving ferry. We focus in our recipe on the simple but luscious combination of figs and spice, a straightforward pairing worthy on its own of Okracoke's passion.

- 2 cups unbleached all-purpose flour
- 1 teaspoon baking soda
- 1 teaspoon salt
- 1 teaspoon ground cinnamon
- 1 teaspoon ground nutmeg
- ½ teaspoon ground cloves
- ¾ cup buttermilk
- 2 teaspoons pure vanilla extract
- 3 large eggs
- 1 cup sugar
- ¾ cup plus 2 tablespoons vegetable oil
- 1 cup Fig Preserves (page 293) or other fig preserves
- 1 cup chopped ripe fresh figs or more fig preserves
- 1 cup chopped pecans, toasted
- Confectioners' sugar

Preheat the oven to 350°F. Grease and flour a 10-inch Bundt cake pan.

Sift together the flour, baking soda, salt, cinnamon, nutmeg, and cloves. Combine the buttermilk and vanilla in a small bowl.

With an electric mixer on high speed, beat together the eggs, sugar, and oil until pale yellow and forming ribbons, about 3 minutes. Reduce the mixer speed to medium, then beat in the buttermilk mixture just until combined. Add in the flour mixture by thirds, stopping as needed to scrape down the sides of the bowl. Mix after each addition just until combined. By hand, stir in the fig preserves, figs, and pecans. Spoon into the prepared pan.

Bake on the oven's middle rack for about 45 minutes, until a toothpick inserted in the center comes out clean. Cool the cake in the pan for about 10 minutes. Then run a knife around the edges, invert it, and remove it from the pan. Finish cooling, top side up, on a baking rack. When cool, dust the whole cake, or individual slices, with confectioners' sugar, sprinkled through a fine sieve. Serve.

Hot Fudge Brownies

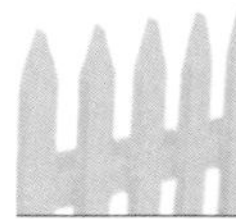

Makes a 9-inch pan of brownies, about 1 dozen

As Richard Sax says in *Classic Home Desserts* (1994), "When all of the flourless chocolate cakes and chocolate mousse or ganache cakes have come and gone, there will still be nothing like a fudgy brownie, dry and crackled on top, moist and dense within." We get nutty in pursuit of that vision, adding several handfuls of toasted walnuts to balance the sweetness of the chocolate and contribute their crunch to the molten goodness within.

2 cups walnut pieces
4 ounces unsweetened chocolate
½ cup (1 stick) unsalted butter
2 teaspoons pure vanilla extract
½ teaspoon salt
2 cups sugar
4 large eggs
1 cup unbleached all-purpose flour
Confectioners' sugar, optional

Preheat the oven to 350°F. Mold a piece of foil around the outside bottom of a 9-inch square baking pan. The foil needs to be large enough that at least two of the sides overhang the edges of the pan. Turn the pan over and arrange the foil inside the pan. (Molding the foil over the outside first cuts down on wrinkles.) Gently grease the foil, preferably with vegetable oil spray, to avoid wrinkling it.

Arrange the walnuts in a single layer on a baking sheet. Bake the walnuts for 6 to 8 minutes, until lightly toasted and fragrant. Set aside to cool.

Melt together the chocolate and butter in a small saucepan over low heat. Remove the chocolate from the heat while a few lumps remain. Continue to stir, finishing the melting with the residual heat of the pan. Scrape the mixture into a medium bowl and let it cool for about 5 minutes. By hand, stir in the vanilla, salt, and sugar, and then the eggs, one at a time. Mix with a minimum of strokes, adding each ingredient just before you have completely incorporated the previous one. Stir in the flour, mixing lightly again, followed by the walnuts. Spoon the batter into the prepared pan and smooth the surface.

Bake for 32 to 35 minutes, until the top looks just lightly set and a toothpick inserted in the center comes out almost but not quite clean. A little chocolate should remain on the toothpick. Avoid overcooking the brownies—when they really look done, they'll be too dry. Cool the brownies in the pan. Remove them from the pan by pulling up on the foil ends, then pull off the foil and cut the brownies to your preferred size. Slicing is easiest if you wipe the knife blade after each cut. If you wish, dust the brownies before serving with confectioners' sugar, sprinkled through a fine sieve.

TECHNIQUE TIP:
If you like frosted brownies, the quickest trick is to use milk-chocolate candy bars. When the brownies are just cooked, remove them from the oven, arrange 4 to 5 thin chocolate bars over the entire surface in one layer, and return to the oven for 30 to 45 seconds. Remove from the oven and immediately smooth the "frosting." When cool, slice the brownies with a serrated knife.

Lemon Squares

MAKES ABOUT 2 DOZEN COOKIES

Cheryl's original Betty Crocker cookbook, a housewarming present when she moved into her first college apartment, flaunts splatters all over the recipe for lemon squares. A type of bar cookie, like the brownie, the squares became one of the hits of that decade, never lasting long at any bake sale. We've revved up the lemon intensity since those days, and firmed up the filling, making them worthy of a few stains on this page.

CRUST

1¾ cups unbleached all-purpose flour

⅔ cup confectioners' sugar

2 tablespoons cornstarch

¾ teaspoon salt

¾ cup (1½ sticks) unsalted butter, cut into small bits, chilled

FILLING

4 eggs

1⅓ cups granulated sugar

¼ cup unbleached all-purpose flour

Pinch of salt

1 to 2 teaspoons minced lemon zest

¾ cup fresh lemon juice (from about 4 lemons)

¼ cup whole milk

¼ cup raspberry or strawberry jam or puréed preserves, warmed, optional

Confectioners' sugar, optional

Preheat the oven to 350°F. Grease a 9-inch × 13-inch baking dish, then lay in it a piece of wax paper about 6 inches longer than the pan. You should have some wax paper overhanging at least two sides of the dish. Grease the wax paper, preferably with vegetable oil spray, to avoid wrinkling it.

Prepare the crust, first combining the flour, confectioners' sugar, cornstarch, and salt in a food processor. Pulse to combine. Scatter the butter over the dry ingredients, then pulse as necessary to form a coarse meal. Using your fingers, press the crust into the prepared dish. Refrigerate the crust for about 30 minutes while you prepare the filling.

Beat the eggs lightly, then add the granulated sugar and beat just until the sugar dissolves. Add the flour, a tablespoon at a time, then the salt, lemon zest and juice, and the milk.

Bake the crust for 20 minutes, until just set and lightly golden. Remove from the oven, give the filling a good stir again, and pour it over the hot crust. Reduce the oven temperature to 325°F and return the pan to the oven. Bake for 18 to 20 additional minutes, until the filling is just firm at its center.

Transfer the lemon squares to a baking rack and let them cool. If you wish to add the jam topping, brush it lightly and evenly across the lemon squares (thinning with the smallest bit of water if needed); then let it cool. Using the overhanging wax paper, gently pull the cookies from the pan. Cut into 1½- to 2-inch squares or rectangles, wiping the knife as necessary to assure clean cuts. Just before serving, top if you wish with confectioners' sugar, sprinkled through a fine sieve.

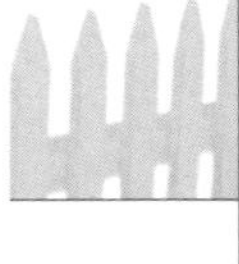

Biscochitos

Makes about 5 dozen cookies

A number of towns and regions across the country boast special holiday cookies. The Pennsylvania Dutch so loved a molasses cookie called brown spice cakes, according to local culinary authority Betty Groff, that the number of people baking them simultaneously at Christmas caused wide fluctuations in the gas-fuel levels reaching homes in the area. That may also have been true at one time in northern New Mexico, where the traditional Christmas cookie is the anise-scented biscochito (also bizcochito). This version comes from our friend Dorothy Montaño, who modified the recipe handed down from her mother, Lydia Garcia, and thereby started a friendly family cookie feud. Don't try to substitute any other fat for the lard; it is essential to the taste and flaky texture of these cookies.

I state, without explanation or apology, that the one gastronomic trait I do not have in common with my fellow Americans is a passion for rich desserts. . . . Americans, naturally, tend to snicker at something so seemingly simple and prosaic as a cookie, but take it from one who regularly bakes his own supply of delicacies, a few well-made cookies not only provide an eminently satisfying alternative to those rich desserts but also do lots less damage to the digestive tract and waistline than a ludicrous slab of apple pie or strawberry shortcake.

James Villas,
American Taste (1982)

COOKIES

3 cups unbleached all-purpose flour
1½ teaspoons baking powder
1 to 1½ teaspoons ground anise
½ teaspoon salt
½ pound lard, softened
½ cup plus 1 tablespoon sugar
1 egg
2 tablespoons sweet white wine, bourbon, or rum

TOPPING

¼ cup sugar
¾ teaspoon ground cinnamon

Sift together the flour, baking powder, anise, and salt.

Beat the lard in an electric mixer, gradually adding the sugar, and cream it until extremely fluffy and light, about 8 minutes. Add the egg, followed by the wine, and continue beating. Mix in the dry ingredients, adding about one-third of the mixture at a time. Stop the mixture as you make each addition and beat no longer than necessary to incorporate the dry ingredients. A stiff pie-crust type of dough is what you're seeking. Chill the dough for about 15 minutes for easy handling.

Preheat the oven to 350°F.

To form her biscochitos, Dorothy uses a cookie press with a *fleur de lis* design. The results are beautiful. If you don't own a cookie press, roll out the dough ¼ inch thick on a floured work surface and cut it with a small cookie cutter. Avoid handling the dough any more than necessary. Transfer the cookies to ungreased cookie sheets.

Bake the cookies for 10 to 12 minutes, until just set and pale golden. While the cookies bake, stir together the topping ingredients. When the cookies are done, cool them for just a minute or two on the baking sheets, then gently dunk the top of each in the cinnamon-sugar. Transfer to absorbent paper to finish cooling. Biscochitos, tightly covered, will keep for at least a week. They also freeze well for up to a month.

Chocolate Chip–Oatmeal Cookies

MAKES ABOUT 4 DOZEN LARGE COOKIES

In an oft-told tale, Ruth Wakefield invented chocolate chip cookies by accident in the 1930s at her Toll House Inn in Massachusetts. Instead of melting chocolate in advance for a batch of popular "butter drop-do" cookies, she put small chips from a bar of chocolate into the batter, thinking they would melt in the cooking. Rather than blending in, the chips stood out just as the cookies have done ever since. With all respect for Wakefield's version, replicated closely on Nestlé packages, we like to make the cookies chewier with the addition of a little oatmeal.

- 1¾ cups unbleached all-purpose flour
- 1 teaspoon baking soda
- ¾ teaspoon salt
- 1 cup (2 sticks) unsalted butter, at very warm room temperature
- 1 cup packed dark brown sugar
- ½ cup granulated sugar
- 2 eggs, beaten
- 1½ teaspoons pure vanilla extract
- 2 cups oats (not the quick-cooking variety)
- 2 cups semisweet chocolate chips (11.5- to 12-ounce bag)
- 1 cup chopped pecans, toasted

Preheat the oven to 350°F.

Sift together the flour, baking soda, and salt. Cream the butter with both sugars in a large bowl, using a sturdy spoon. Mix in the eggs, one at a time, then the vanilla. Stir in the sifted ingredients, about half at a time, mixing just until combined. Stir in the oats, chocolate chips, and pecans, again mixing just until combined. Drop the dough onto ungreased cookie sheets by rounded tablespoons, leaving 1½ to 2 inches between the cookies.

Bake for 10 to 12 minutes, until just lightly browned and set. At the halfway point, exchange the position of the sheets on the racks from top to bottom and from front to back. Avoid overbaking. Cool the cookies on the baking sheets for 1 to 2 minutes, then remove them to baking racks or absorbent paper. Serve warm or at room temperature.

Thumbprint Cookies

MAKES ABOUT 2 DOZEN COOKIES

Like many cakes and cookies, these go by multiple names, including "jelly tots," "bird's nest," and "Polish tea cakes." They vary as well in the kinds of nuts and jams they contain, but always seem to please regardless of the components and appellations.

- 6 tablespoons (¾ stick) unsalted butter, softened
- 2 tablespoons vegetable shortening
- ¼ cup packed light brown sugar
- 1 teaspoon pure vanilla extract
- 1 egg, separated
- 1 cup unbleached all-purpose flour
- ¼ teaspoon salt
- ¾ cup fine-chopped hickory nuts, walnuts, butternuts, or pecans
- Cherry, berry, apricot, or other brightly colored fruit jam

Preheat the oven to 350°F.

Cream together the butter and shortening with the brown sugar, by hand or with an electric mixer. Stir in the vanilla and egg yolk, then add the flour and salt. The dough will be very soft. Roll into 1-inch balls, handling each no longer than necessary.

Whisk the egg white in a small bowl until foamy. Dip the balls into the egg white, then roll them in the nuts. Arrange them 1 inch apart on an ungreased cookie sheet. Bake for 3 minutes, then remove them from the oven and make a deep even indention with your thumb or the small end of a melon baller in the middle of each cookie. Return them to the oven and continue baking for 7 to 8 additional minutes, until lightly colored and softly set. Cool them for 10 minutes on the cookie sheet. Then remove the cookies and spoon jam into the cavity of each. Cool completely before serving.

Short List of Our Favorite American Cookie Names

- Animal Crackers
- Billy Goat Date Cakes
- Cherry Winks
- Hello Dollies
- Hermits
- Joe Froggers
- Jumbles
- Lizzies
- Moon Pies
- Stage Planks
- Snickerdoodles

Double Chocolate Fudge

MAKES A 9-INCH PAN, ABOUT 3 DOZEN PIECES

In the late nineteenth century, students at New England women's colleges adopted fudge as their own special candy, cooking it initially over gas lamps in dormitory rooms. They probably provided the name too, meaning to cheat a little, since they made the fudge at parties after "lights out." We've tried innumerable chocolate versions—using recipes from Vassar and Wellesley colleges, Irma Rombauer, Mamie Eisenhower, Maida Heatter, and our dental hygienist, Joanne Stenzhorn. We've liked them all, even many of the widely circulated shortcut variations, but we haven't found any to compare ultimately with the classic boiled, beaten, and slab-kneaded fudge featured here. (If you're content with the classic single chocolate fudge, simply ignore the white chocolate marbled topping.)

6 ounces high-quality bittersweet or semisweet chocolate, chopped
2 cups sugar
½ cup whipping cream
½ cup half-and-half
3 tablespoons light corn syrup
Pinch of salt
2 tablespoons unsalted butter, softened
1 tablespoon bourbon or light rum
1 teaspoon pure vanilla extract
4 ounces high-quality white chocolate
1 cup chopped pecans, walnuts, or hazelnuts (skins removed), toasted

Mold a piece of foil around the outside bottom of a 9-inch square pan. The foil needs to be large enough that at least two of the sides overhang the edges of the pan. Turn the pan over and arrange the foil inside the pan. (Molding the foil over the outside first cuts down on wrinkles.) Gently grease the foil, preferably with vegetable oil spray, to avoid wrinkling it.

Combine the chocolate, sugar, cream, half-and-half, corn syrup, and salt in a large heavy saucepan. Warm over medium heat, scraping up from the bottom a few times to combine the mixture as the sugar dissolves and the chocolate melts. Bring to a boil, then continue cooking without stirring until it reaches 236°F to 240°F, the "soft ball" stage. Immediately remove from the heat, then place on top of the mixture, without stirring, the butter, bourbon, and vanilla. Allow the fudge to cool to between 100°F and 115°F.

While the mixture cools, melt the white chocolate over low heat and keep it warm.

When the fudge has reached the proper temperature, stir in the butter, bourbon, and vanilla. Mix in the nuts. If you have a marble pastry board or cool stone counter, spoon the fudge out onto it. Less preferable, but still acceptable, is just to leave it in the saucepan. Knead the fudge with a candy or dough scraper, turning

If French cooking is balanced, orderly, and classic, American cooking is its opposite. . . . American cooking is romantic, absurd, full of excess, extravagance, given to self-parody and bizarre contradictions. . . .

If our sugar fixation has produced the world's best dentists, so, too, our health fixation has produced the world's best equipped kitchens. If we have bred a race of amateur engineers, we have also bred a race of professional home cooks on an unprecedented scale and of unparalleled quality.

Betty Fussell, *Masters of American Cookery* (1983)

it over on itself until it begins to hold its shape and lose its shine, about 5 minutes. The fudge also begins to make a snapping noise when it reaches the proper point. If your fudge is in the saucepan, stir briskly with a wooden spoon until it reaches this point. Immediately turn the fudge into the prepared pan and smooth the surface.

Quickly spoon the white chocolate in dollops over the fudge. With a knife, swirl the white chocolate into the fudge in a marble pattern. Let the fudge cool and set for at least 2 hours before slicing it. Invert the pan and peel away the foil. The fudge can be cut into any size portions, though we usually cut it into 6 slices across and down, for 36 pieces. The fudge keeps for a week to 10 days stored airtight at room temperature. If you stack the fudge, separate it with wax paper in between the layers. In warm weather, it keeps better stored in the refrigerator.

TECHNIQUE TIP: One of the best uses for a microwave is melting chocolate. One to two minutes at 50 percent power will soften most oversize chocolate bars or a 12-ounce bag of chips. Stir and use.

Divinity

MAKES 3 TO 4 DOZEN PIECES

We once had a neighbor who did little cooking but took enormous pride in her divinity, carefully picking a day of low humidity for cooking and then proceeding with the discipline of an alchemist. Like our neighbor, we always include nuts in the corn syrup–egg white concoction to counterbalance the sweetness, but avoid over-the-top additions such as maraschino cherries.

2 large egg whites, at room temperature

2 cups sugar

6 tablespoons light corn syrup

1 teaspoon pure vanilla extract

¾ cup to 1 cup black walnut or English walnut pieces, toasted

Top a cookie sheet with wax paper and grease the paper.

Beat the egg whites with a heavy-duty electric mixer until they form stiff but still glossy peaks.

Combine the sugar and corn syrup with ½ cup of water in a heavy medium saucepan. Stir over medium-low heat just until the sugar dissolves. Raise the heat to high and, without stirring, bring the mixture to a boil. Lower the heat to medium and continue cooking until a candy thermometer reaches 250°F to 255°F, the "hard ball" stage.

Beating continuously, pour the syrup directly from the pan in a slow, steady stream into the egg whites. Only pour out the syrup that flows freely, discarding the crystallized syrup that sticks to the edges of the pan. Beat in the vanilla and continue beating until the mixture loses it shiny, gooey, melted-marshmallow appearance and becomes fudgy. This might take as long as 10 to 15 minutes, the reason a heavy-duty mixer is required. When ready, the mixture will hold its shape loosely and will have changed from bright white to a slightly more muted cream tone. Immediately stir in the nuts.

Quickly drop the mixture by rounded spoonfuls onto the wax paper. (We prefer about 2 teaspoons of mixture per candy, but the size is up to you.) Let the divinity cool completely. A friend's grandmother offers that "if made properly, the candy will be firm enough to hold but quite creamy inside." Store it in an airtight container for up to a week.

Candied Grapefruit Peel

MAKES ABOUT 2 CUPS

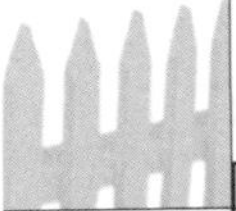

From Florida's Indian River to Texas's Rio Grande Valley, candied grapefruit peel still climaxes many a holiday meal. Some people call the strips "Pamelas," which may come, as Bill Neal suggested, from the French word for grapefruit, *pamplemousse.*

- 2 whole thin-skinned grapefruit
- 1¾ cups sugar plus about ½ cup more for coating

Scrub the grapefruit well. Halve them and squeeze out the juice, reserving both the shells and juice. Slice each half into two sections and with a sharp knife, cut away the membranes and the white pith, leaving just the thin yellow or pink exterior peel. (The pile of discards will be much larger than the peels you keep.) Slice the peel into ⅓- to ½-inch strips. In a large heavy saucepan, cover the peels with several inches of water. Bring them to a boil and boil for 2 minutes.

Drain off the water and repeat the process with three more changes of water, to eliminate bitterness. Pour the grapefruit juice and 1¾ cups sugar into the saucepan, and stir to dissolve the sugar. Bring the mixture to a boil, then reduce the heat to a simmer. Continue cooking for 30 to 40 minutes, until much of the liquid has evaporated and the strips of peel have become somewhat translucent.

Remove the peel from the syrup with a slotted spoon and transfer it to wax paper. Spoon the remaining ½ cup sugar onto a plate. When the peel slices are cool enough to handle, roll each in sugar and place it on another piece of wax paper. Let the peel air-dry until no longer gooey, which could be a couple of hours or a full day, depending on the humidity. We prefer them with a little moistness remaining, so that they are chewy rather than crisp. Serve the peel or store it airtight, between layers of wax paper, for up to 2 weeks.

Caramel Apples

SERVES 8

In the innocent days of Halloween trick-or-treating, before parents worried about X-raying handouts, nothing was as prized as a caramel apple. Skewered onto a popsicle stick, it remains the quintessential autumn treat. Some people opt for store-bought caramels for the coating, but it is almost as easy and much tastier to make the coating from scratch.

8 large red apples, such as Red Delicious or Winesap

2 cups granulated sugar

1 cup packed light brown sugar

1½ cups whipping cream

1 cup light corn syrup

¼ teaspoon salt

3 tablespoons unsalted butter

1½ teaspoons pure vanilla extract

Coarsely chopped salted peanuts or honey-roasted peanuts, optional

Oil a sheet of wax paper large enough to hold the apples without crowding. Insert a popsicle stick or candy stick in the stem end of each apple.

Combine the granulated sugar, brown sugar, whipping cream, corn syrup, and salt in a large heavy saucepan with ½ cup of warm water. Bring the mixture to a boil over medium-high heat, stirring frequently, and cook until the caramel mixture reaches 236°F to 240°F, the "soft ball" stage. Remove from the heat and stir in the butter and vanilla. Keep stirring for several minutes to speed the cooling. When the caramel begins to drip slowly from the spoon instead of just sheeting off, it's ready to coat the apples.

Quickly dunk each apple into the hot caramel, turning to coat evenly, then pausing briefly over the pan for excess caramel to drip back into the pan. If you wish, roll each apple in chopped nuts. Place the apples on the wax paper as they are finished and allow them to cool. Caramel apples can be kept refrigerated for several days. Cover them in a way that avoids touching the caramel, perhaps with a layer cake plate cover or inverted plastic tub.

CHERRY SHRUBS TO Mint Juleps

The Pilgrims landed at Plymouth partially because of a beer shortage. Instead of searching farther in the icy winter of 1620 for a sunnier home, they pulled into a Massachusetts harbor, as one voyager explained, on account of their "victuals being much spent, especially our beere." They had no relief from thirst, knowing salt water caused illness and suspecting the same of fresh water, a common source of health problems in European cities. In the circumstances, it was beer or bust.

The colonists made their own home brews using a wide variety of materials, including spruce bark, corn, and pumpkins. They showed similar resourcefulness with wine, producing it from native fruits, berries, and weeds. As soon as apple seeds arrived from England in the 1630s, farmers planted orchards, and their wives turned the fruit into cider and applejack, drinks enjoyed, like beer, by everyone regardless of age, sex, or religion. Prosperous colonists imported port, Madeira, and French wines, while the less affluent consumed generous quantities of New England rum. Home distillers were making rye whiskey by the mid-seventeenth century, and in 1789, Baptist minister Elijah Craig blessed the country with the first true bourbon, an American original.

Within a few decades Craig's colleagues turned on his spirited inspiration and all other forms of "demon rum." Evangelical Protestants began preaching total abstinence from alcoholic beverages, blaming them for all manner of social ills. By the Civil War, over a dozen states had prohibition laws, and shortly after the conflict, antiliquor crusaders brought their quest to national politics. They won their way in 1920 with the passage of the Eighteenth Amendment to the Constitution, perhaps the most quixotic legislation ever enacted outside a fundamentalist theocracy.

Virtually the only good that came of Prohibition, which ended in 1933, was iced tea. We started drinking much more of it and other distinctively American nonalcoholic beverages, a trend that continues today. We even quaff lots of water now, though like the Pilgrims, many of us still settle in only where the beer flows.

The Republic of Soft Drinks

Beer remains the national beverage of Britain, just as wine reigns in France, but in "the land of the brave" we're softies to the core. We invented modern soft drinks and consume them at an astonishing rate—at meals, between meals, and even before meals, mixed in cocktails. The bottle-cap counters say that we drink more "soda water" than real water. No other country matches us in that thirst.

It's a short step from a cherry shrub to a cherry soda. You omit the brandy to appeal to abstainers, cut costs by cutting the cherry flavor, and replace the cold water with carbonated water, which was being produced commercially by the early nineteenth century. Then you advertise, the creative part of the endeavor and the biggest success factor in the business from the beginning. Waverley Root speculates that the first sex-sells ad dates to a soft-drink promoter in the 1830s; and soon afterward Charles Hires struck another resonant chord by billing his root beer as "the National Temperance Drink."

Coca-Cola was created in an Atlanta pharmacy in 1886 as a hangover and headache cure, and became a hit as a beverage only after the inventor sold out his interest for two thousand dollars. Pepsi-Cola and Dr Pepper also made their debuts in southern pharmacies around the same period. Caleb Bradham developed Pepsi in New Bern, North Carolina, naming it originally "Brad's Drink." Charles Alderton took a different tack with his Waco, Texas, concoction, calling it Dr Pepper in honor of his prospective father-in-law, whose ungrateful daughter never married him.

Cherry Shrub

SERVES 6 OR MORE

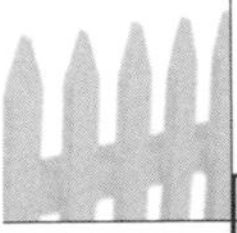

From the colonial period to the nineteenth century, fruit shrubs played a role similar to soft drinks today—even though they typically included the hard stuff. The cook first made juice by boiling down or mashing cherries, currants, raspberries, or other fruit, and then added brandy, rum, or sometimes just steeped the fruit in vinegar. After bottling, as Mary Randolph said in the 1820s, a shrub "will keep all summer, in a dry cool place, and is delicious mixed with water."

- 5 cups sweet cherries, fresh or frozen
- 2 cups sugar
- 1 to 1½ cups brandy
- Small lemon wedges
- Fresh stem-on sweet cherries or mint sprigs, or both, optional

Combine the cherries and sugar in a saucepan with ¼ cup of water. Cook over medium heat until the cherries have disintegrated and let off most of their juice. Strain the juice through a fine sieve or several layers of cheesecloth into a pitcher or large jar. Press lightly to release more juice, but not hard enough to press the pulp through. This has yielded us about 2½ cups juice. If your quantity of juice varies, increase or reduce the quantity of brandy. Chill the shrub.

To serve, fill a tall glass with ice, then fill it halfway with cold water or sparkling water. Add a squeeze of lemon, then toss in the lemon wedge. Top off with cherry shrub and, if you wish, garnish with a cherry or mint sprig. Repeat with the remaining servings. Unused shrub can be kept refrigerated for weeks.

Rum, n. Generically, fiery liquors that produce madness in total abstainers.

AMBROSE BIERCE,
THE DEVIL'S DICTIONARY (1911)

Stone Fence

SERVES 2

In his burlesque *History of New York* (1809), Washington Irving gives local Dutch settlers credit for inventing "recondite" drinks like the cocktail and the stone fence. New Englanders too, loved the latter, partially because it provided a double dose of their abundant apple juice, some alcoholic and some not. You won't find it at the center of many Manhattan or Boston happy hours today, but the stone fence still appears in standard bartender guides.

½ cup applejack (see Ingredient tip)
Dashes of Angostura bitters, optional
About 2 cups apple cider

Pour ¼ cup of applejack into each of two tall glasses, and add a dash of bitters to each if you wish. Add several ice cubes or cracked ice, fill each glass with cider, and serve.

INGREDIENT TIP: Applejack is the traditional American name for fermented cider or apple brandy. Large liquor stores usually carry Laird's, the only widely available commercial American brand, but you can also substitute French calvados.

Dry Martini

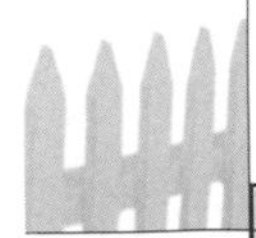

SERVES 2

The chief virtue of cocktails is their informal quality. They loosen tongues and unbutton the reserves of the socially diffident. Serve them by all means, preferably in the living room, and the sooner the better.

IRMA ROMBAUER,
JOY OF COOKING (1943)

Neither gin nor vermouth by itself proffers much in American credentials, but together they constitute the mythic martini, the sophisticate's choice at cocktail parties since the end of Prohibition. The roots of the drink remain obscure, though it seems likely that a bartender first poured one in the mid-nineteenth century in San Francisco. The original name, we know, was Martinez or Martine, related and common family names in the Southwest. "Martini" came later, lifted from the label of an Italian vermouth bottle. Early versions of the cocktail contained a considerable amount of vermouth, but by the 1920s a persistent pursuit of dryness practically eliminated the namesake component.

Lemon peel twists
5 ounces premium gin
Up to ½ ounce premium dry vermouth
2 to 4 green olives or cocktail onions, optional

Rub a lemon peel twist around the rim of two 3-ounce martini glasses. Chill the glasses until they are frosty.

Fill a martini pitcher or other small pitcher halfway with cracked ice. Pour the gin over the ice to "smoke" it for a few seconds. Add the vermouth and stir. Strain the martinis into the glasses, garnish each with a fresh lemon twist and, if you wish, an olive or two. Serve immediately.

Mint Julep

SERVES 1

Plantation breakfasts in the Old South sometimes started with a mint julep, touted as a antidote to heat and malaria both. The earliest versions featured brandy rather than bourbon, and some iconoclasts still prefer it that way. That's a minor point of contention, however, compared to the big issue of bruising the mint. According to Frances Parkinson Keyes, one of the last admonitions of a Virginia gentleman on his deathbed is never to crush the mint in a julep. Kentuckians swear that that must be done, but gently so, and that the sprigs should go immediately into a silver goblet, the only suitable serving glass. In Mississippi, meanwhile, some connoisseurs practically shred the mint and then boil it into a syrup. Though seldom given to moderation in such serious matters, we take the middle path here.

1 teaspoon, more or less, granulated or confectioners' sugar
4 to 8 fresh mint leaves
3 to 4 ounces bourbon or other American whiskey
Fresh mint sprig

In the bottom of a silver julep goblet or a medium glass, combine the sugar and mint leaves with 1 teaspoon of cold water. Crush the mint lightly with a spoon or bar muddler and dissolve the sugar. Fill the goblet with crushed ice. As soon as frost forms on the goblet, pour in the bourbon slowly to fill the glass and top the julep with a mint sprig. Avoid touching the sides of the goblet if possible because it disrupts the lovely frosted appearance. Serve immediately.

TECHNIQUE TIP: The mint syrup approach works particularly well when you're making juleps for a crowd. Combine 1 cup each of sugar and water in a saucepan, and bring the mixture to a boil over medium-high heat. Simmer without stirring for 5 minutes. Remove the pan from the heat and add 1 cup of packed mint leaves. Cool, refrigerate for 8 to 12 hours, and strain out the mint. The syrup is ready to use or can be kept refrigerated for 2 to 3 weeks. Use ½ to 1 tablespoon of the syrup per julep.

Bottling Your Corn

We owe the birth of bourbon to the ease of raising corn. Most farmers grew the crop for income as well as sustenance, which presented major marketing problems on the frontier and in other isolated areas. Turning the corn to liquor was one of the simplest solutions, so effective you could entice buyers to come to you rather than trying to find and ship to them. Many farmers made corn whiskey before Elijah Craig, but he generally gets the credit for refining the taste into bourbon, which is aged in charred oak barrels.

Early home distillers in western Pennsylvania provided the first real challenge to the federal government, rising up in the Whiskey Rebellion of 1794 against a tax on their profits. Some of the defeated rebels moved afterward into the remote hills of Appalachia, switching from rye to corn liquor and continuing their trade in greater secrecy. They became the legendary moonshiners of the region, a breed of romantic outlaws as American as bourbon itself. However clandestine and daring they were, at least in legend, their motives remained economic, turning corn to cash. Sidney Saylor Farr, in *More than Moonshine* (1983), tells the story from the perspective of her family, noting that they could sell a bushel of corn for a few bucks, but bring in hundreds of dollars by making it into raw, unaged whiskey. She demonstrates that the Saylors took pride in their craft, certainly more than can be said for many legally correct food producers.

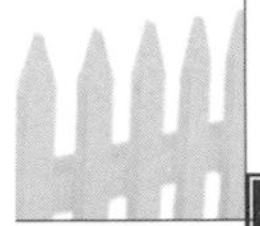

A mint julep is not the product of a formula. It is a ceremony and must be performed by a gentleman possessing a true sense of the artistic, a deep reverence for the ingredients and a proper appreciation of the occasion. It is a rite that must not be entrusted to a novice, a statistician nor a Yankee. It is a heritage of the old South, an emblem of hospitality and a vehicle in which noble minds can travel together upon the flower-strewn paths of happy and congenial thought.

S. B. Buckner, Jr., quoted in *Maryland's Way* (1963)

Orange Sangaree

Serves 8 to 12

Spanish sangria became a popular party drink in the 1960s and 1970s, when all things foreign were fashionable. Few of the revelers realized—or cared—that an old American version existed, a lighter concoction with a similar name, from the Spanish heritage in Florida and New Orleans.

- ½ cup sugar
- 1 cup fresh orange juice plus 1 sliced orange
- ½ cup fresh lemon juice plus 1 sliced lemon
- 1 bottle dry red wine
- 1 heaping teaspoon whole allspice, lightly bruised
- Several cinnamon sticks
- Sparkling water
- Additional orange slices
- Fresh mint or lemon verbena sprigs, optional

Combine the sugar, fruit juices, and fruit slices in a pitcher, and stir until the sugar dissolves. Let the mixture sit at room temperature for 30 minutes to 1 hour. Pour in the wine and add the allspice and cinnamon sticks. Chill for at least 1 hour and up to a day.

Fill tall glasses with ice. Pour each glass about two-thirds full of the wine mixture, straining the fruit slices and spices, then top off with sparkling water. Garnish each glass with a fresh orange slice, and crown the sangaree with a mint sprig if you wish.

Home-Steeped Southern Succor

MAKES ABOUT 1 QUART

The idea of steeped cordials came from Europe, particularly France, at an early period. Home cooks found them easy to make, involving little more than infusing alcohol with fruit pulp or pits, herbs, or rose petals. Based on bourbon and peaches, with a hint of orange, this rendition tastes like a peachy version of Southern Comfort, the Janis Joplin favorite. Try it over Peach Ice Cream (page 391) or as a glaze on grilled pork chops.

6 medium to large peaches, halved
Minced zest and juice of 1 orange
750-milliliter bottle bourbon or other American whiskey
⅔ cup sugar

Place the peaches and the orange zest in a large glass jar or crock. Cover with the orange juice and the bourbon. Cover and let sit in a cool, dark place for 5 to 6 weeks.

Strain the bourbon mixture through a fine sieve or several layers of cheesecloth. Press lightly to release more liquid from the peaches, but not hard enough to press the fruit pulp through. Discard the peaches and orange zest. Return the bourbon mixture to the jar.

Combine the sugar in a small saucepan with ⅓ cup of water and bring to a boil over medium-high heat. Stir until the sugar dissolves, then cool to room temperature. Mix the sugar syrup into the bourbon, cover it again, and return it to a cool, dark place for at least 2 additional weeks. After the brief aging, the drink can be stored at room temperature indefinitely. Serve with ice or straight-up in small glasses.

In the department of amour, I daresay, the first effect of Prohibition will be to raise up impediments to marriage. It was alcohol, in the past, that was the primary cause of perhaps a majority of alliances among civilized folk. The man, priming himself with cocktails to achieve boldness, found himself suddenly bogged in sentimentality. . . . Absolutely sober men will be harder to snare.

H. L. MENCKEN, PREJUDICES; SECOND SERIES (1920)

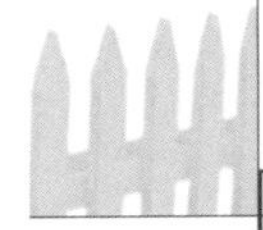

If Berks County could be called the heart of German Pennsylvania, then it follows that whiskey was its lifeblood. By whiskey, we mean *rye* whiskey, which was so common and so cheap in Pennsylvania that it was dispensed free to field-hands, to customers in stores, to the crowds at "vendues," to the mourners at funerals, and to just about anyone who deserved special treatment. . . .

The great funeral banquet in particular was something Pennsylvania Germans looked forward to all their lives. In one grand debut, a simple farmer could make his mark in this world by leaving it. Tongues flapped, obituaries waxed poetic, and the Dutchman's soul, as one wag put it, was usually too soused to get into Heaven until after the vendue of his worldly goods.

WILLIAM WOYS WEAVER, SAUERKRAUT YANKEES (1983)

Fish House Punch

MAKES ABOUT 2 RATHER LETHAL QUARTS

Trader Vic made his name with an irreverent approach to tradition, but even he talked about this venerable punch in earnest tones, suggesting that anyone "without due regard for its historical significance should be made to stand in the corner for one hour with nothing but a bottle of Pepsi-Cola to comfort him." It's a concoction dreamed up by Philadelphia's famed fishing and cooking club, the State in Schuylkill, founded during the reign of George II in 1732. In *The Dictionary of American Food and Drink* (1994), John Mariani says the exclusive membership of thirty open every meeting with the punch and always close with a toast to George Washington, who reportedly dined at the club once and left so speechless that he ignored his diary for days.

- ¾ cup superfine sugar
- 1¾ to 2 cups fresh lime juice
- 1 quart light rum
- 1 cup good but not great cognac
- ¼ cup peach brandy
- A little more rum, cognac, or peach brandy, for good measure

Prepare the punch a few hours ahead of when you plan to serve it because "ripening" it at room temperature is considered important to its potency. Combine the sugar and the lime juice in a punch bowl or other large container. Stir to dissolve the sugar, then pour in the rum, cognac, brandy, and a cup of water. Give it another good splash of rum, cognac, or peach brandy as suits you. Let the punch sit for at least 2 hours and up to twice as long. Add ice, preferably an ice ring, and serve in punch cups.

Spiked Eggnog

SERVES 8 TO 12 OR MORE

Before we knew more than any of us wanted to about compromised immune systems, well-wishers used to prepare eggnog for the ill, often during the Christmas season. The use of uncooked eggs in the beverage makes it a poor choice for the sick, but for the hardy it remains a robust and warming winter drink. The bourbon and rum versions of today developed from a British toddy based on "nog," a strong ale.

- 6 eggs, separated
- ½ cup sugar
- 2 cups half-and-half
- 2 cups bourbon or other American whiskey or light rum
- ½ cup light rum
- 2 cups whipping cream
- Grated nutmeg

Beat the egg yolks and sugar together with an electric mixer over medium speed until light in color and texture. Continue beating as you pour in the half-and-half, bourbon, and rum.

In a separate bowl, beat the whipping cream for several minutes until it forms soft peaks. Beat the egg whites in another clean bowl with clean beaters until they form stiff, glossy peaks. Fold both into the egg yolk–liquor mixture. Refrigerate for 1 to 2 days to settle the eggnog.

Pour the eggnog into a punch bowl and serve chilled in cups, topped with nutmeg.

A Cup of Java

Europeans started drinking coffee about the time they settled North America, just a few decades before the East India Company introduced tea in England. The colonists drank both beverages by the turn of the eighteenth century, though high prices for the imported products limited consumption. First the Revolutionary War and then the War of 1812 turned the country increasingly toward coffee, simply because the British dominated the tea trade at the time.

As the cost of coffee dropped—with help from the nascent A&P chain—it became an American passion, as big as booze on the frontier and as acceptable as a soft drink to an urban teetotaler. We gave it the exotic nickname of "java," from the Indonesian source of some of the beans, and bragged on our brews as being "black as night, sweet as love, and hot as hell." Until the advent of the insidious electric percolator, virtually every cookbook delved into its secrets, treating it as "sheer black magic," in the words of Louis P. De Gouy. We now consume half of the world's supply of coffee, and though hurry-up methods of making it have seriously diluted the flavor and the aura in many cases, we still serve a better cup than the British.

Iced Tea

SERVES 2 TO 4

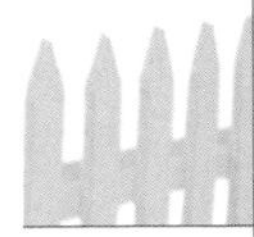

After the colonists threw that tax-tainted tea into the Boston harbor in 1773, patriotic Americans started shunning the beverage in favor of coffee. Tea consumption spiked again in the mid-nineteenth century, when people started drinking it cold and the Great Atlantic and Pacific Tea Company (later A&P) cut prices drastically. The idea of tea iced caught on slowly at first until electric refrigerators became common in kitchens decades later. Since then, it has become an American institution, as cherished a part of our heritage as that Tea Party long ago.

2 heaping tablespoons loose black tea, preferably orange pekoe, or 6 black tea bags (see Ingredient Tip)
Sugar, optional
Hefty lemon wedges
Fresh mint sprigs, optional

Place the tea or tea bags in a large teapot.

Pour 1 quart of fresh cold water into a tea kettle or saucepan. Bring the water to a vigorous boil. Just as soon as it boils, pour it immediately over the tea. Cover the teapot with its lid, and let the tea steep for about 5 minutes. The tea should get quite dark, since it will be diluted by a good bit of ice.

Discard the tea bags or, if you are using loose tea, strain it out before serving. Let the tea cool briefly at least. Pour it over ice into large tall glasses. Sweeten to taste, if you insist. Garnish with lemon wedges and, if available, mint sprigs.

INGREDIENT TIP: The American Classic Tea Company (843-559-0383) in South Carolina sells the only tea grown in the United States. Both tea bags and loose tea are available in a growing number of specialty food shops or by mail order. Among all the flavored teas made today—many just soda pop—we particularly like those from Paradise Tea and The Republic of Tea, both now widely distributed.

ICED TEA

Prepare tea in the morning, making it stronger and sweeter than usual; strain and pour into a clean stone jug or glass bottle, and set aside in the ice-chest until ready to use. Drink from goblets without cream. Serve ice broken in small pieces on a platter nicely garnished with well-washed grape-leaves. . . . [It] makes a delightful drink.

BUCKEYE COOKERY AND PRACTICAL HOUSEKEEPING (1880)

Sassafras Tea

MAKES 1 CUP

In the passion for herbal teas today, many people overlook sassafras tea, a related traditional beverage known in the Appalachias and elsewhere as a spring tonic. Contemporary cooks use sassafras primarily in the form of filé powder in Cajun and Creole dishes, but brewed in a warm drink it is perky both in flavor and pick-me-up power.

- 1 tablespoon or more dried sassafras-root pieces or ¼ to ½ teaspoon ground sassafras root
- Honey or sugar
- Cinnamon sticks, optional

Bring the sassafras just to a boil with 1 cup of water. Set aside to steep 1 to 2 minutes. Strain, add honey to taste, and serve like an herbal tea. (The ground root needs no straining.) Cheryl's great-grandmother would roll her eyes, but a cinnamon stick makes a festive stirrer and adds a bit of its own compatible flavor. The sassafras-root pieces, allowed to dry, can be used once or twice more, but will lose a bit in pungency with successive boilings.

Sassafras Beer

The same sassafras used to make tea was also the original root in root beer. Self-sufficient farm families boiled numerous wild and cultivated plants to extract their flavors for home brews, adding sugar and yeast for fermentation and carbonation. They controlled the alcohol content by bottling their beverages sooner or later in the fermentation process, allowing them to make a range of beers of varying strengths. Home-crafted root beers contained alcohol, but only in minimal amounts compared with the brews that fermented longer.

The earliest commercial root beers continued to rely on sassafras, but ultimately a laboratory rat ate too much of it and got sick, raising carcinogenic concerns. The FDA forbade its use in processed foods and drinks, but allowed natural foods and herbal stores to continue carrying it in a raw form for making tea and other purposes. For a rooty root beer today you have to return to the home-brewing tradition, which Stephen Cresswell explains adeptly in *Homemade Root Beer, Soda & Pop* (1998).

Lemonade

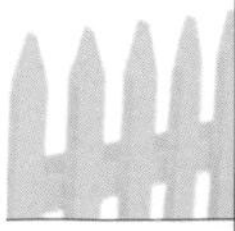

Serves 6 or more

The suffix "ade" simply denotes a fruit drink and Americans made plenty of them—from tamarind, rhubarb, apples, and oranges. None quenched the thirst quite like lemonade, the only antidote to a sweltering summer day.

1 cup sugar

2 cups fresh lemon juice (from about 10 medium lemons) (see Ingredient Tip)

Juice of 1 small orange

Lemon slices

Lemon verbena sprigs or fresh mint sprigs, optional

Boil the sugar together with 1 cup of water in a small saucepan for several minutes until the sugar dissolves and the liquid is clear. Cool briefly and then pour the syrup into a large pitcher. Stir in the lemon juice and orange juice. Add 3 to 4 cups of cold water, keeping in mind that the ice will further dilute the lemonade.

Pour the lemonade into tall glasses over ice. Garnish with lemon slices and, if you wish, lemon verbena. Drink up.

INGREDIENT TIP: To get the most juice from lemons, let them come to room temperature, if refrigerated, or set them in a sunny window. Before cutting the lemons, roll them around on a counter, using moderate pressure, to further stimulate the flow of juices.

Raspberry Switchel

Serves 2

The Graves family of Becket, Massachusetts, who sell their farm products under the Berkshire Berries label, introduced us to switchel, a vintage New England drink with the same refreshing powers as lemonade. Don't be put off by the vinegar base, which adds a zesty tartness rather than any bitterness. Some farmers like to spike the beverage with applejack, giving it an extra-sharp edge.

- ¼ cup raspberry vinegar (see Ingredient Tip)
- ¼ cup sugar or more to taste
- 1 teaspoon grated or minced fresh ginger
- 2 medium lemon wedges

Combine the vinegar, sugar, and ginger with 1 to 1½ cups of water or sparkling water. Refrigerate until very cold. Stir up from the bottom and serve in tall glasses over ice with lemon wedges.

INGREDIENT TIP: A distilled raspberry vinegar will make a tarter version of switchel than an infused variety, where the fruit has steeped in the vinegar to flavor it. Both types of vinegar yield good results, though a bit different. We especially enjoy switchel made with nationally distributed Consorzio raspberry vinegar, a very fruity infused product.

> **Beer is a good family drink. A handful of hops, to a pailful of water, and a half-pint of molasses, makes good hop beer. Spruce mixed with hops is pleasanter than hops alone. Boxberry, fever-bush, sweet fern, and horseradish make a good and healthy diet-drink.**
>
> Lydia Maria Child, The American Frugal Housewife (1832)

Indio Date Shake

Serves 2 to 4

The southern California burg of Indio, in the heart of the desert date country, put its stamp on this luscious version of the American milk shake. We like it by itself as a quick lunch or a hearty snack, not as an accompaniment to food.

- 1 cup chopped pitted dates, preferably Medjool
- 1 cup milk
- 3 cups premium vanilla ice cream or vanilla frozen yogurt, unthawed (see Ingredient Tip)

Combine the dates and the milk in a blender. Purée until smooth but with flecks of date throughout. Add the ice cream or yogurt, and again purée until smooth. Pour into tall glasses and serve with iced tea spoons.

INGREDIENT TIP: Using frozen yogurt instead of ice cream adds tang to the blend, balancing the honeyed richness of the dates.

Acknowledgments

ANY BOOK ON A SHARED TRADITION must share most of the credit. We're indebted in particular to the hundreds of cooks and commentators mentioned in the text and bibliography, but well beyond those people known to us, we owe our ability even to conceive this project to the countless Americans who shaped our common culinary legacy over the centuries past. We wrapped a few words around the food, but we received the food as a gift.

Some friends and colleagues participated more directly in our effort, giving guidance and support that helped mold the book. Among those, our editor, Harriet Bell, and our agent, Doe Coover, contributed in the broadest ways, embracing the concept from the beginning and believing in us in our moments of doubt. Culinary historian Sandra Oliver graciously provided detailed commentary on the manuscript, alerting us to numerous mistakes in our original draft. John Martin Taylor also read key sections of the manuscript and offered some provocative thoughts. All remaining errors of fact and deficiencies in perspective are entirely our own.

Dozens of librarians assisted us in our research. We're especially grateful to Dawn Letson, Ann Barton, and the rest of the staff in the Women's Collection at Texas Woman's University, and to Barbara Haber at the Schlesinger Library of Radcliffe College. The reference staff at the Santa Fe Public Library kept us correct on numerous details. Book lovers and sellers Jan Longone, Johan Mathiesen, and Greg Ohlsen searched for works we wanted to have at hand while we worked.

In research trips across the country, we got important help from Janie Hibler in the Pacific Northwest, Jacquie McMahan in California, and from Donna Jung and Cathy Pescaia Sharpe in Hawaii. In the South our many delightful guides included Ella Brennan and Ti Brennan Martin in New Orleans, John Martin Taylor and Sue Taylor Highfield in Charleston, Damon Lee Fowler and Jim King in Savannah, and Julie and John Brueggeman in North Carolina. We also gained perspective from the speakers at the University of Mississippi's 1998 Southern Foodways Symposium, particularly John Egerton, Betty Fussell, and Jessica Harris.

Betty Groff and Glenn and Karen Brendle gave us an inside peek at Pennsylvania Dutch country; and in New England, Ruth Bauer and Nina Simonds helped light our path. For navigators in the Midwest, we relied heavily on Patrick Geoghegan, Robin Perrine, Myrna and John Richard, and Cheryl's parents, Betty and M. M. Alters, who reminisced for us on everything from morels to milk cows.

We're always thankful for our local food suppliers, from the talented vendors at the Santa Fe Area Farmers' Market to friends who fish, forage, hunt, and grow foods that they share with us. The latter benefactors include Karen Berlanti, Lawry Babbitt, Rob Coffland, Stefan Dobusvynsky and Geoffrey Landis, Jana Edmondson, Gayther and Susie Gonzales, John Loehr, and Jim Neale. For farm produce and food advice alike, we seek out Lé Adams, Don and Blanca Bustos, Marion Carter and Ric Gaudet, Eremita and Margaret Campos, Stan and Rose Mary Crawford, David and Loretta Fresquez, the Harrison-Ingliss family, Kahsia Hartwell, Lynda Prim, Jake and Leona West, and many other New Mexico growers. Among commercial suppliers, we're grateful to Seva Dubuar at The Forager; Art Pacheco and his crew of meatcutters at Kaune's; Nancy Chavez at Albuquerque's Nantucket Shoals seafood market; Grace Graham and the MarketPlace gang; Susan and Nicole Curtis and the rest of the Santa Fe School of Cooking team; Shirley Pisacane, Robert Wichter, and the staff at Kokoman Circus; and Kathleen Craig, Ann Lower, and Michael McLaughlin at Cookworks.

Selected Bibliography

AN EXTRAORDINARY WEALTH of books exists on American home cooking. From just our family collection and the two much more extensive and professional collections at the Schlesinger Library of Radcliffe College and Texas Woman's University, we amassed a bibliography that runs on for fifty-one single-spaced pages, and that includes only works that inspired us to take notes. We cut that list severely to produce this selection, honed to the books we used the most and would recommend to others interested in a deeper immersion in the subject. We include culinary essays and historical tomes as well as cookbooks, but not the literary works or even some of the cookbooks quoted or cited in the preceding pages. The most general and comprehensive histories, unfortunately, tend to be the most speculative and unreliable, though they still deserve a look for broadening the boundaries of our perspective.

The American Heritage Cookbook and Illustrated History of American Eating & Drinking. New York: American Heritage Publishing, 1964.

Anderson, Jean. *The American Century Cookbook: The Most Popular Recipes of the 20th Century.* New York: Clarkson Potter, 1997.

———. *The Grass Roots Cookbook.* New York: Times Books, 1974.

[Andrews, Julie C.]. *Breakfast, Dinner, and Tea: Viewed Classically, Poetically, and Practically.* New York: Appleton and Company, 1865.

Barr, Nancy Verde. *We Called It Macaroni: An American Heritage of Southern Italian Cooking.* New York: Alfred A. Knopf, 1990.

Batchelder, Ann. *Ann Batchelder's Own Cook Book.* New York: M. Barrows & Company, 1949.

Beard, James. *Delights & Prejudices: The Autobiographical Journal of America's Most Noted Food Authority.* New York: Atheneum, 1964.

———. *James Beard's American Cookery.* Boston: Little, Brown and Company, 1972.

Beecher, Catharine. *Miss Beecher's Domestic Receipt Book.* New York: Harper & Brothers, 1849.

Berolzheimer, Ruth, ed. *The United States Regional Cook Book.* Chicago: Culinary Arts Institute, 1947.

Blot, Pierre. *Hand-Book of Practical Cookery.* 1867. Reprint, New York: Arno Press, 1973.

Brown, Cora, Rose, and Bob. *America Cooks.* New York: W. W. Norton & Co., 1940.

Brown, Dale. *American Cooking.* New York: Time-Life Books, 1968.

———. *American Cooking: The Northwest.* New York: Time-Life Books, 1970.

Brown, Helen Evans. *West Coast Cook Book.* 1952. Reprint, Cookbook Collectors Library, n.d.

Bryan, Lettice. *The Kentucky Housewife.* 1839. Reprint, Columbia, SC: University of South Carolina Press, 1991.

Buckeye Cookery and Practical Housekeeping. 1880. Reprint, St. Paul, MN: Minnesota Historical Society Press, 1988.

Callahan, Genevieve. *The New California Cook Book.* New York: M. Barrows & Company, 1955.

Carson, Jane. *Colonial Virginia Cookery.* Williamsburg, VA: Colonial Williamsburg Foundation, 1968.

Chadwick, Mrs. J. *Home Cookery.* 1852. Reprint, Birmingham, AL: Oxmoor House, 1984.

Child, Lydia Maria. *The American Frugal Housewife.* 1832. Reprint, Bedford, MA: Applewood Books, n.d.

Church of the Brethren. *The Inglenook Cook Book.* Elgin, IL: Brethren Publishing, 1911.

Claiborne, Craig. *A Feast Made for Laughter: A Memoir with Recipes.* New York: Holt, Rinehart and Winston, 1982.

Cleveland, Bess. *Alaskan Cookbook.* Berkeley, CA: Howell-North, 1960.

Coffin, Robert P. Tristram. *Mainstays of Maine.* New York: Macmillan Company, 1945.

Colquitt, Harriet Ross. *The Savannah Cook Book.* New York: Farrar & Rinehart, 1933.

Colwin, Laurie. *Home Cooking: A Writer in the Kitchen.* New York: HarperPerennial, 1988.

Cook, Margaret. *America's Charitable Cooks: A Bibliography of Fund-Raising Cook Books Published in the United States, 1861–1915.* Kent, OH: N.p., 1971.

Cornelius, Mrs. [Mary]. *The Young Housekeeper's Friend.* Boston: Whittemore, Niles, and Hall, 1856.

[Crowen, Mrs. T. J.]. *The American Lady's System of Cookery.* New York: Derby and Miller, 1852.

Cunningham, Marion. *The Fannie Farmer Cookbook.* New York: Bantam Books, 1990.

Cushing, C. H., and Mrs. B. Gray. *The Kansas Home Cook-book.* 1886. Reprint, New York: Arno Press, 1973.

Dean, Sidney W. *Cooking American.* New York: Hill and Wang, 1957.

De Gouy, Louis P. *The Gold Cook Book.* Philadelphia: Chilton Books, 1947.

Dull, Mrs. S. R. *Southern Cooking.* New York: Grosset & Dunlap, 1941.

Dupree, Nathalie. *New Southern Cooking.* New York: Alfred A. Knopf, 1986.

DuSablon, Mary Anna. *America's Collectible Cookbooks: The History, the Politics, the Recipes.* Athens, OH: Ohio University Press, 1994.

Early, Eleanor. *New England Cook Book.* New York: Random House, 1954.

Egerton, John. *Southern Food.* New York: Alfred A. Knopf, 1987.

———. *Side Orders.* Atlanta: Peachtree Publishers, 1990.

Farmer, Fannie Merritt. *The Boston Cooking-School Cook Book.* 1896. Reprint, Mineola, NY: Dover Publications, 1997.

Farr, Sidney Saylor. *More than Moonshine.* Pittsburgh: University of Pittsburgh Press, 1983.

Farrington, Doris. *Fireside Cooks & Black Kettle Recipes.* Indianapolis: Bobbs-Merrill Company, 1976.

Fisher, Abby. *What Mrs. Fisher Knows about Old Southern Cooking*. 1881. Reprint, Bedford, MA: Applewood Books, 1995.

Fisher, M.F.K. *The Art of Eating*. New York: Vintage Books, 1976. Five books in one: *Serve It Forth* (1937); *Consider the Oyster* (1941); *How to Cook a Wolf* (1942); *The Gastronomical Me* (1943); and *An Alphabet for Gourmets* (1949).

———. *With Bold Knife and Fork*. New York: Smithmark, 1968.

Fowler, Damon Lee. *Classical Southern Cooking*. New York: Crown Publishers, 1995.

Frederick, J. George. *The Pennsylvania Dutch Cook Book*. 1935. Reprint, New York: Dover Publishing, 1971.

———. *Long Island Seafood Cook Book*. 1939. Reprint, New York: Dover Publishing, 1971.

Fussell, Betty. *I Hear America Cooking*. New York: Viking, 1986.

———. *Masters of American Cookery*. New York: Times Books, 1983.

———. *The Story of Corn*. New York: Alfred A. Knopf, 1992.

Given, Meta. *Modern Encyclopedia of Cooking*. Chicago: J. G. Ferguson Publishing Company, 1959.

Glenn, Camille. *The Heritage of Southern Cooking*. New York: Workman Publishing, 1986.

Greene, Bert. *Honest American Fare*. Chicago: Contemporary Books, 1981.

Groff, Betty. *Betty Groff's Pennsylvania Dutch Cookbook*. New York: Galahad Books, 1990.

Grosvenor, Vertamae. *Vibration Cooking*. New York: Ballantine Books, 1970.

Hachten, Harva. *The Flavor of Wisconsin*. Madison, WI: State Historical Society of Wisconsin, 1981.

Hale, Mrs. Sarah Josepha. *The Good Housekeeper*. 1841. Reprint, Mineola, NY: Dover Publications, 1996.

———. *Mrs. Hale's Receipts for the Millions*. Philadelphia: T. B. Peterson, 1857.

Harland, Marion. *Common Sense in the Household*. New York: Charles Scribner's Sons, 1871.

———. *Marion Harland's Complete Cook Book*. Indianapolis: Bobbs-Merrill Company, 1906.

Harris, Jessica B. *The Welcome Table: African-American Heritage Cooking*. New York: Simon & Schuster, 1995.

Hearn, Lafcadio. *Lafcadio Hearn's Creole Cook Book*. 1885, under the original title *La Cuisine Créole*. Reprint, Gretna, LA: Pelican Publishing, 1967.

Heatter, Maida. *Maida Heatter's Book of Great American Desserts*. New York: Alfred A. Knopf, 1985.

Hess, John and Karen. *The Taste of America*. New York: Penguin Books, 1977.

Hess, Karen. *The Carolina Rice Kitchen: The African Connection*. Columbia, SC: University of South Carolina Press, 1992.

Hess, Karen, ed. *Martha Washington's Booke of Cookery and Booke of Sweetmeats*. N.d. Reprint with extensive commentary, New York: Columbia University Press, 1981.

Heth, Edward Harris. *Wisconsin Country Cookbook and Journal.* 1956, under the original title *The Wonderful World of Cooking.* Reprint, Madison, WI: Tamarack Press, 1979.

Hibben, Sheila. *American Regional Cookery.* New York: Gramercy Publishing Company, 1946. Taken largely from *The National Cookbook,* below.

———. *The National Cookbook: A Kitchen Americana.* New York: Harper & Brothers, 1932.

Hibler, Janie. *Dungeness Crabs and Blackberry Cobblers: The Northwest Heritage Cookbook.* New York: Alfred A. Knopf, 1991.

———. *Wild About Game.* New York: Broadway Books, 1998.

Hill, Annabella P. *Mrs. Hill's Southern Practical Cookery and Receipt Book.* 1872. Reprint, Columbia, SC: University of South Carolina Press, 1995.

Hooker, Richard J. *Food and Drink in America: A History.* Indianapolis: Bobbs-Merrill Company, 1981.

Ingle, Schuyler, and Sharon Kramis. *Northwest Bounty.* New York: Simon & Schuster, 1988.

Jones, Evan. *American Food: The Gastronomic Story.* New York: Vintage Books, 1974.

Junior League of Charleston. *Charleston Receipts.* Charleston, SC: Walker Evans & Cogswell Co., 1950.

Kander, Lizzie Black, and Mrs. Henry Schoenfeld. *The Way to a Man's Heart: "The Settlement" Cook Book.* 1903. Reprint, Bedford, MA: Applewood Books, 1996.

Kaufman, Edna, ed. *Melting Pot of Mennonite Cookery, 1874–1974.* North Newton, KS: Bethel College Women's Association, 1974.

Kent, Louise A., and Elizabeth Kent Gray. *Cooking with Mrs. Appleyard.* New Canaan, CT: Keats Publishing, 1993. Three books in one: *Mrs. Appleyard's Kitchen* (1942); *Mrs. Appleyard's Summer Kitchen* (1957); and *Mrs. Appleyard's Winter Kitchen* (1962).

King, Irene. *Culinary Gems from the Kitchens of Old Virginia.* New York: Dodd, Mead & Company, 1952.

Ladies Auxiliary of the Homestead Welfare Club. *A Collection of Traditional Amana Recipes.* Homestead, IA: N.p., 1948.

Laudan, Rachel. *The Food of Paradise.* Honolulu: University of Hawaii Press, 1996.

Leonard, Jonathan Norton. *American Cooking: The Great West.* New York: Time-Life Books, 1971.

Leslie, Eliza. *Directions for Cookery.* 1837. Reprint of 1848 edition, New York: Arno Press, 1973.

———. *Miss Leslie's New Cookery Book.* Philadelphia: T. B. Peterson, 1857.

———. *Seventy-five Receipts for Pastry, Cakes, and Sweetmeats.* Boston: C. S. Francis, 1828.

Levenstein, Harvey. *Paradox of Plenty: A Social History of Eating in Modern America.* New York: Oxford University Press, 1993.

———. *Revolution at the Table: The Transformation of the American Diet.* New York: Oxford University Press, 1988.

Lewis, Edna. *The Taste of Country Cooking.* New York: Alfred A. Knopf, 1977.

Lincoln, Mary J. *Boston Cooking School Cook Book.* 1884, under the original title *Mrs. Lincoln's Boston Cook Book.* Reprint, Mineola, NY: Dover Publications, 1996.

Longone, Janice B., and Daniel T. *American Cookbooks and Wine Books, 1797–1950.* Ann Arbor, MI: N.p., 1984.

Lovegren, Sylvia. *Fashionable Food: Seven Decades of Food Fads.* New York: Macmillan, 1995.

Lowenstein, Eleanor. *Bibliography of American Cookery Books, 1742–1860.* Worcester, MA: American Antiquarian Society, 1972.

Lukins, Sheila. *U.S.A. Cookbook.* New York: Workman Publishing, 1997.

Madison, Deborah. *America: The Vegetarian Table.* San Francisco: Chronicle Books, 1996.

Mariani, John. The *Dictionary of American Food and Drink.* New York: Hearst Books, 1994.

Maryland's Way. Annapolis, MD: Hammond-Harwood House Association, 1963.

McCulloch-Williams, Martha. *Dishes and Beverages of the Old South.* New York: McBride, Nast & Company, 1913.

McLaren, L. L., ed. *High Living: Recipes from Southern Climes.* San Francisco: Paul Elder and Company, 1904.

McMahan, Jacqueline Higuera. *California Rancho Cooking.* Lake Hughes, CA: Olive Press, 1988.

Miller, Amy Bess, and Persis Fuller. *The Best of Shaker Cooking.* New York: Collier Books, 1985.

Mosser, Marjorie. *Good Maine Food.* New York: Doubleday, Doran & Co., 1939.

Nathan, Joan. *Jewish Cooking in America.* New York: Alfred A. Knopf, 1994.

National Council of Negro Women. *The Black Family Reunion Cookbook: Recipes and Food Memories.* Memphis, TN: Tradery House, 1991.

Neal, Bill. *Bill Neal's Southern Cooking.* Chapel Hill, NC: University of North Carolina Press, 1985.

———. *Biscuits, Spoonbread, and Sweet Potato Pie.* New York: Alfred A. Knopf, 1990.

Oliver, Sandra L. *Saltwater Foodways: New Englanders and Their Food, at Sea and Ashore, in the 19th Century.* Mystic, CT: Mystic Seaport Museum, 1995.

O'Neill, Molly. *The New York Cookbook.* New York: Workman Publishing, 1992.

Paddleford, Clementine. *How America Eats.* New York: Charles Scribner's Sons, 1960.

Parloa, Maria. *Miss Parloa's Appledore Cook Book.* Boston: DeWolfe, Fiske and Company, 1877.

———. *Miss Parloa's Kitchen Companion.* Boston: Estes and Lauriat, 1887.

Pellegrini, Angelo. *The Unprejudiced Palate.* 1948. Reprint, San Francisco: North Point Press, 1984.

The Picayune's Creole Cook Book. 1901. Reprint, New York: Dover Publications, 1993.

Pixley, Aristene. *The Green Mountain Cook Book.* Brattleboro, VT: Stephen Daye, 1934.

Platt, June. *The June Platt Cook Book.* New York: Alfred A. Knopf, 1958.

Porter, Mrs. M. F. *Mrs. Porter's New Southern Cookery Book.* 1871. Reprint, New York: Arno Press, 1973.

Putnam, Mrs. E. *Mrs. Putnam's Receipt Book.* Boston: Ticknor, Reed, and Fields, 1849.

Randolph, Mary. *The Virginia Housewife: or Methodical Cook.* 1824. Reprint of 1860 edition, New York: Dover Publications, 1993.

Rawlings, Marjorie Kinnan. *Cross Creek Cookery.* New York: Simon & Schuster, 1942.

Rector, George. *Dine at Home with Rector: A Book on What Men Like, Why They Like It, and How to Cook It.* New York: E. P. Dutton & Co, 1934.

Rhett, Blanche. *200 Years of Charleston Cooking.* New York: Harrison Smith & Robert Haas, 1930.

Rombauer, Irma. *Joy of Cooking.* Indianapolis: Bobbs-Merrill Company, 1943.

Root, Waverly, and Richard de Rochemont. *Eating in America: A History.* New York: Ecco Press, 1976.

Rorer, Sarah Tyson. *Mrs. Rorer's New Cook Book.* Philadelphia: Arnold and Company, 1902.

———. *Philadelphia Cook Book.* Philadelphia: George H. Buchanan and Company, 1886.

Rutledge, Sarah. *The Carolina Housewife.* 1847. Reprint, Columbia, SC: University of South Carolina Press, 1979.

Schulz, Phillip Stephen. *As American as Apple Pie.* New York: Simon & Schuster, 1990.

Scott, Natalie. *200 Years of New Orleans Cooking.* New York: Jonathan Cape & Harrison Smith, 1931.

Shapiro, Laura. *Perfection Salad: Women and Cooking at the Turn of the Century.* New York: Henry Holt and Company, 1986.

Shields, John. *Chesapeake Bay Cooking with John Shields.* New York: Broadway Books, 1998.

Showalter, Mary Emma. *Mennonite Community Cookbook.* Scottdale, PA: Herald Press, 1950.

Shute, Miss T. S. *The American Housewife Cook Book.* Philadelphia: George T. Lewis and Menzies Company, 1880.

Simmons, Amelia. *American Cookery.* 1796. Reprint, Bedford, MA: Applewood Books, 1996.

Smith, Grace and Beverly, and Charles Morrow Wilson. *Through the Kitchen Door.* New York: Stackpole Sons, 1938.

Sokolov, Raymond. *Fading Feast: A Compendium of Disappearing American Regional Foods.* New York: E. P. Dutton, 1983.

Spencer, Evelene, and John Cobb. *Fish Cookery.* Boston: Little Brown and Company, 1927.

Stern, Jane and Michael. *American Gourmet.* New York: HarperPerennial, 1991.

Stevens, Rose Budd. *From Rose Budd's Kitchen.* Jackson, MS: University of Mississippi Press, 1988.

Stieff, Frederick. *Eat, Drink & Be Merry in Maryland.* New York: G. P. Putnam's Sons, 1932.

Szathmary, Louis, ed. *Along the Northern Border: Cookery in Idaho, Minnesota, and North Dakota.* New York: Arno Press, 1973. Three books in one: *Choice Recipes by Moscow Women* (Moscow, ID, 1931); *Library Ann's Cook Book* (Minneapolis, 1928); and *Y.M.C.A. Cook Book* (Grand Forks, ND, 1924).

———, ed. *Fifty Years of Prairie Cooking.* New York: Arno Press, 1973. Four books in one: *A Collection of Choice Recipes* (Des Moines, IA, 1903); *Dorcas Cook Book*

(Sioux City, IA, 1939); *Patriotic Food Show* (St. Louis, MO, 1918); and *Priscilla Cook Book* (Overton, NE, 1954).

———, ed. *Midwestern Home Cookery.* New York: Promontory Press, 1974. Two books in one: *Presbyterian Cook Book* (Dayton, OH, 1875) and *Capital City Cook Book* (Madison, WI, 1906).

———, ed. *Southwestern Cooking: Indian and Spanish Influences.* New York: Arno Press, 1973. Five books in one: *Favorite Recipes of Colfax County Club Women* (Colfax County, NM, 1946); *The Garfield Woman's Club Cook Book* (Garfield, UT, 1916); *Choctaw Indian Dishes* (Tuskahoma, OK, 1955); *The Indian Cook Book* (Tulsa, OK, 1933); and *The Junior League of Dallas Cook Book* (Dallas, n.d.).

Tartan, Beth. *North Carolina & Old Salem Cookery.* Chapel Hill, NC: University of North Carolina Press, 1992).

Tatum, Billy Joe. *Billy Joe Tatum's Wild Foods Cookbook & Field Guide.* New York: Workman Publishing, 1976.

Taylor, John Martin. *Hoppin' John's Lowcountry Cooking.* New York: Bantam Books, 1992.

———. *The New Southern Cook.* New York: Bantam Books, 1995.

Thorne, John. *Outlaw Cook.* New York: North Point Press, 1992.

———. *Serious Pig: An American Cook in Search of His Roots.* New York: North Point Press, 1996.

———. *Simple Cooking.* New York: Penguin Books, 1987.

Vaughan, Beatrice. *Yankee Hill-Country Cooking.* Brattleboro, VT: Stephen Greene Press, 1963.

Villas, James. *American Taste: A Celebration of Gastronomy Coast-to-Coast.* New York: Arbor House, 1982.

———. *Stews, Bogs & Burgoos: Recipes from the Great American Stewpot.* New York: William Morrow and Company, 1997.

Voltz, Jeanne. *The Flavor of the South.* New York: Gramercy Publishing, 1977.

———, and Caroline Stuart. *The Florida Cookbook: From Gulf Coast Gumbo to Key Lime Pie.* New York: Alfred A. Knopf, 1993.

Walter, Eugene. *American Cooking: Southern Style.* New York: Time-Life Books, 1971.

Weaver, William Woys, ed. *A Quaker Woman's Cookbook; The* Domestic Cookery *of Elizabeth Ellicott Lea.* 1856. Reprint with extensive commentary, Philadelphia: University of Pennsylvania Press, 1982.

———. *Heirloom Vegetable Gardening.* New York: Henry Holt and Company, 1997.

———. *Pennsylvania Dutch Country Cooking.* New York: Abbeville Press, 1993.

———. *Sauerkraut Yankees.* Philadelphia: University of Pennsylvania Press, 1983.

[Webster, Mrs. A. L.]. *The Improved Housewife.* 1845. Reprint, New York: Arno Press, 1973.

Williams, Jacqueline. *The Way We Ate: Pacific Northwest Cooking, 1843–1900.* Pullman, WA: Washington State University Press, 1996.

Wilson, José. *American Cooking: The Eastern Heartland.* New York: Time-Life Books, 1971.

Wolcott, Imogene B. *The New England Yankee Cook Book.* New York: Coward-McCann, 1939.

Ziemann, Hugo, and Mrs. F. L. Gillette. *The White House Cookbook.* 1898. Reprint, New York: Smithmark, 1995.

Index

African-American influence in American home cooking, 8, 36, 115, 149, 279, 319
Alabama Fried Catfish Sandwich, 58
Alaskan Cookbook (Cleveland), 343
Alciatore, Jules, 67
Alice, Let's Eat (Trillin), 91, 170
Allen, Ida Bailey, 159
Almond (Pie) Crust, 364–65
Alters, Betty, 205
Amendola, Joseph, 371
America Cooks (Brown, Brown & Brown), 45, 69, 205, 246, 362
American Century Cookbook, The (Anderson), 106, 404
American Cookbooks and Wine Books (Longone & Longone), 383
American Cookery (Simmons), 19, 359, 399
American cooking, 2–3
  backyard cooking, 12. *See also* Outdoor Grilling
  breakfast cereal, 11
  contemporary, 12–13
  corn and, 7, 8
  food processing industry, 10
  hearth for, 3, 6
  history, colonial, 5–9
  home cooking defined, 2, 3
  praise for, 419
  preserves and putting food up, 288
  regional and cultural diversity, 7–9
  science and technological influences, 9–11
  supermarkets, 270
  TV chefs, 282
American Cooking: The Eastern Heartland (Wilson), 28
American Cooking: The Great West (Leonard), 209
American Cooking: The Northwest, 128
American Cooking: Southern Style (Walter), 248
American Food (Jones), 173
American Friend (Trillin), 123
American Frugal Housewife, The (Child), 43, 137, 198, 312, 379, 436
American Housewife Cook Book, The (Shute), 310
American Lady's System of Cookery, The (Crowen), 68
American Regional Cookery (Hibben), 3
American Table, The (Johnson), 183
American Taste (Villas), 119, 415
Anderson, Jean, 106, 367, 404
Angel Food Cake with Boiled Custard, 402–3
Appetizers
  Bacon-Horseradish Dip, 78
  Boiled Peanuts, 84
  Cajun Crawfish Balls, 71
  Calcuttas, 79
  Cheese Straws, 83
  Chopped Chicken Liver, 75
  Deviled Eggs, 82
  Ham Biscuits, 80–81
  history, 65–66, 67, 68
  Honolulu Poke, 72
  Marinated Salmon Bits, 73
  Olympia Oyster-Stuffed Mushrooms, 68
  Pico de Callo, 77
  Prairie Fire Dip, 76
  Salted Green Soybeans, 85
  Scalloped Oysters, 67
  Shrimp Cocktail, 69
  Shrimp Rémoulade, 70
  Smoked Trout Spread, 74
  surf and turf cocktails, history, 69
Apple
  Baked, with, -Glazed Bacon, 42–43
  boiled-down cider, buying, 185
  Butter, 289
  Caramel, 422
  cider, buying tip, 128
  Cider-Baked City Ham, 174–75
  -Cranberry Pie, 362–63
  Crisp, 380
  and ham, 174
  Pandowdy, 382
  Sweet Potato-, Sauce, 184–85
Applejack
  buying, 426
  Stone Fence, 426

Arizona
Chile Verde, 190
Chimichanga, 206–7
Artichokes
California Fettuccine with, and Garlic, 338
New Orleans, 253
Veal Francese, 233
Asian influences in American cooking, 9, 72, 133, 150, 158, 252, 324, 334
Asparagus, Skillet, 254
Autobiography of Mark Twain, The (Neider, ed.), 51, 222, 352

Bacon
Baked Apples with Apple-Glazed, 42–43
BLT or BCLT with green tomatoes, 246
buying tip and source for, 43
Calcuttas, 79
Denver (Western) Sandwich, 60
Georgia Bits and Grits Waffles, 17
Greens with Pot Liquor, 260
-Horseradish Dip, 78
Santa Fe Breakfast Burritos, 41
Summer's Best BLT, 49
Wilted Greens with Hot, Dressing, 256
Bagels, 35
Baked Apples with Apple-Glazed Bacon, 42–43
Baked Cranberry Sauce, 297
Baked Ham and Cauliflower Casserole, 171
Baked Vidalia Onions, 284
Banana
Calcuttas, 79
history, 388
Pudding, 388
Barbecue(d)
Bandera, Sauce, 202–3
Beer Mop, 202–3
Dry Rub, 202–3
Kansas City Sugar-and-Spice Spareribs, 186–87
Marinade, 121
Mississippi, Chicken, 154
Mop, 52–53
Piedmont Country 'Q, 52–53
Sauces, 52–53, 154, 186
Shrimp, 121
Texas, Brisket, 202–3
Barr, Nancy Verde, 338
Basil Mayonnaise, 49
Batchelder, Ann, 213
Beach Plum Jam, 292
Beans, dried
Boston Baked, 276
Camellia red, buying, 277
Hoppin' John, 319
Picante Pintos, 278
Prairie Fire Dip, 76
Red Beans and Rice, 277
soaking versus not soaking, 101
soup, history, 102
Spanish Bean Soup, 101
Springfield Chilli, 215
Stewed Black-eyed Peas, 279
Texas Caviar, 280
Beard, James, 4, 12, 60, 76, 77, 88, 266, 282
Beecher, Catharine, 346, 403
Beef
Boliche, 204
Bowl of Red (chili), 214
Chicken-Fried Steak, 208–9
Chimichanga, 206–7
Classic Backyard Burger, 50–51
corning, 198
Glaze, 200
Glazed Corned, 200
Grilled T-bone with Horseradish Butter, 196–97
ground chuck, tip on, 51
history, 193–94, 204
Meat Loaf, 216
New England Boiled Dinner, 198–99
Pan-Fried Rib Eye, 195
Pot Roast with Root Vegetables, 201
Red Flannel Hash, 37
skirt steak, buying, 211
smoking brisket, 203
Springfield Chilli, 215
steak, buying and mail source, 195
Stew with Savory Popovers, 212–13
Swiss Steak, 205
Texas Barbecued Brisket, 202–3
Vaquero Fajitas, 210–11
Beer
in America, 436
Mop, 202–3
Beets
mixing types for color, 304
Red Flannel Hash, 37
"Red Turnip" Pickles, 304
Bell, Harriet, 208
Benedictine Spread, 64
Bennell, Julie, 408

Best Loved Recipes of the American People (Allen), 159
Best of Shaker Cooking, The (Miller & Fuller), 232
Between Meals (Liebling), 197
Beverages
  alcoholic, 423–24, 430
  beer, 436
  Cherry Shrub, 425
  coffee, drinking in America, 432
  Dry Martini, 427
  Fish House Punch, 431
  Fresh Fruit Smoothie, 44
  Home-Steeped Southern Succor, 430
  Iced Tea, 433
  Indio Date Shake, 437
  Lemonade, 435
  Mint Julep, 428
  Orange Sangaree, 429
  Raspberry Switchel, 436
  Sassafras Tea, 434
  soft drinks, 424
  Spiked Eggnog, 432
  Stone Fence, 426
Beverly, Robert, 109, 143
Bienvenu, Marcelle, 366
Bierce, Ambrose, 182, 281, 345, 425
Biscochitos, 415
Biscuits
  about American, 348, 349
  Buttermilk, with Country Ham and Red-eye Gravy, 32–33
  Buttermilk Benne, 80–81
  Cream, 348
  flour for, buying/source, 81
  Shortcakes, 386–87
  'Simmon, 349
  technique tip, 81
Biscuits, Spoonbread, and Sweet Potato Pie (Neal), 401
Blackberry
  Catahoula Sweet-Dough Pies, 366–67
  Cobbler, 379
  Jam, 291
  Sauce, 155
Blot, Pierre, 370
Blueberry(-ies)
  Down East, Toast and Butter Pudding, 390
  wild, 390
Blue-Flower Featherbed, 30
Boiled Peanuts, 84
Boliche, 204
Boston
  Baked Beans, 276
  Brown Bread, 346
Boston Cooking School Cook Book, The (Farmer), 17, 60, 102, 215, 360
Bourbon
  -and-Butter Pecan Pie, 372–73
  history, 428
  Mint Julep, 428
  Spiked Eggnog, 432
Bourque, Emma Lou, 366
Bowl of Red (chili), A, 214
Bowl of Red, A (Tolbert), 214
Bran-Date Muffins, 31
Brandy, 424
  California Brandied Dates, 330
  Cherry Shrub, 425
Bread. *See also* Biscuits; Cornmeal
  Boston Brown, 346
  Caramel Pecan Sticky Buns, 356–57
  Crusty San Francisco Sourdough, 341–43
  Dinner Rolls, 350–51
  home making, 339–40
  Maui Mango, 358
  Multi-Grain, 344–45
  New Orleans, Pudding, 389
  piki bread, about, 353
  Rice, 354–55
  short list of American favorite fried, 355
  sourdough starter, 343
  sourdough technique tip, 341
  toasting, 35
  yeast tip, 345
Bread and Butter Pickles, 305
Breakfast
  about American, 15–16, 27–28, 44–45
  Baked Apples with Apple-Glazed Bacon, 42–43
  Blue-Flower Featherbed, 30
  Bran-Date Muffins, 31
  Buckwheats, 24–25
  Buttermilk Biscuits with Country Ham and Red-eye Gravy, 32–33
  Buttermilk Flapjacks with Warm Fruit Sauce, 20–21
  French Quarter Veal Grillades, 40
  Fresh Fruit Smoothie, 44
  Fried Cornmeal Mush with Sorghum Syrup, 36
  Georgia Bits and Grits Waffles, 17

Breakfast (*cont.*)
Minnesota Breakfast Cereal of Wild Rice and Oatmeal, 45
Narragansett Jonnycakes, 18–19
Red Flannel Hash, 37
Rice and Cornmeal Griddle Cakes with Nutmeg Syrup, 22–23
Santa Fe Breakfast Burritos, 41
Shirred Eggs with Indiana Farm Breakfast Sausage, 26–27
South Carolina Shrimp and Grits, 38–39
Tex-Mex Migas, 29
Traverse City Cherry French Toast, 34–35
Weatherberry Scramble, 28
Brendle, Glenn, 289
Brennan, Ella, 277
Brennan, Ralph and Cindy, 121
British influence on American cooking, 5, 7, 79, 100, 102, 127, 128, 144, 192, 193, 314, 335, 360, 397
Broccoli-Rice Casserole, 255
Broiled Petrale Fillets, 137
Brown, Cora, Rose, and Bob, 45, 60, 69, 205, 246, 362
Brown, Helen Evans, 68
Brownies, Hot Fudge, 413
frosting tip, 413
Brown Oyster Stew with Benne, 96
Brunn, Gustav C., 111
Brunswick Stew with Rabbit, 228
Bryan, Lettice, 73, 130, 282, 378, 397
Buckeye Cookery and Practical Housekeeping, 199, 295, 433
Buckner, S. B., Jr., 429
Buckwheats, 24–25
Burritos, Santa Fe Breakfast, 41
Burt, Mrs. C. C., 208
Butter Beans, Fresh, 248. *See also* Lima Beans
Buttermilk
-Bathed Pan-Fried Chicken, 142–43
Benne Biscuits, 80–81
Biscuits with Country Ham and Red-eye Gravy, 32–33
Cast-Iron-Baked, Cornbread, 352
Flapjacks with Warm Fruit Sauce, 20–21
Byrd, William, 173

Cabbage
Coleslaw, 282
New England Boiled Dinner, 198–99
Sandwich Coleslaw, 52–53
Stewed, 281
Cahn, Joe, 389
Cajun cooking, 8
Crawfish Balls, 71
Crawfish Étouffée, 122–23
Cake
Angel Food, with Boiled Custard, 402–3
butter-sugar creaming technique, 407
Carrot, 410–11
Cornmeal Pound, 397
Devil's Food, with Chocolate Butter Frosting, 406–7
Edwardian extravagance, 401
egg whites, using, 403
extracts, tip, 399
frosting technique, 400
German Chocolate, 408–9
Ginger Pear Upside-Down, 404–5
Hartford Election, 398–99
history of, in American cooking, 395–96, 403
Hot Fudge Brownies, 413
Lady Baltimore, with Seven-Minute Frosting, 400–401
Okracoke Fig, 412
steps to remember in making, 408
Calabacitas, New Mexico, 239
Calcuttas, 79
Calico Corn Relish, 312
California
Brandied Dates, 330
Conejo, 227
Crusty San Francisco Sourdough, 341–43
Fettuccine with Artichokes and Garlic, 338
Fishermen's Mussels, 117
Onion and Olive Enchiladas, 285
California Rancho Cooking (McMahan), 285
Callahan, Genevieve, 102
Campbell, Joseph, 10, 88
Candied Grapefruit Peel, 421
Candied Sweet Potatoes, 274
Candies
Candied Grapefruit Peel, 421
Caramel Apples, 422
Divinity, 420
Double Chocolate Fudge, 418–19
Cane syrup, buying/source, 373

Cantaloupe Pickles, Gingered, 301
Caramel
Apples, 422
Pecan Sticky Buns, 356–57
Carolina. *See also* Charleston; North Carolina; South Carolina
Gold (rice), about, 321
Red Rice, 326
Carolina Housewife, The (Rutledge), 73, 326
Carolina Rice Kitchen, The (Hess), 319
Carrot
Cake, 410–11
Pot Roast with Root Vegetables, 201
Carver, George Washington, 48
Cast-Iron-Baked Buttermilk Cornbread, 352
Catahoula Sweet-Dough Pies, 366–67
Catfish
Alabama Fried Sandwich, 58
Crunchy, with Heavenly Hush Puppies, 130–31
Cauliflower Casserole, Baked Ham and, 171
Cereal
history of, in America, 11
Minnesota Breakfast, of Wild Rice and Oatmeal, 45
Charleston, 8
Benne Chicken, 157
Lady Baltimore Cake with Seven-Minute Frosting, 400–401
Scarlet Pepper Jelly, 290
She-Crab Soup, 91
Charleston Receipts (Junior League), 73, 91, 290
Chaurice with Tomato Gravy, 191
Cheese
American-made, 82
Benedictine Spread, 64
BLT or BCLT with green tomatoes, 246
Blue-Flower Featherbed, 30
Broccoli-Rice Casserole, 255
buying/source for Cheddar, 100
buying/source for Crowley, 62
Cheddar (Pie) Crust, 362–63
Creamy Jalapeño Spinach, 264
Golden Grilled, 62
Grits, 328
Macaroni and Wisconsin, Sauce, 335
Maytag Blue Dressing, 258–59
Onion and Olive Enchiladas, 285
Oregon Hot Crab and Cheddar Sandwich, 57
Pea Salad, 263
Pimiento, Sandwich, 63
Prairie Fire Dip, 76
Rutabaga-Colby, Casserole, 283
Santa Fe Breakfast Burritos, 41
sapsago, 180
sauces, 57, 171
Sour Braised Loin with Cherries, 180
Straws, 83
Tex-Mex Migas, 29
Twice Baked Potatoes, 271
Wisconsin, Soup, 100
Yellow Squash Casserole, 249
Cherry(-ies)
Door County Sour, Pie, 364–65
Sauce, 166–67
Shrub, 425
Sour Braised Loin with, 180
Sweet and Sour, 180
Traverse City, French Toast, 34–35
Chesapeake Bay
Blue Crab Cakes, 110–11
Ham and Oyster Pie, 176–77
Chesapeake Bay Cooking (Shields), 247
Chestnuts
Roast Chicken with Nut Sauce, 148–49
Sweet Potato-, Purée, 275
Chicken
Breasts Stuffed with Smithfield Ham, 156
Buttermilk-Bathed Pan-Fried Chicken, 142–43
buying/source for premium, 151
Charleston Benne, 157
Chopped, Liver, 75
Chop Suey, 158
Chow-Chow, Salad, 159
and Dumplings, 146–47
fat (schmaltz) preparation and use, 75
Fricassee over Cornbread Toast, 141
frying and seasoning tips, 143, 149
Georgia Country Captain, 151
history of, in America, 140
King Ranch, 152–53
Lancaster County, -Corn Soup, 98–99
Long Rice, 150
Mississippi Barbecued, 154
Pie, 144–45
Roast, with Nut Sauce, 148–49
Willamette Valley Grilled, with Blackberry Sauce, 155

Chicken-Fried Steak, 208–9
Chickpeas
  Spanish Bean Soup, 101
Chicos, 330
Child, Julia, 12, 282
Child, Lydia Maria, 43, 137, 198, 312, 379, 436
Chile(s)
  Arizona, Verde, 190
  buying/source for, 189
  Calico Corn Relish, 312
  Chimichanga, 206–7
  Creamy Jalapeño Spinach, 264
  Green, sauce, 41
  Hawaii Chili Pepper Water, 315
  Jalapeño Cornbread, 353
  King Ranch Chicken, 152–53
  New Mexico Calabacitas, 239
  Onion and Olive Enchiladas, 285
  Pico de Callo, 77
  Prairie Fire Dip, 76
  Pueblo Lamb Stew with Green, and Posole, 231
  sauce, 189
  Scarlet Pepper Jelly, 290
Chili
  A Bowl of Red, 214
  molé, buying, 214
  Springfield Chilli, 215
  Venison, 223
Chimayó Carne Adovada, 189
Chimichanga, 206–7
Chives
  Blue-Flower Featherbed, 30
Chocolate
  Chip-Oatmeal Cookies, 416
  Devil's Food Cake with, Butter Frosting, 406–7
  Double, Fudge, 418–19
  German, Cake, 408–9
  Hot Fudge Brownies, 413
  microwave melting, 419
Chopped Chicken Liver, 75
Chop Suey, Chicken, 158
Chow-Chow, 310–11
  caramelizing sugar for, 311
  Chicken Salad, 159
Chowder
  history, 89
  Landlubbers Cod, 90
  New England Clam, 89
  Summer Corn, 105
Chutney
  Peach, 80–81
  Pear, 172–73
  Tomato, 296
Cider-Baked City Ham, 174–75
Cioppino, 92–93
Claiborne, Craig, 153, 328
Clam(s)
  Cioppino, 92–93
  clambake, revival of, 116
  and Garlic Sauce, 188
  juice, use of, 96
  New England, Chowder, 89
  Old Sour Seafood Salad, 124–25
  Posillipo, 116
  tip, using for chowder, 89
Clambake (Newstadt), 116
Classical Southern Cooking (Fowler), 84, 335
Classic Thanksgiving Turkey with Sage Dressing, 162–64
Cleveland, Bess, 343
Cobblers
  Blackberry, 379
  Peach, 378
Cocktail sauce, 69
Cocktail snacks, 66, 75, 77. *See also* Appetizers
  Olympia Oyster-Stuffed Mushrooms, 68
Coconut-Pecan Frosting, 408–9
Cod
  Creamy, Cakes, 129
  history of use, 90
  Landlubbers Chowder, 90
  salted, preparation tip, 129
Coffee, 432
Coffin, Robert P. Tristram, 187
Coleslaw, 282
  Sandwich, 52–53
Collard
  Greens with Pot Liquor, 260
  preparation tip, 260
Colquitt, Harriet Ross, 97, 150, 348
Colwin, Laurie, 48, 142, 264, 409
Common Sense in the Household (Harland), 228
Conch, use of, 124, 125
Condiments, buying traditional, source, 294
Convalescent eating, 43
Cook, Doris, 120
Cook, Margaret, 383

Cook, Sid, 100
Cookbooks, charitable, 383
Cookies
  Biscochitos, 415
  Chocolate Chip-Oatmeal, 416
  favorite names list, 417
  Thumbprint, 417
Cooking American (Dean), 19, 302, 303, 358, 387
Cooking techniques
  frying, 142, 143
  grilling fish, 136
  planking, 127
Cook It Outdoors (Beard), 76
Cook Not Mad or Rational Cookery, The, 131
Cooper, Joe, 215
Corbitt, Helen, 76, 280
Corn
  Calico, Relish, 312
  Chicos, 330
  dried, history and buying/source, 330
  history, 7, 8
  hominy, 330
  Lancaster County Chicken-, Soup, 98–99
  Maque Choux, 242
  Nantucket, Pudding, 241
  New Mexico Calabacitas, 239
  Pennsylvania Dutch Noodles with, and Tomatoes, 333
  posole, 330
  Summer, Chowder, 105
  Summer Succotash, 240
  technique tip, off-cob, 240
Cornbread
  Cast-Iron-Baked Buttermilk, 352
  Jalapeño, 353
Cornelius, Mary, 201, 332, 342
Cornmeal
  buying, storing, and sources for, 19, 58, 352
  Cast-Iron-Baked Buttermilk Cornbread, 352
  Fried, Mush with Sorghum Syrup, 36
  Hush Puppies, 130–31
  Narragansett Jonnycakes, 18–19
  Pound Cake, 397
  Rice and, Griddle Cakes with Nutmeg Syrup, 22–23
  Spoonbread, 329
  White Cap flint corn, 19
Country Sausage with Wild Rice Bake, 192
Courtney, W. B., 178
Crab
  blue, crabmeat, buying, 111
  blue, female, buying, 91
  Chesapeake Bay Blue, Cakes, 110–11
  Cioppino, 92–93
  cleaning tip, 112
  Cracked Dungeness, 112
  Dungeness, buying/source, 57
  Old Bay Seasoning for, 111
  Oregon Hot, and Cheddar Sandwich, 57
  Pan-Fried Soft-Shell, 109
  Seafood-Stuffed Eggplant, 126
  She-, Soup, 91
  types of, 112
Crabapples, Spiced, 299
Cracked Dungeness Crab, 112
Craig, Elijah, 424
Cranberry
  Apple-, Pie, 362–63
  Baked, Sauce, 297
  bog, visits, 297
  Glaze, 179
  Orange Relish, 56
Crawfish
  buying and cooking tips, 71, 123
  Cajun Balls, 71
  Étouffée, 122–23
Cream Biscuits, 348
Cream Gravy, 142–43
Creamy Cod Cakes, 129
Creamy Jalapeño Spinach, 264
Creole cooking, 8, 135, 251. *See also* New Orleans
Cresswell, Stephen, 434
Crocker, Betty, 304
Croly, Mrs. J. C., 212
Cross Creek Cookery (Rawlings), 58, 94, 232, 328, 354
Crowen, T. J., 68
Crunchy Catfish with Heavenly Hush Puppies, 130–31
Crusty San Francisco Sourdough, 341–43
Cucumber
  Benedictine Spread, 64
  Bread and Butter Pickles, 305
  Dill Crock Pickles, 306-7
  Pensacola Gazpachee, 244
Cushing, C. H., 164

Dagwood (sandwich), 55
Dandelion Greens, Wilted, 229
Date(s)
  Bran-, Muffins, 31
  buying California, source, 300
  California Brandied, 330
  Indio, Shake, 437
Dean, Sidney, 19, 302, 303, 358, 387
DeGiulio, Joe, 234
De Gouy, Louis P., 17, 432
Delights and Prejudices (Beard), 266
Denver (Western) Sandwich, 60
Des Moines Missionary Sewing School, A Collection of Choice Recipes, 64
Desserts. *See also* Cake; Candies; Cobblers; Cookies; Pie; Pudding
  American love of, 359–60
  Apple Crisp, 380
  Apple Pandowdy, 382
  Banana Pudding, 388
  Caramel Apples, 422
  Divinity, 420
  Down East Blueberry Toast and Butter Pudding, 390
  fruit and pastry favorites, 380
  Hot Fudge Brownies, 413
  Lemon Cream Sherbet, 392
  Lemon Squares, 414
  New Orleans Bread Pudding, 389
  Peach Ice Cream, 391
  Pear Crisp, 381
  Rhubarb Brown Betty, 384
  Strawberry Shortcake, 386–87
  Watermelon Ice, 393
Deviled Eggs, 82
Devil's Dictionary, The (Bierce), 182, 281, 345
Devil's Food Cake with Chocolate Butter Frosting, 406–7
Devine, Nancy Faidley, 110
Dictionary of American Food and Drink, The (Mariani), 26, 116, 431
Dill Crock Pickles, 306-7
Dine at Home with Rector (Rector), 25, 349, 373
Dinner Rolls, 350–51
Dips
  Bacon-Horseradish, 78
  Pico de Callo, 77
  Prairie Fire, 76
Directions for Cookery (Leslie), 196, 197, 222
Dishes and Beverage of the Old South (McCulloch-Williams), 298
Door County Sour Cherry Pie, 364–65
Double Chocolate Fudge, 418–19
Down East Blueberry Toast and Butter Pudding, 390
Dressings and vinaigrettes
  Bacon dressing and variation, 256
  Lemon, 112
  Maytag Blue, 258–59
  Simple Garlic, 257
Duck
  Leelanau Peninsula Roast, with Cherry Sauce, 166–67
  and Sausage Jambalaya, 322–23
Dumplings, 146–47
Dungeness Crabs and Blackberry Cobbler (Hibler), 102

Eat, Drink, and Be Merry in Maryland (Stieff), 173
Egerton, John, 115, 230, 260, 320
Eggplant, Seafood-Stuffed, 126
Eggs
  about American breakfast use, 26
  Blue-Flower Featherbed, 30
  Denver (Western) Sandwich, 60
  Deviled, 82
  Divinity, 420
  Shelby County, Salad Sandwich, 61
  Shirred, with Indiana Farm Breakfast Sausage, 26–27
  Spiked Eggnog, 432
  technique tip, 27
  Tex-Mex Migas, 29
  Weatherberry Scramble, 28
  whites, whipping tip, 403
  Yellow Squash Casserole, 249
Eisenhower, Mamie, 418
Elena's Favorite Foods California Style (Zelayeta), 300
Ellison, Ralph, 274
Emerson, Ralph Waldo, 42, 219
Enchiladas, Onion and Olive, 285
Equipment
  Donvier ice cream maker, 391
  kitchen syringe, 165
  pickle plucker, 307
  tortilla roller, 347
Esquire's Handbook for Hosts, 79, 212
Essence of Tomato Salad, 243

Fading Feast (Sokolov), 228, 363
Fajitas, Vaquero, 210–11
Fannie Farmer Cookbook, The (Farmer), 60, 213
Farmer, Fannie, 17, 60, 102, 159, 215, 360, 407
Farr, Sidney Sailor, 428
Fashionable Food (Lovegren), 158
Fashions in Foods in Beverly Hills, 71
Favorite Recipes of Colfax County Club Women, 314
Fearless Frying Cookbook, The (Taylor), 120
Feast Made for Laughter, A (Clairborne), 153
Fettuccine, California, with Artichokes and Garlic, 338
Fifty-Two Meat Loaves (McLaughlin), 216
Fig
  Okracoke, Cake, 412
  Preserves 293
Filé, 95
Fish. *See also* Clam(s); Crab; Lobster; Mussels; Oysters; Shrimp
  Alabama Fried Catfish Sandwich, 58
  breakfast, 39
  Broiled Petrale Fillets, 137
  Cioppino, 92–93
  Creamy Cod Cakes, 129
  Crunchy Catfish with Heavenly Hush Puppies, 130–31
  fried, American love of, 131
  Great Lakes Smoked Whitefish Salad Sandwich, 59
  Grilled Whole Pompano, 136
  history of American eating, 107–8
  Honolulu Poke, 72
  Landlubbers Cod Chowder, 90
  New Orleans Court Bouillon, 135
  Old Sour Seafood Salad, 124–25
  pickling, 73
  Rocky Mountain Pan-Fried Trout, 132
  Salmon Poached in Hard Cider, 128
  Seafood-Stuffed Eggplant, 126
  Seared Tuna Steaks, 134
  Smoked Pacific Salmon, 127
  Smoked Trout Spread, 74
  smoking, 59, 127
  stock, technique tip, 135
  Sweet-and-Sour Mahi-Mahi, 133
Fisher, Abby, 220, 221, 311
Fisher, M.F.K, 2, 4, 11, 92, 227, 256, 285, 323
Fish House Punch, 431
Fitzgerald, Zelda, 35
Florida
  Boliche, 204
  Chow-Chow Chicken Salad, 159
  conch use, 124
  Grilled Whole Pompano, 136
  Key Lime Pie, 375
  Old Sour Seafood Salad, 124–25
  Pensacola Gazpachee, 244
  Spanish Bean Soup, 101
Florida Cookbook, The (Voltz), 159
Flour Tortillas, 247
Food and Drink in America (Hooker), 270
Food of Paradise, The (Laudan), 72, 334
Foods of Old New England (Mosser), 337
Forgione, Larry, 12
Fowler, Damon Lee, 84, 335
Frederick, J. George, 330
French Quarter Veal Grillades, 40
French Toast, Traverse City Cherry, 34–35
Fresh Butter Beans, 248
Fresh Fruit Smoothie, 44
Fried Green Tomatoes, 246
Fried Okra, 262
Fried Oysters, 114–15
Fried Rabbit Quarters, 226
Fried Rice, 324
From Rose Budd's Kitchen (Willoughby), 83, 279
Frost, Robert, 390
Frosting
  Brownie, quick, 413
  Chocolate Butter, 406–7
  Coconut-Pecan, 408–9
  Cream Cheese, 410–11
  Seven-Minute, 400–401
Fruit. *See also specific fruits*
  dessert favorites, with pastry, 380
  dried, 296
  Fresh, Smoothie, 44
  Warm, Sauce, 20–21
Fudge, Double Chocolate, 418–19
Fuller, Persis, 232
Fussell, Betty, 4, 98, 419

Gaido, Mike and Paul, 109
Game
  Brunswick Stew with Rabbit, 228

Game (*cont.*)
buffalo, history, 225
buying/sources, 219, 225, 226
California Conejo, 227
Fried Rabbit Quarters, 226
Grilled Buffalo Steak, 225
Grilled Elk Backstrap with Spiced Plum Sauce, 220–21
history of, in American cooking, 217–18
Hunter's, Sausage, 224
Silver Dollar Venison Medallions, 219
thawing venison, 219
Venison Chili, 223
Venison Pot Roast with Kitchen Pepper, 222
Garcia, Lydia, 415
Gardener's Wife Salad, 251
Garlic
California Fettuccine with Artichokes and, 338
Clam and, Sauce, 188
Simple, Vinaigrette, 257
Gastronomical Me, The (Fisher), 2, 256
Gentile, Maria, 338
Georgia, 150
Baked Vidalia Onions, 284
Bits and Grits Waffles, 17
Country Captain, 151
Spoonbread, 329
German, Samuel, 408
German Chocolate Cake, 408–9
Gin
Dry Martini, 427
Gingered Cantaloupe Pickles, 301
Ginger Pear Upside-Down Cake, 404–5
Given, Meta, 48
Glazed Corned Beef, 200
Godey's Lady's Book, 163
Gold Cook Book, The (De Gouy), 17
Golden Grilled Cheese (sandwich), 62
Good Housekeeper, The (Hale), 163
Good Housekeeping Everyday Cook Book, 406
Gould, John, 145
Graham, Sylvester, 9, 10, 11
Graham Cracker Pie Crust, 375
Grains, 317–18
Grape
Concord, history, 368
Slip-Skin Concord, Pie, 368–69
Grapefruit, Candied Peel, 421
Grass Roots Cookbook, The (Anderson), 367
Gravy
Chaurice with Tomato, 191
Cream, 142, 208
Red-eye, 32–33
Shrimp, 38–39
Turkey, 162
Gray, Elizabeth Kent, 200, 255
Gray, Mrs. B., 164
Great American Writers' Cookbook (Price), 63
Great Lakes Smoked Whitefish Salad Sandwich, 59
Green Beans with Country Ham and Peanuts, 247
Greens with Pot Liquor, 260
Griffith, Jason, 61
Grilled Buffalo Steak, 225
Grilled Pork Tenderloin with Sweet Potato-Apple Sauce, 184–85
Grilled T-bone with Horseradish Butter, 196–97
Grilled Whole Pompano, 136
Grits
buying/source and cooking tip, 39, 328
Cheese, 328
Georgia Bits and, Waffles, 17
South Carolina Shrimp and, 38–39
Groff, Betty, 289, 372, 415
Grosvenor, Vertamae, 97, 134, 250, 260

Hale, Sarah Joseph, 163, 339
Ham, 170
Baked, and Cauliflower Casserole, 171
Biscuits, 80–81
Buttermilk Biscuits with Country, and Red-eye Gravy, 32–33
Chesapeake Bay, and Oyster Pie, 176–77
Chicken Breasts Stuffed with Smithfield, 156
Cider-Baked City, 174–75
Duck and Sausage Jambalaya, 322–23
Fried Rice, 324
Glazes, 172–73, 174–75, 178
Green Beans with Country, and Peanuts, 247
handcrafted, 173
Hoppin' John, 319
Loaf with Jezebel Glaze, 178
Red Beans and Rice, 277

Sautéed Sweetbreads on Country, 235
Smithfield, 172
sources to buy, 33, 172, 175
Stewed Black-eyed Peas, 279
Virginia Country, 172–73
Weatherberry Scramble, 28
Hamburger
Classic Backyard Burger, 50–51
Hand-Book of Practical Cookery (Blot), 370
Harland, Marion, 33, 213, 215, 228, 391
Harris, Jessica, 149
Hartford Election Cake, 398–99
Hash, Red Flannel, 37
Hash Browns, 268
Hawaii
Chicken Long Rice, 150
Chili Pepper Water, 315
Honolulu Poke, 72
Maui Mango Bread, 358
Saimin, 334
Sweet-and-Sour Mahi-Mahi, 133
Hearn, Lafcadio, 43, 94, 95, 112
Heatter, Maida, 410, 418
Heinz, Henry J., 10
Heirloom Vegetable Gardening (Weaver), 249
Hess, Karen, 148, 319
Heth, Edward Harris, 103, 171, 306
Heyward, DuBose, 131
Hibben, Sheila, 3, 4, 13, 108, 136, 300, 320
Hibler, Janie, 102, 225, 379
Hickman, Zelma, 120
High Living, 106
Hill, Joe, 377
History and Present State of Virginia, The (Beverly), 109, 143
Home canning basics, 288
low-acid foods, 293
Home Cooking (Colwin), 48, 142, 264
Home Fries, 267
Homemade Root Beer, Soda & Pop (Cresswell), 434
Home-Steeped Southern Succor, 430
Honolulu Poke, 72
Hooker, Richard, 270
Hoppin' John, 319
about, 318
Hoppin' John's Lowcountry Cooking (Taylor), 38
Hors d'Oeuvre and Canapés (Beard), 76, 77
Horseradish
Bacon-, Dip, 78
Butter, 196–97
Hot Fudge Brownies, 413
How to Cook and Eat in Chinese (Buwei Yang), 252
How to Cook a Wolf (Fisher), 11, 92, 285
Hunter's Game Sausage, 224
Hush Puppies, 130–31
Husted, Majorie, 304

Iceberg Wedge with Maytag Blue Dressing, 258–59
seeds to grow lettuce, 259
Ice Cream
Donvier ice cream maker, 391
history in American cooking, 391
Indio Date Shake, 437
Peach, 391
Iced Tea, 433
Idaho, Mashed Russets, 269
In Defense of Women (Mencken), 223
Indiana
Shirred Eggs with, Farm Breakfast Sausage, 26–27
Indian Cook Book, The (Lewis), 102
Indio Date Shake, 437
Inglenook Cook Book, The, 147
Invisible Man (Ellison), 274
Iowa Skinny (sandwich), 54
Italian Cook Book, The (Gentile), 338
Italian cooking in America, 338

Jacksboro Fried Shrimp, 120
Jalapeño. *See also* Chile(s)
Cornbread, 353
Creamy, Spinach, 264
Scarlet Pepper Jelly, 290
Jambalaya, Duck and Sausage, 322–23
James Beard's American Cookery, 76
Jams
Beach Plum, 292
Blackberry, 291
making, tip, 291
Thumbprint Cookies, 417
Jefferson, Thomas, 90, 173, 327, 372
Jelly, Scarlet Pepper, 290
Jennie June's American Cookery Book (Croly), 212

Jerusalem Artichoke
preserving tip, 313
Relish, 313
Soup, 104
Jewish Cooking in America (Nathan), 35, 268
Jezebel Glaze, 178
Johnnycakes, 19
Narragansett Jonnycakes, 18–19
Johnson, Lady Bird, 213
Johnson, Ronald, 183
Jones, Evan, 173
Joy of Cooking (Rombauer), 17, 184, 185, 213, 245, 292, 374, 381, 427
June Platt Cook Book, The (Platt), 275

Kander, Lizzie, 4, 69, 383, 384, 385
Kansas City Sugar-and-Spice Spareribs, 186–87
Kansas Home Cook-Book, The (Cushing & Gray), 164
Karo Syrup, 372
Kellogg, Ella Eaton, 10
Kellogg, William, 11
Kent, Louise Andrews, 200, 255
Kentucky
Leg of Lamb with Mint Julep Sauce, 230
Louisville, Brown Hotel in, 56
Louisville Benedictine (sandwich), 64
Mint Julep, 428
Weatherberry Scramble, 28
Kentucky Housewife, The (Bryan), 73, 130, 282, 378, 397
Kerr, Graham, 282
Ketchup, Tomato, 314
King, Jim, 401
King Ranch Chicken, 152–53
Kitchen Manual, A (Hibben), 108, 320
Kitchen Pepper, 222

La Cuisine Creole (Hearn), 43, 94, 95
Lady Baltimore Cake with Seven-Minute Frosting, 400–401
Lagasse, Emeril, 282
Lamb
buying/source, 230
Leg of, with Mint Julep Sauce, 230
Oven-Braised, Shanks, 232
Pan-Seared, Chops with Wilted Dandelion Greens, 229
Pueblo, Stew with Green Chile and Posole, 231
Lancaster County Chicken-Corn Soup, 98–99
Landlubbers Cod Chowder, 90
Lard, 177
Lasorda, Tommy, 276
Laudan, Rachel, 72, 334
Leeks
Chicken Pie, 144–45
Leelanau Peninsula Roast Duck with Cherry Sauce, 166–67
Leg of Lamb with Mint Julep Sauce, 230
Lemon
Cream Sherbet, 392
Dressing, 112
egg whites, using for pie, 403
juicing, 435
Meringue Pie, 374
Squares, 414
weeping, technique tip for pie, 374
Lemonade, 435
Leonard, Jonathan Norton, 209
Leslie, Eliza, 4, 88, 130, 148, 151, 196, 197, 201, 222, 397
Letters from an American Farmer (Crèvecoeur), 362
Lettuce. *See also* Salad(s)
Iceberg Wedge with Maytag Blue Dressing, 258–59
seeds for heirloom varieties, 259
Levenstein, Harvey, 11, 13
Lewis, Edna, 4, 39, 114, 175, 254, 361, 389
Lewis, Mrs. S. R., 102
Library Ann's Cook Book, 338
Liebling, A. J., 198
Lima Beans
Brunswick Stew with Rabbit, 228
Fresh Butter Beans, 248
Summer Succotash, 240
Lime
buying/source, Key limes, 375
Key, Pie, 375
Old Sour, 124–25
Lincoln, Abraham, 88, 372
Lincoln, Mary, 235, 277, 407
Lobster
choosing, tip, 119
Steamed Maine, 118–19
Loin Roast with Cranberry Glaze, 179

Longone, Janice and Daniel, 383
Louisiana
  Catahoula Sweet-Dough Pies, 366–67
  Duck and Sausage Jambalaya, 322–23
  Maque Choux, 242
  "Pie Day," 367
Louisville Benedictine (sandwich), 64
Lovegren, Sylvia, 158
Lundberg, Donald E., 371
Luuwai, Boogie and Violet, 150

Macadamia nuts
  Maui Mango Bread, 358
Macaroni and Wisconsin Cheese Sauce, 335
  with eggs, 335
Madeira Sauce, 160–61
Maine
  Down East Blueberry Toast and Butter Pudding, 390
  Lobster, Steamed, 118–19
  salt pork, 187
Mainstays of Maine (Coffin), 187
Mango, Maui Bread, 358
Maque Choux, 242
Mariani, John, 26, 116, 431
Marinade (Asian style), 134
Marinated Salmon Bits, 73
Marion Harland's Complete Cook Book (Harland), 33, 213, 215
Marjorie Mosser's Good Maine Food, 190
Martha Washington's Booke of Cookery, 148
Martini, Dry, 427
Maryland's Way, 149, 178, 234, 429
Mashed Idaho Russets, 269
Mason, John Landis, 288
Massachusetts
  Concord grapes, history, 368
  Oven-Braised Lamb Shanks, 232
  Pork Cutlets with Clam and Garlic Sauce, 188
  Slip-Skin Concord Grape Pie, 368–69
Masters of American Cookery (Fussell), 98, 419
Maui Mango Bread, 358
Mayberry, Alicia Rhett, 400
Mayonnaise, Basil, 49
Maxcy, Mrs. Virgil, 149
McCullers, Carson, 318
McCulloch-Williams, Martha, 298
McLaughlin, Michael, 48, 216
McMahan, Jacqueline Higuera, 285
Meat Loaf, 216
Melville, Herman, 88
Member of the Wedding (McCullers), 318
Mencken, H. L., 223, 430
Mennonite Community Cookbook (Showalter), 311
Mexican Rice, 325
Meyer, Gertrude, 261
Michigan
  Traverse City Cherry French Toast, 34–35
Miles Standish, 56
Miller, Amy Bess, 232
Miller, Mark, 12
Minnesota
  Breakfast Cereal of Wild Rice and Oatmeal, 45
  Wild Rice Medley, 332
Mint
  Chilled Fresh Pea Soup with, 102
  Julep, 428, 429
  Julep Sauce, 230
  syrup, 428
Miss Beecher's Domestic Receipt Book (Beecher), 346, 403
Mississippi Barbecued Chicken, 154
Miss Leslie's New Cookery Book (Leslie), 151, 197
Miss Parloa's Appledore Cook Book (Parloa), 116, 407
Miss Parloa's Kitchen Companion (Parloa), 407
Miss Parloa's New Cook Book and Marketing Guide (Parloa), 407
Mixed Salad of Greens, Nasturtiums, and Herbs, 257
Mixed Vegetable Stir-Fry, 252
Moby Dick (Melville), 88
Molé, buying/source, 214
Monstrous Depravity (Gould), 145
Monta–o, Dorothy, 415
More Than Moonshine (Farr), 428
Morrow, Charles, 4
Mosser, Marjorie, 190, 337
Mrs. Appleyard's Summer Kitchen (Kent & Gray), 200, 255
Mrs. Lincoln's Boston Cook Book, 235, 277
Mrs. Rorer's New Cook Book, 215, 258, 259, 278
Muffins, Bran-Date, 31
Multi-Grain Bread, 344–45

Mushrooms
  Chicken Fricassee over Cornbread Toast, 141
  morels, buying/source, 261
  Olympia Oyster-Stuffed, 68
  Sugar Creek Fried Morels, 261
  Wild Rice Medley, 332
Mussels, California Fishermen's, 117
Mustard Dressing, 58
Myhre, Helen, 361

Nancy Drew Cookbook, 182
Nantucket Corn Pudding, 241
Narragansett Jonnycakes, 18–19
Nash, Ogden, 150
Nathan, Joan, 35, 268
National Cookbook, The (Hibben), 13, 136, 300
Native Americans, contributions to American cooking, 3, 5, 6, 104, 108, 240, 297, 332
Neal, Bill, 401, 421
Neale, Jim and Sandy, 278
Neighborhood Cook Book, The, 75
Nelsen, Lynne, 283
New California Cook Book, The (Callahan), 102
New England
  Apple Pandowdy, 382
  Boiled Dinner, 198–99
  Boston Baked Beans, 276
  Boston Brown Bread, 346
  Clam Chowder, 89
  cod use in, 90, 129
  Hartford Election Cake, 398–99
  Landlubbers Cod Chowder, 90
  Raspberry Switchel, 436
  Stone Fence, 426
  Sweet Potato-Chestnut Puree, 275
New England Yankee Cookbook, The (Wolcott), 174
New Mexico
  Biscochitos, 415
  Calabacitas, 239
  Chicos, 330
  Chimayó Carne Adovada, 189
  Flour Tortillas, 247
New Orleans, 8
  Artichokes, 253
  Bread Pudding, 389
  Chaurice with Tomato Gravy, 191
  Court Bouillon, 135
  Crawfish Étouffée, 122–23
  French Quarter Veal Grillades, 40
  Galatoire's restaurant, 122
  Gardener's Wife Salad, 251
  muffaletta, 55
  New Potatoes à la Diable, 272
  oyster loaf, 55
  Red Beans and Rice, 277
  Scalloped Oysters, 67
  Seafood Gumbo, 94–95
  Shrimp Rémoulade, 70
New Potatoes à la Diable, 272
Newstadt, Kathy, 116
Noodles
  making, 333
  Pennsylvania Dutch, with Corn and Tomatoes, 333
  Saimin, 334
North Carolina
  Okracoke Fig Cake, 412
  Piedmont County 'Q, 52–53
Novarro, Ramon, 325
Nutmeg Syrup, 22–23

Oatmeal
  Chocolate Chip-, Cookies, 416
  Minnesota Breakfast Cereal of Wild Rice and, 45
Oats
  Pear Crisp, 381
Oils
  peanut for frying, buying, 115
  recommended cooking, 280
Okra
  Fried, 262
  Gumbo Soup, 97
  Pickled, 308
  Seafood Gumbo, 94–95
Okracoke Fig Cake, 412
Old Bay Seasoning, 111
Olive, Onion and, Enchiladas, 285
Oliver, Sandra, 89, 108
Olympia Oyster-Stuffed Mushrooms, 68
Onion(s)
  Baked Vidalia, 284
  and Olive Enchiladas, 285
  Pot Roast with Root Vegetables, 201
  -Smothered Smoked Pork Chops, 182
  Vidalia, serving whole, storing, buying/source, 284
Orange
  Charleston Benne Chicken, 157

Cranberry, Relish, 56
-flower water, 399
Sangaree, 429
Oregon Hot Crab and Cheddar Sandwich, 57
Outdoor grilling
Classic Backyard Burger, 50–51
Grilled Buffalo Steak, 225
Grilled Elk Backstrap with Spiced Plum Sauce, 220–21
Grilled Pork Tenderloin with Sweet Potato-Apple Sauce, 184–85
Grilled T-bone with Horseradish Butter, 196–97
history, 12
Hunter's Game Sausage, 224
Kansas City Sugar-and-Spice Spareribs, 186–87
technique tip, 197
Texas Barbecued Brisket, 202–3
Vaquero Fajitas, 210–11
Willamette Valley Grilled Chicken with Blackberry Sauce, 155
Oven-Braised Lamb Shanks, 232
Oysters
Brown, Stew with Benne, 96
Chesapeake Bay Ham and, Pie, 176–77
Fried, 114–15
history, 67, 68
New Orleans loaf, 55
Olympia, -Stuffed Mushrooms, 68
Pan Roast, 113
peanut oil to fry, buying, 115
recommended type, 113
Scalloped, 67
Seafood Gumbo, 94–95
Ozarks Black Walnut Conserve, 295

Pancakes
American development of, 25
Buckwheats, 24–25
Buttermilk Flapjacks with Warm Fruit Sauce, 20–21
Rice and Cornmeal Griddle Cakes with Nutmeg Syrup, 22–23
technique tip, 21
Pan-Fried Rib Eye, 195
Pan-Fried Soft-Shell Crabs, 109
Pan-Seared Lamp Chops with Wilted Dandelion Greens, 229
Paradox of Plenty (Levenstein), 13
Parloa, Maria, 118, 228, 406, 407
Pasta Primavera, 336–37
Patout, Alex, 122
Patriotic Food Show, 226
Peach(es)
Chutney, 80–81
Cobbler, 378
history of American use, 298
Home-Steeped Southern Succor, 430
Ice Cream, 391
Pickled, 298
ripeness, 391
varieties (clingstone or freestone) 378
Peanut butter
history, 48
Tidewater Peanut Soup, 106
Peanut oil, cooking with, 115
Peanuts
Boiled, 84
Fried Rabbit Quarters, 226
Green Beans with Country Ham and, 247
history, 48
Single Pie Crust, 376–77
Pear
Chutney, 172–73
Crisp, 381
Ginger, Upside-Down Cake, 404–5
Pea(s)
Chilled Fresh, Soup with Mint, 102
Salad, 263
Pecan
Bourbon-and-Butter, Pie, 372–73
Caramel, Sticky Buns, 356–57
Coconut-, Frosting, 408–9
history, 372
Okracoke Fig Cake, 412
Pear Crisp, 381
Thumbprint Cookies, 417
Pellegrini, Angelo, 6, 128, 305
Pennsylvania Dutch, 7, 88, 99
Angel Food Cake with Boiled Custard, 402–3
Apple Butter, 289
Botboi, 147
Chicken and Dumplings, 146–47
cookie-making and, 415
green apple pap, 149
Lancaster County Chicken-Corn Soup, 98–99
Noodles with Corn and Tomatoes, 333
preserves and putting food by, 288
Rhubarb Custard Pie, 370
sapsago cheese, 180

Pennsylvania Dutch (*cont.*)
schnitz und kneppe, 174, 289
scrapple, 27
Sour Braised Loin with Cherries, 180
Spelt Salad with Corn, 331
Pennsylvania Dutch Cook Book (Frederick), 330
Pennsylvania Dutch Cookbook (Groff), 289
Pennsylvania Dutch Country Cooking (Weaver), 99, 180
Pensacola Gazpachee, 244
Peppers (sweet bell)
Pickled, 309
Scarlet Pepper Jelly, 290
Veal and, 234
Perfection Salad (Shapiro), 250
Persimmons
buying and storing tip, 349
'Simmon Biscuits, 349
Philadelphia Cook Book (Rorer), 82, 201, 258
Picante Pintos, 278
Picayune's Creole Cook Book, The, 40, 55, 67, 161, 235, 251, 272
Pickett, Anne, 82
Pickled Okra, 308
Pickled Peaches, 298
Pickled Peppers, 309
Pickles
Bread and Butter, 305
Chow-Chow, 310–11
Dill Crock, 306-7
Gingered Cantaloupe, 301
Pickled Lily (piccalilli), about, 311
"Red Turnip," 304
technique tip, 307
Watermelon-Rind, 302-3
Pickling, 73
Marinated Salmon Bits, 73
Pico de Gallo, 77
Pie. *See also* Pie Crust
Apple-Cranberry, 362–63
Bourbon-and-Butter Pecan, 372–73
cane syrup, buying/source, 373
Catahoula Sweet-Dough, 366–67
Chesapeake Bay Ham and Oyster, 176–77
Chicken, 144–45
Door County Sour Cherry, 364–65
Key Lime, 375
Lemon Meringue, 374
Rhubarb Custard, 370–71
Shoo, Fly! and related pies, 372
Slip-Skin Concord Grape, 368–69
Sour Cream-Raisin, 361
Sweet Potato, 376–77
testing doneness, custard, 371
Pie Crust, 144–45
Almond, 364–65
Buttery Double, 368–69
Buttery Single, 370–71
Cheddar, 362–63
Graham Cracker, 375
lard-based, 276–77
Peanut Single, 376–77
Superbly Flaky Single, 372–73
Sweet Dough, 366–67
"Pie in the Sky" (song), 377
Piedmont Country 'Q, 52–53
Piki Bread, about, 353
Pilau
with Pistachios and Pine Nuts, 327
Shrimp, 320-21
Pimiento Cheese Sandwich, 63
Pistachios, Pilau with, and Pine Nuts, 327
Platt, June, 275
Plum
Beach, Jam, 292
Spiced, Sauce, 220–21
Popovers, 212–13
technique tip, 213
Pork. *See also* Ham; Sausage
Arizona Chile Verde, 190
and beans, 276
Boston Baked Beans, 276
buying chops tip, 183
Carolina Dry Rub for, 52–53
Chimayó Carne Adovada, 189
Chops Braised with Quinces, 183
Cutlets with Clam and Garlic Sauce, 188
Grilled, Tenderloin with Sweet Potato-Apple Sauce, 184–85
history of use in America, 7, 169–70
Iowa Skinny, 54
Kansas City Sugar-and-Spice Spareribs, 186–87
Loin Roast with Cranberry Glaze, 179
Onion-Smothered Smoked, Chops, 182
pickled, buying information, 277
Piedmont County 'Q, 52–53
presmoked, 182
salt, 187
Sour Braised Loin with Cherries, 180
Stuffed, Chops, 181
Posole, buying/source, 231

Post, Charles W., 11
Potato(es)
Brunswick Stew with Rabbit, 228
Creamy Cod Cakes, 129
Hash Browns, 268
history of American use, 265–66
Home Fries, 267
Mashed Idaho Russets, 269
New, à la Diable, 272
New England Boiled Dinner, 198–99
pancakes (*latkes*), history of, 268
Pot Roast with Root Vegetables, 201
Red Bliss, Salad, 270
Red Flannel Hash, 37
Santa Fe Breakfast Burritos, 41
Scalloped, 272
Spanish Bean Soup, 101
Summer Corn Chowder, 105
Twice Baked, 271
Weatherberry Scramble, 28
Pot Roast
with Root Vegetables, 201
Venison with Kitchen Pepper, 222–23
Poultry, 139–40. *See also* Chicken; Turkey
Prairie Fire Dip, 76
Prejudice: Second Series (Mencken), 430
Preserves
Fig, 293
Pumpkin Chip, 294
Price, Reynolds, 63
Priscilla Cook Book (Burt), 208
Prudhomme, Paul, 12
Prunes
Calcuttas, 79
Pudding
Banana, 388
Down East Blueberry Toast and Butter, 390
Nantucket Corn, 241
New Orleans Bread, 389
Pueblo Lamb Stew with Green Chile and Posole, 231
Pumpkin
buying preserves, 294
Chip Preserves, 294
Pyles, Stephan, 12

Quail, Smothered, 168
Quinces
comeback of, 289
Pork Chops Braised with, 183

Rabbit. *See* Game
Raisin
Hartford Election Cake, 398–99
Sour Cream-, Pie, 361
Randolph, Mary, 4, 66, 67, 73, 102, 142, 149, 244, 314, 335, 391, 392, 425
Raspberry
Switchel, 436
vinegar, 436
Rawlings, Marjorie Kinnan, 58, 94, 232, 328, 354
Rector, George, 25, 349, 373
Red Beans and Rice, 277
Red Bliss Potato Salad, 270
Red-eye Gravy, 32–33
Red Flannel Hash, 37
Red Rice, 326
Relish
Calico Corn, 312
Cranberry Orange, 56
Jerusalem Artichoke, 313
Revolution at the Table (Levenstein), 11
Rhett, Blanche, 400
Rhode Island
Narragansett Jonnycakes, 18–19
Rhubarb
Brown Betty, 384
Custard Pie, 370–71
Rice
in American cooking, 8, 255
Bread, 354–55
Broccoli-, Casserole, 255
Carolina Gold, about, 321
cooking tip, 321
and Cornmeal Griddle Cakes with Nutmeg Syrup, 22–23
Duck and Sausage Jambalaya, 322–23
Fried, 324
Hoppin' John, 319
Mexican, 325
Minnesota Breakfast Cereal of Wild, and Oatmeal, 45
Pilau with Pistachios and Pine Nuts, 327
Red, 326
Red Beans and, 277
Shrimp Pilau, 320-21
varieties, 319
Roast Chicken with Nut Sauce, 148–49
Roasted Wild Turkey with Madeira Sauce, 160–61
Roberts, Kenneth, 190, 337
Rocky Mountain Pan-Fried Trout, 132

Rogers, Will, 71
Rombauer, Irma, 4, 17, 184, 185, 245, 292, 374, 380, 418, 427
Roosevelt, Eleanor, 372
Root, Waverly, 424
Rorer, Sarah Tyson, 60, 82, 201, 215, 228, 258, 259, 278
Rose water, 399
Rutabaga-Colby Cheese Casserole, 283
Rutledge, Sarah, 73, 326

Sage Dressing, 162–64
Saimin, 334
Salad(s)
  bacon dressing, variation, 256
  Chow-Chow Chicken, 159
  dressing, amount needed, 257
  edible flowers for, tip, 257
  Essence of Tomato, 243
  Gardener's Wife, 251
  Iceberg Wedge with Maytag Blue Dressing, 258–59
  Jailed, or gelatin, 250
  mayonnaise and, 263
  Mixed, of Greens, Nasturtiums, and Herbs, 257
  Old Sour Seafood, 124–25
  Pea, 263
  Red Bliss Potato Salad, 270
  Shelby County Egg, Sandwich, 61
  Smoked Whitefish, 59
  Spelt, with Corn, 331
  technique tip, vegetables, 251
  Waldorf, origin of, 263
  Wilted Greens with Hot Bacon Dressing, 256
Salmon
  Marinated, Bits, 73
  Poached in Hard Cider, 128
  Smoked Pacific, 127
Salsa
  Pico de Gallo, 77
  Sandy's Cooked, 278
Salted Green Soybeans, 85
Saltwater Foodways (Oliver), 108
Sandwiches
  Alabama Fried Catfish, 58
  BLT or BCLT with green tomatoes, 246
  Classic Backyard Burger, 50–51
  Coleslaw, 52–53
  Dagwood, 55
  Denver, 60
  Golden Grilled Cheese, 62
  Great Lakes Smoked Whitefish Salad, 59
  history, 47–48
  Iowa Skinny, 54
  Louisville Benedictine, 64
  Miles Standish, 56
  Oregon Hot Crab and Cheddar Sandwich, 57
  peanut butter, 48
  Piedmont County 'Q, 52–53
  Pimiento Cheese, 63
  Po'Boys, 55
  Shelby County Egg Salad, 61
  Summer's Best BLT, 49
Sandwiches (Tyson), 60
Santa Fe Breakfast Burritos, 41
Sassafras
  beer, 434
  Tea, 434
Sauces
  Baked Cranberry, 297
  Bandera Barbecue, 202–3
  Barbecue, 52–53, 154, 186
  Blackberry, 155
  Boiled Custard, 402–3
  Cheese, 57, 171, 335
  Cherry, 166–67
  Chile, 189
  Clam and Garlic, 188
  Cocktail, 69
  Crystal, buying/source, 277
  Dipping (Asian style), 134
  Enchilada, 285
  Green Chile, 41
  Hawaii Chili Pepper Water, 315
  King Ranch Chicken, 152–53
  Madeira, 160–61
  Mint Julep, 230
  Nut, 148–49
  Old Sour, 124–25
  Rémoulade, 70
  Spiced Plum Sauce, 220–21
  Stir-fry, 252
  Whiskey, 389
Sauerkraut Yankees (Weaver), 431
Sausage, 192
  casings, tip, 224
  Chaurice with Tomato Gravy, 191
  Country, with Wild Rice Bake, 192
  Duck and, Jambalaya, 322–23
  Hunter's Game, 224
  Mexican Rice, 325

Shirred Eggs with Indiana Farm Breakfast, 26–27
Spanish Bean Soup, 101
Tex-Mex Migas, 29
Sautéed Sweetbreads on Country Ham, 235
Savannah Cook Book, The (Colquitt), 97, 150, 348
Scalloped Oysters, 67
Scalloped Potatoes, 272
Jansson's Temptation, 273
Scallops
Old Sour Seafood Salad, 124–25
Scarlet Pepper Jelly, 290
Schulze, Patricia, 321
Science in the Kitchen (Kellogg), 10
Scott, Ed and Edna, 130
Scott, Natalie, 191
Scrapple, 27
Seafood Gumbo, 94–95
Seafood-Stuffed Eggplant, 126
Seared Tuna Steaks, 134
Seaweed (nori), 72
Serious Pig (Thorne), 8, 267, 319, 329
Serve It Forth (Fisher), 227
Sesame seeds (Benne), 81
Brown Oyster Stew with Benne, 96
Buttermilk Benne Biscuits, 80–81
Charleston Benne Chicken, 157
Settlement Cookbook, The, 22, 69, 383, 385
Seventy-five Receipts for Pastry, Cakes, and Sweetmeats (Leslie), 197
Shapiro, Laura, 250
She-Crab Soup, 91
Shelby County Egg Salad Sandwich, 61
Sherbet, Lemon Cream, 392
Shields, John, 247
Shirred Eggs with Indiana Farm Breakfast Sausage, 26–27
Shortcakes, 386–87
Showalter, Mary Emma, 311
Shrimp
Barbecued, 121
Cioppino, 92–93
Cocktail, 69
Jacksboro Fried, 120
Old Sour Seafood Salad, 124–25
Pilau, 320-21
Rémoulade, 70
Seafood Gumbo, 94–95
South Carolina, and Grits, 38–39
Shute, Miss T. S., 310, 391
Side Orders (Egerton), 115
Silver Dollar Venison Medallions, 219
Simmons, Amelia, 3, 19, 302, 359, 362, 399
Skillet Asparagus, 254
Slip-Skin Concord Grape Pie, 368–69
Smith, Andrew, 243
Smith, Grace and Beverly, 4, 70, 324
Smoke & Spice (Jamison & Jamison), 74, 335
Smoked Pacific Salmon, 127
Smoked Trout Spread, 74
Smoked Turkey Breast, 165
Smothered Quail, 168
Sokolov, Raymond, 228, 363
Sorghum
buying tip and source, 36
Syrup, Fried Cornmeal Mush with, 36
Soups
bean, history, 102
Brown Oyster Stew with Benne, 96
Chilled Fresh Pea, with Mint, 102
Cioppino, 92–93
Croutons, 100
filé as okra substitute, 95
fish stock, technique tip, 135
freezing, history of, 104
Gumbo, 97
history, 87–88
Jerusalem Artichoke, 104
Lancaster County Chicken-Corn Soup, 98–99
Landlubbers Cod Chowder, 90
New England Clam Chowder, 89
New Orleans Court Bouillon, 135
Saimin, 334
Seafood Gumbo, 94–95
seafood tip, shells on, 93
She-Crab, 91
Spanish Bean, 101
stock, making or buying, 96
Summer Corn Chowder, 105
Tidewater Peanut, 106
Tomato, 102
turtle, history of, 97
Wisconsin Cheese, 100
Sour Braised Loin with Cherries, 180
Sour Cream-Raisin Pie, 361
South Carolina, 22. *See also* Charleston
Hoppin' John, 319
Jacksboro Fried Shrimp, 120
Shrimp and Grits, 38–39
Southern Food (Egerton), 230, 320

Southwest. *See also specific states*
piki bread, about, 353
Spanish influence, 8
Soybeans, Salted Green, 85
Spanish Bean Soup, 101
Spareribs, Kansas City Sugar-and-Spice, 186–87
Spelt Salad with Corn, 331
buying/source, 331
Spiced Acorn Squash, 250
Spiced Crabapples, 299
Spiked Eggnog, 432
Spinach
Creamy Jalapeño, 264
Wilted Greens with Hot Bacon Dressing, 256
Spoonbread, 329
Spreads
Benedictine, 64
Smoked Trout, 74
Springfield Chilli, 215
Squash, summer
New Mexico Calabacitas, 239
Yellow, Casserole, 249
Squash, winter
Spiced Acorn, 250
Steamed Maine Lobster, 118–19
Stenzhorn, Joanne, 418
Stew
Beef, with Savory Popovers, 212–13
Brown Oyster with Benne, 96
Brunswick, with Rabbit, 228
history, 228
Oyster Pan Roast, 113
Pueblo Lamb, with Green Chile and Posole, 231
Stewed Black-eyed Peas, 279
Stewed Cabbage, 281
Stewed Tomatoes, 245
Stews, Bogs & Burgoos (Villas), 229
Sticky Buns, Caramel Pecan, 356–57
Stieff, Frederick, 173
Stir-fry, Mixed Vegetable, 252
Stone Fence, 426
Strata (egg-and-bread casserole), Blue-Flower Featherbed, 30
Strawberry Shortcake, 386–87
Stuffed Pork Chops, 181
Sugar
caramelizing, 311
Crackle Topping, 398–99
Sugar Creek Fried Morels, 261
Summer Corn Chowder, 105
Summer's Best BLT, 49
Summer Succotash, 240
Sweet-and-Sour Mahi-Mahi, 133
Sweetbreads, Sautéed on Country Ham, 235
Sweet Potato(es)
-Apple Sauce, 184–85
Candied, 274
-Chestnut Purée, 275
history, 274
Pie, 376–77
Swiss Steak, 205
Syrup
about maple, 25
Nutmeg, 22–23
about sorghum, 36

Tapia family, 347
Taste of Country Cooking, The (Lewis), 39, 114, 175, 254, 361, 389
Taylor, John Martin, 38, 39, 120
Tea
American-grown, source, 433
Iced, 433
Sassafras, 434
Texas
Barbecued Brisket, 202–3
Caviar, 280
Jalapeño Cornbread, 353
King Ranch Chicken, 152–53
Pico de Gallo, 77
Prairie Fire Dip, 76
Shelby County Egg Salad Sandwich, 61
Texas Home Cooking (Jamison & Jamison), 61, 264
Tex-Mex Migas, 29
Thanksgiving
Classic, Turkey with Sage Dressing, 162–64
menu, 161, 164
Thoreau, Henry David, 20, 239
Thorne, John, 4, 8, 267, 319, 329
Through the Kitchen Door (Smith, Smith, & Wilson), 4, 70, 324
Thumbprint Cookies, 417
Tidewater Peanut Soup, 106
Tolbert, Frank X., 214
Tomato(es)
Arizona Chile Verde, 190
canned, brand recommended, 296
Chaurice with, Gravy, 191
Chimichanga, 206–7

Chutney, 296
Cioppino, 92–93
Clams Posillipo, 116
Essence of, Salad, 243
freezing tip, 278
Fried Green, 246
Georgia Country Captain, 151
Gumbo Soup, 97
history, 243
Ketchup, 314
New Orleans Court Bouillon, 135
Pennsylvania Dutch Noodles with Corn and Tomatoes, 333
Pensacola Gazpachee, 244
Pico de Gallo, 77
Red Rice, 326
Sandy's Cooked Salsa, 278
Shrimp Pilau, 320-21
Soup, 103
Springfield Chilli, 215
Stewed, 245
Summer's Best BLT, 49
technique tip, broiling, 77
Veal and Peppers, 234
Tortillas, Flour, 247
Trader Vic's Book of Food and Drink, 75
Tramp Abroad, A (Twain), 195
Treatise on Domestic Economy, A (Beecher), 346
Tremper, Kate, 192
Trillin, Calvin, 91, 123, 170
Trout
Rocky Mountain Pan-Fried, 132
Smoked, Spread, 74
Tschirky, Oscar, 263
Tuna, 134
Seared, Steaks, 134
Turkey
Classic Thanksgiving, with Sage Dressing, 162–64
cooking tip for wild, 160
hot sandwich, 56
Miles Standish (sandwich), 56
Roasted Wild, with Madeira Sauce, 160–61
roasting tip, 162
Smoked, Breast, 165
Twain, Mark, 42, 51, 195, 222, 352, 393
Twice Baked Potatoes, 271
200 Years of Charleston Cooking (Rhett), 400
200 Years of New Orleans Cooking (Scott), 191
Tyler, Susie and Bill, 28

Understanding Baking (Amendola & Lundberg), 371
Unprejudiced Palate, The (Pellegrini), 6, 128, 305

Vaquero Fajitas, 210–11
Vaughan, Beatrice, 104
Veal
Francese, 233
French Quarter, Grillades, 40
and Peppers, 234
Sautéed Sweetbreads on Country Ham, 235
Vegetables, garden, 237–38. *See also specific vegetables*
Gardener's Wife Salad, 251
list of American favorites, 243
Mixed, Stir-Fry, 252
Pasta Primavera, 336–37
Venison. *See* Game
Vibration Cooking (Grosvenor), 97, 134, 250, 260
Villas, James, 4, 119, 228, 229, 415
Vinaigrettes. *See* Dressings and vinaigrettes
Virginia
Brunswick Stew with Rabbit, 228
Calcuttas, 79
Country Ham, 172–73
Fried Rabbit Quarters, 226
ham, buying/sources, 172
Sweet Potato Pie, 376–77
Tidewater Peanut Soup, 106
Virginia Housewife, The (Randolph), 66, 67, 73, 102, 142, 244, 314, 335, 391
Voltz, Jeanne, 159

Waffles
Georgia Bits and Grits, 17
history, 17
Wakefield, Ruth, 416
Waldorf Salad, origin of, 263
Walnut
black, storing and source for, 295
Divinity, 420

Walnut (*cont.*)
Hot Fudge Brownies, 413
Ozarks Black, Conserve, 295
Thumbprint Cookies, 417
Walter, Eugene, 248
Washington, George, 372
Water chestnuts
buying tip, 158
Chicken Chop Suey, 158
Watercress
Benedictine Spread, 64
Watermelon
choosing, 303
Ice, 393
-Rind Pickles, 302-3
Waters, Alice, 12
Way We Ate, The (Williams), 296
We Called It Macaroni (Barr), 338
Weaver, William Woys, 99, 180, 249, 310, 431
Weiss, Joe, 112
Welcome Table, The (Harris), 149
West, Deborah and Richard, 307
West Coast. *See also specific states*
Broiled Petrale Fillets, 137
outdoor grilling, 155
West Coast Cook Book (Brown), 68
What Mrs. Fisher Knows About Old Southern Cooking (Fisher), 220, 311
Whiskey
Home-Steeped Southern Succor, 430
Sauce, 389
White, Jasper, 12
White Sauce, 192
Who's Your Mama . . . (Bienvenu), 366
Wild About Game (Hibler), 225
Wild Foods Cookbook & Field Guide (Tatum), 295
Wild Rice
Bake, Country Sausage with, 192
buying/source, 332
Medley, 332
Willamette Valley Grilled Chicken with Blackberry Sauce, 155
Williams, Jacqueline B., 296
Willoughby, Mamie Davis (Rose Budd), 83, 279
Wilson, Charles Morrow, 4, 70, 324
Wilson, José, 28
Wine
Orange Sangaree, 429
Wisconsin
Cheese Soup, 100
Door County Sour Cherry Pie, 364–65
Macaroni and, Cheese Sauce, 335
Wisconsin Country Cookbook (Heth), 103, 171, 306
With Bold Knife and Fork (Fisher), 323
With or Without Beans (Cooper), 215
Witty, Helen, 241
Wolcott, Imogene, 174

Yankee Hill-Country Cooking (Vaughan), 104
Yellow Squash Casserole, 249
Y.M.C.A. Cook Book, 43
Young Housekeeper's Friend, The (Cornelius), 201, 332, 342

Zelayeta, Elena, 300